WILLIAM SHAKESPEARE

THE COMPLETE WORKS

Volume – 1

Introductions by

R.S. Sharma
Ratri Ray

PEACOCK BOOKS

Published by
PEACOCK BOOKS
7/22, Ansari Road, Darya Ganj, New Delhi-110 002
Phones : +91-11-40775252, 2327 3880, 2327 5880, 2328 0451
Fax : +91-11-2328 5873
E-mail : orders@atlanticbooks.com
Web : www.atlanticbooks.com

Branch Office
5, Nallathambi Street, Wallajah Road,
Chennai-600 002
Phones : +91-44-6461 1085, 3241 3319
E-mail : chennai@atlanticbooks.com

Peacock Books is an imprint of
Atlantic Publishers and Distributors (P) Ltd.

Printed in India at Chaman Enterprises, 1603, Pataudi House, Darya Ganj, New Delhi-110 002

Contents

CONTENTS

INTRODUCTION-I

1. A Symbol of Culture

Introducing Shakespeare to the general reader, G.B. Harrison begins his book with the following statement:

> No household in the English-speaking world is properly furnished unless it contains copies of the *Holy Bible* and of *The Works of William Shakespeare*. It is not always thought necessary that these books should be read in maturer years, but they must be present as symbols of Religion and Culture.

Not only in the English speaking world, but everywhere, acquaintance with Shakespeare's plays is regarded as a mark of culture; and there is hardly any language-community in the civilized world, which does not possess Shakespeare in translation. He is a member of that universal brotherhood of luminaries which defines humanity's distinctive progress towards excellence; he belongs to the whole human race. In his well-known dialogue on civilization, when C.E.M. Joad thought of prompting Lucy to name a civilized person, the word 'Shakespeare' leapt to his pen. Lucy, of course, is too young to be able to understand Shakespeare. Yet she can guess that the man and his plays have a great deal to do with civilization.

We must also distinguish the senses in which Shakespeare is regarded as a symbol of culture. This seems desirable in view of the fact that 'culture' and 'civilization' each has several meanings and is employed in a high as well as a low sense, in a general as well as a specific signification. On the superficial or low level culture simply means observing good manners and fulfilling the expectations of the general as a social group. It is in this sense that many people keep copies of Shakespeare's works without ever caring to enrich their minds by reading them, and it is this idea of culture being pursued when "In the room the women come and go/Talking of Michaelangelo." In a higher but limited sense culture comprises the ideas, beliefs, arts, and customs of a particular society in time, and in this aspect it is a major component of a civilization, the latter being more inclusive and expressive of advancement in a certain direction. Thus we can speak of the culture of a tribal group, but not of their civilization.

There is a third meaning of 'culture' which defines it in terms of certain human attainments. This will be clear from the following definitions randomly picked up from dictionaries:

(a) refined understanding of the arts and other human intellectual achievement;
(b) cultivation: the state of being cultivated: refinement: the result of cultivation;
(c) intellectual and artistic activity; intellectual and social refinement resulting from such activity;
(d) intellectual or moral discipline and training; civilized tastes and values.

These meanings, which focus on intellectual activity, refinement, and arts, are closest to the original metaphorical meaning of the word. In fact, etymologically speaking, both 'culture' and 'cultivation' are ultimately derived from the Latin verb, 'colere', meaning 'to till (land)'. Tilling involves such operations as ploughing, harrowing and fertilizing of the soil. On the metaphorical plane, these find their correlates in stimulation and enrichment of the mind. Both 'culture' and 'cultivation' have retained in modern English the literal as well as the metaphorical meaning—we are concerned with the latter.

Shakespeare imparts to us culture in the above senses because his works stimulate and enrich our mind; they sharpen and refine and develop our sensibility for perception and enjoyment of Beauty and for the recognition of the Good. They offer us the intellectual and emotional fare of a superior kind; they grant us a vision of the inner reality of man and nature and reveal to us the mysteries of love, laughter and tears.

Shakespeare's literary achievement represents a peak in man's creative thinking: it is of "the best that has been said and thought in the world"—to know this is culture according to Matthew Arnold, for he regards literature (the best that has been said and thought in the world) as the type of culture. It is in this broad sense of human enrichment and accomplishment that Shakespeare is a symbol of culture and not in any time-bound or nation-bound sense.

But Shakespeare is more than a symbol; he was a man of flesh and blood who led a hectic life of body and mind. We cannot, however, totally ignore a line of thinking which argues that the works assigned to Shakespeare were actually composed by Francis Bacon, or some other educated person of rank. Now this must come as a shock to any Shakespeare-lover; but instead of enquiring into this approach directly, we shall postpone it until we have seen what knowledge we can gather about his life.

2. Life

Anyone looking for reliable historical information about Shakespeare is bound to meet with disappointment. We get very little help from his contemporaries in the form of recorded reference allusion, or memoirs, Shakespeare himself is completely silent about himself, and as regards his works, he has consumed himself into them so perfectly that it is very risky to draw any clear inferences from his works—except, perhaps, the sonnets, some of which, departing from the convention, appear to be expressing personal experience. We do, however, get some definite information from the parish register, legal documents and town records.

At first sight, it may appear astonishing that such a great writer as Shakespeare should have received no notice from his contemporaries and that no attempt should have been made to preserve every bit of the records associated with his life. But a second look at the state of affairs and attitude to biography prevailing in that period will mollify our uneasiness. The Elizabethans, generally, were indifferent to biographical and autobiographical notes and memoirs; even the biography of the most important personage, Queen Elizabeth herself, is full of gaps and guesses. It should, in fact, be gratifying that we possess more of authentic information about Shakespeare than about any of his contemporary writers excepting Ben Jonson. Moreover, Shakespeare, until very late in his life, was a very ordinary individual belonging to the socially unwelcome profession of actor; and the playwrights, too, were not much distinguished in the society. The critical response to his work was not unmixed high praise until the end of the eighteenth century. It was only in the beginning of the nineteenth century that Shakespeare became established as a great writer who must be spoken of with a feeling of reverence. But during the intervening centuries, he had been steadily moving towards the highest position, and as this process advanced, his admirers became overenthusiastic to complete his biography. The result was an infusion of a great deal of guesswork aggrandisement and romanticising. In such a situation, the best policy will be to keep close to the attested facts and reasonable inferences, except in cases where a highly dubious anecdote may, nevertheless, indicate some important turn in the dramatist's life.

Our author, William Shakespeare—the surname is found spelled in various other ways, which was not unusual in those days—was the son of John Shakespeare of Stratford-on-Avon. In 1556 John Shakespeare bought a house in Henley Street. In 1552, he, along with two neighbours, had been fined for keeping an unauthorized dunghill on Henley Street, which means he had been dwelling there for some years before he bought the house. In 1557 he married Mary Arden, the daughter of Robert Arden, a land-owning farmer who lived in Wilmcote, a small village two miles from Stratford. Mary brought with her an inheritance of sixty acres of land.

In those days, Stratford-on-Avon was an important urban centre in Warwickshire. The south-eastern half of Warwickshire, lying between the Avon and Edgehill, was covered with open fields, producing large quantity of corn and other agricultural goods, the other half, to the north-west of Avon, was deep woodland with its pastoral settlements: this was the Forest of Arden, so beautifully pictured by Shakespeare in *As You Like It* (and not the Forest of Arden, i.e. Ardennes of France). G.M. Trevelyan in his *English Social History* has commented on this unique situation:

> Thus the winding Avon, spanned by Stratford's famous bridge of 'fourteen arches of stone', divided the lonely forest from the populous cornlands. One born and bred in the town upon its banks saw, in his boyhood's

rambles, what was best in wild nature on one side of the river, and what was most characteristic of man upon the other.

John Shakespeare was a glove maker and dealer in wool, he may have at one time or another, pursued some other trades as well. He was a prosperous citizen of Stratford and one of its notables. Prior to 1566, he was assigned various municipal functions with, it may be assumed, corresponding advancement of his financial status: he was one of the "tasters" of the borough of Stratford, he served as a juror, a constable, and an assessor of fines, in 1561 he was associated with the superintendence of municipal finances; and in 1566 he was elected Alderman. He entered the highest municipal office, that of High Bailiff (mayor in modern terms) in 1568 and in 1571 when his term came to an end, he was chosen Chief Alderman to the High Bailiff.

John Shakespeare, although a man of property and high social status, still belonged to the yeoman class and had no right to call himself a gentleman, i.e. member of the gentry. He applied to the College of Heralds for a coat of arms and for upranking in 1576. He did not succeed. Around 1577, his financial condition began to deteriorate rapidly for which there is sufficient proof, but the cause is unknown and the reasons, including recusancy, advanced by scholars cannot be asserted with certainty.

In the year of William Shakespeare's birth, however, his father was a prosperous businessman who was also a man of substance and of social standing. William, the third and surviving child of John and Mary Shakespeare was baptized on 26 April 1564. Allowing the usual period of three days between birth and baptism, it is generally assumed that William Shakespeare was born on 23 April 1564, which is also the day of the feast of St. George, the patron saint of England—and this is also the day on which Shakespeare breathed his last. The Shakespeares had five more children. It requires no documentary evidence to say that Shakespeare during his childhood observed and absorbed the life of town and village surging all around him and, possessing a rare talent, he stored in his mind sights, sounds, scenes and characters, which, combined with his experience of London, would prove a rich material at the forge of his creativity, when he came to write poems and plays.

There is no valid reason to doubt that William was enrolled in the local grammar school when he was six or seven years old. His father was still a prominent citizen and an important member of the borough councing. But the school records for the period are not available. Nicholas Rowe, who brought out the first edited collection of Shakespeare's plays, wrote in his introduction that the boy studied in a free school where "it is probable, he acquired what Latin he was master of, but the narrowness of his circumstances, and the want of his assistance at home, forced his father to withdraw him from thence, and unhappily prevented his further proficiency in that language". John Aubrey a seventeenth-century antiquarian and biographer, in his *Brief Lives* published posthumously in 1813, informs us that Shakespeare had been a school master in a country school.

Whatever the truth, the dramatist at least in two places makes specific references to items in the school curriculum. In *The Merry Wives of Windsor*, Act IV, Sc.l, Mrs. Page complaints to Sir Hugh Evans that her son, William "profits nothing in the world at his book". Sir Hugh then proceeds to ask the boy some questions on Latin words and declensions of the pronouns *hie* and *qui*—the kind of things that a grammar school boy would learn from the course book, *Grammatica Latina* by Lily. The syllabus also included some Latin literature: Terence, Plautus, Virgil, Ovid, Baptista Spagnuoli. There is a reference to Spagnuoli in *Love's Labour's Lost* and to Ovid's *Metamorphoses* in *Titus Andronicus*, Irving Ribner is inclined to the view that such allusions to Elizabethan school books reflect "Shakespeare's recent experience in teaching from these books, rather than as his less likely recollection of them from his own days in the Stratford grammar school". What Shakespeare was doing after completing his school education, or after being withdrawn from school, is anybody's guess. The most convincing possibility is that he would have been apprenticed to his father's trade or might have started a new line in business.

There is, however, no confusion regarding his early marriage to Anne Hathaway, who was about eight years his senior. There is another snag: Anne was already pregnant at the time of marriage and this, in the lack of definite background information, has given rise to a lot of speculation. Shakespeare and Anne may have lived together on the basis of the marriage contract before the actual ceremony. One thing that can be safely inferred is that Shakespeare was an impetuous and highly romantic young man and this conclusion gets ample support in the essential nature of all his writings—they are romantic through and through. There might also have been some foul play or coercion.

On 28 November 1582, the Bishop of Worcester (Stratford was in the diocese of Warcester) issued a licence authorizing the marriage of 'William Shakespeare' and 'Anne Hathaway of Stratford' after one asking of banns rather than the customary three. On 26th May 1583, their first issue Susanna was baptized in Stratford and two years later, the twins, Hamnet and Judith were born and christened on 2 February 1585. Of these children of Shakespeare, Hamnet died in 1596, Susanna married a physician named John Hall and inherited a major portion of her father's assets, Judith married Thomas Quiney.

The period from 1585 to 1592 in Shakespeare's life is known as the "dark years" or "lost years" from the biographer's point of view. For this period we have no authentic information about the family apart from a single reference to John Shakespeare in 1588 in connection with a legal dispute over a sum of money. There is, however, no dearth of legend and hearsay. According to Nicholas Rowe, Shakespeare incurred the wrath of the local landlord, Sir Thomas Lucy for stealing deer in his park and was, as a result, obliged to flee to London. John Aubrey, in his *Brief Lives*, wrote that Shakespeare in his younger years had been a school master; his informant was William Beaston, whose father had been an actor in Shakespeare's company. There are many other conjectures: he worked as a clerk in a lawyer's office; was a scrivener; did soldiering in the Low Countries; visited Italy. Any one or more of such guesses may be true; but apart from these, what sounds most credible is that Shakespeare attached himself to one of the touring theatrical companies that visited the countryside during the period under consideration. Three such companies, the Earl of Worcester's Men, the Earl of Oxford's Men and the Earl of Essex's Men, were giving performances at Stratford in 1581 and in 1585 the town people were entertained by an unidentified company. In 1587, the year in which Shakespeare most probably left his hometown, the Earl of Essex's Men and the Earl of Leicester's Men were in Stratford; he might have accompanied one of these groups to London.

Judging by the quality and magnitude of his achievement, we can be fairly certain that Shakespeare, as a young man, was fully aware of the poetic talent lodged within him and he must have been fired by the ambition to do great things in literature. Like Milton in the next century, he must have resolved to go beyond the existing models. In order to accomplish his aim, the poet was prepared to take all the necessary pains. In dedicating his first poem *Venus and Adonis* to Henry Wrio-thesley, the young Earl of Southampton, Shakespeare vowed "to take advantage of all idle hours, till I have honoured you with some graver labour." By that time he had already taken a big step. In the midst of financial and other problems besetting the family, joining a company of actors must have appealed to Shakespeare as a good expedient because it would bring some wages as well as give him an access to the literary world of London. And it is also likely that his decision to become an actor must have disturbed his father who had with great effort gained social respectability; it might even have caused temporary estrangement between father and son—actors were commonly regarded as a disreputable lot.

The other more unfavourable reports may not be grounded in truth, but they too, are not devoid of significance to a biographer. They suggest something important. Again from the nature and tenor of Shakespeare's oevre, the circumstances of his marriage and his departure for London—from all these, it is not unreasonable to infer that Shakespeare was a highly romantic adventurous youth. It is, therefore, quite probable that he got himself involved in some misadventure, rash action, social scandal, or personal shock. One does not leave one's home, wife and children just for a whim unless it be an overpowering passion or ambition.

However, any such suggestion of a seemingly negative factor in the life of our author is anathema to most Shakespeare scholars and they react to it angrily; they dismiss the unflattering reports as idle gossip and replace them by idealising—even idolising—speculation without actually dispelling any bit the darkness of the "dark years". This attitude of the adoring scholars since the days of Coleridge has completely plugged the possibility of any fresh conjecture based on a negative event in the poet's life; and yet, as evidenced in the life of many a great writer, it is often a tragic experience, or a wound in the psyche, that provides the necessary heat required for the flowering of the creative genius. Shakespeare's moving treatments of human anguish and suffering as well as evil and fate are best explained by assuming that he had himself taken a deep blow some time, somewhere and his songs of joy, his celebration of life, are, to be interpreted as testimony of his power to turn grief into gold. Furthermore, his portrayal of the masses and low and lowly characters along with their doings indicates that he must have been subject to the rough and tumble of life. The story that Shakespeare's first employment in London was to wait outside the play house and tend the horses of those that had no servants may be mere gossip, but what it purports is perfectly sensible: that he must have been engaged in an ordinary job which placed him at a vantage point enabling him to observe closely every variety of people and manners, both low and high. No biography of Shakespeare can be regarded as satisfactory that chooses to gloss over his immersion into the boiling cauldron of Elizabethan society, it was his knowledge and experience of life that made him "naturally learned" and not his talent alone.

By 1592 Shakespeare's struggle had begun to bear fruit; in that year he was worthy enough to arouse the jealousy of another playwright, Robert Greene, one of the University Wits. In a letter addressed to his fellow writers and appended to a pamphlet called *Greene's Groatsworth of Wit Bought with a Million of Repentance* he made a scurrilous attack on Shakespeare for presuming to be not only an actor but the best playwright:

> Yes trust them not: for there is an upstart crow beautified with our feathers, that with his tiger's heart wrapped in a player's hide, supposes he is as well able to bombast out a blank verse as the best of you: and being an absolute Johannes fac totem, is in his own conceit the only Shake-scene in a country.

The phrase "tiger's heart wrapped in a player's hide" is a parody of a line from Duke of York's speech in Shakespeare's *King Henry the Sixth, Part Three*, Act I, Scene IV, which runs: "O tiger's heart wrapp'd in a woman's hide. This makes it fairly certain that Shake-scene is a sarcastic reference to Shakespeare. It is clear that by 1592 Shakespeare had established himself in London as an actor and dramatist: he had completed at least the three plays comprising the *Henry VI* trilogy; he had also probably been improving and retouching existing plays and there might have been some talk of his writing then in progress. Some scholars have argued that he had also completed or was about to complete *The Two Gentlemen of Verona, The Comedy of Errors, The Taming of the Shrew, Richard III, Titus Andronicus* and *Love's Labour's Lost.*

The next year, 1593, saw the publication of a long narrative poem, *Venus and Adonis,* with a signed dedication to Henry Wriothesley, the third Earl of Southampton: "Your Honour's in all duty, William Shakespeare". In the following year came out another poem, *The Rape of Lucrece,* also dedicated to the same lord. This was the period during which the London theatres remained closed on account of the plague; that Shakespeare did not waste his time, but was busy writing poetry shows with what earnestness he pursued his aim of achieving literary renown. He had also started writing his sonnets during this period and some scholars have suggested that the group of sonnets addressed to a young man had the Earl of Southampton for their inspirator.

The theatres reopened in 1594 and staging of plays including some by Shakespeare began. We find that he is already an important member of Lord Chamberlain's company as disclosed by the following entry in the Chamber Accounts:

> To William Kemp, William Shakespeare, and Richard Burbage, servants to the Lord Chamberlain, upon the Council's warrant dated at Whitehall 15 March 1594 (-5) for two several comedies or interludes showed by them before her Majesty in Christmas time last past, viz. upon St. Stephen's day and Innocent's day, £ 13 6s, 8d., and by way of her Majesty's reward £ 6 13 s, 4d.

From recorded references, allusions and lists of actors prefixed to printed plays, we gather that Shakespeare continued to act on the stage at least up to 1603 and if we rely on his fellow-actors, John Heminge and Henry Condell, who edited the First Folio edition of his plays in 1623, up to 1611. He is said to have played kingly roles including the Ghost in *Hamlet* but he also acted the part of old servant Adam in *As You Like* It. According to Aubrey, he "did act exceedingly well".

All the while, Shakespeare was making steady progress in writing plays and in earning money and fame. During 1595-96, five of his new plays were produced: *Richard II, Romeo and Juliet, King John, A Midsummer Night's Dream*, and *The Merchant of Venice*. During the latter year there was a tragedy in the family: his only son Hamnet died in August 1596. In the same year, there was some more trouble for Shakespeare: according to a reference discovered by Leslie Hotson in 1931, one William Wayt claimed sureties of the peace against William Shakespeare and some other persons including Francis Langley then owner of the Swan Theatre. But his financial position was quite sound. He was living in a large house in Bishopsgate as the tax-rolls indicate, perhaps his family also stayed with him for brief periods. There is evidence of his purchase of property in London and in his hometown. On 20 October 1596 John Shakespeare was granted a coat of arms which gave him and his descendants the right to call themselves gentlemen. The motto chosen was *Non sanz droict*, meaning 'not without right'—which, again, suggests some hurdle, some personal, social or religious problem: hence the implied challenge to the slanderers. It may be recalled that John Shakespeare's application for coat of arms on an earlier occasion had been allowed to lapse; but this time his son's personal influence must have been at work.

While living in London, Shakespeare appears to have maintained good links with his native place and its people. His narrative poems had been printed by Richard Field who had migrated from Stratford. In 1597 Shakespeare bought the largest house in Stratford, called New Place, from William Underhill for a sum of £ 60. On 25 October 1598, Richard Quiney a Stratford man who was visiting London wrote a letter to Shakespeare requesting a loan of £ 30. In 1599 the famous actor, Richard Burbage and his brother Cuthbert set up a new playhouse on the Bankside, called the Globe. Since they could not finance the project on their own, they invited some other members of their company, Lord Chamberlain's Men, to become shareholders. Shakespeare thus became a part-owner of the Globe, entitled to ten per cent of the profits. He enjoyed the unique privilege of being a dramatist, actor and businessman.

By 1598 Shakespeare had risen to a great height of fame as a poet and dramatist with several poems and plays to his credit—so distinguished that one could think of comparing him with the great writers of Rome. Francis Meres, a highly educated clergyman living in London, wrote in his book, *Palladis Tamia* that the soul of Ovid lived in "Mellifluous and honey-tongued Shakespeare", that as Plautus and Seneca were regarded the best Roman writers of comedy and tragedy, so Shakespeare among the English "is the most excellent in both kinds for the stage".

During the period 1597-99 six more plays comprising comedies and plays on English history were produced: *Merry Wives of Windsor, Much Ado About Nothing, As You Like It, Henry IV-Part One, Henry IV-Part Two*, and *Henry V*, and probably *Julius Caesar* also had its first staging in 1599.

The new century opened with a personal tragedy to Shakespeare: his father died in 1601. It also brought him to the threshold of his tragic vision—the truest and profoundest ever presented to a theatre audiences and to the readers of the world. Before the death of Queen Elizabeth in 1603, the greatest tragedy of personal dilemma *Hamlet* had its first performance. His finest comedy, *Twelfth Night* and the 'problem play' *Troilus and Cressida* were also produced before 1603. With the accession of King James to the English throne, Lord Chamberlain's Men, evidently regarded as the best company of actors, was taken under royal patronage and was renamed King's Men. The letters patent issued on 19 May 1603 mention William Shakespeare along with some other members of the company including Heminge and Condell, the future editors of the first edition of his *Collected Plays*. The actors of the company became eligible to special privileges; records indicate that they were often called upon to present plays before the Court and to participate in royal pageats and procession—several Shakespeare plays were performed at the Court. In March 1604, when King James made a 'royal proceeding' through the city of London, Shakespeare—as well as each of his fellow players—was given four yards of red cloth for his livery.

On the plane of worldly affairs too, Shakespeare was faring very well. In May 1602 he purchased one hundred and seven acres of arable land in the parish of old Stratford and in September he acquired a cottage in Chapel Lane, Stratford-on-Avon. A fellow actor, Augustine Phillipps, when he made his will in May 1605, mentioned Shakespeare first among the recipients of his bequests of gold pieces: "I give and bequeath to my fellow, William Shakespeare, a thirty-shilling piece in gold." Two years later in 1607 his favourite daughter Susanna, married the physician John Hall and in February 1608 their daughter Elizabeth was born. It is almost certain that Edmond Shakespeare whose burial is recorded in the registers of the Church of St. Saviours in Southwark was the poet's brother. Shakespeare's mother died in 1608.

There is an interesting piece of information about Shakespeare's social activity around the year 1604, furnished by a case, Bellott vs. Mountjoy, of 1612. At that time Shakespeare was living in the house of Christopher Mountjoy, a maker of head-dresses. Mountjoy's one-time apprentice, Stephen Bellott, married the former's daughter on 19 November 1604 on the condition that he would receive a dowry of £ 60 and also a bequest of £ 200 in Mountjoy's will. Shakespeare was one of the match-makers. Eight years later, Bellott feared that Mountjoy was squandering his money and nothing would be left to pay the bequest: hence the lawsuit. In his attestation Shakespeare identified himself as

> William Shakespeare of Stratford upon Avon, in the Country of Warwick, gentleman, of the age of forty-eight years or thereabouts, sworn and examined the day and year above said, deposeth and saith.

Shakespeare cleverly stated that he was a witness to the contract in 1604 but did not remember the amount Mountjoy had promised to bequeath to Bellott. Shakespeare signed his name clearly at the bottom of the statement. We also know from this deposition that in 1612 Shakespeare was living in Stratford.

In the theatre world, too, Shakespeare had won recognition as a great craftsman and a sagacious writer—a master of the dramatic art, even before his great tragedies came into public view. An index of his stature as a playwright is provided by the curious history of a manuscript known as *The Book of Sir Thomas More* to which Shakespeare made an addition probably around 1601. The original text of this stage-play (which was neither staged nor printed during Shakespeare's lifetime) was written by Antony Munday. Since the play contained political matter including the subject of insurrection, it became a sensitive issue for the Master of the Revels, Sir Edmund Tilney, who repeatedly called for revision. Some other writers were therefore invited to improve the draft. Each assisting author wrote his contribution in his own hand, and we have the specimens designated as Hands A, B, C, D and E. It is argued that hand D is that of Shakespeare, adding three autographed pages in a scene in which Sir Thomas More makes a long speech to a crowd of turbulent citizens. Shakespeare's authorship of this addition is established on the basis of style of writing, spelling and literary evidence, the last of which according to Harrison, is the strongest for "the crowd scenes in Sir Thomas More can be paralleled closely with other crowd scenes in Shakespeare's own plays".

In Shakespeare's literary output, the period 1604-1608 is the period of great tragedies: *Othello, Macbeth, King Lear, Antony and Cleopatra* and *Cariolanus*. The other plays first produced during this period are: *Measure for Measure, All is Well That Ends Well* and *Timon of Athens*. Some scholars, however, believe that *All's Well That Ends Well* is an early play, perhaps *Love's Labour's Won*, (no copies of the play are known to have survived, mentioned by Francis Meres in his *Palladis Tamia* (1598).

In 1608 the King's Men took over the Blackfriars, an indoor theatre where Henry Evans's children's company had been staging plays since 1600. Shakespeare thus began writing plays for both Blackfriars and the Globe. He appears to have adjusted himself to the conditions and upper class audiences at the Blackfriars. Otherwise too, Shakespeare about this time had emerged from the inferno of human and supernatural evil. He had explored the genesis, nature, working and consequences of evil and expressed them in the best of utterance. Now in the last phase of his career, he turned to superior kinds of solutions. Evil keeps raising its head, but it is confronted by higher human nature and is overthrown without waste or destruction. This is the tenor of his last plays: *Pericles, Cymbeline, The Winter's Tale,* and *The Tempest*.

William Shakespeare had made his life a grand success: whatever wrongs, malice, envy or injury he had suffered were behind him; he had become rich and respected; thousands of human hearts had been moved to laughter and tears by the magic of his lines; he had learnt the last lesson in human wisdom.

Around 1611 Shakespeare contentedly retired to Stratford. His remaining two younger brothers, Gilbert and Richard died in 1612 and 1613 respectively. John Combe, one of his closest friends also died in 1613 leaving him a bequest of £ 5. On

10 March 1613, he bought the Blackfriar's Gate House.

Shakespeare did not break his relations completely with his company; he also kept visiting London from time to time. The last two plays which he wrote in collaboration with John Fletcher are *Henry VIII* and *The Two Noble Kinsmen*, but his heart wasn't there; they suffer in execution and in imaginative power. Shakespeare's health began to deteriorate after 1613. According to one report some time in 1616 Drayton and Ben Jonson came down to visit him and they had a merry meeting. His will was drawn up in January 1616. Since his younger daughter Judith got married to Thomas Qiney on 10 February the will was revised and executed by him on 25 March.

In his will, Shakespeare bequeathed nearly all his property to his elder daughter Susanna Hall and her husband; Judith his younger daughter received very little in comparison. Perhaps Shakespeare was not happy with Judith's marriage to Thomas Quiney about whom there was some scandal, or, he feared any fixed assets made over to her would not remain secure, but he made provision for yearly payment of some money to her. This apparent lack of balance on the part of Shakespeare is bound to remind us of his own creation King Lear.

Another matter which causes surprise is the bequest to his wife, She is not mentioned by name and Shakespeare appears to have added one sentence about her as an afterthought: "I give unto my wife my second best bed with the furniture". Those who defend Shakespeare on this issue argue that the best bed in the house would be reserved for guests, that he gave her the second best bed because it carried past associations since this must have been the bed the couple used to sleep in. It is also true that Anne's dower rights already stood protected by law; she must have continued to live in New Place until her death in 1623. And yet, when all this has been said, one cannot help feeling that this slighting gesture on the part of Shakespeare indicates that something had gone sour in their relations.

He left something to each of his relations: niece Elizabeth Hall, sister Joan and her three sons; he did not forget his friends and the poor of Stratford, to whom he bequeathed ten pounds. It is to be noted that he gave 26s. 8d. each to his former fellow actors, John Heminge, Richard Burbage and Henry Condell for buying mourning rings.

Shakespeare died on 23 April, 1616, but Death could not be proud of this, for in black ink his name still shines bright. A monument representing the poet in the act of writing with a quill was installed some time between his death and the year 1623. This is the famous bust with which the whole world has become familiar. The other authentic likeness is Martin Droeshout's engraving on the title page of the First Folio *Collection of Shakespeare's Plays*, which is equally familiar to readers. The epitaph inscribed under the bust praises Shakespeare as a writer.

> With whome
> Quick nature dide; whose name doth deck this tombe
> Far more than cost, sith all yt He hath writ
> Leaves living art, but page, to serve his witt.

3. Sweet Shakespeare

Those who knew Shakespeare during his lifetime and those who gathered information about him after his death generally allude to his sweet nature, affability and handsome personality. And sweetness is the virtue equally well applied to his poetry by various commentators. It is true that the first comment that has come down to us is full of venom, but Henry Chettle, who had been instrumental in the publication of Robert Greene's pamphlet apologized for the attack as if it had been his fault. Referring to Shakespeare, he wrote in the Preface to his *Kind-Harts Dreame*;

> ....myself have seen his demeanor no less civil than he excellent in the qualities he professes: Besides diverse of worship have reported his uprightness of dealing, which argues his honesty, and his facetious grace in writing, that approves his art.

This clearly indicates that Shakespeare was not only found to be a decent person and a good writer by Chettle, but he was also held in high esteem by many respectable citizens of London—and that was as early as 1592.

We have already noted that Francis Menes in 1598 declared that Shakespeare was as great in English drama as Plautus and Seneca among the Roman authors. He observed that "the sweet witty soul" of Ovid lived in "mellifluous and honey-tongued Shakespeare". In 1602, when Shakespeare was still alive and active in the theatre world, a barrister named John Manningham recorded in his diary an anecdote in which Richard Burbage is outmanoeuvred by William Shakespeare. The story is perhaps no more than a fabricated joke, but it is eloquent in telling the reader how people wished Shakespeare to be a winner.

The First Folio edition of Shakespeare's plays published in 1623—just seven years after his death—is prefaced with memorial poems by several persons. Referring the reader to the picture of Shakespeare, one poem begins:

> This Figure, that thou here seest put,
> It was for gentle Shakespeare cut

Ben Jonson in his tribute spoke rightly of Shakespeare's natural gift and his art and called him "my gentle Shakespeare" and "sweet swan of Avon". And even in his notes and casual comments published after his death, where he called attention to Shakespeare's lapses, he spoke endearingly about the man; he remarked that he loved the man and honoured his memory, adding that "he was (indeed) honest, and of an open and free nature: had an excellent phantasy; brave notions, and gentle expression."

In the next century, John Aubrey in his notes on Shakespeare tells us that the poet was "a handsome, well-shaped man: very good company, and of a very ready and pleasant smooth wit." This information was conveyed to Aubrey by William Beeston, whose father had been one of Shakespeare's fellow actors. The first brief biography of the dramatist was written by Nicholas Rowe who included it in the introduction to his famous edition of Shakespeare's collected plays published in 1709. His chief source was a famous actor and also a dramatist of the Restoration period, Thomas Betterton, who personally visited Stratford-on-Avon for gathering information. Rowe writes:

> Besides the advantages of his wit, he was in himself a good-natured man, of great sweetness in his manners, and a most agreeable companion; so that it is no wonder, if, with so many good qualities, he made himself acquainted with the best conversations of those times.

Rowe's Edition may be said to have proclaimed Shakespeare—what he had already become in the public mind—a classic. Thereafter the man and his works became coalesced into a single whole, specially in the imagination of the poets who felt inspired to write poems about him. Milton opens his poem "On Shakespeare" with the affectionate reference "my Shakespeare" and avers that the marvellous experience imparted by his art is the best monument to him:

> Thou in our wonder and astonishment
> Hast built thyself a livelong monument.

And in "L'Allegro" Milton implores the spirit of mirth to take him

> Then to the well-trod stage anon,
> If Jonson's learned sock be on,
> Or sweetest Shakespeare, fancy's child,
> Warble his native wood-notes wild.

To Mathew Arnold Shakespeare is an embodiment of the highest wisdom; he is the kindly spirit of life which knows man's limitations and remains unassailable:

> Others abide our question. Thou art free.
> We ask and ask. Thou smilest and art still,
> Out-topping knowledge.

4. Anti-Stratfordians

After gaining so much knowledge about Shakespeare, is it not disturbing to be told that the plays generally assigned to Shakespeare were written not by him but by another more learned individual? Since the mooting of this idea a number of candidates have been sponsored for the authorship of Shakespeare's plays: Francis Bacon, Christopher Marlowe, Edward de Vere (Earl of Oxford), Queen Elizabeth and William Stanley (Earl of Derby).

Many scholars have reacted to the anti-Stratfordian proposals with great resentment. Referring to these ideas in his book, *Introducing Shakespeare*, Harrison asserted it as a fact that "so far no reputable scholar with first-hand knowledge of the Elizabethan age and its literature has ever supported the claim". S. Schoenbaum, a noted Shakespeare scholar, sarcastically observes: "Shakespeare never proceeded to university, a consideration that has prompted anti-Stratfordian fantasies respecting the authorship of the canon, as has the fact that blue blood did not course in his veins." George Sampson in *The Concise Cambridge History of English Literature* is equally acerbic:

> ...The cranks who have declared that the plays of Shakespeare are too good for an actor to have written have never noticed that they are too bad for a Lord Chancellor to have written. What we know definitely about Shakespeare's education is that he studied in two great seats of learning, the theatre and the world.

The statements cited above, apart from angry protest, contain sound points for the rejection of the anti-Stratfordian position. Readers will also be able to form their own judgement from the foregoing pages in which an account of Shakespeare's life, character and fame has been presented on the basis of recorded evidence and reliable information. Ben Jonson and several other contemporaries knew Shakespeare of Stratford personally as the author of the plays. In less than seven years after his death, a bust of the poet was set up and this solid likeness caused no surprise. The First Folio edition of Shakespeare's plays was issued in 1623 when scores of writers and play goers who had seen him must have been alive; the plays were collected by his former theatre associates, Heminge and Condell, whom he had mentioned in his will in 1616. Several of his plays had been printed under his name during his lifetime and nobody raised any doubts. By 1602, when Queen Elizabeth and Bacon both were alive, Shakespeare had already covered himself with immortal glory, had the plays been authored by any other person, he would have kicked the throne in order to claim the plays. In the face of these grounds if someone says the plays attributed to Shakespeare were not really written by him, he is insisting on the unbelievable.

5. Imagination and the World

Shakespeare in his works has given us a world which strikes us as real and solid—a vast range of characters and situations which bring into operation our empathy and sympathy to the fullest extent so that we begin to feel them from inside and outside. His characters are so real to us that we take them to be men and women of flesh and blood about whom we can talk and argue as if they were our acquaintances.

One such character is Sir John Falstaff whose mysterious personality has been arousing the interest of theatre audiences and readers ever since his creation by Shakespeare. If Nicholas Rowe has reported the truth, then the first person to be impressed by this character was Queen Elizabeth herself; according to him "Elizabeth was so taken with Falstaff that she commanded Shakespeare to continue with him for one more play and show him in love"—and the dramatist obeyed her by writing *The Merry Wives of Windsor*. In 1777 Maurice Morgann published his "Essay on the Dramatic Character of Sir John Falstaff" trying to prove that Sir John was not a coward and in 1796 James White brought out "Original Letters of Sir John, and his friends; now first made public by a Gentleman, a Descendant of Dame Quickly." Similarly, Hamlet, Macbeth, Lady Macbeth, Iago, Othello and a host of other Shakespeare characters exercise our feelings, reason, and imagination as if they had actually lived in this world.

This attitude to character has been regarded by some critics as wrong and false; it is wrong because it sidetracks the central and integrating factor in a Shakespeare play, namely, its poetic conception; and it is false because the characters in Shakespeare in fact do not conform to reality. Everything in a Shakespeare play is invented and characters are as much a part of the poetic design as plot, situation or ideas.

There is no doubt some substance in this argument; yet we somehow feel that the characters of Shakespeare are more lifelike than those of any other playwright. And then how do we account for the reader-audience psychology of treating Shakespeare's characters as real persons and of getting involved in their affairs? The answer is that Shakespeare requires us to reconsider our concept of realism. We must cease thinking in terms of the photographic image because it can capture only the superficial aspect of life—it is even unable to represent a three dimensional object. A human being has not only a face and a figure; he or she is a personality endowed with will, emotion, thoughts, ambition, and a capacity to adopt, yield, withstand, resist, change and grow. To imitate this complexity of human life is no easy task; only a great poet by means of deep realism can 'translate' it into the medium of art—and Shakespeare has done it. He has embodied the vast variety of human nature—from pauper to king, from pure villain to saint, from most selfish to the most selfless, from treacherous to steadfast, from idiot to wise clown—in its essence and in its complexity, in such a way that we have more 'knowledge' for example, about Julius Caesar, the Shakespearean character than about this prototype: Shakespeare's Caesar is more real to us than the historical personage.

There is no doubt that the characters in literature are fictions, just as every man when dead is a fiction, strictly speaking; but these fictions in Shakespeare stand invested with life; these offsprings of his imagination are rooted in life. And the whole process is beautifully described by Shakespeare himself.

The poet's eye, in a fine frenzy rolling,
Doth glance from heaven to earth, from earth to heaven;
And as imagination bodies forth
The forms of things unknown, the poet's pen
Turns them to shapes, and gives to airy nothing
A local habitation and a name.

(*A Midsummer Night's Dream,* **Act V, I**)

Shakespeare is a master painter of human passions, longings and wishes that inhabit the deep recesses of the mind and provided the motive force for action. Be it feelings of love, hatred and disgust, jealousy, sorrow or joy—they all find their supreme utterance in his plays and poetry. The story of Romeo and Juliet had been known already, but the youthful love received its immortal articulation only when it was dramatised by Shakespeare, and since then its fascination has never grown weaker. Meeting and parting of young lovers receive their classic expression in *Romeo and Juliet*:

Rom. (To Juliet) If I profane with my unworthiest hand
This holy shrine, the gentle fine is this:
My lips, two blushing pilgrims, ready stand
To smooth that rough touch with a tender kiss.

(*Romeo and Juliet,* **Act I, V**)

Jul. Sweet so would I,
Yet I should kill thee with much cherishing
Good night, good night! Parting is such sweet sorrow
That I shall say good night till it be morrow.

(*Romeo and Juliet,* **Act II, III**)

In the comedies we get glimpses of the joyous and sunnier aspects of love and in *Antony and Cleopatra* it becomes the all-engrossing passion of middleaged lovers who are prepared to sacrifice to it everything including their lives. In the sonnets Shakespeare most probably encoded his personal experience of love for it is clear that he is not a respecter of the prevailing convention. He in fact made bold departures from the stereotyped theme and in this connection Sonnet No.144 is of special importance from thematic as well as autobiographical points of view.

King Lear's outbursts against his ungrateful daughters, Goneril and Regan, are well known, and here is Queen Margaret raging at the killer of her husband and son:

No sleep close up that deadly eye of thine
Unless it be while some tormenting dream
Affrights thee with a hell of ugly devils!
Thou elvish mark'd, abortive, rooting hog,
Thou that wast seal'd in the nativity
The slave of nature and the son of hell,
Thou slander of thy heavy mother's womb,
Thou loathed issue of the father's loins,
Thou rag of honour, thou detested—

(*King Richard III,* **Act I, III**)

Othello is not a jealous man by nature but when jealousy is craftily induced in him it poisons his whole being and allows him no rest no respite:

I had been happy if the general camp,
Pioneers and all, had tasted her sweet body,
So I had nothing known. O, now, for ever
Farewell the tranquil mind! Farewell content!
Farewell the plumed troops and the big wars
That makes ambition virtue! O, farewell!
Farewell the neighing steed, and the shrill trump,
The spirit-stirring drum, th'ear piercing fife,
The royal banner, and all quality,
Pride, pomp and circumstance of glorious war!
And, O ye mortal engines, whose rude throats
Th' immortal Jove's dread clamours counterfeit,
Farewell! Othello's occupation's gone.

(*Othello,* **Act III, III**)

Man's sorrows, common and personal, received their inimitable expression in Shakespeare's work; no writer has so far equalled him in the poignancy, poetic power and depth of his utterances on this theme. When Antony dies, Cleopatra realises that everything of value has gone:

Cleo. Noblest of man, woo't die?
Hast thou no care of me? Shall I abide
In this dull world, which in thy absence is
No better than a sty? O, see, my women,

(Antony dies)

The crown O' th'earth doth melt, My lord!
O, wither'd is the garland of the war,
The soldier's pole is fall'n! Young boys and girls
Are level now with men. The odds is gone,
And there is nothing left remarkable
Beneath the visiting moon.

(*Antony and Cleopatra,* **Act V, I**)

A much deeper sorrow resides in Lear's simple lament over Cordelia lying dead in his arms:

And my poor fool is hang'd! No, no, no life!
Why should a dog, a horse, a rat have life,

And thou no breath at all? Thou'lt come no moro,
Never, never, never, never, never.

(*King Lear*, Act V, III)

Man's earthly existence is beset by many kinds of ills and vagaries of forces beyond his control; Shakespeare's characters reflect on them in their moments of sorrow and pain and their reflections put us in a pensive mood. But greater than these, is death and still greater, the fear of what may follow death. In the words of Claudio:

The weariest and most loathed worldly life
That age, ache, penury, and imprisonment,
Can lay on nature is a paradise
To what we fear of death.

(*Measure for Measure*, Act III, I)

And here is Hamlet on the dreadful mystery:

Who would fardels bear,
To grunt and sweat under a weary life,
But that the dread of something after death,
The undiscovered country from whose bourn
No traveller returns, puzzles the will.
And makes us rather bear those ills we have
Than fly to others that we know not of?

(*Hamlet*, Act III, I)

At the other end of the spectrum we call life, lie joy and gaiety. Shakespeare's powerful fancy, naturally inclined to soaring flights, often transports us to dreamlands where all is love, mirth and sunshine. Not that malice, lust and greed have altogether vanished, they are always visible, even present, but they are kept under check or rendered harmless. Some people have criticised Shakespeare for his forced syphoning off of evil, but it may be said in his defence that he knew life better; beacuase in real life every situation has a comic and a tragic potentiality and chance is a deciding factor more often than we believe.

Shakespeare is most inventive in exploiting comic possibilities such as confusing similarity of appearance, disguise, cleverness and wit, simplicity, eccentricity and idosyncrasy, buffonnery and wise clowning, mischance, and many other devices. These no doubt afford us fun and make us laugh, but the deep feeling of joy is provided in situations where men and nature meet in happy camaraderie. For this felicity Shakespeare moves the action to a forest where nature is beautiful and benignant and the rigours of weather seem a light matter as compared to the evils of human society. We are rewarded with beautiful natural descriptions and lovely songs, which are rare things in world literature. The woods are more free from peril than the envious court,

And this our life, exempt from public haunt,
Finds tongues in trees, books in the running brooks,
Sermons in stones, and good in every thing:
I would not change it.

(*As You Like It*, Act II, I)

Nature was still fresh and fair and a good deal of "merry England" remained. Shakespeare evidently had fully enjoyed the company of nature: he is so familiar with the flora and fauna—knows their shapes and sounds intimately. He also knows well the chores of pastoral life. And he possessed an imagination so fertile that it could weave the objects and creatures of nature in haunting patterns of beauty. In *A Midsummer Night's Dream*, Lysander discloses to Helena that he and Hermia would steal to the woods at night when "Phoebe doth behold/ Her silver visage in the wat'ry glass,/Decking with liquid pearl the bladed grass", and Hermia reminds her of the faint primrose beds on which both the girls used to lie, "Emptying our bosoms of their counsel sweet". Answering Puck's question where she was wandering, a fairy, in her natural language of music and poetry, replies:

Over hill, over dale,
Thorough bush, thorough brier,
Over park, over pale,
Thorough flood, thorough fire,
I do wander everywhere,
Swifter than the moon's sphere;
And I serve the Fairy Queen,
To dew her orbs upon the green.
The cowslips tall her pensioners be;
In their gold coats spots you see;
Those be rubies, fairy favours,
In those freckles live their savours.
I must go seek some dewdrops here,
And hang a pearl in every cowslip's ear.

(*A Midsummer Night's Dream*, Act II, I)

And then we have the songs studded like gems in the plays, in which the lights of nature and love mingle to produce in our heart the prismatic mornings of sweet joy and sweat pain: "Under the Greenwood Tree", "Blow, Blow, Thou Winter Wind", "When That I was and a Little Tiny Boy", "Come Away, Come Away, Death", "Oh Mistress Mine", "Where the Bee Sucks, There Suck I", and many others.

A true product of the Renaissance, Shakespeare was puzzled and fascinated by man and his condition in the universe. To the innocent Miranda who had been brought up in a secluded island, human beings are simply marvellous:

> O, wonder!
> How many goodly creatures are there here!
> How beauteous mankind is ! O brave new world
> That has such people in't.
>
> (*The Tempest*, Act V, I)

To the philosophic mind of Hamlet man is a big riddle—so much glory and yet dust (and dirt):

> What a piece of work
> is a man! How noble in reason! how
> infinite in faculty in form, moving,
> how express and admirable! in action how like
> an angel! in apprehension how like a god!
> the beauty of the world! the paragon of animals!
> And yet, to me, what is this quintessence of dust?
>
> (*Hamlet*, Act II, II)

Confronted with his wife's death, Macbeth, whose overweening ambition had led him into the ways of evil, conceives life cynically as devoid of any meaning:

> Life's but a walking shadow, a poor player
> That struts and frets his hour upon the stage,
> And then is heard no more; it is a tale
> Told by an idiot, full of sound and fury,
> Signifying nothing,
>
> (*Macbeth*, Act V, V)

Finally, Prospero, who had commanded the elements of nature and spirits of the air looks at life from a great height in space and time. Like the things raised by his magic,

> The cloud-capp'd towers, the gorgeous palaces,
> The solemn temples, the great globe itself,
> Yea, all which it inherit, shall dissolve,
> And, like this insubstantial pageant faded,
> Leave not a rack behind. We are such stuff
> As dreams are made on; and our little life
> Is rounded with a sleep,
>
> (*The Tempest*, Act IV, I)

6. The Moral World

Some eighteenth century critics of Shakespeare found him lacking in moral purpose and argued that in drama evil and good ought to be depicted in a different way. "He sacrifices virtue to convenience" wrote Samual Johnson "and is so much more careful to please than to instruct, that he seems to write without any moral purpose". Some say Shakespeare bowed to the demands of the groundlings, while other complain that he held the common people in contempt.

All these charges maybe shown to be applicable at places, but that does not amount to lack of moral purpose, although the moral centre of Shakespeare's world may look quite disconcerting to the conventional mind. Shakespeare's basic commitment is to the realities of life, however unwelcome they may be to us. He appears to be saying to us: Face the sorrows, injustices, evils of human existence, nothing is gained by averting the eyes from what is in front and around you. In his works we find evil getting the upper hand, the virtuous in misery, the simple being duped and mere chance bringing about a tragedy. But can we deny that the same things are true in the human society? Perhaps in the present age, we are in a better position to understand Shakespeare's moral world.

When we look more closely at Shakespeare's tragedies, we discover that he has brought out a fundamental truth about good and evil in this world. Evil is sedulously shown to be self-destructive: it hasn't the slightest chance of survival and abiding success unless it changes its nature—unless there is a change of heart. But in the process of evil's working, so much goodness and so much virtue are destroyed. And that again is an important truth whether we like it or not. Shakespeare in his tragedies is eloquent and most moving in making us aware of what we should value in human life and of how much sacrifice is involved in man's struggle against evil. He is too much of a realist to resort to facile solutions and poetic justice.

And mankind is not without its redeemers: those minor characters in the plays whose motives for succour arise from sympathy, love, charity, loyalty, friendship and abhorrence of evil and inequity—not from any selfish interest. To leave them out of consideration is to distort the picture.

Furthermore, life is not without its joys and its blessings: the experience of love, of beauty in man and nature. In the comedies, evil is absent or overthrown; and music, dance and song, laughter and merriment gladden the heart of man and convince him that there is more to life than tears of sorrow, that it is worthliving. As regards

Shakespeare's attitude to the common people, he was conscious of their good and bad qualities: the cruelty and mindlessness of the degenerate mobs as well as the deep humanity of the simple fold and that is the reality also.

In the last phase of his career, Shakespeare developed a new approach to the problem of evil. In the course of exploring the worst in human nature, he must have realised that evil countered by evil multiplies evil and causes general destruction. Therefore, in the 'romances'—*Pericles, Cymbeline, The Winter's Tale* and *The Tempest*—he put forward a new solution, similar to that preached by the sages of the world. Not that malice, greed, lust and pride have disappeared; no, they are still there, but now they are met with a superior moral force and are neutralised through the agency of children. As David Daiches has noted in his *A Critical History of English Literature*, all these plays "deal in one way or another with evil and innocence, guilt and atonement, uncorrupted youth undoing original sin and starting life afresh".

7. Other Worlds

Most educated people probably no longer believe in the existence of witches and fairies, beings which play a significant role in some of the best plays of Shakespeare. In his time, it was not so. There has come down a story that once, while Marlowe's *Doctor Faustus* was being performed, a certain number of actors impersonating the devils noticed that there was one devil too many, and this caused such a fright that they all dispersed without completing the performance; Edward Alleyn, the famous tragedian, who was acting Doctor Faustus, had to take an early retirement from the stage, on account of this intrusion of a real devil.

Even today, the supernatural world created by Shakespeare retains its dramatic effect and function, although its ontological status is in doubt. In most of the scenes the witches, ghosts and fairies, have a symbolic and psychological meaning; they represent the forces of good and evil as well as the fears and wishes that lie deep below the threshold of consciousness;

> Such tricks hath strong imagination
> That, if it would but apprehend some joy,
> It comprehends some bringer of that joy,
> Or in the night, imagining some fear,
> How easy is a bush supposed a bear?
>
> (*A Midsummer Night's Dream*, Act V, I)

The next leap of the imagination is the supernatural. Secondly these creations are so impressive and some of them so lovable that we do not like to part company with them. Thirdly, their words—even the most sinister—share the magic of Shakespeare's tongue:

> Fair is foul, and foul is fair:
> Hover through the fog and filthy air.

And finally, they remind us that there may exist other worlds, other forms of being besides ours—there may be influences that defy our reason.

8. Shakespeare's Art

Ben Jonson in his memorial poem on Shakespeare wrote:

> Yet must I not give Nature all. Thy Art,
> My gentle Shakespeare, must enjoy a part.

But the art of Shakespeare is such as would not commend itself to the classically minded. He was too steeped in real life to rigorously isolate and rearrange its stuff in a neat pattern. He knew that while a great tragedy is happening, somebody might be joking or singing; he knew that individuals in reality do not live in airtight quarters, other persons and events following their own courses impinge on them, act and react, produce unexpected effects, and thus is woven the intriguing web of life.

His imagination is most fertile and inventive in producing complex plots in which tears and laughter mingle; several strands of life are hooked together in a grand design. And yet his plays retain their unity—most of them. The small play within *Hamlet* is an integral part of the play and like every other device employed by Hamlet serves the purpose of confirming the king's guilt. Given Hamlet's philosophical temperament and the situation, every incident and character in the play has relevance to the central theme of Hamlet's revenge. In *A Midsummer Night's Dream* the stories of the Athenian lovers, rehearsal of a play by the artisans and the quarrel of Oberon and Titania are made to interpenetrate in such a way that to change or remove the one is to destroy the others. The effect of this kind of planning is that the audience get a view of life as it is; they feel that there have been no forced cutting and clipping.

It is true that in some plays Shakespeare's imagination runs to excess, and there what saves the play from failure is powerful character creation and poetry of the highest order. *Cymbeline* has been cited as an example of Shakespeare's badly planned plot: Dr. Johnson severely criticised it for "folly of the fiction, the absurdity of the conduct, the confusion of the names and manners of different times, and the impossibility of the events in any system of life"—and yet the play is safe: quite safe, if for nothing else, for Imogen, who according to the poet Swinburne is "the woman best beloved in all the world of song and all the tide of time", and for the gem of a dirge beginning:

Fear no more the heat o' th' sun
Nor the furious winter's rages,
Thou thy worldly task hast done,
Home art gone and ta'en thy wages.
Golden lads and girls all must,
As chimney sweepers come to dust.
(*Cymbeline*, **Act IV, II**)

As distinguished from high poetry, what unified a Shakespeare plot is its poetic conception. For unity in a play by Shakespeare, we should not concentrate on action, time, place and character (for all these have a disappointing diversity) but on pattern of imagery and symbolism of characters and situations—this is what many modern critics have urged in their in-depth studies of the plays, "A Shakespeare play is a dramatic poem" says L.C. Knights and "its end is to communicate a rich and controlled experience by means of words". According to G. Wilson Knight each play should be regarded "as a visionary whole, close-knit in personification, atmospheric suggestion, and direct poetic symbolism".

9. The Voice of Poetry

Shakespeare was not only "naturally learned", he was also a born poet. Francis Mere's wrote:

> As Epius Stola said, that the Muses would speak with Plautus' tongue, if they would speak Latin, so I say that the Muses would speak with Shakespeare's fine filed phrase, if they would speak English.

Whether he is dealing with sorrow or joy, with love or beauty, with time or death, with nature or human qualities, he provides us with specimens of superb poetry which is the hallmark of the unique Shakespeare touch and which is the most valuable guide for identifying Shakespeare's texts. Many of his sonnets have been favourites of poetry-lovers and anthologists: "Shall I Compare Thee to a Summer's Day?", "When to the Sessions of Sweet Silent Thought", "That Time of Year Thou Mayst in Me Behold", "Let me not to the Marriage of True Minds", and many others. Secondly, who has not felt the charm of scores of lovely songs and lyrics and the pathos of many dirges scattered here and there in the plays? And then there are passages of great poetic power in the dialogues and speeches. In such passages much more than craftsmanship is involved; they take us to the heart of the thing described or to its mystery; when Shakespeare describes something, we more than see it. Let us be content with a few examples:

Now o'er the one half-world
Nature seems dead, and wicked dreams abuse
The curtain'd sleep; now witchcraft celebrates
Pale Hecate's offerings; and wither'd murder,
Alarm'd by his sentinel, the wolf,
Whose howl's his watch, thus with his stealthy pace,
With Tarquin's ravishing strides, towards his design
Moves like a ghost.
(*Macbeth*, **Act II, I**)

Age cannot wither her, nor custom stale
Her infinite variety. Other women cloy
The appetites they feed, but she makes hungry
Where most she satisfies.
(*Antony and Cleopatra*, **Act II, II**)

That strain again! It had a dying fall;
O! it came o'er my ear like the sweet sound
That breathes upon a bank of violets,
Stealing and giving odour.
(*Twelfth Night*, **Act I, I**)

The quality of mercy is not strained;
It droppeth as the gentle rain from heaven
Upon the place beneath; it is twice blest:
It blesseth him that gives, and him that takes;
Tis mightiest in the mightiest; it becomes,
The throned monarch better than his crown.
(*The Merchant of Venice*, **Act IV, I**)

10. Goldmine of Quotables

H.C. Bunner paid his homage to Shakespeare by saying:

Shake was a dramatist of note;
He lived by writing things to quote.

Shakespeare is the greatest single contributor to the hoard of quotables in English—this is easily seen in any book of quotations one may like to consult. And his statements carry a greater weight of truth and insight than those of the other principal contributors, who make their point through word-play, witticism, anticlimax, paradox, facetiousness, or some other superficial device.

Shakespeare supplies us quotations—idiomatic, proverbial, poetic—for a large variety of occasions, moods, temperaments, and also for truths of life, which we find being used consciously or unconsciously by every class of people from learned professors to laymen. But this widespread employment of Shakespeare's quotables has entailed an unintended wrong to the great author himself. For example, we often hear: "Shakespeare has said, 'Frailty, thy name is woman'." In our feminist age, the statement will be regarded scandalous. So let us not forget that it is Hamlet speaking—Hamlet who suspects that his father has been foully done to death and whose mother has married his uncle Claudius in an unseemly haste. We should also not ignore the fact that a Shakespeare character is independent of the author: he lives his own life, feels his own feelings and thinks his own thoughts. He is not like a Shavian creature—shall we say counter—who thinks what Shaw wants him to think. The views of Shakespeare's characters should not be confused with those of Shakespeare himself— at least that is generally true. Let us now turn to a random sampling of quotations taken from Shakespeare. It will be a pleasant pastime to locate them in his works and discover the setting, character and mood involved in each case:

(1) All that glisters (glitters) is not gold.
(2) Sweet are the uses of adversity;
Which, like the toad, ugly and venomous,
Wears yet a precious jewel in his head.
(3) Since brevity is the soul of wit,
And tediousness the limbs and outward flourishes,
I will be brief.
(4) How sharper than a serpent's tooth it is
To have a thankless child.
(5) Thus conscience does make cowards of us all.
(6) Cowards die many times before their deaths; The valiant never taste of death but once.
(7) it is a custom
More honour'd in the breach than the observance.
(8) How far that little candle throws his (its) beams!
So shines a good deed in a naughty world.
(9) The prince of darkness is a gentleman.
(10) The better part of valour is discretion.
(11) The evil that men do lives after them. The good is oft interred with their bones.
(12) What stronger breastplate than a heart untainted!
(13) All the world's a stage,
And all the men and women merely players.
(14) To be or not to be: that is the question:
Whether 'tis nobler in the mind to suffer
The slings and arrows of outrageous fortune,
Or to take arms against a sea of troubles,
And by opposing end them.
(15) There is a tide in the affairs of men,
Which, taken at the flood, leads on to fortune.
Omitted, all the voyage of their life
Is bound in shallows and in miseries.
(16) To thine own self be true,
And it must follow, as the night the day,
Thou canst not then be false to any man.
(17) His speech was like a tangled chain, nothing impaired, but all disordered.
(18) Our doubts are traitors
And make us lose the good we oft might win
By fearing to attempt.
(19) Uneasy lies the head that wears a crown.
(20) For her own person,
It begger'd all description.

11. Prospero

Shakespeare died in 1616 at the age of fiftythree, but he had withdrawn himself from London's theatrical life in around 1611.

Within a period of less than thirty years, he had produced at least 35 plays, two poems and 154 sonnets. He had also been acting on the stage and participating in other affairs of the theatres, the Globe and the Blackfriars. Why he decided to retire early from the stage at the age of fortyseven or thereabouts is not known, but it is clear that the 'composition' of his literary career found its most appropriate finale in the writing of the romances, in which all the earlier themes are present in a happy blend. His imagination had laughed the laughter of carefree lovers, witnessed the tragedy of passionate love, seen the machinations of power politics, like Dante explored the hell of the human heart and, as the mature fruit of these experiences, come to the final conclusion that forgiveness and employment of superior knowledge for benevolent purposes provided a better solution to human ills than revenge and murder—and that is the theme of *The Tempest*. As a writer he had mastered the world of the imagination, held the audiences spellbound, and now (it is most satisfying to think), through the character of Prospero he bids farewell to the stage. Towards the end of his life, Shakespeare—the best and most comprehensive mind that the English race has produced—must have come to the profound realisation that imagination cannot be a substitute for action: it must lead to action, he therefore relinquished the stage in order to practise forgiveness and benevolence that he had embodied in the character of Prospero:

Graves at my command
Have wak'd their sleepers, op'd and let'em forth,
By my so potent art.
But this rough magic
I here abjure: and, when I have requir'd
Some heavenly music which even now I do–
To work mine end upon their senses that
This airy charm is for, I'll break my staff
Bury it certain fathoms in the earth
And deeper than did ever plummet sound
I'll drown my book.

R.S. Sharma

Introduction-II

As the centuries roll on, some names and reputations are ground to dust, and a few emerge with diamond-like purity and clarity. Shakespeare's is one such name. He indeed is the archetypal poet who speaks to us across the manifold barriers of language and religion, of space and time. It is generally thought that the greatness of a genius is recognized by posterity, not by his contemporaries and, what is more, he generally lives in poverty and dies in obscurity. Such indeed has been the fate of many, but Shakespeare is not one of them. He had been recognized by his own peers and others for what he was—a powerful dramatist who produced works of unparalleled excellence not only in the field of drama but in other spheres also, whether it be songs, sonnets or narrative poems. His plays were highly successful on the stage, so that he could buy a share in the company that staged them and also bought land and house in his birthplace. He died one of the most prosperous men of his town. This is proof enough of his fame, social security and the wealth he had acquired.

According to his own time he lived to a ripe old age. He produced such a wealth of plays, poems and sonnets that has not been equaled by any other dramatist of his time. There were many rules and conventions, classical and Elizabethan, literary and performance-wise, that he had to follow. Sometimes he deigned to follow them, as in *The Tempest* and at others, throwing them to the four winds, he wrote with a sovereign disregard for them, yet producing work that has triumphantly stood the test of time. The more one reads his plays, the more do they grow on one-word like "sublimity", "universality", "esemplastic imagination", "defamiliarization", etc. can but catch a few feathers of this unique and immortal phoenix. He remains an enigma.

It should be remembered that he was versatile to an unprecedented extent. He has written plays of all kinds—tragedies, comedies, chronicles and romances. Marlowe, who had the genius to have rivaled him, wrote only tragedies, and Ben Jonson was successful only in satiric comedies. Within the three main varieties of tragedies, comedies and chronicles, there is more variety in Shakespeare than in any other dramatist. All the four main kinds of tragedies can be found in his works, as well as all the varieties of comedy. While speaking of different genres, one should always keep in mind that his plays are far too complex to be contained within just one category. He took up a popular genre, brought it to perfection and elevated it far beyond its limits. Whatever he wrote, whether tragedy or comedy, he always upheld positive virtues. The French critic Henri Fluchire has pointed this out:

> What has always appealed to him with constant tenacity is the haunting sense of order and equilibrium which can be attained only by crushing the forces of evil by the triumph of the good.[1]

EDITIONS OF HIS WORKS

Two friends of Shakespeare, John Heminge (d.1630) and Henry Condell (d.1627) published the First Folio of the *Works of Shakespeare* in 1623. Then came the Second Folio in 1632 which corrected some errors and modernized the spelling. The Third Folio was printed by Thomas Cotes in 1663, which included several plays that are now known as not having been written by Shakespeare. The Fourth Folio (1685) is but a reprint of the Third with some correction and modernization.

These are not scholarly or critical editions. Nicholas Rowe's edition (1709) was the first scholarly edition and included a Life of Shakespeare as its Preface. He had chosen the text of the Fourth Folio and not only modernized the spelling but also made emendations on a few obscure passages. He also added lists of dramatists personae to the plays, which had not been there before, put in scene and act divisions and gave stage directions about exits and entrances which have been accepted by later editors.

Pope's edition of the works, published in 1723 was not at all faithful to the text. In fact he altered it according to his own will. These alterations and corrections have become notorious. Lewis Theobald, a classical scholar, not only attacked Pope but published his own edition of the works in 1733. Then in 1743-44 Sir Thomas Hanmer published a six-volume edition. Bishop William Warburton, basing his edition on Pope's made some corrections and published an eight volume edition in 1747. Dr. Johnson criticized his corrections:

> The worst of Warburton is that he has a rage for saying something when there is nothing to be said.[2]

After this, in 1765, came Dr. Johnson's own edition of *The Plays of William Shakespeare...* to which are added notes by Sam Johnson, in eight octavo volumes. He aimed at clarity and intelligibility and therefore he modified the punctuation, modernized the spelling and added a few more stage directions. It is not, however, for these that his edition is valued, but for his comments on the individual plays, these days published independently as *Preface to Shakespeare* which establishes him as the first serious, systematic and scholarly critic of Shakespeare.

The next important editor of Shakespeare is Edward Capell who published his edition after almost twenty years of devoted labour in 1768, in ten volumes. He had collated his text from a most scholarly study of all the Quartos and the Folios that had been published earlier. His textural commentary entitled *Notes and Various Readings to Shakespeare* which appeared in 1783 is a most valuable contribution to academic works on Shakespeare.

In 1773, a ten-volume edition was published as the joint venture of Dr. Johnson and George Steevens, and was revised in 1778. It was revised once more by Isaac Reed and published again in 1785, and another 15-volume edition appeared in 1793. Reed's edition was reprinted in 1803 and 1813. Edmund Malone's ten-volume edition of Shakespeare in 1790 is one of the most important editions of this century.

In 1821 James Boswell, the son of Dr. Johnson's biographer, published an edition following the revisions made by Malone. This was the Third Variorum edition. After this, throughout the nineteenth century, many editions of Shakespeare's works were published, among which the edition of Dyce and the Cambridge edition are the most important.

One of the most important editions published in the twentieth century was the one edited by W.J. Craig, usually known as the Oxford Standard Edition published in 1905. It is indeed a definitive text. The editor has depended for the text on the seventeen early Quartos and the Folio of 1623. In the Preface, the editor says that he has tried to avoid the danger of altering passages that seem to be obscure:

> I have only adopted a change after convincing myself that the characteristics of Shakespeare's vocabulary or literary style failed to justify the original reading.[3]

So many editions of his works have been published in the twentieth century, both in single volume editions and in multiple volumes, that it is difficult to keep track of them. George Harrison's edition published by Harcourt, Brace, Jovanovich in 1952 was a very good single volume edition and so was the one edited by Sylvan Barnett, published by Signet in 1972. Stanley Wells edited a single volume edition in 1988, published by Clarendon, and the Arden edition edited by Richard Proudfoot in 1998 is a definitive edition. Many illustrated editions have also been published. Among these, special mention has to be made of the *Illustrated Stratford Shakespeare* because, though it is in only one volume, *its* jacket says:

> More than 450 exquisite black and white drawings illuminate his thirty-seven plays.[4]

(a) The Social Setting

Society is the soil from which each individual springs. An individual and/or his work cannot be separated from his background. It is with this idea in mind that Donne had declared, "No man is an island". It is very necessary that the socio-political background of a writer be taken into account if his work is to be understood and appreciated. As it is not possible to mention all the multifarious details of the political, social, economic, religious and literary details of a time in a brief introduction, a chronological table of all these events has been given at the end of the introduction. It will help the reader to know easily, and at a glance, about the main events in a particular year.

Queen Elizabeth's position was a very precarious one when Shakespeare was born. Plots against her were being continually hatched at home and there was continuous warfare with the nations in the continent. It took Queen Elizabeth quite a few years to settle down firmly and securely on the throne of England. Mary Queen of Scots, throughout her meteoric and tumultuous though brief life, was a continual source of trouble. It was only after plotting against the Queen who was, after all, her cousin, she met with the fate proper for a traitor, that Queen Elizabeth was without a serious rival and could feel more or less secure. She was not only a good ruler, but a very good diplomat as well—patriotic and courageous. She was very wise in her religious policies and this was very important as religion was a burning issue of the time—more important, if possible, than politics. Her tolerant policies put an end to the religious controversies that were tearing the land apart. G.M. Trevelyan points out:

> In the years in which the Queen succeeded her sister Mary, Puritanism was mainly a foreign doctrine imported from Geneva and Rhineland; when she died it was rootedly and characteristically English.[5]

This was the time when Anglicanism drove deep roots into the country. This could happen only because of her tolerance, and the peace and prosperity of her long reign. The English people, be it rural or urban, rich or poor, had accepted Anglicanism heart and soul:

> At the end of her reign it had become a real religion; its services were dear to many, after more than forty years of use in the ancient churches of England.[6]

There had been problems regarding succession before Queen Elizabeth acceded to the throne, and likewise there were problems towards the end of her reign. It had been foreseen for many years, as there could be no direct or obvious heir to the throne after her. While she lived, however, she gave security and prosperity to her country by her wisdom and moderation.

The Elizabethan Age was remarkable for its continuous growth and expansion. The very social structure fostered the spirit of expansion. It is true that, it being a feudal society, class barriers were most prominent, but they were accepted, not resented. Nothing hampers growth so much as friction between the classes and as this did not exist, society continued to develop. The feudal lords existed along with the working class, but there was not much oppression of the latter by the former. Equality did not matter so-significantly as the freedom of opportunity. In this respect, Elizabethan England had left mediaeval England much behind, for in the middle ages there was lot of difference between the lord of the manor and the peasantry which did not exist at this time:

> In Tudor England such rigid lines were rendered impossible by the number and variety of men in intermediate classes and occupations, who were closely connected, in the business and amusements of daily life, with those above and those below them in social status...such was the England known and approved by Shakespeare.[7]

The concept of dignity of labour did not have to be argued about—it was not a mere theory but a proven fact. Everyone worked honestly and efficiently and earned a fair wage for the work done. This naturally fostered a spirit of self-reliance and self-respect in the mind of everyone. No one looked down upon anyone. Each had a respected place in society.

As a major part of the population consisted of responsible and self-respecting citizens there was a general sense of responsibility towards the poor and the disabled. The passing of the Poor Law in 1597 is a landmark in the history of social awareness. The system of appointing a Justice of Peace for parishes was also stored which assured speedy justice administered by local persons who knew the ins and outs of each case. These Justices of Peace were, in their turn, controlled by the Privy Council, a highly respected organization concerned with law and order.

The factory system had started by this time, which gave a much-needed boost to economy, bringing in industrial prosperity. Mining improved to a remarkable extent so that many metals like lead, copper, tin, etc. became easily available. Coal became cheaper, so homes became warmer. They also became better lighted as window-panes of glass became available.

Patriotism received a boost as the great explorer Sir Francis Drake brought national glory by circumnavigating the world and defeating the Spanish Armada. This last was of immeasurable benefit to the nation as it put an end to threats from the sea. A few years later a second Armada was sent which perished in a storm. This gave the entire nation a confirmation in her faith that the English were the chosen of God, specially favoured above other nations. These were halcyon days of prosperity and security, of expansion and enthusiasm. G.M. Trevelyan declares:

> By the end of Elizabeth's reign not only was English commerce and finance thus reviving the expanding on a modern basis but her ancient rivals were in rapid decline.[8]

The Jacobean Age did not lag behind in economic progress. London continued to grow (it had been only one square mile in area when Shakespeare had arrived there) and industry flourished. That much-coveted luxury article, silk, started being manufactured in 1604. Not many significant changes took place in the first forty years, for those changes that did take place were political ones, not agricultural or industrial changes and therefore did not much affect the common people. When Queen Elizabeth died in 1603 King James VI of Scotland who was her distant cousin acceded to the throne of England as James I of England. This brought about a union of the royal families of the two nations. The King tried very hard to bring the two nations politically together but it was not to be. Culturally also, Scotland was much nearer to England than Holland, yet the latter was of far more influence than the former.

One of the important achievements of King James was that in the very first year of his reign he made peace with Spain, thus removing all obstacles for maritime trade as well as other journeys by the sea. Once the seas were safe, overseas colonization started with great enthusiasm. English settlers started on their journeys to the fabled lands of Virginia, New England, etc. This was the time that the seeds of the British Empire were being sown. Emigrations were organized by the Virginia Company and the Massachusetts Bay Company. The pioneer settlers were motivated by a high religious ideal.

During the reign of King James religious issues became very much bound up with politics. They also affected more people than had formerly been the case, and the emotions stirred up were far more intense. Queen Elizabeth had steered the middle course between Catholicism and Protestantism. This had brought peace and prosperity to the country but had lost the sympathies of those who used to take an avoid interest in religion. King James was himself quite tolerant, but as Catholic conspiracies went on and the number of recusants increased, his patience was much abused, and he reinforced old penal laws about religion. Some Puritan priests were banished from the churches. This in turn precipitated the Gunpowder Plot which aimed at blowing up Parliament House. The King became alarmed and tightened penal laws against recusants and enforced a new Oath of Allegiance to the Church in 1606, which is the year when *King Lear* was written.

King James was Scottish, and always remained a stranger. Even then, there were many who had the ability to appreciate the religious and economic stability he was trying to bring to England. Fuller, the famous historian of the time, had observed:

> Indeed all the Reign of King James was better for one to live under than to write of, consisting of a Champion of constant tranquility without any tumours of trouble to entertain posterity with.[9]

All these events give but a sketchy account of the vibrant, tumultuous times in which Shakespeare lived and wrote. These are of interest to the historian. Posterity remembers the name: Shakespeare. G.M. Trevelyan, connecting the time with the man, observes:

> His works could never have been produced in any other period than those Late Elizabethan and Early Jacobean times in which it was his luck to live.[10]

(b) The Literary Background

E.M.W. Tillyard, in his thought-provoking book *English Renaissance: Fact or Fiction* had observed that while in Italy the spirit of the Renaissance expressed itself through painting and sculpture, in England it manifested itself through literature. Not just a star, not even a constellation, but an entire galaxy of poets, dramatists and prose-writers were living and writing at this time. Shakespeare's work, thus, was rooted in fertile soil. A chronological table, given at the end of this Introduction, will show that the few years from Sidney's birth in 1554 to Shakespeare's death in 1616 cover the best time of literary efflorescence in England. The most familiar names of Elizabethan and Jacobean times come later than Sidney. The Tudor dynasty had a rose as its emblem and if the literature of the Renaissance can be compared with a rose then it can be said that what Sidney saw in his lifetime was only a bud that later opened out to unequalled beauty and fragrance.

The plays that were being written and performed in Sidney's time were nothing in comparison to those that Shakespeare and the other playwrights of his time were to write, but it cannot be denied that they prepared the ground for their followers. Keeping in view the fact that drama, which is the glory of the time, had barely made a beginning, it is not surprising that Sidney had condemned contemporary drama, excepting Gorboduc:

> Our tragedies and comedies not without cause cried out against, observing rules neither of honest civility nor of skilful poetry; excepting *Gorboduc*... which notwithstanding as it is full of stately speeches and well-sounding phrases, climbing to the height of Seneca's style, and as full of notable morality, which it doth most delightfully teach, and so obtain the very end of poesy.[11]

This play, which is the only one he found worthy of praising, today has more the standing of a work of historical interest than one of literary merit. *Ralph Roister Doister*, a rollicking comedy had been staged ten years before Shakespeare's birth. Such works have only historical importance rather than literary merit.

Turning to narrative poetry, the prospect is little better than that of drama, or songs or sonnets, in all of which Shakespeare was to excel a few years later. Spenser's *Shepheard's Calendar* and parts of *Faerie Queene* had been published before Shakespeare's own narrative poems. Tottlel had published his famous *Miscellany* which included the sonnets of Wyatt and Surrey. The famous sequences of Elizabethan love—sonnets started being written by the end of the sixteenth century, reaching their climax in Shakespeare's sequence. The most flourishing genre was that of the lyric. The best lyrics were written by the "Elizabethan nest of singing-birds" from 1580 to 1620 and were being collected and published at this time under attractive and inspiring names like *The Paradise of Dainty Devices* (1576), *A Gorgeous Gallery of Gallant Inventions* (1578) etc. Shakespeare's plays are full of songs and in writing them he took the help of these collections, adopting the words to suit his own requirements. These were mostly light-hearted love-songs:

> The song-lyric, as developed in accord with the musical art of the time, is too light an instrument to utter the deeper notes of passion and its theme is fanciful love.[12]

The literary output became more and more prolific as well as dazzling as the Elizabethan Age advanced. Discursive poetry on serious philosophical and religious themes, narrative poems based mainly on classical myths, lyric poetry—all flourished in a manner but hardly equaled before or since. Prose, which is of much less importance to us (only as sources of Shakespeare's plays) was developed not only in the romances of Sidney, Lyly and others, but also in the philosophical works of writers like Bacon, Hooker and others.

Drama was undoubtedly the most important of the literary genres. The University Wits took London by storm by starting with Kyd's *The Spanish Tragedy*, a revenge tragedy in the Senecan mode which at once became all the rage. Indeed, this play became the proto-type for all the revenge tragedies written later. Marlowe's very first attempt *Tamburlaine* (which belongs to the genre of conqueror tragedy) became so popular that he hurriedly wrote the second part to it. As theatres were established, by Burbage and Henslowe, plays were in great demand. The dramatists had ample opportunity for experimenting with different varieties of plays so that they could find the form that suited them the best. Shakespeare was specially versatile, so much so that no one could rival him in the range of his plays, or indeed, in any other matter, but each of the dramatists could find their own form and settle down with it, such was the great demand for plays. Ben Jonson, for example, brought the form of the humour comedy to perfection at the same time that Beaumont and Fletcher achieved success with quite another kind, the tragic-comedy—a literary genre that blends both tragic and comic elements.

The influence of classical dramatists, specially of Seneca, was the most pervasive influence at the time. It was Kyd who set the example in this direction:

> It was the genius of Thomas Kyd that seized upon the essential effects of Senecan action and adapted them, with much relation of rules, to the conditions of the public stage.[13]

These tragedies are usually known as the Blood-and-Thunder Tragedies. They have been divided into four divisions: Conqueror tragedy (*Tamburlaine, Macbeth,* etc.), Revenge tragedy (*The Spanish Tragedy, Hamlet,* etc.), Villain tragedy (*The Changeling, Othello,* etc.), and Domestic tragedy (*A Woman Killed with Kindness, Romeo and Juliet,* etc.). There are many tragedies that cannot be contained within just one group. Webster's *The Duchess of Malfi*, for example, is a revenge tragedy as well as a domestic tragedy. Shakespeare's *Othello* is a villain tragedy as well as a domestic tragedy.

Comedy flourished in the hands of Lyly, Peele, Greene, Shakespeare, Ben Jonson and others. M.C. Bradbrook has divided Elizabethan society into three categories, the Court, the Country and the City, and ascribed different kinds of comedy to each. The comedies of Shakespeare come mostly under the first of these and those of Ben Jonson under the third. There is great variety within the genre of comedy. There are the romantic comedies, satirical comedies, problem comedies, tragi-comedies and romances.

Besides these there are also the chronicles or the history plays in which Shakespeare excelled though many others wrote this kind of play. Marlowe's *Edward II*, for example, is a historical play as well as a tragedy. One of the very first plays *Misfortunes of King Arthur*, written by eight scholars for the entertainment of the Queen, was a play of this kind.

Another kind of play that is outside all these categories is that of masques. These were used mainly for courtly entertainment. Those of Ben Jonson were specially successful. Shakespeare used this device quite frequently in his plays. It can be found in a very simple form in one of his earliest plays, *Love's Labour's Lost*, and in an elaborate form in his last play, *The Tempest*.

His work, thus, was firmly rooted in the soil of Elizabethan England and he is the ideal product of his milieu. Another poet, four centuries later, points out the relevance of this background:

> No poet, no artist of any art, has his complete meaning along. His significance, his appreciation is the appreciation of his relation to the dead poets and artists.[14]

(c) The Elizabethan Theatre

It is one of the achievements of the Elizabethan Age that permanent theatre halls were built at this time, for nothing like them had existed before. When Queen Elizabeth acceded to the throne there were no specially designed theatre halls in the whole of England. Troupes of actors roamed the country and performed their plays in villages and towns, sometimes on hastily built temporary stages, sometimes in the halls of the lord of the manor, or any open space. There are records of performances held in churches, in inn yards, in town halls, in the town Square, wherever a crowd could be accommodated. As F.E. Schelling has noted:

> Acting in the yards of inns and other public places … must have been old when parliament adopted, in 1543, stringent measures.[15]

There were troupes or companies of actors patronised by the great noblemen of the time who performed seasonally in various places all over England. This was from before the Queen's time. These became the foundations for the professional players who performed on the Elizabethan stage. The tourings of these players gradually replaced the performances of the Mystery and the Morality plays by local players. These touring companies were, in their turn, replaced by professional companies with noble patrons.

The authorities of the City of London were, in general, hostile to theatrical shows. The Queen, however, liked to see plays and the Privy Council also supported her. So theatres were established in the suburbs as the mayor's powers ended at the gates to the city. The position has been clarified admirably by Schelling:

> The earliest playhouses were built beyond the walls … in Shoreditch … where the Theatre, first structure of its kind in England, dating 1576, and the Curtain … were erected; or across the river at the Bankside, where in the nineties there arose the Globe, the Rose, the Hope and the Swan.[16]

The companies, aware of the hostile attitude of the London Council, maintained a pretence that their public performances were just rehearsals for the performances before the Queen. This definitely granted prestige, but the public performances were the real success of the income that professional actors and dramatists needed. The drama was a focus of unification, for the highest (the Court) watched it as well as the common people. As the private theatres developed, drama became more and more oriented towards the taste of the audience.

The success of Elizabethan drama is to a large extent due to the establishment of commodious and profitable public theatres. Once they were in smooth and economically viable operation drama was in a position to become a settled feature of society rather than just a transitory or seasonal phenomenon. The Theatre, established in 1576 was promptly followed by the Curtain, the Rose, the Swan, the Globe, the Fortune and the Red Bull. Archaeological excavations on the foundations of the Rose and the Globe showed that though the theatres had individual differences, their common function necessitated a general plan which had to be more or less the same.

The tearm "theatre" which today is applied to all purposely built halls solely intended for theatrical performances was the name of the first such building in England "The Theatre". The design had been based on bull-baiting and bear-baiting yards. It seems to have been of wood and polygonal and may have had three galleries of seats one above another. The main area of the theatre was open to the sky. There was a large yard for those of the audience to stand in who could not afford to buy a seat:

> On the fourth side of the yard and opposite to the entrance door was situated the stage, a platform jutting far out into the middle of the yard so that the audience there might stand on three sides of it.[17]

The Globe was definitely the most famous of the theatres, but there were many others as well. As they were built of timber and lath and plaster and had thatched roofs these theatres were very vulnerable to fire. It was imperative, in the interests of the public, that they be replaced with stronger buildings. The Globe was burnt down in 1613 and was given a tile roof when rebuilt. Then in 1621 the Fortune got burnt down and was rebuilt in brick. The second Globe was demolished in 1644 after the playhouses were closed in 1642 by the Puritans.

The cast was always an all-male one. There were social stigmas attached to women appearing on the stage. English travelers abroad were surprised as well as amused at the continental custom that required women to play female roles. Elizabethan actors followed a rigorous schedule of rehearsals and performances. Usually six different plays were performed in the six-day week and a specially successful play would be repeated within a month or so. The income of the actor varied according to his position in the company. Shakespeare earned quite a lot so that he gradually became one of the most affluent men in his native town.

The stage was left more or less bare, only a few significant props being used. Thus it was in the costumes that the visual appeal of the plays lay. These were rich and brightly coloured. As the costumes were quite expensive the actors did not try to be faithful to the costumes necessary for a period piece, wearing contemporary clothes instead. The leading actor might occasionally wear a proper costume, but not the minor ones. This might be seen as a limitation, but these days a positive attitude is taken:

> The chief characteristic of the Elizabethan stage was its neutrality, and its corresponding virtue, flexibility. There was no inevitable scenic background or any other localising factor, such as the Chorus provides.[18]

This is the technique which modern directors would call minimalism. Yet this is not, strictly speaking, true. The Elizabethans used more sophisticated props, costumes and stage effects than is usually supposed. Strict laws existed about the costume of different social classes. It would be immediately obvious to the Elizabethan audience that actors wearing particular types of clothes were enacting the roles of people of particular background and types. Heavy make-up was used, particularly for boys enacting female roles as was but necessary.

The Elizabethan theatre was virtually without any lighting effects. Torches carried by the actors served to indicate that that particular scene was a night scene, but from a practical point of view it made little difference because actually it was day. It was left to the spectator's imagination. Colours helped substantially in indicating the nature of the scene that was being presented:

> The mere fact that public playhouse performances generally took place by day light meant that the spectators were on show to one another.[19]

This meant that visual appeal mattered very much, for the spectators themselves were dazzlingly colourful. Besides this, colours were important for another reason. Different colours depicted the specific mood of the play. Tragedy and comedy could be clearly indicated with appropriate colours:

> As the stage was hung with black for tragedies, it was used for mourning and for funerals ... white symbolised innocence and purity; it was worn by angels and good spirits.[20]

As the end of the Elizabethan Age drew near the rising puritan movement became more and more hostile to the theatre, for the puritans thought it promoted immorality. One of their most common complaints was the practice of boys playing female roles. From a political point of view dramatists and actors depended on the royalty and the aristocracy and therefore supported them. But the puritan factions gained control over London quite early in the Civil War and closed the halls down. Up till then the Elizabethan mode had endured. When they reopened after the Restoration it was on a different kind of world. The years during the end of the Elizabethan and the beginning of the Jacobean ages (Shakespeare's time) were the best times for the theatre.

(d) A Short Biography

As usually happens in the case of well-known figures, Shakespeare became invested with an aura of glory, all the more pronounced as this renown was not posthumous but attained during his lifetime. In the seventeenth century Fuller wrote a brief life in his famous *Worthies* (1662) and John Aubrey included him in his *Lives of Eminent Men.* The first modern editor Nicholas Rowe took material from many other sources as well in the life given in his edition of the plays. Much more intensive research work has been done by modern scholars and more material on his life has come to light.

The exact date of his birth is not known, as the Register of Baptism maintained by the parish church did not record the date of birth but of baptism only. As the official language of the time was Latin, the entry in the Register says:

> 1564, Apr. 26, Culielmus Filius Johannes Shakespeare.[21]

It was the custom those days to baptise a baby three days after its birth. It is therefore assumed that he was born on the twenty-third of April, in the village of Stratford-upon-Avon, the country being Warwickshire. This was a lucky day as it was St. George's day, England's patron saint.

Not much is known about his childhood days but it can be taken for granted that he spent a happy and secure childhood. His father was in trade and therefore did not have the status of the landed gentry, but he became the alderman when the village expanded enough to have one, in 1565. His mother was from a socially higher family.

His father was a justice of peace (a J.P.) as well as the High Bailiff. As such he had to execute many duties connected with the law courts and Shakespeare, being the eldest son, often accompanied him. He thus gained intimate knowledge of legal proceedings, as can be seen in the Trial Scene of *The Merchant of Venice*.

Queen Elizabeth had established Grammar Schools all over England in order to educate the common people. Shakespeare was duly admitted to the local school. He was perhaps seven at this time and did not take kindly to it at all. Boys of the aristocracy went to expensive schools where they got classical education which Shakespeare could not get. But this does not mean that he did not get any grounding in the classics. Ben Jonson's ridicule of his "Small Latin and Less Greek" is most misleading. All the schools followed the same curriculum which included the poetry of Virgil and Horace, and Ovid, the prose of caesar, Livy and Cicero and the plays of Seneca, Plautus and Terence. Shakespeare thus acquired a solid foundation in Latin literature. One of his biographers remarks:

> Today all scholars are agreed that Shakespeare was a well-educated man of his times, that he certainly continued to further his education by wide reading throughout his life.[22]

Shakespeare left the school in his teens but it is not known exactly when. Nor is it known whether he had completed his education by that time or not.

It was during these highly formative years that he came into contact with stage performances. As has already been clarified, itinerant groups patronised by the great noblemen of the time used to roam all over England to present traditional as well as new plays. There are records of the groups visiting the different towns and of the plays they presented.

More important than this was the event of his falling in love with Anne Hathaway, a much sought-after girl fully eight years older than him. He was not yet nineteen when they got married in 1582. Their first girl-child Susanna was born next year, and two years later the twins Hamnet and Judith were born. Hamnet died in 1596, leaving no one to carry on the line.

Shakespeare was now, at barely twenty-one, a man with a family to support and with no visible means of earning a livelihood. What he was doing at this time is not known for sure, though the story concerning Sir Thomas Lucy is the most widely known. It seems Shakespeare was caught poaching in Sir Thomas's deer park. Unpleasant results followed and it is believed that this incident prompted him to leave for London. There are many stories about this time. In any case, it is thought that he left for London in 1586.

Little is known of the time from 1586 to 1592 and the years are known as the Dark Years. Again, there are many legends but nothing is known for sure. We hear of him in 1593 when Richard Field, a fellow villager, who had become an established printer, published his *Venus and Adonis* and *The Rape of Lucrece* in 1594.

Both of these became instantly popular. Narrative poems were very popular at this time and his literary career, thus, began with them.

In the field of drama his only serious rival was Marlowe. They had both been born the same year and reached London at the same time. The decade of the eighties was a stimulating and prosperous one. That group of learned young men, the University Wits was consolidating in London. Sidney's *Astrophel* and Stella and Spenser's *Faerie Queene* were being composed Lyly's *Euphues* was already in every drawing-room. Marlowe's *Tamburlaine* was presented 1587. F.E. Halliday observes:

> Shakespeare had arrived in London at the most thrilling moment in its history.[23]

Shakespeare was watching and learning. He quickly became important enough to be noticed by such a well-established person as Greene, the first contemporary to have mentioned Shakespeare's name. He wrote a pamphlet which is known today chiefly for this reference:

> There is an upstart crow, beautified with our feathers that with his Tyger's heart wrapt in a Player's hyde, supposes he is as well able to bombast out a blank verse as the best of you: and being an absolute Johannes factotum, is in his own conceit the only Shake-scene in a country.[24]

This famous sentence has two clear clues. The line "Tyger's heart wrapt in a player's hide" is a deliberate misquotation of a line from *Henry VI, Pt.III*, and of course there is the word "Shake-scene", referring to Shakespeare.

At this time he was still learning his craft and these are known as the years of apprenticeship. The sonnets, the two narrative poems, the *Henry VI* trilogy, *Richard III*, *Titus Andronicus*, *The Comedy of Errors*, *The Two Gentlemen of Verona*, and *The Taming of the Shrew* were all written at this time, all highly successful, *Titus Andronicus* particularly so, a Senecan tragedy.

This list shows that Shakespeare had not confined himself to just one genre. Kyd and Marlowe had written only tragedies. Shakespeare, from the very beginning produced successful literary works of all kinds. By 1594 Marlowe had already been killed and Shakespeare had proved his versatility as well as his stage-worthiness.

By this time he had joined the group of Lord Chamberlain's men and become an important member of it. He remained with it till the very end of his life. He had also paid a visit to his family. It is thought the poem *Venus and Adonis* and *Richard III* were written during this four month visit, a very fruitful one.

Venus and Adonis was dedicated to the Earl of Southampton. He was lucky to get this patron and a deep and intense friendship grew between the two. The sonnets speak eloquently of this relationship though the Earl is not mentioned anywhere. He is designated as Mr. W.H. in the Dedication. The sonnets also describe a nameless Dark Lady and most painful triangular situation is described. How much of this is true cannot be known for sure, but Shakespeare shows himself as a master of the sonnet form and the mode of Courtly Love. The *Dedication* to *The Rape of Lucrece* indicates his attitude clearly:

> The Love I dedicate to your Lordship is without end...what I have done is yours, what I have to do is yours, being part in all I have devoted yours.[25]

This patronage enabled him to buy a share in his company. A.L. Rowse has remarked:

> It meant all the difference between the dreadful insecurity poor Greene had, and others, died of, and having firm ground under his feet.[26]

In 1597 he lost his son Hamnet. The same year his application at the Herald's College for a coat-of-arms was granted so that now his family would have the status of a gentleman—a matter of moment in feudal society. He had also taken new place which was the second best house in Stratford which had expanded into a town.

By 1598 he was acknowledged as a master-dramatist. A well-known document of the time, named "Palladis Tamia" written by Francis Meres gives an eulogistic account of his works. Meres's attitude is a pointer to the high esteem in which Shakespeare was held. He asserts that Shakespeare was the contemporary equivalent of Plautus and Terence in comedy and of Seneca in tragedy, and Orid in poetry and lyrics.

When King James acceded to the throne in 1603 he took Shakespeare's company under his own patronage and it became known as the King's Men. This was the highest honour for any group. There are many records of Shakespeare's life from this point onwards, particularly of Court performances. We come also to know of the houses and the land he had bought at this time.

His great tragedies were now produced. Except for *Hamlet* all the other tragedies, the Problem Plays and many of the Chronicles were products of the Jacobean Age. A sombre evaluation of life and persons succeeded the exuberance of the Elizabethan Age. A valuable observation has been made in this connection by T. Spencer:

> The earlier Renaissance had emphasised man's potentialities by comparing him with the angels; the later Renaissance emphasised their destruction by comparing man with the animals.[27]

As the years passed he left the turbulent waters of the problem comedies and the tragedies behind him and emerged into the deep serenity of the last romances. In 1611 he retired to Stratford, though he continued coming to London on matters of business. At the end of 1612 *The Tempest* was performed to celebrate a royal betrothal. It is said that he himself enacted the role of Prospero and blessed the royal couple himself.

In 1616 his will was drawn up and can still be seen in Somerset House. This was in February and two short months later, on 23rd April which was his birthday, he passed away at fifty-two years of age, a ripe old age.

His tomb is quite an ornate one, with many rich and complex symbols adorning it. There is a bust of himself with a quill in his hand, signifying that he was a writer. His coat-of-arms is placed between the two allegorical figures of Rest and Labour. The whole thing is surmounted by a skull. The grave bears an epitaph in the form of a quatrain. It is thought that this was written by the poet himself, though many critics think it to be too crude to have been his own work. This is how it goes:

> Good friend, for Jesus sake forbeare
> To dig the dust enclosed here!
> Blest be the man yt spares these stones,
> And curst be he yt moves my bones.[28]

(e) Shakespeare's Works

Shakespearean critics and scholars have, after much research, drawn up a tentative scheme of his works. This has been based on contemporary documents like the "Diary" kept by Henslowe, the Stationer's Register and some others. These record the dates of the performances on stage, not those of composition or publications. In addition to this, the performance dates of many of the plays are not known and, to make the whole thing quite confusing, some of the plays (like, for example, *Titus Andronicus*) were published quite early and some much later. In spite of these difficulties, a scheme has been roughly made up, though the stages are not clearly demarcated:

Phase I

1591	–	*The Comedy of Errors*
1592	–	*The Two Gentlemen of Verona, Henry VI, Pts. I, II & III*
1593	–	*Richard III, Romeo and Juliet, Venus and Adonis*

Phase II

1594	–	*The Rape of Lucrece, The Sonnets, Titus Andronicus, Richard II, Midsummer Night's Dream, Love's Labour's Lost, King John, The Taming of the Shrew*
1595	–	*The Merchant of Venice*
1597	–	*Henry IV, Pt. I*
1598	–	*Henry VI, Pt. II, The Merry Wives of Windsor*
1599	–	*Henry V, Much Ado About Nothing, Julius Caesar*
1600	–	*As You like It, Twelfth Night*

Phase III

1602	–	*Hamlet, Troilus and Cressida, All's Well That Ends Well*
1604	–	*Measure for Measure, Othello*
1605	–	*King Lear*
1606	–	*Macbeth*
1607	–	*Antony and Cleopatra*

1608 – *Coriolanus, Timon of Athens, Pericles*

Phase IV

1610 – *Cymbeline, The Winter's Tale, The Tempest*

1611 – *Henry VIII* (the authorship was doubtful for long)

The Two Noble Kinsmen (in collaboration with Fletcher).

Shakespeare's career has been roughly divided into the phases given above though they are not by any means mutually exclusive. The different phases often overlap, as for example, some critics would say that the works up till *Love's Labour's Lost* belong to the first phase and some say that *Pericles* belongs to the last phase, not the third. As a rough estimate however, his career can be divided into the four phases given above. The first phase is known as the phase of Experiment, from 1591 to 1594 or perhaps to 1595. This was the time when he was learning his craft by mostly revising and reconstructing plays that were already in existence. During this early period he made occasional use of rhyming and end-stopped lines. This can be seen in *A Mid-summer Night's Dream* as well. There is much exuberant playing with words, as in *Love's Labour's Lost*. The art of characterization has yet developed noticeably.

The second period, that of Development, is from 1594-95 to 1601. The Chronicle plays and the Golden Comedies were written during this time. By now he has attained mastery over the poetic medium, i.e. dramatic blank verse. As far as characterization goes, he has started plumbing the depths of the human mind. The plots are managed in a masterly way.

The third period ended in 1608. There is a remarkable change in mood in the plays of this time. The exuberance of wit, the light-hearted characters have gone. Instead there is sombre contemplation of evil in human nature as well as in Nature. In this he reflects the spirit of the age superlatively well:

> The conflict between good and evil, ugliness and beauty, innocence and crime, purity and impurity, hope and disgust, love and hate, order and disorder, natural laws and the anarchy produced by the passions—all is resolved in Shakespeare's so-called "dark period" with an infinite despair.

The Great Tragedies and the Problem Comedies, also known as the Dark Comedies, belong to this stage.

The last phase, or the Romance period, goes on to 1612 and the last four Romances belong to this time. Here we see a calm and serene Shakespeare, who has reconciled himself to the existence of evil and hands over the future to a younger and purer generation:

> As his career draws to a close Shakespeare turned back to his youth, and his implicit theme is always that of fertility, resurrection, joy of life.

These four plays were succeeded by two more. There was some controversy about *Henry VIII*, but it has now been ascribed to him, and *The Two Noble Kinsmen* is a work of collaboration with Fletcher.

(f) Brief Notes on His Works

The Comedy of Errors

The shortest of his plays, many critics take it to be his first. It was performed at Court in 1594 but it is not known whether this was the first staging or not. The plot is taken from Plautus's *The Menaechmi*. He has but one pair of twins in it and Shakespeare has two. So the intrigues, mistaken identities etc. are doubled. The theme of the relationship between husband and wife, which Shakespeare will take up in *The Taming of the Shrew*, gains prominence here. The dramatist presents both the sides—that of the husband as well as that of the wife.

The Two Gentlemen of Verona

Critics usually regard this play as the first of his Romantic Comedies. There are two pairs of lovers, two servants and two fathers, making a symmetrical pattern. The theme is of the conflict between love and friendship, with the emphasis falling on the latter. Along with this there is the theme of forgiveness and reconciliation. This appears in this play for the first time and will go on appearing till in the last plays it dominates the entire work. Many features of his mature comedies are also present, as crossed love, disguised heroines, exile and flight. Julia is a precursor of Rosalind and Portia, just as Silvia foreshadows. Juliet and Lance the later jesters.

Henry VI, Pts. I, II & III

This trilogy is the first of the Chronicles, which are a class by themselves. No other Elizabethan dramatist wrote so many. He wrote ten of them, including *Henry VIII*. The pomp and pageantry of royalty captivated his imagination. The serious issues of the duties of Kings and their human aspects, all fascinated him. The spirit of patriotism cast a glory over everything else—king and country.

The plays were based on the famous *Chronicles* of Raphael Holinshed, and staged in 1592. It became so popular that this trilogy was staged three times in eight days. It presents a world of ferocity and betrayal and ends in regicide. Greene had referred to one of its lines.

Richard III

This play belongs more to the genre of tragedy than to chronicles. The *Henry VI* trilogy shows the influence of Marlowe and in this play it is even more intense. The hero, King Richard III, is a Marlovian figure but far more complex than the typical heroes of Marlowe. This play, except for *Hamlet*, is Shakespeare's longest and is very stage-worthy. The figure of the King dominates the entire play and thus his tragic end makes the play more of a tragedy than a history. This is the main difference between this play and the *Henry VI* trilogy. Many critics tend to group this play with the trilogy and call the whole sequence a tetralogy. As far as the time covered is concerned, this can be done quite easily but usually they are treated separately.

Romeo and Juliet

This play tells one of the most popular stories of the time—a story of family feuds and star-crossed love. As till now, Shakespeare's tragedies are tragedies of fate, and family feud takes the place of fate. It controls the lives of the two young lovers, placing insuperable difficulties along their way. The kind of hero for whom "Character is destiny" has yet to be formed. This has happened because he has followed the original story very closely in it. Some of the scenes, particularly the Balcony scene, have become classics, to the extent of being parodied. Shakespeare's genius expresses itself, if not through the characters, then through its blank verse, which is of great lyrical beauty. The character of Mercutio is said to be marginally autobiographical.

Venus and Adonis

This is the first of his narrative poems. Based on classical mythology, the story is taken from Ovid. The poem was so successful that it ran through ten or eleven editions in his own lifetime. Narrative poetry was a new experiment for him, but he had excellent models to guide him, specially Marlowe's *Hero and Leander*. It is so highly sensuous that it can be classed as erotica. He has used a stanza of six lines in it, a quatrain followed by a couplet. It is a pattern highly suitable for narrative poetry, being a smoothly flowing metre and simpler than the Spenserian stanza.

The Rape of Lucrece

This too, like *Venus and Adonis*, is a narrative poem based on classical myths, and like it, is dedicated to the Earl of Southampton. It is not as light-hearted a poem as the former one for here he explores the feeling of guilt in Tarquin. It is thus a rather sombre poem and these psychological complexities raise it above the level of a merely narrative poem. Tarquin has become a tragic figure. The poet has used the rhyme royal stanza in it; seven iambic pentameter lines rhyming a b a b b c c. He manages this complex form in a masterly manner.

The Sonnets

This sequence of hundred and fifty-four sonnets is dedicated to Mr. W.H., named as "the onlie begetter". The sonnets, in their intensity of passion as well as their beauty of expression, are unique and supposed to be autobiographical. Out of these hundred and fifty-four sonnets, the first 126 are addressed to Mr. W.H., who is supposed to be Henry, Wriothesley, the Earl of Southampton. The remaining twenty-eight are addressed, except for the last three, to the Dark Lady, who was perhaps Mary Fitton, one of the maids of honour of Queen Elizabeth. This is a unique feature, for the sequence is addressed to two persons, one of them a man, whereas the other sonnet-sequences of the time were addressed to just one person, a lady. The sonnets explore the relationships involved in such a triangular situation, very intensely.

Titus Andronicus

This falls within the genre of Revenge Tragedies and is also the first of the Roman tragedies. As such, it is a typical blood-and-thunder tragedy and follows Kyd's *The Spanish Tragedy*. It contains a parody of one of the most famous passages of Kyd. It was highly popular at the time (vide Shakespeare's life, supra).

Richard II

Shakespeare's plays do not, usually have much topical relevance, but this play is an exception. Ireland was posing a great problem and this is the theme of the play. It reflects the political situation of the time so well that the Queen had become extremely angry on seeing it. "I am Richard II, know ye that?" she had exclaimed, "This tragedy is played forty times in open streets and houses". The play shows the deposition of King Richard II. This was such a sensitive issue that the deposition-scene had to be omitted when the play was staged. The character of Richard II is supposed to be a study in weakness and has been depicted with great sympathy. Shakespeare shows himself to be able already to handle characters in a most delicate manner.

A Midsummer Night's Dream

The best of the early plays, this is the work which is called a fairy-tale. It has been a popular work from the very beginning, with adults as well as school children, particularly because of the supernatural element in it, as in *The Tempest*.

Love's Labour's Lost

Produced in 1594, this play is brilliant for its sparkling dialogues, specially those of Lord Berowne and Lady Rosaline. There are four pairs of courtly lovers and a few humble characters have also been brought in. Lord Berowne, the wittiest of the Lords is supposed to be slightly autobiographical. He, in a famous passage renounces flowery diction:

> Taffeta phrases, silken terms precise
> Three-piled, hyperboles, spruce affectations
> Figures pedantical: those summer flies
> Have blown me full of maggot ostentation
> I do forswear them.

This marks a significant development in the poet's dramatic career.

King John

Though this play is an entirely historical one, yet it has contemporary relevance as well, in an indirect manner. Shakespeare, as a rule, avoided the controversial issue of religion, yet in this play he has taken it up. It is the only such play. King John had carried on a life-long struggle with the Roman Catholic Church and the supremacy of the Pope. Queen Elizabeth had done the same, to the extent that she was excommunicated by the Pope (vide Ch.2, Socio-Political Background, supra). It is not, however, a religious play but a patriotic one and foreign policy is the central theme.

The Taming of the Shrew

Many critics hold that this is the first of his plays to have an Italian setting. It was performed in 1594. Though an early play, the two main characters are strongly delineated. Katharine, the Shrew of the title and Petruchio the tamer, are both strong, credible characters. The main theme is the relationship between husband and wife and the conflict for supremacy between them. This was a very valid theme for the audience of his day. In all, it is a rollicking play, highly stageworthy. Shakespeare has created another female character as foil for the shrew, which throws both the characters into relief.

The Merchant of Venice

The great age of the Golden Comedies starts with this play. The merchant after whom the play is named is Antonio, but he cannot claim the title of the hero. This is because the position of the most important character has to be given to Shylock who is the villain of the piece. He is a class by himself. The heroine Portia is one of the most important female characters he has created. The Elizabethan convention of disguise is used most effectively in this play for each one of the three female characters adopts disguises, though for short durations only. His poetic style has reached a high standard of excellence. There is solemn, thoughtful poetry in the mercy-speech and lyrically beautiful poetry in the moonlight scene.

Henry IV – Pts. 1 and 2

The English Chronicle play reached its highest point in these two plays. Falstaff whom Queen Elizabeth called "the fat knight" is the main attraction of the play. His rejection by King Henry V is one of the most moving scenes. The rejection, however, is fully justified, for that part of his life has come to an end. King Henry V cannot roister about with Sir John the way Prince Hal did. The play is about the duties and responsibilities of kingship and the King has to shoulder his burdens. The first part with the amusing doings of Falstaff, is entertaining, but the second part is of more psychological interest. However, Falstaff remains immortal. Everything might be forgotten, but Falstaff is remembered as one of the greatest comic figures ever created.

The Merry Wives of Windsor

This play was specially ordered for by the Queen. She liked Sir John Falstaff so much that she wanted a play to be written about "the fat knight in love". The play is hilarious and begins at the point where Sir John was left at the end of *Henry IV, Pt.2.* The play, otherwise unimportant, gains special significance because it is thought that Shakespeare had poked fun at Ben Jonson's humour characters. This is said particularly with corporal Nym in mind, who makes an inordinate use of the word "humour" in every second sentence he speaks in the play.

King Henry V

This play presents the dramatist's concept of the ideal king. There are two main themes that rule the play—kingship and patriotism. Shakespeare presents the positive as well as the negative side of war—bravery and endurance on one hand, and death and destruction on the other. King Henry, the boisterous Prince. Hal of the earlier plays, is presented as the ideal king, with all the qualities necessary for leadership. The historical triumph at Agincourt is shown in a vivid and graphic manner, with Henry V manifesting himself as a strict but just king. Falstaff goes to Arthur's bosom in this play, a babbling of green fields.

Much Ado About Nothing

This is the second of Shakespeare's four Golden Comedies. It is double-plotted, and the theme is love. This theme, too, is treated in two different ways. There is physical love based on appearances which in this case prove to be deceptive. The Hero-Claudio plot takes up this aspect of love and the Benedick-Beatrice plot takes up the theme of the rejection of married love which makes its appearance again and again in the works. His craftsmanship shows itself to better advantage than in *The Merchant of Venice*, for here the main plot is easily differentiable from the sub-plot. As in the other romantic comedies the lovers move towards a higher consciousness of love and responsibly, integrating themselves within the framework of society.

Julius Caesar

This Roman Tragedy is definitely the most political play of Shakespeare. The plot is extremely with but little comedy in it. The central theme is the opposition between tyranny and liberty. Characterisation shows itself in the creations of persons who project themselves as living, three-dimensional individuals. The play is eminently stage-worthy, specially the Forum Scene. Lord North's translation of Plutarch's *Lives* supplied the story and Shakespeare shows his economy and resourcefulness by adapting many of the prose passages in this book into appropriate blank verse. He makes use of the supernatural element by introducing the Ghost of Caesar.

As You Like It

This is acknowledged to be the cheeriest and the sunniest of the Romantic Comedies. The major part of the play is located in the Forest of Arden. There are four pairs of lovers, taken from different levels of society and illustrating different types of love. They are all neatly paired off in the end. There is the courtly love of Rosalind and Orlando, as well as the more down-to-earth love of the shepherds. One of the most charming heroines of Shakespeare, Rosalind, enlivens the play with her wit. The convention of disguise plays a prominent part in the play. The famous passage about the seven stages of man as well as the equally famous lyric "Under the greenwood tree" occurs in this play.

Twelfth Night

This is the fourth and the last of his Golden Comedies. It contains all the usual ingredients of popular comedies like disguises, mistaken, identities, the separation and unions of siblings, etc. Plot-structure presents the usual features—a main plot with courtly love and aristocratic characters and a comic sub-plot. Sir Toby is a diluted version of Falstaff and Malvolio is a puritan melancholic. He was extremely popular with the audience. This play presents one of the most important Fools or court jesters in Shakespeare. Feste is highly accomplished and in dramatic importance is second only to the Fool in *King Lear*. The disguise-convention has been used to provide much entertainment.

Hamlet

This is perhaps the best-known play of Shakespeare. It is the first of the four Great Tragedies. It follows the basic pattern of a revenge tragedy but the character of the hero, Hamlet, that like a giant, dominates the play to such an extent that the other features of the play are often neglected. He is today looked upon not as just a hero with the flow of indecision in his nature, but also as a typical intellectual. Shakespeare has shown us that the crude blood-and-thunder tragedy of Kyd can be sublimated to such an extent that the limitations of the revenge tragedy are left far behind and play becomes a sophisticated one with the quality of true sublimity and universality.

Troilus And Cressida

The Problem Comedies of Shakespeare all present a highly serious treatment of the seamy side of life and human nature and tremble on the verge of tragedy. This play is as close to a satire as Shakespeare even came. It gives a satirical view of the themes of love and war. Ulysses is character who is said to come very close to the poet.

All's Well That Ends Well

This too, is a Problem Comedy. The basic theme is the conflict between virtue and nobility as in the Bertram-Helena plot, but there are several sub-themes, i.e. the conflict between old and young generations. Shakespeare shows himself far less able to endure the follies and vices of humanity as the difference between the braggart soldier Parolles and Falstaff clearly illustrates.

Measure for Measure

This too, like the two Problem Comedies preceding it, is a sombre play. Paradoxically enough it is the only other play, besides *As You Like It*, to have four marriages in it. Forcing a man to marriage by trickery was present in *All's Well That Ends Well* and here also makes its appearance. The sole ruler of a country withdraws from the state after having appointed a deputy and comes back to observe the state of affairs in disguise. This is an old theme and along with it goes the theme of justice, which is a recurring theme in these later plays. This play contains the famous song "Take O take those lips away" about which A.E. Housman had said that it was nonsense, but ravishing poetry.

Othello

This is Shakespeare's first Jacobean play, as Hamlet is the last of his Elizabethan tragedies. It has been labeled as the *Romeo and Juliet* of his later phase and is a study in jealousy. Othello and King Leontes in *The Winter's Tale* are both studies in jealousy but the outcome is tragic here and otherwise in the later play. The character of Iago, about whom Coleridge has used the famous phrase "motiveless malignity", is one of the unforgettable villains of Shakespeare. Desdemona the heroine is one of the most pathetic creations of the poet. As the play affects a limited family circle, it has been classified as a domestic tragedy and insofar as the tragedy is the result of the plotting of Iago it is a villain tragedy.

King Lear

This play now vies for the place of the greatest of his tragedies with *Hamlet*. It has been called a Cosmic drama, showing man's place in the universe. The story is taken from several sources, like the old play of *King Leir*, *The Mirror for Magistrates* and Sir Philip Sidney's *Arcadia*. The poet has woven all these diverse strands together to produce a unique play of elemental passions. A primitive legend is transformed into a terrible tragedy that, nonetheless, has the quality of universality. The word which is usually applied to it is "sublime". The character of the Fool is unique. He is not only the wisest Fool but also serves many other complex purposes. The play has been compared with Dante's *The Divine Comedy*.

Macbeth

This is the darkest of the Tragedies, a play of gloom and horror. Shakespeare was paying a tribute to the Scottish king by choosing a story from Scottish history. He has given the unique character of Lady Macbeth and has made use of the supernatural element in many different ways in this play.

Antony and Cleopatra

This Roman Tragedy forms a sequel to *Julius Caesar*, though it is entirely different in theme. Here the theme of love predominates. The unforgettable character of Cleopatra dominates the play. The play is so complex that critics cannot decide whether to call it a history, a symphony, a political play or a tragedy.

Coriolanus

This is the last of the Tragedies, a political and a Roman Tragedy. So it is usually grouped with the two other Roman Tragedies. The hero's noble nature is in conflict with society. He hates the populace and this brings tragic doom on him, for he is rejected by the mob and joins the enemy, to bring ruin upon his country and himself.

Timon of Athens

This is not a finished product and for that very reason affords insight into the poet's creative processes. The play ends with hero's withdrawal from society, yet there is a sense of its being an unfinished work. This is usually classed as a Problem Comedy.

Pericles, Cymbeline, The Winter's Tale, and *The Tempest*

This quartet of plays is known as the Last Romances and in all of them the theme is the same—sin and repentance leading to forgiveness, and the tainted older generation giving way to a purer new generation. *The Tempest* is the last play of Shakespeare and Prospero's renunciation of magic is thought to be the poet's farewell to the theatre.

Henry VIII

The authorship of this play had been disputed for a long time but now it is attributed to Shakespeare. It is a history play, but ends with the assurance of the continuity of life, as the last Romances do. It is a study on the theme of patience in adversity. Not only does the King learn patience, but so do the others.

The Two Noble Kinsmen

This is a dramatization of *The Knight's Tale* in Chaucer's *Canterbury Tales* and is a collaboration with Fletcher. Shakespeare wrote the major parts of Act I and parts of Act III and V. When, however Fletcher brought in a rather vulgar sub-plot Shakespeare left off collaboration. He did not write any other work in collaboration with others, as many of his contemporaries had done.

(g) A Chronological Table

Only the most significant events have been given under different heads. The table starts with the performance of the first English play and ends with Shakespeare's death. Different events have been given under different heads which have been mentioned under the first date, i.e. 1554. Events concerned with Shakespeare have been entered separately, under no. 4.

1554	–	1. *Political events*—Lady Jane Gray, rival to the throne, is executed.
		2. *Social and Religious events*—Roman Catholicism restored.
		3. *Literary events*—Sir Philip Sidney and Lyly born, *Ralph Roister Doister* staged.
1557	–	1. England supports Spain in war against France.
		3. Tottel's *Miscellany.*
1558	–	1. Queen Mary I dies, Elizabeth I succeeds, Mary Queen of Scots marries the French Dauphin.
		3. Kyd, Lodge, Greene, Peele born.
1559	–	1. Mary Queen of Scots declares herself the Queen of England and Scotland.
		2. Church of England established on a firm basis.
1561	–	1. Mary Queen of Scots returns from France and clashes with the Calvinists.
		3. Gorboduc performed, Bacon born.
1564	–	1. Anglo-French war ends. England at war with Spain.
		2. The Thirty-Nine Articles adopted by Church of England. Queen Elizabeth tries to enforce religious unity.
		4. Shakespeare born. Marlowe also born.
1567	–	1. Mary Queen of Scots abdicates.
		3. Cambion and Nashe born. Painter's *Palace of Pleasure.*
1568	–	1. Mary Queen of Scots flees to England and is held captive by Queen Elizabeth.
1570	–	2. Pope Pius V excommunicates Queen Elizabeth.

1574 – 3. Roger Ascham's *The Schoolmaster*, Burbage gets license to build the first theatre in London.

1575 – 3. Heywood and Tourneur born. *Apius and Virginia*, *Gammer Gurton's Needle* staged.

1576 – 3. Burbage opens the first theatre of England at Shoreditch. *Paradyse of Daynty Devises.*

1577 – 1. England makes treaty with the Dutch.

2. Sir Francis Drake begins circumnavigation of the globe in The Pelican.

3. The Curtain, the second theatre built at Moorfields. Holinshed's *Chronicles.* Translation of Ovid's *Heroic Epistles.*

1578 – 3. Lyly's *Euphues.*

1579 – 3. Spenser's *Shepheard's Calendar*, Lord North's translation of Plutarch's *Lives*, Stephen Gosson's *The School of Abuse.*

1581 – 2. Conversion to Roman Catholicism is declared to be a treasonable offence.

1582 – 3. Haktuyt's *Voyages.*

4. Shakespeare marries Anne Hathaway.

1583 – 1. Plot against the Queen.

2. Humphrey Gilbert takes possession of Newfoundland.

4. Birth of Shakespeare's first daughter Susanna.

1584 – 2. Sir Walter Raleigh discovers names and starts to colonize Virginia.

1585 – 3. Kyd's *The Spanish Tragedy.*

4. Shakespeare's twins Hamnet and Judith born.

1586 – 1. England wins the battle of Zutphen in which Sir Philip Sidney gets fatally wounded. Mary Queen of Scots implicated in plot against the Queen and is convicted of treason.

3. Lyly's *Endimion.*

4. Shakespeare leaves for London.

1587 – 1. Mary Queen of Scots executed for treason.

3. Rose Theatre built by Henslowe. Marlowe's *Tamburlaine*, Lyly's *Gallathea.*

1588 – 2. Defeat of the Spanish Armada by Sir Fancis Drake.

1589 – 3. Marlowe's *The Jew of Malta*, Puttenham's *The Arte of English Poesie.*

1590 – 3. *Faerie Queene* Books I-III, Lodge's *Rosalynde.*

1591 – 3. Sidney's *Astrophel and Stella*, Marlowe's *Edward II.*

1592 – 2. John Davies discovers Falkland Island.

3. Sidney's *Arcadia*, Daniel's *To Delia* (sonnets), Marlowe's *Hero and Leander*; *Arden of Feversham* (anon).

4. *Henry VI*, Pts. I, II & III, *Richard III.*

1593 – 2. Absence from the church on Sundays made punishable by law.

3. Kyd dies.

4. *Venus and Adonis* published by Richard Field.

1594 – 4. *Titus Andronicus*, *The Taming of the Shrew*, *Rape of Lucrece.*

1595 – 2. Southwell the Roman Catholic mystical poet executed for celebrating Mass.

3. Spenser's *Amoretti* (sonnets), Sidney's *Apology for Poetry.*

4. *A Midsummer Night's Dream.*

1596 – 1. England, France and the Netherlands form alliance against Spain.

2. Peasant revolt in Oxfordshire.

4. *The Sonnets.* Only son Hamnet dies.

1597 – 1. The second Spanish Armada sent against England destroyed by a storm.

2. Beggary made illegal. Statutory provisions for Poor Relief.
4. *The Merchant of Venice.* Buys New Place.

1598 – 2. The Bodleian Library begun.
3. Globe Theatre opened. Francis Meres's *Palladis Tamia.* Ben Jonson's *Every Man in His Humour*, Sidney's *Defense of Poesy.*

1599 – 3. John Davies's *Nosce Teipsum*, Ben Jonson's *Every Man Out of His Humour*. Spenser dies.
4. *Much Ado About Nothing, As You Like It, Twelfth Night, Henry V, Julius Caesar.* Buys Shares in Globe Theatre.

1600 – 2. East India Company founded.
3. England's *Helicon, England's Parnassus*, Jonson's Cynthia's *Revels*, Dekker's *The Shoemaker's Holiday.*

1601 – 1. The Earl of Essex raises rebellion against the Queen and is executed.
2. East India Company despatches its first trading fleet to Sumatra.
3. Jonson's *The Poetaster.* Dekker & Marston's *Satiromastix.*

1602 – 1. End of Irish Rebellion.
2. Boleian Library opened.
4. *All's Well That Ends Well, Troilus and Cressida, Hamlet.* He buys 107 acres of land. The birth of his first grandchild.

1603 – 1. Queen Elizabeth dies. Accession of James VI of Scotland as James I of England.
2. East India Company sends trade mission to India.
3. Dowland's *Third Book of Songs*, Heywood's *A Woman Killed with Kindness*, Jonson's *Sejanus.*

1604 – 1. Peace with Spain.
2. Banishment of Roman Catholic priests provokes Gunpowder Plot. Silk manufacture begins.
3. Champan's *Bussy D'Ambois*, Marston's *The Malcontent.*
4. *Measure for Measure, Othello*, His company comes under Royal patronage and is named The King's Men.

1605 – 1. Gunpowder Plot discovered and Guy Fawkes arrested.
2. English colonists land at Barbodos.
3. Drayton's *Collected Poems*, Bacon's *Advancement of Learning.*
4. *Macbeth.*

1606 – 1. James I imposes customs duty without the sanction of the Parliament.
3. Lyly dies. *A Yorkshire Tragedy* (anon.), Jonson's *Volpone Tourneur's The Revenger's Tragedy.*
4. *King Lear.*

1607 – 2. The first permanent settlement, Jamestown founded in America.
3. Beaumont and Fletcher's *The Knight of the Burning Pestle.*
4. *Timon of Athens.*

1608 – 1. Failure of plan for union with Scotland.
3. Fuller and Milton born. Chapman's *Duke of Byron.*

1609 – 3. Beaumont and Fletcher's *Philaster*, Fulke Greville's *Mustapha*, Tourneur's *The Atheist's Tragedy.*
4. *Coriolanus* published, *The Sonnets* published.

1610 – 1. Judiciary decision against royal proclamations.
3. Ben Jonson's *The Alchemist.*

1611 – 1. Parliament dissolved.
2. Land granted in northern Ireland to Scottish and English Protestants.
3. Spenser's *Collected Works. The Authorized Version of the Bible.* Ben Jonson's *Catiline* (tragedy).

4. *The Winter's Tale*. He retires to Stratford.

1612 – 1. Alliance with German Protestant princes.
2. Last recorded execution for heresy—witches hanged in Lancashire.
3. Chapman's *Iliad*, Webster's *The White Devil*.
4. *Henry VIII* (Possibly in collaboration with Fletcher).

1613 – 1. Princess Elizabeth marries Elector Frederick V.
3. Globe Theatre burnt down, Purchas's *Pilgrimage*.
4. *The Tempest* performed at royal betrothal.

1614 – 3. Sir John Querbury's *Characters*, Lodge's *Works of Seneca*, Sir Walter Raleigh's *History of the World*, Jonson's *Bartholomew Fair*, Webster's *The Duchess of Malfi*.

1616 – 3. Ben Jonson given royal pension, *Works* printed.
4. Shakespeare dies.

1623 – 4. *First Folio* printed.

1632 – 4. *Second Folio* printed.

1642 – Theatres closed.

Ratri Ray

Notes

1. Henri Fluchere, *Shakespeare*, London, Longmans, Green & Co., 1953, p. 264.
2. C.T. Thomas, ed., Samuel Johnson: *Preface to Shakespeare*, Macmillan India Ltd., 1986, p. xxiv.
3. W.J. Craig, ed., *The Complete Works of William Shakespeare*, London, Oxford University Press, 1957 rpt., p. v.
4. *The Illustrated Stratford Shakespeare*, London, Chancellor Press, 1982.
5. G.M. Trevelyan, *Illustrated English Social History*, Vol. 2, Harmondsworth, Penguin Books Ltd., 1964, p. 86.
6. *Ibid.*
7. *Ibid.*, p. 62.
8. *Ibid.*, p. 123.
9. Douglas, Quoted in Bush, *English Literature in the Earlier Seventeenth Century*, Oxford, At the Clarendon Press, 1946, p. 4.
10. Trevelyan, *op. cit.*, p. 125.
11. D.J. Enright and Ernst de Chickera, ed., *English Critical Texts: 16th Century to 20th Century*, Oxford, the University Press, 2002 rpt., p. 40.
12. Frederick Ives Carpenter, *English Lyric Poetry: 1500-1700*, London, Blackie & Sons Ltd., no date, p. xlvii.
13. Hardin Craid, *The Literature of the English Renaissance: 1485-1660*. New York, Collier Books, 1962, p. 80.
14. T.S. Eliot, *Three Essays*, Calcutta, Oxford University Press, 1979, p. 17.
15. F.E. Schelling, *English Drama*, New Delhi, S. Chand & Co., 1963, p. 49.
16. *Ibid.*, p. 53.
17. *Ibid.*
18. M.C. Bradbrook, *A History of Elizabethan Drama*, Cambridge University Press, 1981 rpt., p. 8.
19. Michael Hattaway, *Elizabethan Popular Theatre: Plays in Performance*. London, Routtedge, 2005, p. 46.
20. M.C. Bradbrook, *op. cit.*, p. 16.
21. F.E. Cited in Halliday, *The Life of Shakespeare*, London, Gerald Duckworth & Co. Ltd., 1961, p. 20.
22. Irving Ribner, *William Shakespeare: Life, Times and Theatre*, London, John Wiley & Sons, 1969, p. 38.
23. Halliday, *op. cit.*, p. 60.
24. Quoted in Ribner, I., *op. cit.*, p. 45.
25. Quoted in Halliday, *op. cit.*, pp. 102-03.
26. A.L. Rowse, *William Shakespeare: A Biography, London*, Macmillan & Co. Ltd., 1963, p. 100.
27. Theodore Spencer, *Shakespeare and the Nature of Man*, New York, Macmillan, 1945, p. 49.
28. Quoted in Ribner, *op. cit.*, p. 64 and by many others.

COMEDY

ALL'S WELL THAT ENDS WELL

DRAMATIS PERSONÆ

THE KING OF FRANCE
THE DUKE OF FLORENCE
BERTRAM, *Count of Rousillon*
LAFEU, *an old lord*
PAROLLES, *a follower of Bertram*
Two French Lords, *serving with Bertram*
Steward servants to the Countess of Rousillon
LAVACHE, a clown
A Page,
COUNTESS OF ROUSILLON, mother to Bertram
HELENA, a gentlewoman protected by the Countess
A Widow of Florence
DIANA, daughter to the Widow
VIOLENTA, MARIANA, neighbours and friends to the Widow
Lords, Officers, Soldiers, etc., French and Florentine

THE SCENE: Rousillon; Paris; Florence; Marseilles

ACT I

SCENE I—*Rousillon: The Count's palace*

Enter BERTRAM, the COUNTESS OF ROUSILLON, HELENA, and LAFEU, all in black

COUNTESS: In delivering my son from me, I bury a second husband.

BERTRAM: And I in going, madam, weep o'er my father's death anew; but I must attend his majesty's command, to whom I am now in ward, evermore in subjection.

LAFEU: You shall find of the king a husband, madam; you, sir, a father. He that so generally is at all times good must of necessity hold his virtue to you, whose worthiness would stir it up where it wanted, rather than lack it where there is such abundance.

COUNTESS: What hope is there of his majesty's amendment?

LAFEU: He hath abandoned his physicians, madam; under whose practises he hath persecuted time with hope, and finds no other advantage in the process but only the losing of hope by time.

COUNTESS: This young gentlewoman had a father—O, that 'had', how sad a passage 'tis!—whose skill was almost as great as his honesty; had it stretched so far, would have made nature immortal, and death should have play for lack of work. Would, for the king's sake, he were living! I think it would be the death of the king's disease.

LAFEU: How called you the man you speak of, madam?

COUNTESS: He was famous, sir, in his profession, and it was his great right to be so—Gerard de Narbon.

LAFEU: He was excellent indeed, madam; the king very lately spoke of him admiringly and mourningly: he was skilful enough to have lived still, if knowledge could be set up against mortality.

BERTRAM: What is it, my good lord, the king languishes of?

LAFEU: A fistula, my lord.

BERTRAM: I heard not of it before.

LAFEU: I would it were not notorious. Was this gentlewoman the daughter of Gerard de Narbon?

COUNTESS: His sole child, my lord, and bequeathed to my overlooking. I have those hopes of her good that her education promises; her dispositions she inherits, which makes fair gifts fairer; for where an unclean mind carries virtuous qualities, there commendations go with pity—they are virtues and traitors too. In her they are the better for their simpleness; she derives her honesty, and achieves her goodness.

LAFEU: Your commendations, madam, get from her tears.

COUNTESS: 'Tis the best brine a maiden can season her praise in. The remembrance of her father never approaches her heart but the tyranny of her sorrows takes all livelihood from her cheek. No more of this, Helena; go to, no more; lest it be rather thought you affect a sorrow than to have—.

HELENA: I do affect a sorrow indeed, but I have it too.

LAFEU: Moderate lamentation is the right of the dead: excessive grief the enemy to the living.

COUNTESS: If the living be enemy to the grief, the excess makes it soon mortal.

BERTRAM: Madam, I desire your holy wishes.

LAFEU: How understand we that?

COUNTESS: Be thou blest, Bertram, and succeed thy father
In manners, as in shape! Thy blood and virtue
Contend for empire in thee, and thy goodness
Share with thy birthright! Love all, trust a few,
Do wrong to none; be able for thine enemy
Rather in power than use, and keep thy friend
Under thy own life's key; be check'd for silence,
But never tax'd for speech. What heaven more will,
That thee may furnish, and my prayers pluck down,
Fall on thy head! Farewell. My lord,
'Tis an unseason'd courtier; good my lord,
Advise him.

LAFEU: He cannot want the best
That shall attend his love.

COUNTESS: Heaven bless him! Farewell, Bertram.

Exit COUNTESS

BERTRAM: The best wishes that can be forged in your thoughts be servants to you! [*To Helena*] Be comfortable to my mother, your mistress, and make much of her.

LAFEU: Farewell, pretty lady; you must hold the credit of your father.

Exeunt BERTRAM and LAFEU

HELENA: O, were that all! I think not on my father;
And these great tears grace his remembrance more
Than those I shed for him. What was he like?
I have forgot him: my imagination
Carries no favour in't but Bertram's.
I am undone; there is no living, none,
If Bertram be away. 'Twere all one
That I should love a bright particular star
And think to wed it, he is so above me.
In his bright radiance and collateral light
Must I be comforted, not in his sphere.
The ambition in my love thus plagues itself:
The hind that would be mated by the lion
Must die for love. 'Twas pretty, though a plague,
To see him every hour; to sit and draw
His arched brows, his hawking eye, his curls,
In our heart's table—heart too capable
Of every line and trick of his sweet favour.
But now he's gone, and my idolatrous fancy
Must sanctify his relics. Who comes here?

Enter PAROLLES

[*Aside*] One that goes with him. I love him for his sake;
And yet I know him a notorious liar,
Think him a great way fool, solely a coward;
Yet these fixed evils sit so fit in him
That they take place, when virtue's steely bones
Look bleak i' the cold wind; withal, full oft we see
Cold wisdom waiting on superfluous folly.

PAROLLES: Save you, fair queen!

HELENA: And you, monarch!

PAROLLES: No.

HELENA: And no.

PAROLLES: Are you meditating on virginity?

HELENA: Ay. You have some stain of soldier in you; let me ask you a question. Man is enemy to virginity; how may we barricado it against him?

PAROLLES: Keep him out.

HELENA: But he assails; and our virginity, though valiant in the defence, yet is weak. Unfold to us some warlike resistance.

PAROLLES: There is none. Man, setting down before you, will undermine you and blow you up.

HELENA: Bless our poor virginity from underminers and blowers-up! Is there no military policy how virgins might blow up men?

PAROLLES: Virginity being blown down, man will quicklier be blown up; marry, in blowing him down again, with the breach yourselves made, you lose your city. It is not politic in the commonwealth of nature to preserve virginity. Loss of virginity is rational increase; and there was never virgin got till virginity was first lost. That you were made of is metal to make virgins. Virginity by being once lost may be ten times found; by being ever kept, it is ever lost. 'Tis too cold a companion; away with't.

HELENA: I will stand for 't a little, though therefore I die a virgin.

PAROLLES: There's little can be said in't; 'tis against the rule of nature. To speak on the part of virginity is to accuse your mothers; which is most infallible disobedience. He that hangs himself is a virgin: virginity murders itself, and should be buried in highways, out of all sanctified limit, as a desperate offendress against nature. Virginity breeds mites, much like a cheese; consumes itself to the very paring, and so dies with feeding his own stomach. Besides, virginity is peevish, proud, idle, made of self-love, which is the most inhibited sin in the canon. Keep it not; you cannot choose but lose by't. Out with 't. Within ten year it will make itself ten, which is a goodly increase; and the principal itself not much the worse. Away with 't.

HELENA: How might one do, sir, to lose it to her own liking?

PAROLLES: Let me see. Marry, ill to like him that ne'er it likes. 'Tis a commodity will lose the gloss with lying; the longer kept, the less worth. Off with 't while 'tis vendible; answer the time of request. Virginity, like an old courtier, wears her cap out of fashion: richly suited but unsuitable; just like the brooch and the tooth-pick, which wear not now. Your date is better in your pie and your porridge than in your cheek. And your virginity, your old virginity, is like one of our French withered pears: it looks ill, it eats drily; marry, 'tis a withered pear; it was formerly better; marry, yet 'tis a withered pear. Will you anything with it?

HELENA: Not my virginity yet.
There shall your master have a thousand loves,
A mother, and a mistress, and a friend,
A phoenix, captain and an enemy,
A guide, a goddess, and a sovereign,
A counsellor, a traitress, and a dear;
His humble ambition, proud humility,
His jarring concord, and his discord dulcet,
His faith, his sweet disaster; with a world
Of pretty, fond, adoptious christendoms
That blinking Cupid gossips. Now shall he—
I know not what he shall. God send him well!
The court's a learning-place, and he is one—

PAROLLES: What one, i' faith?

HELENA: That I wish well. 'Tis pity—

PAROLLES: What's pity?

HELENA: That wishing well had not a body in't
Which might be felt; that we, the poorer born,
Whose baser stars do shut us up in wishes,
Might with effects of them follow our friends
And show what we alone must think, which never
Return us thanks.

Enter PAGE

PAGE: Monsieur Parolles, my lord calls for you.

Exit PAGE

PAROLLES: Little Helen, farewell; if I can remember thee, I will think of thee at court.

HELENA: Monsieur Parolles, you were born under a charitable star.

PAROLLES: Under Mars, I.

HELENA: I especially think, under Mars.

PAROLLES: Why under Mars?

HELENA: The wars have so kept you under that you must needs be born under Mars.

PAROLLES: When he was predominant.

HELENA: When he was retrograde, I think, rather.

PAROLLES: Why think you so?

HELENA: You go so much backward when you fight.

PAROLLES: That's for advantage.

HELENA: So is running away, when fear proposes the safety; but the composition that your valour and fear makes in you is a virtue of a good wing, and I like the wear well.

PAROLLES: I am so full of businesses I cannot answer thee acutely. I will return perfect courtier; in the which my instruction shall serve to naturalize thee, so thou wilt be capable of a courtier's counsel, and understand what advice shall thrust upon thee; else thou diest in thine unthankfulness, and thine ignorance makes thee away: farewell. When thou hast leisure, say thy prayers; when thou hast none, remember thy friends. Get thee a good husband, and use him as he uses thee; so, farewell.

Exit

HELENA: Our remedies oft in ourselves do lie,
Which we ascribe to heaven. The fated sky
Gives us free scope, only doth backward pull
Our slow designs when we ourselves are dull.
What power is it which mounts my love so high,
That makes me see, and cannot feed mine eye?
The mightiest space in fortune nature brings
To join like likes, and kiss like native things.
Impossible be strange attempts to those
That weigh their pains in sense, and do suppose
What hath been cannot be. Who ever strove
To show her merit that did miss her love?
The king's disease—my project may deceive me,
But my intents are fixed, and will not leave me.

Exit

SCENE II—*Paris: The King's palace*

Flourish of cornets. Enter the KING OF FRANCE, with letters, and divers Attendants

KING: The Florentines and Senoys are by the ears;
Have fought with equal fortune, and continue
A braving war.

FIRST LORD: So 'tis reported, sir.

KING: Nay, 'tis most credible; we here received it
A certainty, vouch'd from our cousin Austria,
With caution that the Florentine will move us
For speedy aid; wherein our dearest friend
Prejudicates the business and would seem
To have us make denial.

FIRST LORD: His love and wisdom,
Approved so to your majesty, may plead
For amplest credence.

KING: He hath arm'd our answer,
And Florence is denied before he comes;
Yet, for our gentlemen that mean to see
The Tuscan service, freely have they leave
To stand on either part.

SECOND LORD: It well may serve
A nursery to our gentry, who are sick
For breathing and exploit.

KING: What's he comes here?

Enter BERTRAM, LAFEU, and PAROLLES

FIRST LORD: It is the Count Rousillon, my good lord,
Young Bertram.

KING: Youth, thou bear'st thy father's face;
Frank nature, rather curious than in haste,
Hath well composed thee. Thy father's moral parts
Mayst thou inherit too! Welcome to Paris.

BERTRAM: My thanks and duty are your majesty's.

KING: I would I had that corporal soundness now,
As when thy father and myself in friendship
First tried our soldiership. He did look far
Into the service of the time, and was
Discipled of the bravest. He lasted long;
But on us both did haggish age steal on,
And wore us out of act. It much repairs me
To talk of your good father. In his youth
He had the wit which I can well observe
To-day in our young lords; but they may jest
Till their own scorn return to them unnoted
Ere they can hide their levity in honour.
So like a courtier, contempt nor bitterness
Were in his pride or sharpness; if they were,
His equal had awaked them, and his honour,
Clock to itself, knew the true minute when
Exception bid him speak, and at this time
His tongue obey'd his hand. Who were below him
He used as creatures of another place;
And bow'd his eminent top to their low ranks,
Making them proud of his humility
In their poor praise he humbled. Such a man
Might be a copy to these younger times;

Which, followed well, would demonstrate them now
But goers backward.
BERTRAM: His good remembrance, sir,
Lies richer in your thoughts than on his tomb;
So in approof lives not his epitaph
As in your royal speech.
KING: Would I were with him! He would always say—
Methinks I hear him now; his plausive words
He scatter'd not in ears, but grafted them
To grow there, and to bear—'Let me not live'—
This his good melancholy oft began,
On the catastrophe and heel of pastime,
When it was out—'Let me not live' quoth he,
'After my flame lacks oil, to be the snuff
Of younger spirits, whose apprehensive senses
All but new things disdain; whose judgments are
Mere fathers of their garments; whose constancies
Expire before their fashions.' This he wish'd;
I, after him, do after him wish too,
Since I nor wax nor honey can bring home,
I quickly were dissolved from my hive,
To give some labourers room.
SECOND LORD: You are loved, sir;
They that least lend it you shall lack you first.
KING: I fill a place, I know't. How long is't, count,
Since the physician at your father's died?
He was much famed.
BERTRAM: Some six months since, my lord.
KING: If he were living, I would try him yet—
Lend me an arm—the rest have worn me out
With several applications. Nature and sickness
Debate it at their leisure. Welcome, count;
My son's no dearer.
BERTRAM: Thank your majesty.

Exeunt Flourish

SCENE III—*Rousillon: The Count's palace*

Enter COUNTESS, STEWARD, and CLOWN

COUNTESS: I will now hear; what say you of this gentlewoman?

STEWARD: Madam, the care I have had to even your content I wish might be found in the calendar of my past endeavours; for then we wound our modesty, and make foul the clearness of our deservings, when of ourselves we publish them.

COUNTESS: What does this knave here? Get you gone, sirrah. The complaints I have heard of you I do not all believe: 'tis my slowness that I do not, for I know you lack not folly to commit them and have ability enough to make such knaveries yours.

CLOWN: 'Tis not unknown to you, madam, I am a poor fellow.

COUNTESS: Well, sir.

CLOWN: No, madam, 'tis not so well that I am poor, though many of the rich are damned; but if I may have your ladyship's good will to go to the world, Isbel the woman and I will do as we may.

COUNTESS: Wilt thou needs be a beggar?

CLOWN: I do beg your good will in this case.

COUNTESS: In what case?

CLOWN: In Isbel's case and mine own. Service is no heritage; and I think I shall never have the blessing of God till I have issue o' my body; for they say barnes are blessings.

COUNTESS: Tell me thy reason why thou wilt marry.

CLOWN: My poor body, madam, requires it. I am driven on by the flesh; and he must needs go that the devil drives.

COUNTESS: Is this all your worship's reason?

CLOWN: Faith, madam, I have other holy reasons, such as they are.

COUNTESS: May the world know them?

CLOWN: I have been, madam, a wicked creature, as you and all flesh and blood are; and, indeed, I do marry that I may repent.

COUNTESS: Thy marriage, sooner than thy wickedness.

CLOWN: I am out o' friends, madam. and I hope to have friends for my wife's sake.

COUNTESS: Such friends are thine enemies, knave.

CLOWN: You're shallow, madam—in great friends; for the knaves come to do that for me which I am aweary of. He that ears my land spares my team and gives me leave to in the crop. If I be his cuckold, he's my drudge. He that comforts my wife is the cherisher of my flesh and blood; he that cherishes my flesh and blood loves my flesh and blood; he that loves my flesh and blood is my friend: ergo, he that kisses my wife is my friend. If men could be contented to be what they are, there were no fear in marriage; for young Charbon the

Puritan and old Poysam the Papist, howsome'er their hearts are severed in religion, their heads are both one: they may jowl horns together like any deer i' the herd.

COUNTESS: Wilt thou ever be a foul-mouthed and calumnious knave?

CLOWN: A prophet I, madam; and I speak the truth the next way:

For I the ballad will repeat,
Which men full true shall find:
Your marriage comes by destiny,
Your cuckoo sings by kind.

COUNTESS: Get you gone, sir; I'll talk with you more anon.

STEWARD: May it please you, madam, that he bid Helen come to you. Of her I am to speak.

COUNTESS: Sirrah, tell my gentlewoman I would speak with her; Helen, I mean.

CLOWN: [*Sings*] Was this fair face the cause, quoth she

'Why the Grecians sacked Troy?
Fond done, done fond,
Was this King Priam's joy?'
With that she sighed as she stood,
With that she sighed as she stood,
And gave this sentence then:
'Among nine bad if one be good,
Among nine bad if one be good,
There's yet one good in ten'.

COUNTESS: What, one good in ten? you corrupt the song, sirrah.

CLOWN: One good woman in ten, madam; which is a purifying o' the song. Would God would serve the world so all the year! We'd find no fault with the tithe-woman, if I were the parson. One in ten, quoth 'a! An we might have a good woman born every blazing star, or at an earthquake, 'twould mend the lottery well: a man may draw his heart out, ere 'a pluck one.

COUNTESS: You'll be gone, sir knave, and do as I command you.

CLOWN: That man should be at woman's command, and yet no hurt done! Though honesty be no puritan, yet it will do no hurt; it will wear the surplice of humility over the black gown of a big heart. I am going, forsooth. The business is for Helen to come hither.

Exit

COUNTESS: Well, now.

STEWARD: I know, madam, you love your gentlewoman entirely.

COUNTESS: Faith, I do. Her father bequeathed her to me; and she herself, without other advantage, may lawfully make title to as much love as she finds. There is more owing her than is paid; and more shall be paid her than she'll demand.

STEWARD: Madam, I was very late more near her than I think she wished me. Alone she was, and did communicate to herself her own words to her own ears; she thought, I dare vow for her, they touched not any stranger sense. Her matter was, she loved your son. Fortune, she said, was no goddess, that had put such difference betwixt their two estates; Love no god, that would not extend his might only where qualities were level; Diana no queen of virgins, that would suffer her poor knight surprised, without rescue in the first assault, or ransom afterward. This she delivered in the most bitter touch of sorrow that e'er I heard virgin exclaim in; which I held my duty speedily to acquaint you withal; sithence, in the loss that may happen, it concerns you something to know it.

COUNTESS: You have discharged this honestly; keep it to yourself. Many likelihoods informed me of this before, which hung so tottering in the balance that I could neither believe nor misdoubt. Pray you leave me. Stall this in your bosom; and I thank you for your honest care: I will speak with you further anon.

Exit STEWARD

Enter HELENA

Even so it was with me when I was young.
If ever we are nature's, these are ours; this thorn
Doth to our rose of youth rightly belong;
Our blood to us, this to our blood is born.
It is the show and seal of nature's truth,
Where love's strong passion is impress'd in youth.
By our remembrances of days foregone,
Such were our faults, or then we thought them none.
Her eye is sick on't; I observe her now.

HELENA: What is your pleasure, madam?

COUNTESS: You know, Helen,
I am a mother to you.

HELENA: Mine honourable mistress.

COUNTESS: Nay, a mother.
Why not a mother? When I said 'a mother',
Methought you saw a serpent. What's in 'mother',
That you start at it? I say, I am your mother,
And put you in the catalogue of those
That were enwombed mine. 'Tis often seen
Adoption strives with nature and choice breeds
A native slip to us from foreign seeds.
You ne'er oppress'd me with a mother's groan,
Yet I express to you a mother's care.
God's mercy, maiden! does it curd thy blood
To say I am thy mother? What's the matter,
That this distemper'd messenger of wet,
The many-colour'd Iris, rounds thine eye?
Why, that you are my daughter?
HELENA: That I am not.
COUNTESS: I say, I am your mother.
HELENA: Pardon, madam;
The Count Rousillon cannot be my brother:
I am from humble, he from honoured name;
No note upon my parents, his all noble.
My master, my dear lord he is; and I
His servant live, and will his vassal die.
He must not be my brother.
COUNTESS: Nor I your mother?
HELENA: You are my mother, madam; would you were—
So that my lord your son were not my brother—
Indeed my mother! Or were you both our mothers,
I care no more for than I do for heaven,
So I were not his sister. Can't no other,
But, I your daughter, he must be my brother?
COUNTESS: Yes, Helen, you might be my daughter-in-law.
God shield you mean it not! 'daughter' and 'mother'
So strive upon your pulse. What! pale again?
My fear hath catch'd your fondness. Now I see
The mystery of your loneliness, and find
Your salt tears' head. Now to all sense 'tis gross
You love my son; invention is ashamed,
Against the proclamation of thy passion,
To say thou dost not. Therefore tell me true;
But tell me then, 'tis so; for, look thy cheeks
Confess it, th' one to th' other; and thine eyes
See it so grossly shown in thy behaviours
That in their kind they speak it; only sin
And hellish obstinacy tie thy tongue,
That truth should be suspected. Speak, is't so?
If it be so, you have wound a goodly clew;
If it be not, forswear't: howe'er, I charge thee,
As heaven shall work in me for thine avail,
To tell me truly.
HELENA: Good madam, pardon me!
COUNTESS: Do you love my son?
HELENA: Your pardon, noble mistress!
COUNTESS: Love you my son?
HELENA: Do not you love him, madam?
COUNTESS: Go not about; my love hath in't a bond.
Whereof the world takes note. Come, come, disclose
The state of your affection; for your passions
Have to the full appeach'd.
HELENA: Then, I confess,
Here on my knee, before high heaven and you,
That before you, and next unto high heaven,
I love your son.
My friends were poor, but honest; so's my love.
Be not offended; for it hurts not him
That he is loved of me; I follow him not
By any token of presumptuous suit,
Nor would I have him till I do deserve him;
Yet never know how that desert should be.
I know I love in vain, strive against hope;
Yet in this captious and intenible sieve
I still pour in the waters of my love,
And lack not to lose still. Thus, Indian-like,
Religious in mine error, I adore
The sun that looks upon his worshipper,
But knows of him no more. My dearest madam,
Let not your hate encounter with my love,
For loving where you do; but if yourself,
Whose aged honour cites a virtuous youth,
Did ever in so true a flame of liking
Wish chastely and love dearly that your Dian
Was both herself and love; O, then, give pity
To her, whose state is such that cannot choose
But lend and give where she is sure to lose;
That seeks not to find that her search implies,
But riddle-like, lives sweetly where she dies!
COUNTESS: Had you not lately an intent—speak truly—
To go to Paris?

HELENA: Madam, I had.
COUNTESS: Wherefore? tell true.
HELENA: I will tell truth; by grace itself I swear.
You know my father left me some prescriptions
Of rare and proved effects, such as his reading
And manifest experience had collected
For general sovereignty; and that he will'd me
In heedfull'st reservation to bestow them,
As notes whose faculties inclusive were
More than they were in note. Amongst the rest,
There is a remedy, approved, set down,
To cure the desperate languishings whereof
The king is render'd lost.
COUNTESS: This was your motive
For Paris, was it? Speak.
HELENA: My lord your son made me to think of this,
Else Paris, and the medicine, and the king,
Had from the conversation of my thoughts
Haply been absent then.
COUNTESS: But think you, Helen,
If you should tender your supposed aid,
He would receive it? He and his physicians
Are of a mind: he, that they cannot help him;
They, that they cannot help. How shall they credit
A poor unlearned virgin, when the schools,
Embowell'd of their doctrine, have left off
The danger to itself?
HELENA: There's something in't
More than my father's skill, which was the greatest
Of his profession, that his good receipt
Shall for my legacy be sanctified
By the luckiest stars in heaven; and, would your honour
But give me leave to try success, I'd venture
The well-lost life of mine on his grace's cure
By such a day and hour.
COUNTESS: Dost thou believe't?
HELENA: Ay, madam, knowingly.
COUNTESS: Why, Helen, thou shalt have my leave and love,
Means and attendants and my loving greetings
To those of mine in court. I'll stay at home,
And pray God's blessing into thy attempt.
Be gone to-morrow; and be sure of this,
What I can help thee to thou shalt not miss.
Exeunt

Act II

Scene I—*Paris: The King's palace*

Flourish of cornets. Enter the KING with divers young Lords taking leave for the Florentine war; BERTRAM, and PAROLLES; Attendants.

KING: Farewell, young lords; these warlike principles
Do not throw from you. And you, my lords, farewell;
Share the advice betwixt you; if both gain all,
The gift doth stretch itself as 'tis received,
And is enough for both.

FIRST LORD: 'Tis our hope, sir,
After well-enter'd soldiers, to return
And find your grace in health.

KING: No, no, it cannot be; and yet my heart
Will not confess he owes the malady
That doth my life besiege. Farewell, young lords;
Whether I live or die, be you the sons
Of worthy Frenchmen; let higher Italy—
Those bated that inherit but the fall
Of the last monarchy—see that you come
Not to woo honour, but to wed it; when
The bravest questant shrinks, find what you seek,
That fame may cry you loud. I say, farewell.

SECOND LORD: Health, at your bidding, serve your majesty!

KING: Those girls of Italy, take heed of them:
They say our French lack language to deny,
If they demand, beware of being captives,
Before you serve.

BOTH: Our hearts receive your warnings.

KING: Farewell. [*To Attendants*] Come hither to me.

The King retires attended

FIRST LORD: O my sweet lord, that you will stay behind us!

PAROLLES: 'Tis not his fault, the spark.

SECOND LORD: O, 'tis brave wars!

PAROLLES: Most admirable! I have seen those wars.

BERTRAM: I am commanded here and kept a coil with
'Too young' and 'the next year' and ''tis too early'.

PAROLLES: An thy mind stand to 't, boy, steal away bravely.

BERTRAM: I shall stay here the forehorse to a smock,
Creaking my shoes on the plain masonry,
Till honour be bought up, and no sword worn
But one to dance with. By heaven, I'll steal away.

FIRST LORD: There's honour in the theft.

PAROLLES: Commit it, Count.

SECOND LORD: I am your accessary; and so farewell.

BERTRAM: I grow to you, and our parting is a tortured body.

FIRST LORD: Farewell, Captain.

SECOND LORD: Sweet Monsieur Parolles!

PAROLLES: Noble heroes, my sword and yours are kin. Good sparks and lustrous, a word, good metals: you shall find in the regiment of the Spinii one Captain Spurio, with his cicatrice, an emblem of war, here on his sinister cheek; it was this very sword entrenched it. Say to him, I live; and observe his reports for me.

FIRST LORD: We shall, noble captain.

[*Exeunt Lords*]

PAROLLES: Mars dote on you for his novices! What will ye do?

Re-enter the King

BERTRAM: Stay; the king.

PAROLLES: Use a more spacious ceremony to the noble lords; you have restrained yourself within the list of too cold an adieu. Be more expressive to them; for they wear themselves in the cap of the time; there do muster true gait; eat, speak, and move, under the influence of the most received star; and though the devil lead the measure, such are to be followed. After them, and take a more dilated farewell.

BERTRAM: And I will do so.

PAROLLES: Worthy fellows; and like to prove most sinewy sword-men.

Exeunt BERTRAM and PAROLLES

Enter LAFEU

LAFEU: [*Kneeling*] Pardon, my lord, for me and for my tidings.

KING: I'll fee thee to stand up.

LAFEU: Then here's a man stands that has brought his pardon.
I would you had kneel'd, my lord, to ask me mercy;
And that at my bidding you could so stand up.

KING: I would I had; so I had broke thy pate,
And ask'd thee mercy for't.

LAFEU: Good faith, across! But, my good lord 'tis thus: will you be cured of your infirmity?

KING: No.

LAFEU: O, will you eat
No grapes, my royal fox?
Yes, but you will
My noble grapes, an if my royal fox
Could reach them: I have seen a medicine
That's able to breathe life into a stone,
Quicken a rock, and make you dance canary
With spritely fire and motion; whose simple touch
Is powerful to araise King Pepin, nay,
To give great Charlemain a pen in's hand,
And write to her a love-line.

KING: What her is this?

LAFEU: Why, Doctor She! My lord, there's one arrived,
If you will see her. Now, by my faith and honour,
If seriously I may convey my thoughts
In this my light deliverance, I have spoke
With one that, in her sex, her years, profession,
Wisdom, and constancy, hath amazed me more
Than I dare blame my weakness. Will you see her,
For that is her demand, and know her business?
That done, laugh well at me.

KING: Now, good Lafeu,
Bring in the admiration, that we with thee
May spend our wonder too, or take off thine
By wondering how thou took'st it.

LAFEU: Nay, I'll fit you,
And not be all day neither.

Exit LAFEU

KING: Thus he his special nothing ever prologues.

Re-enter LAFEU, with HELENA

LAFEU: Nay, come your ways.

KING: This haste hath wings indeed.

LAFEU: Nay, come your ways;
This is his majesty; say your mind to him:
A traitor you do look like; but such traitors
His majesty seldom fears: I am Cressid's uncle,
That dare leave two together. Fare you well.

Exit

KING: Now, fair one, does your business follow us?

HELENA: Ay, my good lord.
Gerard de Narbon was my father,
In what he did profess, well found.

KING: I knew him.

HELENA: The rather will I spare my praises towards him;
Knowing him is enough. On's bed of death
Many receipts he gave me; chiefly one,
Which, as the dearest issue of his practise,
And of his old experience the oily darling,
He bade me store up as a triple eye,
Safer than mine own two, more dear. I have so
And, hearing your high majesty is touch'd
With that malignant cause wherein the honour
Of my dear father's gift stands chief in power,
I come to tender it, and my appliance
With all bound humbleness.

KING: We thank you, maiden;
But may not be so credulous of cure,
When our most learned doctors leave us, and
The congregated college have concluded
That labouring art can never ransom nature
From her inaidable estate—I say we must not
So stain our judgment, or corrupt our hope,
To prostitute our past-cure malady
To empirics; or to dissever so
Our great self and our credit to esteem
A senseless help, when help past sense we deem.

HELENA: My duty then shall pay me for my pains.
I will no more enforce mine office on you,
Humbly entreating from your royal thoughts
A modest one to bear me back again.

KING: I cannot give thee less, to be call'd grateful.
Thou thought'st to help me; and such thanks I give
As one near death to those that wish him live.
But what at full I know, thou know'st no part,
I knowing all my peril, thou no art.

HELENA: What I can do can do no hurt to try,
Since you set up your rest 'gainst remedy.
He that of greatest works is finisher
Oft does them by the weakest minister.
So holy writ in babes hath judgment shown,
When judges have been babes. Great floods have flown
From simple sources, and great seas have dried
When miracles have by the greatest been denied.
Oft expectation fails and most oft there
Where most it promises, and oft it hits
Where hope is coldest, and despair most fits.

KING: I must not hear thee. Fare thee well, kind maid;
Thy pains, not used, must by thyself be paid;
Proffers not took reap thanks for their reward.

HELENA: Inspired merit so by breath is barr'd.
It is not so with Him that all things knows,
As 'tis with us that square our guess by shows;
But most it is presumption in us when
The help of heaven we count the act of men.
Dear sir, to my endeavours give consent;
Of heaven, not me, make an experiment.
I am not an impostor, that proclaim
Myself against the level of mine aim;
But know I think, and think I know most sure,
My art is not past power nor you past cure.

KING: Art thou so confident? Within what space
Hopest thou my cure?

HELENA: The great'st grace lending grace,
Ere twice the horses of the sun shall bring
Their fiery torcher his diurnal ring,
Ere twice in murk and occidental damp
Moist Hesperus hath quench'd his sleepy lamp,
Or four and twenty times the pilot's glass
Hath told the thievish minutes how they pass,
What is infirm from your sound parts shall fly,
Health shall live free, and sickness freely die.

KING: Upon thy certainty and confidence
What darest thou venture?

HELENA: Tax of impudence,
A strumpet's boldness, a divulged shame
Traduced by odious ballads; my maiden's name
Sear'd otherwise; ne worse of worst—extended
With vilest torture let my life be ended.

KING: Methinks in thee some blessed spirit doth speak
His powerful sound within an organ weak;
And what impossibility would slay
In common sense, sense saves another way.
Thy life is dear; for all that life can rate
Worth name of life in thee hath estimate:
Youth, beauty, wisdom, courage, all
That happiness and prime can happy call.
Thou this to hazard needs must intimate
Skill infinite or monstrous desperate.
Sweet practiser, thy physic I will try,
That ministers thine own death if I die.

HELENA: If I break time, or flinch in property
Of what I spoke, unpitied let me die,
And well deserved. Not helping, death's my fee;
But, if I help, what do you promise me?

KING: Make thy demand.

HELENA: But will you make it even?

KING: Ay, by my sceptre and my hopes of heaven.

HELENA: Then shalt thou give me with thy kingly hand
What husband in thy power I will command.
Exempted be from me the arrogance
To choose from forth the royal blood of France,
My low and humble name to propagate
With any branch or image of thy state;
But such a one, thy vassal, whom I know
Is free for me to ask, thee to bestow.

KING: Here is my hand; the premises observed,
Thy will by my performance shall be served.
So make the choice of thy own time, for I,
Thy resolved patient, on thee still rely.
More should I question thee, and more I must,
Though more to know could not be more to trust,
From whence thou camest, how tended on. But rest
Unquestion'd welcome and undoubted blest.
Give me some help here, ho! If thou proceed
As high as word, my deed shall match thy deed.

Flourish. Exeunt

SCENE II—*Rousillon: The Count's palace*

Enter COUNTESS and CLOWN

COUNTESS: Come on, sir; I shall now put you to the height of your breeding.

CLOWN: I will show myself highly fed and lowly taught: I know my business is but to the court.

COUNTESS: To the court! Why, what place make you special, when you put off that with such contempt? But to the court!

CLOWN: Truly, madam, if God have lent a man any manners, he may easily put it off at court. He that cannot make a leg, put off's cap, kiss his hand, and say nothing, has neither leg, hands, lip, nor cap; and indeed such a fellow, to say precisely, were not for the court; but for me, I have an answer will serve all men.

COUNTESS: Marry, that's a bountiful answer that fits all questions.

CLOWN: It is like a barber's chair that fits all buttocks—the pin buttock, the quatch buttock, the brawn buttock, or any buttock.

COUNTESS: Will your answer serve fit to all questions?

Clown: As fit as ten groats is for the hand of an attorney, as your French crown for your taffety punk, as Tib's rush for Tom's forefinger, as a pancake for Shrove Tuesday, a morris for Mayday, as the nail to his hole, the cuckold to his horn, as a scolding queen to a wrangling knave, as the nun's lip to the friar's mouth; nay, as the pudding to his skin.

COUNTESS: Have you, I say, an answer of such fitness for all questions?

CLOWN: From below your duke to beneath your constable, it will fit any question.

COUNTESS: It must be an answer of most monstrous size that must fit all demands.

CLOWN: But a trifle neither, in good faith, if the learned should speak truth of it. Here it is, and all that belongs to't. Ask me if I am a courtier: it shall do you no harm to learn.

COUNTESS: To be young again, if we could, I will be a fool in question, hoping to be the wiser by your answer. I pray you, sir, are you a courtier?

CLOWN: O Lord, sir!—There's a simple putting off. More, more, a hundred of them.

COUNTESS: Sir, I am a poor friend of yours, that loves you.

CLOWN: O Lord, sir!—Thick, thick; spare not me.

COUNTESS: I think, sir, you can eat none of this homely meat.

CLOWN: O Lord, sir!—Nay, put me to't, I warrant you.

COUNTESS: You were lately whipped, sir, as I think.

CLOWN: O Lord, sir!—Spare not me.

COUNTESS: Do you cry, 'O Lord, sir!' at your whipping, and 'spare not me?' Indeed your 'O Lord, sir!' is very sequent to your whipping. You would answer very well to a whipping, if you were but bound to't.

CLOWN: I ne'er had worse luck in my life in my 'O Lord, sir!' I see things may serve long, but not serve ever.

COUNTESS: I play the noble housewife with the time,
To entertain it so merrily with a fool.

CLOWN: O Lord, sir!—Why, there't serves well again.

COUNTESS: An end, sir! To your business: give Helen this,
And urge her to a present answer back;
Commend me to my kinsmen and my son.
This is not much.

CLOWN: Not much commendation to them.

COUNTESS: Not much employment for you. You understand me?

CLOWN: Most fruitfully; I am there before my legs.

COUNTESS: Haste you again.

Exeunt

SCENE III—*Paris: The King's palace*

Enter BERTRAM, LAFEU, and PAROLLES

LAFEU: They say miracles are past; and we have our philosophical persons, to make modern and familiar, things supernatural and causeless. Hence is it that we make trifles of terrors, ensconcing ourselves into seeming knowledge when we should submit ourselves to an unknown fear.

PAROLLES: Why, 'tis the rarest argument of wonder that hath shot out in our latter times.

BERTRAM: And so 'tis.

LAFEU: To be relinquish'd of the artists,—

PAROLLES: So I say—both of Galen and Paracelsus.

LAFEU: Of all the learned and authentic fellows—

PAROLLES: Right; so I say.

LAFEU: That gave him out incurable—

PAROLLES: Why, there 'tis; so say I too.

LAFEU: Not to be helped—

PAROLLES: Right; as 'twere a man assured of a—

LAFEU: Uncertain life, and sure death.

PAROLLES: Just, you say well; so would I have said.

LAFEU: I may truly say, it is a novelty to the world.

PAROLLES: It is, indeed. If you will have it in showing, you shall read it in what do you call there?

LAFEU: [*Reading the ballad title*] 'A Showing of a Heavenly Effect in an Earthly Actor'.

PAROLLES: That's it; I would have said the very same.

LAFEU: Why, your dolphin is not lustier. Fore me, I speak in respect—

PAROLLES: Nay, 'tis strange, 'tis very strange, that is the brief and the tedious of it; and he's of a most facinerious spirit that will not acknowledge it to be the—

LAFEU: Very hand of heaven.

PAROLLES: Ay; so I say.

LAFEU: In a most weak—

PAROLLES: And debile minister, great power, great transcendence; which should, indeed, give us a further use to be made than alone the recovery of the king, as to be—

LAFEU: Generally thankful.

Enter KING, HELENA, and Attendants

PAROLLES: I would have said it; you say well. Here comes the king.

LAFEU: Lustig, as the Dutchman says. I'll like a maid the better, whilst I have a tooth in my head. Why, he's able to lead her a coranto.

PAROLLES: Mort du vinaigre! Is not this Helen?

LAFEU: Fore God, I think so.

KING: Go, call before me all the lords in court.

Exit an Attendant

Sit, my preserver, by thy patient's side;
And with this healthful hand, whose banish'd sense
Thou hast repeal'd, a second time receive
The confirmation of my promised gift,
Which but attends thy naming.

Enter three or four Lords

Fair maid, send forth thine eye. This youthful parcel
Of noble bachelors stand at my bestowing,
O'er whom both sovereign power and father's voice
I have to use. Thy frank election make;
Thou hast power to choose, and they none to forsake.

HELENA: To each of you one fair and virtuous mistress
Fall, when love please. Marry, to each, but one!

LAFEU: I'd give bay Curtal and his furniture
My mouth no more were broken than these boys',
And writ as little beard.

KING: Peruse them well.
Not one of those but had a noble father.

HELENA: Gentlemen,
Heaven hath through me restored the king to health.

All. We understand it, and thank heaven for you.

HELENA: I am a simple maid, and therein wealthiest.
That I protest I simply am a maid.
Please it your majesty, I have done already.
The blushes in my cheeks thus whisper me:
'We blush that thou shouldst choose; but, be refused,
Let the white death sit on thy cheek for ever,
We'll ne'er come there again.'

KING: Make choice and see:
Who shuns thy love shuns all his love in me.

HELENA: Now, Dian, from thy altar do I fly,
And to imperial Love, that god most high,
Do my sighs stream. Sir, will you hear my suit?

FIRST LORD: And grant it.

HELENA: Thanks, sir; all the rest is mute.

LAFEU: I had rather be in this choice than throw ames-ace for my life.

HELENA: The honour, sir, that flames in your fair eyes,
Before I speak, too threateningly replies:
Love make your fortunes twenty times above
Her that so wishes and her humble love!

SECOND LORD: No better, if you please.

HELENA: My wish receive,
Which great Love grant; and so, I take my leave.

LAFEU: Do all they deny her? An they were sons of mine I'd have them whipt; or I would send them to the Turk, to make eunuchs of.

HELENA: Be not afraid that I your hand should take;
I'll never do you wrong for your own sake.
Blessing upon your vows; and in your bed
Find fairer fortune, if you ever wed!

LAFEU: These boys are boys of ice, they'll none have her. Sure, they are bastards to the English; the French ne'er got 'em.

HELENA: You are too young, too happy, and too good,
To make yourself a son out of my blood.

Fourth Lord: Fair one, I think not so.

LAFEU: There's one grape yet; I am sure thy father drunk wine—but if thou be'st not an ass, I am a youth of fourteen; I have known thee already.

HELENA: [*To BERTRAM*] I dare not say I take you; but I give
Me and my service, ever whilst I live,
Into your guiding power. This is the man.

KING: Why, then, young Bertram, take her; she's thy wife.

BERTRAM: My wife, my liege! I shall beseech your highness,
In such a business give me leave to use
The help of mine own eyes.

KING: Know'st thou not, Bertram,
What she has done for me?

BERTRAM: Yes, my good lord;
But never hope to know why I should marry her.

KING: Thou know'st she has raised me from my sickly bed.

BERTRAM: But follows it, my lord, to bring me down
Must answer for your raising? I know her well:
She had her breeding at my father's charge.
A poor physician's daughter my wife! Disdain
Rather corrupt me ever!

KING: 'Tis only title thou disdain'st in her, the which
I can build up. Strange is it that our bloods,
Of colour, weight, and heat, pour'd all together,
Would quite confound distinction, yet stand off
In differences so mighty. If she be
All that is virtuous—save what thou dislikest,
A poor physician's daughter—thou dislikest
Of virtue for the name; but do not so.
From lowest place when virtuous things proceed,
The place is dignified by the doer's deed;
Where great additions swell 's, and virtue none,
It is a dropsied honour. Good alone
Is good without a name. Vileness is so:
The property by what it is should go,
Not by the title. She is young, wise, fair;
In these to nature she's immediate heir,
And these breed honour. That is honour's scorn
Which challenges itself as honour's born
And is not like the sire. Honours thrive
When rather from our acts we them derive
Than our foregoers. The mere word's a slave.
Debauch'd on every tomb, on every grave
A lying trophy, and as oft is dumb
Where dust and damn'd oblivion is the tomb
Of honour'd bones indeed. What should be said?
If thou canst like this creature as a maid,
I can create the rest. Virtue and she
Is her own dower; honour and wealth from me.

BERTRAM: I cannot love her, nor will strive to do't.

KING: Thou wrong'st thyself, if thou shouldst strive to choose.

HELENA: That you are well restored, my lord, I'm glad.
Let the rest go.

KING: My honour's at the stake; which to defeat,
I must produce my power. Here, take her hand,
Proud scornful boy, unworthy this good gift,
That dost in vile misprision shackle up
My love and her desert; that canst not dream
We, poising us in her defective scale,
Shall weigh thee to the beam; that wilt not know
It is in us to plant thine honour where
We please to have it grow. Check thy contempt;
Obey our will, which travails in thy good;
Believe not thy disdain, but presently
Do thine own fortunes that obedient right
Which both thy duty owes and our power claims;
Or I will throw thee from my care for ever
Into the staggers and the careless lapse
Of youth and ignorance; both my revenge and hate
Loosing upon thee, in the name of justice,
Without all terms of pity. Speak; thine answer.

BERTRAM: Pardon, my gracious lord; for I submit
My fancy to your eyes. When I consider

What great creation and what dole of honour
Flies where you bid it, I find that she which late
Was in my nobler thoughts most base, is now
The praised of the king; who, so ennobled,
Is as 'twere born so.

KING: Take her by the hand,
And tell her she is thine; to whom I promise
A counterpoise, if not to thy estate
A balance more replete.

BERTRAM: I take her hand.

KING: Good fortune and the favour of the king
Smile upon this contract; whose ceremony
Shall seem expedient on the now-born brief,
And be perform'd to-night. The solemn feast
Shall more attend upon the coming space,
Expecting absent friends. As thou lovest her,
Thy love's to me religious; else, does err.

Exeunt all but LAFEU and PAROLLES who stay behind, commenting of this wedding

LAFEU: [*Advancing*] Do you hear, monsieur? A word with you.

PAROLLES: Your pleasure, sir?

LAFEU: Your lord and master did well to make his recantation.

PAROLLES: Recantation! My lord! my master!

LAFEU: Ay; is it not a language I speak?

PAROLLES: A most harsh one, and not to be understood without bloody succeeding. My master!

LAFEU: Are you companion to the Count Rousillon?

PAROLLES: To any count, to all counts, to what is man.

LAFEU: To what is count's man: count's master is of another style.

PAROLLES: You are too old, sir; let it satisfy you, you are too old.

LAFEU: I must tell thee, sirrah, I write man; to which title age cannot bring thee.

PAROLLES: What I dare too well do, I dare not do.

LAFEU: I did think thee, for two ordinaries, to be a pretty wise fellow; thou didst make tolerable vent of thy travel; it might pass. Yet the scarfs and the bannerets about thee did manifoldly dissuade me from believing thee a vessel of too great a burthen. I have now found thee; when I lose thee again, I care not; yet art thou good for nothing but taking up; and that thou'rt scarce worth.

PAROLLES: Hadst thou not the privilege of antiquity upon thee—

LAFEU: Do not plunge thyself too far in anger, lest thou hasten thy trial; which if—Lord have mercy on thee for a hen! So, my good window of lattice, fare thee well; thy casement I need not open, for I look through thee. Give me thy hand.

PAROLLES: My lord, you give me most egregious indignity.

LAFEU: Ay, with all my heart; and thou art worthy of it.

PAROLLES: I have not, my lord, deserved it.

LAFEU: Yes, good faith, every dram of it; and I will not bate thee a scruple.

PAROLLES: Well, I shall be wiser.

LAFEU: Even as soon as thou canst, for thou hast to pull at a smack o' the contrary. If ever thou be'st bound in thy scarf and beaten, thou shalt find what it is to be proud of thy bondage. I have a desire to hold my acquaintance with thee, or rather my knowledge, that I may say in the default, 'he is a man I know'.

PAROLLES: My lord, you do me most insupportable vexation.

LAFEU: I would it were hell-pains for thy sake, and my poor doing eternal; for doing I am past, as I will by thee, in what motion age will give me leave.

Exit

PAROLLES: Well, thou hast a son shall take this disgrace off me: scurvy, old, filthy, scurvy lord! Well, I must be patient; there is no fettering of authority. I'll beat him, by my life, if I can meet him with any convenience, an he were double and double a lord. I'll have no more pity of his age than I would of—I'll beat him, an if I could but meet him again.

Re-enter LAFEU

LAFEU: Sirrah, your lord and master's married; there's news for you; you have a new mistress.

PAROLLES: I most unfeignedly beseech your lordship to make some reservation of your wrongs. He is my good lord: whom I serve above is my master.

LAFEU: Who? God?

PAROLLES: Ay, sir.

LAFEU: The devil it is that's thy master. Why dost thou garter up thy arms o' this fashion? Dost make hose of sleeves? Do other servants so? Thou wert best set thy lower part where thy nose stands. By mine honour, if I were but two hours younger, I'd beat thee. Methink'st, thou art a general offence, and every man should beat thee. I think thou wast created for men to breathe themselves upon thee.

PAROLLES: This is hard and undeserved measure, my lord.

LAFEU: Go to, sir; you were beaten in Italy for picking a kernel out of a pomegranate; you are a vagabond and no true traveler; you are more saucy with lords and honourable personages than the commission of your birth and virtue gives you heraldry. You are not worth another word, else I'd call you knave. I leave you.

Exit

Enter BERTRAM

PAROLLES: Good, very good, it is so then. Good, very good; let it be concealed awhile.

BERTRAM: Undone, and forfeited to cares for ever!

PAROLLES: What's the matter, sweet-heart?

BERTRAM: Although before the solemn priest I have sworn,
I will not bed her.

PAROLLES: What, what, sweet-heart?

BERTRAM: O my Parolles, they have married me!
I'll to the Tuscan wars, and never bed her.

PAROLLES: France is a dog-hole, and it no more merits
The tread of a man's foot. To the wars!

BERTRAM: There's letters from my mother; what the import is
I know not yet.

PAROLLES: Ay, that would be known. To the wars, my boy, to the wars!
He wears his honour in a box unseen,
That hugs his kicky-wicky here at home,
Spending his manly marrow in her arms,
Which should sustain the bound and high curvet
Of Mars's fiery steed. To other regions!
France is a stable; we that dwell in't jades;
Therefore, to the war!

BERTRAM: It shall be so; I'll send her to my house,
Acquaint my mother with my hate to her,
And wherefore I am fled; write to the king
That which I durst not speak. His present gift
Shall furnish me to those Italian fields
Where noble fellows strike. War is no strife
To the dark house and the detested wife.

PAROLLES: Will this capriccio hold in thee, art sure?

BERTRAM: Go with me to my chamber and advise me.
I'll send her straight away. To-morrow
I'll to the wars, she to her single sorrow.

PAROLLES: Why, these balls bound; there's noise in it. 'Tis hard:
A young man married is a man that's marr'd.
Therefore away, and leave her bravely; go.
The king has done you wrong; but, hush, 'tis so.

Exeunt

SCENE IV—*Paris: The King's palace*

Enter HELENA and CLOWN

HELENA: My mother greets me kindly; is she well?

Clown: She is not well; but yet she has her health; she's very merry; but yet she is not well. But thanks be given, she's very well and wants nothing i' the world; but yet she is not well.

HELENA: If she be very well, what does she ail that she's not very well?

Clown: Truly, she's very well indeed, but for two things.

HELENA: What two things?

Clown: One, that she's not in heaven, whither God send her quickly! The others that she's in earth, from whence God send her quickly!

Enter PAROLLES

PAROLLES: Bless you, my fortunate lady!

HELENA: I hope, sir, I have your good will to have mine own good fortunes.

PAROLLES: You had my prayers to lead them on; and to keep them on, have them still. O, my knave, how does my old lady?

CLOWN: So that you had her wrinkles and I her money, I would she did as you say.

PAROLLES: Why, I say nothing.

CLOWN: Marry, you are the wiser man; for many a man's tongue shakes out his master's undoing. To say nothing, to do nothing, to know nothing, and to have nothing, is to be a great part of your title; which is within a very little of nothing.

PAROLLES: Away! Th'art a knave.

CLOWN: You should have said, sir, 'Before a knave th'art a knave'; that's, 'Before me th'art a knave'. This had been truth, sir.

PAROLLES: Go to, thou art a witty fool; I have found thee.

CLOWN: Did you find me in yourself, sir? or were you
taught to find me? The search, sir, was profitable; and much fool may you find in you, even to the world's pleasure and the increase of laughter.

PAROLLES: A good knave, I' faith, and well fed.
Madam, my lord will go away to-night:
A very serious business calls on him.
The great prerogative and rite of love,
Which, as your due, time claims, he does acknowledge;
But puts it off to a compell'd restraint;
Whose want, and whose delay, is strew'd with sweets,
Which they distil now in the curbed time,
To make the coming hour o'erflow with joy
And pleasure drown the brim.

HELENA: What's his will else?

PAROLLES: That you will take your instant leave o' the king,
And make this haste as your own good proceeding,
Strengthen'd with what apology you think
May make it probable need.

HELENA: What more commands he?

PAROLLES: That, having this obtain'd, you presently
Attend his further pleasure.

HELENA: In every thing I wait upon his will.

PAROLLES: I shall report it so.

HELENA: I pray you. [*Exit Parolles*] Come, sirrah.

Exeunt

SCENE V—*Paris: The King's palace*

Enter LAFEU and BERTRAM

LAFEU: But I hope your lordship thinks not him a soldier.

BERTRAM: Yes, my lord, and of very valiant approof.

LAFEU: You have it from his own deliverance.

BERTRAM: And by other warranted testimony.

LAFEU: Then my dial goes not true: I took this lark for a bunting.

BERTRAM: I do assure you, my lord, he is very great in knowledge and accordingly valiant.

LAFEU: I have then sinned against his experience and transgressed against his valour; and my state that way is dangerous, since I cannot yet find in my heart to repent. Here he comes: I pray you, make us friends; I will pursue the amity.

Enter PAROLLES

PAROLLES: [*To BERTRAM*] These things shall be done, sir.

LAFEU: Pray you, sir, who's his tailor?

PAROLLES: Sir?

LAFEU: O, I know him well, Ay, sir; he, sir, 's a good workman, a very good tailor.

BERTRAM: [*Aside to PAROLLES*] Is she gone to the king?

PAROLLES: She is.

BERTRAM: Will she away to-night?

PAROLLES: As you'll have her.

BERTRAM: I have writ my letters, casketed my treasure,
Given order for our horses; and to-night,
When I should take possession of the bride,
End ere I do begin.

LAFEU: A good traveller is something at the latter end of a dinner; but one that lies three thirds and uses a known truth to pass a thousand nothings with, should be once heard and thrice beaten. God save you, captain.

BERTRAM: Is there any unkindness between my lord and you, monsieur?

PAROLLES: I know not how I have deserved to run into my lord's displeasure.

LAFEU: You have made shift to run into 't, boots and spurs and all, like him that leaped into the custard; and out of it you'll run again, rather than suffer question for your residence.

BERTRAM: It may be you have mistaken him, my lord.

LAFEU: And shall do so ever, though I took him at's prayers. Fare you well, my lord; and believe this of me: there can be no kernel in this light nut; the soul of this man is his clothes; trust him not in matter of heavy consequence; I have kept of them tame, and know their natures. Farewell, monsieur; I have spoken better of you than you have or will to deserve at my hand; but we must do good against evil.

Exit

PAROLLES: An idle lord. I swear.

BERTRAM: I think so.

PAROLLES: Why, do you not know him?

BERTRAM: Yes, I do know him well, and common speech
Gives him a worthy pass. Here comes my clog.

Enter HELENA

HELENA: I have, sir, as I was commanded from you,
Spoke with the king and have procured his leave
For present parting; only he desires
Some private speech with you.

BERTRAM: I shall obey his will.
You must not marvel, Helen, at my course,
Which holds not colour with the time, nor does
The ministration and required office
On my particular. Prepared I was not
For such a business; therefore am I found
So much unsettled. This drives me to entreat you
That presently you take our way for home;
And rather muse than ask why I entreat you;
For my respects are better than they seem
And my appointments have in them a need
Greater than shows itself at the first view
To you that know them not. This to my mother.

Giving a letter

'Twill be two days ere I shall see you; so
I leave you to your wisdom.

HELENA: Sir, I can nothing say
But that I am your most obedient servant.

BERTRAM: Come, come, no more of that.

HELENA: And ever shall
With true observance seek to eke out that
Wherein toward me my homely stars have fail'd
To equal my great fortune.

BERTRAM: Let that go.
My haste is very great. Farewell; hie home.

HELENA: Pray, sir, your pardon.

BERTRAM: Well, what would you say?

HELENA: I am not worthy of the wealth I owe,
Nor dare I say 'tis mine, and yet it is;
But, like a timorous thief, most fain would steal
What law does vouch mine own.

BERTRAM: What would you have?

HELENA: Something; and scarce so much; nothing, indeed.
I would not tell you what I would, my lord.
Faith yes:
Strangers and foes do sunder, and not kiss.

BERTRAM: I pray you, stay not, but in haste to horse.

HELENA: I shall not break your bidding, good my lord.

BERTRAM: Where are my other men, monsieur? Farewell!

Exit HELENA

Go thou toward home; where I will never come
Whilst I can shake my sword or hear the drum.
Away, and for our flight.

PAROLLES: Bravely, coragio!

Exeunt

Act III

Scene I—*Florence: The Duke's palace*

Flourish. Enter the DUKE OF FLORENCE attended; two French Lords, with a Troop of Soldiers

DUKE: So that from point to point, now have you heard
The fundamental reasons of this war,
Whose great decision hath much blood let forth
And more thirsts after.

FIRST LORD: Holy seems the quarrel
Upon your grace's part; black and fearful
On the opposer.

DUKE: Therefore we marvel much our cousin France
Would in so just a business shut his bosom
Against our borrowing prayers.

SECOND LORD: Good my lord,
The reasons of our state I cannot yield,
But like a common and an outward man.
That the great figure of a council frames
By self-unable motion; therefore dare not
Say what I think of it, since I have found
Myself in my incertain grounds to fail.
As often as I guess'd.

DUKE: Be it his pleasure.

FIRST LORD: But I am sure the younger of our nature,
That surfeit on their ease, will day by day
Come here for physic.

DUKE: Welcome shall they be;
And all the honours that can fly from us
Shall on them settle. You know your places well;
When better fall, for your avails they fell.
To-morrow to the field.

Flourish. Exeunt

Scene II—*Rousillon: The Count's palace*

Enter COUNTESS and CLOWN

COUNTESS: It hath happened all as I would have had it, save that he comes not along with her.

CLOWN: By my troth, I take my young lord to be a very melancholy man.

COUNTESS: By what observance, I pray you?

CLOWN: Why, he will look upon his boot and sing; mend the ruff and sing; ask questions and sing; pick his teeth and sing. I know a man that had this trick of melancholy sold a goodly manor for a song.

COUNTESS: Let me see what he writes, and when he means to come.

Opening a letter

CLOWN: I have no mind to Isbel since I was at court. Our old ling and our Isbels o' the country are nothing like your old ling and your Isbels o' the court. The brains of my Cupid's knocked out; and I begin to love, as an old man loves money, with no stomach.

COUNTESS: What have we here?

CLOWN: E'en that you have there.

Exit

COUNTESS: [*Reads*] 'I have sent you a daughter-in-law; she hath recovered the king, and undone me. I have wedded her, not bedded her; and sworn to make the "not" eternal. You shall hear I am run away; know it before the report come. If there be breadth enough in the world, I will hold a long distance. My duty to you. Your unfortunate son, Bertram'.
This is not well, rash and unbridled boy,
To fly the favours of so good a king,
To pluck his indignation on thy head
By the misprising of a maid too virtuous
For the contempt of empire.

Re-enter CLOWN

CLOWN: O madam, yonder is heavy news within between two soldiers and my young lady.

COUNTESS: What is the matter?

CLOWN: Nay, there is some comfort in the news, some comfort; your son will not be killed so soon as I thought he would.

COUNTESS: Why should he be killed?

CLOWN: So say I, madam, if he run away, as I hear he does; the danger is in standing to 't; that's the loss of men, though it be the getting of children. Here they come will tell you more. For my part, I only hear your son was run away.

Exit

Enter HELENA, and two French Gentlemen

SECOND GENTLEMAN: Save you, good madam.

HELENA: Madam, my lord is gone, for ever gone.

FIRST GENTLEMAN: Do not say so.

COUNTESS: Think upon patience. Pray you, gentlemen—
I have felt so many quirks of joy and grief,
That the first face of neither, on the start,
Can woman me unto 't. Where is my son, I pray you?

FIRST GENTLEMAN: Madam, he's gone to serve the duke of Florence.
We met him thitherward; for thence we came,
And, after some dispatch in hand at court,
Thither we bend again.

HELENA: Look on his letter, madam; here's my passport.
[*Reads*] 'When thou canst get the ring upon my finger which never shall come off, and show me a child begotten of thy body that I am father to, then call me husband; but in such a "then" I write a "never". This is a dreadful sentence.

COUNTESS: Brought you this letter, gentlemen?

FIRST GENTLEMAN: Ay, madam;
And for the contents' sake are sorry for our pain.

COUNTESS: I prithee, lady, have a better cheer;
If thou engrossest all the griefs are thine,
Thou robb'st me of a moiety. He was my son;
But I do wash his name out of my blood,
And thou art all my child. Towards Florence is he?

FIRST GENTLEMAN: Ay, madam.

COUNTESS: And to be a soldier?

FIRST GENTLEMAN: Such is his noble purpose; and, believe 't,
The Duke will lay upon him all the honour
That good convenience claims.

COUNTESS: Return you thither?

SECOND GENTLEMAN: Ay, madam, with the swiftest wing of speed.

HELENA: [*Reads*] 'Till I have no wife, I have nothing in France.'
'Tis bitter.

COUNTESS: Find you that there?

HELENA: Ay, madam.

SECOND GENTLEMAN: 'Tis but the boldness of his hand, haply, which his heart was not consenting to.

COUNTESS: Nothing in France until he have no wife!
There's nothing here that is too good for him
But only she; and she deserves a lord
That twenty such rude boys might tend upon,
And call her hourly mistress. Who was with him?

SECOND GENTLEMAN: A servant only, and a gentleman
Which I have sometime known.

COUNTESS: Parolles, was it not?

SECOND GENTLEMAN: Ay, my good lady, he.

COUNTESS: A very tainted fellow, and full of wickedness.
My son corrupts a well-derived nature
With his inducement.

SECOND GENTLEMAN: Indeed, good lady,
The fellow has a deal of that too much
Which holds him much to have.

COUNTESS: You're welcome, gentlemen.
I will entreat you, when you see my son,
To tell him that his sword can never win
The honour that he loses. More I'll entreat you
Written to bear along.

FIRST GENTLEMAN: We serve you, madam,
In that and all your worthiest affairs.

COUNTESS: Not so, but as we change our courtesies.
Will you draw near!

Exeunt COUNTESS and Gentlemen

HELENA: 'Till I have no wife, I have nothing in France.'
Nothing in France, until he has no wife!
Thou shalt have none, Rousillon, none in France;
Then hast thou all again. Poor lord! Is't I
That chase thee from thy country and expose
Those tender limbs of thine to the event

Of the none-sparing war? And is it I
That drive thee from the sportive court, where thou
Wast shot at with fair eyes, to be the mark
Of smoky muskets? O you leaden messengers,
That ride upon the violent speed of fire,
Fly with false aim; move the still-piecing air,
That sings with piercing; do not touch my lord.
Whoever shoots at him, I set him there;
Whoever charges on his forward breast,
I am the caitiff that do hold him to't;
And though I kill him not, I am the cause
His death was so effected. Better 'twere
I met the ravin lion when he roar'd
With sharp constraint of hunger; better 'twere
That all the miseries which nature owes
Were mine at once. No, come thou home, Rousillon,
Whence honour but of danger wins a scar,
As oft it loses all. I will be gone.
My being here it is that holds thee hence.
Shall I stay here to do't? No, no, although
The air of paradise did fan the house,
And angels officed all. I will be gone,
That pitiful rumour may report my flight
To consolate thine ear. Come, night; end, day.
For with the dark, poor thief, I'll steal away.

Exit

SCENE III—*Florence: Before the Duke's palace*

Flourish. Enter the DUKE OF FLORENCE, BERTRAM, PAROLLES, Soldiers, drum, and trumpets

DUKE: The general of our horse thou art; and we,
Great in our hope, lay our best love and credence
Upon thy promising fortune.

BERTRAM: Sir, it is
A charge too heavy for my strength, but yet
We'll strive to bear it for your worthy sake
To the extreme edge of hazard.

DUKE: Then go thou forth;
And fortune play upon thy prosperous helm,
As thy auspicious mistress!

BERTRAM: This very day,
Great Mars, I put myself into thy file;
Make me but like my thoughts, and I shall prove
A lover of thy drum, hater of love.

Exeunt

SCENE IV—*Rousillon: The Count's palace*

Enter COUNTESS and STEWARD

COUNTESS: Alas! and would you take the letter of her?
Might you not know she would do as she has done,
By sending me a letter? Read it again.

STEWARD: [Reads] 'I am Saint Jaques' pilgrim, thither gone.
Ambitious love hath so in me offended
That barefoot plod I the cold ground upon,
With sainted vow my faults to have amended.
Write, write, that from the bloody course of war
My dearest master, your dear son, may hie.
Bless him at home in peace, whilst I from far
His name with zealous fervor sanctify.
His taken labours bid him me forgive;
I, his despiteful Juno, sent him forth
From courtly friends, with camping foes to live,
Where death and danger dogs the heels of worth.
He is too good and fair for death and me;
Whom I myself embrace to set him free.'

COUNTESS: Ah, what sharp stings are in her mildest words!
Rinaldo, you did never lack advice so much,
As letting her pass so; had I spoke with her,
I could have well diverted her intents,
Which thus she hath prevented.

STEWARD: Pardon me, madam;
If I had given you this at over-night,
She might have been o'erta'en; and yet she writes
Pursuit would be but vain.

COUNTESS: What angel shall
Bless this unworthy husband? He cannot thrive,
Unless her prayers, whom heaven delights to hear
And loves to grant, reprieve him from the wrath
Of greatest justice. Write, write, Rinaldo,
To this unworthy husband of his wife;
Let every word weigh heavy of her worth
That he does weigh too light. My greatest grief,

Though little he do feel it, set down sharply.
Dispatch the most convenient messenger:
When haply he shall hear that she is gone,
He will return; and hope I may that she,
Hearing so much, will speed her foot again,
Led hither by pure love. Which of them both
Is dearest to me I have no skill in sense
To make distinction. Provide this messenger.
My heart is heavy, and mine age is weak;
Grief would have tears, and sorrow bids me speak.

Exeunt

SCENE V—*Without the walls of Florence*

A tucket afar off. Enter an old Widow of Florence, DIANA, VIOLENTA, and MARIANA, with other Citizens

WIDOW: Nay, come; for if they do approach the city, we shall lose all the sight.

DIANA: They say the French count has done most honourable service.

WIDOW: It is reported that he has taken their greatest commander; and that with his own hand he slew the duke's brother. [*Tucket*] We have lost our labour; they are gone a contrary way. Hark! you may know by their trumpets.

MARIANA: Come, let's return again, and suffice ourselves with the report of it. Well, Diana, take heed of this French earl; the honour of a maid is her name, and no legacy is so rich as honesty.

WIDOW: I have told my neighbour how you have been solicited by a gentleman his companion.

MARIANA: I know that knave, hang him! one Parolles; a filthy officer he is in those suggestions for the young earl. Beware of them, Diana: their promises, enticements, oaths, tokens, and all these engines of lust, are not the things they go under; many a maid hath been seduced by them; and the misery is, example, that so terrible shows in the wreck of maidenhood, cannot for all that dissuade succession, but that they are limed with the twigs that threaten them. I hope I need not to advise you further; but I hope your own grace will keep you where you are, though there were no further danger known but the modesty which is so lost.

DIANA: You shall not need to fear me.

Enter HELENA in the dress of a pilgrim

WIDOW: I hope so. Look, here comes a pilgrim. I know she will lie at my house: thither they send one another. I'll question her. God save you, pilgrim! Whither are bound?

HELENA: To Saint Jaques le Grand.
Where do the palmers lodge, I do beseech you?

WIDOW: At the Saint Francis here, beside the port.

HELENA: Is this the way? [*A march afar*].

WIDOW: Ay, marry, is't. Hark you! they come this way.
If you will tarry, holy pilgrim,
But till the troops come by,
I will conduct you where you shall be lodged;
The rather, for I think I know your hostess
As ample as myself.

HELENA: Is it yourself?

WIDOW: If you shall please so, pilgrim.

HELENA: I thank you, and will stay upon your leisure.

WIDOW: You came, I think, from France?

HELENA: I did so.

WIDOW: Here you shall see a countryman of yours
That has done worthy service.

HELENA: His name, I pray you.

DIANA: The Count Rousillon: know you such a one?

HELENA: But by the ear, that hears most nobly of him;
His face I know not.

DIANA: Whatsome'er he is,
He's bravely taken here. He stole from France,
As 'tis reported, for the king had married him
Against his liking. Think you it is so?

HELENA: Ay, surely, mere the truth; I know his lady.

DIANA: There is a gentleman that serves the Count
Reports but coarsely of her.

HELENA: What's his name?

DIANA: Monsieur Parolles.

HELENA: O, I believe with him,
In argument of praise, or to the worth
Of the great count himself, she is too mean
To have her name repeated; all her deserving
Is a reserved honesty, and that
I have not heard examined.

DIANA: Alas, poor lady!
'Tis a hard bondage to become the wife
Of a detesting lord.

WIDOW: I weet, good creature, wheresoe'er she is
Her heart weighs sadly. This young maid might do her
A shrewd turn, if she pleased.

HELENA: How do you mean?
May be the amorous Count solicits her
In the unlawful purpose.

WIDOW: He does, indeed;
And brokes with all that can in such a suit
Corrupt the tender honour of a maid;
But she is arm'd for him and keeps her guard
In honestest defence.

Enter, with drum and colours BERTRAM, PAROLLES, and the whole Army

MARIANA: The gods forbid else!

WIDOW: So, now they come.
That is Antonio, the Duke's eldest son;
That, Escalus.

HELENA: Which is the Frenchman?

DIANA: He—
That with the plume; 'tis a most gallant fellow.
I would he loved his wife; if he were honester
He were much goodlier. Isn't not a handsome gentleman?

HELENA: I like him well.

DIANA: 'Tis pity he is not honest. Yond's that same knave
That leads him to these places; were I his lady
I would poison that vile rascal.

HELENA: Which is he?

DIANA: That jack-an-apes with scarfs. Why is he melancholy?

HELENA: Perchance he's hurt i' the battle.

PAROLLES: Lose our drum! well.

MARIANA: He's shrewdly vexed at something. Look, he has spied us.

WIDOW: Marry, hang you!

MARIANA: And your courtesy, for a ring-carrier!

Exeunt BERTRAM, PAROLLES, and army

WIDOW: The troop is past. Come, pilgrim, I will bring you
Where you shall host. Of enjoin'd penitents
There's four or five, to great Saint Jacques bound,
Already at my house.

HELENA: I humbly thank you.
Please it this matron and this gentle maid
To eat with us to-night; the charge and thanking
Shall be for me, and, to requite you further,
I will bestow some precepts of this virgin,
Worthy the note.

BOTH: We'll take your offer kindly.

Exeunt

SCENE VI—*Camp before Florence*

Enter BERTRAM and the two French Lords

SECOND LORD: Nay, good my lord, put him to't; let him have his way.

FIRST LORD: If your lordship find him not a hilding, hold me no more in your respect.

SECOND LORD: On my life, my lord, a bubble.

BERTRAM: Do you think I am so far deceived in him?

SECOND LORD: Believe it, my lord, in mine own direct knowledge, without any malice, but to speak of him as my kinsman, he's a most notable coward, an infinite and endless liar, an hourly promise-breaker, the owner of no one good quality worthy your lordship's entertainment.

FIRST LORD: It were fit you knew him; lest, reposing too far in his virtue, which he hath not, he might at some great and trusty business in a main danger fail you.

BERTRAM: I would I knew in what particular action to try him.

FIRST LORD: None better than to let him fetch off his drum, which you hear him so confidently undertake to do.

SECOND LORD: I, with a troop of Florentines will suddenly surprise him; such I will have whom I am sure he knows not from the enemy. We will bind and hoodwink him so that he shall suppose no other but that he is carried into the leaguer of the adversaries, when we bring him to our own tents. Be but your lordship present at his examination; if he do not, for the promise of his life and in the highest compulsion of base fear, offer to betray you and deliver all the intelligence in his power against you, and that with the divine forfeit of his soul upon oath, never trust my judgment in anything.

FIRST LORD: O, for the love of laughter, let him fetch his drum; he says he has a stratagem for't: when your lordship sees the bottom of his success in't, and to what metal this counterfeit lump of ore will be melted, if you give him not John Drum's entertainment, your inclining cannot be removed. Here he comes.

Enter PAROLLES

SECOND LORD: O, for the love of laughter, hinder not the honour of his design; let him fetch off his drum in any hand.

BERTRAM: How now, monsieur! this drum sticks sorely in your disposition.

FIRST LORD: A pox on't; let it go; 'tis but a drum.

PAROLLES: But a drum! Is't but a drum? A drum so lost! There was excellent command: to charge in with our horse upon our own wings, and to rend our own soldiers!

FIRST LORD: That was not to be blamed in the command of the service; it was a disaster of war that Caesar himself could not have prevented, if he had been there to command.

BERTRAM: Well, we cannot greatly condemn our success. Some dishonour we had in the loss of that drum; but it is not to be recovered.

PAROLLES: It might have been recovered.

BERTRAM: It might, but it is not now.

PAROLLES: It is to be recovered. But that the merit of service is seldom attributed to the true and exact performer, I would have that drum or another, or 'hic jacet.'

BERTRAM: Why, if you have a stomach, to't, monsieur. If you think your mystery in stratagem can bring this instrument of honour again into his native quarter, be magnanimous in the enterprise and go on; I will grace the attempt for a worthy exploit. If you speed well in it, the Duke shall both speak of it and extend to you what further becomes his greatness, even to the utmost syllable of your worthiness.

PAROLLES: By the hand of a soldier, I will undertake it.

BERTRAM: But you must not now slumber in it.

PAROLLES: I'll about it this evening; and I will presently pen down my dilemmas, encourage myself in my certainty, put myself into my mortal preparation; and by midnight look to hear further from me.

BERTRAM: May I be bold to acquaint his grace you are gone about it?

PAROLLES: I know not what the success will be, my lord; but the attempt I vow.

BERTRAM: I know th'art valiant; and, to the possibility of thy soldiership, will subscribe for thee. Farewell.

PAROLLES: I love not many words.

Exit

SECOND LORD: No more than a fish loves water. Is not this a strange fellow, my lord, that so confidently seems to undertake this business, which he knows is not to be done; damns himself to do, and dares better be damned than to do't.

FIRST LORD: You do not know him, my lord, as we do. Certain it is that he will steal himself into a man's favour, and for a week escape a great deal of discoveries; but when you find him out, you have him ever after.

BERTRAM: Why, do you think he will make no deed at all of this that so seriously he does address himself unto?

SECOND LORD: None in the world; but return with an invention, and clap upon you two or three probable lies. But we have almost embossed him. You shall see his fall to-night; for indeed he is not for your lordship's respect.

FIRST LORD: We'll make you some sport with the fox ere we case him. He was first smoked by the old Lord Lafeu. When his disguise and he is parted, tell me what a sprat you shall find him; which you shall see this very night.

SECOND LORD: I must go look my twigs; he shall be caught.

BERTRAM: Your brother, he shall go along with me.

SECOND LORD: As't please your lordship. I'll leave you.

Exit

BERTRAM: Now will I lead you to the house, and show you
The lass I spoke of.

FIRST LORD: But you say she's honest.

BERTRAM: That's all the fault. I spoke with her but once,
And found her wondrous cold; but I sent to her,
By this same coxcomb that we have I' the wind,
Tokens and letters which she did re-send;
And this is all I have done. She's a fair creature;
Will you go see her?

FIRST LORD: With all my heart, my lord.

Exeunt

Scene VII—*Florence: The Widow's house*

Enter HELENA and WIDOW

HELENA: If you misdoubt me that I am not she,
I know not how I shall assure you further
But I shall lose the grounds I work upon.

WIDOW: Though my estate be fallen, I was well born,
Nothing acquainted with these businesses;
And would not put my reputation now
In any staining act.

HELENA: Nor would I wish you.
First, give me trust the Count he is my husband,
And what to your sworn counsel I have spoken
Is so from word to word; and then you cannot,
By the good aid that I of you shall borrow,
Err in bestowing it.

WIDOW: I should believe you;
For you have show'd me that which well approves
You're great in fortune.

HELENA: Take this purse of gold,
And let me buy your friendly help thus far,
Which I will over-pay and pay again
When I have found it. The Count he wooes your daughter,
Lays down his wanton siege before her beauty,
Resolved to carry her. Let her in fine consent,
As we'll direct her how 'tis best to bear it.
Now his important blood will nought deny
That she'll demand. A ring the county wears,
That downward hath succeeded in his house
From son to son some four or five descents
Since the first father wore it. This ring he holds
In most rich choice; yet, in his idle fire,
To buy his will, it would not seem too dear,
Howe'er repented after.

WIDOW: Now I see
The bottom of your purpose.

HELENA: You see it lawful, then. It is no more,
But that your daughter, ere she seems as won,
Desires this ring; appoints him an encounter;
In fine, delivers me to fill the time,
Herself most chastely absent. After this,
To marry her, I'll add three thousand crowns
To what is passed already.

WIDOW: I have yielded.
Instruct my daughter how she shall persever,
That time and place with this deceit so lawful
May prove coherent. Every night he comes
With musics of all sorts and songs composed
To her unworthiness. It nothing steads us
To chide him from our eaves, for he persists
As if his life lay on't.

HELENA: Why then to-night
Let us assay our plot; which, if it speed,
Is wicked meaning in a lawful deed,
And lawful meaning in a lawful act;
Where both not sin, and yet a sinful fact.
But let's about it.

Exeunt

Act IV

Scene I—*Without the Florentine camp*

Enter Second French Lord with five or six other Soldiers in ambush

SECOND LORD: He can come no other way but by this hedge-corner. When you sally upon him, speak what terrible language you will; though you understand it not yourselves, no matter; for we must not seem to understand him, unless some one among us, whom we must produce for an interpreter.

FIRST SOLDIER: Good captain, let me be the interpreter.

SECOND LORD: Art not acquainted with him? knows he not thy voice?

FIRST SOLDIER: No, sir, I warrant you.

SECOND LORD: But what linsey-woolsey hast thou to speak to us again?

FIRST SOLDIER: E'en such as you speak to me.

SECOND LORD: He must think us some band of strangers i' the adversary's entertainment. Now he hath a smack of all neighbouring languages; therefore we must every one be a man of his own fancy; not to know what we speak one to another, so we seem to know, is to know straight our purpose: choughs' language, gabble enough, and good enough. As for you, interpreter, you must seem very politic. But couch, ho! here he comes, to beguile two hours in a sleep, and then to return and swear the lies he forges.

Enter PAROLLES

PAROLLES: Ten o'clock. Within these three hours 'twill be time enough to go home. What shall I say I have done? It must be a very plausive invention that carries it. They begin to smoke me; and disgraces have of late knocked too often at my door. I find my tongue is too foolhardy; but my heart hath the fear of Mars before it, and of his creatures, not daring the reports of my tongue.

SECOND LORD: This is the first truth that e'er thine own tongue was guilty of.

PAROLLES: What the devil should move me to undertake the recovery of this drum, being not ignorant of the impossibility, and knowing I had no such purpose? I must give myself some hurts, and say I got them in exploit. Yet slight ones will not carry it. They will say, 'Came you off with so little?' And great ones I dare not give. Wherefore, what's the instance? Tongue, I must put you into a butter-woman's mouth and buy myself another of Bajazet's mule, if you prattle me into these perils.

SECOND LORD: Is it possible he should know what he is, and be that he is?

PAROLLES: I would the cutting of my garments would serve the turn, or the breaking of my Spanish sword.

SECOND LORD: We cannot afford you so.

PAROLLES: Or the baring of my beard; and to say it was in stratagem.

SECOND LORD: 'Twould not do.

PAROLLES: Or to drown my clothes, and say I was stripped.

SECOND LORD: Hardly serve.

PAROLLES: Though I swore I leaped from the window of the citadel—

SECOND LORD: How deep?

PAROLLES: Thirty fathom.

SECOND LORD: Three great oaths would scarce make that be believed.

PAROLLES: I would I had any drum of the enemy's; I would swear I recovered it.

SECOND LORD: You shall hear one anon.

Alarum within

PAROLLES: A drum now of the enemy's!

SECOND LORD: Throca movousus, cargo, cargo, cargo.

ALL: Cargo, cargo, cargo, villianda par corbo, cargo.

PAROLLES: O, ransom, ransom! Do not hide mine eyes.

They blindfold him

FIRST SOLDIER: Boskos thromuldo boskos.

PAROLLES: I know you are the Muskos' regiment,
And I shall lose my life for want of language.
If there be here German, or Dane, low Dutch,
Italian, or French, let him speak to me; I'll
discover that which shall undo the Florentine.

FIRST SOLDIER: Boskos vauvado. I understand thee, and can speak thy tongue. Kerely-bonto, sir, betake thee to thy faith, for seventeen poniards are at thy bosom.

PAROLLES: O!

FIRST SOLDIER: O, pray, pray, pray! Manka revania dulche.

SECOND LORD: Oscorbidulchos volivorco.

FIRST SOLDIER: The general is content to spare thee yet;
And, hoodwink'd as thou art, will lead thee on
To gather from thee. Haply thou mayst inform
Something to save thy life.

PAROLLES: O, let me live!
And all the secrets of our camp I'll show,
Their force, their purposes. Nay, I'll speak that
Which you will wonder at.

FIRST SOLDIER: But wilt thou faithfully?

PAROLLES: If I do not, damn me.

FIRST SOLDIER: Acordo linta.
Come on; thou art granted space.

Exit, with PAROLLES guarded.
A short alarum within

SECOND LORD: Go, tell the Count Rousillon, and my brother.
We have caught the woodcock, and will keep him muffled
Till we do hear from them.

SECOND SOLDIER: Captain, I will.

SECOND LORD: 'A will betray us all unto ourselves—
Inform on that.

SECOND SOLDIER: So I will, sir.

SECOND LORD: Till then I'll keep him dark and safely lock'd.

Exeunt

SCENE II—*Florence: The Widow's house*

Enter BERTRAM and DIANA

BERTRAM: They told me that your name was Fontibell.

DIANA: No, my good lord, Diana.

BERTRAM: Titled goddess;
And worth it, with addition! But, fair soul,
In your fine frame hath love no quality?
If the quick fire of youth light not your mind,
You are no maiden, but a monument;
When you are dead, you should be such a one
As you are now, for you are cold and stem;
And now you should be as your mother was
When your sweet self was got.

DIANA: She then was honest.

BERTRAM: So should you be.

DIANA: No.
My mother did but duty; such, my lord,
As you owe to your wife.

BERTRAM: No more o' that!
I prithee do not strive against my vows.
I was compell'd to her; but I love thee
By love's own sweet constraint, and will for ever
Do thee all rights of service.

DIANA: Ay, so you serve us
Till we serve you; but when you have our roses
You barely leave our thorns to prick ourselves
And mock us with our bareness.

BERTRAM: How have I sworn!

DIANA: 'Tis not the many oaths that makes the truth,
But the plain single vow that is vow'd true.
What is not holy, that we swear not by,
But take the High'st to witness. Then, pray you, tell me,
If I should swear by Jove's great attributes
I loved you dearly, would you believe my oaths
When I did love you ill? This has no holding,
To swear by him whom I protest to love
That I will work against him. Therefore your oaths
Are words and poor conditions, but unseal'd—
At least in my opinion.

BERTRAM: Change it, change it;
Be not so holy-cruel. Love is holy;
And my integrity ne'er knew the crafts
That you do charge men with. Stand no more off,
But give thyself unto my sick desires,
Who then recovers. Say thou art mine, and ever
My love as it begins shall so persever.

DIANA: I see that men make ropes in such a scarre
That we'll forsake ourselves. Give me that ring.

BERTRAM: I'll lend it thee, my dear, but have no power
To give it from me.

DIANA: Will you not, my lord?

BERTRAM: It is an honour 'longing to our house,
Bequeathed down from many ancestors;
Which were the greatest obloquy i' the world
In me to lose.

DIANA: Mine honour's such a ring:
My chastity's the jewel of our house,
Bequeathed down from many ancestors;
Which were the greatest obloquy i' the world
In me to lose. Thus your own proper wisdom
Brings in the champion Honour on my part
Against your vain assault.

BERTRAM: Here, take my ring;
My house, mine honour, yea, my life, be thine,
And I'll be bid by thee.

DIANA: When midnight comes, knock at my chamber-window;
I'll order take my mother shall not hear.
Now will I charge you in the band of truth,
When you have conquer'd my yet maiden bed,
Remain there but an hour, nor speak to me:
My reasons are most strong; and you shall know them
When back again this ring shall be deliver'd:
And on your finger in the night I'll put
Another ring, that what in time proceeds
May token to the future our past deeds.
Adieu till then; then fail not. You have won
A wife of me, though there my hope be done.

BERTRAM: A heaven on earth I have won by wooing thee.

Exit

DIANA: For which live long to thank both heaven and me!
You may so in the end.
My mother told me just how he would woo,
As if she sat in's heart; she says all men
Have the like oaths. He had sworn to marry me
When his wife's dead; therefore I'll lie with him
When I am buried. Since Frenchmen are so braid,
Marry that will, I live and die a maid.
Only in this disguise, I think't no sin
To cozen him that would unjustly win.

Exit

SCENE III—*The Florentine camp*

Enter the two French Lords and two or three Soldiers

SECOND LORD: You have not given him his mother's letter?

FIRST LORD: I have delivered it an hour since. There is something in't that stings his nature; for on the reading it he changed almost into another man.

SECOND LORD: He has much worthy blame laid upon him for shaking off so good a wife and so sweet a lady.

FIRST LORD: Especially he hath incurred the everlasting displeasure of the king, who had even tuned his bounty to sing happiness to him. I will tell you a thing, but you shall let it dwell darkly with you.

SECOND LORD: When you have spoken it, 'tis dead, and I am the grave of it.

FIRST LORD: He hath perverted a young gentlewoman here in Florence, of a most chaste renown; and this night he fleshes his will in the spoil of her honour. He hath given her his monumental ring, and thinks himself made in the unchaste composition.

SECOND LORD: Now, God delay our rebellion! As we are ourselves, what things are we!

FIRST LORD: Merely our own traitors. And as in the common course of all treasons, we still see them reveal themselves till they attain to their abhorred ends; so he that in this action contrives against his own nobility, in his proper stream, o'erflows himself.

SECOND LORD: Is it not meant damnable in us to be trumpeters of our unlawful intents? We shall not then have his company to-night?

FIRST LORD: Not till after midnight; for he is dieted to his hour.

SECOND LORD: That approaches apace. I would gladly have him see his company anatomized, that he might take a measure of his own judgments, wherein so curiously he had set this counterfeit.

FIRST LORD: We will not meddle with him till he come; for his presence must be the whip of the other.

SECOND LORD: In the meantime, what hear you of these wars?

FIRST LORD: I hear there is an overture of peace.

SECOND LORD: Nay, I assure you, a peace concluded.

FIRST LORD: What will Count Rousillon do then? Will he travel higher, or return again into France?

SECOND LORD: I perceive, by this demand, you are not altogether of his counsel.

FIRST LORD: Let it be forbid, sir! So should I be a great deal of his act.

SECOND LORD: Sir, his wife, some two months since, fled from his house. Her pretence is a pilgrimage to Saint Jaques le Grand; which holy undertaking with most austere sanctimony she accomplished; and, there residing the tenderness of her nature became as a prey to her grief; in fine, made a groan of her last breath, and now she sings in heaven.

FIRST LORD: How is this justified?

SECOND LORD: The stronger part of it by her own letters, which makes her story true even to the point of her death. Her death itself, which could not be her office to say is come, was faithfully confirmed by the rector of the place.

FIRST LORD: Hath the Count all this intelligence?

SECOND LORD: Ay, and the particular confirmations, point from point, to the full arming of the verity.

FIRST LORD: I am heartily sorry that he'll be glad of this.

SECOND LORD: How mightily sometimes we make us comforts of our losses!

FIRST LORD: And how mightily some other times we drown our gain in tears! The great dignity that his valour hath here acquired for him shall at home be encountered with a shame as ample.

SECOND LORD: The web of our life is of a mingled yarn, good and ill together. Our virtues would be proud, if our faults whipped them not; and our crimes would despair if they were not cherished by our virtues.

Enter a Messenger

How now? Where's your master?

SERVANT: He met the Duke in the street, sir; of whom he hath taken a solemn leave. His lordship will next morning for France. The Duke hath offered him letters of commendations to the king.

SECOND LORD: They shall be no more than needful there, if they were more than they can commend.

FIRST LORD: They cannot be too sweet for the king's tartness. Here's his lordship now.

Enter BERTRAM

How now, my lord! Is't not after midnight?

BERTRAM: I have to-night dispatched sixteen businesses, a month's length apiece; by an abstract of success: I have congied with the duke, done my adieu with his nearest; buried a wife, mourned for her; writ to my lady mother I am returning; entertained my convoy; and between these main parcels of dispatch effected many nicer needs. The last was the greatest, but that I have not ended yet.

SECOND LORD: If the business be of any difficulty, and this morning your departure hence, it requires haste of your lordship.

BERTRAM: I mean the business is not ended, as fearing to hear of it hereafter. But shall we have this dialogue between the Fool and the Soldier? Come, bring forth this counterfeit module has deceived me like a double-meaning prophesier.

SECOND LORD: Bring him forth [*Exeunt Soldiers*] Has sat I' the stocks all night, poor gallant knave.

BERTRAM: No matter; his heels have deserved it, in usurping his spurs so long. How does he carry himself?

SECOND LORD: I have told your lordship already the stocks carry him. But to answer you as you would be understood: he weeps like a wench that had shed her milk; he hath confessed himself to Morgan, whom he supposes to be a friar, from the time of his remembrance to this very instant disaster of his setting i' the stocks. And what think you he hath confessed?

BERTRAM: Nothing of me, has a'?

SECOND LORD: His confession is taken, and it shall be read to his face; if your lordship be in't, as I believe you are, you must have the patience to hear it.

Enter PAROLLES guarded, and First Soldier as interpreter

BERTRAM: A plague upon him! Muffled. He can say nothing of me.

SECOND LORD: Hush, hush! Hoodman comes! Portotartarossa.

FIRST SOLDIER: He calls for the tortures: What will you say without 'em?

PAROLLES: I will confess what I know without constraint; if ye pinch me like a pasty, I can say no more.

FIRST SOLDIER: Bosko chimurcho.
SECOND LORD: Boblibindo chicurmurco.
FIRST SOLDIER: You are a merciful general. Our General bids you answer to what I shall ask you out of a note.
PAROLLES: And truly, as I hope to live.
FIRST SOLDIER: 'First demand of him how many horse the Duke is strong.' What say you to that?
PAROLLES: Five or six thousand; but very weak and unserviceable. The troops are all scattered, and the commanders very poor rogues, upon my reputation and credit, and as I hope to live.
FIRST SOLDIER: Shall I set down your answer so?
PAROLLES: Do; I'll take the sacrament on't, how and which way you will.
BERTRAM: All's one to him. What a past-saving slave is this!
SECOND LORD: You're deceived, my lord; this is Monsieur Parolles, the gallant militarist—that was his own phrase—that had the whole theoric of war in the knot of his scarf, and the practice in the chape of his dagger.
FIRST LORD: I will never trust a man again for keeping his sword clean; nor believe he can have everything in him by wearing his apparel neatly.
FIRST SOLDIER: Well, that's set down.
PAROLLES: 'Five or six thousand horse' I said—I will say true—'or thereabouts' set down, for I'll speak truth.
SECOND LORD: He's very near the truth in this.
BERTRAM: But I con him no thanks for't in the nature he delivers it.
PAROLLES: 'Poor rogues' I pray you say.
FIRST SOLDIER: Well, that's set down.
PAROLLES: I humbly thank you, sir. A truth's a truth—the rogues are marvellous poor.
FIRST SOLDIER: 'Demand of him of what strength they are a-foot.' What say you to that?
PAROLLES: By my troth, sir, if I were to live this present hour, I will tell true. Let me see: Spurio, a hundred and fifty; Sebastian, so many; Corambus, so many; Jaques, so many; Guiltian, Cosmo, Lodowick, and Gratii, two hundred and fifty each; mine own company, Chitopher, Vaumond, Bentii, two hundred and fifty each; so that the muster-file, rotten and sound, upon my life, amounts not to fifteen thousand poll; half of the which dare not shake snow from off their cassocks, lest they shake themselves to pieces.
BERTRAM: What shall be done to him?
SECOND LORD: Nothing, but let him have thanks. Demand of him my condition, and what credit I have with the Duke.
FIRST SOLDIER: Well, that's set down. 'You shall demand of him whether one Captain Dumain be i' the camp, a Frenchman; what his reputation is with the Duke; what his valour, honesty, and expertness in wars; or whether he thinks it were not possible, with well-weighing sums of gold, to corrupt him to revolt.' What say you to this? What do you know of it?
PAROLLES: I beseech you, let me answer to the particular of the inter'gatories. Demand them singly.
FIRST SOLDIER: Do you know this Captain Dumain?
PAROLLES: I know him: 'a was a botcher's prentice in Paris, from whence he was whipt for getting the shrieve's fool with child—a dumb innocent, that could not say him nay.
BERTRAM: Nay, by your leave, hold your hands; though I know his brains are forfeit to the next tile that falls.
FIRST SOLDIER: Well, is this captain in the Duke of Florence's camp?
PAROLLES: Upon my knowledge, he is, and lousy.
SECOND LORD: Nay look not so upon me; shall hear of your lordship anon.
FIRST SOLDIER: What is his reputation with the Duke?
PAROLLES: The Duke knows him for no other but a poor officer of mine; and writ to me this other day to turn him out o' the band. I think I have his letter in my pocket.
FIRST SOLDIER: Marry, we'll search.
PAROLLES: In good sadness, I do not know; either it is there, or it is upon a file with the Duke's other letters in my tent.
FIRST SOLDIER: Here 'tis; here's a paper. Shall I read it to you?
PAROLLES: I do not know if it be it or no.
BERTRAM: Our interpreter does it well.
SECOND LORD: Excellently.
FIRST SOLDIER: [*Reads*] 'Dian, the Count's a fool, and full of gold'.
PAROLLES: That is not the Duke's letter, sir; that is an advertisement to a proper maid in Florence, one Diana, to take heed of the allurement of one Count

Rousillon, a foolish idle boy, but for all that very ruttish. I pray you, sir, put it up again.

FIRST SOLDIER: Nay, I'll read it first, by your favour.

PAROLLES: My meaning in't, I protest, was very honest in the behalf of the maid; for I knew the young Count to be a dangerous and lascivious boy, who is a whale to virginity and devours up all the fry it finds.

BERTRAM: Damnable both-sides rogue!

FIRST SOLDIER: [*Reads*] 'When he swears oaths, bid him drop gold, and take it;

After he scores, he never pays the score.

Half won is match well made; match, and well make it;

He ne'er pays after-debts, take it before.

And say a soldier, Dian, told thee this;

Men are to mell with, boys are not to kiss;

For count of this, the Count's a fool, I know it,

Who pays before, but not when he does owe it.

Thine, as he vowed to thee in thine ear,

PAROLLES.'

BERTRAM: He shall be whipt through the army with this rhyme in's forehead.

FIRST LORD: This is your devoted friend, sir, the manifold linguist and the armipotent soldier.

BERTRAM: I could endure anything before but a cat, and now he's a cat to me.

FIRST SOLDIER: I perceive, sir, by the General's looks, we shall be fain to hang you.

PAROLLES: My life, sir, in any case! Not that I am afraid to die, but that, my offences being many, I would repent out the remainder of nature. Let me live, sir, in a dungeon, i' the stocks, or any where, so I may live.

FIRST SOLDIER: We'll see what may be done, so you confess freely; therefore, once more to this Captain Dumain: you have answered to his reputation with the Duke and to his valour; what is his honesty?

PAROLLES: He will steal, sir, an egg out of a cloister; for rapes and ravishments he parallels Nessus. He professes not keeping of oaths; in breaking 'em he is stronger than Hercules. He will lie, sir, with such volubility, that you would think truth were a fool. Drunkenness is his best virtue, for he will be swine-drunk; and in his sleep he does little harm, save to his bedclothes about him; but they know his conditions and lay him in straw. I have but little more to say, sir, of his honesty. He has everything that an honest man should not have; what an honest man should have he has nothing.

SECOND LORD: I begin to love him for this.

BERTRAM: For this description of thine honesty? A pox upon him. For me, he's more and more a cat.

FIRST SOLDIER: What say you to his expertness in war?

PAROLLES: Faith, sir, he has led the drum before the English tragedians—to belie him—I will not—and more of his soldiership I know not, except in that country he had the honour to be the officer at a place there called Mile-end to instruct for the doubling of files—I would do the man what honour I can—but of this I am not certain.

SECOND LORD: He hath out-villained villainy so far that the rarity redeems him.

BERTRAM: A pox on him! he's a cat still.

FIRST SOLDIER: His qualities being at this poor price, I need not to ask you if gold will corrupt him to revolt.

PAROLLES: Sir, for a cardecue he will sell the fee-simple of his salvation, the inheritance of it; and cut the entail from all remainders and a perpetual succession for it perpetually.

FIRST SOLDIER: What's his brother, the other Captain Dumain?

FIRST LORD: Why does be ask him of me?

FIRST SOLDIER: What's he?

PAROLLES: E'en a crow o' the same nest; not altogether so great as the first in goodness, but greater a great deal in evil. He excels his brother for a coward, yet his brother is reputed one of the best that is. In a retreat he outruns any lackey: marry, in coming on he has the cramp.

FIRST SOLDIER: If your life be saved, will you undertake to betray the Florentine?

PAROLLES: Ay, and the Captain of his Horse, Count Rousillon.

FIRST SOLDIER: I'll whisper with the general, and know his pleasure.

PAROLLES: [*Aside*] I'll no more drumming; a plague of all drums! Only to seem to deserve well, and to beguile the supposition of that lascivious young boy the Count, have I run into this danger. Yet who would have suspected an ambush where I was taken?

FIRST SOLDIER: There is no remedy, sir, but you must die. The General says you that have so traitorously discovered the secrets of your army, and made such pestiferous reports of men very nobly held, can serve the world for no honest use; therefore you must die. Come, headsman, off with his head.

PAROLLES: O Lord, sir, let me live, or let me see my death!

FIRST SOLDIER: That shall you, and take your leave of all your friends.

Unmuffling him

So look about you; know you any here?

BERTRAM: Good morrow, noble Captain.

FIRST LORD: God bless you, Captain Parolles.

SECOND LORD: God save you, noble Captain.

FIRST LORD: Captain, what greeting will you to my Lord Lafeu? I am for France.

SECOND LORD: Good Captain, will you give me a copy of the sonnet you writ to Diana in behalf of the Count Rousillon? An I were not a very coward, I'ld compel it of you; but fare you well.

Exeunt BERTRAM and Lords

FIRST SOLDIER: You are undone, captain, all but your scarf; that has a knot on't yet.

PAROLLES: Who cannot be crushed with a plot?

FIRST SOLDIER: If you could find out a country where but women were that had received so much shame, you might begin an impudent nation. Fare ye well, sir; I am for France too; we shall speak of you there.

Exit with Soldiers

PAROLLES: Yet am I thankful. If my heart were great,
'Twould burst at this. Captain I'll be no more;
But I will eat, and drink, and sleep as soft
As captain shall. Simply the thing I am
Shall make me live. Who knows himself a braggart,
Let him fear this, for it will come to pass
that every braggart shall be found an ass.
Rust, sword; cool, blushes; and, Parolles, live
Safest in shame. Being fool'd, by foolery thrive.
There's place and means for every man alive.
I'll after them.

Exit

SCENE IV—*Florence: The Widow's house*

Enter HELENA, Widow, and DIANA

HELENA: That you may well perceive I have not wrong'd you,
One of the greatest in the Christian world
Shall be my surety; fore whose throne 'tis needful,
Ere I can perfect mine intents, to kneel.
Time was, I did him a desired office,
Dear almost as his life; which gratitude
Through flinty Tartar's bosom would peep forth,
And answer, thanks. I duly am inform'd
His grace is at Marseilles; to which place
We have convenient convoy. You must know
I am supposed dead. The army breaking,
My husband hies him home; where, heaven aiding,
And by the leave of my good lord the king,
We'll be before our welcome.

WIDOW: Gentle madam,
You never had a servant to whose trust
Your business was more welcome.

HELENA: Nor you, mistress,
Ever a friend whose thoughts more truly labour
To recompense your love. Doubt not but heaven
Hath brought me up to be your daughter's dower,
As it hath fated her to be my motive
And helper to a husband. But, O strange men!
That can such sweet use make of what they hate,
When saucy trusting of the cozen'd thoughts
Defiles the pitchy night. So lust doth play
With what it loathes, for that which is away.
But more of this hereafter. You, Diana,
Under my poor instructions yet must suffer
Something in my behalf.

DIANA: Let death and honesty
Go with your impositions, I am yours
Upon your will to suffer.

HELENA: Yet, I pray you:
But with the word the time will bring on summer,
When briers shall have leaves as well as thorns
And be as sweet as sharp. We must away;
Our wagon is prepared, and time revives us.
All's Well that Ends Well; Still the fine's the crown.
Whate'er the course, the end is the renown.

Exeunt

SCENE V—*Rousillon: The Count's palace*

Enter COUNTESS, LAFEU, and CLOWN

LAFEU: No, no, no, your son was misled with a snipt-taffeta fellow there, whose villanous saffron would have made all the unbaked and doughy youth of a nation in his colour. Your daughter-in-law had been alive at this hour, and your son here at home, more advanced by the King than by that red-tailed humble-bee I speak of.

COUNTESS: I would I had not known him; it was the death of the most virtuous gentlewoman that ever nature had praise for creating. If she had partaken of my flesh, and cost me the dearest groans of a mother, I could not have owed her a more rooted love.

LAFEU: 'Twas a good lady, 'twas a good lady. We may pick a thousand sallets ere we light on such another herb.

CLOWN: Indeed, sir, she was the sweet-marjoram of the sallet, or rather, the herb of grace.

LAFEU: They are not sallet-herbs, you knave; they are nose-herbs.

CLOWN: I am no great Nebuchadnezzar, sir; I have not much skill in grass.

LAFEU: Whether dost thou profess thyself—a knave or a fool?

CLOWN: A fool, sir, at a woman's service, and a knave at a man's.

LAFEU: Your distinction?

CLOWN: I would cozen the man of his wife, and do his service.

LAFEU: So you were a knave at his service, indeed.

CLOWN: And I would give his wife my bauble, sir, to do her service.

LAFEU: I will subscribe for thee; thou art both knave and fool.

CLOWN: At your service.

LAFEU: No, no, no.

CLOWN: Why, sir, if I cannot serve you, I can serve as great a prince as you are.

LAFEU: Who's that? A Frenchman?

CLOWN: Faith, sir, 'a has an English name; but his fisnomy is more hotter in France than there.

LAFEU: What prince is that?

CLOWN: The Black Prince, sir; alias, the Prince of Darkness; alias, the devil.

LAFEU: Hold thee, there's my purse. I give thee not this to suggest thee from thy master thou talkest of; serve him still.

CLOWN: I am a woodland fellow, sir, that always loved a great fire; and the master I speak of ever keeps a good fire. But, sure, he is the prince of the world; let his nobility remain in's court. I am for the house with the narrow gate, which I take to be too little for pomp to enter. Some that humble themselves may; but the many will be too chill and tender; and they'll be for the flowery way that leads to the broad gate and the great fire.

LAFEU: Go thy ways, I begin to be aweary of thee; and I tell thee so before, because I would not fall out with thee. Go thy ways; let my horses be well looked to, without any tricks.

CLOWN: If I put any tricks upon 'em, sir, they shall be jades' tricks, which are their own right by the law of nature.

Exit

LAFEU: A shrewd knave, and an unhappy.

COUNTESS: So 'a is. My lord that's gone made himself much sport out of him. By his authority he remains here, which he thinks is a patent for his sauciness; and, indeed, he has no pace, but runs where he will.

LAFEU: I like him well; 'tis not amiss. And I was about to tell you, since I heard of the good lady's death, and that my lord your son was upon his return home, I moved the king my master to speak in the behalf of my daughter; which, in the minority of them both, his majesty, out of a self-gracious remembrance, did first propose. His highness hath promised me to do it; and, to stop up the displeasure he hath conceived against your son, there is no fitter matter. How does your ladyship like it?

COUNTESS: With very much content, my lord; and I wish it happily effected.

LAFEU: His highness comes post from Marseilles, of as able body as when he numbered thirty; 'a will be here to-morrow, or I am deceived by him that in such intelligence hath seldom failed.

COUNTESS: It rejoices me, that I hope I shall see him ere I die. I have letters that my son will be here to-night. I shall beseech your lordship to remain with me till they meet together.

LAFEU: Madam, I was thinking with what manners I might safely be admitted.

COUNTESS: You need but plead your honourable privilege.

LAFEU: Lady, of that I have made a bold charter; but, I thank my God, it holds yet.

Re-enter CLOWN

CLOWN: O madam, yonder's my lord your son with a patch of velvet on's face; whether there be a scar under't or no, the velvet knows; but 'tis a goodly patch of velvet. His left cheek is a cheek of two pile and a half, but his right cheek is worn bare.

LAFEU: A scar nobly got, or a noble scar, is a good livery of honour; so belike is that.

CLOWN: But it is your carbonadoed face.

LAFEU: Let us go see your son, I pray you; I long to talk with the young noble soldier.

CLOWN: Faith there's a dozen of 'em, with delicate fine hats, and most courteous feathers, which bow the head and nod at every man.

Exeunt

Act V

Scene I—*Marseilles: A street*

Enter HELENA, WIDOW, and DIANA, with two Attendants

HELENA: But this exceeding posting day and night
Must wear your spirits low; we cannot help it.
But since you have made the days and nights as one,
To wear your gentle limbs in my affairs,
Be bold you do so grow in my requital
As nothing can unroot you.

Enter a Gentleman

In happy time!
This man may help me to his majesty's ear,
If he would spend his power. God save you, sir.

GENTLEMAN: And you.

HELENA: Sir, I have seen you in the court of France.

GENTLEMAN: I have been sometimes there.

HELENA: I do presume, sir, that you are not fallen
From the report that goes upon your goodness;
And therefore, goaded with most sharp occasions,
Which lay nice manners by, I put you to
The use of your own virtues, for the which
I shall continue thankful.

GENTLEMAN: What's your will?

HELENA: That it will please you
To give this poor petition to the king,
And aid me with that store of power you have
To come into his presence.

GENTLEMAN: The king's not here.

HELENA: Not here, sir!

GENTLEMAN: Not, indeed.
He hence removed last night, and with more haste
Than is his use.

WIDOW: Lord, how we lose our pains!

HELENA: All's Well That Ends Well yet,
Though time seem so adverse and means unfit.
I do beseech you, whither is he gone?

GENTLEMAN: Marry, as I take it, to Rousillon;
Whither I am going.

HELENA: I do beseech you, sir,
Since you are like to see the king before me,
Commend the paper to his gracious hand;
Which I presume shall render you no blame,
But rather make you thank your pains for it.
I will come after you with what good speed
Our means will make us means.

GENTLEMAN: This I'll do for you.

HELENA: And you shall find yourself to be well thank'd,
Whate'er falls more. We must to horse again;
Go, go, provide.

Exeunt

Scene II—*Rousillon: The Inner Court of the Count's palace*

Enter CLOWN, and PAROLLES

PAROLLES: Good Monsieur Lavache, give my Lord Lafeu this letter. I have ere now, sir, been better known to you, when I have held familiarity with fresher clothes; but I am now, sir, muddied in fortune's mood, and smell somewhat strong of her strong displeasure.

CLOWN: Truly, fortune's displeasure is but sluttish, if it smell so strongly as thou speakest of. I will henceforth eat no fish of fortune's buttering. Prithee, allow the wind.

PAROLLES: Nay, you need not to stop your nose, sir; I spake but by a metaphor.

CLOWN: Indeed, sir, if your metaphor stink, I will stop my nose; or against any man's metaphor. Prithee, get thee further.

PAROLLES: Pray you, sir, deliver me this paper.

CLOWN: Foh! prithee stand away. A paper from fortune's close-stool to give to a nobleman! Look, here he comes himself.

Enter LAFEU

Here is a pur of fortune's, sir, or of fortune's cat, but not a musk-cat, that has fallen into the unclean fishpond of her displeasure, and, as he says, is muddied withal. Pray you, sir, use the carp as you may; for he looks like a poor, decayed, ingenious, foolish, rascally knave. I do pity his distress in my similes of comfort and leave him to your lordship.

Exit

PAROLLES: My lord, I am a man whom fortune hath cruelly scratched.

LAFEU: And what would you have me to do? 'Tis too late to pare her nails now. Wherein have you played the knave with fortune, that she should scratch you, who of herself is a good lady and would not have knaves thrive long under her? There's a cardecue for you. Let the justices make you and fortune friends; I am for other business.

PAROLLES: I beseech your honour to hear me one single word.

LAFEU: You beg a single penny more; come, you shall ha't; save your word.

PAROLLES: My name, my good lord, is Parolles.

LAFEU: You beg more than word then. Cox my passion! give me your hand. How does your drum?

PAROLLES: O my good lord, you were the first that found me!

LAFEU: Was I, in sooth? And I was the first that lost thee.

PAROLLES: It lies in you, my lord, to bring me in some grace, for you did bring me out.

LAFEU: Out upon thee, knave! Dost thou put upon me at once both the office of God and the devil? One brings thee in grace, and the other brings thee out. [*Trumpets sound*] The king's coming; I know by his trumpets. Sirrah, inquire further after me; I had talk of you last night. Though you are a fool and a knave, you shall eat. Go to; follow.

PAROLLES: I praise God for you.

Exeunt

SCENE III—*Rousillon: The Count's palace*

Flourish. Enter KING, COUNTESS, LAFEU, the two French Lords, with Attendants

KING: We lost a jewel of her; and our esteem
Was made much poorer by it; but your son,
As mad in folly, lack'd the sense to know
Her estimation home.

COUNTESS: 'Tis past, my liege;
And I beseech your majesty to make it
Natural rebellion, done I' the blaze of youth,
When oil and fire, too strong for reason's force,
O'erbears it and burns on.

KING: My honour'd lady,
I have forgiven and forgotten all;
Though my revenges were high bent upon him,
And watch'd the time to shoot.

LAFEU: This I must say—
But first, I beg my pardon: the young lord
Did to his majesty, his mother, and his lady,
Offence of mighty note; but to himself
The greatest wrong of all. He lost a wife
Whose beauty did astonish the survey
Of richest eyes, whose words all ears took captive,
Whose dear perfection hearts that scorn'd to serve
Humbly call'd mistress.

KING: Praising what is lost
Makes the remembrance dear. Well, call him hither;
We are reconciled, and the first view shall kill
All repetition. Let him not ask our pardon;
The nature of his great offence is dead,
And deeper than oblivion do we bury
The incensing relics of it; let him approach,
A stranger, no offender; and inform him
So 'tis our will he should.

GENTLEMAN: I shall, my liege.

Exit Gentleman

KING: What says he to your daughter? Have you spoke?

LAFEU: All that he is hath reference to your highness.

KING: Then shall we have a match. I have letters sent me

That sets him high in fame.

Enter BERTRAM

LAFEU: He looks well on't.

KING: I am not a day of season,
For thou mayst see a sunshine and a hail
In me at once. But to the brightest beams
Distracted clouds give way; so stand thou forth;
The time is fair again.

BERTRAM: My high-repented blames,
Dear sovereign, pardon to me.

KING: All is whole;
Not one word more of the consumed time.
Let's take the instant by the forward top;
For we are old, and on our quick'st decrees
The inaudible and noiseless foot of Time
Steals ere we can effect them. You remember
The daughter of this lord?

BERTRAM: Admiringly, my liege. At first
I stuck my choice upon her, ere my heart
Durst make too bold a herald of my tongue;
Where the impression of mine eye infixing,
Contempt his scornful perspective did lend me,
Which warp'd the line of every other favour,
Scorn'd a fair colour, or express'd it stolen,
Extended or contracted all proportions
To a most hideous object. Thence it came
That she whom all men prais'd and whom myself,
Since I have lost, have loved, was in mine eye
The dust that did offend it.

KING: Well excused:
That thou didst love her, strikes some scores away
From the great compt; but love that comes too late,
Like a remorseful pardon slowly carried,
To the great sender turns a sour offence,
Crying, 'That's good that's gone'. Our rash faults
Make trivial price of serious things we have,
Not knowing them until we know their grave.
Oft our displeasures, to ourselves unjust,
Destroy our friends, and after weep their dust;
Our own love waking cries to see what's done,
While shameful hate sleeps out the afternoon.
Be this sweet Helen's knell. And now forget her.
Send forth your amorous token for fair Maudlin.
The main consents are had; and here we'll stay
To see our widower's second marriage-day.

COUNTESS: Which better than the first, O dear heaven, bless!
Or, ere they meet, in me, O nature, cesse!

LAFEU: Come on, my son, in whom my house's name
Must be digested; give a favour from you,
To sparkle in the spirits of my daughter,
That she may quickly come.

BERTRAM gives a ring

By my old beard,
And every hair that's on't, Helen, that's dead,
Was a sweet creature; such a ring as this,
The last that e'er I took her at court,
I saw upon her finger.

BERTRAM: Hers it was not.

KING: Now, pray you, let me see it; for mine eye,
While I was speaking, oft was fasten'd to't.
This ring was mine; and, when I gave it Helen
I bade her, if her fortunes ever stood
Necessitied to help, that by this token
I would relieve her. Had you that craft, to reave her
Of what should stead her most?

BERTRAM: My gracious sovereign,
Howe'er it pleases you to take it so,
The ring was never hers.

COUNTESS: Son, on my life,
I have seen her wear it; and she reckon'd it
At her life's rate.

LAFEU: I am sure I saw her wear it.

BERTRAM: You are deceived, my lord; she never saw it.
In Florence was it from a casement thrown me,
Wrapp'd in a paper, which contain'd the name
Of her that threw it. Noble she was, and thought
I stood engaged; but when I had subscribed
To mine own fortune, and inform'd her fully
I could not answer in that course of honour
As she had made the overture, she ceased,
In heavy satisfaction, and would never
Receive the ring again.

KING: Plutus himself,

That knows the tinct and multiplying medicine,
Hath not in nature's mystery more science
Than I have in this ring. 'Twas mine, 'twas Helen's,
Whoever gave it you. Then, if you know
That you are well acquainted with yourself,
Confess 'twas hers, and by what rough enforcement
You got it from her. She call'd the saints to surety
That she would never put it from her finger
Unless she gave it to yourself in bed—
Where you have never come—or sent it us
Upon her great disaster.

BERTRAM: She never saw it.

KING: Thou speak'st it falsely, as I love mine honour;
And makest conjectural fears to come into me
Which I would fain shut out. If it should prove
That thou art so inhuman—'twill not prove so.—
And yet I know not—thou didst hate her deadly,
And she is dead; which nothing, but to close
Her eyes myself, could win me to believe
More than to see this ring. Take him away.

Guards seize BERTRAM

My fore-past proofs, howe'er the matter fall,
Shall tax my fears of little vanity,
Having vainly fear'd too little. Away with him.
We'll sift this matter further.

BERTRAM: If you shall prove
This ring was ever hers, you shall as easy
Prove that I husbanded her bed in Florence,
Where yet she never was.

Exit guarded

KING: I am wrap'd in dismal thinkings.

Enter a Gentleman

GENTLEMAN: Gracious sovereign,
Whether I have been to blame or no, I know not:
Here's a petition from a Florentine,
Who hath, for four or five removes, come short
To tender it herself. I undertook it,
Vanquish'd thereto by the fair grace and speech
Of the poor suppliant, who by this, I know
Is here attending; her business looks in her
With an importing visage; and she told me
In a sweet verbal brief it did concern
Your Highness with herself.

KING: [*Reads the letter*] 'Upon his many protestations to marry me when his wife was dead, I blush to say it, he won me. Now is the Count Rousillon a widower; his vows are forfeited to me, and my honour's paid to him. He stole from Florence, taking no leave, and I follow him to his country for justice. Grant it me, O king! in you it best lies; otherwise a seducer flourishes, and a poor maid is undone.

DIANA CAPILET.'

LAFEU: I will buy me a son-in-law in a fair, and toll for this. I'll none of him.

KING: The heavens have thought well on thee, Lafeu,
To bring forth this discovery. Seek these suitors.
Go speedily and bring again the Count.

Exeunt Attendants

I am afeard the life of Helen, lady,
Was foully snatch'd.

COUNTESS: Now, justice on the doers!

Re-enter BERTRAM, guarded

KING: I wonder, sir, sith wives are monsters to you,
And that you fly them as you swear them lordship,
Yet you desire to marry.

Enter Widow and DIANA

What woman's that?

DIANA: I am, my lord, a wretched Florentine,
Derived from the ancient Capilet.
My suit, as I do understand, you know,
And therefore know how far I may be pitied.

WIDOW: I am her mother, sir, whose age and honour
Both suffer under this complaint we bring,
And both shall cease, without your remedy.

KING: Come hither, Count; do you know these women?

BERTRAM: My lord, I neither can nor will deny
But that I know them. Do they charge me further?

DIANA: Why do you look so strange upon your wife.

BERTRAM: She's none of mine, my lord.

DIANA: If you shall marry,

You give away this hand, and that is mine;
You give away heaven's vows, and those are mine;
You give away myself, which is known mine;
For I by vow am so embodied yours
That she which marries you must marry me,
Either both or none.

LAFEU: [*To Bertram*] Your reputation comes too short for my daughter; you are no husband for her.

BERTRAM: My lord, this is a fond and desperate creature
Whom sometime I have laugh'd with. Let your Highness
Lay a more noble thought upon mine honour
Than for to think that I would sink it here.

KING: Sir, for my thoughts, you have them ill to friend
Till your deeds gain them. Fairer prove your honour
Than in my thought it lies!

DIANA: Good my lord,
Ask him upon his oath if he does think
He had not my virginity.

KING: What say'st thou to her?

BERTRAM: She's impudent, my lord,
And was a common gamester to the camp.

DIANA: He does me wrong, my lord; if I were so
He might have bought me at a common price.
Do not believe him. O, behold this ring,
Whose high respect and rich validity
Did lack a parallel; yet for all that,
He gave it to a commoner o' the camp,
If I be one.

COUNTESS: He blushes, and 'tis it.
Of six preceding ancestors, that gem
Conferr'd by testament to the sequent issue,
Hath it been owed and worn. This is his wife:
That ring's a thousand proofs.

KING: Methought you said
You saw one here in court could witness it.

DIANA: I did, my lord, but loath am to produce
So bad an instrument; his name's Parolles.

LAFEU: I saw the man to-day, if man he be.

KING: Find him, and bring him hither.

Exit an Attendant

BERTRAM: What of him?
He's quoted for a most perfidious slave,
With all the spots o' th' world tax'd and debauch'd,
Whose nature sickens but to speak a truth.
Am I or that or this for what he'll utter
That will speak any thing?

KING: She hath that ring of yours.

BERTRAM: I think she has. Certain it is I liked her,
And boarded her i' the wanton way of youth.
She knew her distance, and did angle for me,
Madding my eagerness with her restraint,
As all impediments in fancy's course
Are motives of more fancy; and, in fine,
Her infinite cunning, with her modern grace
Subdued me to her rate. She got the ring;
And I had that which any inferior might
At market-price have bought.

DIANA: I must be patient.
You that have turn'd off a first so noble wife
May justly diet me. I pray you yet—
Since you lack virtue, I will lose a husband—
Send for your ring, I will return it home,
And give me mine again.

BERTRAM: I have it not.

KING: What ring was yours, I pray you?

DIANA: Sir, much like
The same upon your finger.

KING: Know you this ring? This ring was his of late.

DIANA: And this was it I gave him, being abed.

KING: The story, then, goes false you threw it him
Out of a casement.

DIANA: I have spoke the truth.

Enter PAROLLES

BERTRAM: My lord, I do confess the ring was hers.

KING: You boggle shrewdly; every feather starts you.
Is this the man you speak of?

DIANA: Ay, my lord.

KING: Tell me, sirrah—but tell me true I charge you,
Not fearing the displeasure of your master,
Which, on your just proceeding I'll keep off—
By him and by this woman here what know you?

PAROLLES: So please your Majesty, my master hath been an honourable gentleman: tricks he hath had in him, which gentlemen have.

KING: Come, come, to the purpose. Did he love this woman?

PAROLLES: Faith, sir, he did love her; but how?

KING: How, I pray you?

PAROLLES: He did love her, sir, as a gentleman loves a woman.

KING: How is that?

PAROLLES: He loved her, sir, and loved her not.

KING: As thou art a knave, and no knave. What an equivocal companion is this!

PAROLLES: I am a poor man, and at your majesty's command.

LAFEU: He's a good drum, my lord, but a naughty orator.

DIANA: Do you know he promised me marriage?

PAROLLES: Faith, I know more than I'll speak.

KING: But wilt thou not speak all thou knowest?

PAROLLES: Yes, so please your majesty. I did go between them, as I said; but more than that, he loved her—for indeed he was mad for her, and talked of Satan and of Limbo and of Furies, and I know not what. Yet I was in that credit with them at that time that I knew of their going to bed; and of other motions, as promising her marriage, and things which would derive me ill will to speak of; therefore I will not speak what I know.

KING: Thou hast spoken all already, unless thou canst say they are married: but thou art too fine in thy evidence; therefore stand aside.

This ring, you say, was yours?

DIANA: Ay, my good lord.

KING: Where did you buy it? or who gave it you?

DIANA: It was not given me, nor I did not buy it.

KING: Who lent it you?

DIANA: It was not lent me neither.

KING: Where did you find it then?

DIANA: I found it not.

KING: If it were yours by none of all these ways,
How could you give it him?

DIANA: I never gave it him.

LAFEU: This woman's an easy glove, my lord; she goes off and on at pleasure.

KING: This ring was mine, I gave it his first wife.

DIANA: It might be yours or hers, for aught I know.

KING: Take her away, I do not like her now;
To prison with her. And away with him.
Unless thou tell'st me where thou hadst this ring,
Thou diest within this hour.

DIANA: I'll never tell you.

KING: Take her away.

DIANA: I'll put in bail, my liege.

KING: I think thee now some common customer.

DIANA: By Jove, if ever I knew man, 'twas you.

KING: Wherefore hast thou accused him all this while?

DIANA: Because he's guilty, and he is not guilty.
He knows I am no maid, and he'll swear to't:
I'll swear I am a maid, and he knows not.
Great king, I am no strumpet, by my life;
I am either maid, or else this old man's wife.

Pointing to LAFEU

KING: She does abuse our ears: to prison with her.

DIANA: Good mother, fetch my bail. Stay, royal sir;

Exit Widow

The jeweller that owes the ring is sent for,
And he shall surety me. But for this lord
Who hath abused me as he knows himself,
Though yet he never harm'd me, here I quit him.
He knows himself my bed he hath defiled;
And at that time he got his wife with child.
Dead though she be, she feels her young one kick:
So there's my riddle: one that's dead is quick—
And now behold the meaning.

Re-enter Widow with HELENA

KING: Is there no exorcist
Beguiles the truer office of mine eyes?
Is't real that I see?

HELENA: No, my good lord;
'Tis but the shadow of a wife you see,
The name and not the thing.

BERTRAM: Both, both; O, pardon!

HELENA: O, my good lord, when I was like this maid,
I found you wondrous kind. There is your ring;
And, look you, here's your letter. This it says:
'When from my finger you can get this ring,
And are by me with child,' & c. This is done.
Will you be mine now you are doubly won?

BERTRAM: If she, my liege, can make me know this clearly,
I'll love her dearly, ever, ever dearly.

HELENA: If it appear not plain and prove untrue,
Deadly divorce step between me and you!
O my dear mother, do I see you living?

LAFEU: Mine eyes smell onions; I shall weep anon.

To PAROLLES

Good Tom Drum, lend me a handkercher. So, I thank thee. Wait on me home, I'll make sport with thee; let thy courtsies alone, they are scurvy ones.

KING: Let us from point to point this story know,
To make the even truth in pleasure flow.
[*To DIANA*] If thou beest yet a fresh uncropped flower,
Choose thou thy husband, and I'll pay thy dower;
For I can guess that by thy honest aid
Thou keep'st a wife herself, thyself a maid—
Of that and all the progress, more or less,
Resolvedly more leisure shall express,
All yet seems well; and if it end so meet,
The bitter past, more welcome is the sweet.

Flourish

EPILOGUE

The King's a beggar, now the play is done:
All is well ended, if this suit be won,
That you express content; which we will pay,
With strife to please you, day exceeding day.
Ours be your patience then, and yours our parts;
Your gentle hands lend us, and take our hearts.

Exeunt omnes

As You Like It

DRAMATIS PERSONÆ

DUKE, *living in exile*
FREDERICK, his brother, and usurper of his dominions
AMIENS, JAQUES, *lords attending on the banished Duke*
LE BEAU, *a courtier attending upon Frederick*
CHARLES, *a wrestler to Frederick*
OLIVER, JAQUES, ORLANDO, *sons of Sir Rowland de Boys*
ADAM, DENNIS, *servants to oliver*
TOUCHSTONE, *the court jestes*
SIR OLIVER MARTEXT, *a vicar*
CORIN, SILVIUS, *shepherds*
WILLIAM, *a country fellow, in love with Audrey*
A person representing HYMEN
ROSALIND, daughter to the banished Duke
CELIA, daughter to Frederick
PHEBE, a shepherdess
AUDREY, a country wench
Lords, Pages, Foresters, and Attendants

THE SCENE: *Oliver's house; Frederick's Court; and in the Forest of Arden*

Act I

Scene I—*Orchard of Oliver's house*

Enter ORLANDO and ADAM

ORLANDO: As I remember, Adam, it was upon this fashion bequeathed me by will but poor a thousand crowns, and, as thou sayest, charged my brother, on his blessing, to breed me well; and there begins my sadness. My brother Jaques he keeps at school, and report speaks goldenly of his profit. For my part, he keeps me rustically at home, or, to speak more properly, stays me here at home unkept; for call you that keeping for a gentleman of my birth, that differs not from the stalling of an ox? His horses are bred better; for, besides that they are fair with their feeding, they are taught their manage, and to that end riders dearly hired; but I, his brother, gain nothing under him but growth; for the which his animals on his dunghills are as much bound to him as I. Besides this nothing that he so plentifully gives me, the something that nature gave me his countenance seems to take from me. He lets me feed with his hinds, bars me the place of a brother, and as much as in him lies, mines my gentility with my education. This is it, Adam, that grieves me; and the spirit of my father, which I think is within me, begins to mutiny against this servitude. I will no longer endure it, though yet I know no wise remedy how to avoid it.

Enter OLIVER

ADAM: Yonder comes my master, your brother.

ORLANDO: Go apart, Adam, and thou shalt hear how he will shake me up.

Adam Retires

OLIVER: Now, sir! what make you here?

ORLANDO: Nothing; I am not taught to make any thing.

OLIVER: What mar you then, sir?

ORLANDO: Marry, sir, I am helping you to mar that which God made, a poor unworthy brother of yours, with idleness.

OLIVER: Marry, sir, be better employed, and be nought awhile.

ORLANDO: Shall I keep your hogs, and eat husks with them? What prodigal portion have I spent that I should come to such penury?

OLIVER: Know you where you are, sir?

ORLANDO: O, sir, very well; here in your orchard.

OLIVER: Know you before whom, sir?

ORLANDO: Ay, better than him I am before knows me. I know you are my eldest brother; and, in the gentle condition of blood, you should so know me. The courtesy of nations allows you my better in that you are the first-born; but the same tradition takes not away my blood, were there twenty brothers betwixt us. I have as much of my father in me as you, albeit I confess your coming before me is nearer to his reverence.

Strikes Him

OLIVER: What, boy!

ORLANDO: Come, come, elder brother, you are too young in this.

OLIVER: Wilt thou lay hands on me, villain?

ORLANDO: I am no villain; I am the youngest son of Sir Rowland de Boys. He was my father; and he is thrice a villain that says such a father begot villains. Wert thou not my brother, I would not take this hand from thy throat till this other had pulled out thy tongue for saying so. Thou has railed on thyself.

ADAM: [*Coming forward*] Sweet masters, be patient; for your father's remembrance, be at accord.

OLIVER: Let me go, I say.

ORLANDO: I will not, till I please; you shall hear me. My father charged you in his will to give me good education: you have trained me like a peasant, obscuring and hiding from me all gentleman-like qualities. The spirit of my father grows strong in me, and I will no longer endure it; therefore allow me such exercises as may become a gentleman, or give me the poor allottery my father left me by testament; with that I will go buy my fortunes.

OLIVER: And what wilt thou do? Beg, when that is spent? Well, sir, get you in. I will not long be troubled with you; you shall have some part of your will. I pray you leave me.

ORLANDO: I will no further offend you than becomes me for my good.

OLIVER: Get you with him, you old dog.

ADAM: Is 'old dog' my reward? Most true, I have lost my teeth in your service. God be with my old master! He would not have spoke such a word.

Exeunt ORLANDO and ADAM

OLIVER: Is it even so? Begin you to grow upon me? I will physic your rankness, and yet give no thousand crowns neither. Holla, Dennis!

Enter DENNIS

DENNIS: Calls your worship?

OLIVER: Was not Charles, the Duke's wrestler, here to speak with me?

DENNIS: So please you, he is here at the door and importunes access to you.

OLIVER: Call him in.

Exit DENNIS

'Twill be a good way; and to-morrow the wrestling is.

Enter CHARLES

CHARLES: Good morrow to your worship.

OLIVER: Good Monsieur Charles! What's the new news at the new court?

CHARLES: There's no news at the court, sir, but the old news; that is, the old Duke is banished by his younger brother the new Duke; and three or four loving lords have put themselves into voluntary exile with him, whose lands and revenues enrich the new Duke; therefore he gives them good leave to wander.

OLIVER: Can you tell if Rosalind, the Duke's daughter, be banished with her father?

CHARLES: O, no; for the Duke's daughter, her cousin, so loves her, being ever from their cradles bred together, that she would have followed her exile, or have died to stay behind her. She is at the court, and no less beloved of her uncle than his own daughter; and never two ladies loved as they do.

OLIVER: Where will the old Duke live?

CHARLES: They say he is already in the Forest of Arden, and a many merry men with him; and there they live like the old Robin Hood of England. They say many young gentlemen flock to him every day, and fleet the time carelessly, as they did in the golden world.

OLIVER: What, you wrestle to-morrow before the new Duke?

CHARLES: Marry, do I, sir; and I came to acquaint you with a matter. I am given, sir, secretly to understand that your younger brother, Orlando, hath a disposition to come in disguised against me to try a fall. To-morrow, sir, I wrestle for my credit; and he that escapes me without some broken limb shall acquit him well. Your brother is but young and tender; and, for your love, I would be loath to foil him, as I must, for my own honour, if he come in; therefore, out of my love to you, I came hither to acquaint you withal, that either you might stay him from his intendment, or brook such disgrace well as he shall run into, in that it is a thing of his own search and altogether against my will.

OLIVER: Charles, I thank thee for thy love to me, which thou shalt find I will most kindly requite. I had myself notice of my brother's purpose herein, and have by underhand means laboured to dissuade him from it; but he is resolute. I'll tell thee, Charles, it is the stubbornest young fellow of France; full of ambition, an envious emulator of every man's good parts, a secret and villainous contriver against me his natural brother. Therefore use thy discretion: I had as lief thou didst break his neck as his finger. And thou wert best look to't; for if thou dost him any slight disgrace, or if he do not mightily grace himself on thee, he will practise against thee by poison, entrap thee by some treacherous device, and never leave thee till he hath ta'en thy life by some indirect means or other; for, I assure thee, and almost with tears I speak it, there is not one so young and so villainous this day living. I speak but brotherly of him; but should I anatomize him to thee as he is, I must blush and weep, and thou must look pale and wonder.

CHARLES: I am heartily glad I came hither to you. If he come to-morrow I'll give him his payment. If ever he go alone again, I'll never wrestle for prize more. And so, God keep your worship!

Exit CHARLES

OLIVER: Farewell, good Charles. Now will I stir this gamester. I hope I shall see an end of him; for my soul, yet I know not why, hates nothing more than he. Yet he's gentle; never schooled and yet learned; full of noble device; of all sorts enchantingly beloved; and indeed, so much in the heart of the world, and especially of my own people, who best know him, that I am altogether misprised. But it shall not be so long; this wrestler shall clear all. Nothing remains but that I kindle the boy thither, which now I'll go about.

Exit

SCENE II—A *Lawn before the Duke's palace*

Enter CELIA and ROSALIND

CELIA: I pray thee, Rosalind, sweet my coz, be merry.

ROSALIND: Dear Celia, I show more mirth than I am mistress of; and would you yet I were merrier? Unless you could teach me to forget a banished father, you must not learn me how to remember any extraordinary pleasure.

CELIA: Herein I see thou lovest me not with the full weight that I love thee. If my uncle, thy banished father, had banished thy uncle, the Duke my father, so thou hadst been still with me, I could have taught my love to take thy father for mine; so wouldst thou, if the truth of thy love to me were so righteously tempered as mine is to thee.

ROSALIND: Well, I will forget the condition of my estate, to rejoice in yours.

CELIA: You know my father hath no child but I, nor none is like to have; and, truly, when he dies thou shalt be his heir; for what he hath taken away from thy father perforce, I will render thee again in affection. By mine honour, I will; and when I break that oath, let me turn monster; therefore, my sweet Rose, my dear Rose, be merry.

ROSALIND: From henceforth I will, coz, and devise sports. Let me see; what think you of falling in love?

CELIA: Marry, I prithee, do, to make sport withal; but love no man in good earnest, nor no further in sport neither than with safety of a pure blush thou mayst in honour come off again.

ROSALIND: What shall be our sport, then?

CELIA: Let us sit and mock the good housewife Fortune from her wheel, that her gifts may henceforth be bestowed equally.

ROSALIND: I would we could do so; for her benefits are mightily misplaced; and the bountiful blind woman doth most mistake in her gifts to women.

CELIA: 'Tis true; for those that she makes fair she scarce makes honest; and those that she makes honest she makes very ill-favouredly.

ROSALIND: Nay; now thou goest from Fortune's office to Nature's: Fortune reigns in gifts of the world, not in the lineaments of Nature.

Enter TOUCHSTONE

CELIA: No; when Nature hath made a fair creature, may she not by Fortune fall into the fire? Though Nature hath given us wit to flout at Fortune, hath not Fortune sent in this fool to cut off the argument?

ROSALIND: Indeed, there is Fortune too hard for Nature, when Fortune makes Nature's natural the cutter-off of Nature's wit.

CELIA: Peradventure this is not Fortune's work neither, but Nature's, who perceiveth our natural wits too dull to reason of such goddesses, and hath sent this natural for our whetstone; for always the dullness of the fool is the whetstone of the wits. How now, wit! Whither wander you?

TOUCHSTONE: Mistress, you must come away to your father.

CELIA: Were you made the messenger?

TOUCHSTONE: No, by mine honour; but I was bid to come for you.

ROSALIND: Where learned you that oath, fool?

TOUCHSTONE: Of a certain knight that swore by his honour they were good pancakes, and swore by his honour the mustard was naught. Now I'll stand to it, the pancakes were naught and the mustard was good, and yet was not the knight forsworn.

CELIA: How prove you that, in the great heap of your knowledge?

ROSALIND: Ay, marry, now unmuzzle your wisdom.

TOUCHSTONE: Stand you both forth now: stroke your chins, and swear by your beards that I am a knave.

CELIA: By our beards, if we had them, thou art.

TOUCHSTONE: By my knavery, if I had it, then I were. But if you swear by that that is not, you are not forsworn; no more was this knight, swearing by his honour, for he never had any; or if he had, he had sworn it away before ever he saw those pancakes or that mustard.

CELIA: Prithee, who is't that thou meanest?

TOUCHSTONE: One that old Frederick, your father, loves.

CELIA: My father's love is enough to honour him. Enough. speak no more of him; you'll be whippt for taxation one of these days.

TOUCHSTONE: The more pity that fools may not speak wisely what wise men do foolishly.

CELIA: By my troth, thou sayest true; for since the little wit that fools have was silenced, the little foolery that wise men have makes a great show. Here comes Monsieur Le Beau.

Enter LE BEAU

ROSALIND: With his mouth full of news.

CELIA: Which he will put on us as pigeons feed their young.

ROSALIND: Then shall we be news-crammed.

CELIA: All the better; we shall be the more marketable. Bon jour, Monsieur Le Beau. What's the news?

LE BEAU: Fair princess, you have lost much good sport.

CELIA: Sport! of what colour?

LE BEAU: What colour, madam? How shall I answer you?

ROSALIND: As wit and fortune will.

TOUCHSTONE: Or as the Destinies decrees.

CELIA: Well said; that was laid on with a trowel.

TOUCHSTONE: Nay, if I keep not my rank—

ROSALIND: Thou losest thy old smell.

LE BEAU: You amaze me, ladies. I would have told you of good wrestling, which you have lost the sight of.

ROSALIND: You tell us the manner of the wrestling.

LE BEAU: I will tell you the beginning; and, if it please your ladyships, you may see the end; for the best is yet to do; and here, where you are, they are coming to perform it.

CELIA: Well, the beginning that is dead and buried.

LE BEAU: There comes an old man and his three sons—

CELIA: I could match this beginning with an old tale.

LE BEAU: Three proper young men, of excellent growth and presence.

ROSALIND: With bills on their necks: 'Be it known unto all men by these presents.'—

LE BEAU: The eldest of the three wrestled with Charles, the Duke's wrestler; which Charles in a moment threw him, and broke three of his ribs, that there is little hope of life in him. So he served the second, and so the third. Yonder they lie; the poor old man, their father, making such pitiful dole over them that all the beholders take his part with weeping.

ROSALIND: Alas!

TOUCHSTONE: But what is the sport, monsieur, that the ladies have lost?

LE BEAU: Why, this that I speak of.

TOUCHSTONE: Thus men may grow wiser every day. It is the first time that ever I heard breaking of ribs was sport for ladies.

CELIA: Or I, I promise thee.

ROSALIND: But is there any else longs to see this broken music in his sides? Is there yet another dotes upon rib-breaking? Shall we see this wrestling, cousin?

LE BEAU: You must, if you stay here; for here is the place appointed for the wrestling, and they are ready to perform it.

CELIA: Yonder, sure, they are coming. Let us now stay and see it.

Flourish. Enter DUKE FREDERICK, Lords, ORLANDO, CHARLES, and Attendants

DUKE FREDERICK: Come on; since the youth will not be entreated, his own peril on his forwardness.

ROSALIND: Is yonder the man?

LE BEAU: Even he, madam.

CELIA: Alas, he is too young; yet he looks successfully.

DUKE FREDERICK: How now, daughter and cousin! Are you crept hither to see the wrestling?

ROSALIND: Ay, my liege, so please you give us leave.

DUKE FREDERICK: You will take little delight in it, I can tell you; there is such odds in the man. In pity of the challenger's youth I would fain dissuade him, but he will not be entreated. Speak to him, ladies; see if you can move him.

CELIA: Call him hither, good Monsieur Le Beau.

DUKE FREDERICK: Do so; I'll not be by.

[*Duke Frederick goes apart*]

LE BEAU: Monsieur the Challenger, the Princess calls for you.

ORLANDO: I attend them with all respect and duty.

ROSALIND: Young man, have you challenged Charles the wrestler?

ORLANDO: No, fair princess; he is the general challenger. I come but in, as others do, to try with him the strength of my youth.

CELIA: Young gentleman, your spirits are too bold for your years. You have seen cruel proof of this man's strength; if you saw yourself with your eyes, or knew yourself with your judgment, the fear of your adventure would counsel you to a more equal enterprise. We pray you, for your own sake, to embrace your own safety and give over this attempt.

ROSALIND: Do, young sir; your reputation shall not therefore be misprised: we will make it our suit to the Duke that the wrestling might not go forward.

ORLANDO: I beseech you, punish me not with your hard thoughts; wherein I confess me much guilty to deny so fair and excellent ladies any thing. But let your fair eyes and gentle wishes go with me to my trial; wherein if I be foiled, there is but one shamed that was never gracious; if killed, but one dead that was willing to be so. I shall do my friends no wrong, for I have none to lament me, the world no injury, for in it I have nothing; only in the world I fill up a place, which may be better supplied when I have made it empty.

ROSALIND: The little strength that I have, I would it were with you.

CELIA: And mine, to eke out hers.

ROSALIND: Fare you well. Pray heaven I be deceived in you!

CELIA: Your heart's desires be with you!

CHARLES: Come, where is this young gallant that is so desirous to lie with his mother earth?

ORLANDO: Ready, sir; but his will hath in it a more modest working.

DUKE FREDERICK: You shall try but one fall.

CHARLES: No, I warrant your Grace, you shall not entreat him to a second, that have so mightily persuaded him from a first.

ORLANDO: You mean to mock me after, you should not have mocked me before; but come your ways.

ROSALIND: Now, Hercules be thy speed, young man!

CELIA: I would I were invisible, to catch the strong fellow by the leg.

They wrestle

ROSALIND: O excellent young man!

CELIA: If I had a thunderbolt in mine eye, I can tell who should down.

Shout. CHARLES is thrown

DUKE FREDERICK: No more, no more.

ORLANDO: Yes, I beseech your Grace; I am not yet well breathed.

DUKE FREDERICK: How dost thou, Charles?

LE BEAU: He cannot speak, my lord.

DUKE FREDERICK: Bear him away. What is thy name, young man?

ORLANDO: Orlando, my liege; the youngest son of Sir Rowland de Boys.

DUKE FREDERICK: I would thou hadst been son to some man else.
The world esteemed thy father honourable,
But I did find him still mine enemy.
Thou shouldst have better pleased me with this deed,
Hadst thou descended from another house.
But fare thee well; thou art a gallant youth;
I would thou hadst told me of another father.

Exeunt DUKE FREDERICK, Train, and LE BEAU

CELIA: Were I my father, coz, would I do this?

ORLANDO: I am more proud to be Sir Rowland's son,
His youngest son—and would not change that calling
To be adopted heir to Frederick.

ROSALIND: My father loved Sir Rowland as his soul,
And all the world was of my father's mind;
Had I before known this young man his son,
I should have given him tears unto entreaties
Ere he should thus have ventured.

CELIA: Gentle cousin,
Let us go thank him, and encourage him;
My father's rough and envious disposition
Sticks me at heart. Sir, you have well deserved;
If you do keep your promises in love
But justly as you have exceeded all promise,
Your mistress shall be happy.

ROSALIND: Gentleman,

Giving him a chain from her neck

Wear this for me, one out of suits with fortune,
That could give more, but that her hand lacks means.
Shall we go, coz?

CELIA: Ay. Fare you well, fair gentleman.

ORLANDO: Can I not say 'I thank you'? My better parts
Are all thrown down, and that which here stands up
Is but a quintain, a mere lifeless block.

ROSALIND: He calls us back. My pride fell with my fortunes;
I'll ask him what he would. Did you call, sir?
Sir, you have wrestled well, and overthrown
More than your enemies.

CELIA: Will you go, coz?

ROSALIND: Have with you. Fare you well.

Exeunt ROSALIND and CELIA

ORLANDO: What passion hangs these weights upon my tongue?
I cannot speak to her, yet she urged conference.
O poor Orlando, thou art overthrown!
Or Charles or something weaker masters thee.

Re-enter LE BEAU

LE BEAU: Good sir, I do in friendship counsel you
To leave this place. Albeit you have deserved
High commendation, true applause, and love,
Yet such is now the Duke's condition
That he misconstrues all that you have done.
The Duke is humorous; what he is, indeed
More suits you to conceive than I to speak of.

ORLANDO: I thank you, sir; and, pray you tell me this:
Which of the two was daughter of the Duke
That here was at the wrestling?

LE BEAU: Neither his daughter, if we judge by manners;
But yet, indeed, the smaller is his daughter;
The other is daughter to the banished Duke,
And here detained by her usurping uncle,
To keep his daughter company; whose loves
Are dearer than the natural bond of sisters.
But I can tell you that of late this Duke
Hath taken displeasure against his gentle niece,
Grounded upon no other argument
But that the people praise her for her virtues
And pity her for her good father's sake;
And, on my life, his malice against the lady
Will suddenly break forth. Sir, fare you well.
Hereafter, in a better world than this,
I shall desire more love and knowledge of you.

ORLANDO: I rest much bounden to you; fare you well.

Exit LE BEAU

Thus must I from the smoke into the smother;
From tyrant Duke unto a tyrant brother.
But heavenly Rosalind!

Exit

SCENE III—*The Duke's palace*

Enter CELIA and ROSALIND

CELIA: Why, cousin! why, Rosalind! Cupid have mercy! Not a word?

ROSALIND: Not one to throw at a dog.

CELIA: No, thy words are too precious to be cast away upon curs; throw some of them at me; come, lame me with reasons.

ROSALIND: Then there were two cousins laid up; when the one should be lamed with reasons and the other mad without any.

CELIA: But is all this for your father?

ROSALIND: No, some of it is for my child's father. O, how full of briers is this working-day world!

CELIA: They are but burs, cousin, thrown upon thee in holiday foolery; if we walk not in the trodden paths, our very petticoats will catch them.

ROSALIND: I could shake them off my coat: these burs are in my heart.

CELIA: Hem them away.

ROSALIND: I would try, if I could cry 'hem' and have him.

CELIA: Come, come, wrestle with thy affections.

ROSALIND: O, they take the part of a better wrestler than myself.

CELIA: O, a good wish upon you! You will try in time, in despite of a fall. But, turning these jests out of service, let us talk in good earnest. Is it possible, on such a sudden, you should fall into so strong a liking with old Sir Rowland's youngest son?

ROSALIND: The Duke my father loved his father dearly.

CELIA: Doth it therefore ensue that you should love his son dearly? By this kind of chase I should hate him, for my father hated his father dearly; yet I hate not Orlando.

ROSALIND: No, faith, hate him not, for my sake.

CELIA: Why should I not? Doth he not deserve well?

Enter DUKE FREDERICK, with Lords

ROSALIND: Let me love him for that, and do you love him because I do. Look, here comes the Duke.

CELIA: With his eyes full of anger.

DUKE FREDERICK: Mistress, dispatch you with your safest haste,
And get you from our court.

ROSALIND: Me, uncle?

DUKE FREDERICK: You, cousin.
Within these ten days if that thou beest found
So near our public court as twenty miles,
Thou diest for it.

ROSALIND: I do beseech your Grace,
Let me the knowledge of my fault bear with me.
If with myself I hold intelligence,
Or have acquaintance with mine own desires,
If that I do not dream, or be not frantic—
As I do trust I am not—then, dear uncle,
Never so much as in a thought unborn
Did I offend your Highness.

DUKE FREDERICK: Thus do all traitors;
If their purgation did consist in words,
They are as innocent as grace itself.
Let it suffice thee that I trust thee not.

ROSALIND: Yet your mistrust cannot make me a traitor.
Tell me whereon the likelihood depends.

DUKE FREDERICK: Thou art thy father's daughter; there's enough.

ROSALIND: So was I when your Highness took his dukedom;
So was I when your Highness banished him.
Treason is not inherited, my lord;
Or, if we did derive it from our friends,
What's that to me? My father was no traitor.
Then, good my liege, mistake me not so much
To think my poverty is treacherous.

CELIA: Dear sovereign, hear me speak.

DUKE FREDERICK: Ay, Celia; we stayed her for your sake,
Else had she with her father ranged along.

CELIA: I did not then entreat to have her stay;
It was your pleasure, and your own remorse;
I was too young that time to value her;
But now I know her. If she be a traitor,
Why so am I: we still have slept together,
Rose at an instant, learned, played, eat together,

And wheresoever we went, like Juno's swans,
Still we went coupled and inseparable.

DUKE FREDERICK: She is too subtle for thee; and her smoothness,
Her very silence and her patience,
Speak to the people, and they pity her.
Thou art a fool. She robs thee of thy name;
And thou wilt show more bright and seem more virtuous
When she is gone. Then open not thy lips.
Firm and irrevocable is my doom
Which I have passed upon her; she is banished.

CELIA: Pronounce that sentence, then, on me, my liege;
I cannot live out of her company.

DUKE FREDERICK: You are a fool. You, niece, provide yourself.
If you outstay the time, upon mine honour,
And in the greatness of my word, you die.

Exeunt DUKE FREDERICK and Lords

CELIA: O my poor Rosalind! Whither wilt thou go?
Wilt thou change fathers? I will give thee mine.
I charge thee be not thou more grieved than I am.

ROSALIND: I have more cause.

CELIA: Thou hast not, cousin.
Prithee be cheerful. Knowest thou not the Duke
Hath banished me, his daughter?

ROSALIND: That he hath not.

CELIA: No, hath not? Rosalind lacks, then, the love
Which teacheth thee that thou and I am one.
Shall we be sundered? Shall we part, sweet girl?
No; let my father seek another heir.
Therefore devise with me how we may fly,
Whither to go, and what to bear with us;
And do not seek to take your change upon you,
To bear your griefs yourself, and leave me out;
For, by this heaven, now at our sorrows pale,
Say what thou canst, I'll go along with thee.

ROSALIND: Why, whither shall we go?

CELIA: To seek my uncle in the Forest of Arden.

ROSALIND: Alas, what danger will it be to us,
Maids as we are, to travel forth so far!
Beauty provoketh thieves sooner than gold.

CELIA: I'll put myself in poor and mean attire,
And with a kind of umber smirch my face;
The like do you; so shall we pass along,
And never stir assailants.

ROSALIND: Were it not better,
Because that I am more than common tall,
That I did suit me all points like a man?
A gallant curtle-axe upon my thigh,
A boar spear in my hand; and—in my heart
Lie there what hidden woman's fear there will—
We'll have a swashing and a martial outside,
As many other mannish cowards have
That do outface it with their semblances.

CELIA: What shall I call thee when thou art a man?

ROSALIND: I'll have no worse a name than Jove's own page;
And therefore look you call me Ganymede.
But what will you be called?

CELIA: Something that hath a reference to my state:
No longer Celia, but Aliena.

ROSALIND: But, cousin, what if we assayed to steal
The clownish fool out of your father's court?
Would he not be a comfort to our travel?

CELIA: He'll go along over the wide world with me;
Leave me alone to woo him. Let's away,
And get our jewels and our wealth together,
Devise the fittest time and safest way
To hide us from pursuit that will be made
After my flight. Now go we in content
To liberty, and not to banishment.

Exeunt

Act II

Scene I—*The forest of Arden*

Enter DUKE SENIOR, AMIENS, and two or three Lords, like foresters

DUKE SENIOR: Now, my co-mates and brothers in exile,
Hath not old custom made this life more sweet
Than that of painted pomp? Are not these woods
More free from peril than the envious court?
Here feel we not the penalty of Adam,
The seasons' difference, as the icy fang
And churlish chiding of the winter's wind,
Which when it bites and blows upon my body,
Even till I shrink with cold, I smile and say
'This is no flattery; these are counsellors
That feelingly persuade me what I am.'
Sweet are the uses of adversity,
Which, like the toad, ugly and venomous,
Wears yet a precious jewel in his head;
And this our life, exempt from public haunt,
Finds tongues in trees, books in the running brooks,
Sermons in stones, and good in everything.
I would not change it.

AMIENS: Happy is your Grace,
That can translate the stubbornness of fortune
Into so quiet and so sweet a style.

DUKE SENIOR: Come, shall we go and kill us venison?
And yet it irks me the poor dappled fools,
Being native burghers of this desert city,
Should, in their own confines, with forked heads
Have their round haunches gored.

FIRST LORD: Indeed, my lord,
The melancholy Jaques grieves at that,
And, in that kind, swears you do more usurp
Than doth your brother that hath banished you.
To-day my Lord of Amiens and myself
Did steal behind him as he lay along
Under an oak whose antique root peeps out
Upon the brook that brawls along this wood!
To the which place a poor sequestered stag,
That from the hunter's aim had taken a hurt,
Did come to languish, and indeed, my lord,
The wretched animal heaved forth such groans
That their discharge did stretch his leathern coat
Almost to bursting, and the big round tears
Coursed one another down his innocent nose
In piteous chase; and thus the hairy fool,
Much marked of the melancholy Jaques,
Stood on the extremest verge of the swift brook,
Augmenting it with tears.

DUKE SENIOR: But what said Jaques?
Did he not moralize this spectacle?

FIRST LORD: O, yes, into a thousand similes.
First, for his weeping into the needless stream:
'Poor deer,' quoth he, 'thou makest a testament
As worldlings do, giving thy sum of more
To that which had too much'. Then, being there alone,
Left and abandoned of his velvet friends:
''Tis right' quoth he; 'thus misery doth part
The flux of company'. Anon, a careless herd,
Full of the pasture, jumps along by him
And never stays to greet him. 'Ay', quoth Jaques
'Sweep on, you fat and greasy citizens;
'Tis just the fashion. Wherefore do you look
Upon that poor and broken bankrupt there?'
Thus most invectively he pierceth through
The body of the country, city, court,
Yea, and of this our life, swearing that we
Are mere usurpers, tyrants and what's worse,
To fright the animals, and to kill them up
In their assigned and native dwelling-place.

DUKE SENIOR: And did you leave him in this contemplation?

SECOND LORD: We did, my lord, weeping and commenting
Upon the sobbing deer.

DUKE SENIOR: Show me the place;
I love to cope him in these sullen fits,
For then he's full of matter.

FIRST LORD: I'll bring you to him straight.

Exeunt

SCENE II—*The Duke's palace*

Enter DUKE FREDERICK, with Lords

DUKE FREDERICK: Can it be possible that no man saw them?
It cannot be; some villains of my court
Are of consent and sufferance in this.

FIRST LORD: I cannot hear of any that did see her.
The ladies, her attendants of her chamber,
Saw her abed, and in the morning early
They found the bed untreasured of their mistress.

SECOND LORD: My lord, the roynish clown, at whom so oft
Your Grace was wont to laugh, is also missing.
Hisperia, the Princess' gentlewoman,
Confesses that she secretly overheard
Your daughter and her cousin much commend
The parts and graces of the wrestler
That did but lately foil the sinewy Charles;
And she believes, wherever they are gone,
That youth is surely in their company.

DUKE FREDERICK: Send to his brother; fetch that gallant hither.
If he be absent, bring his brother to me;
I'll make him find him. Do this suddenly,
And let not search and inquisition quail
To bring again these foolish runaways.

Exeunt

SCENE III—*Before Oliver's house*

Enter ORLANDO and ADAM, meeting

ORLANDO: Who's there?

ADAM: What, my young master? O, my gentle master!
O my sweet master! O you memory
Of old Sir Rowland! Why, what make you here?
Why are you virtuous? Why do people love you?
And wherefore are you gentle, strong and valiant?
Why would you be so fond to overcome
The bonny prizer of the humorous Duke?
Your praise is come too swiftly home before you.
Know you not, master, to some kind of men
Their graces serve them but as enemies?
No more do yours. Your virtues, gentle master,
Are sanctified and holy traitors to you.
O, what a world is this, when what is comely
Envenoms him that bears it!

ORLANDO: Why, what's the matter?

ADAM: O unhappy youth!
Come not within these doors; within this roof
The enemy of all your graces lives.
Your brother—no, no brother; yet the son—
Yet not the son, I will not call him son
Of him I was about to call his father—
Hath heard your praises, and this night he means
To burn the lodging where you use to lie,
And you within it. If he fail of that,
He will have other means to cut you off.
I overheard him and his practises.
This is no place; this house is but a butchery:
Abhor it, fear it, do not enter it.

ORLANDO: Why, whither, Adam, wouldst thou have me go?

ADAM: No matter whither, so you come not here.

ORLANDO: What, wouldst thou have me go and beg my food?
Or with a base and boisterous sword enforce
A thievish living on the common road?
This I must do, or know not what to do:
Yet this I will not do, do how I can.
I rather will subject me to the malice
Of a diverted blood and bloody brother.

ADAM: But do not so. I have five hundred crowns,
The thrifty hire I saved under your father,
Which I did store to be my foster-nurse
When service should in my old limbs lie lame,
And unregarded age in corners thrown.
Take that, and He that doth the ravens feed,
Yea, providently caters for the sparrow,

Be comfort to my age! Here is the gold;
All this I give you. Let me be your servant;
Though I look old, yet I am strong and lusty;
For in my youth I never did apply
Hot and rebellious liquors in my blood,
Nor did not with unbashful forehead woo
The means of weakness and debility;
Therefore my age is as a lusty winter,
Frosty, but kindly. Let me go with you;
I'll do the service of a younger man
In all your business and necessities.

ORLANDO: O good old man, how well in thee appears
The constant service of the antique world,
When service sweat for duty, not for meed!
Thou art not for the fashion of these times,
Where none will sweat but for promotion,
And having that do choke their service up
Even with the having; it is not so with thee.
But, poor old man, thou prunest a rotten tree
That cannot so much as a blossom yield
In lieu of all thy pains and husbandry.
But come thy ways; well go along together,
And ere we have thy youthful wages spent
We'll light upon some settled low content.

ADAM: Master, go on, and I will follow thee
To the last gasp, with truth and loyalty.
From seventeen years till now almost fourscore
Here lived I, but now live here no more.
At seventeen years many their fortunes seek;
But at fourscore it is too late a week:
Yet fortune cannot recompense me better
Than to die well and not my master's debtor.

Exeunt

SCENE IV—*The forest of Arden*

Enter ROSALIND for Ganymede, CELIA for Aliena, and Clown Alias TOUCHSTONE

ROSALIND: O Jupiter, how weary are my spirits!

TOUCHSTONE: I care not for my spirits, if my legs were not weary.

ROSALIND: I could find in my heart to disgrace my man's apparel; and to cry like a woman; but I must comfort the weaker vessel, as doublet and hose ought to show itself courageous to petticoat: therefore, courage, good Aliena!

CELIA: I pray you bear with me; I cannot go no further.

TOUCHSTONE: For my part, I had rather bear with you than bear you; yet I should bear no cross if I did bear you, for I think you have no money in your purse.

ROSALIND: Well, this is the Forest of Arden.

TOUCHSTONE: Ay, now am I in Arden; the more fool I; when I was at home I was in a better place: but travelers must be content.

Enter CORIN and SILVIUS

ROSALIND: Ay, be so, good Touchstone. Look you, who comes here; a young man and an old in solemn talk.

CORIN: That is the way to make her scorn you still.

SILVIUS: O Corin, that thou knewest how I do love her!

CORIN: I partly guess; for I have loved ere now.

SILVIUS: No, Corin, being old, thou canst not guess,
Though in thy youth thou wast as true a lover
As ever sighed upon a midnight pillow.
But if thy love were ever like to mine,
As sure I think did never man love so,
How many actions most ridiculous
Hast thou been drawn to by thy fantasy?

CORIN: Into a thousand that I have forgotten.

SILVIUS: O, thou didst then never love so heartily!
If thou rememberest not the slightest folly
That ever love did make thee run into,
Thou hast not loved;
Or if thou hast not sat as I do now,
Wearing thy hearer in thy mistress' praise,
Thou hast not loved.
Or if thou hast not broke from company
Abruptly, as my passion now makes me,
Thou hast not loved.
O Phebe, Phebe, Phebe!

Exit Silvius

ROSALIND: Alas, poor shepherd! searching of thy wound,
I have by hard adventure found mine own.

TOUCHSTONE: And I mine. I remember, when I was in love, I broke my sword upon a stone, and bid him take that for coming a-night to Jane Smile; and I remember the kissing of her batler, and the cow's dugs that her pretty chopt hands had milked; and I remember the wooing of a peascod instead of her, from whom I took two cods, and, giving her them again, said with weeping tears 'Wear these for my sake.' We that are true lovers run into strange capers; but as all is mortal in nature, so is all nature in love mortal in folly.

ROSALIND: Thou speakest wiser than thou art ware of.

TOUCHSTONE: Nay, I shall never be ware of mine own wit till I break my shins against it.

ROSALIND: Jove, Jove! this shepherd's passion
Is much upon my fashion.

TOUCHSTONE: And mine; but it grows something stale with me.

CELIA: I pray you, one of you question yond man
If he for gold will give us any food:
I faint almost to death.

TOUCHSTONE: Holla, you clown!

ROSALIND: Peace, fool: he's not thy kinsman.

CORIN: Who calls?

TOUCHSTONE: Your betters, sir.

CORIN: Else are they very wretched.

ROSALIND: Peace, I say. Good even to you, friend.

CORIN: And to you, gentle sir, and to you all.

ROSALIND: I prithee, shepherd, if that love or gold
Can in this desert place buy entertainment,
Bring us where we may rest ourselves and feed.
Here's a young maid with travel much oppressed,
And faints for succour.

CORIN: Fair sir, I pity her,
And wish, for her sake more than for mine own,
My fortunes were more able to relieve her;
But I am shepherd to another man,
And do not shear the fleeces that I graze.
My master is of churlish disposition,
And little recks to find the way to heaven
By doing deeds of hospitality.
Besides, his cote, his flocks, and bounds of feed,
Are now on sale, and at our sheepcote now,
By reason of his absence, there is nothing
That you will feed on; but what is, come see,
And in my voice most welcome shall you be.

ROSALIND: What is he that shall buy his flock and pasture?

CORIN: That young swain that you saw here but erewhile,
That little cares for buying any thing.

ROSALIND: I pray thee, if it stand with honesty,
Buy thou the cottage, pasture, and the flock,
And thou shalt have to pay for it of us.

CELIA: And we will mend thy wages. I like this place,
And willingly could waste my time in it.

CORIN: Assuredly the thing is to be sold.
Go with me: if you like upon report
The soil, the profit, and this kind of life,
I will your very faithful feeder be,
And buy it with your gold right suddenly.

Exeunt

SCENE V—*Another part of the forest*

Enter AMIENS, JAQUES, and Others

Song

AMIENS: Under the greenwood tree
Who loves to lie with me,
And turn his merry note
Unto the sweet bird's throat,
Come hither, come hither, come hither.
Here shall he see
No enemy
But winter and rough weather.

JAQUES: More, more, I prithee, more.

AMIENS: It will make you melancholy, Monsieur Jaques.

JAQUES: I thank it. More, I prithee, more. I can suck melancholy out of a song, as a weasel sucks eggs. More, I prithee, more.

AMIENS: My voice is ragged: I know I cannot please you.

JAQUES: I do not desire you to please me; I do desire you to sing. Come, more; another stanza. Call you 'em stanzos?

AMIENS: What you will, Monsieur Jaques.

JAQUES: Nay, I care not for their names; they owe me nothing. Will you sing?

AMIENS: More at your request than to please myself.

JAQUES: Well then, if ever I thank any man, I'll thank you; but that they call compliment is like the encounter of two dog-apes, and when a man thanks me heartily, methinks I have given him a penny, and he renders me the beggarly thanks. Come, sing; and you that will not, hold your tongues.

AMIENS: Well, I'll end the song: Sirs, cover the while; the Duke will drink under this tree. He hath been all this day to look you.

JAQUES: And I have been all this day to avoid him. He is too disputable for my company. I think of as many matters as he, but I give heaven thanks, and make no boast of them. Come, warble, come.

Song
All together here

Who doth ambition shun
And loves to live i' the sun,
Seeking the food he eats,
And pleased with what he gets,
Come hither, come hither, come hither.
Here shall he see
No enemy
But winter and rough weather.

JAQUES: I'll give you a verse to this note that I made yesterday in despite of my invention.

AMIENS: And I'll sing it.

JAQUES: Thus it goes:—

If it do come to pass
That any man turn ass,
Leaving his wealth and ease,
A stubborn will to please,
Ducdame, ducdame, ducdame:
Here shall he see
Gross fools as he,
An if he will come to me.

AMIENS: What's that 'ducdame'?

JAQUES: 'Tis a Greek invocation, to call fools into a circle. I'll go sleep, if I can; if I cannot, I'll rail against all the first-born of Egypt.

AMIENS: And I'll go seek the Duke: his banquet is prepared.

Exeunt severally

Scene VI—*The forest*

Enter ORLANDO and ADAM

ADAM: Dear master, I can go no further. O, I die for food! Here lie I down, and measure out my grave. Farewell, kind master.

ORLANDO: Why, how now, Adam! No greater heart in thee? Live a little; comfort a little; cheer thyself a little. If this uncouth forest yield anything savage, I will either be food for it or bring it for food to thee. Thy conceit is nearer death than thy powers. For my sake be comfortable; hold death awhile at the arm's end. I will here be with thee presently; and if I bring thee not something to eat, I will give thee leave to die; but if thou diest before I come, thou art a mocker of my labour. Well said! thou lookest cheerly, and I'll be with thee quickly. Yet thou liest in the bleak air. Come, I will bear thee to some shelter; and thou shalt not die for lack of a dinner, if there live any thing in this desert. Cheerly, good Adam!

Exeunt

Scene VII—*The forest*

A table set out. Enter DUKE SENIOR, AMIENS, and Lords, like outlaws

DUKE SENIOR: I think he be transformed into a beast;
For I can no where find him like a man.

FIRST LORD: My lord, he is but even now gone hence;
Here was he merry, hearing of a song.

DUKE SENIOR: If he, compact of jars, grow musical,
We shall have shortly discord in the spheres.
Go seek him: tell him I would speak with him.

Enter JAQUES

FIRST LORD: He saves my labour by his own approach.

DUKE SENIOR: Why, how now, monsieur! what a life is this,
That your poor friends must woo your company?
What, you look merrily!

JAQUES: A fool, a fool! I met a fool in the forest,
A motley fool. A miserable world!
As I do live by food, I met a fool,
Who laid him down and basked him in the sun,
And railed on Lady Fortune in good terms,
In good set terms—and yet a motley fool.
'Good morrow, fool' quoth I; 'No, sir,' quoth he
'Call me not fool till heaven hath sent me fortune.'
And then he drew a dial from his poke,
And, looking on it with lack-lustre eye,
Says very wisely 'It is ten o'clock:
Thus we may see' quoth he 'how the world wags:
'Tis but an hour ago since it was nine,
And after one hour more 'twill be eleven;
And so, from hour to hour, we ripe and ripe,
And then, from hour to hour, we rot and rot;
And thereby hangs a tale.' When I did hear
The motley fool thus moral on the time,

My lungs began to crow like chanticleer
That fools should be so deep contemplative,
And I did laugh sans intermission
An hour by his dial. O noble fool!
A worthy fool! Motley's the only wear.

DUKE SENIOR: What fool is this?

JAQUES: O worthy fool! One that hath been a courtier,
And says, if ladies be but young and fair,
They have the gift to know it: and in his brain,
Which is as dry as the remainder biscuit
After a voyage, he hath strange places crammed
With observation, the which he vents
In mangled forms. O that I were a fool!
I am ambitious for a motley coat.

DUKE SENIOR: Thou shalt have one.

JAQUES: It is my only suit;
Provided that you weed your better judgments
Of all opinion that grows rank in them
That I am wise. I must have liberty
Withal, as large a charter as the wind,
To blow on whom I please; for so fools have;
And they that are most galled with my folly,
They most must laugh. And why, sir, must they so?
The why is plain as way to parish church:
He that a fool doth very wisely hit
Doth very foolishly, although he smart,
Not to seem senseless of the bob: if not,
The wise man's folly is anatomized
Even by the squandering glances of the fool.
Invest me in my motley; give me leave
To speak my mind, and I will through and through
Cleanse the foul body of the infected world,
If they will patiently receive my medicine.

DUKE SENIOR: Fie on thee! I can tell what thou wouldst do.

JAQUES: What, for a counter, would I do but good?

DUKE SENIOR: Most mischievous foul sin, in chiding sin:
For thou thyself hast been a libertine,
As sensual as the brutish sting itself;
And all the embossed sores and headed evils
That thou with licence of free foot hast caught
Wouldst thou disgorge into the general world.

JAQUES: Why, who cries out on pride
That can therein tax any private party?
Doth it not flow as hugely as the sea,
Till that the wearer's very means do ebb?
What woman in the city do I name
When that I say the city-woman bears
The cost of princes on unworthy shoulders?
Who can come in and say that I mean her,
When such a one as she such is her neighbour?
Or what is he of basest function
That says his bravery is not of my cost,
Thinking that I mean him, but therein suits
His folly to the mettle of my speech?
There then! how then? what then? Let me see wherein
My tongue hath wronged him: if it do him right,
Then he hath wronged himself; if he be free,
Why then my taxing like a wild-goose flies,
Unclaimed of any man. But who comes here?

Enter ORLANDO, with his sword drawn

ORLANDO: Forbear, and eat no more.

JAQUES: Why, I have eat none yet.

ORLANDO: Nor shalt not, till necessity be served.

JAQUES: Of what kind should this cock come of?

DUKE SENIOR: Art thou thus boldened, man, by thy distress,
Or else a rude despiser of good manners,
That in civility thou seemest so empty?

ORLANDO: You touched my vein at first: the thorny point
Of bare distress hath taken from me the show
Of smooth civility: yet am I inland bred,
And know some nurture. But forbear, I say:
He dies that touches any of this fruit
Till I and my affairs are answered.

JAQUES: An you will not be answered with reason, I must die.

DUKE SENIOR: What would you have? Your gentleness shall force
More than your force move us to gentleness.

ORLANDO: I almost die for food; and let me have it.

DUKE SENIOR: Sit down and feed, and welcome to our table.

ORLANDO: Speak you so gently? Pardon me, I pray you:
I thought that all things had been savage here;
And therefore put I on the countenance

Of stern commandment. But whatever you are
That in this desert inaccessible,
Under the shade of melancholy boughs,
Lose and neglect the creeping hours of time;
If ever you have looked on better days,
If ever been where bells have knolled to church,
If ever sat at any good man's feast,
If ever from your eyelids wiped a tear,
And know what 'tis to pity and be pitied,
Let gentleness my strong enforcement be:
In the which hope I blush, and hide my sword.

DUKE SENIOR: True is it that we have seen better days,
And have with holy bell been knolled to church
And sat at good men's feasts, and wiped our eyes
Of drops that sacred pity hath engendered:
And therefore sit you down in gentleness,
And take upon command what help we have
That to your wanting may be ministered.

ORLANDO: Then but forbear your food a little while,
Whiles, like a doe, I go to find my fawn
And give it food. There is an old poor man
Who after me hath many a weary step
Limped in pure love: till he be first sufficed,
Oppressed with two weak evils, age and hunger,
I will not touch a bit.

DUKE SENIOR: Go find him out.
And we will nothing waste till you return.

ORLANDO: I thank ye; and be blest for your good comfort!

Exit

DUKE SENIOR: Thou seest we are not all alone unhappy:
This wide and universal theatre
Presents more woeful pageants than the scene
Wherein we play in.

JAQUES: All the world's a stage,
And all the men and women merely players:
They have their exits and their entrances;
And one man in his time plays many parts,
His acts being seven ages. At first the infant,
Mewling and puking in the nurse's arms.
Then the whining school-boy, with his satchel
And shining morning face, creeping like snail
Unwillingly to school. And then the lover,
Sighing like furnace, with a woeful ballad
Made to his mistress' eyebrow. Then a soldier,
Full of strange oaths, and bearded like the pard,
Jealous in honour, sudden and quick in quarrel,
Seeking the bubble reputation
Even in the cannon's mouth. And then the justice,
In fair round belly with good capon lined,
With eyes severe and beard of formal cut,
Full of wise saws and modern instances;
And so he plays his part. The sixth age shifts
Into the lean and slippered pantaloon,
With spectacles on nose and pouch on side,
His youthful hose, well saved, a world too wide
For his shrunk shank; and his big manly voice,
Turning again toward childish treble, pipes
And whistles in his sound. Last scene of all,
That ends this strange eventful history,
Is second childishness and mere oblivion,
Sans teeth, sans eyes, sans taste, sans everything.

Re-enter ORLANDO with ADAM

DUKE SENIOR: Welcome. Set down your venerable burden,
And let him feed.

ORLANDO: I thank you most for him.

ADAM: So had you need:
I scarce can speak to thank you for myself.

DUKE SENIOR: Welcome; fall to. I will not trouble you
As yet to question you about your fortunes.
Give us some music; and, good cousin, sing.

Song

AMIENS: Blow, blow, thou winter wind,
Thou art not so unkind
As man's ingratitude;
Thy tooth is not so keen,
Because thou art not seen,
Although thy breath be rude.
Heigh-ho! sing heigh-ho! unto the green holly.
Most friendship is feigning, most loving mere folly.
Then, heigh-ho, the holly!
This life is most jolly.
Freeze, freeze, thou bitter sky,
That dost not bite so nigh
As benefits forgot:

Though thou the waters warp,
Thy sting is not so sharp
As friend remembered not.
Heigh-ho! sing, & c.

DUKE SENIOR: If that you were the good Sir Rowland's son,
As you have whispered faithfully you were,
And as mine eye doth his effigies witness
Most truly limned and living in your face,
Be truly welcome hither. I am the Duke
That loved your father. The residue of your fortune,
Go to my cave and tell me. Good old man,
Thou art right welcome as thy master is.
Support him by the arm. Give me your hand,
And let me all your fortunes understand.

Exeunt

ACT III

SCENE I—*The palace*

Enter DUKE FREDERICK, Lords, and OLIVER

DUKE FREDERICK: Not see him since! Sir, sir, that cannot be.
But were I not the better part made mercy,
I should not seek an absent argument
Of my revenge, thou present. But look to it:
Find out thy brother wheresoever he is;
Seek him with candle; bring him dead or living
Within this twelvemonth, or turn thou no more
To seek a living in our territory.
Thy lands and all things that thou dost call thine
Worth seizure do we seize into our hands,
Till thou canst quit thee by thy brother's mouth
Of what we think against thee.

OLIVER: O that your Highness knew my heart in this!
I never loved my brother in my life.

DUKE FREDERICK: More villain thou. Well, push him out of doors;
And let my officers of such a nature
Make an extent upon his house and lands.
Do this expediently, and turn him going.

Exeunt

SCENE II—*The forest*

Enter ORLANDO, with a paper

ORLANDO: Hang there, my verse, in witness of my love:
And thou, thrice-crowned Queen of Night, survey
With thy chaste eye, from thy pale sphere above,
Thy huntress' name that my full life doth sway.

O Rosalind! these trees shall be my books,
And in their barks my thoughts I'll character;
That every eye which in this forest looks
Shall see thy virtue witnessed every where
Run, run, Orlando; carve on every tree,
The fair, the chaste, and unexpressive she.

Exit

Enter CORIN and TOUCHSTONE

CORIN: And how like you this shepherd's life, Master Touchstone?

TOUCHSTONE: Truly, shepherd, in respect of itself, it is a good life, but in respect that it is a shepherd's life, it is nought. In respect that it is solitary, I like it very well; but in respect that it is private, it is a very vile life. Now, in respect it is in the fields, it pleaseth me well; but in respect it is not in the court, it is tedious. As is it a spare life, look you, it fits my humour well; but as there is no more plenty in it, it goes much against my stomach. Hast any philosophy in thee, shepherd?

CORIN: No more but that I know the more one sickens the worse at ease he is; and that he that wants money, means, and content, is without three good friends; that the property of rain is to wet, and fire to burn; that good pasture makes fat sheep, and that a great cause of the night is lack of the sun; that he that hath learned no wit by nature nor art may complain of good breeding, or comes of a very dull kindred.

TOUCHSTONE: Such a one is a natural philosopher. Wast ever in court, shepherd?

CORIN: No, truly.

TOUCHSTONE: Then thou art damned.

CORIN: Nay, I hope.

TOUCHSTONE: Truly, thou art damned, like an ill-roasted egg, all on one side.

CORIN: For not being at court? Your reason.

TOUCHSTONE: Why, if thou never wast at court thou never sawest good manners; if thou never sawest good manners, then thy manners must be wicked; and wickedness is sin, and sin is damnation. Thou art in a parlous state, shepherd.

CORIN: Not a whit, Touchstone. Those that are good manners at the court are as ridiculous in the country as the behavior of the country is most mockable at the court. You told me you salute not at the court, but you kiss your hands: that courtesy would be uncleanly if courtiers were shepherds.

TOUCHSTONE: Instance, briefly; come, instance.

CORIN: Why, we are still handling our ewes, and their fells, you know, are greasy.

TOUCHSTONE: Why, do not your courtier's hands sweat? And is not the grease of a mutton as wholesome as the sweat of a man? Shallow, shallow. A better instance, I say; come.

CORIN: Besides, our hands are hard.

TOUCHSTONE: Your lips will feel them the sooner. Shallow again. A more sounder instance, come.

CORIN: And they are often tarred over with the surgery of our sheep: and would you have us kiss tar? The courtier's hands are perfumed with civet.

TOUCHSTONE: Most shallow man! thou worm's meat in respect of a good piece of flesh indeed! Learn of the wise, and perpend: civet is of a baser birth than tar—the very uncleanly flux of a cat. Mend the instance, shepherd.

CORIN: You have too courtly a wit for me: I'll rest.

TOUCHSTONE: Wilt thou rest damned? God help thee, shallow man! God make incision in thee! thou art raw.

CORIN: Sir, I am a true labourer: I earn that I eat, get that I wear, owe no man hate, envy no man's happiness, glad of other men's good, content with my harm, and the greatest of my pride is to see my ewes graze and my lambs suck.

TOUCHSTONE: That is another simple sin in you, to bring the ewes and the rams together, and to offer to get your living by the copulation of cattle; to be bawd to a bell-wether, and to betray a she-lamb of a twelvemonth to a crooked-pated, old, cuckoldly ram, out of all reasonable match. If thou beest not damned for this, the devil himself will have no shepherds; I cannot see else how thou shouldst scape.

CORIN: Here comes young Master Ganymede, my new mistress's brother.

Enter ROSALIND, reading a paper

ROSALIND: From the east to western Inde
No jewel is like Rosalinde.
Her worth, being mounted on the wind,
Through all the world bears Rosalinde.
All the pictures fairest lined
Are but black to Rosalinde
Let no fair be kept in mind
But the fair of Rosalinde.

TOUCHSTONE: I'll rhyme you so eight years together, dinners, and suppers, and sleeping-hours, excepted. It is the right butter-women's rank to market.

ROSALIND: Out, fool!

TOUCHSTONE: For a taste:
If a hart do lack a hind,
Let him seek out Rosalinde.
If the cat will after kind,
So be sure will Rosalinde.
Winter garments must be lined,
So must slender Rosalinde.
They that reap must sheaf and bind;
Then to cart with Rosalinde.
Sweetest nut hath sourest rind,
Such a nut is Rosalinde.
He that sweetest rose will find
Must find love's prick and Rosalinde.

This is the very false gallop of verses: why do you infect yourself with them?

ROSALIND: Peace, you dull fool! I found them on a tree.

TOUCHSTONE: Truly, the tree yields bad fruit.

ROSALIND: I'll graff it with you, and then I shall graff it with a medlar. Then it will be the earliest fruit in the country; for you'll be rotten ere you be half ripe, and that's the right virtue of the medlar.

TOUCHSTONE: You have said; but whether wisely or no, let the forest judge.

Enter CELIA, with a writing

ROSALIND: Peace! Here comes my sister, reading: stand aside.

CELIA: [*Reads*]
Why should this a desert be?
For it is unpeopled? No:
Tongues I'll hang on every tree
That shall civil sayings show:
Some, how brief the life of man
Runs his erring pilgrimage,
That the stretching of a span
Buckles in his sum of age;
Some, of violated vows
'Twixt the souls of friend and friend:
But upon the fairest boughs,

Or at every sentence end,
Will I Rosalinda write,
Teaching all that read to know
The quintessence of every sprite
Heaven would in little show.
Therefore Heaven Nature charged
That one body should be filled
With all graces wide-enlarged:
Nature presently distilled
Helen's cheek, but not her heart,
Cleopatra's majesty,
Atalanta's better part,
Sad Lucretia's modesty.
Thus Rosalinde of many parts
By heavenly synod was devised,
Of many faces, eyes, and hearts,
To have the touches dearest prized.
Heaven would that she these gifts should have,
And I to live and die her slave.

ROSALIND: O most gentle pulpiter! What tedious homily of love have you wearied your parishioners withal, and never cried 'Have patience, good people!'

CELIA: How now! Back, friends; shepherd, go off a little; go with him, sirrah.

TOUCHSTONE: Come, shepherd, let us make an honourable retreat; though not with bag and baggage, yet with scrip and scrippage.

Exeunt CORIN and TOUCHSTONE

CELIA: Didst thou hear these verses?

ROSALIND: O, yes, I heard them all, and more too; for some of them had in them more feet than the verses would bear.

CELIA: That's no matter: the feet might bear the verses.

ROSALIND: Ay, but the feet were lame, and could not bear themselves without the verse and therefore stood lamely in the verse.

CELIA: But didst thou hear without wondering how thy name should be hanged and carved upon these trees?

ROSALIND: I was seven of the nine days out of the wonder before you came; for look here what I found on a palm-tree. I was never so berhymed since Pythagoras' time that I was an Irish rat, which I can hardly remember.

CELIA: Trow you who hath done this?

ROSALIND: Is it a man?

CELIA: And a chain, that you once wore, about his neck. Change you colour?

ROSALIND: I prithee, who?

CELIA: O Lord, Lord! it is a hard matter for friends to meet; but mountains may be removed with earthquakes, and so encounter.

ROSALIND: Nay, but who is it?

CELIA: Is it possible?

ROSALIND: Nay, I prithee now, with most petitionary vehemence, tell me who it is.

CELIA: O wonderful, wonderful, and most wonderful wonderful, and yet again wonderful, and after that, out of all whooping!

ROSALIND: Good my complexion! dost thou think, though I am caparisoned like a man, I have a doublet and hose in my disposition? One inch of delay more is a South Sea of discovery. I prithee, tell me who is it quickly, and speak apace. I would thou couldst stammer, that thou mightst pour this concealed man out of thy mouth, as wine comes out of a narrow-mouthed bottle—either too much at once or none at all. I prithee take the cork out of thy mouth that may drink thy tidings.

CELIA: So you may put a man in your belly.

ROSALIND: Is he of God's making? What manner of man? Is his head worth a hat or his chin worth a beard?

CELIA: Nay, he hath but a little beard.

ROSALIND: Why, God will send more if the man will be thankful. Let me stay the growth of his beard, if thou delay me not the knowledge of his chin.

CELIA: It is young Orlando, that tripped up the wrestler's heels and your heart both in an instant.

ROSALIND: Nay, but the devil take mocking! Speak, sad brow and true maid.

CELIA: I' faith, coz, 'tis he.

ROSALIND: Orlando?

CELIA: Orlando.

ROSALIND: Alas the day! what shall I do with my doublet and hose? What did he when thou sawest him? What said he? How looked he? Wherein went he? What makes him here? Did he ask for me? Where remains he? How parted he with thee? And when shalt thou see him again? Answer me in one word.

CELIA: You must borrow me Gargantua's mouth first: 'tis a word too great for any mouth of this age's size. To say ay and no to these particulars is more than to answer in a catechism.

ROSALIND: But doth he know that I am in this forest, and in man's apparel? Looks he as freshly as he did the day he wrestled?

CELIA: It is as easy to count atomies as to resolve the propositions of a lover; but take a taste of my finding him, and relish it with good observance. I found him under a tree, like a dropped acorn.

ROSALIND: It may well be called Jove's tree, when it drops forth such fruit.

CELIA: Give me audience, good madam.

ROSALIND: Proceed.

CELIA: There lay he, stretched along like a wounded knight.

ROSALIND: Though it be pity to see such a sight, it well becomes the ground.

CELIA: Cry 'Holla' to thy tongue, I prithee; it curvets unseasonably. He was furnished like a hunter.

ROSALIND: O, ominous! he comes to kill my heart.

CELIA: I would sing my song without a burden: thou bringest me out of tune.

ROSALIND: Do you not know I am a woman? When I think, I must speak. Sweet, say on.

CELIA: You bring me out. Soft! comes he not here?

Enter ORLANDO and JAQUES

ROSALIND: 'Tis he: slink by, and note him.

JAQUES: I thank you for your company; but, good faith, I had as lief have been myself alone.

ORLANDO: And so had I; but yet, for fashion sake, I thank you too for your society.

JAQUES: God buy you: let's meet as little as we can.

ORLANDO: I do desire we may be better strangers.

JAQUES: I pray you mar no more trees with writing lovesongs in their barks.

ORLANDO: I pray you mar no more of my verses with reading them ill-favouredly.

JAQUES: Rosalind is your love's name?

ORLANDO: Yes, just.

JAQUES: I do not like her name.

ORLANDO: There was no thought of pleasing you when she was christened.

JAQUES: What stature is she of?

ORLANDO: Just as high as my heart.

JAQUES: You are full of pretty answers. Have you not been acquainted with goldsmiths' wives, and conned them out of rings?

ORLANDO: Not so; but I answer you right painted cloth, from whence you have studied your questions.

JAQUES: You have a nimble wit: I think 'twas made of Atalanta's heels. Will you sit down with me? And we two will rail against our mistress the world, and all our misery.

ORLANDO: I will chide no breather in the world but myself, against whom I know most faults.

JAQUES: The worst fault you have is to be in love.

ORLANDO: 'Tis a fault I will not change for your best virtue. I am weary of you.

JAQUES: By my troth, I was seeking for a fool when I found you.

ORLANDO: He is drowned in the brook: look but in, and you shall see him.

JAQUES: There I shall see mine own figure.

ORLANDO: Which I take to be either a fool or a cipher.

JAQUES: I'll tarry no longer with you; farewell, good Signior Love.

ORLANDO: I am glad of your departure: adieu, good Monsieur Melancholy.

Exit JAQUES

ROSALIND: [*Aside to CELIA*] I will speak to him like a saucy lackey, and under that habit play the knave with him.—Do you hear, forester?

ORLANDO: Very well: what would you?

ROSALIND: I pray you, what is't o'clock?

ORLANDO: You should ask me what time o' day: there's no clock in the forest.

ROSALIND: Then there is no true lover in the forest; else sighing every minute and groaning every hour would detect the lazy foot of Time as well as a clock.

ORLANDO: And why not the swift foot of Time? Had not that been as proper?

ROSALIND: By no means, sir. Time travels in divers paces with divers persons. I'll tell you who Time ambles withal, who Time trots withal, who Time gallops withal, and who he stands still withal.

ORLANDO: I prithee, who doth he trot withal?

ROSALIND: Marry, he trots hard with a young maid between the contract of her marriage and the day it is solemnized; if the interim be but a seennight, Time's pace is so hard that it seems the length of seven year.

ORLANDO: Who ambles Time withal?

ROSALIND: With a priest that lacks Latin and a rich man that hath not the gout, for the one sleeps easily because he cannot study, and the other lives merrily because he feels no pain, the one lacking the burden of lean and wasteful learning, the other knowing no burden of heavy tedious penury; these Time ambles withal.

ORLANDO: Who doth he gallop withal?

ROSALIND: With a thief to the gallows, for though he go as softly as foot can fall, he thinks himself too soon there.

ORLANDO: Who stays it still withal?

ROSALIND: With lawyers in the vacation, for they sleep between term and term, and then they perceive not how Time moves.

ORLANDO: Where dwell you, pretty youth?

ROSALIND: With this shepherdess, my sister; here in the skirts of the forest, like fringe upon a petticoat.

ORLANDO: Are you native of this place?

ROSALIND: As the cony that you see dwell where she is kindled.

ORLANDO: Your accent is something finer than you could purchase in so removed a dwelling.

ROSALIND: I have been told so of many: but indeed an old religious uncle of mine taught me to speak, who was in his youth an inland man; one that knew courtship too well, for there he fell in love. I have heard him read many lectures against it, and I thank God I am not a woman, to be touched with so many giddy offences as he hath generally taxed their whole sex withal.

ORLANDO: Can you remember any of the principal evils that he laid to the charge of women?

ROSALIND: There were none principal; they were all like one another as half-pence are, every one fault seeming monstrous till his fellow fault came to match it.

ORLANDO: I prithee, recount some of them.

ROSALIND: No, I will not cast away my physic but on those that are sick. There is a man haunts the forest, that abuses our young plants with carving 'Rosalind' on their barks; hangs odes upon hawthorns and elegies on brambles, all, forsooth, deifying the name of Rosalind: if I could meet that fancy-monger I would give him some good counsel, for he seems to have the quotidian of love upon him.

ORLANDO: I am he that is so love-shaked: I pray you tell me your remedy.

ROSALIND: There is none of my uncle's marks upon you: he taught me how to know a man in love; in which cage of rushes I am sure you are not prisoner.

ORLANDO: What were his marks?

ROSALIND: A lean cheek, which you have not, a blue eye and sunken, which you have not, an unquestionable spirit, which you have not, a beard neglected, which you have not; but I pardon you for that, for simply your having in beard is a younger brother's revenue: then your hose should be ungartered, your bonnet unbanded, your sleeve unbuttoned, your shoe untied and every thing about you demonstrating a careless desolation; but you are no such man; you are rather point-device in your accoutrements as loving yourself than seeming the lover of any other.

ORLANDO: Fair youth, I would I could make thee believe I love.

ROSALIND: Me believe it! you may as soon make her that you love believe it; which, I warrant, she is apter to do than to confess she does: that is one of the points in the which women still give the lie to their consciences. But, in good sooth, are you he that hangs the verses on the trees, wherein Rosalind is so admired?

ORLANDO: I swear to thee, youth, by the white hand of Rosalind, I am that he, that unfortunate he.

ROSALIND: But are you so much in love as your rhymes speak?

ORLANDO: Neither rhyme nor reason can express how much.

ROSALIND: Love is merely a madness, and, I tell you, deserves as well a dark house and a whip as madmen do; and the reason why they are not so punished and cured is, that the lunacy is so ordinary that the whippers are in love too. Yet I profess curing it by counsel.

ORLANDO: Did you ever cure any so?

ROSALIND: Yes, one, and in this manner. He was to imagine me his love, his mistress; and I set him every day to woo me; at which time would I, being but a moonish youth, grieve, be effeminate, changeable, longing and liking, proud, fantastical, apish, shallow, inconstant, full of tears, full of smiles; for every passion something and for no passion truly anything, as boys and women are for the most part cattle of this colour; would now like him, now loathe him; then entertain him, then forswear him; now weep for him, then spit at him; that I drave my suitor from his mad humour of love to a living humour of madness; which was, to forswear the full stream of the world, and to live in a nook merely monastic. And thus I cured him; and this way will I take upon me to wash your liver as clean as a sound sheep's heart, that there shall not be one spot of love in't.

ORLANDO: I would not be cured, youth.

ROSALIND: I would cure you, if you would but call me Rosalind and come every day to my cote and woo me.

ORLANDO: Now, by the faith of my love, I will: tell me where it is.

ROSALIND: Go with me to it and I'll show it you; and by the way, you shall tell me where in the forest you live. Will you go?

ORLANDO: With all my heart, good youth.

ROSALIND: Nay you must call me Rosalind. Come, sister, will you go?

Exeunt

SCENE III—*The forest*

Enter TOUCHSTONE and AUDREY; JAQUES behind

TOUCHSTONE: Come apace, good Audrey: I will fetch up your goats, Audrey. And how, Audrey, am I the man yet? doth my simple feature content you?

AUDREY: Your features! Lord warrant us! What features!

TOUCHSTONE: I am here with thee and thy goats, as the most capricious poet, honest Ovid, was among the Goths.

JAQUES: [*Aside*] O knowledge ill-inhabited, worse than Jove in a thatched house!

TOUCHSTONE: When a man's verses cannot be understood, nor a man's good wit seconded with the forward child understanding, it strikes a man more dead than a great reckoning in a little room. Truly, I would the gods had made thee poetical.

AUDREY: I do not know what 'poetical' is: is it honest in deed and word? is it a true thing?

TOUCHSTONE: No, truly; for the truest poetry is the most feigning; and lovers are given to poetry, and what they swear in poetry may be said as lovers they do feign.

AUDREY: Do you wish then that the gods had made me poetical?

TOUCHSTONE: I do, truly; for thou swearest to me thou art honest: now, if thou wert a poet, I might have some hope thou didst feign.

AUDREY: Would you not have me honest?

TOUCHSTONE: No, truly, unless thou wert hard-favoured; for honesty coupled to beauty is to have honey a sauce to sugar.

JAQUES: [*Aside*] A material fool!

AUDREY: Well, I am not fair; and therefore I pray the gods make me honest.

TOUCHSTONE: Truly, and to cast away honesty upon a foul slut were to put good meat into an unclean dish.

AUDREY: I am not a slut, though I thank the gods I am foul.

TOUCHSTONE: Well, praised be the gods for thy foulness! sluttishness may come hereafter. But be it as it may be, I will marry thee, and to that end I have been with Sir Oliver Martext, the vicar of the next village, who hath promised to meet me in this place of the forest and to couple us.

JAQUES: [*Aside*] I would fain see this meeting.

AUDREY: Well, the gods give us joy!

TOUCHSTONE: Amen. A man may, if he were of a fearful heart, stagger in this attempt; for here we have no temple but the wood, no assembly but horn-beasts. But what though? Courage! As horns are odious, they are necessary. It is said, 'many a man knows no end of his goods:' right; many a man has good horns, and knows no end of them. Well, that is the dowry of his wife; 'tis none of his own getting. Horns? Even so. Poor men alone? No, no; the noblest deer hath them as huge as the rascal. Is the single man therefore blessed? No: as a walled town is more worthier than a village, so is the forehead of a married man more honourable than the bare brow of a bachelor; and by how much defence is better than no skill, by so much is a horn more precious than to want. Here comes Sir Oliver.

Enter SIR OLIVER MARTEXT

Sir Oliver Martext, you are well met: will you dispatch us here under this tree, or shall we go with you to your chapel?

SIR OLIVER MARTEXT: Is there none here to give the woman?

TOUCHSTONE: I will not take her on gift of any man.

SIR OLIVER MARTEXT: Truly, she must be given, or the marriage is not lawful.

JAQUES: [*Discovering himself*] Proceed, proceed; I'll give her.

TOUCHSTONE: Good even, good Master What-ye-call't; how do you, sir? You are very well met. Goddild you for your last company. I am very glad to see you: even a toy in hand here, sir: nay, pray be covered.

JAQUES: Will you be married, motley?

TOUCHSTONE: As the ox hath his bow, sir, the horse his curb and the falcon her bells, so man hath his desires; and as pigeons bill, so wedlock would be nibbling.

JAQUES: And will you, being a man of your breeding, be married under a bush like a beggar? Get you to church, and have a good priest that can tell you what marriage is: this fellow will but join you together as they join wainscot; then one of you will prove a shrunk panel and, like green timber, warp, warp.

TOUCHSTONE: [*Aside*] I am not in the mind but I were better to be married of him than of another; for he is not like to marry me well; and not being well married, it will be a good excuse for me hereafter to leave my wife.

JAQUES: Go thou with me, and let me counsel thee.

TOUCHSTONE: Come, sweet Audrey;
We must be married, or we must live in bawdry.
Farewell, good Master Oliver: not—
O sweet Oliver,
O brave Oliver,
Leave me not behind thee: but—
Wind away,
Begone, I say,
I will not to wedding with thee.

Exeunt JAQUES, TOUCHSTONE and AUDREY

SIR OLIVER MARTEXT: 'Tis no matter: ne'er a fantastical knave of them all shall flout me out of my calling.

Exit

SCENE IV—*The forest*

Enter ROSALIND and CELIA

ROSALIND: Never talk to me; I will weep.

CELIA: Do, I prithee; but yet have the grace to consider that tears do not become a man.

ROSALIND: But have I not cause to weep?

CELIA: As good cause as one would desire; therefore weep.

ROSALIND: His very hair is of the dissembling colour.

CELIA: Something browner than Judas's. Marry, his kisses are Judas's own children.

ROSALIND: I' faith, his hair is of a good colour.

CELIA: An excellent colour: your chestnut was ever the only colour.

ROSALIND: And his kissing is as full of sanctity as the touch of holy bread.

CELIA: He hath bought a pair of cast lips of Diana: a nun of winter's sisterhood kisses not more religiously; the very ice of chastity is in them.

ROSALIND: But why did he swear he would come this morning, and comes not?

CELIA: Nay, certainly, there is no truth in him.

ROSALIND: Do you think so?

CELIA: Yes; I think he is not a pick-purse nor a horse-stealer, but for his verity in love, I do think him as concave as a covered goblet or a worm-eaten nut.

ROSALIND: Not true in love?

CELIA: Yes, when he is in; but I think he is not in.

ROSALIND: You have heard him swear downright he was.

CELIA: 'Was' is not 'is'; besides, the oath of a lover is no stronger than the word of a tapster; they are both the confirmer of false reckonings. He attends here in the forest on the Duke, your father.

ROSALIND: I met the Duke yesterday and had much question with him: he asked me of what parentage I was; I told him, of as good as he; so he laughed and let me go. But what talk we of fathers, when there is such a man as Orlando?

CELIA: O, that's a brave man! he writes brave verses, speaks brave words, swears brave oaths and breaks them bravely, quite traverse, athwart the heart of his lover; as a puisny tilter, that spurs his horse but on one side, breaks his staff like a noble goose: but all's brave that youth mounts and folly guides. Who comes here?

Enter CORIN

CORIN: Mistress and master, you have oft inquired
After the shepherd that complain'd of love,
Who you saw sitting by me on the turf,
Praising the proud disdainful shepherdess
That was his mistress.

CELIA: Well, and what of him?

CORIN: If you will see a pageant truly play'd,
Between the pale complexion of true love
And the red glow of scorn and proud disdain,
Go hence a little and I shall conduct you,
If you will mark it.

ROSALIND: O, come, let us remove!
The sight of lovers feedeth those in love.
Bring us to this sight, and you shall say
I'll prove a busy actor in their play.

Exeunt

SCENE V—*Another part of the forest*

Enter SILVIUS and PHEBE

SILVIUS: Sweet Phebe, do not scorn me; do not, Phebe;
Say that you love me not, but say not so
In bitterness. The common executioner,
Whose heart the accustom'd sight of death makes hard,
Falls not the axe upon the humbled neck
But first begs pardon: will you sterner be
Than he that dies and lives by bloody drops?

Enter ROSALIND, CELIA, and CORIN, behind

PHEBE: I would not be thy executioner;
I fly thee, for I would not injure thee.
Thou tell'st me there is murder in mine eye.
'Tis pretty, sure, and very probable,
That eyes, that are the frail'st and softest things,
Who shut their coward gates on atomies,
Should be call'd tyrants, butchers, murderers!
Now I do frown on thee with all my heart;
And if mine eyes can wound, now let them kill thee,
Now counterfeit to swoon; why now fall down;
Or if thou canst not, O, for shame, for shame,
Lie not, to say mine eyes are murderers!
Now show the wound mine eye hath made in thee.
Scratch thee but with a pin, and there remains
Some scar of it; lean but upon a rush,
The cicatrice and capable impressure
Thy palm some moment keeps; but now mine eyes,
Which I have darted at thee, hurt thee not,
Nor, I am sure, there is no force in eyes
That can do hurt.

SILVIUS: O dear Phebe,
If ever—as that ever may be near—
You meet in some fresh cheek the power of fancy,
Then shall you know the wounds invisible
That love's keen arrows make.

PHEBE: But till that time
Come not thou near me; and when that time comes,
Afflict me with thy mocks, pity me not;
As till that time I shall not pity thee.

ROSALIND: [*Advancing*] And why, I pray you? Who might be your mother,
That you insult, exult, and all at once,
Over the wretched? What though you have no beauty—
As, by my faith, I see no more in you
Than without candle may go dark to bed—
Must you be therefore proud and pitiless?
Why, what means this? Why do you look on me?
I see no more in you than in the ordinary
Of nature's sale-work. 'Od's my little life,
I think she means to tangle my eyes too!
No, faith, proud mistress, hope not after it:
'Tis not your inky brows, your black silk hair,
Your bugle eyeballs, nor your cheek of cream,
That can entame my spirits to your worship.
You foolish shepherd, wherefore do you follow her,
Like foggy south puffing with wind and rain?
You are a thousand times a properer man
Than she a woman: 'tis such fools as you
That makes the world full of ill-favour'd children:
'Tis not her glass, but you, that flatters her;
And out of you she sees herself more proper
Than any of her lineaments can show her.
But, mistress, know yourself: down on your knees,
And thank heaven, fasting, for a good man's love;
For I must tell you friendly in your ear,
Sell when you can: you are not for all markets.
Cry the man mercy; love him; take his offer;
Foul is most foul, being foul to be a scoffer.
So take her to thee, shepherd: fare you well.

PHEBE: Sweet youth, I pray you, chide a year together;
I had rather hear you chide than this man woo.

ROSALIND: He's fallen in love with your foulness and she'll fall in love with my anger. If it be so, as fast as she answers thee with frowning looks, I'll sauce her with bitter words. Why look you so upon me?

PHEBE: For no ill will I bear you.

ROSALIND: I pray you, do not fall in love with me,
For I am falser than vows made in wine:
Besides, I like you not. If you will know my house,
'Tis at the tuft of olives here hard by.
Will you go, sister? Shepherd, ply her hard.
Come, sister. Shepherdess, look on him better,
And be not proud; though all the world could see,
None could be so abused in sight as he.
Come, to our flock.

Exeunt ROSALIND, CELIA and CORIN

PHEBE: Dead Shepherd, now I find thy saw of might,
'Who ever loved that loved not at first sight?'
SILVIUS: Sweet Phebe—
PHEBE: Ha, what say'st thou, Silvius?
SILVIUS: Sweet Phebe, pity me.
PHEBE: Why, I am sorry for thee, gentle Silvius.
SILVIUS: Wherever sorrow is, relief would be.
If you do sorrow at my grief in love,
By giving love your sorrow and my grief
Were both extermined.
PHEBE: Thou hast my love: is not that neighbourly?
SILVIUS: I would have you.
PHEBE: Why, that were covetousness.
Silvius, the time was that I hated thee,
And yet it is not that I bear thee love;
But since that thou canst talk of love so well,
Thy company, which erst was irksome to me,
I will endure, and I'll employ thee too.
But do not look for further recompense
Than thine own gladness that thou art employ'd.
SILVIUS: So holy and so perfect is my love,
And I in such a poverty of grace,
That I shall think it a most plenteous crop
To glean the broken ears after the man
That the main harvest reaps; loose now and then
A scatter'd smile, and that I'll live upon.
PHEBE: Know'st thou the youth that spoke to me erewhile?
SILVIUS: Not very well, but I have met him oft;
And he hath bought the cottage and the bounds
That the old carlot once was master of.
PHEBE: Think not I love him, though I ask for him;
'Tis but a peevish boy; yet he talks well.
But what care I for words? yet words do well
When he that speaks them pleases those that hear.
It is a pretty youth: not very pretty;
But, sure, he's proud, and yet his pride becomes him.
He'll make a proper man: the best thing in him
Is his complexion; and faster than his tongue
Did make offence, his eye did heal it up.
He is not very tall; yet for his years he's tall;
His leg is but so-so; and yet 'tis well.
There was a pretty redness in his lip,
A little riper and more lusty red
Than that mix'd in his cheek; 'twas just the difference
Between the constant red and mingled damask.
There be some women, Silvius, had they mark'd him
In parcels as I did, would have gone near
To fall in love with him; but, for my part,
I love him not nor hate him not; and yet
I have more cause to hate him than to love him;
For what had he to do to chide at me?
He said mine eyes were black and my hair black,
And, now I am remember'd, scorn'd at me.
I marvel why I answer'd not again;
But that's all one: omittance is no quittance.
I'll write to him a very taunting letter,
And thou shalt bear it: wilt thou, Silvius?
SILVIUS: Phebe, with all my heart.
PHEBE: I'll write it straight;
The matter's in my head and in my heart;
I will be bitter with him and passing short.
Go with me, Silvius.

Exeunt

ACT IV

SCENE I—*The forest*

Enter ROSALIND, CELIA, and JAQUES

JAQUES: I prithee, pretty youth, let me be better acquainted with thee.

ROSALIND: They say you are a melancholy fellow.

JAQUES: I am so; I do love it better than laughing.

ROSALIND: Those that are in extremity of either are abominable fellows and betray themselves to every modern censure worse than drunkards.

JAQUES: Why, 'tis good to be sad and say nothing.

ROSALIND: Why then, 'tis good to be a post.

JAQUES: I have neither the scholar's melancholy, which is emulation; nor the musician's, which is fantastical; nor the courtier's, which is proud; nor the soldier's, which is ambitious; nor the lawyer's, which is politic; nor the lady's, which is nice; nor the lover's, which is all these: but it is a melancholy of mine own, compounded of many simples, extracted from many objects, and indeed, the sundry's contemplation of my travels, in which my often rumination wraps me in a most humorous sadness.

ROSALIND: A traveller! By my faith, you have great reason to be sad. I fear you have sold your own lands to see other men's; then, to have seen much and to have nothing, is to have rich eyes and poor hands.

JAQUES: Yes, I have gained my experience.

ROSALIND: And your experience makes you sad. I had rather have a fool to make me merry than experience to make me sad; and to travel for it too!

Enter ORLANDO

ORLANDO: Good day and happiness, dear Rosalind!

JAQUES: Nay, then, God be wi' you, an you talk in blank verse.

Exit JAQUES

ROSALIND: Farewell, Monsieur Traveller; look you lisp and wear strange suits, disable all the benefits of your own country, be out of love with your nativity and almost chide God for making you that countenance you are, or I will scarce think you have swam in a gondola. Why, how now, Orlando! where have you been all this while? You a lover! An you serve me such another trick, never come in my sight more.

ORLANDO: My fair Rosalind, I come within an hour of my promise.

ROSALIND: Break an hour's promise in love! He that will divide a minute into a thousand parts and break but a part of the thousandth part of a minute in the affairs of love, it may be said of him that Cupid hath clapped him o' the shoulder, but I'll warrant him heart-whole.

ORLANDO: Pardon me, dear Rosalind.

ROSALIND: Nay, an you be so tardy, come no more in my sight. I had as lief be wooed of a snail.

ORLANDO: Of a snail?

ROSALIND: Ay, of a snail; for though he comes slowly, he carries his house on his head: a better jointure, I think, than you make a woman: besides he brings his destiny with him.

ORLANDO: What's that?

ROSALIND: Why, horns, which such as you are fain to be beholding to your wives for; but he comes armed in his fortune and prevents the slander of his wife.

ORLANDO: Virtue is no horn-maker; and my Rosalind is virtuous.

ROSALIND: And I am your Rosalind.

CELIA: It pleases him to call you so; but he hath a Rosalind of a better leer than you.

ROSALIND: Come, woo me, woo me; for now I am in a holiday humour and like enough to consent. What would you say to me now, an I were your very very Rosalind?

ORLANDO: I would kiss before I spoke.

ROSALIND: Nay, you were better speak first, and when you were gravelled for lack of matter, you might take occasion to kiss. Very good orators, when they are out, they will spit; and for lovers lacking—God warn us!—matter, the cleanliest shift is to kiss.

ORLANDO: How if the kiss be denied?

ROSALIND: Then she puts you to entreaty, and there begins new matter.

ORLANDO: Who could be out, being before his beloved mistress?

ROSALIND: Marry, that should you, if I were your mistress, or I should think my honesty ranker than my wit.

ORLANDO: What, of my suit?

ROSALIND: Not out of your apparel, and yet out of your suit. Am not I your Rosalind?

ORLANDO: I take some joy to say you are, because I would be talking of her.

ROSALIND: Well in her person I say I will not have you.

ORLANDO: Then, in mine own person I die.

ROSALIND: No, faith, die by attorney. The poor world is almost six thousand years old, and in all this time there was not any man died in his own person, videlicit, in a love-cause. Troilus had his brains dashed out with a Grecian club; yet he did what he could to die before, and he is one of the patterns of love. Leander, he would have lived many a fair year, though Hero had turned nun, if it had not been for a hot midsummer night; for, good youth, he went but forth to wash him in the Hellespont and being taken with the cramp, was drowned and the foolish chroniclers of that age found it was 'Hero of Sestos'. But these are all lies: men have died from time to time and worms have eaten them, but not for love.

ORLANDO: I would not have my right Rosalind of this mind, for, I protest, her frown might kill me.

ROSALIND: By this hand, it will not kill a fly. But come, now I will be your Rosalind in a more coming-on disposition, and ask me what you will. I will grant it.

ORLANDO: Then love me, Rosalind.

ROSALIND: Yes, faith, will I, Fridays and Saturdays and all.

ORLANDO: And wilt thou have me?

ROSALIND: Ay, and twenty such.

ORLANDO: What sayest thou?

ROSALIND: Are you not good?

ORLANDO: I hope so.

ROSALIND: Why then, can one desire too much of a good thing? Come, sister, you shall be the priest and marry us. Give me your hand, Orlando. What do you say, sister?

ORLANDO: Pray thee, marry us.

CELIA: I cannot say the words.

ROSALIND: You must begin, 'Will you, Orlando—'

CELIA: Go to. Will you, Orlando, have to wife this Rosalind?

ORLANDO: I will.

ROSALIND: Ay, but when?

ORLANDO: Why, now; as fast as she can marry us.

ROSALIND: Then you must say 'I take thee, Rosalind, for wife'.

ORLANDO: I take thee, Rosalind, for wife.

ROSALIND: I might ask you for your commission; but I do take thee, Orlando, for my husband: there's a girl goes before the priest; and certainly, a woman's thought runs before her actions.

ORLANDO: So do all thoughts; they are winged.

ROSALIND: Now tell me how long you would have her after you have possessed her.

ORLANDO: For ever and a day.

ROSALIND: Say 'a day,' without the 'ever'. No, no, Orlando; men are April when they woo, December when they wed; maids are May when they are maids, but the sky changes when they are wives. I will be more jealous of thee than a Barbary cock-pigeon over his hen, more clamorous than a parrot against rain, more new-fangled than an ape, more giddy in my desires than a monkey. I will weep for nothing, like Diana in the fountain, and I will do that when you are disposed to be merry; I will laugh like a hyen, and that when thou art inclined to sleep.

ORLANDO: But will my Rosalind do so?

ROSALIND: By my life, she will do as I do.

ORLANDO: O, but she is wise.

ROSALIND: Or else she could not have the wit to do this: the wiser, the waywarder. Make the doors upon a woman's wit and it will out at the casement; shut that and 'twill out at the key-hole; stop that, 'twill fly with the smoke out at the chimney.

ORLANDO: A man that had a wife with such a wit, he might say 'Wit, whither wilt?'

ROSALIND: Nay, you might keep that check for it till you met your wife's wit going to your neighbour's bed.

ORLANDO: And what wit could wit have to excuse that?

ROSALIND: Marry, to say she came to seek you there. You shall never take her without her answer, unless you take her without her tongue. O, that woman that cannot make her fault her husband's occasion, let her never nurse her child herself, for she will breed it like a fool!

ORLANDO: For these two hours, Rosalind, I will leave thee.

ROSALIND: Alas! dear love, I cannot lack thee two hours.

ORLANDO: I must attend the Duke at dinner; by two o'clock I will be with thee again.

ROSALIND: Ay, go your ways, go your ways, I knew what you would prove; my friends told me as much, and I thought no less: that flattering tongue of yours won me: 'tis but one cast away, and so, come death! Two o'clock is your hour?

ORLANDO: Ay, sweet Rosalind.

ROSALIND: By my troth, and in good earnest, and so God mend me, and by all pretty oaths that are not dangerous, if you break one jot of your promise or come one minute behind your hour, I will think you the most pathetical break-promise and the most hollow lover and the most unworthy of her you call Rosalind that may be chosen out of the gross band of the unfaithful. Therefore beware my censure and keep your promise.

ORLANDO: With no less religion than if thou wert indeed my Rosalind; so adieu.

ROSALIND: Well, Time is the old justice that examines all such offenders, and let Time try: adieu.

Exit ORLANDO

CELIA: You have simply misused our sex in your love-prate: we must have your doublet and hose plucked over your head, and show the world what the bird hath done to her own nest.

ROSALIND: O coz, coz, coz, my pretty little coz, that thou didst know how many fathom deep I am in love! But it cannot be sounded: my affection hath an unknown bottom, like the Bay of Portugal.

CELIA: Or rather, bottomless, that as fast as you pour affection in, it runs out.

ROSALIND: No, that same wicked bastard of Venus that was begot of thought, conceived of spleen and born of madness, that blind rascally boy that abuses every one's eyes because his own are out: let him be judge how deep I am in love. I'll tell thee, Aliena, I cannot be out of the sight of Orlando: I'll go find a shadow and sigh till he come.

CELIA: And I'll sleep.

Exeunt

SCENE II—*The forest*

Enter JAQUES, Lords, in the habit of Foresters

JAQUES: Which is he that killed the deer?

LORD: Sir, it was I.

JAQUES: Let's present him to the Duke, like a Roman conqueror; and it would do well to set the deer's horns upon his head, for a branch of victory. Have you no song, forester, for this purpose?

LORD: Yes, sir.

JAQUES: Sing it; 'tis no matter how it be in tune, so it make noise enough.

Song

What shall he have that kill'd the deer?
His leather skin and horns to wear.
Then sing him home.

The rest shall bear this burden

Take thou no scorn to wear the horn;
It was a crest ere thou wast born.
Thy father's father wore it,
And thy father bore it.
The horn, the horn, the lusty horn
Is not a thing to laugh to scorn.

Exeunt

SCENE III—*The forest*

Enter ROSALIND and CELIA

ROSALIND: How say you now? Is it not past two o'clock? And here much Orlando!

CELIA: I warrant you, with pure love and troubled brain, he hath ta'en his bow and arrows and is gone forth—to sleep. Look, who comes here.

Enter SILVIUS

SILVIUS: My errand is to you, fair youth;
My gentle Phebe bid me give you this.
I know not the contents; but, as I guess
By the stern brow and waspish action
Which she did use as she was writing of it,
It bears an angry tenor. Pardon me,
I am but as a guiltless messenger.

ROSALIND: Patience herself would startle at this letter
And play the swaggerer; bear this, bear all:

She says I am not fair, that I lack manners;
She calls me proud, and that she could not love me,
Were man as rare as phoenix. 'Od's my will!
Her love is not the hare that I do hunt;
Why writes she so to me? Well, shepherd, well,
This is a letter of your own device.

SILVIUS: No, I protest, I know not the contents;
Phebe did write it.

ROSALIND: Come, come, you are a fool
And turn'd into the extremity of love.
I saw her hand; she has a leathern hand.
A freestone-colour'd hand; I verily did think
That her old gloves were on, but 'twas her hands;
She has a huswife's hand; but that's no matter.
I say she never did invent this letter;
This is a man's invention and his hand.

SILVIUS: Sure, it is hers.

ROSALIND: Why, 'tis a boisterous and a cruel style.
A style for-challengers; why, she defies me,
Like Turk to Christian. Women's gentle brain
Could not drop forth such giant-rude invention
Such Ethiope words, blacker in their effect
Than in their countenance. Will you hear the letter?

SILVIUS: So please you, for I never heard it yet;
Yet heard too much of Phebe's cruelty.

ROSALIND: She Phebes me: mark how the tyrant writes.

Reads

Art thou god to shepherd turn'd,
That a maiden's heart hath burn'd?
Can a woman rail thus?

SILVIUS: Call you this railing?

ROSALIND: Why, thy godhead laid apart,
Warr'st thou with a woman's heart?
Did you ever hear such railing?
Whiles the eye of man did woo me,
That could do no vengeance to me.
Meaning me a beast.
If the scorn of your bright eyne
Have power to raise such love in mine,
Alack, in me what strange effect
Would they work in mild aspect!
Whiles you chid me, I did love;
How then might your prayers move!
He that brings this love to thee
Little knows this love in me;
And by him seal up thy mind;
Whether that thy youth and kind
Will the faithful offer take
Of me and all that I can make;
Or else by him my love deny,
And then I'll study how to die.

SILVIUS: Call you this chiding?

CELIA: Alas, poor shepherd!

ROSALIND: Do you pity him? No, he deserves no pity. Wilt thou love such a woman? What, to make thee an instrument and play false strains upon thee! Not to be endured! Well, go your way to her, for I see love hath made thee a tame snake, and say this to her: that if she love me, I charge her to love thee; if she will not, I will never have her unless thou entreat for her. If you be a true lover, hence, and not a word; for here comes more company.

Exit SILVIUS

Enter OLIVER

OLIVER: Good morrow, fair ones; pray you, if you know,
Where in the purlieus of this forest stands
A sheep-cote fenced about with olive trees?

CELIA: West of this place, down in the neighbour bottom
The rank of osiers by the murmuring stream
Left on your right hand brings you to the place.
But at this hour the house doth keep itself;
There's none within.

OLIVER: If that an eye may profit by a tongue,
Then should I know you by description;
Such garments and such years: 'The boy is fair,
Of female favour, and bestows himself
Like a ripe sister; the woman low
And browner than her brother.' Are not you
The owner of the house I did inquire for?

CELIA: It is no boast, being ask'd, to say we are.

OLIVER: Orlando doth commend him to you both,
And to that youth he calls his Rosalind
He sends this bloody napkin. Are you he?

ROSALIND: I am: what must we understand by this?

OLIVER: Some of my shame; if you will know of me
What man I am, and how, and why, and where
This handkercher was stain'd.

CELIA: I pray you, tell it.

OLIVER: When last the young Orlando parted from you
He left a promise to return again
Within an hour, and pacing through the forest,
Chewing the food of sweet and bitter fancy,
Lo, what befell! he threw his eye aside,
And mark what object did present itself.
Under an oak, whose boughs were moss'd with age
And high top bald with dry antiquity,
A wretched ragged man, o'ergrown with hair,
Lay sleeping on his back: about his neck
A green and gilded snake had wreathed itself,
Who with her head nimble in threats approach'd
The opening of his mouth; but suddenly,
Seeing Orlando, it unlink'd itself,
And with indented glides did slip away
Into a bush; under which bush's shade
A lioness, with udders all drawn dry,
Lay couching, head on ground, with catlike watch,
When that the sleeping man should stir; for 'tis
The royal disposition of that beast
To prey on nothing that doth seem as dead.
This seen, Orlando did approach the man
And found it was his brother, his elder brother.

CELIA: O, I have heard him speak of that same brother;
And he did render him the most unnatural
That lived amongst men.

OLIVER: And well he might so do,
For well I know he was unnatural.

ROSALIND: But, to Orlando: did he leave him there,
Food to the suck'd and hungry lioness?

OLIVER: Twice did he turn his back and purposed so;
But kindness, nobler ever than revenge,
And nature, stronger than his just occasion,
Made him give battle to the lioness,
Who quickly fell before him; in which hurtling
From miserable slumber I awaked.

CELIA: Are you his brother?

ROSALIND: Wast you he rescued?

CELIA: Was't you that did so oft contrive to kill him?

OLIVER: 'Twas I; but 'tis not I. I do not shame
To tell you what I was, since my conversion
So sweetly tastes, being the thing I am.

ROSALIND: But, for the bloody napkin?

OLIVER: By and by.
When from the first to last betwixt us two
Tears our recountments had most kindly bathed,
As how I came into that desert place—
In brief, he led me to the gentle Duke,
Who gave me fresh array and entertainment,
Committing me unto my brother's love;
Who led me instantly unto his cave,
There stripp'd himself, and here upon his arm
The lioness had torn some flesh away,
Which all this while had bled; and now he fainted
And cried, in fainting, upon Rosalind.
Brief, I recover'd him, bound up his wound;
And, after some small space, being strong at heart,
He sent me hither, stranger as I am,
To tell this story, that you might excuse
His broken promise, and to give this napkin
Dyed in his blood unto the shepherd youth
That he in sport doth call his Rosalind.

ROSALIND swoons

CELIA: Why, how now, Ganymede! sweet Ganymede!

OLIVER: Many will swoon when they do look on blood.

CELIA: There is more in it. Cousin Ganymede!

OLIVER: Look, he recovers.

ROSALIND: I would I were at home.

CELIA: We'll lead you thither.
I pray you, will you take him by the arm?

OLIVER: Be of good cheer, youth: you a man! You lack a man's heart.

ROSALIND: I do so, I confess it. Ah, sirrah, a body would think this was well counterfeited! I pray you, tell your brother how well I counterfeited. Heigh-ho!

OLIVER: This was not counterfeit: there is too great testimony in your complexion that it was a passion of earnest.

ROSALIND: Counterfeit, I assure you.

OLIVER: Well then, take a good heart and counterfeit to be a man.

ROSALIND: So I do; but, i' faith, I should have been a woman by right.

CELIA: Come, you look paler and paler; pray you, draw homewards. Good sir, go with us.

OLIVER: That will I, for I must bear answer back
How you excuse my brother, Rosalind.

ROSALIND: I shall devise something; but, I pray you, commend my counterfeiting to him. Will you go?

Exeunt

Act V

Scene I—*The forest*

Enter TOUCHSTONE and AUDREY

TOUCHSTONE: We shall find a time, Audrey; patience, gentle Audrey.

AUDREY: Faith, the priest was good enough, for all the old gentleman's saying.

TOUCHSTONE: A most wicked Sir Oliver, Audrey, a most vile Martext. But, Audrey, there is a youth here in the forest lays claim to you.

AUDREY: Ay, I know who 'tis; he hath no interest in me in the world: here comes the man you mean.

TOUCHSTONE: It is meat and drink to me to see a clown: by my troth, we that have good wits have much to answer for; we shall be flouting; we cannot hold.

Enter WILLIAM

WILLIAM: Good even, Audrey.

AUDREY: God ye good even, William.

WILLIAM: And good even to you, sir.

TOUCHSTONE: Good even, gentle friend. Cover thy head, cover thy head; nay, prithee, be covered. How old are you, friend?

WILLIAM: Five and twenty, sir.

TOUCHSTONE: A ripe age. Is thy name William?

WILLIAM: William, sir.

TOUCHSTONE: A fair name. Wast born i' the forest here?

WILLIAM: Ay, sir, I thank God.

TOUCHSTONE: 'Thank God;' a good answer. Art rich?

WILLIAM: Faith, sir, so so.

TOUCHSTONE: 'So so' is good, very good, very excellent good; and yet it is not; it is but so so. Art thou wise?

WILLIAM: Ay, sir, I have a pretty wit.

TOUCHSTONE: Why, thou sayest well. I do now remember a saying, 'The fool doth think he is wise, but the wise man knows himself to be a fool.' The heathen philosopher, when he had a desire to eat a grape, would open his lips when he put it into his mouth; meaning thereby that grapes were made to eat and lips to open. You do love this maid?

WILLIAM: I do, sir.

TOUCHSTONE: Give me your hand. Art thou learned?

WILLIAM: No, sir.

TOUCHSTONE: Then learn this of me: to have, is to have; for it is a figure in rhetoric that drink, being poured out of a cup into a glass, by filling the one doth empty the other; for all your writers do consent that ipse is he; now, you are not ipse, for I am he.

WILLIAM: Which he, sir?

TOUCHSTONE: He, sir, that must marry this woman. Therefore, you clown, abandon—which is in the vulgar leave—the society—which in the boorish is company—of this female—which in the common is woman; which together is, abandon the society of this female, or, clown, thou perishest; or, to thy better understanding, diest; or, to wit I kill thee, make thee away, translate thy life into death, thy liberty into bondage. I will deal in poison with thee, or in bastinado, or in steel; I will bandy with thee in faction; I will o'errun thee with policy; I will kill thee a hundred and fifty ways; therefore tremble and depart.

AUDREY: Do, good William.

WILLIAM: God rest you merry, sir.

Exit

Enter CORIN

CORIN: Our master and mistress seeks you; come away, away!

TOUCHSTONE: Trip, Audrey! trip, Audrey! I attend, I attend.

Exeunt

Scene II—*The forest*

Enter ORLANDO and OLIVER

ORLANDO: Is't possible that on so little acquaintance you should like her? that but seeing you should love her? and loving woo? and, wooing, she should grant? and will you persever to enjoy her?

OLIVER: Neither call the giddiness of it in question, the poverty of her, the small acquaintance, my sudden wooing, nor her sudden consenting; but say with me, I love Aliena; say with her that she loves me; consent with both that we may enjoy each other: it shall be to your good; for my father's house and all the revenue that was old Sir Rowland's will I estate upon you, and here live and die a shepherd.

ORLANDO: You have my consent. Let your wedding be to-morrow: thither will I invite the Duke and all's contented followers. Go you and prepare Aliena; for look you, here comes my Rosalind.

Enter ROSALIND

ROSALIND: God save you, brother.

OLIVER: And you, fair sister.

Exit

ROSALIND: O, my dear Orlando, how it grieves me to see thee wear thy heart in a scarf!

ORLANDO: It is my arm.

ROSALIND: I thought thy heart had been wounded with the claws of a lion.

ORLANDO: Wounded it is, but with the eyes of a lady.

ROSALIND: Did your brother tell you how I counterfeited to swoon when he showed me your handkerchief?

ORLANDO: Ay, and greater wonders than that.

ROSALIND: O, I know where you are: nay, 'tis true. There was never any thing so sudden but the fight of two rams and Caesar's thrasonical brag of 'I came, saw, and overcame.' For your brother and my sister no sooner met but they looked, no sooner looked but they loved, no sooner loved but they sighed, no sooner sighed but they asked one another the reason, no sooner knew the reason but they sought the remedy; and in these degrees have they made a pair of stairs to marriage which they will climb incontinent, or else be incontinent before marriage. They are in the very wrath of love and they will together; clubs cannot part them.

ORLANDO: They shall be married to-morrow, and I will bid the Duke to the nuptial. But, O, how bitter a thing it is to look into happiness through another man's eyes! By so much the more shall I to-morrow be at the height of heart-heaviness, by how much I shall think my brother happy in having what he wishes for.

ROSALIND: Why then, to-morrow I cannot serve your turn for Rosalind?

ORLANDO: I can live no longer by thinking.

ROSALIND: I will weary you then no longer with idle talking. Know of me then, for now I speak to some purpose, that I know you are a gentleman of good conceit. I speak not this that you should bear a good opinion of my knowledge, insomuch I say I know you are; neither do I labour for a greater esteem than may in some little measure draw a belief from you, to do yourself good and not to grace me. Believe then, if you please, that I can do strange things. I have, since I was three year old, conversed with a magician, most profound in his art and yet not damnable. If you do love Rosalind so near the heart as your gesture cries it out, when your brother marries Aliena, shall you marry her. I know into what straits of fortune she is driven; and it is not impossible to me, if it appear not inconvenient to you, to set her before your eyes tomorrow human as she is, and without any danger.

ORLANDO: Speakest thou in sober meanings?

ROSALIND: By my life, I do; which I tender dearly, though I say I am a magician. Therefore, put you in your best array: bid your friends; for if you will be married to-morrow, you shall, and to Rosalind, if you will.

Enter SILVIUS and PHEBE

Look, here comes a lover of mine and a lover of hers.

PHEBE: Youth, you have done me much ungentleness,
To show the letter that I write to you.

ROSALIND: I care not if I have: it is my study
To seem despiteful and ungentle to you.
You are there followed by a faithful shepherd;
Look upon him, love him; he worships you.

PHEBE: Good shepherd, tell this youth what 'tis to love.

SILVIUS: It is to be all made of sighs and tears;
And so am I for Phebe.

PHEBE: And I for Ganymede.

ORLANDO: And I for Rosalind.

ROSALIND: And I for no woman.

SILVIUS: It is to be all made of faith and service;
And so am I for Phebe.

PHEBE: And I for Ganymede.
ORLANDO: And I for Rosalind.
ROSALIND: And I for no woman.
SILVIUS: It is to be all made of fantasy,
All made of passion and all made of wishes,
All adoration, duty, and observance,
All humbleness, all patience and impatience,
All purity, all trial, all observance;
And so am I for Phebe.
PHEBE: And so am I for Ganymede.
ORLANDO: And so am I for Rosalind.
ROSALIND: And so am I for no woman.
PHEBE: If this be so, why blame you me to love you?
SILVIUS: If this be so, why blame you me to love you?
ORLANDO: If this be so, why blame you me to love you?
ROSALIND: Who do you speak too, 'Why blame you me to love you?'
ORLANDO: To her that is not here, nor doth not hear.
ROSALIND: Pray you, no more of this; 'tis like the howling of Irish wolves against the moon. (*To SILVIUS*) I will help you, if I can: (*To PHEBE*) I would love you, if I could. To-morrow meet me all together. (*To PHEBE*) I will marry you, if ever I marry woman, and I'll be married to-morrow. (*To ORLANDO*) I will satisfy you, if ever I satisfied man, and you shall be married to-morrow: (*To SILVIUS*) I will content you, if what pleases you contents you, and you shall be married to-morrow. (*To ORLANDO*) As you love Rosalind, meet. (*To SILVIUS*) As you love Phebe, meet: and as I love no woman, I'll meet. So fare you well: I have left you commands.
SILVIUS: I'll not fail, if I live.
PHEBE: Nor I.
ORLANDO: Nor I.

Exeunt

SCENE III—*The forest*

Enter TOUCHSTONE and AUDREY

TOUCHSTONE: To-morrow is the joyful day, Audrey; to-morrow will we be married.
AUDREY: I do desire it with all my heart; and I hope it is no dishonest desire to desire to be a woman of the world. Here comes two of the banished Duke's pages.

Enter two Pages

FIRST PAGE: Well met, honest gentleman.
TOUCHSTONE: By my troth, well met. Come, sit, sit, and a song.
SECOND PAGE: We are for you; sit i' the middle.
FIRST PAGE: Shall we clap into't roundly, without hawking or spitting or saying we are hoarse, which are the only prologues to a bad voice?
SECOND PAGE: I'faith, i'faith; and both in a tune, like two gipsies on a horse.

Song

It was a lover and his lass,
With a hey, and a ho, and a hey nonino,
That o'er the green corn-field did pass
In the spring time, the only pretty ring time,
When birds do sing, hey ding a ding, ding:
Sweet lovers love the spring.
Between the acres of the rye,
With a hey, and a ho, and a hey nonino
These pretty country folks would lie,
In spring time, & c.
This carol they began that hour,
With a hey, and a ho, and a hey nonino,
How that a life was but a flower
In spring time, & c.
And therefore take the present time,
With a hey, and a ho, and a hey nonino;
For love is crowned with the prime
In spring time, & c.

TOUCHSTONE: Truly, young gentlemen, though there was no great matter in the ditty, yet the note was very untuneable.
FIRST PAGE: You are deceived, sir: we kept time, we lost not our time.
TOUCHSTONE: By my troth, yes; I count it but time lost to hear such a foolish song. God buy you; and God mend your voices. Come, Audrey.

Exeunt

SCENE IV—*The forest*

Enter DUKE SENIOR, AMIENS, JAQUES, ORLANDO, OLIVER, and CELIA

DUKE SENIOR: Dost thou believe, Orlando, that the boy
Can do all this that he hath promised?
ORLANDO: I sometimes do believe, and sometimes do not;
As those that fear they hope, and know they fear.

Enter ROSALIND, SILVIUS, and PHEBE

ROSALIND: Patience once more, whiles our compact is urged:

You say, if I bring in your Rosalind,
You will bestow her on Orlando here?

DUKE SENIOR: That would I, had I kingdoms to give with her.

ROSALIND: And you say, you will have her, when I bring her?

ORLANDO: That would I, were I of all kingdoms king.

ROSALIND: You say, you'll marry me, if I be willing?

PHEBE: That will I, should I die the hour after.

ROSALIND: But if you do refuse to marry me,
You'll give yourself to this most faithful shepherd?

PHEBE: So is the bargain.

ROSALIND: You say, that you'll have Phebe, if she will?

SILVIUS: Though to have her and death were both one thing.

ROSALIND: I have promised to make all this matter even.

Keep you your word, O Duke, to give your daughter;
You yours, Orlando, to receive his daughter;
Keep your word, Phebe, that you'll marry me,
Or else refusing me, to wed this shepherd;
Keep your word, Silvius, that you'll marry her.
If she refuse me; and from hence I go,
To make these doubts all even.

Exeunt ROSALIND and CELIA

DUKE SENIOR: I do remember in this shepherd boy
Some lively touches of my daughter's favour.

ORLANDO: My lord, the first time that I ever saw him
Methought he was a brother to your daughter.
But, my good lord, this boy is forest-born,
And hath been tutor'd in the rudiments
Of many desperate studies by his uncle,
Whom he reports to be a great magician,
Obscured in the circle of this forest.

Enter TOUCHSTONE and AUDREY

JAQUES: There is, sure, another flood toward, and these couples are coming to the ark. Here comes a pair of very strange beasts, which in all tongues are called fools.

TOUCHSTONE: Salutation and greeting to you all!

JAQUES: Good my lord, bid him welcome. This is the motley-minded gentleman that I have so often met in the forest: he hath been a courtier, he swears.

TOUCHSTONE: If any man doubt that, let him put me to my purgation. I have trod a measure; I have flattered a lady; I have been politic with my friend, smooth with mine enemy; I have undone three tailors; I have had four quarrels, and like to have fought one.

JAQUES: And how was that ta'en up?

TOUCHSTONE: Faith, we met, and found the quarrel was upon the seventh cause.

JAQUES: How seventh cause? Good my lord, like this fellow.

DUKE SENIOR: I like him very well.

TOUCHSTONE: God 'ild you, sir; I desire you of the like. I press in here, sir, amongst the rest of the country copulatives, to swear and to forswear, according as marriage binds and blood breaks. A poor virgin, sir, an ill-favoured thing, sir, but mine own; a poor humour of mine, sir, to take that that no man else will. Rich honesty dwells like a miser, sir, in a poor house; as your pearl in your foul oyster.

DUKE SENIOR: By my faith, he is very swift and sententious.

TOUCHSTONE: According to the fool's bolt, sir, and such dulcet diseases.

JAQUES: But, for the seventh cause; how did you find the quarrel on the seventh cause?

TOUCHSTONE: Upon a lie seven times removed:—bear your body more seeming, Audrey:—as thus, sir. I did dislike the cut of a certain courtier's beard; he sent me word, if I said his beard was not cut well, he was in the mind it was: this is called the Retort Courteous. If I sent him word again 'it was not well cut', he would send me word, he cut it to please himself: this is called the Quip Modest. If again 'it was not well cut,' he disabled my judgment: this is called the Reply Churlish. If again 'it was not well cut,' he would answer, I spake not true: this is called the Reproof Valiant. If again 'it was not well cut,' he would say I lied: this is called the Counter-cheque Quarrelsome: and so to the Lie Circumstantial and the Lie Direct.

JAQUES: And how oft did you say his beard was not well cut?

TOUCHSTONE: I durst go no further than the Lie Circumstantial, nor he durst not give me the Lie Direct; and so we measured swords and parted.

JAQUES: Can you nominate in order now the degrees of the lie?

TOUCHSTONE: O sir, we quarrel in print, by the book; as you have books for good manners. I will name you the degrees. The first, the Retort Courteous; the second, the Quip Modest; the third, the Reply Churlish; the fourth, the Reproof Valiant; the fifth, the Countercheque Quarrelsome; the sixth, the Lie with Circumstance; the seventh, the Lie Direct. All these you may avoid but the Lie Direct; and you may avoid that too, with an If. I knew when seven justices could not take up a quarrel, but when the parties were met themselves, one of them thought but of an If, as, 'If you said so, then I said so'; and they shook hands and swore brothers. Your If is the only peacemaker; much virtue in If.

JAQUES: Is not this a rare fellow, my lord? he's as good at any thing and yet a fool.

DUKE SENIOR: He uses his folly like a stalking-horse and under the presentation of that he shoots his wit.

Enter HYMEN, ROSALIND, and CELIA

Still Music

HYMEN: Then is there mirth in heaven,
When earthly things made even Atone together.
Good duke, receive thy daughter
Hymen from heaven brought her,
Yea, brought her hither,
That thou mightst join her hand with his
Whose heart within his bosom is.

ROSALIND: [*To DUKE SENIOR*] To you I give myself, for I am yours. (*To ORLANDO*) To you I give myself, for I am yours.

DUKE SENIOR: If there be truth in sight, you are my daughter.

ORLANDO: If there be truth in sight, you are my Rosalind.

PHEBE: If sight and shape be true,
Why then, my love adieu!

ROSALIND: I'll have no father, if you be not he;
I'll have no husband, if you be not he;
Nor ne'er wed woman, if you be not she.

HYMEN: Peace, ho! I bar confusion;
'Tis I must make conclusion
Of these most strange events.
Here's eight that must take hands
To join in Hymen's bands,
If truth holds true contents.
You and you no cross shall part;
You and you are heart in heart
You to his love must accord,
Or have a woman to your lord;
You and you are sure together,
As the winter to foul weather.
Whiles a wedlock-hymn we sing,
Feed yourselves with questioning;
That reason wonder may diminish,
How thus we met, and these things finish.

Song

Wedding is great Juno's crown;
O blessed bond of board and bed!
'Tis Hymen peoples every town;
High wedlock then be honoured;
Honour, high honour and renown,
To Hymen, god of every town!

DUKE SENIOR: O my dear niece, welcome thou art to me!
Even daughter, welcome, in no less degree.

PHEBE: I will not eat my word, now thou art mine;
Thy faith my fancy to thee doth combine.

Enter JAQUES DE BOYS

JAQUES DE BOYS: Let me have audience for a word or two.
I am the second son of old Sir Rowland,
That bring these tidings to this fair assembly.
Duke Frederick, hearing how that every day
Men of great worth resorted to this forest,
Address'd a mighty power; which were on foot,
In his own conduct, purposely to take
His brother here and put him to the sword;
And to the skirts of this wild wood he came;
Where meeting with an old religious man,
After some question with him, was converted
Both from his enterprise and from the world,
His crown bequeathing to his banish'd brother,
And all their lands restored to them again
That were with him exiled. This to be true,
I do engage my life.

DUKE SENIOR: Welcome, young man;
Thou offer'st fairly to thy brothers' wedding:
To one his lands withheld, and to the other
A land itself at large, a potent dukedom.

First, in this forest, let us do those ends
That here were well begun and well begot:
And after, every of this happy number,
That have endured shrewd days and nights with us,
Shall share the good of our returned fortune,
According to the measure of their states.
Meantime, forget this new-fall'n dignity,
And fall into our rustic revelry.
Play, music! And you, brides and bridegrooms all,
With measure heap'd in joy, to the measures fall.

JAQUES: Sir, by your patience. If I heard you rightly,
The Duke hath put on a religious life,
And thrown into neglect the pompous court.

JAQUES DE BOYS: He hath.

JAQUES: To him will I : out of these convertites
There is much matter to be heard and learn'd.
(*To DUKE SENIOR*) You to your former honour I bequeath;
Your patience and your virtue well deserves it.
(*To ORLANDO*) You to a love that your true faith doth merit;
(*To OLIVER*) You to your land and love and great allies:
(*To SILVIUS*) You to a long and well-deserved bed;
(*To TOUCHSTONE*) And you to wrangling; for thy loving voyage
Is but for two months victuall'd. So, to your pleasures;
I am for other than for dancing measures.

DUKE SENIOR: Stay, Jaques, stay.

JAQUES: To see no pastime I. What you would have
I'll stay to know at your abandon'd cave.

Exit

DUKE SENIOR: Proceed, proceed: we will begin these rites,
As we do trust they'll end, in true delights.

A dance. Exeunt

EPILOGUE

ROSALIND: It is not the fashion to see the lady the epilogue; but it is no more unhandsome than to see the lord the prologue. If it be true that good wine needs no bush, 'tis true that a good play needs no epilogue; yet to good wine they do use good bushes, and good plays prove the better by the help of good epilogues. What a case am I in then, that am neither a good epilogue nor cannot insinuate with you in the behalf of a good play! I am not furnished like a beggar, therefore to beg will not become me: my way is to conjure you; and I'll begin with the women. I charge you, O women, for the love you bear to men, to like as much of this play as please you; and I charge you, O men, for the love you bear to women—as I perceive by your simpering, none of you hates them—that between you and the women the play may please. If I were a woman I would kiss as many of you as had beards that pleased me, complexions that liked me, and breaths that I defied not; and, I am sure, as many as have good beards or good faces or sweet breaths will, for my kind offer, when I make curtsy, bid me farewell.

THE COMEDY OF ERRORS

DRAMATIS PERSONÆ

SOLINUS, *Duke of Ephesus*
AEGEON, *a merchant of Syracuse*
ANTIPHOLUS of Ephesus, ANTIPHOLUS of Syracuse, *twin brothers, and sons to Ægeon and Æmilia*
DROMIO of Ephesus, DROMIO of Syracuse, *twin brothers, and attendants on the two Antipholuses*
BALTHAZAR, *a merchant*
ANGELO, *a goldsmith*
First Merchant, *friend to Antipholus of Syracuse*
Second merchant, *to whom Angelo is a debtor*
PINCH, *a schoolmaster*
ÆMILIA, *wife to Aegeon, an abbess at Ephesus*
ADRIANA, *wife to Antipholus of Ephesus*
LUCIANA, *her sister*
LUCE, *servant to Adriana*
A Courtezan
Gaoler, Officers, Attendants

THE SCENE: Ephesus

ACT I

SCENE I—*A hall in Duke Solinus's palace*

Enter DUKE SOLINUS, AEGEON, the Merchant of Syracusa, Gaoler, Officers, and other Attendants

AEGEON: Proceed, Solinus, to procure my fall
And by the doom of death end woes and all.

DUKE SOLINUS: Merchant of Syracusa, plead no more;
I am not partial to infringe our laws.
The enmity and discord which of late
Sprung from the rancorous outrage of your Duke
To merchants, our well-dealing countrymen,
Who wanting guilders to redeem their lives
Have seal'd his rigorous statutes with their bloods,
Excludes all pity from our threatening looks.
For, since the mortal and intestine jars
'Twixt thy seditious countrymen and us,
It hath in solemn synods been decreed
Both by the Syracusians and ourselves,
To admit no traffic to our adverse towns;
Nay, more,
If any born at Ephesus
Be seen at any Syracusian marts and fairs;
Again, if any Syracusian born
Come to the bay of Ephesus, he dies,
His goods confiscate to the Duke's dispose,
Unless a thousand marks be levied,
To quit the penalty and to ransom him.
Thy substance, valued at the highest rate,

Cannot amount unto a hundred marks;
Therefore by law thou art condemned to die.

AEGEON: Yet this my comfort: when your words are done,
My woes end likewise with the evening sun.

DUKE SOLINUS: Well, Syracusian, say in brief the cause
Why thou departed'st from thy native home,
And for what cause thou camest to Ephesus.

AEGEON: A heavier task could not have been imposed
Than I to speak my griefs unspeakable;
Yet, that the world may witness that my end
Was wrought by nature, not by vile offence,
I'll utter what my sorrows gives me leave.
In Syracusa was I born, and wed
Unto a woman, happy but for me,
And by me, had not our hap been bad.
With her I lived in joy; our wealth increased
By prosperous voyages I often made
To Epidamnum; till my factor's death
And the great care of goods at random left
Drew me from kind embracements of my spouse;
From whom my absence was not six months old
Before herself, almost at fainting under
The pleasing punishment that women bear,
Had made provision for her following me,
And soon and safe arrived where I was.
There had she not been long, but she became
A joyful mother of two goodly sons;
And, which was strange, the one so like the other,
As could not be distinguish'd but by names.
That very hour, and in the self-same inn,
A meaner woman was delivered
Of such a burden, male twins, both alike.
Those, for their parents were exceeding poor,
I bought and brought up to attend my sons.
My wife, not meanly proud of two such boys,
Made daily motions for our home return;
Unwilling I agreed. Alas! too soon,
We came aboard.
A league from Epidamnum had we sail'd,
Before the always wind-obeying deep
Gave any tragic instance of our harm;
But longer did we not retain much hope;
For what obscured light the heavens did grant
Did but convey unto our fearful minds
A doubtful warrant of immediate death;
Which though myself would gladly have embraced,
Yet the incessant weepings of my wife,
Weeping before for what she saw must come,
And piteous plainings of the pretty babes,
That mourn'd for fashion, ignorant what to fear,
Forced me to seek delays for them and me.
And this it was, for other means was none:
The sailors sought for safety by our boat,
And left the ship, then sinking-ripe, to us:
My wife, more careful for the latter-born,
Had fasten'd him unto a small spare mast,
Such as sea-faring men provide for storms;
To him one of the other twins was bound,
Whilst I had been like heedful of the other:
The children thus disposed, my wife and I,
Fixing our eyes on whom our care was fix'd,
Fasten'd ourselves at either end the mast;
And floating straight, obedient to the stream,
Was carried towards Corinth, as we thought.
At length the sun, gazing upon the earth,
Dispersed those vapours that offended us;
And by the benefit of his wished light,
The seas wax'd calm, and we discovered
Two ships from far making amain to us,
Of Corinth that, of Epidaurus this.
But ere they came—O, let me say no more!
Gather the sequel by that went before.

DUKE SOLINUS: Nay, forward, old man; do not break off so;
For we may pity, though not pardon thee.

AEGEON: O, had the gods done so, I had not now
Worthily term'd them merciless to us!
For, ere the ships could meet by twice five leagues,
We were encounterd by a mighty rock;
Which being violently borne upon,
Our helpful ship was splitted in the midst;
So that, in this unjust divorce of us,
Fortune had left to both of us alike
What to delight in, what to sorrow for.
Her part, poor soul! seeming as burdened
With lesser weight but not with lesser woe,

Was carried with more speed before the wind;
And in our sight they three were taken up
By fishermen of Corinth, as we thought.
At length, another ship had seized on us;
And, knowing whom it was their hap to save,
Gave healthful welcome to their shipwreck'd guests;
And would have reft the fishers of their prey,
Had not their bark been very slow of sail;
And therefore homeward did they bend their course.
Thus have you heard me sever'd from my bliss;
That by misfortunes was my life prolong'd,
To tell sad stories of my own mishaps.

DUKE SOLINUS: And for the sake of them thou sorrowest for,
Do me the favour to dilate at full
What hath befall'n of them and thee till now.

AEGEON: My youngest boy, and yet my eldest care,
At eighteen years became inquisitive
After his brother, and importuned me
That his attendant—so his case was like,
Reft of his brother, but retain'd his name—
Might bear him company in the quest of him;
Whom whilst I labour'd of a love to see,
I hazarded the loss of whom I loved.
Five summers have I spent in furthest Greece,
Roaming clean through the bounds of Asia,
And, coasting homeward, came to Ephesus;
Hopeless to find, yet loath to leave unsought
Or that or any place that harbours men.
But here must end the story of my life;
And happy were I in my timely death,
Could all my travels warrant me they live.

DUKE SOLINUS: Hapless AEgeon, whom the fates have mark'd
To bear the extremity of dire mishap!
Now, trust me, were it not against our laws,
Against my crown, my oath, my dignity,
Which princes, would they, may not disannul,
My soul would sue as advocate for thee.
But, though thou art adjudged to the death
And passed sentence may not be recall'd
But to our honour's great disparagement,
Yet I will favour thee in what I can.
Therefore, merchant, I'll limit thee this day
To seek thy help by beneficial hap.
Try all the friends thou hast in Ephesus;
Beg thou, or borrow, to make up the sum,
And live; if no, then thou art doom'd to die.
Gaoler, take him to thy custody.

Gaoler: I will, my lord.

AEGEON: Hopeless and helpless doth AEgeon wend,
But to procrastinate his lifeless end.

Exeunt

SCENE II—*The mart*

Enter Antipholus of Syracuse, Dromio of Syracuse, and First Merchant

FIRST MERCHANT: Therefore give out you are of Epidamnum,
Lest that your goods too soon be confiscate.
This very day a Syracusian merchant
Is apprehended for arrival here;
And, not being able to buy out his life,
According to the statute of the town,
Dies ere the weary sun set in the west.
There is your money that I had to keep.

ANTIPHOLUS OF SYRACUSE: Go bear it to the Centaur, where we host,
And stay there, Dromio, till I come to thee.
Within this hour it will be dinner-time;
Till that, I'll view the manners of the town,
Peruse the traders, gaze upon the buildings,
And then return and sleep within mine inn,
For with long travel I am stiff and weary.
Get thee away.

DROMIO OF SYRACUSE: Many a man would take you at your word,
And go indeed, having so good a mean.

Exit Dromio of Syracuse

ANTIPHOLUS OF SYRACUSE: A trusty villain, sir, that very oft,
When I am dull with care and melancholy,
Lightens my humour with his merry jests.
What, will you walk with me about the town,
And then go to my inn and dine with me?

FIRST MERCHANT: I am invited, sir, to certain merchants,
Of whom I hope to make much benefit;
I crave your pardon. Soon at five o'clock,
Please you, I'll meet with you upon the mart
And afterward consort you till bed-time.
My present business calls me from you now.

ANTIPHOLUS OF SYRACUSE: Farewell till then. I will go lose myself,

And wander up and down to view the city.

FIRST MERCHANT: Sir, I commend you to your own content.

Exit First Merchant

ANTIPHOLUS OF SYRACUSE: He that commends me to mine own content

Commends me to the thing I cannot get.
I to the world am like a drop of water
That in the ocean seeks another drop,
Who, falling there to find his fellow forth,
Unseen, inquisitive, confounds himself.
So I, to find a mother and a brother,
In quest of them, unhappy, lose myself.

Enter DROMIO of Ephesus

Here comes the almanac of my true date.
What now? How chance thou art return'd so soon?

DROMIO OF EPHESUS: Return'd so soon! rather approach'd too late.

The capon burns, the pig falls from the spit,
The clock hath strucken twelve upon the bell:
My mistress made it one upon my cheek;
She is so hot because the meat is cold;
The meat is cold because you come not home;
You come not home because you have no stomach;
You have no stomach having broke your fast;
But we that know what 'tis to fast and pray
Are penitent for your default to-day.

ANTIPHOLUS OF SYRACUSE: Stop in your wind, sir: tell me this, I pray:

Where have you left the money that I gave you?

DROMIO OF EPHESUS: O—sixpence, that I had a Wednesday last

To pay the saddler for my mistress' crupper?
The saddler had it, sir; I kept it not.

ANTIPHOLUS OF SYRACUSE: I am not in a sportive humour now;

Tell me, and dally not, where is the money?
We being strangers here, how darest thou trust
So great a charge from thine own custody?

DROMIO OF EPHESUS: I pray you jest, air, as you sit at dinner.

I from my mistress come to you in post;
If I return, I shall be post indeed,
For she will score your fault upon my pate.
Methinks your maw, like mine, should be your clock,
And strike you home without a messenger.

ANTIPHOLUS OF SYRACUSE: Come, Dromio, come, these jests are out of season;

Reserve them till a merrier hour than this.
Where is the gold I gave in charge to thee?

DROMIO OF EPHESUS: To me, sir? why, you gave no gold to me.

ANTIPHOLUS OF SYRACUSE: Come on, sir knave, have done your foolishness,

And tell me how thou hast disposed thy charge.

DROMIO OF EPHESUS: My charge was but to fetch you from the mart

Home to your house, the Phoenix, sir, to dinner.
My mistress and her sister stays for you.

ANTIPHOLUS OF SYRACUSE: Now, as I am a Christian, answer me

In what safe place you have bestow'd my money,
Or I shall break that merry sconce of yours
That stands on tricks when I am undisposed.
Where is the thousand marks thou hadst of me?

DROMIO OF EPHESUS: I have some marks of yours upon my pate,

Some of my mistress' marks upon my shoulders,
But not a thousand marks between you both.
If I should pay your worship those again,
Perchance you will not bear them patiently.

ANTIPHOLUS OF SYRACUSE: Thy mistress' marks? what mistress, slave, hast thou?

DROMIO OF EPHESUS: Your worship's wife, my mistress at the Phoenix;

She that doth fast till you come home to dinner,
And prays that you will hie you home to dinner.

ANTIPHOLUS OF SYRACUSE: What, wilt thou flout me thus unto my face,

Being forbid? There, take you that, sir knave.

DROMIO OF EPHESUS: What mean you, sir? For God's sake, hold your hands!

Nay, and you will not, sir, I'll take my heels.

Exit Dromio of Ephesus

ANTIPHOLUS OF SYRACUSE: Upon my life, by some device or other

The villain is o'er-raught of all my money.
They say this town is full of cozenage,

As, nimble jugglers that deceive the eye,
Dark-working sorcerers that change the mind,
Soul-killing witches that deform the body,
Disguised cheaters, prating mountebanks,
And many such-like liberties of sin:
If it prove so, I will be gone the sooner.
I'll to the Centaur, to go seek this slave.
I greatly fear my money is not safe.

Exit

Act II

Scene I—*The house of Antipholus of Ephesus*

Enter ADRIANA and LUCIANA

ADRIANA: Neither my husband nor the slave return'd,
That in such haste I sent to seek his master!
Sure, Luciana, it is two o'clock.

LUCIANA: Perhaps some merchant hath invited him,
And from the mart he's somewhere gone to dinner.
Good sister, let us dine and never fret.
A man is master of his liberty;
Time is their master, and, when they see time,
They'll go or come: if so, be patient, sister.

ADRIANA: Why should their liberty than ours be more?

LUCIANA: Because their business still lies out o' door.

ADRIANA: Look, when I serve him so, he takes it ill.

LUCIANA: O, know he is the bridle of your will.

ADRIANA: There's none but asses will be bridled so.

LUCIANA: Why, headstrong liberty is lash'd with woe.
There's nothing situate under heaven's eye
But hath his bound, in earth, in sea, in sky.
The beasts, the fishes, and the winged fowls,
Are their males' subjects and at their controls.
Men, more divine, the masters of all these,
Lords of the wide world and wild watery seas,
Indued with intellectual sense and souls,
Of more preeminence than fish and fowls,
Are masters to their females, and their lords;
Then let your will attend on their accords.

ADRIANA: This servitude makes you to keep unwed.

LUCIANA: Not this, but troubles of the marriage-bed.

ADRIANA: But, were you wedded, you would bear some sway.

LUCIANA: Ere I learn love, I'll practise to obey.

ADRIANA: How if your husband start some other where?

LUCIANA: Till he come home again, I would forbear.

ADRIANA: Patience unmoved! no marvel though she pause;
They can be meek that have no other cause.
A wretched soul, bruised with adversity,
We bid be quiet when we hear it cry;
But were we burdened with like weight of pain,
As much or more would we ourselves complain.
So thou, that hast no unkind mate to grieve thee,
With urging helpless patience wouldst relieve me,
But, if thou live to see like right bereft,
This fool-begg'd patience in thee will be left.

LUCIANA: Well, I will marry one day, but to try.
Here comes your man; now is your husband nigh.

Enter DROMIO of Ephesus

ADRIANA: Say, is your tardy master now at hand?

DROMIO OF EPHESUS: Nay, he's at two hands with me, and that my two ears can witness.

ADRIANA: Say, didst thou speak with him? know'st thou his mind?

DROMIO OF EPHESUS: Ay, ay, he told his mind upon mine ear.
Beshrew his hand, I scarce could understand it.

LUCIANA: Spake he so doubtfully, thou couldst not feel his meaning?

DROMIO OF EPHESUS: Nay, he struck so plainly, I could too well feel his blows; and withal so doubtfully that I could scarce understand them.

ADRIANA: But say, I prithee, is he coming home?
It seems he hath great care to please his wife.

DROMIO OF EPHESUS: Why, mistress, sure my master is horn-mad.

ADRIANA: Horn-mad, thou villain!

DROMIO OF EPHESUS: I mean not cuckold-mad;
But, sure, he is stark mad.
When I desired him to come home to dinner,
He ask'd me for a thousand marks in gold.
''Tis dinner-time,' quoth I; 'My gold!' quoth he.
'Your meat doth burn,' quoth I; 'My gold!' quoth he.
'Will you come home?' quoth I; 'My gold!' quoth he.
'Where is the thousand marks I gave thee, villain?'
'The pig,' quoth I, 'is burn'd;' 'My gold!' quoth he.
'My mistress, sir' quoth I; 'Hang up thy mistress!
I know not thy mistress; out on thy mistress! '

LUCIANA: Quoth who?

DROMIO OF EPHESUS: Quoth my master.
'I know,' quoth he, 'no house, no wife, no mistress.'
So that my errand, due unto my tongue,
I thank him, I bare home upon my shoulders;
For, in conclusion, he did beat me there.

ADRIANA: Go back again, thou slave, and fetch him home.

DROMIO OF EPHESUS: Go back again, and be new beaten home?
For God's sake, send some other messenger.

ADRIANA: Back, slave, or I will break thy pate across.

DROMIO OF EPHESUS: And he will bless that cross with other beating;
Between you I shall have a holy head.

ADRIANA: Hence, prating peasant! fetch thy master home.

DROMIO OF EPHESUS: Am I so round with you as you with me,
That like a football you do spurn me thus?
You spurn me hence, and he will spurn me hither;
If I last in this service, you must case me in leather.

Exit

LUCIANA: Fie, how impatience loureth in your face!

ADRIANA: His company must do his minions grace,
Whilst I at home starve for a merry look.
Hath homely age the alluring beauty took
From my poor cheek? then he hath wasted it.
Are my discourses dull? barren my wit?
If voluble and sharp discourse be marr'd,
Unkindness blunts it more than marble hard.
Do their gay vestments his affections bait?
That's not my fault: he's master of my state.
What ruins are in me that can be found,
By him not ruin'd? then is he the ground
Of my defeatures. My decayed fair
A sunny look of his would soon repair.
But, too unruly deer, he breaks the pale
And feeds from home; poor I am but his stale.

LUCIANA: Self-harming jealousy! fie, beat it hence!

ADRIANA: Unfeeling fools can with such wrongs dispense.
I know his eye doth homage otherwhere,
Or else what lets it but he would be here?
Sister, you know he promised me a chain;
Would that alone, a love he would detain,
So he would keep fair quarter with his bed!
I see the jewel best enamelled
Will lose his beauty; yet the gold bides still,
That others touch, and often touching will
Wear gold; and no man that hath a name,
By falsehood and corruption doth it shame.
Since that my beauty cannot please his eye,
I'll weep what's left away, and weeping die.

LUCIANA: How many fond fools serve mad jealousy!

Exeunt

SCENE II—*The mart*

Enter ANTIPHOLUS of Syracuse

ANTIPHOLUS OF SYRACUSE: The gold I gave to Dromio is laid up
Safe at the Centaur, and the heedful slave
Is wander'd forth, in care to seek me out
By computation and mine host's report.
I could not speak with Dromio since at first
I sent him from the mart. See, here he comes.

Enter DROMIO of Syracuse

How now, sir! is your merry humour alter'd?
As you love strokes, so jest with me again.
You know no Centaur? You received no gold?
Your mistress sent to have me home to dinner?
My house was at the Phoenix? Wast thou mad,
That thus so madly thou didst answer me?

DROMIO OF SYRACUSE: What answer, sir? When spake I such a word?

ANTIPHOLUS OF SYRACUSE: Even now, even here, not half an hour since.

DROMIO OF SYRACUSE: I did not see you since you sent me hence,
Home to the Centaur, with the gold you gave me.

ANTIPHOLUS OF SYRACUSE: Villain, thou didst deny the gold's receipt,
And told'st me of a mistress and a dinner;
For which, I hope, thou felt'st I was displeased.

DROMIO OF SYRACUSE: I am glad to see you in this merry vein.
What means this jest? I pray you, master, tell me.

ANTIPHOLUS OF SYRACUSE: Yea, dost thou jeer and flout me in the teeth?
Think'st thou I jest? Hold, take thou that, and that.

Beating him

DROMIO OF SYRACUSE: Hold, sir, for God's sake! Now your jest is earnest.
Upon what bargain do you give it me?

ANTIPHOLUS OF SYRACUSE: Because that I familiarly sometimes
Do use you for my fool and chat with you,
Your sauciness will jest upon my love,
And make a common of my serious hours.
When the sun shines let foolish gnats make sport,
But creep in crannies when he hides his beams.
If you will jest with me, know my aspect,
And fashion your demeanor to my looks,
Or I will beat this method in your sconce.

DROMIO OF SYRACUSE: Sconce call you it? So you would leave battering, I had rather have it a head. An you use these blows long, I must get a sconce for my head and ensconce it too; or else I shall seek my wit in my shoulders. But, I pray, sir why am I beaten?

ANTIPHOLUS OF SYRACUSE: Dost thou not know?

DROMIO OF SYRACUSE: Nothing, sir, but that I am beaten.

ANTIPHOLUS OF SYRACUSE: Shall I tell you why?

DROMIO OF SYRACUSE: Ay, sir, and wherefore; for they say every why hath a wherefore.

ANTIPHOLUS OF SYRACUSE: Why, first for flouting me; and then, wherefore,
For urging it the second time to me.

DROMIO OF SYRACUSE: Was there ever any man thus beaten out of season,
When in the why and the wherefore is neither rhyme nor reason?
Well, sir, I thank you.

ANTIPHOLUS OF SYRACUSE: Thank me, sir, for what?

DROMIO OF SYRACUSE: Marry, sir, for this something that you gave me for nothing.

ANTIPHOLUS OF SYRACUSE: I'll make you amends next, to give you nothing for something. But say, sir, is it dinner-time?

DROMIO OF SYRACUSE: No, sir; I think the meat wants that I have.

ANTIPHOLUS OF SYRACUSE: In good time, sir; what's that?

DROMIO OF SYRACUSE: Basting.

ANTIPHOLUS OF SYRACUSE: Well, sir, then 'twill be dry.

DROMIO OF SYRACUSE: If it be, sir, I pray you eat none of it.

ANTIPHOLUS OF SYRACUSE: Your reason?

DROMIO OF SYRACUSE: Lest it make you choleric, and purchase me another dry basting.

ANTIPHOLUS OF SYRACUSE: Well, sir, learn to jest in good time: there's a time for all things.

DROMIO OF SYRACUSE: I durst have denied that, before you were so choleric.

ANTIPHOLUS OF SYRACUSE: By what rule, sir?

DROMIO OF SYRACUSE: Marry, sir, by a rule as plain as the plain bald pate of Father Time himself.

ANTIPHOLUS OF SYRACUSE: Let's hear it.

DROMIO OF SYRACUSE: There's no time for a man to recover his hair that grows bald by nature.

ANTIPHOLUS OF SYRACUSE: May he not do it by fine and recovery?

DROMIO OF SYRACUSE: Yes, to pay a fine for a periwig and recover the lost hair of another man.

ANTIPHOLUS OF SYRACUSE: Why is Time such a niggard of hair, being, as it is, so plentiful an excrement?

DROMIO OF SYRACUSE: Because it is a blessing that he bestows on beasts, and what he hath scanted men in hair he hath given them in wit.

ANTIPHOLUS OF SYRACUSE: Why, but there's many a man hath more hair than wit.

DROMIO OF SYRACUSE: Not a man of those but he hath the wit to lose his hair.

ANTIPHOLUS OF SYRACUSE: Why, thou didst conclude hairy men plain dealers without wit.

DROMIO OF SYRACUSE: The plainer dealer, the sooner lost; yet he loseth it in a kind of jollity.

ANTIPHOLUS OF SYRACUSE: For what reason?

DROMIO OF SYRACUSE: For two; and sound ones too.

ANTIPHOLUS OF SYRACUSE: Nay, not sound, I pray you.

DROMIO OF SYRACUSE: Sure ones, then.

ANTIPHOLUS OF SYRACUSE: Nay, not sure, in a thing falsing.

DROMIO OF SYRACUSE: Certain ones then.

ANTIPHOLUS OF SYRACUSE: Name them.

DROMIO OF SYRACUSE: The one, to save the money that he spends in tiring; the other, that at dinner they should not drop in his porridge.

ANTIPHOLUS OF SYRACUSE: You would all this time have proved there is no time for all things.

DROMIO OF SYRACUSE: Marry, and did, sir; namely, no time to recover hair lost by nature.

ANTIPHOLUS OF SYRACUSE: But your reason was not substantial, why there is no time to recover.

DROMIO OF SYRACUSE: Thus I mend it: Time himself is bald and therefore to the world's end will have bald followers.

ANTIPHOLUS OF SYRACUSE: I knew 'twould be a bald conclusion.

But, soft! who wafts us yonder?

Enter ADRIANA and LUCIANA

ADRIANA: Ay, ay, Antipholus, look strange and frown.
Some other mistress hath thy sweet aspects;
I am not Adriana, nor thy wife.
The time was once when thou unurged wouldst vow
That never words were music to thine ear,
That never object pleasing in thine eye,
That never touch well welcome to thy hand,
That never meat sweet-savor'd in thy taste,
Unless I spake, or look'd, or touch'd, or carved to thee.
How comes it now, my husband, O, how comes it,
That thou art then estranged from thyself?
Thyself I call it, being strange to me,
That, undividable, incorporate,
Am better than thy dear self's better part.
Ah, do not tear away thyself from me;
For know, my love, as easy mayest thou fall
A drop of water in the breaking gulf,
And take unmingled thence that drop again,
Without addition or diminishing,
As take from me thyself, and not me too.
How dearly would it touch me to the quick,
Shouldst thou but hear I were licentious,
And that this body, consecrate to thee,
By ruffian lust should be contaminate!
Wouldst thou not spit at me and spurn at me,
And hurl the name of husband in my face,
And tear the stain'd skin off my harlot-brow,
And from my false hand cut the wedding-ring.
And break it with a deep-divorcing vow?
I know thou canst, and therefore see thou do it.
I am possess'd with an adulterate blot;
My blood is mingled with the crime of lust:
For if we too be one and thou play false,
I do digest the poison of thy flesh,
Being strumpeted by thy contagion.
Keep then fair league and truce with thy true bed;
I live unstain'd, thou undishonoured.

ANTIPHOLUS OF SYRACUSE: Plead you to me, fair dame? I know you not:
In Ephesus I am but two hours old,
As strange unto your town as to your talk,
Who, every word by all my wit being scann'd,
Want wit in all one word to understand.

LUCIANA: Fie, brother, how the world is changed with you!
When were you wont to use my sister thus?
She sent for you by Dromio home to dinner.

ANTIPHOLUS OF SYRACUSE: By Dromio?

DROMIO OF SYRACUSE: By me?

ADRIANA: By thee; and this thou didst return from him—
That he did buffet thee, and in his blows
Denied my house for his, me for his wife.

ANTIPHOLUS OF SYRACUSE: Did you converse, sir, with this gentlewoman?
What is the course and drift of your compact?

DROMIO OF SYRACUSE: I, sir? I never saw her till this time.

ANTIPHOLUS OF SYRACUSE: Villain, thou liest; for even her very words
Didst thou deliver to me on the mart.

DROMIO OF SYRACUSE: I never spake with her in all my life.

ANTIPHOLUS OF SYRACUSE: How can she thus, then call us by our names,

Unless it be by inspiration?

ADRIANA: How ill agrees it with your gravity
To counterfeit thus grossly with your slave,
Abetting him to thwart me in my mood!
Be it my wrong you are from me exempt,
But wrong not that wrong with a more contempt.
Come, I will fasten on this sleeve of thine:
Thou art an elm, my husband, I a vine,
Whose weakness, married to thy stronger state,
Makes me with thy strength to communicate.
If aught possess thee from me, it is dross,
Usurping ivy, brier, or idle moss;
Who all, for want of pruning, with intrusion
Infect thy sap and live on thy confusion.

ANTIPHOLUS OF SYRACUSE: To me she speaks; she moves me for her theme.
What, was I married to her in my dream?
Or sleep I now and think I hear all this?
What error drives our eyes and ears amiss?
Until I know this sure uncertainty,
I'll entertain the offer'd fallacy.

LUCIANA: Dromio, go bid the servants spread for dinner.

DROMIO OF SYRACUSE: O, for my beads! I cross me for a sinner.
This is the fairy land. O spite of spites!
We talk with goblins, owls and sprites.
If we obey them not, this will ensue;
They'll suck our breath, or pinch us black and blue.

LUCIANA: Why pratest thou to thyself, and answer'st not?
Dromio, thou drone, thou snail, thou slug, thou sot!

DROMIO OF SYRACUSE: I am transformed, master, am I not?

ANTIPHOLUS OF SYRACUSE: I think thou art in mind, and so am I.

DROMIO OF SYRACUSE: Nay, master, both in mind and in my shape.

ANTIPHOLUS OF SYRACUSE: Thou hast thine own form.

DROMIO OF SYRACUSE: No, I am an ape.

LUCIANA: If thou art changed to aught, 'tis to an ass.

DROMIO OF SYRACUSE: 'Tis true; she rides me and I long for grass.
'Tis so, I am an ass; else it could never be
But I should know her as well as she knows me.

ADRIANA: Come, come, no longer will I be a fool,
To put the finger in the eye and weep,
Whilst man and master laugh my woes to scorn.
Come, sir, to dinner. Dromio, keep the gate.
Husband, I'll dine above with you to-day,
And shrive you of a thousand idle pranks.
Sirrah, if any ask you for your master,
Say he dines forth, and let no creature enter.
Come, sister. Dromio, play the porter well.

ANTIPHOLUS OF SYRACUSE: Am I in earth, in heaven, or in hell?
Sleeping or waking, mad or well-advised?
Known unto these, and to myself disguised!
I'll say as they say and persever so,
And in this mist at all adventures go.

DROMIO OF SYRACUSE: Master, shall I be porter at the gate?

ADRIANA: Ay; and let none enter, lest I break your pate.

LUCIANA: Come, come, Antipholus, we dine too late.

Exeunt

ACT III

SCENE I—*Before the house of Antipholus of Ephesus*

Enter ANTIPHOLUS of Ephesus, DROMIO of Ephesus, ANGELO, and BALTHAZAR

ANTIPHOLUS OF EPHESUS: Good Signior Angelo, you must excuse us all;

My wife is shrewish when I keep not hours.

Say that I linger'd with you at your shop

To see the making of her carcanet,

And that to-morrow you will bring it home.

But here's a villain that would face me down

He met me on the mart, and that I beat him,

And charged him with a thousand marks in gold,

And that I did deny my wife and house.

Thou drunkard, thou, what didst thou mean by this?

DROMIO OF EPHESUS: Say what you will, sir, but I know what I know;

That you beat me at the mart, I have your hand to show;

If the skin were parchment, and the blows you gave were ink,

Your own handwriting would tell you what I think.

ANTIPHOLUS OF EPHESUS: I think thou art an ass.

DROMIO OF EPHESUS: Marry, so it doth appear

By the wrongs I suffer and the blows I bear.

I should kick, being kick'd; and, being at that pass,

You would keep from my heels and beware of an ass.

ANTIPHOLUS OF EPHESUS: You're sad, Signior Balthazar; pray God our cheer

May answer my good will and your good welcome here.

BALTHAZAR: I hold your dainties cheap, sir, and your welcome dear.

ANTIPHOLUS OF EPHESUS: O, Signior Balthazar, either at flesh or fish,

A table full of welcome makes scarce one dainty dish.

BALTHAZAR: Good meat, sir, is common; that every churl affords.

ANTIPHOLUS OF EPHESUS: And welcome more common; for that's nothing but words.

BALTHAZAR: Small cheer and great welcome makes a merry feast.

ANTIPHOLUS OF EPHESUS: Ay, to a niggardly host, and more sparing guest.

But though my cates be mean, take them in good part;

Better cheer may you have, but not with better heart.

But, soft! my door is lock'd. Go bid them let us in.

DROMIO OF EPHESUS: Maud, Bridget, Marian, Cicely, Gillian, Ginn!

DROMIO OF SYRACUSE: [*Within*] Mome, malt-horse, capon, coxcomb, idiot, patch!

Either get thee from the door, or sit down at the hatch.

Dost thou conjure for wenches, that thou call'st for such store,

When one is one too many? Go, get thee from the door.

DROMIO OF EPHESUS: What patch is made our porter? My master stays in the street.

DROMIO OF SYRACUSE: [*Within*] Let him walk from whence he came, lest he catch cold on 's feet.

ANTIPHOLUS OF EPHESUS: Who talks within there? Ho, open the door!

DROMIO OF SYRACUSE: [*Within*] Right, sir; I'll tell you when, an you will tell me wherefore.

ANTIPHOLUS OF EPHESUS: Wherefore? For my dinner: I have not dined to-day.

DROMIO OF SYRACUSE: [*Within*] Nor to-day here you must not; come again when you may.

ANTIPHOLUS OF EPHESUS: What art thou that keepest me out from the house I owe?

DROMIO OF SYRACUSE: [*Within*] The porter for this time, sir, and my name is Dromio.

DROMIO OF EPHESUS: O villain! thou hast stolen both mine office and my name.

The one ne'er got me credit, the other mickle blame.

If thou hadst been Dromio to-day in my place,

Thou wouldst have changed thy face for a name or thy name for an ass.

Enter LUCE, within

LUCE: [*Within*] What a coil is there, Dromio? Who are those at the gate?

DROMIO OF EPHESUS: Let my master in, Luce.

LUCE: [*Within*] Faith, no; he comes too late;
And so tell your master.

DROMIO OF EPHESUS: O Lord, I must laugh!

Have at you with a proverb—Shall I set in my staff?

LUCE: [*Within*] Have at you with another; that's—

When? can you tell?

DROMIO OF SYRACUSE: [*Within*] If thy name be call'd Luce-Luce, thou hast answered him well.

ANTIPHOLUS OF EPHESUS: Do you hear, you minion? you'll let us in, I hope?

LUCE: [*Within*] I thought to have asked you.

DROMIO OF SYRACUSE: [*Within*] And you said no.

DROMIO OF EPHESUS: So, come, help: well struck! there was blow for blow.

ANTIPHOLUS OF EPHESUS: Thou baggage, let me in.

LUCE: [*Within*] Can you tell for whose sake?

DROMIO OF EPHESUS: Master, knock the door hard.

LUCE: [*Within*] Let him knock till it ache.

ANTIPHOLUS OF EPHESUS: You'll cry for this, minion, if I beat the door down.

LUCE: [*Within*] What needs all that, and a pair of stocks in the town?

Enter ADRIANA within

ADRIANA: [*Within*] Who is that at the door that keeps all this noise?

DROMIO OF SYRACUSE: [*Within*] By my troth, your town is troubled with unruly boys.

ANTIPHOLUS OF EPHESUS: Are you there, wife? You might have come before.

ADRIANA: [*Within*] Your wife, sir knave! Go get you from the door.

DROMIO OF EPHESUS: If you went in pain, master, this 'knave' would go sore.

ANGELO: Here is neither cheer, sir, nor welcome: we would fain have either.

BALTHAZAR: In debating which was best, we shall part with neither.

DROMIO OF EPHESUS: They stand at the door, master; bid them welcome hither.

ANTIPHOLUS OF EPHESUS: There is something in the wind, that we cannot get in.

DROMIO OF EPHESUS: You would say so, master, if your garments were thin.

Your cake here is warm within; you stand here in the cold:

It would make a man mad as a buck, to be so bought and sold.

ANTIPHOLUS OF EPHESUS: Go fetch me something: I'll break ope the gate.

DROMIO OF SYRACUSE: [*Within*] Break any breaking here, and I'll break your knave's pate.

DROMIO OF EPHESUS: A man may break a word with you, sir, and words are but wind,

Ay, and break it in your face, so he break it not behind.

DROMIO OF SYRACUSE: [*Within*] It seems thou want'st breaking: out upon thee, hind!

DROMIO OF EPHESUS: Here's too much 'out upon thee!' I pray thee, let me in.

DROMIO OF SYRACUSE: [*Within*] Ay, when fowls have no feathers and fish have no fin.

ANTIPHOLUS OF EPHESUS: Well, I'll break in: go borrow me a crow.

DROMIO OF EPHESUS: A crow without feather? Master, mean you so?

For a fish without a fin, there's a fowl without a feather;

If a crow help us in, sirrah, we'll pluck a crow together.

ANTIPHOLUS OF EPHESUS: Go get thee gone; fetch me an iron crow.

BALTHAZAR: Have patience, sir; O, let it not be so!
Herein you war against your reputation
And draw within the compass of suspect
The unviolated honour of your wife.
Once this—your long experience of her wisdom,
Her sober virtue, years and modesty,
Plead on her part some cause to you unknown:
And doubt not, sir, but she will well excuse
Why at this time the doors are made against you.

Be ruled by me: depart in patience,
And let us to the Tiger all to dinner,
And about evening come yourself alone
To know the reason of this strange restraint.
If by strong hand you offer to break in
Now in the stirring passage of the day,
A vulgar comment will be made of it,
And that supposed by the common rout
Against your yet ungalled estimation
That may with foul intrusion enter in
And dwell upon your grave when you are dead;
For slander lives upon succession,
For ever housed where it gets possession.

ANTIPHOLUS OF EPHESUS: You have prevailed: I will depart in quiet,
And, in despite of mirth, mean to be merry.
I know a wench of excellent discourse,
Pretty and witty; wild, and yet, too, gentle;
There will we dine. This woman that I mean,
My wife—but, I protest, without desert—
Hath oftentimes upbraided me withal;
To her will we to dinner. [*To Angelo*] Get you home
And fetch the chain; by this I know 'tis made.
Bring it, I pray you, to the Porpentine;
For there's the house: that chain will I bestow—
Be it for nothing but to spite my wife—
Upon mine hostess there: good sir, make haste.
Since mine own doors refuse to entertain me,
I'll knock elsewhere, to see if they'll disdain me.

ANGELO: I'll meet you at that place some hour hence.

ANTIPHOLUS OF EPHESUS: Do so. This jest shall cost me some expense.

Exeunt

SCENE II—*The same*

Enter LUCIANA and ANTIPHOLUS of Syracuse

LUCIANA: And may it be that you have quite forgot
A husband's office? shall, Antipholus.
Even in the spring of love, thy love-springs rot?
Shall love, in building, grow so ruinous?
If you did wed my sister for her wealth,
Then for her wealth's sake use her with more kindness;
Or if you like elsewhere, do it by stealth;
Muffle your false love with some show of blindness;
Let not my sister read it in your eye;
Be not thy tongue thy own shame's orator;
Look sweet, be fair, become disloyalty;
Apparel vice like virtue's harbinger;
Bear a fair presence, though your heart be tainted;
Teach sin the carriage of a holy saint;
Be secret-false: what need she be acquainted?
What simple thief brags of his own attaint?
'Tis double wrong, to truant with your bed
And let her read it in thy looks at board;
Shame hath a bastard fame, well managed;
Ill deeds are doubled with an evil word.
Alas, poor women! make us but believe,
Being compact of credit, that you love us;
Though others have the arm, show us the sleeve;
We in your motion turn and you may move us.
Then, gentle brother, get you in again;
Comfort my sister, cheer her, call her wife.
'Tis holy sport to be a little vain,
When the sweet breath of flattery conquers strife.

ANTIPHOLUS OF SYRACUSE: Sweet mistress—what your name is else, I know not,
Nor by what wonder you do hit of mine—
Less in your knowledge and your grace you show not
Than our earth's wonder, more than earth divine.
Teach me, dear creature, how to think and speak;
Lay open to my earthy-gross conceit,
Smother'd in errors, feeble, shallow, weak,
The folded meaning of your words' deceit.
Against my soul's pure truth why labour you
To make it wander in an unknown field?
Are you a god? would you create me new?
Transform me then, and to your power I'll yield.
But if that I am I, then well I know
Your weeping sister is no wife of mine,
Nor to her bed no homage do I owe
Far more, far more to you do I decline.
O, train me not, sweet mermaid, with thy note,
To drown me in thy sister's flood of tears.

Sing, siren, for thyself and I will dote;
Spread o'er the silver waves thy golden hairs,
And as a bed I'll take them and there lie,
And in that glorious supposition think
He gains by death that hath such means to die.
Let Love, being light, be drowned if she sink!

LUCIANA: What, are you mad, that you do reason so?

ANTIPHOLUS OF SYRACUSE: Not mad, but mated; how, I do not know.

LUCIANA: It is a fault that springeth from your eye.

ANTIPHOLUS OF SYRACUSE: For gazing on your beams, fair sun, being by.

LUCIANA: Gaze where you should, and that will clear your sight.

ANTIPHOLUS OF SYRACUSE: As good to wink, sweet love, as look on night.

LUCIANA: Why call you me love? call my sister so.

ANTIPHOLUS OF SYRACUSE: Thy sister's sister.

LUCIANA: That's my sister.

ANTIPHOLUS OF SYRACUSE: No;
It is thyself, mine own self's better part,
Mine eye's clear eye, my dear heart's dearer heart,
My food, my fortune and my sweet hope's aim,
My sole earth's heaven and my heaven's claim.

LUCIANA: All this my sister is, or else should be.

ANTIPHOLUS OF SYRACUSE: Call thyself sister, sweet, for I am thee;
Thee will I love and with thee lead my life;
Thou hast no husband yet nor I no wife.
Give me thy hand.

LUCIANA: O, soft, sir! hold you still;
I'll fetch my sister, to get her good will.

Exit LUCIANA

Enter DROMIO of Syracuse

ANTIPHOLUS OF SYRACUSE: Why, how now, Dromio! where runn'st thou so fast?

DROMIO OF SYRACUSE: Do you know me, sir? Am I Dromio? Am I your man? Am I myself?

ANTIPHOLUS OF SYRACUSE: Thou art Dromio, thou art my man, thou art thyself.

DROMIO OF SYRACUSE: I am an ass, I am a woman's man and besides myself.

ANTIPHOLUS OF SYRACUSE: What woman's man, and how besides thyself?

DROMIO OF SYRACUSE: Marry, sir, besides myself, I am due to a woman: one that claims me, one that haunts me, one that will have me.

ANTIPHOLUS OF SYRACUSE: What claim lays she to thee?

DROMIO OF SYRACUSE: Marry sir, such claim as you would lay to your horse; and she would have me as a beast: not that, I being a beast, she would have me; but that she, being a very beastly creature, lays claim to me.

ANTIPHOLUS OF SYRACUSE: What is she?

DROMIO OF SYRACUSE: A very reverent body; ay, such a one as a man may not speak of without he say 'Sir-reverence.' I have but lean luck in the match, and yet is she a wondrous fat marriage.

ANTIPHOLUS OF SYRACUSE: How dost thou mean a fat marriage?

DROMIO OF SYRACUSE: Marry, sir, she's the kitchen-wench and all grease; and I know not what use to put her to but to make a lamp of her and run from her by her own light. I warrant, her rags and the tallow in them will burn a Poland winter: if she lives till doomsday, she'll burn a week longer than the whole world.

ANTIPHOLUS OF SYRACUSE: What complexion is she of?

DROMIO OF SYRACUSE: Swart, like my shoe, but her face nothing like so clean kept: for why, she sweats; a man may go over shoes in the grime of it.

ANTIPHOLUS OF SYRACUSE: That's a fault that water will mend.

DROMIO OF SYRACUSE: No, sir, 'tis in grain; Noah's flood could not do it.

ANTIPHOLUS OF SYRACUSE: What's her name?

DROMIO OF SYRACUSE: Nell, sir; but her name and three quarters, that's an ell and three quarters, will not measure her from hip to hip.

ANTIPHOLUS OF SYRACUSE: Then she bears some breadth?

DROMIO OF SYRACUSE: No longer from head to foot than from hip to hip: she is spherical, like a globe; I could find out countries in her.

ANTIPHOLUS OF SYRACUSE: In what part of her body stands Ireland?

DROMIO OF SYRACUSE: Marry, in her buttocks: I found it out by the bogs.

ANTIPHOLUS OF SYRACUSE: Where Scotland?

DROMIO OF SYRACUSE: I found it by the barrenness; hard in the palm of the hand.

ANTIPHOLUS OF SYRACUSE: Where France?
DROMIO OF SYRACUSE: In her forehead; armed and reverted, making war against her heir.
ANTIPHOLUS OF SYRACUSE: Where England?
DROMIO OF SYRACUSE: I looked for the chalky cliffs, but I could find no whiteness in them; but I guess it stood in her chin, by the salt rheum that ran between France and it.
ANTIPHOLUS OF SYRACUSE: Where Spain?
DROMIO OF SYRACUSE: Faith, I saw it not; but I felt it hot in her breath.
ANTIPHOLUS OF SYRACUSE: Where America, the Indies?
DROMIO OF SYRACUSE: Oh, sir, upon her nose all o'er embellished with rubies, carbuncles, sapphires, declining their rich aspect to the hot breath of Spain; who sent whole armadoes of caracks to be ballast at her nose.
ANTIPHOLUS OF SYRACUSE: Where stood Belgia, the Netherlands?
DROMIO OF SYRACUSE: Oh, sir, I did not look so low. To conclude, this drudge, or diviner, laid claim to me, call'd me Dromio; swore I was assured to her; told me what privy marks I had about me, as, the mark of my shoulder, the mole in my neck, the great wart on my left arm, that I amazed ran from her as a witch.

And, I think, if my breast had not been made of faith and my heart of steel, She had transform'd me to a curtal dog and made me turn i' the wheel.

ANTIPHOLUS OF SYRACUSE: Go hie thee presently, post to the road;
An if the wind blow any way from shore,
I will not harbour in this town to-night.
If any bark put forth, come to the mart,
Where I will walk till thou return to me.
If every one knows us and we know none,
'Tis time, I think, to trudge, pack and be gone.
DROMIO OF SYRACUSE: As from a bear a man would run for life,
So fly I from her that would be my wife.

Exit

ANTIPHOLUS OF SYRACUSE: There's none but witches do inhabit here;
And therefore 'tis high time that I were hence.
She that doth call me husband, even my soul
Doth for a wife abhor. But her fair sister,
Possess'd with such a gentle sovereign grace,
Of such enchanting presence and discourse,
Hath almost made me traitor to myself;
But, lest myself be guilty to self-wrong,
I'll stop mine ears against the mermaid's song.

Enter ANGELO with the chain

ANGELO: Master Antipholus—
ANTIPHOLUS OF SYRACUSE: Ay, that's my name.
ANGELO: I know it well, sir, lo, here is the chain.
I thought to have ta'en you at the Porpentine;
The chain unfinish'd made me stay thus long.
ANTIPHOLUS OF SYRACUSE: What is your will that I shall do with this?
ANGELO: What please yourself, sir: I have made it for you.
ANTIPHOLUS OF SYRACUSE: Made it for me, sir! I bespoke it not.
ANGELO: Not once, nor twice, but twenty times you have.
Go home with it and please your wife withal;
And soon at supper-time I'll visit you
And then receive my money for the chain.
ANTIPHOLUS OF SYRACUSE: I pray you, sir, receive the money now,
For fear you ne'er see chain nor money more.
ANGELO: You are a merry man, sir: fare you well.

Exit

ANTIPHOLUS OF SYRACUSE: What I should think of this, I cannot tell;
But this I think, there's no man is so vain
That would refuse so fair an offer'd chain.
I see a man here needs not live by shifts,
When in the streets he meets such golden gifts.
I'll to the mart, and there for Dromio stay
If any ship put out, then straight away.

Exit

Act IV

Scene I—*A public place*

Enter Second Merchant, ANGELO, and an Officer

SECOND MERCHANT: You know since Pentecost the sum is due,

And since I have not much importuned you;
Nor now I had not, but that I am bound
To Persia, and want guilders for my voyage;
Therefore make present satisfaction,
Or I'll attach you by this officer.

ANGELO: Even just the sum that I do owe to you
Is growing to me by Antipholus,
And in the instant that I met with you
He had of me a chain: at five o'clock
I shall receive the money for the same.
Pleaseth you walk with me down to his house,
I will discharge my bond and thank you too.

Enter ANTIPHOLUS of Ephesus and DROMIO of Ephesus from the courtezan's

OFFICER: That labour may you save: see where he comes.

ANTIPHOLUS OF EPHESUS: While I go to the goldsmith's house, go thou
And buy a rope's end; that will I bestow
Among my wife and her confederates,
For locking me out of my doors by day.
But, soft! I see the goldsmith. Get thee gone;
Buy thou a rope and bring it home to me.

DROMIO OF EPHESUS: I buy a thousand pound a year; I buy a rope.

Exit DROMIO

ANTIPHOLUS OF EPHESUS: A man is well holp up that trusts to you:
I promised your presence and the chain;
But neither chain nor goldsmith came to me.
Belike you thought our love would last too long,
If it were chain'd together, and therefore came not.

ANGELO: Saving your merry humour, here's the note
How much your chain weighs to the utmost carat,
The fineness of the gold and chargeful fashion.
Which doth amount to three odd ducats more
Than I stand debted to this gentleman.
I pray you, see him presently discharged,
For he is bound to sea and stays but for it.

ANTIPHOLUS OF EPHESUS: I am not furnish'd with the present money;
Besides, I have some business in the town.
Good signior, take the stranger to my house,
And with you take the chain and bid my wife
Disburse the sum on the receipt thereof.
Perchance I will be there as soon as you.

ANGELO: Then you will bring the chain to her yourself?

ANTIPHOLUS OF EPHESUS: No; bear it with you, lest I come not time enough.

ANGELO: Well, sir, I will. Have you the chain about you?

ANTIPHOLUS OF EPHESUS: An if I have not, sir, I hope you have;
Or else you may return without your money.

ANGELO: Nay, come, I pray you, sir, give me the chain;
Both wind and tide stays for this gentleman,
And I, to blame, have held him here too long.

ANTIPHOLUS OF EPHESUS: Good Lord! you use this dalliance to excuse
Your breach of promise to the Porpentine.
I should have chid you for not bringing it,
But, like a shrew, you first begin to brawl.

SECOND MERCHANT: The hour steals on; I pray you, sir, dispatch.

ANGELO: You hear how he importunes me—the chain!

ANTIPHOLUS OF EPHESUS: Why, give it to my wife and fetch your money.

ANGELO: Come, come, you know I gave it you even now.

Either send the chain or send me by some token.

ANTIPHOLUS OF EPHESUS: Fie, now you run this humour out of breath! Come, where's the chain? I pray you, let me see it.

SECOND MERCHANT: My business cannot brook this dalliance.

Good sir, say whether you'll answer me or no;
If not, I'll leave him to the officer.

ANTIPHOLUS OF EPHESUS: I answer you! what should I answer you?

ANGELO: The money that you owe me for the chain.

ANTIPHOLUS OF EPHESUS: I owe you none till I receive the chain.

ANGELO: You know I gave it you half an hour since.

ANTIPHOLUS OF EPHESUS: You gave me none: you wrong me much to say so.

ANGELO: You wrong me more, sir, in denying it.
Consider how it stands upon my credit.

SECOND MERCHANT: Well, officer, arrest him at my suit.

OFFICER: I do; and charge you in the Duke's name to obey me.

ANGELO: This touches me in reputation.
Either consent to pay this sum for me
Or I attach you by this officer.

ANTIPHOLUS OF EPHESUS: Consent to pay thee that I never had!
Arrest me, foolish fellow, if thou darest.

ANGELO: Here is thy fee; arrest him, officer,
I would not spare my brother in this case,
If he should scorn me so apparently.

OFFICER: I do arrest you, sir: you hear the suit.

ANTIPHOLUS OF EPHESUS: I do obey thee till I give thee bail.
But, sirrah, you shall buy this sport as dear
As all the metal in your shop will answer.

ANGELO: Sir, sir, I will have law in Ephesus,
To your notorious shame; I doubt it not.

Enter DROMIO of Syracuse, from the bay

DROMIO OF SYRACUSE: Master, there is a bark of Epidamnum
That stays but till her owner comes aboard,
And then, sir, she bears away. Our fraughtage, sir,
I have convey'd aboard; and I have bought
The oil, the balsamum and aqua-vitae.
The ship is in her trim; the merry wind
Blows fair from land: they stay for nought at all
But for their owner, master, and yourself.

ANTIPHOLUS OF EPHESUS: How now! a madman! Why, thou peevish sheep,
What ship of Epidamnum stays for me?

DROMIO OF SYRACUSE: A ship you sent me to, to hire waftage.

ANTIPHOLUS OF EPHESUS: Thou drunken slave, I sent thee for a rope;
And told thee to what purpose and what end.

DROMIO OF SYRACUSE: You sent me for a rope's end as soon:
You sent me to the bay, sir, for a bark.

ANTIPHOLUS OF EPHESUS: I will debate this matter at more leisure
And teach your ears to list me with more heed.
To Adriana, villain, hie thee straight;
Give her this key, and tell her, in the desk
That's cover'd o'er with Turkish tapestry,
There is a purse of ducats; let her send it.
Tell her I am arrested in the street
And that shall bail me; hie thee, slave, be gone!
On, officer, to prison till it come.

Exeunt Second Merchant, Angelo, Officer, and Antipholus of Ephesus

DROMIO OF SYRACUSE: To Adriana! that is where we dined,
Where Dowsabel did claim me for her husband.
She is too big, I hope, for me to compass.
Thither I must, although against my will,
For servants must their masters' minds fulfil.

Exit

SCENE II—*The house of Antipholus of Ephesus*

Enter ADRIANA and LUCIANA

ADRIANA: Ah, Luciana, did he tempt thee so?
Mightst thou perceive austerely in his eye
That he did plead in earnest? yea or no?
Look'd he or red or pale, or sad or merrily?

What observation madest thou in this case
Of his heart's meteors tilting in his face?

LUCIANA: First he denied you had in him no right.

ADRIANA: He meant he did me none; the more my spite.

LUCIANA: Then swore he that he was a stranger here.

ADRIANA: And true he swore, though yet forsworn he were.

LUCIANA: Then pleaded I for you.

ADRIANA: And what said he?

LUCIANA: That love I begg'd for you he begg'd of me.

ADRIANA: With what persuasion did he tempt thy love?

LUCIANA: With words that in an honest suit might move.
First he did praise my beauty, then my speech.

ADRIANA: Didst speak him fair?

LUCIANA: Have patience, I beseech.

ADRIANA: I cannot, nor I will not, hold me still;
My tongue, though not my heart, shall have his will.
He is deformed, crooked, old and sere,
Ill-faced, worse bodied, shapeless everywhere;
Vicious, ungentle, foolish, blunt, unkind;
Stigmatical in making, worse in mind.

LUCIANA: Who would be jealous then of such a one?
No evil lost is wail'd when it is gone.

ADRIANA: Ah, but I think him better than I say,
And yet would herein others' eyes were worse.
Far from her nest the lapwing cries away;
My heart prays for him, though my tongue do curse.

Enter DROMIO of Syracuse

DROMIO OF SYRACUSE: Here go—the desk, the purse. Sweet now, make haste.

LUCIANA: How hast thou lost thy breath?

DROMIO OF SYRACUSE: By running fast.

ADRIANA: Where is thy master, Dromio? Is he well?

DROMIO OF SYRACUSE: No, he's in Tartar limbo, worse than hell.
A devil in an everlasting garment hath him;
One whose hard heart is button'd up with steel;
A fiend, a fury, pitiless and rough;
A wolf, nay, worse, a fellow all in buff;
A back-friend, a shoulder-clapper, one that countermands
The passages of alleys, creeks and narrow lands;
A hound that runs counter and yet draws dryfoot well;
One that before the judgement carries poor souls to hell.

ADRIANA: Why, man, what is the matter?

DROMIO OF SYRACUSE: I do not know the matter: he is 'rested on the case.

ADRIANA: What, is he arrested? Tell me, at whose suit?

DROMIO OF SYRACUSE: I know not at whose suit he is arrested well;
But he's in a suit of buff which 'rested him, that can I tell.
Will you send him, mistress, redemption, the money in his desk?

ADRIANA: Go fetch it, sister.

Exit Luciana

This I wonder at,
That he, unknown to me, should be in debt.
Tell me, was he arrested on a band?

DROMIO OF SYRACUSE: Not on a band, but on a stronger thing;
A chain, a chain! Do you not hear it ring?

ADRIANA: What, the chain?

DROMIO OF SYRACUSE: No, no, the bell: 'tis time that I were gone:
It was two ere I left him, and now the clock strikes one.

ADRIANA: The hours come back! that did I never hear.

DROMIO OF SYRACUSE: O, yes; if any hour meet a sergeant, 'a turns back for very fear.

ADRIANA: As if Time were in debt! how fondly dost thou reason!

DROMIO OF SYRACUSE: Time is a very bankrupt, and owes more than he's worth, to season.
Nay, he's a thief too: have you not heard men say
That Time comes stealing on by night and day?
If Time be in debt and theft, and a sergeant in the way,
Hath he not reason to turn back an hour in a day?

Re-enter LUCIANA with a purse

ADRIANA: Go, Dromio; there's the money, bear it straight;

And bring thy master home immediately.
Come, sister: I am press'd down with conceit—
Conceit, my comfort and my injury.

Exeunt

SCENE III—*The mart*

Enter ANTIPHOLUS of Syracuse

ANTIPHOLUS OF SYRACUSE: There's not a man I meet but doth salute me

As if I were their well-acquainted friend;
And every one doth call me by my name.
Some tender money to me; some invite me;
Some other give me thanks for kindnesses;
Some offer me commodities to buy;
Even now a tailor call'd me in his shop
And show'd me silks that he had bought for me,
And therewithal took measure of my body.
Sure, these are but imaginary wiles
And Lapland sorcerers inhabit here.

Enter DROMIO of Syracuse

DROMIO OF SYRACUSE: Master, here's the gold you sent me for. What, have you got the picture of old Adam new-apparelled?

ANTIPHOLUS OF SYRACUSE: What gold is this? What Adam dost thou mean?

DROMIO OF SYRACUSE: Not that Adam that kept the Paradise but that Adam that keeps the prison: he that goes in the calf's skin that was killed for the Prodigal; he that came behind you, sir, like an evil angel, and bid you forsake your liberty.

ANTIPHOLUS OF SYRACUSE: I understand thee not.

DROMIO OF SYRACUSE: No? why, 'tis a plain case: he that went, like a bass-viol, in a case of leather; the man, sir, that, when gentlemen are tired, gives them a sob and 'rests them; he, sir, that takes pity on decayed men and gives them suits of durance; he that sets up his rest to do more exploits with his mace than a morris-pike.

ANTIPHOLUS OF SYRACUSE: What, thou meanest an officer?

DROMIO OF SYRACUSE: Ay, sir, the sergeant of the band, he that brings any man to answer it that breaks his band; one that thinks a man always going to bed, and says, 'God give you good rest!'

ANTIPHOLUS OF SYRACUSE: Well, sir, there rest in your foolery. Is there any ship puts forth to-night? May we be gone?

DROMIO OF SYRACUSE: Why, sir, I brought you word an hour since that the bark Expedition put forth to-night; and then were you hindered by the sergeant, to tarry for the hoy Delay. Here are the angels that you sent for to deliver you.

ANTIPHOLUS OF SYRACUSE: The fellow is distract, and so am I;

And here we wander in illusions.
Some blessed power deliver us from hence!

Enter a Courtezan

COURTEZAN: Well met, well met, Master Antipholus.

I see, sir, you have found the goldsmith now.
Is that the chain you promised me to-day?

ANTIPHOLUS OF SYRACUSE: Satan, avoid! I charge thee, tempt me not.

DROMIO OF SYRACUSE: Master, is this Mistress Satan?

ANTIPHOLUS OF SYRACUSE: It is the devil.

DROMIO OF SYRACUSE: Nay, she is worse, she is the devil's dam; and here she comes in the habit of a light wench: and thereof comes that the wenches say 'God damn me;' that's as much to say 'God make me a light wench'. It is written, they appear to men like angels of light: light is an effect of fire, and fire will burn; ergo, light wenches will burn. Come not near her.

COURTEZAN: Your man and you are marvellous merry, sir.

Will you go with me? We'll mend our dinner here?

DROMIO OF SYRACUSE: Master, if you do, expect spoon-meat; or bespeak a long spoon.

ANTIPHOLUS OF SYRACUSE: Why, Dromio?

DROMIO OF SYRACUSE: Marry, he must have a long spoon that must eat with the devil.

ANTIPHOLUS OF SYRACUSE: Avoid then, fiend! what tell'st thou me of supping?

Thou art, as you are all, a sorceress;
I conjure thee to leave me and be gone.

COURTEZAN: Give me the ring of mine you had at dinner,

Or, for my diamond, the chain you promised,
And I'll be gone, sir, and not trouble you.

DROMIO OF SYRACUSE: Some devils ask but the parings of one's nail,

A rush, a hair, a drop of blood, a pin,
A nut, a cherry-stone;
But she, more covetous, would have a chain.
Master, be wise; an if you give it her,
The devil will shake her chain and fright us with it.

COURTEZAN: I pray you, sir, my ring, or else the chain;
I hope you do not mean to cheat me so.

ANTIPHOLUS OF SYRACUSE: Avaunt, thou witch! Come, Dromio, let us go.

DROMIO OF SYRACUSE: 'Fly pride,' says the peacock: mistress, that you know.

Exeunt ANTIPHOLUS of Syracuse and DROMIO of Syracuse

COURTEZAN: Now, out of doubt, Antipholus is mad,
Else would he never so demean himself.
A ring he hath of mine worth forty ducats,
And for the same he promised me a chain:
Both one and other he denies me now.
The reason that I gather he is mad,
Besides this present instance of his rage,
Is a mad tale he told to-day at dinner,
Of his own doors being shut against his entrance.
Belike his wife, acquainted with his fits,
On purpose shut the doors against his way.
My way is now to hie home to his house,
And tell his wife that, being lunatic,
He rush'd into my house and took perforce
My ring away. This course I fittest choose;
For forty ducats is too much to lose.

Exit

SCENE IV—*A street*

Enter ANTIPHOLUS of Ephesus and the Officer

ANTIPHOLUS OF EPHESUS: Fear me not, man; I will not break away.
I'll give thee, ere I leave thee, so much money,
To warrant thee, as I am 'rested for.
My wife is in a wayward mood to-day,
And will not lightly trust the messenger.
That I should be attach'd in Ephesus,
I tell you, 'twill sound harshly in her ears.

Enter DROMIO of Ephesus with a rope's-end

Here comes my man; I think he brings the money.
How now, sir! have you that I sent you for?

DROMIO OF EPHESUS: Here's that, I warrant you, will pay them all.

ANTIPHOLUS OF EPHESUS: But where's the money?

DROMIO OF EPHESUS: Why, sir, I gave the money for the rope.

ANTIPHOLUS OF EPHESUS: Five hundred ducats, villain, for a rope?

DROMIO OF EPHESUS: I'll serve you, sir, five hundred at the rate.

ANTIPHOLUS OF EPHESUS: To what end did I bid thee hie thee home?

DROMIO OF EPHESUS: To a rope's-end, sir; and to that end am I returned.

ANTIPHOLUS OF EPHESUS: And to that end, sir, I will welcome you.

Beating him

OFFICER: Good sir, be patient.

DROMIO OF EPHESUS: Nay, 'tis for me to be patient; I am in adversity.

Officer: Good, now, hold thy tongue.

DROMIO OF EPHESUS: Nay, rather persuade him to hold his hands.

ANTIPHOLUS OF EPHESUS: Thou whoreson, senseless villain!

DROMIO OF EPHESUS: I would I were senseless, sir, that I might not feel your blows.

ANTIPHOLUS: Thou art sensible in nothing but blows, and so is an ass.

DROMIO OF EPHESUS: I am an ass, indeed; you may prove it by my long ears. I have served him from the hour of my nativity to this instant, and have nothing at his hands for my service but blows. When I am cold, he heats me with beating. when I am warm, he cools me with beating. I am waked with it when I sleep; raised with it when I sit; driven out of doors with it when I go from home; welcomed home with it when I return; nay, I bear it on my shoulders, as a beggar wont her brat; and, I think when he hath lamed me, I shall beg with it from door to door.

ANTIPHOLUS OF EPHESUS: Come, go along; my wife is coming yonder.

Enter ADRIANA, LUCIANA, the Courtezan, and PINCH

DROMIO OF EPHESUS: Mistress, 'respice finem', respect your end; or rather, the prophecy like the parrot, 'beware the rope's-end'.

ANTIPHOLUS OF EPHESUS: Wilt thou still talk?

Beating him

COURTEZAN: How say you now? Is not your husband mad?

ADRIANA: His incivility confirms no less.
Good Doctor Pinch, you are a conjurer;
Establish him in his true sense again,
And I will please you what you will demand.

LUCIANA: Alas, how fiery and how sharp he looks!

COURTEZAN: Mark how he trembles in his ecstasy!

PINCH: Give me your hand and let me feel your pulse.

ANTIPHOLUS OF EPHESUS: There is my hand, and let it feel your ear.

Striking him

PINCH: I charge thee, Satan, housed within this man,
To yield possession to my holy prayers
And to thy state of darkness hie thee straight.
I conjure thee by all the saints in heaven!

ANTIPHOLUS OF EPHESUS: Peace, doting wizard, peace! I am not mad.

ADRIANA: O, that thou wert not, poor distressed soul!

ANTIPHOLUS OF EPHESUS: You minion, you, are these your customers?
Did this companion with the saffron face
Revel and feast it at my house to-day,
Whilst upon me the guilty doors were shut
And I denied to enter in my house?

ADRIANA: O husband, God doth know you dined at home;
Where would you had remain'd until this time,
Free from these slanders and this open shame!

ANTIPHOLUS OF EPHESUS: Dined at home! Thou villain, what sayest thou?

DROMIO OF EPHESUS: Sir, sooth to say, you did not dine at home.

ANTIPHOLUS OF EPHESUS: Were not my doors lock'd up and I shut out?

DROMIO OF EPHESUS: Perdie, your doors were lock'd and you shut out.

ANTIPHOLUS OF EPHESUS: And did not she herself revile me there?

DROMIO OF EPHESUS: Sans fable, she herself reviled you there.

ANTIPHOLUS OF EPHESUS: Did not her kitchen-maid rail, taunt, and scorn me?

DROMIO OF EPHESUS: Certes, she did; the kitchen-vestal scorn'd you.

ANTIPHOLUS OF EPHESUS: And did not I in rage depart from thence?

DROMIO OF EPHESUS: In verity you did; my bones bear witness,
That since have felt the vigour of his rage.

ADRIANA: Is't good to soothe him in these contraries?

PINCH: It is no shame: the fellow finds his vein,
And yielding to him humours well his frenzy.

ANTIPHOLUS OF EPHESUS: Thou hast suborn'd the goldsmith to arrest me.

ADRIANA: Alas, I sent you money to redeem you,
By Dromio here, who came in haste for it.

DROMIO OF EPHESUS: Money by me! Heart and goodwill you might;
But surely master, not a rag of money.

ANTIPHOLUS OF EPHESUS: Went'st not thou to her for a purse of ducats?

ADRIANA: He came to me and I deliver'd it.

LUCIANA: And I am witness with her that she did.

DROMIO OF EPHESUS: God and the rope-maker bear me witness
That I was sent for nothing but a rope!

PINCH: Mistress, both man and master is possess'd;
I know it by their pale and deadly looks.
They must be bound and laid in some dark room.

ANTIPHOLUS OF EPHESUS: Say, wherefore didst thou lock me forth to-day?
And why dost thou deny the bag of gold?

ADRIANA: I did not, gentle husband, lock thee forth.

DROMIO OF EPHESUS: And, gentle master, I received no gold;
But I confess, sir, that we were lock'd out.

ADRIANA: Dissembling villain, thou speak'st false in both.

ANTIPHOLUS OF EPHESUS: Dissembling harlot, thou art false in all;
And art confederate with a damned pack
To make a loathsome abject scorn of me;
But with these nails I'll pluck out these false eyes
That would behold in me this shameful sport.

Enter three or four, and offer to bind him. He strives

ADRIANA: O, bind him, bind him! let him not come near me.

PINCH: More company! The fiend is strong within him.

LUCIANA: Ay me, poor man, how pale and wan he looks!

ANTIPHOLUS OF EPHESUS: What, will you murder me? Thou gaoler, thou,

I am thy prisoner: wilt thou suffer them
To make a rescue?

OFFICER: Masters, let him go;

He is my prisoner, and you shall not have him.

PINCH: Go bind this man, for he is frantic too.

They offer to bind Dromio of Ephesus

ADRIANA: What wilt thou do, thou peevish officer?

Hast thou delight to see a wretched man
Do outrage and displeasure to himself?

OFFICER: He is my prisoner: if I let him go,

The debt he owes will be required of me.

ADRIANA: I will discharge thee ere I go from thee;

Bear me forthwith unto his creditor,
And, knowing how the debt grows, I will pay it.
Good master doctor, see him safe convey'd
Home to my house. O most unhappy day!

ANTIPHOLUS OF EPHESUS: O most unhappy strumpet!

DROMIO OF EPHESUS: Master, I am here entered in bond for you.

ANTIPHOLUS OF EPHESUS: Out on thee, villain! Wherefore dost thou mad me?

DROMIO OF EPHESUS: Will you be bound for nothing?

Be mad, good master: cry 'The devil!'

LUCIANA: God help, poor souls, how idly do they talk!

ADRIANA: Go bear him hence. Sister, go you with me.

Exeunt all but Adriana, Luciana, Officer and Courtezan

Say now, whose suit is he arrested at?

OFFICER: One Angelo, a goldsmith: do you know him?

ADRIANA: I know the man. What is the sum he owes?

OFFICER: Two hundred ducats.

ADRIANA: Say, how grows it due?

OFFICER: Due for a chain your husband had of him.

ADRIANA: He did bespeak a chain for me, but had it not.

COURTEZAN: When as your husband, all in rage, to-day

Came to my house and took away my ring—
The ring I saw upon his finger now—
Straight after did I meet him with a chain.

ADRIANA: It may be so, but I did never see it.

Come, gaoler, bring me where the goldsmith is;
I long to know the truth hereof at large.

Enter ANTIPHOLUS of Syracuse with his rapier drawn, and DROMIO of Syracuse

LUCIANA: God, for thy mercy! they are loose again.

ADRIANA: And come with naked swords.

Let's call more help to have them bound gain.

OFFICER: Away! they'll kill us.

Exeunt all but Antipholus of Syracuse and Dromio of Syracuse as fast as may be, frighted

ANTIPHOLUS OF SYRACUSE: I see these witches are afraid of swords.

DROMIO OF SYRACUSE: She that would be your wife now ran from you.

ANTIPHOLUS OF SYRACUSE: Come to the Centaur; fetch our stuff from thence:

I long that we were safe and sound aboard.

DROMIO OF SYRACUSE: Faith, stay here this night; they will surely do us no harm: you saw they speak us fair, give us gold: methinks they are such a gentle nation that, but for the mountain of mad flesh that claims marriage of me, I could find in my heart to stay here still and turn witch.

ANTIPHOLUS OF SYRACUSE: I will not stay to-night for all the town;

Therefore away, to get our stuff aboard.

Exeunt

ACT V

SCENE I—*A street before a Priory*

Enter Second Merchant and ANGELO

ANGELO: I am sorry, sir, that I have hinder'd you;
But, I protest, he had the chain of me,
Though most dishonestly he doth deny it.

SECOND MERCHANT: How is the man esteemed here in the city?

ANGELO: Of very reverend reputation, sir,
Of credit infinite, highly beloved,
Second to none that lives here in the city;
His word might bear my wealth at any time.

SECOND MERCHANT: Speak softly; yonder, as I think, he walks.

Enter ANTIPHOLUS of Syracuse and DROMIO of Syracuse

ANGELO: 'Tis so; and that self chain about his neck
Which he forswore most monstrously to have.
Good sir, draw near to me, I'll speak to him.
Signior Antipholus, I wonder much
That you would put me to this shame and trouble;
And, not without some scandal to yourself,
With circumstance and oaths so to deny
This chain which now you wear so openly.
Beside the charge, the shame, imprisonment,
You have done wrong to this my honest friend,
Who, but for staying on our controversy,
Had hoisted sail and put to sea to-day.
This chain you had of me; can you deny it?

ANTIPHOLUS OF SYRACUSE: I think I had; I never did deny it.

SECOND MERCHANT: Yes, that you did, sir, and forswore it too.

ANTIPHOLUS OF SYRACUSE: Who heard me to deny it or forswear it?

SECOND MERCHANT: These ears of mine, thou know'st did hear thee.
Fie on thee, wretch! 'tis pity that thou livest
To walk where any honest man resort.

ANTIPHOLUS OF SYRACUSE: Thou art a villain to impeach me thus;
I'll prove mine honour and mine honesty
Against thee presently, if thou darest stand.

SECOND MERCHANT: I dare, and do defy thee for a villain.

They draw

Enter ADRIANA, LUCIANA, the Courtezan, and others

ADRIANA: Hold, hurt him not, for God's sake! he is mad.
Some get within him, take his sword away;
Bind Dromio too, and bear them to my house.

DROMIO OF SYRACUSE: Run, master, run; for God's sake, take a house!
This is some priory. In, or we are spoil'd!

Exeunt Antipholus of Syracuse and Dromio of Syracuse to the Priory

Enter the Lady Abbess

ABBESS: Be quiet, people. Wherefore throng you hither?

ADRIANA: To fetch my poor distracted husband hence.
Let us come in, that we may bind him fast
And bear him home for his recovery.

ANGELO: I knew he was not in his perfect wits.

SECOND MERCHANT: I am sorry now that I did draw on him.

ABBESS: How long hath this possession held the man?

ADRIANA: This week he hath been heavy, sour, sad,
And much different from the man he was;
But till this afternoon his passion
Ne'er brake into extremity of rage.

ABBESS: Hath he not lost much wealth by wreck of sea?
Buried some dear friend? Hath not else his eye
Stray'd his affection in unlawful love?

A sin prevailing much in youthful men,
Who give their eyes the liberty of gazing.
Which of these sorrows is he subject to?

ADRIANA: To none of these, except it be the last;
Namely, some love that drew him oft from home.

ABBESS: You should for that have reprehended him.

ADRIANA: Why, so I did.

ABBESS: Ay, but not rough enough.

ADRIANA: As roughly as my modesty would let me.

ABBESS: Haply, in private.

ADRIANA: And in assemblies too.

ABBESS: Ay, but not enough.

ADRIANA: It was the copy of our conference.
In bed he slept not for my urging it;
At board he fed not for my urging it;
Alone, it was the subject of my theme;
In company I often glanced it;
Still did I tell him it was vile and bad.

ABBESS: And thereof came it that the man was mad.
The venom clamours of a jealous woman
Poisons more deadly than a mad dog's tooth.
It seems his sleeps were hinder'd by thy railing,
And therefore comes it that his head is light.
Thou say'st his meat was sauced with thy upbraidings:
Unquiet meals make ill digestions;
Thereof the raging fire of fever bred;
And what's a fever but a fit of madness?
Thou say'st his sports were hinderd by thy brawls.
Sweet recreation barr'd, what doth ensue
But moody and dull melancholy,
Kinsman to grim and comfortless despair,
And at her heels a huge infectious troop
Of pale distemperatures and foes to life?
In food, in sport and life-preserving rest
To be disturb'd, would mad or man or beast.
The consequence is then thy jealous fits
Have scared thy husband from the use of wits.

LUCIANA: She never reprehended him but mildly,
When he demean'd himself rough, rude and wildly.
Why bear you these rebukes and answer not?

ADRIANA: She did betray me to my own reproof.
Good people enter and lay hold on him.

ABBESS: No, not a creature enters in my house.

ADRIANA: Then let your servants bring my husband forth.

ABBESS: Neither; he took this place for sanctuary,
And it shall privilege him from your hands
Till I have brought him to his wits again,
Or lose my labour in assaying it.

ADRIANA: I will attend my husband, be his nurse,
Diet his sickness, for it is my office,
And will have no attorney but myself;
And therefore let me have him home with me.

ABBESS: Be patient; for I will not let him stir
Till I have used the approved means I have,
With wholesome syrups, drugs and holy prayers,
To make of him a formal man again.
It is a branch and parcel of mine oath,
A charitable duty of my order;
Therefore depart and leave him here with me.

ADRIANA: I will not hence and leave my husband here;
And ill it doth beseem your holiness
To separate the husband and the wife.

ABBESS: Be quiet and depart: thou shalt not have him.

Exit Abbess

LUCIANA: Complain unto the Duke of this indignity.

ADRIANA: Come, go, I will fall prostrate at his feet;
And never rise until my tears and prayers
Have won his grace to come in person hither
And take perforce my husband from the abbess.

SECOND MERCHANT: By this, I think, the dial points at five;
Anon, I'm sure, the Duke himself in person
Comes this way to the melancholy vale,
The place of death and sorry execution,
Behind the ditches of the abbey here.

ANGELO: Upon what cause?

SECOND MERCHANT: To see a reverend Syracusian merchant,
Who put unluckily into this bay
Against the laws and statutes of this town,
Beheaded publicly for his offence.

ANGELO: See where they come: we will behold his death.

LUCIANA: Kneel to the Duke before he pass the abbey.

Enter DUKE SOLINUS, attended; AEGEON bareheaded; with the Headsman and other Officers

DUKE SOLINUS: Yet once again proclaim it publicly,
If any friend will pay the sum for him,
He shall not die; so much we tender him.

ADRIANA: Justice, most sacred Duke, against the abbess!

DUKE SOLINUS: She is a virtuous and a reverend lady;
It cannot be that she hath done thee wrong.

ADRIANA: May it please your Grace, Antipholus, my husband,
Whom I made lord of me and all I had,
At your important letters—this ill day
A most outrageous fit of madness took him;
That desperately he hurried through the street,
With him his bondman, all as mad as he—
Doing displeasure to the citizens
By rushing in their houses, bearing thence
Rings, jewels, any thing his rage did like.
Once did I get him bound and sent him home,
Whilst to take order for the wrongs I went,
That here and there his fury had committed.
Anon, I wot not by what strong escape,
He broke from those that had the guard of him;
And with his mad attendant and himself,
Each one with ireful passion, with drawn swords,
Met us again and madly bent on us,
Chased us away; till, raising of more aid,
We came again to bind them. Then they fled
Into this abbey, whither we pursued them;
And here the Abbess shuts the gates on us
And will not suffer us to fetch him out,
Nor send him forth that we may bear him hence.
Therefore, most gracious Duke, with thy command
Let him be brought forth and borne hence for help.

DUKE SOLINUS: Long since thy husband served me in my wars,
And I to thee engaged a prince's word,
When thou didst make him master of thy bed,
To do him all the grace and good I could.
Go, some of you, knock at the abbey-gate
And bid the lady Abbess come to me.
I will determine this before I stir.

Enter a Servant

SERVANT: O mistress, mistress, shift and save yourself!
My master and his man are both broke loose,
Beaten the maids a-row and bound the doctor
Whose beard they have singed off with brands of fire;
And ever, as it blazed, they threw on him
Great pails of puddled mire to quench the hair.
My master preaches patience to him and the while
His man with scissors nicks him like a fool,
And sure, unless you send some present help,
Between them they will kill the conjurer.

ADRIANA: Peace, fool! thy master and his man are here,
And that is false thou dost report to us.

SERVANT: Mistress, upon my life, I tell you true;
I have not breathed almost since I did see it.
He cries for you, and vows, if he can take you,
To scorch your face and to disfigure you.

Cry within

Hark, hark! I hear him, mistress. fly, be gone!

DUKE SOLINUS: Come, stand by me; fear nothing. Guard with halberds!

ADRIANA: Ay me, it is my husband! Witness you,
That he is borne about invisible.
Even now we housed him in the abbey here;
And now he's there, past thought of human reason.

Enter ANTIPHOLUS of Ephesus and DROMIO of Ephesus

ANTIPHOLUS OF EPHESUS: Justice, most gracious Duke; O, grant me justice!
Even for the service that long since I did thee,
When I bestrid thee in the wars and took
Deep scars to save thy life; even for the blood
That then I lost for thee, now grant me justice.

AEGEON: Unless the fear of death doth make me dote,
I see my son Antipholus and Dromio.

ANTIPHOLUS OF EPHESUS: Justice, sweet Prince, against that woman there!
She whom thou gavest to me to be my wife,

That hath abused and dishonour'd me
Even in the strength and height of injury!
Beyond imagination is the wrong
That she this day hath shameless thrown on me.

DUKE SOLINUS: Discover how, and thou shalt find me just.

ANTIPHOLUS OF EPHESUS: This day, great Duke, she shut the doors upon me,
While she with harlots feasted in my house.

DUKE SOLINUS: A grievous fault! Say, woman, didst thou so?

ADRIANA: No, my good lord: myself, he and my sister
To-day did dine together. So befall my soul
As this is false he burdens me withal!

LUCIANA: Ne'er may I look on day, nor sleep on night,
But she tells to your Highness simple truth!

ANGELO: O perjured woman! They are both forsworn.
In this the madman justly chargeth them.

ANTIPHOLUS OF EPHESUS: My liege, I am advised what I say,
Neither disturbed with the effect of wine,
Nor heady-rash, provoked with raging ire,
Albeit my wrongs might make one wiser mad.
This woman lock'd me out this day from dinner;
That goldsmith there, were he not pack'd with her,
Could witness it, for he was with me then;
Who parted with me to go fetch a chain,
Promising to bring it to the Porpentine,
Where Balthazar and I did dine together.
Our dinner done, and he not coming thither,
I went to seek him: in the street I met him
And in his company that gentleman.
There did this perjured goldsmith swear me down
That I this day of him received the chain,
Which, God he knows, I saw not; for the which
He did arrest me with an officer.
I did obey, and sent my peasant home
For certain ducats; he with none return'd.
Then fairly I bespoke the officer
To go in person with me to my house.
By the way we met
My wife, her sister, and a rabble more
Of vile confederates. Along with them
They brought one Pinch, a hungry lean-faced villain,
A mere anatomy, a mountebank,
A threadbare juggler and a fortune-teller,
A needy, hollow-eyed, sharp-looking wretch,
A dead-looking man: this pernicious slave,
Forsooth, took on him as a conjurer,
And, gazing in mine eyes, feeling my pulse,
And with no face, as 'twere, outfacing me,
Cries out, I was possess'd. Then all together
They fell upon me, bound me, bore me thence
And in a dark and dankish vault at home
There left me and my man, both bound together;
Till, gnawing with my teeth my bonds in sunder,
I gain'd my freedom, and immediately
Ran hither to your Grace; whom I beseech
To give me ample satisfaction
For these deep shames and great indignities.

ANGELO: My lord, in truth, thus far I witness with him,
That he dined not at home, but was lock'd out.

DUKE SOLINUS: But had he such a chain of thee or no?

ANGELO: He had, my lord, and when he ran in here,
These people saw the chain about his neck.

SECOND MERCHANT: Besides, I will be sworn these ears of mine
Heard you confess you had the chain of him
After you first forswore it on the mart;
And thereupon I drew my sword on you;
And then you fled into this abbey here,
From whence, I think, you are come by miracle.

ANTIPHOLUS OF EPHESUS: I never came within these abbey-walls,
Nor ever didst thou draw thy sword on me;
I never saw the chain, so help me Heaven!
And this is false you burden me withal.

DUKE SOLINUS: Why, what an intricate impeach is this!
I think you all have drunk of Circe's cup.
If here you housed him, here he would have been;

If he were mad, he would not plead so coldly.
You say he dined at home; the goldsmith here
Denies that saying. Sirrah, what say you?

DROMIO OF EPHESUS: Sir, he dined with her there, at the Porpentine.

COURTEZAN: He did, and from my finger snatch'd that ring.

ANTIPHOLUS OF EPHESUS: 'tis true, my liege; this ring I had of her.

DUKE SOLINUS: Saw'st thou him enter at the abbey here?

COURTEZAN: As sure, my liege, as I do see your Grace.

DUKE SOLINUS: Why, this is strange. Go call the Abbess hither.
I think you are all mated or stark mad.

Exit one to Abbess

AEGEON: Most mighty Duke, vouchsafe me speak a word:
Haply I see a friend will save my life
And pay the sum that may deliver me.

DUKE SOLINUS: Speak freely, Syracusian, what thou wilt.

AEGEON: Is not your name, sir, call'd Antipholus?
And is not that your bondman, Dromio?

DROMIO OF EPHESUS: Within this hour I was his bondman sir,
But he, I thank him, gnaw'd in two my cords;
Now am I Dromio and his man unbound.

AEGEON: I am sure you both of you remember me.

DROMIO OF EPHESUS: Ourselves we do remember, sir, by you;
For lately we were bound, as you are now
You are not Pinch's patient, are you, sir?

AEGEON: Why look you strange on me? you know me well.

ANTIPHOLUS OF EPHESUS: I never saw you in my life till now.

AEGEON: O, grief hath changed me since you saw me last,
And careful hours with time's deformed hand
Have written strange defeatures in my face.
But tell me yet, dost thou not know my voice?

ANTIPHOLUS OF EPHESUS: Neither.

AEGEON: Dromio, nor thou?

DROMIO OF EPHESUS: No, trust me, sir, nor I.

AEGEON: I am sure thou dost.

DROMIO OF EPHESUS: Ay, sir, but I am sure I do not; and whatsoever a man denies, you are now bound to believe him.

AEGEON: Not know my voice! O time's extremity,
Hast thou so crack'd and splitted my poor tongue
In seven short years, that here my only son
Knows not my feeble key of untuned cares?
Though now this grained face of mine be hid
In sap-consuming winter's drizzled snow,
And all the conduits of my blood froze up,
Yet hath my night of life some memory,
My wasting lamps some fading glimmer left,
My dull deaf ears a little use to hear;
All these old witnesses—I cannot err—
Tell me thou art my son Antipholus.

ANTIPHOLUS OF EPHESUS: I never saw my father in my life.

AEGEON: But seven years since, in Syracusa, boy,
Thou know'st we parted; but perhaps, my son,
Thou shamest to acknowledge me in misery.

ANTIPHOLUS OF EPHESUS: The Duke and all that know me in the city
Can witness with me that it is not so
I ne'er saw Syracusa in my life.

DUKE SOLINUS: I tell thee, Syracusian, twenty years
Have I been patron to Antipholus,
During which time he ne'er saw Syracusa.
I see thy age and dangers make thee dote.

Re-enter ÆMILIA, with ANTIPHOLUS of Syracuse and DROMIO of Syracuse

ÆMILIA: Most mighty Duke, behold a man much wrong'd.

All gather to see them

ADRIANA: I see two husbands, or mine eyes deceive me.

DUKE SOLINUS: One of these men is Genius to the other;
And so of these. Which is the natural man,
And which the spirit? Who deciphers them?

DROMIO OF SYRACUSE: I, sir, am Dromio; command him away.

DROMIO OF EPHESUS: I, sir, am Dromio; pray, let me stay.

ANTIPHOLUS OF SYRACUSE: Aegeon art thou not? or else his ghost?

DROMIO OF SYRACUSE: O, my old master! who hath bound him here?

ÆMILIA: Whoever bound him, I will loose his bonds
And gain a husband by his liberty.
Speak, old Ægeon, if thou be'st the man
That hadst a wife once call'd Æmilia
That bore thee at a burden two fair sons.
O, if thou be'st the same Ægeon, speak,
And speak unto the same Æmilia!

AEGION: If I dream not, thou art Æmilia.
If thou art she, tell me where is that son
That floated with thee on the fatal raft?

ÆMILIA: By men of Epidamnum he and I
And the twin Dromio all were taken up;
But by and by rude fishermen of Corinth
By force took Dromio and my son from them
And me they left with those of Epidamnum.
What then became of them I cannot tell
I to this fortune that you see me in.

DUKE SOLINUS: Why, here begins his morning story right;
These two Antipholuses, these two so like,
And these two Dromios, one in semblance—
Besides her urging of her wreck at sea—
These are the parents to these children,
Which accidentally are met together.
Antipholus, thou camest from Corinth first?

ANTIPHOLUS OF SYRACUSE: No, sir, not I; I came from Syracuse.

DUKE SOLINUS: Stay, stand apart; I know not which is which.

ANTIPHOLUS OF EPHESUS: I came from Corinth, my most gracious lord.—

DROMIO OF EPHESUS: And I with him.

ANTIPHOLUS OF EPHESUS: Brought to this town by that most famous warrior,
Duke Menaphon, your most renowned uncle.

ADRIANA: Which of you two did dine with me to-day?

ANTIPHOLUS OF SYRACUSE: I, gentle mistress.

ADRIANA: And are not you my husband?

ANTIPHOLUS OF EPHESUS: No; I say nay to that.

ANTIPHOLUS OF SYRACUSE: And so do I; yet did she call me so;
And this fair gentlewoman, her sister here,
Did call me brother. [*To Luciana*] What I told you then,
I hope I shall have leisure to make good;
If this be not a dream I see and hear.

ANGELO: That is the chain, sir, which you had of me.

ANTIPHOLUS OF SYRACUSE: I think it be, sir; I deny it not.

ANTIPHOLUS OF EPHESUS: And you, sir, for this chain arrested me.

ANGELO: I think I did, sir; I deny it not.

ADRIANA: I sent you money, sir, to be your bail,
By Dromio; but I think he brought it not.

DROMIO OF EPHESUS: No, none by me.

ANTIPHOLUS OF SYRACUSE: This purse of ducats I received from you,
And Dromio, my man, did bring them me.
I see we still did meet each other's man,
And I was ta'en for him, and he for me,
And thereupon these errors are arose.

ANTIPHOLUS OF EPHESUS: These ducats pawn I for my father here.

DUKE SOLINUS: It shall not need; thy father hath his life.

COURTEZAN: Sir, I must have that diamond from you.

ANTIPHOLUS OF EPHESUS: There, take it; and much thanks for my good cheer.

ÆMILIA: Renowned Duke, vouchsafe to take the pains
To go with us into the abbey here
And hear at large discoursed all our fortunes;
And all that are assembled in this place,
That by this sympathized one day's error
Have suffer'd wrong, go keep us company,
And we shall make full satisfaction.
Thirty-three years have I but gone in travail
Of you, my sons; and till this present hour
My heavy burden ne'er delivered.
The Duke, my husband and my children both,
And you the calendars of their nativity,
Go to a gossips' feast and go with me;
After so long grief, such festivity!

DUKE SOLINUS: With all my heart, I'll gossip at this feast.

Exeunt all but ANTIPHOLUS of Syracuse, ANTIPHOLUS of Ephesus, DROMIO of Syracuse and DROMIO OF Ephesus

DROMIO OF SYRACUSE: Master, shall I fetch your stuff from shipboard?

ANTIPHOLUS OF EPHESUS: Dromio, what stuff of mine hast thou embark'd?

DROMIO OF SYRACUSE: Your goods that lay at host, sir, in the Centaur.

ANTIPHOLUS OF SYRACUSE: He speaks to me. I am your master, Dromio:

Come, go with us; we'll look to that anon.
Embrace thy brother there; rejoice with him.

Exeunt ANTIPHOLUS of Syracuse and ANTIPHOLUS of Ephesus

DROMIO OF SYRACUSE: There is a fat friend at your master's house,

That kitchen'd me for you to-day at dinner;
She now shall be my sister, not my wife.

DROMIO OF EPHESUS: Methinks you are my glass, and not my brother;

I see by you I am a sweet-faced youth.
Will you walk in to see their gossiping?

DROMIO OF SYRACUSE: Not I, sir; you are my elder.

DROMIO OF EPHESUS: That's a question: how shall we try it?

DROMIO OF SYRACUSE: We'll draw cuts for the senior; till then lead thou first.

DROMIO OF EPHESUS: Nay, then, thus:

We came into the world like brother and brother;
And now let's go hand in hand, not one before another.

Exeunt

Cymbeline

DRAMATIS PERSONÆ

CYMBELINE, *King of Britain*
CLOTEN, *son to the Queen by a former husband*
POSTHUMUS LEONATUS, *a gentleman, husband to Imogen*
BELARIUS, *a banished lord, disguised under the name of MORGAN*
GUIDERIUS, ARVIRAGUS, *sons to Cymbeline, disguised under the names of POLYDORE and CADWAL, supposed sons to Belarius*
PHILARIO, *friend to Posthumus,*
IACHIMO, friend to Philario, Italians
A French Gentleman, *friend to Philario*
CAIUS LUCIUS, *General of the Roman Forces*
A Roman Captain
Two British Captains
PISANIO, *servant to Posthumus*
CORNELIUS, *a physician*
Two Lords *of Cymbeline's court*
Two Gentlemen *of the same*
Two Gaolers

QUEEN, *wife to Cymbeline*
IMOGEN, *daughter to Cymbeline by a former queen*
HELEN, *a lady attending on Imogen*

Apparitions

Lords, Ladies, Roman Senators, Tribunes, a Dutch Gentleman, a Spanish Gentleman, a Soothsayer, Musicians, Officers, Captains, Soldiers, Messengers, and Attendants

THE SCENE: *Britain; Italy*

Act I

Scene I—*Britain: The garden of Cymbeline's palace*

Enter two Gentlemen

FIRST GENTLEMAN: You do not meet a man but frowns; our bloods
No more obey the heavens than our courtiers
Still seem as does the king.

SECOND GENTLEMAN: But what's the` matter?

FIRST GENTLEMAN: His daughter, and the heir of's kingdom, whom
He purposed to his wife's sole son—a widow
That late he married—hath referr'd herself
Unto a poor but worthy gentleman: she's wedded;
Her husband banish'd; she imprison'd: all

Is outward sorrow; though I think the king
Be touch'd at very heart.

SECOND GENTLEMAN: None but the king?

FIRST GENTLEMAN: He that hath lost her too; so is the queen,
That most desired the match; but not a courtier,
Although they wear their faces to the bent
Of the king's look's, hath a heart that is not
Glad at the thing they scowl at.

SECOND GENTLEMAN: And why so?

FIRST GENTLEMAN: He that hath miss'd the princess is a thing
Too bad for bad report; and he that hath her—
I mean, that married her, alack, good man!
And therefore banish'd—is a creature such
As, to seek through the regions of the earth
For one his like, there would be something failing
In him that should compare. I do not think
So fair an outward and such stuff within
Endows a man but he.

SECOND GENTLEMAN: You speak him far.

FIRST GENTLEMAN: I do extend him, sir, within himself,
Crush him together rather than unfold
His measure duly.

SECOND GENTLEMAN: What's his name and birth?

FIRST GENTLEMAN: I cannot delve him to the root; his father
Was call'd Sicilius, who did join his honour
Against the Romans with Cassibelan,
But had his titles by Tenantius whom
He served with glory and admired success,
So gain'd the sur-addition Leonatus;
And had, besides this gentleman in question,
Two other sons, who in the wars o' the time
Died with their swords in hand; for which their father,
Then old and fond of issue, took such sorrow
That he quit being, and his gentle lady,
Big of this gentleman our theme, deceased
As he was born. The king he takes the babe
To his protection, calls him Posthumus Leonatus,
Breeds him and makes him of his bed-chamber,
Puts to him all the learnings that his time
Could make him the receiver of; which he took,
As we do air, fast as 'twas minister'd,
And in's spring became a harvest, lived in court—
Which rare it is to do—most praised, most loved,
A sample to the youngest, to the more mature
A glass that feated them, and to the graver
A child that guided dotards; to his mistress,
For whom he now is banish'd, her own price
Proclaims how she esteem'd him and his virtue;
By her election may be truly read
What kind of man he is.

SECOND GENTLEMAN: I honour him
Even out of your report. But, pray you tell me,
Is she sole child to the king?

FIRST GENTLEMAN: His only child.
He had two sons—if this be worth your hearing,
Mark it: the eldest of them at three years old,
I' the swathing-clothes the other, from their nursery
Were stol'n, and to this hour no guess in knowledge
Which way they went.

SECOND GENTLEMAN: How long is this ago?

FIRST GENTLEMAN: Some twenty years.

SECOND GENTLEMAN: That a king's children should be so convey'd,
So slackly guarded, and the search so slow,
That could not trace them!

FIRST GENTLEMAN: Howsoe'er 'tis strange,
Or that the negligence may well be laugh'd at,
Yet is it true, sir.

SECOND GENTLEMAN: I do well believe you.

FIRST GENTLEMAN: We must forbear: here comes the gentleman,
The queen, and princess.

Exeunt

Enter the QUEEN, POSTHUMUS LEONATUS, and IMOGEN

QUEEN: No, be assured you shall not find me, daughter,
After the slander of most stepmothers,
Evil-eyed unto you: you're my prisoner, but
Your gaoler shall deliver you the keys
That lock up your restraint. For you, Posthumus,
So soon as I can win the offended king,

I will be known your advocate: marry, yet
The fire of rage is in him, and 'twere good
You lean'd unto his sentence with what patience
Your wisdom may inform you.
POSTHUMUS LEONATUS: Please your highness,
I will from hence today.
QUEEN: You know the peril.
I'll fetch a turn about the garden, pitying
The pangs of barr'd affections, though the king
Hath charged you should not speak together.

Exit

IMOGEN Dissembling courtesy! How fine this tyrant
Can tickle where she wounds! My dearest husband,
I something fear my father's wrath; but nothing—
Always reserved my holy duty—what
His rage can do on me, you must be gone;
And I shall here abide the hourly shot
Of angry eyes, not comforted to live,
But that there is this jewel in the world
That I may see again.
POSTHUMUS LEONATUS: My queen! my mistress!
O lady, weep no more, lest I give cause
To be suspected of more tenderness
Than doth become a man. I will remain
The loyal'st husband that did e'er plight troth:
My residence in Rome at one Philario's,
Who to my father was a friend, to me
Known but by letter; thither write, my queen,
And with mine eyes I'll drink the words you send,
Though ink be made of gall.

Re-enter QUEEN

QUEEN: Be brief, I pray you:
If the king come, I shall incur I know not
How much of his displeasure. *Aside*
Yet I'll move him
To walk this way: I never do him wrong,
But he does buy my injuries, to be friends;
Pays dear for my offences.

Exit

POSTHUMUS LEONATUS: Should we be taking leave
As long a term as yet we have to live,
The loathness to depart would grow. Adieu!
IMOGEN: Nay, stay a little:
Were you but riding forth to air yourself,
Such parting were too petty. Look here, love;
This diamond was my mother's; take it, heart;
But keep it till you woo another wife,
When Imogen is dead.
POSTHUMUS LEONATUS: How, how! another?
You gentle gods, give me but this I have,
And sear up my embracements from a next
With bonds of death! (*Putting on the ring*)
Remain, remain thou here
While sense can keep it on. And, sweetest, fairest,
As I my poor self did exchange for you,
To your so infinite loss, so in our trifles
I still win of you. For my sake wear this;
It is a manacle of love; I'll place it
Upon this fairest prisoner.

Putting a bracelet upon her arm

IMOGEN: O the gods!
When shall we see again?

Enter CYMBELINE and Lords

POSTHUMUS LEONATUS: Alack, the king!
CYMBELINE: Thou basest thing, avoid; hence, from my sight!
If after this command thou fraught the court
With thy unworthiness, thou diest. Away!
Thou'rt poison to my blood.
POSTHUMUS LEONATUS: The gods protect you!
And bless the good remainders of the court!
I am gone.

Exit

IMOGEN: There cannot be a pinch in death
More sharp than this is.
CYMBELINE: O disloyal thing,
That shouldst repair my youth, thou heap'st
A year's age on me.
IMOGEN: I beseech you, sir,
Harm not yourself with your vexation
I am senseless of your wrath; a touch more rare
Subdues all pangs, all fears.
CYMBELINE: Past grace? obedience?
IMOGEN: Past hope, and in despair; that way, past grace.
CYMBELINE: That mightst have had the sole son of my queen!
IMOGEN: O blest, that I might not! I chose an eagle,

And did avoid a puttock.
CYMBELINE: Thou took'st a beggar; wouldst have made my throne
A seat for baseness.
IMOGEN: No; I rather added
A lustre to it.
CYMBELINE: O thou vile one!
IMOGEN: Sir,
It is your fault that I have loved Posthumus.
You bred him as my playfellow, and he is
A man worth any woman, overbuys me
Almost the sum he pays.
CYMBELINE: What, art thou mad?
IMOGEN: Almost, sir. Heaven restore me! Would I were
A neat-herd's daughter, and my Leonatus
Our neighbour shepherd's son!

Re-enter QUEEN

CYMBELINE: Thou foolish thing!
They were again together. You have done
Not after our command. Away with her,
And pen her up.
QUEEN: Beseech your patience. Peace,
Dear lady daughter, peace! Sweet sovereign,
Leave us to ourselves; and make yourself some comfort
Out of your best advice.
CYMBELINE: Nay, let her languish
A drop of blood a day; and, being aged,
Die of this folly!

Exeunt CYMBELINE and Lords

QUEEN: Fie! you must give way.

Enter PISANIO

Here is your servant. How now, sir! What news?
PISANIO: My lord your son drew on my master.
QUEEN: Ha!
No harm, I trust, is done?
PISANIO: There might have been,
But that my master rather play'd than fought
And had no help of anger; they were parted
By gentlemen at hand.
QUEEN: I am very glad on't.
IMOGEN: Your son's my father's friend; he takes his part.
To draw upon an exile! O brave sir!
I would they were in Afric both together;
Myself by with a needle, that I might prick
The goer-back. Why came you from your master?
PISANIO: On his command. He would not suffer me
To bring him to the haven; left these notes
Of what commands I should be subject to,
When't pleased you to employ me.
QUEEN: This hath been
Your faithful servant. I dare lay mine honour
He will remain so.
PISANIO: I humbly thank your highness.
QUEEN: Pray, walk awhile.
IMOGEN: About some half-hour hence,
I pray you, speak with me. You shall at least
Go see my lord aboard. For this time leave me.

Exeunt

SCENE II—*Britain: A public place*

Enter CLOTEN and two Lords

FIRST LORD: Sir, I would advise you to shift a shirt; the violence of action hath made you reek as a sacrifice. Where air comes out, air comes in: there's none abroad so wholesome as that you vent.

CLOTEN: If my shirt were bloody, then to shift it. Have I hurt him?

SECOND LORD: [*Aside*] No, faith; not so much as his patience.

FIRST LORD: Hurt him! his body's a passable carcass, if he be not hurt. It is a thoroughfare for steel, if it be not hurt.

SECOND LORD: [*Aside*] His steel was in debt; it went o' the backside the town.

CLOTEN: The villain would not stand me.

SECOND LORD: [*Aside*] No; but he fled forward still, toward your face.

FIRST LORD: Stand you! You have land enough of your own; but he added to your having; gave you some ground.

SECOND LORD: [*Aside*] As many inches as you have oceans. Puppies!

CLOTEN: I would they had not come between us.

SECOND LORD: [*Aside*] So would I, till you had measured how long a fool you were upon the ground.

CLOTEN: And that she should love this fellow and refuse me!

SECOND LORD: [*Aside*] If it be a sin to make a true election, she is damned.

FIRST LORD: Sir, as I told you always, her beauty and her brain go not together: she's a good sign, but I have seen small reflection of her wit.

SECOND LORD: [*Aside*] She shines not upon fools, lest the reflection should hurt her.

CLOTEN: Come, I'll to my chamber. Would there had been some hurt done!

SECOND LORD: [*Aside*] I wish not so; unless it had been the fall of an ass, which is no great hurt.

CLOTEN: You'll go with us?

FIRST LORD: I'll attend your lordship.

CLOTEN: Nay, come, let's go together.

SECOND LORD: Well, my lord.

Exeunt

SCENE III—*Britain: Cymbeline's palace*

Enter IMOGEN and PISANIO

IMOGEN: I would thou grew'st unto the shores o' the haven,
And question'dst every sail: if he should write
And not have it, 'twere a paper lost,
As offer'd mercy is. What was the last
That he spake to thee?

PISANIO: It was his queen, his queen!

IMOGEN: Then waved his handkerchief?

PISANIO: And kiss'd it, madam.

IMOGEN: Senseless Linen! happier therein than I!
And that was all?

PISANIO: No, madam; for so long
As he could make me with his eye or ear
Distinguish him from others, he did keep
The deck, with glove, or hat, or handkerchief,
Still waving, as the fits and stirs of 's mind
Could best express how slow his soul sail'd on,
How swift his ship.

IMOGEN: Thou shouldst have made him
As little as a crow, or less, ere left
To after-eye him.

PISANIO: Madam, so I did.

IMOGEN: I would have broke mine eye-strings; crack'd them, but
To look upon him, till the diminution
Of space had pointed him sharp as my needle,
Nay, follow'd him, till he had melted from
The smallness of a gnat to air, and then
Have turn'd mine eye and wept. But, good Pisanio,
When shall we hear from him?

PISANIO: Be assured, madam,
With his next vantage.

IMOGEN: I did not take my leave of him, but had
Most pretty things to say. Ere I could tell him
How I would think on him at certain hours
Such thoughts and such, or I could make him swear
The shes of Italy should not betray
Mine interest and his honour, or have charged him,
At the sixth hour of morn, at noon, at midnight,
To encounter me with orisons, for then
I am in heaven for him; or ere I could
Give him that parting kiss which I had set
Betwixt two charming words, comes in my father
And like the tyrannous breathing of the north
Shakes all our buds from growing.

Enter a Lady

LADY: The queen, madam,
Desires your highness' company.

IMOGEN: Those things I bid you do, get them dispatch'd.
I will attend the queen.

PISANIO: Madam, I shall.

Exeunt

SCENE IV—*Rome: Philario's house*

Enter PHILARIO, IACHIMO, a Frenchman, a Dutchman, and a Spaniard

IACHIMO: Believe it, sir, I have seen him in Britain: he was then of a crescent note, expected to prove so worthy as since he hath been allowed the name of; but I could then have looked on him without the help of admiration, though the catalogue of his endowments had been tabled by his side and I to peruse him by items.

PHILARIO: You speak of him when he was less furnished than now he is with that which makes him both without and within.

FRENCHMAN: I have seen him in France: we had very many there could behold the sun with as firm eyes as he.

IACHIMO: This matter of marrying his king's daughter, wherein he must be weighed rather by her value than his own, words him, I doubt not, a great deal from the matter.

FRENCHMAN: And then his banishment.

IACHIMO: Ay, and the approbation of those that weep this lamentable divorce under her colours are wonderfully to extend him; be it but to fortify her judgment, which else an easy battery might lay flat, for taking a beggar without less quality. But how comes it he is to sojourn with you? How creeps acquaintance?

PHILARIO: His father and I were soldiers together; to whom I have been often bound for no less than my life. Here comes the Briton. Let him be so entertained amongst you as suits, with gentlemen of your knowing, to a stranger of his quality.

Enter POSTHUMUS LEONATUS

I beseech you all, be better known to this gentleman; whom I commend to you as a noble friend of mine: how worthy he is I will leave to appear hereafter, rather than story him in his own hearing.

FRENCHMAN: Sir, we have known together in Orleans.

POSTHUMUS LEONATUS: Since when I have been debtor to you for courtesies, which I will be ever to pay and yet pay still.

FRENCHMAN: Sir, you o'er-rate my poor kindness. I was glad I did atone my countryman and you; it had been pity you should have been put together with so mortal a purpose as then each bore, upon importance of so slight and trivial a nature.

POSTHUMUS LEONATUS: By your pardon, sir, I was then a young traveller; rather shunned to go even with what I heard than in my every action to be guided by others' experiences; but upon my mended judgment—if I offend not to say it is mended—my quarrel was not altogether slight.

FRENCHMAN: Faith, yes, to be put to the arbitrement of swords, and by such two that would by all likelihood have confounded one the other, or have fallen both.

IACHIMO: Can we, with manners, ask what was the difference?

FRENCHMAN: Safely, I think: 'twas a contention in public, which may, without contradiction, suffer the report. It was much like an argument that fell out last night, where each of us fell in praise of our country mistresses; this gentleman at that time vouching—and upon warrant of bloody affirmation—his to be more fair, virtuous, wise, chaste, constant-qualified and less attemptable than any the rarest of our ladies in France.

IACHIMO: That lady is not now living, or this gentleman's opinion by this worn out.

POSTHUMUS LEONATUS: She holds her virtue still and I my mind.

IACHIMO: You must not so far prefer her fore ours of Italy.

POSTHUMUS LEONATUS: Being so far provoked as I was in France, I would abate her nothing, though I profess myself her adorer, not her friend.

IACHIMO: As fair and as good—a kind of hand-in-hand comparison—had been something too fair and too good for any lady in Britain. If she went before others I have seen, as that diamond of yours outlustres many I have beheld. I could not but believe she excelled many; but I have not seen the most precious diamond that is, nor you the lady.

POSTHUMUS LEONATUS: I praised her as I rated her: so do I my stone.

IACHIMO: What do you esteem it at?

POSTHUMUS LEONATUS: More than the world enjoys.

IACHIMO: Either your unparagoned mistress is dead, or she's outprized by a trifle.

POSTHUMUS LEONATUS: You are mistaken; the one may be sold, or given, if there were wealth enough for the purchase, or merit for the gift: the other is not a thing for sale, and only the gift of the gods.

IACHIMO: Which the gods have given you?

POSTHUMUS LEONATUS: Which, by their graces, I will keep.

IACHIMO: You may wear her in title yours: but, you know, strange fowl light upon neighbouring ponds. Your ring may be stolen too. So your brace of unprizable estimations; the one is but frail and the other casual; a cunning thief, or a that way accomplished courtier, would hazard the winning both of first and last.

POSTHUMUS LEONATUS: Your Italy contains none so accomplished a courtier to convince the honour of my mistress, if, in the holding or loss of that you term her frail. I do nothing doubt you have store of thieves; notwithstanding, I fear not my ring.

PHILARIO: Let us leave here, gentlemen.

POSTHUMUS LEONATUS: Sir, with all my heart. This worthy signior, I thank him, makes no stranger of me; we are familiar at first.
IACHIMO: With five times so much conversation, I should get ground of your fair mistress, make her go back, even to the yielding, had I admittance and opportunity to friend.
POSTHUMUS LEONATUS: No, no.
IACHIMO: I dare thereupon pawn the moiety of my estate to your ring; which, in my opinion, o'ervalues it something: but I make my wager rather against your confidence than her reputation: and, to bar your offence herein too, I durst attempt it against any lady in the world.
POSTHUMUS LEONATUS: You are a great deal abused in too bold a persuasion; and I doubt not you sustain what you're worthy of by your attempt.
IACHIMO: What's that?
POSTHUMUS LEONATUS: A repulse: though your attempt, as you call it, deserve more; a punishment too.
PHILARIO: Gentlemen, enough of this. It came in too suddenly; let it die as it was born, and, I pray you, be better acquainted.
IACHIMO: Would I had put my estate and my neighbour's on the approbation of what I have spoke!
POSTHUMUS LEONATUS: What lady would you choose to assail?
IACHIMO: Yours, whom in constancy you think stands so safe. I will lay you ten thousand ducats to your ring, that, commend me to the court where your lady is, with no more advantage than the opportunity of a second conference, and I will bring from thence that honour of hers which you imagine so reserved.
POSTHUMUS LEONATUS: I will wage against your gold, gold to it. My ring I hold dear as my finger; 'tis part of it.
IACHIMO: You are afraid, and therein the wiser. If you buy ladies' flesh at a million a dram, you cannot preserve it from tainting: but I see you have some religion in you, that you fear.
POSTHUMUS LEONATUS: This is but a custom in your tongue; you bear a graver purpose, I hope.
IACHIMO: I am the master of my speeches, and would undergo what's spoken, I swear.
POSTHUMUS LEONATUS: Will you? I shall but lend my diamond till your return. Let there be covenants drawn between's. My mistress exceeds in goodness the hugeness of your unworthy thinking. I dare you to this match: here's my ring.
PHILARIO: I will have it no lay.
IACHIMO: By the gods, it is one. If I bring you no sufficient testimony that I have enjoyed the dearest bodily part of your mistress, my ten thousand ducats are yours; so is your diamond too. If I come off, and leave her in such honour as you have trust in, she your jewel, this your jewel, and my gold are yours—provided I have your commendation for my more free entertainment.
POSTHUMUS LEONATUS: I embrace these conditions; let us have articles betwixt us. Only, thus far you shall answer: if you make your voyage upon her and give me directly to understand you have prevailed, I am no further your enemy—she is not worth our debate; if she remain unseduced, you not making it appear otherwise, for your ill opinion and the assault you have made to her chastity you shall answer me with your sword.
IACHIMO: Your hand—a covenant! We will have these things set down by lawful counsel, and straight away for Britain, lest the bargain should catch cold and starve. I will fetch my gold and have our two wagers recorded.
POSTHUMUS LEONATUS: Agreed.

Exeunt POSTHUMUS LEONATUS and IACHIMO

FRENCHMAN: Will this hold, think you?
PHILARIO: Signior Iachimo will not from it. Pray, let us follow 'em.

Exeunt

SCENE V—*Britain: Cymbeline's palace*

Enter QUEEN, Ladies, and CORNELIUS

QUEEN: Whiles yet the dew's on ground, gather those flowers;
Make haste; who has the note of them?
First Lady: I, madam.
QUEEN: Dispatch.

Exeunt Ladies

Now, master doctor, have you brought those drugs?
CORNELIUS: Pleaseth your highness, ay. Here they are, madam: (*Presenting a small box*)
But I beseech your grace, without offence—

My conscience bids me ask—wherefore you have
Commanded of me those most poisonous compounds,
Which are the movers of a languishing death;
But though slow, deadly?

QUEEN: I wonder, doctor,
Thou ask'st me such a question. Have I not been
Thy pupil long? Hast thou not learn'd me how
To make perfumes? distil? preserve? yea, so
That our great king himself doth woo me oft
For my confections? Having thus far proceeded—
Unless thou think'st me devilish—is't not meet
That I did amplify my judgment in
Other conclusions? I will try the forces
Of these thy compounds on such creatures as
We count not worth the hanging—but none human—
To try the vigour of them and apply
Allayments to their act, and by them gather
Their several virtues and effects.

CORNELIUS: Your highness
Shall from this practise but make hard your heart;
Besides, the seeing these effects will be
Both noisome and infectious.

QUEEN: O, content thee.

Enter PISANIO

Aside

Here comes a flattering rascal; upon him
Will I first work. He's for his master,
An enemy to my son. How now, Pisanio!
Doctor, your service for this time is ended;
Take your own way.

CORNELIUS: [*Aside*] I do suspect you, madam;
But you shall do no harm.

QUEEN: [*To Pisanio*] Hark thee, a word.

CORNELIUS: [*Aside*] I do not like her. She doth think she has
Strange lingering poisons. I do know her spirit,
And will not trust one of her malice with
A drug of such damn'd nature. Those she has
Will stupefy and dull the sense awhile,
Which first perchance she'll prove on cats and dogs,
Then afterward up higher; but there is
No danger in what show of death it makes,
More than the locking-up the spirits a time,
To be more fresh, reviving. She is fool'd
With a most false effect; and I the truer,
So to be false with her.

QUEEN: No further service, doctor,
Until I send for thee.

CORNELIUS: I humbly take my leave.

Exit

QUEEN: Weeps she still, say'st thou? Dost thou think in time
She will not quench and let instructions enter
Where folly now possesses? Do thou work.
When thou shalt bring me word she loves my son,
I'll tell thee on the instant thou art then
As great as is thy master; greater, for
His fortunes all lie speechless and his name
Is at last gasp. Return he cannot, nor
Continue where he is. To shift his being
Is to exchange one misery with another,
And every day that comes comes to decay
A day's work in him. What shalt thou expect,
To be depender on a thing that leans,
Who cannot be new built, nor has no friends,
So much as but to prop him?

The QUEEN drops the box: PISANIO takes it up

Thou takest up
Thou know'st not what; but take it for thy labour.
It is a thing I made, which hath the king
Five times redeem'd from death. I do not know
What is more cordial. Nay, I prethee, take it;
It is an earnest of a further good
That I mean to thee. Tell thy mistress how
The case stands with her; do't as from thyself.
Think what a chance thou changest on, but think
Thou hast thy mistress still, to boot, my son,
Who shall take notice of thee. I'll move the king
To any shape of thy preferment such
As thou'lt desire; and then myself, I chiefly,
That set thee on to this desert, am bound
To load thy merit richly. Call my women.
Think on my words.

Exit PISANIO

A sly and constant knave,
Not to be shaked; the agent for his master
And the remembrancer of her to hold
The hand-fast to her lord. I have given him that
Which, if he take, shall quite unpeople her
Of liegers for her sweet, and which she after,
Except she bend her humour, shall be assured
To taste of too.

Re-enter PISANIO and Ladies

So, so. Well done, well done.
The violets, cowslips, and the primroses,
Bear to my closet. Fare thee well, Pisanio;
Think on my words.

Exeunt QUEEN and Ladies

PISANIO: And shall do.
But when to my good lord I prove untrue,
I'll choke myself—there's all I'll do for you.

Exit

SCENE VI—*Britain: The palace*

Enter IMOGEN

IMOGEN: A father cruel and a step-dame false;
A foolish suitor to a wedded lady,
That hath her husband banish'd. O, that husband!
My supreme crown of grief! and those repeated
Vexations of it! Had I been thief-stol'n,
As my two brothers, happy! but most miserable
Is the desire that's glorious. Blessed be those,
How mean soe'er, that have their honest wills,
Which seasons comfort. Who may this be? Fie!

Enter PISANIO and IACHIMO

PISANIO: Madam, a noble gentleman of Rome
Comes from my lord with letters.
IACHIMO: Change you, madam?
The worthy Leonatus is in safety
And greets your highness dearly.

Presents a letter

IMOGEN: Thanks, good sir.
You're kindly welcome.
IACHIMO: [*Aside*] All of her that is out of door most rich!
If she be furnish'd with a mind so rare,
She is alone the Arabian bird, and I
Have lost the wager. Boldness be my friend!
Arm me, audacity, from head to foot!
Or, like the Parthian, I shall flying fight;
Rather directly fly.
IMOGEN: [*Reads*] 'He is one of the noblest note, to whose kindnesses I am most infinitely tied. Reflect upon him accordingly, as you value your trust—LEONATUS.'
So far I read aloud;
But even the very middle of my heart
Is warm'd by the rest, and takes it thankfully.
You are as welcome, worthy sir, as I
Have words to bid you, and shall find it so
In all that I can do.
IACHIMO: Thanks, fairest lady.
What, are men mad? Hath nature given them eyes
To see this vaulted arch, and the rich crop
Of sea and land, which can distinguish 'twixt
The fiery orbs above and the twinn'd stones
Upon the number'd beach? and can we not
Partition make with spectacles so precious
'Twixt fair and foul?
IMOGEN: What makes your admiration?
IACHIMO: It cannot be i' the eye, for apes and monkeys
'Twixt two such shes would chatter this way and
Contemn with mows the other; nor i' the judgment,
For idiots in this case of favour would
Be wisely definite; nor i' the appetite;
Sluttery to such neat excellence opposed
Should make desire vomit emptiness,
Not so allured to feed.
IMOGEN: What is the matter, trow?
IACHIMO: The cloyed will—
That satiate yet unsatisfied desire, that tub
Both fill'd and running—ravening first the lamb
Longs after for the garbage.
IMOGEN: What, dear sir,
Thus raps you? Are you well?
IACHIMO: Thanks, madam; well.

To PISANIO

Beseech you, sir, desire
My man's abode where I did leave him. He
Is strange and peevish.

PISANIO: I was going, sir,
To give him welcome.
Exit
IMOGEN: Continues well my lord? His health, beseech you?
IACHIMO: Well, madam.
IMOGEN: Is he disposed to mirth? I hope he is.
IACHIMO: Exceeding pleasant; none a stranger there
So merry and so gamesome: he is call'd
The Briton reveller.
IMOGEN: When he was here,
He did incline to sadness, and oft-times
Not knowing why.
IACHIMO: I never saw him sad.
There is a Frenchman his companion, one
An eminent monsieur, that, it seems, much loves
A Gallian girl at home; he furnaces
The thick sighs from him; whiles the jolly Briton—
Your lord, I mean—laughs from's free lungs, cries 'O,
Can my sides hold, to think that man—who knows
By history, report, or his own proof,
What woman is, yea, what she cannot choose
But must be—will his free hours languish for
Assured bondage?'
IMOGEN: Will my lord say so?
IACHIMO: Ay, madam, with his eyes in flood with laughter.
It is a recreation to be by
And hear him mock the Frenchman. But, heavens know
Some men are much to blame.
IMOGEN: Not he, I hope.
IACHIMO: Not he; but yet heaven's bounty towards him might
Be used more thankfully. In himself, 'tis much;
In you, which I account his beyond all talents,
Whilst I am bound to wonder, I am bound
To pity too.
IMOGEN: What do you pity, sir?
IACHIMO: Two creatures heartily.
IMOGEN: Am I one, sir?
You look on me: what wreck discern you in me
Deserves your pity?
IACHIMO: Lamentable! What,
To hide me from the radiant sun and solace
I' the dungeon by a snuff?
IMOGEN: I pray you, sir,
Deliver with more openness your answers
To my demands. Why do you pity me?
IACHIMO: That others do—
I was about to say—enjoy your—But
It is an office of the gods to venge it,
Not mine to speak on't.
IMOGEN: You do seem to know
Something of me, or what concerns me: pray you—
Since doubling things go ill often hurts more
Than to be sure they do; for certainties
Either are past remedies, or, timely knowing,
The remedy then born—discover to me
What both you spur and stop.
IACHIMO: Had I this cheek
To bathe my lips upon; this hand, whose touch,
Whose every touch, would force the feeler's soul
To the oath of loyalty; this object, which
Takes prisoner the wild motion of mine eye,
Fixing it only here; should I, damn'd then,
Slaver with lips as common as the stairs
That mount the Capitol; join gripes with hands
Made hard with hourly falsehood—falsehood, as
With labour; then by-peeping in an eye
Base and unlustrous as the smoky light
That's fed with stinking tallow; it were fit
That all the plagues of hell should at one time
Encounter such revolt.
IMOGEN: My lord, I fear,
Has forgot Britain.
IACHIMO: And himself. Not I,
Inclined to this intelligence, pronounce
The beggary of his change; but 'tis your graces
That from pay mutest conscience to my tongue
Charms this report out.
IMOGEN: Let me hear no more.
IACHIMO: O dearest soul! your cause doth strike my heart
With pity, that doth make me sick. A lady
So fair, and fasten'd to an empery,

Would make the great'st king double—to be partner'd
With tomboys hired with that self-exhibition
Which your own coffers yield! with diseased ventures
That play with all infirmities for gold
Which rottenness can lend nature! such boil'd stuff
As well might poison poison! Be revenged;
Or she that bore you was no queen, and you
Recoil from your great stock.

IMOGEN: Revenged!
How should I be revenged? If this be true—
As I have such a heart that both mine ears
Must not in haste abuse—if it be true,
How should I be revenged?

IACHIMO: Should he make me
Live like Diana's priest, betwixt cold sheets,
Whiles he is vaulting variable ramps,
In your despite, upon your purse? Revenge it.
I dedicate myself to your sweet pleasure,
More noble than that runagate to your bed,
And will continue fast to your affection,
Still close as sure.

IMOGEN: What, ho, Pisanio!

IACHIMO: Let me my service tender on your lips.

IMOGEN: Away! I do condemn mine ears that have
So long attended thee. If thou wert honourable,
Thou wouldst have told this tale for virtue, not
For such an end thou seek'st, as base as strange.
Thou wrong'st a gentleman, who is as far
From thy report as thou from honour, and
Solicit'st here a lady that disdains
Thee and the devil alike. What ho, Pisanio!
The king my father shall be made acquainted
Of thy assault. If he shall think it fit,
A saucy stranger in his court to mart
As in a Romish stew and to expound
His beastly mind to us, he hath a court
He little cares for and a daughter who
He not respects at all. What, ho, Pisanio!

IACHIMO: O happy Leonatus! I may say
The credit that thy lady hath of thee
Deserves thy trust, and thy most perfect goodness
Her assured credit. Blessed live you long!
A lady to the worthiest sir that ever
Country call'd his! and you his mistress, only
For the most worthiest fit! Give me your pardon.
I have spoke this, to know if your affiance
Were deeply rooted; and shall make your lord,
That which he is, new o'er; and he is one
The truest manner'd; such a holy witch
That he enchants societies into him;
Half all men's hearts are his.

IMOGEN: You make amends.

IACHIMO: He sits 'mongst men like a descended god:
He hath a kind of honour sets him off
More than a mortal seeming. Be not angry,
Most mighty princess, that I have adventured
To try your taking a false report, which hath
Honour'd with confirmation your great judgment
In the election of a sir so rare,
Which you know cannot err. The love I bear him
Made me to fan you thus, but the gods made you,
Unlike all others, chaffless. Pray, your pardon.

IMOGEN: All's well, sir; take my power i' the court for yours.

IACHIMO: My humble thanks. I had almost forgot
To entreat your grace but in a small request,
And yet of moment to, for it concerns
Your lord; myself and other noble friends,
Are partners in the business.

IMOGEN: Pray, what is't?

IACHIMO: Some dozen Romans of us and your lord—
The best feather of our wing—have mingled sums
To buy a present for the emperor
Which I, the factor for the rest, have done
In France. 'Tis plate of rare device, and jewels
Of rich and exquisite form; their values great;
And I am something curious, being strange,
To have them in safe stowage. May it please you
To take them in protection?

IMOGEN: Willingly;
And pawn mine honour for their safety. Since
My lord hath interest in them, I will keep them
In my bedchamber.

IACHIMO: They are in a trunk,

Attended by my men. I will make bold
To send them to you, only for this night;
I must aboard to-morrow.

IMOGEN: O, no, no.

IACHIMO: Yes, I beseech; or I shall short my word
By lengthening my return. From Gallia
I cross'd the seas on purpose and on promise
To see your grace.

IMOGEN: I thank you for your pains.
But not away to-morrow!

IACHIMO: O, I must, madam.
Therefore I shall beseech you, if you please
To greet your lord with writing, do't to-night.
I have outstood my time; which is material
To the tender of our present.

IMOGEN: I will write.
Send your trunk to me; it shall safe be kept
And truly yielded you. You're very welcome.

Exeunt

Act II

Scene I—*Britain: Before Cymbeline's palace*

Enter CLOTEN and two Lords

CLOTEN: Was there ever man had such luck! when I kissed the jack, upon an up-cast to be hit away! I had a hundred pound on't; and then a whoreson jackanapes must take me up for swearing; as if I borrowed mine oaths of him and might not spend them at my pleasure.

FIRST LORD: What got he by that? You have broke his pate with your bowl.

SECOND LORD: [*Aside*] If his wit had been like him that broke it, it would have run all out.

CLOTEN: When a gentleman is disposed to swear, it is not for any standers-by to curtail his oaths, ha?

SECOND LORD: No my lord; [Aside] nor crop the ears of them.

CLOTEN: Whoreson dog! I give him satisfaction? Would he had been one of my rank!

SECOND LORD: [*Aside*] To have smelt like a fool.

CLOTEN: I am not vexed more at any thing in the earth. A pox on't! I had rather not be so noble as I am; they dare not fight with me, because of the queen my mother. Every Jack-slave hath his bellyful of fighting, and I must go up and down like a cock that nobody can match.

SECOND LORD: [*Aside*] You are cock and capon too; and you crow, cock, with your comb on.

CLOTEN: Sayest thou?

SECOND LORD: It is not fit your lordship should undertake every companion that you give offence to.

CLOTEN: No, I know that; but it is fit I should commit offence to my inferiors.

SECOND LORD: Ay, it is fit for your lordship only.

CLOTEN: Why, so I say.

FIRST LORD: Did you hear of a stranger that's come to court to-night?

CLOTEN: A stranger, and I not know on't!

SECOND LORD: [*Aside*] He's a strange fellow himself, and knows it not.

FIRST LORD: There's an Italian come; and, 'tis thought, one of Leonatus' friends.

CLOTEN: Leonatus! a banished rascal; and he's another, whatsoever he be. Who told you of this stranger?

FIRST LORD: One of your lordship's pages.

CLOTEN: Is it fit I went to look upon him? is there no derogation in't?

SECOND LORD: You cannot derogate, my lord.

CLOTEN: Not easily, I think.

SECOND LORD: [*Aside*] You are a fool granted; therefore your issues, being foolish, do not derogate.

CLOTEN: Come, I'll go see this Italian. What I have lost to-day at bowls I'll win to-night of him. Come, go.

SECOND LORD: I'll attend your lordship.

Exeunt CLOTEN and First Lord

That such a crafty devil as is his mother
Should yield the world this ass! A woman that
Bears all down with her brain; and this her son
Cannot take two from twenty, for his heart,
And leave eighteen. Alas, poor princess,
Thou divine Imogen, what thou endurest,
Betwixt a father by thy step-dame govern'd,
A mother hourly coining plots, a wooer
More hateful than the foul expulsion is
Of thy dear husband, than that horrid act
Of the divorce he'ld make! The heavens hold firm
The walls of thy dear honour, keep unshaked
That temple, thy fair mind, that thou mayst stand,
To enjoy thy banish'd lord and this great land!

Exit

SCENE II—*Britain: Imogen's bedchamber in Cymbeline's palace: a trunk in one corner*

IMOGEN in bed, reading; a Lady attending

IMOGEN: Who's there? My woman Helen?
LADY: Please you, madam
IMOGEN: What hour is it?
LADY: Almost midnight, madam.
IMOGEN: I have read three hours then. Mine eyes are weak:
Fold down the leaf where I have left. To bed.
Take not away the taper, leave it burning;
And if thou canst awake by four o' the clock,
I prithee, call me. Sleep hath seized me wholly

Exit Lady

To your protection I commend me, gods.
From fairies and the tempters of the night
Guard me, beseech ye.

Sleeps IACHIMO comes from the trunk

IACHIMO: The crickets sing, and man's o'er-labour'd sense
Repairs itself by rest. Our Tarquin thus
Did softly press the rushes, ere he waken'd
The chastity he wounded. Cytherea,
How bravely thou becomest thy bed, fresh lily,
And whiter than the sheets! That I might touch!
But kiss; one kiss! Rubies unparagon'd,
How dearly they do't! 'Tis her breathing that
Perfumes the chamber thus. The flame o' the taper
Bows toward her, and would under-peep her lids
To see the enclosed lights, now canopied
Under these windows, white and azure laced
With blue of heaven's own tinct. But my design,
To note the chamber. I will write all down:
Such and such pictures; there the window; such
The adornment of her bed; the arras; figures,
Why, such and such; and the contents o' the story.
Ah, but some natural notes about her body,
Above ten thousand meaner moveables
Would testify, to enrich mine inventory.
O sleep, thou ape of death, lie dull upon her!
And be her sense but as a monument,
Thus in a chapel lying! Come off, come off;

Taking off her bracelet

As slippery as the Gordian knot was hard!
'Tis mine; and this will witness outwardly,
As strongly as the conscience does within,
To the madding of her lord. On her left breast
A mole cinque-spotted, like the crimson drops
I' the bottom of a cowslip: here's a voucher,
Stronger than ever law could make; this secret
Will force him think I have pick'd the lock and ta'en
The treasure of her honour. No more. To what end?
Why should I write this down, that's riveted,
Screw'd to my memory? She hath been reading late
The tale of Tereus; here the leaf's turn'd down
Where Philomel gave up. I have enough.
To the trunk again, and shut the spring of it.
Swift, swift, you dragons of the night, that dawning
May bare the raven's eye! I lodge in fear;
Though this a heavenly angel, hell is here.

Clock strikes

One, two, three. Time, time!

Goes into the trunk.

SCENE III—*Cymbeline's palace: An ante-chamber adjoining Imogen's apartments*

Enter CLOTEN and Lords

FIRST LORD: Your lordship is the most patient man in loss, the most coldest that ever turned up ace.
CLOTEN: It would make any man cold to lose.
FIRST LORD: But not every man patient after the noble temper of your lordship. You are most hot and furious when you win.
CLOTEN: Winning will put any man into courage. If I could get this foolish Imogen, I should have gold enough. It's almost morning, is't not?
FIRST LORD: Day, my lord.
CLOTEN: I would this music would come. I am advised to give her music a mornings; they say it will penetrate.

Enter Musicians

Come on, tune. If you can penetrate her with your fingering, so; we'll try with tongue too. If none will do, let her remain; but I'll never give o'er. First, a very excellent good-conceited thing; after, a wonderful sweet air, with admirable rich words to it—and then let her consider.

Song

Hark, hark! the lark at heaven's gate sings,
And Phoebus 'gins arise,
His steeds to water at those springs
On chaliced flowers that lies;
And winking Mary-buds begin
To ope their golden eyes.
With every thing that pretty is,
My lady sweet, arise;
Arise, arise.

CLOTEN: So, get you gone. If this penetrate, I will consider your music the better; if it do not, it is a vice in her ears, which horsehairs and calves'guts' nor the voice of unpaved eunuch to boot, can never amend.

Exeunt Musicians

SECOND LORD: Here comes the king.

CLOTEN: I am glad I was up so late, for that's the reason I was up so early. He cannot choose but take this service I have done fatherly.

Enter CYMBELINE and QUEEN

Good morrow to your majesty and to my gracious mother.

CYMBELINE: Attend you here the door of our stern daughter? Will she not forth?

CLOTEN: I have assailed her with music, but she vouchsafes no notice.

CYMBELINE: The exile of her minion is too new;
She hath not yet forgot him; some more time
Must wear the print of his remembrance out,
And then she's yours.

QUEEN: You are most bound to the king,
Who lets go by no vantages that may
Prefer you to his daughter. Frame yourself
To orderly soliciting, and be friended
With aptness of the season; make denials
Increase your services; so seem as if
You were inspired to do those duties which
You tender to her; that you in all obey her,
Save when command to your dismission tends,
And therein you are senseless.

CLOTEN: Senseless! not so.

Enter a Messenger

Messenger: So like you, sir, ambassadors from Rome;
The one is Caius Lucius.

CYMBELINE: A worthy fellow,
Albeit he comes on angry purpose now;
But that's no fault of his. We must receive him
According to the honour of his sender;
And towards himself, his goodness forespent on us,
We must extend our notice. Our dear son,
When you have given good morning to your mistress,
Attend the queen and us; we shall have need
To employ you towards this Roman. Come, our queen.

Exeunt all but CLOTEN

CLOTEN: If she be up, I'll speak with her; if not,
Let her lie still and dream. (*Knocks*) By your leave, ho!
I know her women are about her; what
If I do line one of their hands? 'Tis gold
Which buys admittance; oft it doth—yea, and makes
Diana's rangers false themselves, yield up
Their deer to the stand o' the stealer; and 'tis gold
Which makes the true man kill'd and saves the thief;
Nay, sometime hangs both thief and true man. what
Can it not do and undo? I will make
One of her women lawyer to me, for
I yet not understand the case myself.
(*Knocks*) By your leave.

Enter a Lady

LADY: Who's there that knocks?

CLOTEN: A gentleman.

LADY: No more?

CLOTEN: Yes, and a gentlewoman's son.

LADY: That's more
Than some, whose tailors are as dear as yours,
Can justly boast of. What's your lordship's pleasure?

CLOTEN: Your lady's person; is she ready?

LADY: Ay,
To keep her chamber.
CLOTEN: There is gold for you;
Sell me your good report.
LADY: How! my good name? or to report of you
What I shall think is good? The princess!

Enter IMOGEN

CLOTEN: Good morrow, fairest sister. Your sweet hand.

Exit Lady

IMOGEN: Good morrow, sir. You lay out too much pains
For purchasing but trouble. The thanks I give
Is telling you that I am poor of thanks
And scarce can spare them.
CLOTEN: Still, I swear I love you.
IMOGEN: If you but said so, 'twere as deep with me.
If you swear still, your recompense is still
That I regard it not.
CLOTEN: This is no answer.
IMOGEN: But that you shall not say I yield being silent,
I would not speak. I pray you spare me. Faith,
I shall unfold equal discourtesy
To your best kindness; one of your great knowing
Should learn, being taught, forbearance.
CLOTEN: To leave you in your madness, 'twere my sin; I will not.
IMOGEN: Fools are not mad folks.
CLOTEN: Do you call me fool?
IMOGEN: As I am mad, I do;
If you'll be patient, I'll no more be mad;
That cures us both. I am much sorry, sir,
You put me to forget a lady's manners,
By being so verbal; and learn now, for all,
That I, which know my heart, do here pronounce,
By the very truth of it, I care not for you,
And am so near the lack of charity
To accuse myself I hate you; which I had rather
You felt than make't my boast.
CLOTEN: You sin against
Obedience, which you owe your father. For
The contract you pretend with that base wretch,
One bred of alms and foster'd with cold dishes,
With scraps o' the court—it is no contract, none.
And though it be allow'd in meaner parties—
Yet who than he more mean?—to knit their souls,
On whom there is no more dependency
But brats and beggary—in self-figured knot,
Yet you are curb'd from that enlargement by
The consequence o' the crown, and must not soil
The precious note of it with a base slave.
A hilding for a livery, a squire's cloth,
A pantler, not so eminent.
IMOGEN: Profane fellow!
Wert thou the son of Jupiter and no more
But what thou art besides, thou wert too base
To be his groom. Thou wert dignified enough,
Even to the point of envy, if 'twere made
Comparative for your virtues, to be styled
The under-hangman of his kingdom, and hated
For being preferred so well.
CLOTEN: The south fog rot him!
IMOGEN: He never can meet more mischance than come
To be but named of thee. His meanest garment,
That ever hath but clipp'd his body, is dearer
In my respect than all the hairs above thee,
Were they all made such men. How now, Pisanio!

Enter PISANIO

CLOTEN: 'His garment!' Now the devil—
IMOGEN: To Dorothy my woman hie thee presently.
CLOTEN: 'His garment!'
IMOGEN: I am sprited with a fool;
Frighted, and anger'd worse. Go bid my woman
Search for a jewel that too casually
Hath left mine arm. It was thy master's; 'shrew me,
If I would lose it for a revenue
Of any king's in Europe. I do think
I saw't this morning: confident I am
Last night 'twas on mine arm; I kiss'd it:
I hope it be not gone to tell my lord
That I kiss aught but he.
PISANIO: 'Twill not be lost.
IMOGEN: I hope so. Go and search.

Exit PISANIO

CLOTEN: You have abused me. 'His meanest garment!'

IMOGEN: Ay, I said so, sir.
If you will make't an action, call witness to 't.

CLOTEN: I will inform your father.

IMOGEN: Your mother too.
She's my good lady, and will conceive, I hope,
But the worst of me. So, I leave you, sir,
To the worst of discontent.

Exit

CLOTEN: I'll be revenged: 'His meanest garment!' Well.

Exit

SCENE IV—*Rome: Philario's house*

Enter POSTHUMUS and PHILARIO

POSTHUMUS LEONATUS: Fear it not, sir; I would I were so sure
To win the king as I am bold her honour
Will remain hers.

PHILARIO: What means do you make to him?

POSTHUMUS LEONATUS: Not any; but abide the change of time,
Quake in the present winter's state and wish
That warmer days would come: in these fear'd hopes,
I barely gratify your love; they failing,
I must die much your debtor.

PHILARIO: Your very goodness and your company
O'erpays all I can do. By this your king
Hath heard of great Augustus. Caius Lucius
Will do's commission thoroughly; and I think
He'll grant the tribute, send the arrearages,
Or look upon our Romans, whose remembrance
Is yet fresh in their grief.

POSTHUMUS LEONATUS: I do believe,
Statist though I am none, nor like to be,
That this will prove a war; and you shall hear
The legions now in Gallia sooner landed
In our not-fearing Britain than have tidings
Of any penny tribute paid. Our countrymen
Are men more order'd than when Julius Caesar
Smiled at their lack of skill, but found their courage
Worthy his frowning at. Their discipline,
Now mingled with their courages, will make known
To their approvers they are people such
That mend upon the world.

Enter IACHIMO

PHILARIO: See! Iachimo!

POSTHUMUS LEONATUS: The swiftest harts have posted you by land,
And winds of all the comers kiss'd your sails,
To make your vessel nimble.

PHILARIO: Welcome, sir.

POSTHUMUS LEONATUS: I hope the briefness of your answer made
The speediness of your return.

IACHIMO: Your lady
Is one of the fairest that I have look'd upon.

POSTHUMUS LEONATUS: And therewithal the best; or let her beauty
Look through a casement to allure false hearts
And be false with them.

IACHIMO: Here are letters for you.

POSTHUMUS LEONATUS: Their tenor good, I trust.

IACHIMO: 'Tis very like.

PHILARIO: Was Caius Lucius in the Britain court
When you were there?

IACHIMO: He was expected then,
But not approach'd.

POSTHUMUS LEONATUS: All is well yet.
Sparkles this stone as it was wont? or is't not
Too dull for your good wearing?

IACHIMO: If I had lost it,
I should have lost the worth of it in gold.
I'll make a journey twice as far, to enjoy
A second night of such sweet shortness which
Was mine in Britain, for the ring is won.

POSTHUMUS LEONATUS: The stone's too hard to come by.

IACHIMO: Not a whit, Your lady being so easy.

POSTHUMUS LEONATUS: Make not, sir,
Your loss your sport. I hope you know that we
Must not continue friends.

IACHIMO: Good sir, we must,
If you keep covenant. Had I not brought
The knowledge of your mistress home, I grant
We were to question further; but I now
Profess myself the winner of her honour,
Together with your ring; and not the wronger

Of her or you, having proceeded but
By both your wills.

POSTHUMUS LEONATUS: If you can make't apparent
That you have tasted her in bed, my hand
And ring is yours; if not, the foul opinion
You had of her pure honour gains or loses
Your sword or mine, or masterless leaves both
To who shall find them.

IACHIMO: Sir, my circumstances,
Being so near the truth as I will make them,
Must first induce you to believe—whose strength
I will confirm with oath; which, I doubt not,
You'll give me leave to spare, when you shall find
You need it not.

POSTHUMUS LEONATUS: Proceed.

IACHIMO: First, her bedchamber,
Where, I confess, I slept not, but profess
Had that was well worth watching—it was hang'd
With tapesty of silk and silver; the story
Proud Cleopatra, when she met her Roman,
And Cydnus swell'd above the banks, or for
The press of boats or pride. A piece of work
So bravely done, so rich, that it did strive
In workmanship and value; which I wonder'd
Could be so rarely and exactly wrought,
Since the true life on't was—

POSTHUMUS LEONATUS: This is true;
And this you might have heard of here, by me,
Or by some other.

IACHIMO: More particulars
Must justify my knowledge.

POSTHUMUS LEONATUS: So they must,
Or do your honour injury.

IACHIMO: The chimney
Is south the chamber, and the chimney-piece
Chaste Dian bathing. Never saw I figures
So likely to report themselves. The cutter
Was as another nature, dumb; outwent her,
Motion and breath left out.

POSTHUMUS LEONATUS: This is a thing
Which you might from relation likewise reap,
Being, as it is, much spoke of.

IACHIMO: The roof o' the chamber
With golden cherubins is fretted: her andirons—
I had forgot them—were two winking Cupids
Of silver, each on one foot standing, nicely
Depending on their brands.

POSTHUMUS LEONATUS: This is her honour!
Let it be granted you have seen all this, and praise
Be given to your remembrance, the description
Of what is in her chamber nothing saves
The wager you have laid.

IACHIMO: Then, if you can,

Showing the bracelet

Be pale. I beg but leave to air this jewel. See!
And now 'tis up again. It must be married
To that your diamond; I'll keep them.

POSTHUMUS LEONATUS: Jove!
Once more let me behold it. Is it that
Which I left with her?

IACHIMO: Sir—I thank her—that.
She stripp'd it from her arm; I see her yet;
Her pretty action did outsell her gift,
And yet enrich'd it too. She gave it me, and said
She prized it once.

POSTHUMUS LEONATUS: May be she pluck'd it off
To send it me.

IACHIMO: She writes so to you, doth she?

POSTHUMUS LEONATUS: O, no, no, no! 'tis true. Here, take this too;

Gives the ring

It is a basilisk unto mine eye,
Kills me to look on't. Let there be no honour
Where there is beauty; truth, where semblance; love,
Where there's another man. The vows of women
Of no more bondage be, to where they are made,
Than they are to their virtues, which is nothing.
O, above measure false!

PHILARIO: Have patience, sir,
And take your ring again; 'tis not yet won.
It may be probable she lost it, or
Who knows if one of her women, being corrupted,
Hath stol'n it from her?

POSTHUMUS LEONATUS: Very true;

And so, I hope, he came by't. Back my ring.
Render to me some corporal sign about her,
More evident than this; for this was stolen.

IACHIMO: By Jupiter, I had it from her arm.

POSTHUMUS LEONATUS: Hark you, he swears; by Jupiter he swears.
'Tis true:—nay, keep the ring—'tis true. I am sure
She would not lose it. Her attendants are
All sworn and honourable—they induced to steal it!
And by a stranger! No, he hath enjoyed her.
The cognizance of her incontinency
Is this: she hath bought the name of whore thus dearly.
There, take thy hire; and all the fiends of hell
Divide themselves between you!

PHILARIO: Sir, be patient;
This is not strong enough to be believed
Of one persuaded well of.

POSTHUMUS LEONATUS: Never talk on't;
She hath been colted by him.

IACHIMO: If you seek
For further satisfying, under her breast—
Worthy the pressing—lies a mole, right proud
Of that most delicate lodging. By my life,
I kiss'd it; and it gave me present hunger
To feed again, though full. You do remember
This stain upon her?

POSTHUMUS LEONATUS: Ay, and it doth confirm
Another stain, as big as hell can hold,
Were there no more but it.

IACHIMO: Will you hear more?

POSTHUMUS LEONATUS: Spare your arithmetic; never count the turns. Once, and a million!

IACHIMO: I'll be sworn—

POSTHUMUS LEONATUS: No swearing.
If you will swear you have not done't, you lie;
And I will kill thee, if thou dost deny
Thou'st made me cuckold.

IACHIMO: I'll deny nothing.

POSTHUMUS LEONATUS: O, that I had her here, to tear her limb-meal!
I will go there and do't, i' the court, before
Her father. I'll do something—

Exit

PHILARIO: Quite besides
The government of patience! You have won.
Let's follow him, and pervert the present wrath
He hath against himself.

IACHIMO: With an my heart.

Exeunt

SCENE V—*Rome: Another room in Philario's house*

Enter POSTHUMUS LEONATUS

POSTHUMUS LEONATUS: Is there no way for men to be but women
Must be half-workers? We are all bastards;
And that most venerable man which I
Did call my father, was I know not where
When I was stamp'd; some coiner with his tools
Made me a counterfeit; yet my mother seem'd
The Dian of that time so doth my wife
The nonpareil of this. O, vengeance, vengeance!
Me of my lawful pleasure she restrain'd
And pray'd me oft forbearance; did it with
A pudency so rosy the sweet view on't
Might well have warm'd old Saturn; that I thought her
As chaste as unsunn'd snow. O, all the devils!
This yellow Iachimo, in an hour—wast not?
Or less, —at first? —perchance he spoke not, but,
Like a full-acorn'd boar, a German one,
Cried 'O!' and mounted; found no opposition
But what he look'd for should oppose and she
Should from encounter guard. Could I find out
The woman's part in me! For there's no motion
That tends to vice in man, but I affirm
It is the woman's part. Be it lying, note it,
The woman's; flattering, hers; deceiving, hers;
Lust and rank thoughts, hers, hers; revenges, hers;
Ambitions, covetings, change of prides, disdain,
Nice longing, slanders, mutability,
All faults that may be named, nay, that hell knows,
Why, hers, in part or all; but rather, all;
For even to vice
They are not constant but are changing still
One vice, but of a minute old, for one
Not half so old as that. I'll write against them,
Detest them, curse them. Yet 'tis greater skill
In a true hate, to pray they have their will:
The very devils cannot plague them better.

Exit

ACT III

SCENE I—*Britain: A hall in Cymbeline's palace*

Enter in state, CYMBELINE, QUEEN, CLOTEN, and Lords at one door, and at another, CAIUS LUCIUS and Attendants

CYMBELINE: Now say, what would Augustus Caesar with us?

CAIUS LUCIUS: When Julius Caesar—whose remembrance yet
Lives in men's eyes and will to ears and tongues
Be theme and hearing ever, was in this Britain
And conquer'd it, Cassibelan, thine uncle,
Famous in Caesar's praises, no whit less
Than in his feats deserving it, for him
And his succession granted Rome a tribute,
Yearly three thousand pounds, which by thee lately
Is left untender'd.

QUEEN: And, to kill the marvel,
Shall be so ever.

CLOTEN: There be many Caesars
Ere such another Julius. Britain is
A world by itself, and we will nothing pay
For wearing our own noses.

QUEEN: That opportunity
Which then they had to take from 's, to resume
We have again. Remember, sir, my liege,
The kings your ancestors, together with
The natural bravery of your isle, which stands
As Neptune's park, ribbed and paled in
With rocks unscalable and roaring waters,
With sands that will not bear your enemies' boats
But suck them up to the topmast. A kind of conquest
Caesar made here; but made not here his brag
Of 'came' and 'saw' and 'overcame'. With shame—
That first that ever touch'd him—he was carried
From off our coast, twice beaten; and his shipping—
Poor ignorant baubles!— upon our terrible seas,
Like egg-shells moved upon their surges, crack'd
As easily 'gainst our rocks; for joy whereof
The famed Cassibelan, who was once at point—
O giglot fortune!—to master Caesar's sword,
Made Lud's town with rejoicing fires bright
And Britons strut with courage.

CLOTEN: Come, there's no more tribute to be paid. Our kingdom is stronger than it was at that time; and, as I said, there is no moe such Caesars. Other of them may have crook'd noses, but to owe such straight arms, none.

CYMBELINE: Son, let your mother end.

CLOTEN: We have yet many among us can gripe as hard as Cassibelan: I do not say I am one; but I have a hand. Why tribute? why should we pay tribute? If Caesar can hide the sun from us with a blanket, or put the moon in his pocket, we will pay him tribute for light; else, sir, no more tribute, pray you now.

CYMBELINE: You must know,
Till the injurious Romans did extort
This tribute from us, we were free. Caesar's ambition,
Which swell'd so much that it did almost stretch
The sides o' the world—against all colour here
Did put the yoke upon 's; which to shake off
Becomes a warlike people, whom we reckon
Ourselves to be.

CLOTEN Lords: We do.

CYMBELINE: Say, then, to Caesar,
Our ancestor was that Mulmutius which
Ordain'd our laws—whose use the sword of Caesar

Hath too much mangled; whose repair and franchise
Shall, by the power we hold, be our good deed,
Though Rome be therefore angry. Mulmutius made our laws,
Who was the first of Britain which did put
His brows within a golden crown, and call'd
Himself a king.

CAIUS LUCIUS: I am sorry, Cymbeline,
That I am to pronounce Augustus Caesar—
Caesar, that hath more kings his servants than
Thyself domestic officers—thine enemy.
Receive it from me, then: war and confusion
In Caesar's name pronounce I 'gainst thee; look
For fury not to be resisted. Thus defied,
I thank thee for myself.

CYMBELINE: Thou art welcome, Caius.
Thy Caesar knighted me; my youth I spent
Much under him; of him I gather'd honour;
Which he to seek of me again, perforce,
Behoves me keep at utterance. I am perfect
That the Pannonians and Dalmatians for
Their liberties are now in arms, a precedent
Which not to read would show the Britons cold;
So Caesar shall not find them.

CAIUS LUCIUS: Let proof speak.

CLOTEN: His majesty bids you welcome. Make pastime with us a day or two, or longer. If you seek us afterwards in other terms, you shall find us in our salt-water girdle. If you beat us out of it, it is yours; if you fall in the adventure, our crows shall fare the better for you; and there's an end.

CAIUS LUCIUS: So, sir.

CYMBELINE: I know your master's pleasure, and he mine;
All the remain is welcome.

Exeunt

SCENE II—*Britain: Another room in the Cymbeline's palace*

Enter PISANIO, with a letter

PISANIO: How? of adultery? Wherefore write you not
What monster's her accuser? Leonatus,
O master! what a strange infection
Is fall'n into thy ear! What false Italian,
As poisonous-tongued as handed, hath prevail'd
On thy too ready hearing? Disloyal! No.
She's punish'd for her truth, and undergoes,
More goddess-like than wife-like, such assaults
As would take in some virtue. O my master!
Thy mind to her is now as low as were
Thy fortunes. How! that I should murder her?
Upon the love and truth and vows which I
Have made to thy command? I, her? her blood?
If it be so to do good service, never
Let me be counted serviceable. How look I,
That I should seem to lack humanity
So much as this fact comes to? (*Reading*)
'Do't. The letter.
That I have sent her, by her own command
Shall give thee opportunity.' O damn'd paper!
Black as the ink that's on thee! Senseless bauble,
Art thou a feodary for this act, and look'st
So virgin-like without? Lo, here she comes.
I am ignorant in what I am commanded.

Enter IMOGEN

IMOGEN: How now, Pisanio!

PISANIO: Madam, here is a letter from my lord.

IMOGEN: Who? thy lord? that is my lord, Leonatus!
O, learn'd indeed were that astronomer
That knew the stars as I his characters—
He'ld lay the future open. You good gods,
Let what is here contain'd relish of love,
Of my lord's health, of his content, yet not
That we two are asunder—let that grieve him!
Some griefs are med'cinable; that is one of them,
For it doth physic love—of his content,
All but in that. Good wax, thy leave. Blest be
You bees that make these locks of counsel! Lovers
And men in dangerous bonds pray not alike;
Though forfeiters you cast in prison, yet
You clasp young Cupid's tables. Good news, gods!

Reads

'Justice, and your father's wrath, should he take me in his dominion, could not be so cruel to me, as you, O the dearest of creatures, would even renew me with your eyes. Take notice that I am in Cambria, at Milford Haven. What your own love will out of this advise you, follow. So he wishes you all happiness, that remains loyal to his vow, and your increasing in love Leonatus Posthumus'.

O, for a horse with wings! Hear'st thou, Pisanio?
He is at Milford-Haven. Read, and tell me
How far 'tis thither. If one of mean affairs
May plod it in a week, why may not I
Glide thither in a day? Then, true Pisanio—
Who long'st, like me, to see thy lord, who long'st,—
O, let me—bate, 'but not like me—yet long'st,
But in a fainter kind—O, not like me,
For mine's beyond beyond—say, and speak thick;
Love's counsellor should fill the bores of hearing,
To the smothering of the sense—how far it is
To this same blessed Milford. And by the way
Tell me how Wales was made so happy as
To inherit such a haven. But first of all,
How we may steal from hence, and for the gap
That we shall make in time, from our hence-going
And our return, to excuse. But first, how get hence.
Why should excuse be born or ere begot?
We'll talk of that hereafter. Prithee, speak,
How many score of miles may we well ride
'Twixt hour and hour?

PISANIO: One score 'twixt sun and sun,
Madam, 's enough for you, and too much too.

IMOGEN: Why, one that rode to's execution, man,
Could never go so slow. I have heard of riding wagers,
Where horses have been nimbler than the sands
That run i' the clock's behalf. But this is foolery.
Go bid my woman feign a sickness; say
She'll home to her father; and provide me presently
A riding suit, no costlier than would fit
A franklin's housewife.

PISANIO: Madam, you're best consider.

IMOGEN: I see before me, man. Nor here, nor here,
Nor what ensues, but have a fog in them,
That I cannot look through. Away, I prithee;
Do as I bid thee. There's no more to say,
Accessible is none but Milford way.

Exeunt

SCENE III—*Wales: A mountainous country with a cave*

Enter, from the cave, BELARIUS; GUIDERIUS, and ARVIRAGUS following

BELARIUS: A goodly day not to keep house, with such
Whose roof's as low as ours! Stoop, boys; this gate
Instructs you how to adore the heavens and bows you
To a morning's holy office. The gates of monarchs
Are arch'd so high that giants may jet through
And keep their impious turbans on without
Good morrow to the sun. Hail, thou fair heaven!
We house i' the rock, yet use thee not so hardly
As prouder livers do.

GUIDERIUS: Hail, heaven!

ARVIRAGUS: Hail, heaven!

BELARIUS: Now for our mountain sport. Up to yond hill,
Your legs are young; I'll tread these flats. Consider,
When you above perceive me like a crow,
That it is place which lessens and sets off;
And you may then revolve what tales I have told you
Of courts, of princes, of the tricks in war.
This service is not service, so being done,
But being so allow'd. To apprehend thus,
Draws us a profit from all things we see;
And often, to our comfort, shall we find
The sharded beetle in a safer hold
Than is the full-wing'd eagle. O, this life
Is nobler than attending for a cheque,
Richer than doing nothing for a bauble,
Prouder than rustling in unpaid-for silk:
Such gain the cap of him that makes him fine,
Yet keeps his book uncross'd. No life to ours.

GUIDERIUS: Out of your proof you speak. We, poor unfledged,
Have never wing'd from view o' the nest, nor know not
What air's from home. Haply this life is best,
If quiet life be best; sweeter to you
That have a sharper known; well corresponding

With your stiff age. But unto us it is
A cell of ignorance; travelling a, bed,
A prison for a debtor, that not dares
To stride a limit.

ARVIRAGUS: What should we speak of
When we are old as you? when we shall hear
The rain and wind beat dark December, how,
In this our pinching cave, shall we discourse
The freezing hours away? We have seen nothing;
We are beastly, subtle as the fox for prey,
Like warlike as the wolf for what we eat.
Our valour is to chase what flies; our cage
We make a quire, as doth the prison'd bird,
And sing our bondage freely.

BELARIUS: How you speak!
Did you but know the city's usuries
And felt them knowingly—the art o' the court
As hard to leave as keep, whose top to climb
Is certain falling, or so slippery that
The fear's as bad as falling; the toil o' the war,
A pain that only seems to seek out danger
I' the name of fame and honour, which dies i' the search,
And hath as oft a slanderous epitaph
As record of fair act; nay, many times,
Doth ill deserve by doing well; what's worse,
Must court'sy at the censure. O boys, this story
The world may read in me; my body's mark'd
With Roman swords, and my report was once
First with the best of note. Cymbeline loved me,
And when a soldier was the theme, my name
Was not far off. Then was I as a tree
Whose boughs did bend with fruit; but in one night,
A storm or robbery, call it what you will,
Shook down my mellow hangings, nay, my leaves,
And left me bare to weather.

GUIDERIUS: Uncertain favour!

BELARIUS: My fault being nothing—as I have told you oft—
But that two villains, whose false oaths prevail'd
Before my perfect honour, swore to Cymbeline
I was confederate with the Romans. So
Follow'd my banishment, and this twenty years
This rock and these demesnes have been my world,
Where I have lived at honest freedom, paid
More pious debts to heaven than in all
The fore-end of my time. But up to the mountains!
This is not hunters' language. He that strikes
The venison first shall be the lord o' the feast;
To him the other two shall minister;
And we will fear no poison, which attends
In place of greater state. I'll meet you in the valleys.

Exeunt GUIDERIUS and ARVIRAGUS

How hard it is to hide the sparks of nature!
These boys know little they are sons to the king,
Nor Cymbeline dreams that they are alive.
They think they are mine; and though train'd up thus meanly
I' the cave wherein they bow, their thoughts do hit
The roofs of palaces, and nature prompts them
In simple and low things to prince it much
Beyond the trick of others. This Polydore,
The heir of Cymbeline and Britain, who
The king his father call'd Guiderius—Jove!
When on my three-foot stool I sit and tell
The warlike feats I have done, his spirits fly out
Into my story; say 'Thus, mine enemy fell,
And thus I set my foot on 's neck;' even then
The princely blood flows in his cheek, he sweats,
Strains his young nerves and puts himself in posture
That acts my words. The younger brother, Cadwal,
Once Arviragus, in as like a figure,
Strikes life into my speech and shows much more
His own conceiving. Hark, the game is roused!
O Cymbeline! heaven and my conscience knows
Thou didst unjustly banish me! Whereon,
At three and two years old, I stole these babes;
Thinking to bar thee of succession as
Thou reft'st me of my lands. Euriphile,
Thou wast their nurse; they took thee for their mother,
And every day do honour to her grave.
Myself, Belarius, that am Morgan call'd,
They take for natural father. The game is up.

Exit

SCENE IV—*Wales, near Milford-Haven*

Enter PISANIO and IMOGEN

IMOGEN: Thou told'st me, when we came from horse, the place
Was near at hand. Ne'er long'd my mother so
To see me first, as I have now. Pisanio! man!
Where is Posthumus? What is in thy mind,
That makes thee stare thus? Wherefore breaks that sigh
From the inward of thee? One, but painted thus,
Would be interpreted a thing perplex'd
Beyond self-explication. Put thyself
Into a havior of less fear, ere wildness
Vanquish my staider senses. What's the matter?
Why tender'st thou that paper to me, with
A look untender? If't be summer news,
Smile to't before; if winterly, thou need'st
But keep that countenance still. My husband's hand!
That drug-damn'd Italy hath out-craftied him,
And he's at some hard point. Speak, man; thy tongue
May take off some extremity, which to read
Would be even mortal to me.

PISANIO: Please you, read,
And you shall find me, wretched man, a thing
The most disdain'd of fortune.

IMOGEN: [*Reads*] 'Thy mistress, Pisanio, hath played the strumpet in my bed, the testimonies whereof lie bleeding in me. I speak not out of weak surmises, but from proof as strong as my grief and as certain as I expect my revenge. That part thou, Pisanio, must act for me, if thy faith be not tainted with the breach of hers. Let thine own hands take away her life; I shall give thee opportunity at Milford-Haven. She hath my letter for the purpose where, if thou fear to strike and to make me certain it is done, thou art the pander to her dishonour and equally to me disloyal.'

PISANIO: What shall I need to draw my sword? The paper
Hath cut her throat already. No, 'tis slander,
Whose edge is sharper than the sword, whose tongue
Outvenoms all the worms of Nile, whose breath
Rides on the posting winds and doth belie
All corners of the world. Kings, queens and states,
Maids, matrons, nay, the secrets of the grave
This viperous slander enters. What cheer, madam?

IMOGEN: False to his bed! What is it to be false?
To lie in watch there and to think on him?
To weep twixt clock and clock? If sleep charge nature,
To break it with a fearful dream of him
And cry myself awake? That's false to's bed, is it?

PISANIO: Alas, good lady!

IMOGEN: I false! Thy conscience witness! Iachimo,
Thou didst accuse him of incontinency;
Thou then look'dst like a villain; now methinks
Thy favour's good enough. Some jay of Italy
Whose mother was her painting, hath betray'd him.
Poor I am stale, a garment out of fashion,
And, for I am richer than to hang by the walls,
I must be ripp'd. To pieces with me! O,
Men's vows are women's traitors! All good seeming,
By thy revolt, O husband, shall be thought
Put on for villany; not born where't grows,
But worn a bait for ladies.

PISANIO: Good madam, hear me.

IMOGEN: True honest men being heard, like false Aeneas,
Were in his time thought false; and Sinon's weeping
Did scandal many a holy tear, took pity
From most true wretchedness. So thou, Posthumus,
Wilt lay the leaven on all proper men;
Goodly and gallant shall be false and perjured
From thy great fall. Come, fellow, be thou honest;
Do thou thy master's bidding; when thou see'st him,
A little witness my obedience. Look!
I draw the sword myself; take it, and hit
The innocent mansion of my love, my heart.
Fear not; 'tis empty of all things but grief;
Thy master is not there, who was indeed
The riches of it. Do his bidding; strike
Thou mayst be valiant in a better cause;
But now thou seem'st a coward.

PISANIO: Hence, vile instrument!
Thou shalt not damn my hand.
IMOGEN: Why, I must die;
And if I do not by thy hand, thou art
No servant of thy master's. Against self-slaughter
There is a prohibition so divine
That cravens my weak hand. Come, here's my heart.
Something's afore't. Soft, soft! we'll no defence;
Obedient as the scabbard. What is here?
The scriptures of the loyal Leonatus
All turn'd to heresy? Away, away,
Corrupters of my faith! you shall no more
Be stomachers to my heart. Thus may poor fools
Believe false teachers: though those that are betray'd
Do feel the treason sharply, yet the traitor
Stands in worse case of woe.
And thou, Posthumus, thou that didst set up
My disobedience 'gainst the king my father
And make me put into contempt the suits
Of princely fellows, shalt hereafter find
It is no act of common passage, but
A strain of rareness; and I grieve myself
To think, when thou shalt be disedged by her
That now thou tirest on, how thy memory
Will then be pang'd by me. Prithee, dispatch.
The lamb entreats the butcher. Where's thy knife?
Thou art too slow to do thy master's bidding,
When I desire it too.
PISANIO: O gracious lady,
Since I received command to do this business
I have not slept one wink.
IMOGEN: Do't, and to bed then.
PISANIO: I'll wake mine eyeballs blind first.
IMOGEN: Wherefore then
Didst undertake it? Why hast thou abused
So many miles with a pretence? This place?
Mine action and thine own? our horses' labour?
The time inviting thee? The perturb'd court,
For my being absent?—whereunto I never
Purpose return. Why hast thou gone so far,
To be unbent when thou hast ta'en thy stand,
The elected deer before thee?
PISANIO: But to win time
To lose so bad employment, in the which
I have consider'd of a course. Good lady,
Hear me with patience.
IMOGEN: Talk thy tongue weary—speak.
I have heard I am a strumpet, and mine ear
Therein false struck, can take no greater wound,
Nor tent to bottom that. But speak.
PISANIO: Then, madam,
I thought you would not back again.
IMOGEN: Most like—
Bringing me here to kill me.
PISANIO: Not so, neither;
But if I were as wise as honest, then
My purpose would prove well. It cannot be
But that my master is abused.
Some villain, ay, and singular in his art.
Hath done you both this cursed injury.
IMOGEN: Some Roman courtezan.
PISANIO: No, on my life.
I'll give but notice you are dead and send him
Some bloody sign of it, for 'tis commanded
I should do so. You shall be miss'd at court,
And that will well confirm it.
IMOGEN: Why good fellow,
What shall I do the where? where bide? how live?
Or in my life what comfort, when I am
Dead to my husband?
PISANIO: If you'll back to the court—
IMOGEN: No court, no father, nor no more ado
With that harsh, noble, simple nothing,
That Cloten, whose love-suit hath been to me
As fearful as a siege.
PISANIO: If not at court,
Then not in Britain must you bide.
IMOGEN: Where then?
Hath Britain all the sun that shines? Day, night,
Are they not but in Britain? I' the world's volume
Our Britain seems as of it, but not n't;
In a great pool a swan's nest. Prithee, think
There's livers out of Britain.
PISANIO: I am most glad
You think of other place. The ambassador,
Lucius the Roman, comes to Milford-Haven
To-morrow. Now, if you could wear a mind

Dark as your fortune is, and but disguise
That which, to appear itself, must not yet be
But by self-danger, you should tread a course
Pretty and full of view; yea, haply, near
The residence of Posthumus; so nigh at least
That though his actions were not visible, yet
Report should render him hourly to your ear
As truly as he moves.

IMOGEN: O, for such means!
Though peril to my modesty, not death on't,
I would adventure.

PISANIO: Well, then, here's the point:
You must forget to be a woman; change
Command into obedience; fear and niceness—
The handmaids of all women, or, more truly,
Woman its pretty self—into a waggish courage;
Ready in gibes, quick-answer'd, saucy and
As quarrelous as the weasel. Nay, you must
Forget that rarest treasure of your cheek,
Exposing it—but, O, the harder heart!
Alack, no remedy!—to the greedy touch
Of common-kissing Titan, and forget
Your laboursome and dainty trims, wherein
You made great Juno angry.

IMOGEN: Nay, be brief;
I see into thy end, and am almost
A man already.

PISANIO: First, make yourself but like one.
Fore-thinking this, I have already fit—
'Tis in my cloak-bag—doublet, hat, hose, all
That answer to them. Would you in their serving,
And with what imitation you can borrow
From youth of such a season, fore noble Lucius
Present yourself, desire his service, tell him
Wherein you're happy—which you'll make him know,
If that his head have ear in music; doubtless
With joy he will embrace you, for he's honourable
And doubling that, most holy. Your means abroad—
You have me, rich; and I will never fail
Beginning nor supplyment.

IMOGEN: Thou art all the comfort
The gods will diet me with. Prithee, away!
There's more to be consider'd; but we'll even
All that good time will give us: this attempt
I am soldier to, and will abide it with
A prince's courage. Away, I prithee.

PISANIO: Well, madam, we must take a short farewell,
Lest, being miss'd, I be suspected of
Your carriage from the court. My noble mistress,
Here is a box; I had it from the queen.
What's in't is precious. If you are sick at sea,
Or stomach-qualm'd at land, a dram of this
Will drive away distemper. To some shade,
And fit you to your manhood. May the gods
Direct you to the best!

IMOGEN: Amen: I thank thee.

Exeunt, severally

SCENE V—*Britain: Cymbeline's palace*

Enter CYMBELINE, QUEEN, CLOTEN, LUCIUS, Lords, and Attendants

CYMBELINE: Thus far; and so farewell.

CAIUS LUCIUS: Thanks, royal sir.
My emperor hath wrote, I must from hence,
And am right sorry that I must report ye
My master's enemy.

CYMBELINE: Our subjects, sir,
Will not endure his yoke; and for ourself
To show less sovereignty than they, must needs
Appear unkinglike.

CAIUS LUCIUS: So, sir. I desire of you
A conduct overland to Milford Haven.
Madam, all joy befal your Grace and you!

CYMBELINE: My lords, you are appointed for that office;
The due of honour in no point omit.
So farewell, noble Lucius.

CAIUS LUCIUS: Your hand, my lord.

CLOTEN: Receive it friendly; but from this time forth
I wear it as your enemy.

CAIUS LUCIUS: Sir, the event
Is yet to name the winner. Fare you well.

CYMBELINE: Leave not the worthy Lucius, good my lords,
Till he have cross'd the Severn. Happiness!

Exeunt LUCIUS and Lords

QUEEN: He goes hence frowning; but it honours us
That we have given him cause.
CLOTEN: 'Tis all the better;
Your valiant Britons have their wishes in it.
CYMBELINE: Lucius hath wrote already to the emperor
How it goes here. It fits us therefore ripely
Our chariots and our horsemen be in readiness.
The powers that he already hath in Gallia
Will soon be drawn to head, from whence he moves
His war for Britain.
QUEEN: 'Tis not sleepy business;
But must be look'd to speedily and strongly.
CYMBELINE: Our expectation that it would be thus
Hath made us forward. But, my gentle queen,
Where is our daughter? She hath not appear'd
Before the Roman, nor to us hath tender'd
The duty of the day. She looks us like
A thing more made of malice than of duty;
We have noted it. Call her before us, for
We have been too slight in sufferance.

Exit an Attendant

QUEEN: Royal sir,
Since the exile of Posthumus, most retired
Hath her life been; the cure whereof, my lord,
'Tis time must do. Beseech your majesty,
Forbear sharp speeches to her; she's a lady
So tender of rebukes that words are strokes
And strokes death to her.

Re-enter Attendant

CYMBELINE: Where is she, sir? How
Can her contempt be answer'd?
ATTENDANT: Please you, sir,
Her chambers are all lock'd, and there's no answer
That will be given to the loudest noise we make.
QUEEN: My lord, when last I went to visit her,
She pray'd me to excuse her keeping close,
Whereto constrain'd by her infirmity,
She should that duty leave unpaid to you,
Which daily she was bound to proffer. This
She wish'd me to make known; but our great court
Made me to blame in memory.
CYMBELINE: Her doors lock'd?
Not seen of late? Grant, heavens, that which I fear
Prove false!

Exit

QUEEN: Son, I say, follow the king.
CLOTEN: That man of hers, Pisanio, her old servant, have not seen these two days.
QUEEN: Go, look after.

Exit CLOTEN

Pisanio, thou that stand'st so for Posthumus!
He hath a drug of mine; I pray his absence
Proceed by swallowing that, for he believes
It is a thing most precious. But for her,
Where is she gone? Haply, despair hath seized her;
Or, wing'd with fervor of her love, she's flown
To her desired Posthumus. Gone she is
To death or to dishonor, and my end
Can make good use of either. She being down,
I have the placing of the British crown.

Re-enter CLOTEN

How now, my son!
CLOTEN: 'Tis certain she is fled.
Go in and cheer the king. He rages; none
Dare come about him.
QUEEN: All the better. May
This night forestall him of the coming day!

Exit

CLOTEN: I love and hate her: for she's fair and royal,
And that she hath all courtly parts more exquisite
Than lady, ladies, woman. From every one
The best she hath, and she, of all compounded,
Outsells them all. I love her therefore: but
Disdaining me and throwing favours on
The low Posthumus slanders so her judgment
That what's else rare is choked; and in that point
I will conclude to hate her, nay, indeed,
To be revenged upon her. For when fools Shall—

Enter PISANIO

Who is here? What, are you packing, sirrah?
Come hither. Ah, you precious pander! Villain,
Where is thy lady? In a word, or else

Thou art straightway with the fiends.
PISANIO: O, good my lord!
CLOTEN: Where is thy lady? Or, by Jupiter—
I will not ask again. Close villain,
I'll have this secret from thy heart, or rip
Thy heart to find it. Is she with Posthumus?
From whose so many weights of baseness cannot
A dram of worth be drawn.
PISANIO: Alas, my lord,
How can she be with him? When was she missed?
He is in Rome.
CLOTEN: Where is she, sir? Come nearer.
No further halting! Satisfy me home
What is become of her.
PISANIO: O, my all-worthy lord!
CLOTEN: All-worthy villain!
Discover where thy mistress is at once,
At the next word. No more of 'worthy lord!'
Speak, or thy silence on the instant is
Thy condemnation and thy death.
PISANIO: Then, sir,
This paper is the history of my knowledge
Touching her flight.

Presenting a letter

CLOTEN: Let's see't. I will pursue her
Even to Augustus' throne.
PISANIO: [*Aside*] Or this or perish.
She's far enough; and what he learns by this
May prove his travel, not her danger.
CLOTEN: Humh!
PISANIO: [*Aside*] I'll write to my lord she's dead. O Imogen,
Safe mayst thou wander, safe return again!
CLOTEN: Sirrah, is this letter true?
PISANIO: Sir, as I think.

CLOTEN: It is Posthumus' hand; I know't. Sirrah, if thou wouldst not be a villain, but do me true service, undergo those employments wherein I should have cause to use thee with a serious industry, that is, what villany soe'er I bid thee do, to perform it directly and truly, I would think thee an honest man; thou shouldst neither want my means for thy relief nor my voice for thy preferment.

PISANIO: Well, my good lord.

CLOTEN: Wilt thou serve me? for since patiently and constantly thou hast stuck to the bare fortune of that beggar Posthumus, thou canst not, in the course of gratitude, but be a diligent follower of mine. Wilt thou serve me?

PISANIO: Sir, I will.

CLOTEN: Give me thy hand; here's my purse. Hast any of thy late master's garments in thy possession?

PISANIO: I have, my lord, at my lodging, the same suit he wore when he took leave of my lady and mistress.

CLOTEN: The first service thou dost me, fetch that suit hither. Let it be thy lint service; go.

PISANIO: I shall, my lord.

Exit

CLOTEN: Meet thee at Milford-Haven! I forgot to ask him one thing; I'll remember't anon. Even there, thou villain Posthumus, will I kill thee. I would these garments were come. She said upon a time—the bitterness of it I now belch from my heart—that she held the very garment of Posthumus in more respect than my noble and natural person together with the adornment of my qualities. With that suit upon my back, will I ravish her; first kill him, and in her eyes. There shall she see my valour, which will then be a torment to her contempt. He on the ground, my speech of insultment ended on his dead body, and when my lust hath dined—which, as I say, to vex her I will execute in the clothes that she so praised—to the court I'll knock her back, foot her home again. She hath despised me rejoicingly, and I'll be merry in my revenge.

Re-enter PISANIO, with the clothes

Be those the garments?

PISANIO: Ay, my noble lord.

CLOTEN: How long is't since she went to Milford-Haven?

PISANIO: She can scarce be there yet.

CLOTEN: Bring this apparel to my chamber; that is the second thing that I have commanded thee. The third is, that thou wilt be a voluntary mute to my design. Be but duteous, and true preferment shall tender itself to thee. My revenge is now at Milford; would I had wings to follow it! Come, and be true.

Exit

PISANIO: Thou bid'st me to my loss; for true to thee
Were to prove false, which I will never be,

To him that is most true. To Milford go,
And find not her whom thou pursuest. Flow, flow,
You heavenly blessings, on her! This fool's speed
Be cross'd with slowness; labour be his meed!

Exit

SCENE VI—*Wales: Before the cave of Belarius*

Enter IMOGEN, in boy's clothes

IMOGEN: I see a man's life is a tedious one.
I have tired myself, and for two nights together
Have made the ground my bed. I should be sick,
But that my resolution helps me. Milford,
When from the mountain-top Pisanio show'd thee,
Thou wast within a ken. O Jove! I think
Foundations fly the wretched; such, I mean,
Where they should be relieved. Two beggars told me
I could not miss my way. Will poor folks lie,
That have afflictions on them, knowing 'tis
A punishment or trial? Yes; no wonder,
When rich ones scarce tell true. To lapse in fullness
Is sorer than to lie for need, and falsehood
Is worse in kings than beggars. My dear lord!
Thou art one o' the false ones. Now I think on thee,
My hunger's gone; but even before, I was
At point to sink for food. But what is this?
Here is a path to't; 'tis some savage hold.
I were best not to call; I dare not call. Yet famine,
Ere clean it o'erthrow nature, makes it valiant,
Plenty and peace breeds cowards; hardness ever
Of hardiness is mother. Ho! who's here?
If any thing that's civil, speak; if savage,
Take or lend. Ho! No answer? Then I'll enter.
Best draw my sword; and if mine enemy
But fear the sword like me, he'll scarcely look on't.
Such a foe, good heavens!

Exit, to the cave

Enter BELARIUS, GUIDERIUS, and ARVIRAGUS

BELARIUS: You, Polydote, have proved best woodman and
Are master of the feast. Cadwal and I
Will play the cook and servant; 'tis our match.
The sweat of industry would dry and die,
But for the end it works to. Come, our stomachs
Will make what's homely savoury; weariness
Can snore upon the flint, when resty sloth
Finds the down pillow hard. Now peace be here,
Poor house, that keep'st thyself!

GUIDERIUS: I am thoroughly weary.

ARVIRAGUS: I am weak with toil, yet strong in appetite.

GUIDERIUS: There is cold meat i' the cave; we'll browse on that,
Whilst what we have kill'd be cook'd.

BELARIUS: [*Looking into the cave*] Stay, come not in.
But that it eats our victuals, I should think
Here were a fairy.

GUIDERIUS: What's the matter, sir?

BELARIUS: By Jupiter, an angel! or, if not,
An earthly paragon! Behold divineness
No elder than a boy!

Re-enter IMOGEN

IMOGEN: Good masters, harm me not.
Before I enter'd here, I call'd, and thought
To have begg'd or bought what I have took. good troth,
I have stol'n nought, nor would not, though I had found
Gold strew'd i' the floor. Here's money for my meat.
I would have left it on the board so soon
As I had made my meal, and parted
With prayers for the provider.

GUIDERIUS: Money, youth?

ARVIRAGUS: All gold and silver rather turn to dirt!
As 'tis no better reckon'd, but of those
Who worship dirty gods.

IMOGEN: I see you're angry.
Know, if you kill me for my fault, I should
Have died had I not made it.

BELARIUS: Whither bound?

IMOGEN: To Milford-Haven.

BELARIUS: What's your name?

IMOGEN: Fidele, sir. I have a kinsman who
Is bound for Italy; he embark'd at Milford;

To whom being going, almost spent with hunger,
I am fall'n in this offence.
BELARIUS: Prithee, fair youth,
Think us no churls, nor measure our good minds
By this rude place we live in. Well encounter'd!
'Tis almost night; you shall have better cheer
Ere you depart, and thanks to stay and eat it.
Boys, bid him welcome.
GUIDERIUS: Were you a woman, youth,
I should woo hard but be your groom. In honesty,
I bid for you as I'd buy.
ARVIRAGUS: I'll make't my comfort
He is a man. I'll love him as my brother;
And such a welcome as I'd give to him
After long absence, such is yours. Most welcome!
Be sprightly, for you fall 'mongst friends.
IMOGEN: 'Mongst friends,
If brothers. [*Aside*] Would it had been so, that they
Had been my father's sons! then had my prize
Been less, and so more equal ballasting
To thee, Posthumus.
BELARIUS: He wrings at some distress.
GUIDERIUS: Would I could free't!
ARVIRAGUS: Or I, whate'er it be,
What pain it cost, what danger. God's!
BELARIUS: [*Whispering*] Hark, boys.
IMOGEN: [*Aside*] Great men,
That had a court no bigger than this cave,
That did attend themselves and had the virtue
Which their own conscience seal'd them, laying by
That nothing-gift of differing multitudes,
Could not out-peer these twain. Pardon me, gods!
I'd change my sex to be companion with them,
Since Leonatus's false.
BELARIUS: It shall be so.
Boys, we'll go dress our hunt. Fair youth, come in.
Discourse is heavy, fasting; when we have supp'd,
We'll mannerly demand thee of thy story,
So far as thou wilt speak it.
GUIDERIUS: Pray, draw near.
ARVIRAGUS: The night to the owl and morn to the lark less welcome.
IMOGEN: Thanks, sir.
ARVIRAGUS: I pray, draw near.

Exeunt

SCENE VII—*Rome: A public place*

Enter two Senators and Tribunes

FIRST SENATOR: This is the tenor of the emperor's writ:
That since the common men are now in action
'Gainst the Pannonians and Dalmatians,
And that the legions now in Gallia are
Full weak to undertake our wars against
The fall'n-off Britons, that we do incite
The gentry to this business. He creates
Lucius proconsul; and to you the tribunes,
For this immediate levy, he commends
His absolute commission. Long live Caesar!
FIRST TRIBUNE: Is Lucius general of the forces?
SECOND SENATOR: Ay.
FIRST TRIBUNE: Remaining now in Gallia?
FIRST SENATOR: With those legions
Which I have spoke of, whereunto your levy
Must be supplyant. The words of your commission
Will tie you to the numbers and the time
Of their dispatch.
FIRST TRIBUNE: We will discharge our duty.

Exeunt

ACT IV

SCENE I—*Wales: Near the cave of Belarius*

Enter CLOTEN

CLOTEN: I am near to the place where they should meet, if Pisanio have mapped it truly. How fit his garments serve me! Why should his mistress, who was made by him that made the tailor, not be fit too? The rather—saving reverence of the word—for 'tis said a woman's fitness comes by fits. Therein I must play the workman. I dare speak it to myself—for it is not vain-glory for a man and his glass to confer in his own chamber—I mean, the lines of my body are as well drawn as his; no less young, more strong, not beneath him in fortunes, beyond him in the advantage of the time, above him in birth, alike conversant in general services, and more remarkable in single oppositions. Yet this imperceiverant thing loves him in my despite. What mortality is! Posthumus, thy head, which now is growing upon thy shoulders, shall within this hour be off; thy mistress enforced; thy garments cut to pieces before thy face; and all this done, spurn her home to her father; who may haply be a little angry for my so rough usage; but my mother, having power of his testiness, shall turn all into my commendations. My horse is tied up safe. Out, sword, and to a sore purpose! Fortune, put them into my hand! This is the very description of their meeting-place; and the fellow dares not deceive me.

Exit

SCENE II—*Wales: Before the cave of Belarius*

Enter, from the cave, BELARIUS, GUIDERIUS, ARVIRAGUS, and IMOGEN

BELARIUS: [To Imogen] You are not well. Remain here in the cave;

We'll come to you after hunting.

ARVIRAGUS: [To Imogen] Brother, stay here

Are we not brothers?

IMOGEN: So man and man should be;

But clay and clay differs in dignity,

Whose dust is both alike. I am very sick.

GUIDERIUS: Go you to hunting; I'll abide with him.

IMOGEN: So sick I am not, yet I am not well;

But not so citizen a wanton as

To seem to die ere sick. So please you, leave me;

Stick to your journal course. The breach of custom

Is breach of all. I am ill, but your being by me

Cannot amend me; society is no comfort

To one not sociable. I am not very sick,

Since I can reason of it. Pray you, trust me here.

I'll rob none but myself; and let me die,

Stealing so poorly.

GUIDERIUS: I love thee; I have spoke it.

How much the quantity, the weight as much,

As I do love my father.

BELARIUS: What! how! how!

ARVIRAGUS: If it be sin to say so, sir, I yoke me

In my good brother's fault. I know not why

I love this youth; and I have heard you say

Love's reason's without reason. The bier at door,

And a demand who is't shall die, I'd say

'My father, not this youth.'

BELARIUS: [*Aside*] O noble strain!

O worthiness of nature! breed of greatness!

Cowards father cowards and base things sire base.

Nature hath meal and bran, contempt and grace.

I'm not their father; yet who this should be,

Doth miracle itself, loved before me.

'Tis the ninth hour o' the morn.

ARVIRAGUS: Brother, farewell.

IMOGEN: I wish ye sport.

ARVIRAGUS: You health. [*To Belarius*] So please you, sir.

IMOGEN: [*Aside*] These are kind creatures. Gods, what lies I have heard!
Our courtiers say all's savage but at court.
Experience, O, thou disprovest report!
The imperious seas breed monsters, for the dish
Poor tributary rivers as sweet fish.
I am sick still; heart-sick. Pisanio,
I'll now taste of thy drug.

Swallows some

GUIDERIUS: I could not stir him.
He said he was gentle, but unfortunate;
Dishonestly afflicted, but yet honest.

ARVIRAGUS: Thus did he answer me; yet said, hereafter
I might know more.

BELARIUS: To the field, to the field!
We'll leave you for this time. Go in and rest.

ARVIRAGUS: We'll not be long away.

BELARIUS: Pray, be not sick,
For you must be our housewife.

IMOGEN: Well or ill,
I am bound to you.

BELARIUS: And shalt be ever.

Exit IMOGEN, to the cave

This youth, how'er distress'd, appears he hath had Good ancestors.

ARVIRAGUS: How angel-like he sings!

GUIDERIUS: But his neat cookery! He cut our roots
In characters,
And sauced our broths, as Juno had been sick
And he her dieter.

ARVIRAGUS: Nobly he yokes
A smiling with a sigh, as if the sigh
Was that it was, for not being such a smile;
The smile mocking the sigh, that it would fly
From so divine a temple, to commix
With winds that sailors rail at.

GUIDERIUS: I do note
That grief and patience, rooted in him both,
Mingle their spurs together.

ARVIRAGUS: Grow, patience!
And let the stinking elder, grief, untwine
His perishing root with the increasing vine!

BELARIUS: It is great morning. Come, away!
Who's there?

Enter CLOTEN

CLOTEN: I cannot find those runagates; that villain
Hath mock'd me. I am faint.

BELARIUS: Those runagates!
Means he not us? I partly know him; 'tis
Cloten, the son o' the queen. I fear some ambush.
I saw him not these many years, and yet
I know 'tis he. We are held as outlaws. Hence!

GUIDERIUS: He is but one: you and my brother search
What companies are near. Pray you, away;
Let me alone with him.

Exeunt BELARIUS and ARVIRAGUS

CLOTEN: Soft! What are you
That fly me thus? Some villain mountaineers?
I have heard of such. What slave art thou?

GUIDERIUS: A thing
More slavish did I ne'er than answering
A slave without a knock.

CLOTEN: Thou art a robber,
A law-breaker, a villain. Yield thee, thief.

GUIDERIUS: To who? To thee? What art thou? Have not I
An arm as big as thine, a heart as big?
Thy words, I grant, are bigger, for I wear not
My dagger in my mouth. Say what thou art,
Why I should yield to thee?

CLOTEN: Thou villain base,
Know'st me not by my clothes?

GUIDERIUS: No, nor thy tailor, rascal,
Who is thy grandfather; he made those clothes,
Which, as it seems, make thee.

CLOTEN: Thou precious varlet,
My tailor made them not.

GUIDERIUS: Hence, then, and thank
The man that gave them thee. Thou art some fool;
I am loath to beat thee.

CLOTEN: Thou injurious thief,
Hear but my name, and tremble.

GUIDERIUS: What's thy name?

CLOTEN: Cloten, thou villain.

GUIDERIUS: Cloten, thou double villain, be thy name,
I cannot tremble at it. Were it toad, or adder, spider,
'Twould move me sooner.

CLOTEN: To thy further fear,
Nay, to thy mere confusion, thou shalt know
I am son to the queen.

GUIDERIUS: I am sorry for 't; not seeming
So worthy as thy birth.

CLOTEN: Art not afeard?

GUIDERIUS: Those that I reverence those I fear—the wise:
At fools I laugh, not fear them.

CLOTEN: Die the death.
When I have slain thee with my proper hand,
I'll follow those that even now fled hence,
And on the gates of Lud's town set your heads:
Yield, rustic mountaineer.

Exeunt, fighting

Re-enter BELARIUS and ARVIRAGUS

BELARIUS: No companies abroad.

ARVIRAGUS: None in the world; you did mistake him, sure.

BELARIUS: I cannot tell; long is it since I saw him,
But time hath nothing blurr'd those lines of favour
Which then he wore; the snatches in his voice,
And burst of speaking, were as his. I am absolute
'Twas very Cloten.

ARVIRAGUS: In this place we left them.
I wish my brother make good time with him,
You say he is so fell.

BELARIUS: Being scarce made up,
I mean to man, he had not apprehension
Of roaring terrors; for the effect of judgment
Is oft the cause of fear. But, see, thy brother.

Re-enter GUIDERIUS, with CLOTEN'S head

GUIDERIUS: This Cloten was a fool, an empty purse;
There was no money in't. Not Hercules
Could have knock'd out his brains, for he had none;
Yet I not doing this, the fool had borne
My head as I do his.

BELARIUS: What hast thou done?

GUIDERIUS: I am perfect what: cut off one Cloten's head,
Son to the queen, after his own report;
Who call'd me traitor, mountaineer, and swore
With his own single hand he'd take us in
Displace our heads where—thank the gods!—they grow,
And set them on Lud's town.

BELARIUS: We are all undone.

GUIDERIUS: Why, worthy father, what have we to lose,
But that he swore to take, our lives? The law
Protects not us; then why should we be tender
To let an arrogant piece of flesh threat us,
Play judge and executioner all himself,
For we do fear the law? What company
Discover you abroad?

BELARIUS: No single soul
Can we set eye on; but in all safe reason
He must have some attendants. Though his humour
Was nothing but mutation—ay, and that
From one bad thing to worse; not frenzy, not
Absolute madness could so far have raved
To bring him here alone. Although perhaps
It may be heard at court that such as we
Cave here, hunt here, are outlaws, and in time
May make some stronger head—the which he hearing,
As it is like him, might break out, and swear
He'd fetch us in; yet is't not probable
To come alone, either he so undertaking,
Or they so suffering. Then on good ground we fear,
If we do fear this body hath a tail
More perilous than the head.

ARVIRAGUS: Let ordinance
Come as the gods foresay it. Howsoe'er,
My brother hath done well.

BELARIUS: I had no mind
To hunt this day; the boy Fidele's sickness
Did make my way long forth.

GUIDERIUS: With his own sword,
Which he did wave against my throat, I have ta'en
His head from him. I'll throw't into the creek
Behind our rock; and let it to the sea,
And tell the fishes he's the queen's son, Cloten.
That's all I reck.

Exit

BELARIUS: I fear 'twill be revenged.
Would, Polydote, thou hadst not done't! though valour

Becomes thee well enough.

ARVIRAGUS: Would I had done't

So the revenge alone pursued me! Polydore,

I love thee brotherly, but envy much

Thou hast robb'd me of this deed. I would revenges,

That possible strength might meet, would seek us through

And put us to our answer.

BELARIUS: Well, 'tis done.

We'll hunt no more to-day, nor seek for danger

Where there's no profit. I prithee, to our rock.

You and Fidele play the cooks; I'll stay

Till hasty Polydote return, and bring him

To dinner presently.

ARVIRAGUS: Poor sick Fidele!

I'll willingly to him; to gain his colour

I'ld let a parish of such Clotens' blood,

And praise myself for charity.

Exit

BELARIUS: O thou goddess,

Thou divine Nature, how thyself thou blazon'st

In these two princely boys! They are as gentle

As zephyrs blowing below the violet,

Not wagging his sweet head; and yet as rough,

Their royal blood enchafed, as the rudest wind,

That by the top doth take the mountain pine,

And make him stoop to the vale. 'Tis wonder

That an invisible instinct should frame them

To royalty unlearn'd, honour untaught,

Civility not seen from other, valour

That wildly grows in them, but yields a crop

As if it had been sow'd. Yet still it's strange

What Cloten's being here to us portends,

Or what his death will bring us.

Re-enter GUIDERIUS

GUIDERIUS: Where's my brother?

I have sent Cloten's clotpoll down the stream,

In embassy to his mother; his body's hostage

For his return.

Solemn music

BELARIUS: My ingenious instrument!

Hark, Polydore, it sounds! But what occasion

Hath Cadwal now to give it motion? Hark!

GUIDERIUS: Is he at home?

BELARIUS: He went hence even now.

GUIDERIUS: What does he mean? Since death of my dear'st mother

It did not speak before. All solemn things

Should answer solemn accidents. The matter?

Triumphs for nothing and lamenting toys

Is jollity for apes and grief for boys.

Is Cadwal mad?

BELARIUS: Look, here he comes,

And brings the dire occasion in his arms

Of what we blame him for!

Re-enter ARVIRAGUS, with IMOGEN, as dead, bearing her in his arms

ARVIRAGUS: The bird is dead

That we have made so much on. I had rather

Have skipp'd from sixteen years of age to sixty,

To have turn'd my leaping-time into a crutch,

Than have seen this.

GUIDERIUS: O sweetest, fairest lily!

My brother wears thee not the one half so well

As when thou grew'st thyself.

BELARIUS: O melancholy!

Who ever yet could sound thy bottom? Find

The ooze, to show what coast thy sluggish crare

Might easiliest harbour in? Thou blessed thing!

Jove knows what man thou mightst have made; but I,

Thou diedst, a most rare boy, of melancholy.

How found you him?

ARVIRAGUS: Stark, as you see;

Thus smiling, as some fly had tickled slumber,

Not as death's dart, being laugh'd at; his right cheek

Reposing on a cushion.

GUIDERIUS: Where?

ARVIRAGUS: O' the floor;

His arms thus leagued. I thought he slept, and put

My clouted brogues from off my feet, whose rudeness

Answer'd my steps too loud.

GUIDERIUS: Why, he but sleeps.

If he be gone, he'll make his grave a bed;

With female fairies will his tomb be haunted,

And worms will not come to thee.

ARVIRAGUS: With fairest flowers

Whilst summer lasts and I live here, Fidele,

I'll sweeten thy sad grave. Thou shalt not lack

The flower that's like thy face, pale primrose, nor

The azured harebell, like thy veins, no, nor
The leaf of eglantine, whom not to slander,
Out-sweeten'd not thy breath. The ruddock would,
With charitable bill—O bill, sore shaming
Those rich-left heirs that let their fathers lie
Without a monument!—bring thee all this;
Yea, and furr'd moss besides, when flowers are none,
To winter-ground thy corse.

GUIDERIUS: Prithee, have done;
And do not play in wench-like words with that
Which is so serious. Let us bury him,
And not protract with admiration what
Is now due debt. To the grave!

ARVIRAGUS: Say, where shall's lay him?

GUIDERIUS: By good Euriphile, our mother.

ARVIRAGUS: Be't so;
And let us, Polydore, though now our voices
Have got the mannish crack, sing him to the ground,
As once our mother; use like note and words,
Save that Euriphile must be Fidele.

GUIDERIUS: Cadwal,
I cannot sing. I'll weep, and word it with thee;
For notes of sorrow out of tune are worse
Than priests and fanes that lie.

ARVIRAGUS: We'll speak it, then.

BELARIUS: Great griefs, I see, medicine the less; for Cloten
Is quite forgot. He was a queen's son, boys;
And though he came our enemy, remember
He was paid for that. Though mean and mighty, rotting
Together, have one dust, yet reverence—
That angel of the world—doth make distinction
Of place 'tween high and low. Our foe was princely
And though you took his life, as being our foe,
Yet bury him as a prince.

GUIDERIUS: Pray You, fetch him hither.
Thersites' body is as good as Ajax',
When neither are alive.

ARVIRAGUS: If you'll go fetch him,
We'll say our song the whilst. Brother, begin.

Exit BELARIUS

GUIDERIUS: Nay, Cadwal, we must lay his head to the east;
My father hath a reason for't.

ARVIRAGUS: 'Tis true.

GUIDERIUS: Come on then, and remove him.

ARVIRAGUS: So. Begin.

Song

GUIDERIUS: Fear no more the heat o' the sun,
Nor the furious winter's rages;
Thou thy worldly task hast done,
Home art gone, and ta'en thy wages.
Golden lads and girls all must,
As chimney-sweepers, come to dust.

ARVIRAGUS: Fear no more the frown o' the great;
Thou art past the tyrant's stroke;
Care no more to clothe and eat;
To thee the reed is as the oak.
The sceptre, learning, physic, must
All follow this, and come to dust.

GUIDERIUS: Fear no more the lightning flash,

ARVIRAGUS: Nor the all-dreaded thunder-stone;

GUIDERIUS: Fear not slander, censure rash;

ARVIRAGUS: Thou hast finish'd joy and moan.

GUIDERIUS AND ARVIRAGUS: All lovers young, all lovers must
Consign to thee and come to dust.

GUIDERIUS: No exorciser harm thee!

ARVIRAGUS: Nor no witchcraft charm thee!

GUIDERIUS: Ghost unlaid forbear thee!

ARVIRAGUS: Nothing ill come near thee!

GUIDERIUS AND ARVIRAGUS: Quiet consummation have,
And renowned be thy grave!

Re-enter BELARIUS, with the body of CLOTEN

GUIDERIUS: We have done our obsequies. Come, lay him down.

BELARIUS: Here's a few flowers; but 'bout midnight, more.
The herbs that have on them cold dew o' the night
Are strewings fitt'st for graves. Upon their faces.
You were as flowers, now wither'd. Even so
These herblets shall, which we upon you strew.
Come on, away. Apart upon our knees.
The ground that gave them first has them again.
Their pleasures here are past, so is their pain.

Exeunt BELARIUS, GUIDERIUS, and ARVIRAGUS

IMOGEN: [*Awaking*] Yes, sir, to Milford-Haven. Which is the way?

I thank you. By yond bush? Pray, how far thither?
'Ods pittikins! can it be six mile yet?
I have gone all night. Faith, I'll lie down and sleep.
But, soft! no bedfellow! O gods and goddesses!

Seeing the body of CLOTEN

These flowers are like the pleasures of the world;
This bloody man, the care on't. I hope I dream;
For so I thought I was a cave-keeper,
And cook to honest creatures. But 'tis not so;
'Twas but a bolt of nothing, shot at nothing,
Which the brain makes of fumes. Our very eyes
Are sometimes like our judgments, blind. Good faith,
I tremble stiff with fear; but if there be
Yet left in heaven as small a drop of pity
As a wren's eye, fear'd gods, a part of it!
The dream's here still. Even when I wake, it is
Without me, as within me; not imagined, felt.
A headless man! The garments of Posthumus!
I know the shape of's leg; this is his hand;
His foot Mercurial; his Martial thigh;
The brawns of Hercules; but his Jovial face—
Murder in heaven?—How!—'Tis gone. Pisanio,
All curses madded Hecuba gave the Greeks,
And mine to boot, be darted on thee! Thou,
Conspired with that irregulous devil, Cloten,
Hast here cut off my lord. To write and read
Be henceforth treacherous! Damn'd Pisanio
Hath with his forged letters,—damn'd Pisanio—
From this most bravest vessel of the world
Struck the main-top! O Posthumus! alas,
Where is thy head? where's that? Ay me! where's that?
Pisanio might have kill'd thee at the heart,
And left this head on. How should this be? Pisanio?
'Tis he and Cloten; malice and lucre in them
Have laid this woe here. O, 'tis pregnant, pregnant!
The drug he gave me, which he said was precious
And cordial to me, have I not found it
Murderous to the senses? That confirms it home.
This is Pisanio's deed, and Cloten. O!
Give colour to my pale cheek with thy blood,
That we the horrider may seem to those
Which chance to find us. O, my lord, my lord!

Falls on the body

Enter LUCIUS, a Captain and a Soothsayer

CAPTAIN: To them the legions garrison'd in Gailia,
After your will, have cross'd the sea, attending
You here at Milford-Haven; with your ships,
They are in readiness.

CAIUS LUCIUS: But what from Rome?

CAPTAIN: The senate hath stirr'd up the confiners
And gentlemen of Italy, most willing spirits,
That promise noble service; and they come
Under the conduct of bold Iachimo,
Syenna's brother.

CAIUS LUCIUS: When expect you them?

CAPTAIN: With the next benefit o' the wind.

CAIUS LUCIUS: This forwardness
Makes our hopes fair. Command our present numbers
Be muster'd; bid the captains look to't. Now, sir,
What have you dream'd of late of this war's purpose?

SOOTHSAYER: Last night the very gods show'd me a vision—
I fast and pray'd for their intelligence—thus:
I saw Jove's bird, the Roman eagle, wing'd
From the spongy south to this part of the west,
There vanish'd in the sunbeams; which portends,
Unless my sins abuse my divination,
Success to the Roman host.

CAIUS LUCIUS: Dream often so,
And never false. Soft, ho! what trunk is here
Without his top? The ruin speaks that sometime
It was a worthy building. How! a page!
Or dead, or sleeping on him? But dead, rather;
For nature doth abhor to make his bed
With the defunct, or sleep upon the dead.
Let's see the boy's face.

CAPTAIN: He's alive, my lord.

CAIUS LUCIUS: He'll then instruct us of this body. Young one,
Inform us of thy fortunes, for it seems
They crave to be demanded. Who is this

Thou makest thy bloody pillow? Or who was he
That, otherwise than noble nature did,
Hath alter'd that good picture? What's thy interest
In this sad wreck? How came it? Who is it?
What art thou?

IMOGEN: I am nothing; or if not,
Nothing to be were better. This was my master,
A very valiant Briton and a good,
That here by mountaineers lies slain. Alas!
There is no more such masters. I may wander
From east to occident, cry out for service,
Try many, all good, serve truly, never
Find such another master.

CAIUS LUCIUS: 'Lack, good youth!
Thou movest no less with thy complaining than
Thy master in bleeding. say his name, good friend.

IMOGEN: Richard du Champ. (*Aside*)
If I do lie and do
No harm by it, though the gods hear, I hope
They'll pardon it.—Say you, sir?

CAIUS LUCIUS: Thy name?

IMOGEN: Fidele, sir.

CAIUS LUCIUS: Thou dost approve thyself the very same;
Thy name well fits thy faith, thy faith thy name.
Wilt take thy chance with me? I will not say
Thou shalt be so well master'd, but, be sure,
No less beloved. The Roman emperor's letters,
Sent by a consul to me, should not sooner
Than thine own worth prefer thee. Go with me.

IMOGEN: I'll follow, sir. But first, an't please the gods,
I'll hide my master from the flies, as deep
As these poor pickaxes can dig; and when
With wild wood-leaves and weeds I ha' strew'd his grave,
And on it said a century of prayers,
Such as I can, twice o'er, I'll weep and sigh;
And leaving so his service, follow you,
So please you entertain me.

CAIUS LUCIUS: Ay, good youth!
And rather father thee than master thee.
My friends,
The boy hath taught us manly duties; let us
Find out the prettiest daisied plot we can,
And make him with our pikes and partisans
A grave. Come, arm him. Boy, he is preferr'd
By thee to us, and he shall be interr'd
As soldiers can. Be cheerful; wipe thine eyes.
Some falls are means the happier to arise.

Exeunt

SCENE III—*Britain: Cymbeline's palace*

Enter CYMBELINE, Lords, PISANIO, and Attendants

CYMBELINE: Again; and bring me word how 'tis with her.

Exit an Attendant

A fever with the absence of her son,
A madness, of which her life's in danger. Heavens,
How deeply you at once do touch me! Imogen,
The great part of my comfort, gone; my queen
Upon a desperate bed, and in a time
When fearful wars point at me; her son gone,
So needful for this present. It strikes me, past
The hope of comfort. But for thee, fellow,
Who needs must know of her departure and
Dost seem so ignorant, we'll enforce it from thee
By a sharp torture.

PISANIO: Sir, my life is yours;
I humbly set it at your will; but, for my mistress,
I nothing know where she remains, why gone,
Nor when she purposes return. Beseech your highness,
Hold me your loyal servant.

FIRST LORD: Good my liege,
The day that she was missing he was here.
I dare be bound he's true and shall perform
All parts of his subjection loyally. For Cloten,
There wants no diligence in seeking him,
And will, no doubt, be found.

CYMBELINE: The time is troublesome.
(*To PISANIO*) We'll slip you for a season; but our jealousy
Does yet depend.

FIRST LORD: So please your majesty,
The Roman legions, all from Gallia drawn,
Are landed on your coast, with a supply
Of Roman gentlemen by the senate sent.

CYMBELINE: Now for the counsel of my son and queen!
I am amazed with matter.
FIRST LORD: Good my liege,
Your preparation can affront no less
Than what you hear of. Come more, for more you're ready.
The want is but to put those powers in motion
That long to move.
CYMBELINE: I thank you. Let's withdraw;
And meet the time as it seeks us. We fear not
What can from Italy annoy us; but
We grieve at chances here. Away!

Exeunt all but PISANIO

PISANIO: I heard no letter from my master since
I wrote him Imogen was slain. 'Tis strange.
Nor hear I from my mistress who did promise
To yield me often tidings. Neither know I
What is betid to Cloten; but remain
Perplex'd in all. The heavens still must work.
Wherein I am false I am honest; not true, to be true.
These present wars shall find I love my country,
Even to the note o' the king, or I'll fall in them.
All other doubts, by time let them be clear'd:
Fortune brings in some boats that are not steer'd.

Exit

SCENE IV—*Wales: Before the cave of Belarius*

Enter BELARIUS, GUIDERIUS, and ARVIRAGUS

GUIDERIUS: The noise is round about us.
BELARIUS: Let us from it.
ARVIRAGUS: What pleasure, sir, find we in life, to lock it
From action and adventure?
GUIDERIUS: Nay, what hope
Have we in hiding us? This way, the Romans
Must or for Britons slay us, or receive us
For barbarous and unnatural revolts
During their use, and slay us after.
BELARIUS: Sons,
We'll higher to the mountains; there secure us.
To the king's party there's no going. Newness
Of Cloten's death—we being not known, not muster'd
Among the bands—may drive us to a render
Where we have lived, and so extort from's that
Which we have done, whose answer would be death
Drawn on with torture.
GUIDERIUS: This is, sir, a doubt
In such a time nothing becoming you,
Nor satisfying us.
ARVIRAGUS: It is not likely
That when they hear the Roman horses neigh,
Behold their quarter'd fires, have both their eyes
And ears so cloy'd importantly as now,
That they will waste their time upon our note,
To know from whence we are.
BELARIUS: O, I am known
Of many in the army. Many years,
Though Cloten then but young, you see, not wore him
From my remembrance. And, besides, the king
Hath not deserved my service nor your loves;
Who find in my exile the want of breeding,
The certainty of this hard life; aye hopeless
To have the courtesy your cradle promised,
But to be still hot summer's tamings and
The shrinking slaves of winter.
GUIDERIUS: Than be so
Better to cease to be. Pray, sir, to the army.
I and my brother are not known; yourself
So out of thought, and thereto so o'ergrown,
Cannot be question'd.
ARVIRAGUS: By this sun that shines,
I'll thither. What thing is it that I never
Did see man die! scarce ever look'd on blood,
But that of coward hares, hot goats, and venison!
Never bestrid a horse, save one that had
A rider like myself, who ne'er wore rowel
Nor iron on his heel! I am ashamed
To look upon the holy sun, to have
The benefit of his blest beams, remaining
So long a poor unknown.
GUIDERIUS: By heavens, I'll go!
If you will bless me, sir, and give me leave,
I'll take the better care, but if you will not,

The hazard therefore due fall on me by
The hands of Romans!
ARVIRAGUS: So say I amen.
BELARIUS: No reason I, since of your lives you set
So slight a valuation, should reserve
My crack'd one to more care. Have with you, boys!
If in your country wars you chance to die,
That is my bed too, lads, an there I'll lie.
Lead, lead. [*Aside*] The time seems long; their blood thinks scorn,
Till it fly out and show them princes born.

Exeunt

Act V

Scene I—*Britain: The Roman camp*

Enter POSTHUMUS, with a bloody handkerchief

POSTHUMUS LEONATUS: Yea, bloody cloth, I'll keep thee, for I wish'd
Thou shouldst be colour'd thus. You married ones,
If each of you should take this course, how many
Must murder wives much better than themselves
For wrying but a little! O Pisanio!
Every good servant does not all commands;
No bond but to do just ones. Gods! if you
Should have ta'en vengeance on my faults, I never
Had lived to put on this; so had you saved
The noble Imogen to repent, and struck
Me, wretch more worth your vengeance. But, alack,
You snatch some hence for little faults; that's love,
To have them fall no more. You some permit
To second ills with ills, each elder worse,
And make them dread it, to the doers' thrift.
But Imogen is your own. Do your best wills,
And make me blest to obey! I am brought hither
Among the Italian gentry, and to fight
Against my lady's kingdom. 'Tis enough
That, Britain, I have kill'd thy mistress; peace!
I'll give no wound to thee. Therefore, good heavens,
Hear patiently my purpose. I'll disrobe me
Of these Italian weeds and suit myself
As does a Briton peasant. So I'll fight
Against the part I come with; so I'll die
For thee, O Imogen, even for whom my life
Is every breath a death. And thus, unknown,
Pitied nor hated, to the face of peril
Myself I'll dedicate. Let me make men know
More valour in me than my habits show.
Gods, put the strength o' the Leonati in me!
To shame the guise o' the world, I will begin
The fashion, less without and more within.

Exit

Scene II—*Britain: Field of battle between the British and Roman camps*

Enter, from one side, LUCIUS, IACHIMO, and the Roman Army: from the other side, the British Army; POSTHUMUS LEONATUS following, like a poor soldier. They march over and go out. Then enter again, in skirmish, IACHIMO and POSTHUMUS LEONATUS he vanquisheth and disarmeth IACHIMO, and then leaves him

IACHIMO: The heaviness and guilt within my bosom
Takes off my manhood. I have belied a lady,
The princess of this country, and the air on't
Revengingly enfeebles me; or could this carl,
A very drudge of nature's, have subdued me
In my profession? Knighthoods and honours, borne
As I wear mine are titles but of scorn.
If that thy gentry, Britain, go before
This lout as he exceeds our lords, the odds
Is that we scarce are men and you are gods.

Exit

The battle continues; the Britons fly; CYMBELINE is taken: then enter, to his rescue, BELARIUS, GUIDERIUS, and ARVIRAGUS

BELARIUS: Stand, stand! We have the advantage of the ground;
The lane is guarded: nothing routs us but
The villany of our fears.

GUIDERIUS AND ARVIRAGUS: Stand, stand, and fight!

Re-enter POSTHUMUS LEONATUS, and seconds the Britons: they rescue CYMBELINE, and exeunt. Then re-enter LUCIUS, and IACHIMO, with IMOGEN

CAIUS LUCIUS: Away, boy, from the troops, and save thyself;

For friends kill friends, and the disorder's such
As war were hoodwink'd.

IACHIMO: 'Tis their fresh supplies.

CAIUS LUCIUS: It is a day turn'd strangely. Or betimes
Let's reinforce or fly.

Exeunt

SCENE III—*Another part of the field*

Enter POSTHUMUS LEONATUS and a British Lord

LORD: Camest thou from where they made the stand?

POSTHUMUS LEONATUS: I did.
Though you, it seems, come from the fliers.

LORD: I did.

POSTHUMUS LEONATUS: No blame be to you, sir; for all was lost,
But that the heavens fought. The king himself
Of his wings destitute, the army broken,
And but the backs of Britons seen, all flying
Through a straight lane; the enemy full-hearted,
Lolling the tongue with slaughtering, having work
More plentiful than tools to do't, struck down
Some mortally, some slightly touch'd, some falling
Merely through fear; that the straight pass was damm'd
With dead men hurt behind, and cowards living
To die with lengthen'd shame.

LORD: Where was this lane?

POSTHUMUS LEONATUS: Close by the battle, ditch'd, and wall'd with turf;
Which gave advantage to an ancient soldier,
An honest one, I warrant; who deserved
So long a breeding as his white beard came to,
In doing this for's country. Athwart the lane,
He, with two striplings—lads more like to run
The country base than to commit such slaughter
With faces fit for masks, or rather fairer
Than those for preservation cased, or shame—
Made good the passage, cried to those that fled,
'Our Britain's harts die flying, not our men.
To darkness fleet souls that fly backwards. Stand;
Or we are Romans and will give you that
Like beasts which you shun beastly, and may save
But to look back in frown. Stand, stand!' These three.
Three thousand confident, in act as many—
For three performers are the file when all
The rest do nothing—with this word 'Stand, stand!'
Accommodated by the place, more charming
With their own nobleness, which could have turn'd
A distaff to a lance, gilded pale looks,
Part shame, part spirit renew'd; that some, turn'd coward
But by example—O, a sin in war,
Damn'd in the first beginners!—gan to look
The way that they did, and to grin like lions
Upon the pikes o' the hunters. Then began
A stop i' the chaser, a retire, anon
A rout, confusion thick. Forthwith they fly
Chickens, the way which they stoop'd eagles; slaves,
The strides they victors made; and now our cowards,
Like fragments in hard voyages, became
The life o' the need. Having found the backdoor open
Of the unguarded hearts, heavens, how they wound!
Some slain before; some dying; some their friends
O'er borne i' the former wave. Ten chased by one
Are now each one the slaughterman of twenty.
Those that would die or ere resist are grown
The mortal bugs o' the field.

LORD: This was strange chance:
A narrow lane, an old man, and two boys.

POSTHUMUS LEONATUS: Nay, do not wonder at it; you are made
Rather to wonder at the things you hear
Than to work any. Will you rhyme upon't,
And vent it for a mockery? Here is one:
'Two boys, an old man twice a boy, a lane,
Preserved the Britons, was the Romans' bane.'

LORD: Nay, be not angry, sir.
POSTHUMUS LEONATUS: 'Lack, to what end?
Who dares not stand his foe, I'll be his friend;
For if he'll do as he is made to do,
I know he'll quickly fly my friendship too.
You have put me into rhyme.
LORD: Farewell; you're angry.

Exit Lord

POSTHUMUS LEONATUS: Still going?
This is a lord! O noble misery,
To be i' the field, and ask 'what news?' of me!
To-day how many would have given their honours
To have saved their carcasses! took heel to do't,
And yet died too! I, in mine own woe charm'd,
Could not find death where I did hear him groan,
Nor feel him where he struck. Being an ugly monster,
'Tis strange he hides him in fresh cups, soft beds,
Sweet words; or hath more ministers than we
That draw his knives i' the war. Well, I will find him
For being now a favourer to the Briton,
No more a Briton, I have resumed again
The part I came in. Fight I will no more,
But yield me to the veriest hind that shall
Once touch my shoulder. Great the slaughter is
Here made by the Roman; great the answer be
Britons must take. For me, my ransom's death;
On either side I come to spend my breath;
Which neither here I'll keep nor bear again,
But end it by some means for Imogen.

Enter two British Captains and Soldiers

FIRST CAPTAIN: Great Jupiter be praised! Lucius is taken.
'Tis thought the old man and his sons were angels.
SECOND CAPTAIN: There was a fourth man, in a silly habit,
That gave the affront with them.
FIRST CAPTAIN: So 'tis reported;
But none of 'em can be found. Stand! who's there?
POSTHUMUS LEONATUS: A Roman,
Who had not now been drooping here, if seconds
Had answer'd him.
SECOND CAPTAIN: Lay hands on him; a dog!
A leg of Rome shall not return to tell
What crows have peck'd them here. He brags his service
As if he were of note. Bring him to the king.

Enter CYMBELINE, BELARIUS, GUIDERIUS, ARVIRAGUS, PISANIO, Soldiers, Attendants, and Roman Captives. The Captains present POSTHUMUS LEONATUS to CYMBELINE, who delivers him over to a Gaoler: then exeunt omnes

SCENE IV—*A British prison*

Enter POSTHUMUS LEONATUS and two Gaolers

FIRST GAOLER: You shall not now be stol'n, you have locks upon you;
So graze as you find pasture.
SECOND GAOLER: Ay, or a stomach.

Exeunt Gaolers

POSTHUMUS LEONATUS: Most welcome, bondage! for thou art away,
I think, to liberty. Yet am I better
Than one that's sick o' the gout; since he had rather
Groan so in perpetuity than be cured
By the sure physician, death, who is the key
To unbar these locks. My conscience, thou art fetter'd
More than my shanks and wrists; you good gods, give me
The penitent instrument to pick that bolt,
Then, free for ever! Is't enough I am sorry?
So children temporal fathers do appease;
Gods are more full of mercy. Must I repent?
I cannot do it better than in gyves,
Desired more than constrain'd. To satisfy,
If of my freedom 'tis the main part, take
No stricter render of me than my all.
I know you are more clement than vile men,
Who of their broken debtors take a third,
A sixth, a tenth, letting them thrive again
On their abatement; that's not my desire.
For Imogen's dear life take mine; and though
'Tis not so dear, yet 'tis a life; you coin'd it.
'Tween man and man they weigh not every stamp;
Though light, take pieces for the figure's sake;

You rather mine, being yours. And so, great powers,
If you will take this audit, take this life,
And cancel these cold bonds. O Imogen!
I'll speak to thee in silence.

Sleeps

Solemn music. Enter, as in an apparition, SICILIUS LEONATUS, father to Posthumus Leonatus, an old man, attired like a warrior; leading in his hand an ancient matron, his wife, and mother to Posthumus Leonatus, with music before them. Then, after other music, follow the two young Leonati, brothers to Posthumus Leonatus, with wounds as they died in the wars. They circle Posthumus Leonatus round, as he lies sleeping

SICILIUS LEONATUS: No more, thou thunder-master, show
Thy spite on mortal flies.
With Mars fall out, with Juno chide,
That thy adulteries
Rates and revenges.
Hath my poor boy done aught but well,
Whose face I never saw?
I died whilst in the womb he stay'd
Attending nature's law;
Whose father then, as men report
Thou orphans' father art,
Thou shouldst have been, and shielded him
From this earth-vexing smart.

MOTHER: Lucina lent not me her aid,
But took me in my throes;
That from me was Posthumus ripp'd
Came crying 'mongst his foes,
A thing of pity.

SICILIUS LEONATUS: Great nature, like his ancestry,
Moulded the stuff so fair,
That he deserved the praise o' the world,
As great Sicilius' heir.

FIRST BROTHER: When once he was mature for man,
In Britain where was he
That could stand up his parallel;
Or fruitful object be
In eye of Imogen, that best
Could deem his dignity?

MOTHER: With marriage wherefore was he mock'd,
To be exiled, and thrown
From Leonati seat, and cast
From her his dearest one,
Sweet Imogen?

SICILIUS LEONATUS: Why did you suffer Iachimo,
Slight thing of Italy,
To taint his nobler heart and brain
With needless jealosy;
And to become the geck and scorn
O' th' other's villany?

SECOND BROTHER: For this from stiller seats we came,
Our parents and us twain,
That striking in our country's cause
Fell bravely and were slain,
Our fealty and Tenantius' right
With honour to maintain.

FIRST BROTHER: Like hardiment Posthumus hath
To Cymbeline perform'd.
Then, Jupiter, thou king of gods,
Why hast thou thus adjourn'd
The graces for his merits due,
Being all to dolours turn'd?

SICILIUS LEONATUS: Thy crystal window ope; look out;
No longer exercise
Upon a valiant race thy harsh
And potent injuries.

MOTHER: Since, Jupiter, our son is good,
Take off his miseries.

SICILIUS LEONATUS: Peep through thy marble mansion. Help;
Or we poor ghosts will cry
To the shining synod of the rest
Against thy deity.

FIRST AND SECOND BROTHER: Help, Jupiter! or we appeal,
And from thy justice fly.

Jupiter descends in thunder and lightning, sitting upon an eagle. He throws a thunderbolt. The Ghosts fall on their knees

JUPITER: No more, you petty spirits of region low,
Offend our hearing; hush! How dare you ghosts
Accuse the thunderer, whose bolt, you know,
Sky-planted batters all rebelling coasts?
Poor shadows of Elysium, hence, and rest
Upon your never-withering banks of flowers.

Be not with mortal accidents opprest:
No care of yours it is; you know 'tis ours.
Whom best I love I cross; to make my gift,
The more delay'd, delighted. Be content;
Your low-laid son our godhead will uplift;
His comforts thrive, his trials well are spent.
Our Jovial star reign'd at his birth, and in
Our temple was he married. Rise, and fade!
He shall be lord of lady Imogen,
And happier much by his affliction made.
This tablet lay upon his breast, wherein
Our pleasure his full fortune doth confine;
And so, away; no further with your din
Express impatience, lest you stir up mine.
Mount, eagle, to my palace crystalline.

Ascends

SICILIUS LEONATUS: He came in thunder; his celestial breath
Was sulphurous to smell; the holy eagle
Stoop'd as to foot us. His ascension is
More sweet than our blest fields. His royal bird
Prunes the immortal wing and cloys his beak,
As when his god is pleased.

ALL: Thanks, Jupiter!

SICILIUS LEONATUS: The marble pavement closes, he is enter'd
His radiant root. Away! and, to be blest,
Let us with care perform his great behest.

Ghosts vanish

POSTHUMUS LEONATUS: [*Waking*] Sleep, thou hast been a grandsire, and begot
A father to me; and thou hast created
A mother and two brothers. But, O scorn!
Gone! They went hence so soon as they were born.
And so I am awake. Poor wretches that depend
On greatness' favour dream as I have done,
Wake and find nothing. But, alas, I swerve;
Many dream not to find, neither deserve,
And yet are steep'd in favours; so am I,
That have this golden chance and know not why.
What fairies haunt this ground? A book? O rare one!
Be not, as is our fangled world, a garment
Nobler than that it covers. Let thy effects
So follow, to be most unlike our courtiers,
As good as promise.

Reads

'When as a lion's whelp shall, to himself unknown, without seeking find, and be embraced by a piece of tender air; and when from a stately cedar shall be lopped branches, which, being dead many years, shall after revive, be jointed to the old stock and freshly grow; then shall Posthumus end his miseries, Britain be fortunate and flourish in peace and plenty.'

'Tis still a dream, or else such stuff as madmen
Tongue and brain not; either both or nothing;
Or senseless speaking or a speaking such
As sense cannot untie. Be what it is,
The action of my life is like it, which
I'll keep, if but for sympathy.

Re-enter First Gaoler

FIRST GAOLER: Come, sir, are you ready for death?

POSTHUMUS LEONATUS: Over-roasted rather; ready long ago.

FIRST GAOLER: Hanging is the word, sir: if you be ready for that, you are well cooked.

POSTHUMUS LEONATUS: So, if I prove a good repast to the spectators, the dish pays the shot.

FIRST GAOLER: A heavy reckoning for you, sir. But the comfort is, you shall be called to no more payments, fear no more tavern-bills; which are often the sadness of parting, as the procuring of mirth. You come in flint for want of meat, depart reeling with too much drink; sorry that you have paid too much, and sorry that you are paid too much; purse and brain both empty; the brain the heavier for being too light, the purse too light, being drawn of heaviness. Of this contradiction you shall now be quit. O, the charity of a penny cord! It sums up thousands in a trice. You have no true debitor and creditor but it; of what's past, is, and to come, the discharge. Your neck, sir, is pen, book and counters; so the acquittance follows.

POSTHUMUS LEONATUS: I am merrier to die than thou art to live.

FIRST GAOLER: Indeed, sir, he that sleeps feels not the tooth-ache. But a man that were to sleep your sleep, and a hangman to help him to bed, I think he would change places with his officer; for, look you, sir, you know not which way you shall go.

POSTHUMUS LEONATUS: Yes, indeed do I, fellow.

FIRST GAOLER: Your death has eyes in 's head then; I have not seen him so pictured. You must either be directed by some that take upon them to know, or do take upon yourself that which I am sure you do not know, or jump the after inquiry on your own peril. And how you shall speed in your journey's end, I think you'll never return to tell one.

POSTHUMUS LEONATUS: I tell thee, fellow, there are none want eyes to direct them the way I am going, but such as wink and will not use them.

First Gaoler: What an infinite mock is this, that a man should have the best use of eyes to see the way of blindness! I am sure hanging's the way of winking.

Enter a Messenger

MESSENGER: Knock off his manacles; bring your prisoner to the king.

POSTHUMUS LEONATUS: Thou bring'st good news; I am called to be made free.

FIRST GAOLER: I'll be hang'd then.

POSTHUMUS LEONATUS: Thou shalt be then freer than a gaoler; no bolts for the dead.

Exeunt POSTHUMUS LEONATUS and Messenger

FIRST GAOLER: Unless a man would marry a gallows and beget young gibbets, I never saw one so prone. Yet, on my conscience, there are verier knaves desire to live, for all he be a Roman; and there be some of them too that die against their wills; so should I, if I were one. I would we were all of one mind, and one mind good. O, there were desolation of gaolers and gallowses! I speak against my present profit, but my wish hath a preferment in't.

Exeunt

SCENE V—*Britain: Cymbeline's tent*

Enter CYMBELINE, BELARIUS, GUIDERIUS, ARVIRAGUS, PISANIO, Lords, Officers, and Attendants

CYMBELINE: Stand by my side, you whom the gods have made
Preservers of my throne. Woe is my heart
That the poor soldier that so richly fought,
Whose rags shamed gilded arms, whose naked breast
Stepp'd before larges of proof, cannot be found.
He shall be happy that can find him, if
Our grace can make him so.

BELARIUS: I never saw
Such noble fury in so poor a thing;
Such precious deeds in one that promises nought
But beggary and poor looks.

CYMBELINE: No tidings of him?

PISANIO: He hath been search'd among the dead and living,
But no trace of him.

CYMBELINE: To my grief, I am
The heir of his reward;
[To BELARIUS, GUIDERIUS, and ARVIRAGUS]
which I will add
To you, the liver, heart and brain of Britain,
By whom I grant she lives. 'Tis now the time
To ask of whence you are. Report it.

BELARIUS: Sir,
In Cambria are we born, and gentlemen;
Further to boast were neither true nor modest,
Unless I add, we are honest.

CYMBELINE: Bow your knees.
Arise my knights o' the battle; I create you
Companions to our person and will fit you
With dignities becoming your estates.

Enter CORNELIUS and Ladies

There's business in these faces. Why so sadly
Greet you our victory? you look like Romans,
And not o' the court of Britain.

CORNELIUS: Hail, great King!
To sour your happiness, I must report
The queen is dead.

CYMBELINE: Who worse than a physician
Would this report become? But I consider,
By medicine life may be prolong'd, yet death
Will seize the doctor too. How ended she?

CORNELIUS: With horror, madly dying, like her life,
Which, being cruel to the world, concluded
Most cruel to herself. What she confess'd
I will report, so please you; these her women
Can trip me, if I err; who with wet cheeks
Were present when she finish'd.

CYMBELINE: Prithee, say.

CORNELIUS: First, she confess'd she never loved you, only
Affected greatness got by you, not you;
Married your royalty, was wife to your place;
Abhorr'd your person.

CYMBELINE: She alone knew this;

And, but she spoke it dying, I would not
Believe her lips in opening it. Proceed.

CORNELIUS: Your daughter, whom she bore in hand to love
With such integrity, she did confess
Was as a scorpion to her sight; whose life,
But that her flight prevented it, she had
Ta'en off by poison.

CYMBELINE: O most delicate fiend!
Who is 't can read a woman? Is there more?

CORNELIUS: More, sir, and worse. She did confess she had
For you a mortal mineral; which, being took,
Should by the minute feed on life and lingering
By inches waste you. In which time she purposed,
By watching, weeping, tendance, kissing, to
O'ercome you with her show, and in time,
When she had fitted you with her craft, to work
Her son into the adoption of the crown;
But, failing of her end by his strange absence,
Grew shameless-desperate; open'd, in despite
Of heaven and men, her purposes; repented
The evils she hatch'd were not effected; so,
Despairing died.

CYMBELINE: Heard you all this, her women?

FIRST LADY: We did, so please your highness.

CYMBELINE: Mine eyes
Were not in fault, for she was beautiful;
Mine ears, that heard her flattery; nor my heart,
That thought her like her seeming. It had been vicious
To have mistrusted her: yet, O my daughter!
That it was folly in me, thou mayst say,
And prove it in thy feeling. Heaven mend all!

Enter LUCIUS, IACHIMO, the Soothsayer, and other Roman Prisoners, guarded; POSTHUMUS LEONATUS behind, and IMOGEN

Thou comest not, Caius, now for tribute; that
The Britons have razed out, though with the loss
Of many a bold one; whose kinsmen have made suit
That their good souls may be appeased with slaughter
Of you their captives, which ourself have granted;
So think of your estate.

CAIUS LUCIUS: Consider, sir, the chance of war. The day
Was yours by accident; had it gone with us,
We should not, when the blood was cool, have threaten'd
Our prisoners with the sword. But since the gods
Will have it thus, that nothing but our lives
May be call'd ransom, let it come. Sufficeth
A Roman with a Roman's heart can suffer.
Augustus lives to think on't; and so much
For my peculiar care. This one thing only
I will entreat; my boy, a Briton born,
Let him be ransom'd. Never master had
A page so kind, so duteous, diligent,
So tender over his occasions, true,
So feat, so nurse-like; let his virtue join
With my request, which I make bold your highness
Cannot deny; he hath done no Briton harm,
Though he have served a Roman. Save him, sir,
And spare no blood beside.

CYMBELINE: I have surely seen him;
His favour is familiar to me. Boy,
Thou hast look'd thyself into my grace,
And art mine own. I know not why, wherefore,
To say 'live, boy'. Ne'er thank thy master; live;
And ask of Cymbeline what boon thou wilt,
Fitting my bounty and thy state, I'll give it;
Yea, though thou do demand a prisoner,
The noblest ta'en.

IMOGEN: I humbly thank your highness.

CAIUS LUCIUS: I do not bid thee beg my life, good lad;
And yet I know thou wilt.

IMOGEN: No, no! alack,
There's other work in hand. I see a thing
Bitter to me as death; your life, good master,
Must shuffle for itself.

CAIUS LUCIUS: The boy disdains me,
He leaves me, scorns me. Briefly die their joys
That place them on the truth of girls and boys.
Why stands he so perplex'd?

CYMBELINE: What wouldst thou, boy?
I love thee more and more; think more and more
What's best to ask. Know'st him thou look'st on? Speak,
Wilt have him live? Is he thy kin? thy friend?

IMOGEN: He is a Roman, no more kin to me

Than I to your Highness; who, being born your vassal,
Am something nearer.
CYMBELINE: Wherefore eyest him so?
IMOGEN: I'll tell you, sir, in private, if you please
To give me hearing.
CYMBELINE: Ay, with all my heart,
And lend my best attention. What's thy name?
IMOGEN: Fidele, sir.
CYMBELINE: Thou'rt my good youth, my page;
I'll be thy master. Walk with me; speak freely.
CYMBELINE and IMOGEN converse apart
BELARIUS: Is not this boy revived from death?
ARVIRAGUS: One sand another
Not more resembles that sweet rosy lad
Who died, and was Fidele. What think you?
GUIDERIUS: The same dead thing alive.
BELARIUS: Peace, peace! see further. He eyes us not; forbear.
Creatures may be alike; were't he, I am sure
He would have spoke to us.
GUIDERIUS: But we saw him dead.
BELARIUS: Be silent; let's see further.
PISANIO: [Aside] It is my mistress.
Since she is living, let the time run on
To good or bad.
CYMBELINE and IMOGEN come forward
CYMBELINE: Come, stand thou by our side;
Make thy demand aloud. [*To IACHIMO*] Sir, step you forth;
Give answer to this boy, and do it freely;
Or, by our greatness and the grace of it,
Which is our honour, bitter torture shall
Winnow the truth from falsehood. On, speak to him.
IMOGEN: My boon is that this gentleman may render
Of whom he had this ring.
POSTHUMUS LEONATUS: [*Aside*] What's that to him?
CYMBELINE: That diamond upon your finger, say
How came it yours?
IACHIMO: Thou'lt torture me to leave unspoken that
Which, to be spoke, would torture thee.
CYMBELINE: How! me?
IACHIMO: I am glad to be constrain'd to utter that
Which torments me to conceal. By villainy
I got this ring: 'twas Leonatus' jewel;
Whom thou didst banish; and—which more may grieve thee,
As it doth me—a nobler sir ne'er lived
'Twixt sky and ground. Wilt thou hear more, my lord?
CYMBELINE: All that belongs to this.
IACHIMO: That paragon, thy daughter,
For whom my heart drops blood, and my false spirits
Quail to remember—Give me leave; I faint.
CYMBELINE: My daughter! what of her? Renew thy strength;
I had rather thou shouldst live while nature will
Than die ere I hear more. Strive, man, and speak.
IACHIMO: Upon a time—unhappy was the clock
That struck the hour!—it was in Rome—accursed
The mansion where!—'twas at a feast—O, would
Our viands had been poison'd, or at least
Those which I heaved to head!—the good Posthumus—
What should I say? he was too good to be
Where ill men were; and was the best of all
Amongst the rarest of good ones—sitting sadly,
Hearing us praise our loves of Italy
For beauty that made barren the swell'd boast
Of him that best could speak, for feature, laming
The shrine of Venus, or straight-pight Minerva.
Postures beyond brief nature, for condition,
A shop of all the qualities that man
Loves woman for, besides that hook of wiving,
Fairness which strikes the eye—
CYMBELINE: I stand on fire.
Come to the matter.
IACHIMO: All too soon I shall,
Unless thou wouldst grieve quickly. This Posthumus,
Most like a noble lord in love and one
That had a royal lover, took his hint;
And, not dispraising whom we praised—therein

He was as calm as virtue—he began
His mistress' picture; which by his tongue being made,
And then a mind put in't, either our brags
Were crack'd of kitchen trolls, or his description
Proved us unspeaking sots.

CYMBELINE: Nay, nay, to the purpose.

IACHIMO: Your daughter's chastity—there it begins.
He spake of her, as Dian had hot dreams,
And she alone were cold; whereat I, wretch,
Made scruple of his praise; and wager'd with him
Pieces of gold, 'gainst this which then he wore
Upon his honour'd finger, to attain
In suit the place of's bed and win this ring
By hers and mine adultery. He, true knight,
No lesser of her honour confident
Than I did truly find her, stakes this ring;
And would so, had it been a carbuncle
Of Phoebus' wheel, and might so safely, had it
Been all the worth of's car. Away to Britain
Post I in this design. Well may you, sir,
Remember me at court; where I was taught
Of your chaste daughter the wide difference
'Twixt amorous and villanous. Being thus quench'd
Of hope, not longing, mine Italian brain
Gan in your duller Britain operate
Most vilely; for my vantage, excellent;
And, to be brief, my practise so prevail'd,
That I return'd with simular proof enough
To make the noble Leonatus mad,
By wounding his belief in her renown
With tokens thus, and thus; averting notes
Of chamber-hanging, pictures, this her bracelet—
O cunning, how I got it!—nay, some marks
Of secret on her person, that he could not
But think her bond of chastity quite crack'd,
I having ta'en the forfeit. Whereupon—
Methinks, I see him now—

POSTHUMUS LEONATUS: [*Advancing*] Ay, so thou dost,
Italian fiend! Ay me, most credulous fool,
Egregious murderer, thief, any thing
That's due to all the villains past, in being,
To come! O, give me cord, or knife, or poison,
Some upright justicer! Thou, king, send out
For torturers ingenious. It is I
That all the abhorred things o' the earth amend
By being worse than they. I am Posthumus,
That kill'd thy daughter; villain-like, I lie—
That caused a lesser villain than myself,
A sacrilegious thief, to do't. The temple
Of virtue was she; yea, and she herself.
Spit, and throw stones, cast mire upon me, set
The dogs o' the street to bay me. Every villain
Be call'd Posthumus Leonitus; and
Be villany less than 'twas! O Imogen!
My queen, my life, my wife! O Imogen,
Imogen, Imogen!

IMOGEN: Peace, my lord. Hear, hear—

POSTHUMUS LEONATUS: Shall's have a play of this? Thou scornful page,
There lie thy part.

Striking her: she falls

PISANIO: O, gentlemen, help!
Mine and your mistress! O, my lord Posthumus!
You ne'er kill'd Imogen til now. Help, help!
Mine honour'd lady!

CYMBELINE: Does the world go round?

POSTHUMUS LEONATUS: How come these staggers on me?

PISANIO: Wake, my mistress!

CYMBELINE: If this be so, the gods do mean to strike me
To death with mortal joy.

PISANIO: How fares thy mistress?

IMOGEN: O, get thee from my sight;
Thou gavest me poison. Dangerous fellow, hence!
Breathe not where princes are.

CYMBELINE: The tune of Imogen!

PISANIO: Lady,
The gods throw stones of sulphur on me, if
That box I gave you was not thought by me
A precious thing! I had it from the queen.

CYMBELINE: New matter still?

IMOGEN: It poison'd me.

CORNELIUS: O gods!
I left out one thing which the queen confess'd.
Which must approve thee honest. 'If Pisanio

Have,' said she, 'given his mistress that confection
Which I gave him for cordial, she is served
As I would serve a rat.'
CYMBELINE: What's this, Comelius?
CORNELIUS: The queen, sir, very oft importuned me
To temper poisons for her, still pretending
The satisfaction of her knowledge only
In killing creatures vile, as cats and dogs,
Of no esteem. I, dreading that her purpose
Was of more danger, did compound for her
A certain stuff, which, being ta'en, would cease
The present power of life, but in short time
All offices of nature should again
Do their due functions. Have you ta'en of it?
IMOGEN: Most like I did, for I was dead.
BELARIUS: My boys,
There was our error.
GUIDERIUS: This is, sure, Fidele.
IMOGEN: Why did you throw your wedded lady from you?
Think that you are upon a rock; and now
Throw me again.

Embracing him

POSTHUMUS LEONATUS: Hang there like a fruit, my soul,
Till the tree die!
CYMBELINE: How now, my flesh, my child!
What, makest thou me a dullard in this act?
Wilt thou not speak to me?
IMOGEN: [*Kneeling*] Your blessing, sir.
BELARIUS: [To GUIDERIUS and ARVIRAGUS] Though you did love this youth, I blame ye not;
You had a motive for't.
CYMBELINE: My tears that fall
Prove holy water on thee! Imogen,
Thy mother's dead.
IMOGEN: I am sorry for't, my lord.
CYMBELINE: O, she was nought; and long of her it was
That we meet here so strangely; but her son
Is gone, we know not how nor where.
PISANIO: My lord,
Now fear is from me, I'll speak troth. Lord Cloten,
Upon my lady's missing, came to me
With his sword drawn; foam'd at the mouth, and swore,
If I discover'd not which way she was gone,
It was my instant death. By accident,
I had a feigned letter of my master's
Then in my pocket; which directed him
To seek her on the mountains near to Milford;
Where, in a frenzy, in my master's garments,
Which he enforced from me, away he posts
With unchaste purpose and with oath to violate
My lady's honour. What became of him
I further know not.
GUIDERIUS: Let me end the story:
I slew him there.
CYMBELINE: Marry, the gods forfend!
I would not thy good deeds should from my lips
Pluck a bard sentence. Prithee, valiant youth,
Deny't again.
GUIDERIUS: I have spoke it, and I did it.
CYMBELINE: He was a prince.
GUIDERIUS: A most incivil one. The wrongs he did me
Were nothing prince-like; for he did provoke me
With language that would make me spurn the sea,
If it could so roar to me. I cut off's head;
And am right glad he is not standing here
To tell this tale of mine.
CYMBELINE: I am sorry for thee.
By thine own tongue thou art condemn'd, and must
Endure our law. Thou'rt dead.
IMOGEN: That headless man
I thought had been my lord.
CYMBELINE: Bind the offender,
And take him from our presence.
BELARIUS: Stay, sir king.
This man is better than the man he slew,
As well descended as thyself; and hath
More of thee merited than a band of Clotens
Had ever scar for. [*To the Guard*] Let his arms alone;
They were not born for bondage.
CYMBELINE: Why, old soldier,
Wilt thou undo the worth thou art unpaid for,
By tasting of our wrath? How of descent
As good as we?

ARVIRAGUS: In that he spake too far.
CYMBELINE: And thou shalt die for't.
BELARIUS: We will die all three;
But I will prove that two on's are as good
As I have given out him. My sons, I must,
For mine own part, unfold a dangerous speech,
Though, haply, well for you.
ARVIRAGUS: Your danger's ours.
GUIDERIUS: And our good his.
BELARIUS: Have at it then, by leave.
Thou hadst, great king, a subject who
Was call'd Belarius.
CYMBELINE: What of him? he is
A banish'd traitor.
BELARIUS: He it is that hath
Assumed this age; indeed a banish'd man;
I know not how a traitor.
CYMBELINE: Take him hence,
The whole world shall not save him.
BELARIUS: Not too hot.
First pay me for the nursing of thy sons;
And let it be confiscate all, so soon
As I have received it.
CYMBELINE: Nursing of my sons!
BELARIUS: I am too blunt and saucy: here's my knee.
Ere I arise, I will prefer my sons;
Then spare not the old father. Mighty sir,
These two young gentlemen, that call me father
And think they are my sons, are none of mine;
They are the issue of your loins, my liege,
And blood of your begetting.
CYMBELINE: How! my issue!
BELARIUS: So sure as you your father's. I, old Morgan,
Am that Belarius whom you sometime banish'd.
Your pleasure was my mere offence, my punishment
Itself, and all my treason; that I suffer'd
Was all the harm I did. These gentle princes—
For such and so they are—these twenty years
Have I train'd up; those arts they have as I
Could put into them. My breeding was, sir, as
Your highness knows. Their nurse, Euriphile,
Whom for the theft I wedded, stole these children
Upon my banishment; I moved her to't,
Having received the punishment before,
For that which I did then. Beaten for loyalty
Excited me to treason. Their dear loss,
The more of you 'twas felt, the more it shaped
Unto my end of stealing them. But, gracious sir,
Here are your sons again; and I must lose
Two of the sweet'st companions in the world.
The benediction of these covering heavens
Fall on their heads like dew! for they are worthy
To inlay heaven with stars.
CYMBELINE: Thou weep'st, and speak'st.
The service that you three have done is more
Unlike than this thou tell'st. I lost my children.
If these be they, I know not how to wish
A pair of worthier sons.
BELARIUS: Be pleased awhile.
This gentleman, whom I call Polydore,
Most worthy prince, as yours, is true Guiderius;
This gentleman, my Cadwal, Arviragus,
Your younger princely son; he, sir, was lapp'd
In a most curious mantle, wrought by the hand
Of his queen mother, which for more probation
I can with ease produce.
CYMBELINE: Guiderius had
Upon his neck a mole, a sanguine star;
It was a mark of wonder.
BELARIUS: This is he;
Who hath upon him still that natural stamp.
It was wise nature's end in the donation,
To be his evidence now.
CYMBELINE: O, what, am I
A mother to the birth of three? Ne'er mother
Rejoiced deliverance more. Blest pray you be,
That, after this strange starting from your orbs,
You may reign in them now! O Imogen,
Thou hast lost by this a kingdom.
IMOGEN: No, my lord;
I have got two worlds by 't. O my gentle brothers,
Have we thus met? O, never say hereafter
But I am truest speaker you call'd me brother,
When I was but your sister; I you brothers,
When we were so indeed.
CYMBELINE: Did you e'er meet?
ARVIRAGUS: Ay, my good lord.

GUIDERIUS: And at first meeting loved;
Continued so, until we thought he died.
CORNELIUS: By the queen's dram she swallow'd.
CYMBELINE: O rare instinct!
When shall I hear all through? This fierce abridgement
Hath to it circumstantial branches, which
Distinction should be rich in. Where? how lived you?
And when came you to serve our Roman captive?
How parted with your brothers? how first met them?
Why fled you from the court? and whither? These,
And your three motives to the battle, with
I know not how much more, should be demanded;
And all the other by-dependencies,
From chance to chance; but nor the time nor place
Will serve our long interogatories. See,
Posthumus anchors upon Imogen,
And she, like harmless lightning, throws her eye
On him, her brother, me, her master, hitting
Each object with a joy; the counterchange
Is severally in all. Let's quit this ground,
And smoke the temple with our sacrifices.
[*To Belarius*] Thou art my brother; so we'll hold thee ever.
IMOGEN: You are my father too, and did relieve me,
To see this gracious season.
CYMBELINE: All o'erjoy'd,
Save these in bonds. Let them be joyful too,
For they shall taste our comfort.
IMOGEN: My good master,
I will yet do you service.
CAIUS LUCIUS: Happy be you!
CYMBELINE: The forlorn soldier, that so nobly fought,
He would have well becomed this place, and graced
The thankings of a king.
POSTHUMUS LEONATUS: I am, sir,
The soldier that did company these three
In poor beseeming; 'twas a fitment for
The purpose I then follow'd. That I was he,
Speak, Iachimo: I had you down and might
Have made you finish.
IACHIMO: [*Kneeling*] I am down again:
But now my heavy conscience sinks my knee,
As then your force did. Take that life, beseech you,
Which I so often owe; but your ring first;
And here the bracelet of the truest princess
That ever swore her faith.
POSTHUMUS LEONATUS: Kneel not to me.
The power that I have on you is to spare you;
The malice towards you to forgive you. Live,
And deal with others better.
CYMBELINE: Nobly doom'd!
We'll learn our freeness of a son-in-law;
Pardon's the word to all.
ARVIRAGUS: You holp us, sir,
As you did mean indeed to be our brother;
Joy'd are we that you are.
POSTHUMUS LEONATUS: Your servant, princes. Good my lord of Rome,
Call forth your soothsayer. As I slept, methought
Great Jupiter, upon his eagle back'd,
Appear'd to me, with other spritely shows
Of mine own kindred. When I waked, I found
This label on my bosom; whose containing
Is so from sense in hardness, that I can
Make no collection of it. Let him show
His skill in the construction.
CAIUS LUCIUS: Philarmonus!
SOOTHSAYER: Here, my good lord.
CAIUS LUCIUS: Read, and declare the meaning.
SOOTHSAYER: [*Reads*] 'When as a lion's whelp shall, to himself unknown, without seeking find, and be embraced by a piece of tender air; and when from a stately cedar shall be lopped branches, which, being dead many years, shall after revive, be jointed to the old stock, and freshly grow; then shall Posthumus end his miseries, Britain be fortunate and flourish in peace and plenty.' Thou, Leonatus, art the lion's whelp; The fit and apt construction of thy name, Being Leonatus, doth import so much.

To CYMBELINE

The piece of tender air, thy virtuous daughter,
Which we call 'mollis aer;' and 'mollis aer'
We term it 'mulier:' which 'mulier' I divine
Is this most constant wife; who, even now,
Answering the letter of the oracle,
Unknown to you, unsought, were clipp'd about
With this most tender air.

CYMBELINE: This hath some seeming.
SOOTHSAYER: The lofty cedar, royal Cymbeline,
Personates thee; and thy lopp'd branches point
Thy two sons forth; who, by Belarius stol'n,
For many years thought dead, are now revived,
To the majestic cedar join'd, whose issue
Promises Britain peace and plenty.
CYMBELINE: Well
My peace we will begin. And, Caius Lucius,
Although the victor, we submit to Caesar,
And to the Roman empire; promising
To pay our wonted tribute, from the which
We were dissuaded by our wicked queen;
Whom heavens, in justice, both on her and hers,
Have laid most heavy hand.
SOOTHSAYER: The fingers of the powers above do tune
The harmony of this peace. The vision
Which I made known to Lucius, ere the stroke
Of this yet scarce-cold battle, at this instant
Is full accomplish'd; for the Roman eagle,
From south to west on wing soaring aloft,
Lessen'd herself, and in the beams o' the sun
So vanish'd: which foreshow'd our princely eagle,
The imperial Caesar, should again unite
His favour with the radiant Cymbeline,
Which shines here in the west.
CYMBELINE: Laud we the gods;
And let our crooked smokes climb to their nostrils
From our blest altars. Publish we this peace
To all our subjects. Set we forward; let
A Roman and a British ensign wave
Friendly together. So through Lud's town march;
And in the temple of great Jupiter
Our peace we'll ratify; seal it with feasts.
Set on there! Never was a war did cease,
Ere bloody hands were wash'd, with such a peace.

Exeunt

Love's Labour's Lost

DRAMATIS PERSONÆ

FERDINAND, *King of Navarre*
BEROWNE, LONGAVILLE, DUMAINE, *lords attending on the King*
BOYET, MARCADE, *lords attending on the Princess of France*
DON ADRIANO DE ARMADO, *a fantastical Spaniard*
SIR NATHANIEL, *a curate*
HOLOFERNES, *a schoolmaster*
DULL, *a constable*
COSTARD, *a clown*
MOTH, *page to Armado*
A Forester
THE PRINCESS OF FRANCE
ROSALINE, MARIA, KATHARINE, *ladies attending on the Princess*
JAQUENETTA, a country *wench*
Lords, Attendants, etc.

THE SCENE: *Navarre*

Act I

Scene I—*Navarre: The King's park*

Enter FERDINAND king of Navarre, BEROWNE, LONGAVILLE and DUMAIN

FERDINAND: Let fame, that all hunt after in their lives,
Live register'd upon our brazen tombs
And then grace us in the disgrace of death;
When, spite of cormorant devouring Time,
The endeavor of this present breath may buy
That honour which shall bate his scythe's keen edge
And make us heirs of all eternity.
Therefore, brave conquerors—for so you are,
That war against your own affections
And the huge army of the world's desires—
Our late edict shall strongly stand in force:
Navarre shall be the wonder of the world;
Our court shall be a little Academe,
Still and contemplative in living art.
You three, Berowne, Dumain, and Longaville,
Have sworn for three years' term to live with me
My fellow-scholars, and to keep those statutes
That are recorded in this schedule here.
Your oaths are pass'd; and now subscribe your names,
That his own hand may strike his honour down
That violates the smallest branch herein.
If you are arm'd to do as sworn to do,
Subscribe to your deep oaths, and keep it too.

LONGAVILLE: I am resolved; 'tis but a three years' fast.
The mind shall banquet, though the body pine.
Fat paunches have lean pates, and dainty bits
Make rich the ribs, but bankrupt quite the wits.

DUMAIN: My loving lord, Dumain is mortified.
The grosser manner of these world's delights
He throws upon the gross world's baser slaves;

To love, to wealth, to pomp, I pine and die;
With all these living in philosophy.

BEROWNE: I can but say their protestation over;
So much, dear liege, I have already sworn,
That is, to live and study here three years.
But there are other strict observances;
As, not to see a woman in that term,
Which I hope well is not enrolled there;
And one day in a week to touch no food
And but one meal on every day beside,
The which I hope is not enrolled there;
And then, to sleep but three hours in the night,
And not be seen to wink of all the day—
When I was wont to think no harm all night
And make a dark night too of half the day—
Which I hope well is not enrolled there.
O, these are barren tasks, too hard to keep,
Not to see ladies, study, fast, not sleep!

FERDINAND: Your oath is pass'd to pass away from these.

BEROWNE: Let me say no, my liege, an if you please:
I only swore to study with your grace
And stay here in your court for three years' space.

LONGAVILLE: You swore to that, Berowne, and to the rest.

BEROWNE: By yea and nay, sir, then I swore in jest.
What is the end of study? let me know.

FERDINAND: Why, that to know, which else we should not know.

BEROWNE: Things hid and barr'd, you mean, from common sense?

FERDINAND: Ay, that is study's godlike recompense.

BEROWNE: Come on, then; I will swear to study so,
To know the thing I am forbid to know,
As thus—to study where I well may dine,
When I to feast expressly am forbid;
Or study where to meet some mistress fine,
When mistresses from common sense are hid;
Or, having sworn too hard a keeping oath,
Study to break it and not break my troth.
If study's gain be thus and this be so,
Study knows that which yet it doth not know.
Swear me to this, and I will ne'er say no.

FERDINAND: These be the stops that hinder study quite
And train our intellects to vain delight.

BEROWNE: Why, all delights are vain; but that most vain,
Which with pain purchased doth inherit pain,
As, painfully to pore upon a book
To seek the light of truth; while truth the while
Doth falsely blind the eyesight of his look.
Light seeking light doth light of light beguile;
So, ere you find where light in darkness lies,
Your light grows dark by losing of your eyes.
Study me how to please the eye indeed
By fixing it upon a fairer eye,
Who dazzling so, that eye shall be his heed
And give him light that it was blinded by.
Study is like the heaven's glorious sun
That will not be deep-search'd with saucy looks;
Small have continual plodders ever won
Save base authority from others' books
These earthly godfathers of heaven's lights
That give a name to every fixed star
Have no more profit of their shining nights
Than those that walk and wot not what they are.
Too much to know is to know nought but fame;
And every godfather can give a name.

FERDINAND: How well he's read, to reason against reading!

DUMAIN: Proceeded well, to stop all good proceeding!

LONGAVILLE: He weeds the corn and still lets grow the weeding.

BEROWNE: The spring is near when green geese are a-breeding.

DUMAIN: How follows that?

BEROWNE: Fit in his place and time.

DUMAIN: In reason nothing.

BEROWNE: Something then in rhyme.

FERDINAND: Berowne is like an envious sneaping frost,
That bites the first-born infants of the spring.

BEROWNE: Well, say I am; why should proud summer boast
Before the birds have any cause to sing?
Why should I joy in any abortive birth?
At Christmas I no more desire a rose
Than wish a snow in May's new-fangled mirth;
But like of each thing that in season grows.
So you, to study now it is too late,
Climb o'er the house to unlock the little gate.

FERDINAND: Well, sit you out: go home, Berowne; adieu.
BEROWNE: No, my good lord; I have sworn to stay with you;
And though I have for barbarism spoke more
Than for that angel knowledge you can say,
Yet confident I'll keep what I have swore
And bide the penance of each three years' day.
Give me the paper; let me read the same;
And to the strict'st decrees I'll write my name.
FERDINAND: How well this yielding rescues thee from shame!
BEROWNE: [*Reads*] 'Item, That no woman shall come within a mile of my court.' Hath this been proclaimed?
LONGAVILLE: Four days ago.
BEROWNE: Let's see the penalty. [*Reads*] '—on pain of losing her tongue.' Who devised this penalty?
LONGAVILLE: Marry, that did I.
BEROWNE: Sweet lord, and why?
LONGAVILLE: To fright them hence with that dread penalty.
BEROWNE: A dangerous law against gentility! [*Reads*]
'Item. If any man be seen to talk with a woman within the term of three years, he shall endure such public shame as the rest of the court can possibly devise.'
This article, my liege, yourself must break;
For well you know here comes in embassy
The French king's daughter with yourself to speak—
A maid of grace and complete majesty—
About surrender up of Aquitaine
To her decrepit, sick and bedrid father;
Therefore this article is made in vain,
Or vainly comes the admired princess hither.
FERDINAND: What say you, lords? Why, this was quite forgot.
BEROWNE: So study evermore is overshot.
While it doth study to have what it would
It doth forget to do the thing it should,
And when it hath the thing it hunteth most,
'Tis won as towns with fire, so won, so lost.
FERDINAND: We must of force dispense with this decree;
She must lie here on mere necessity.
BEROWNE: Necessity will make us all forsworn
Three thousand times within this three years' space;
For every man with his affects is born,
Not by might master'd but by special grace.
If I break faith, this word shall speak for me;
I am forsworn on mere necessity.
So to the laws at large I write my name;
Subscribes
And he that breaks them in the least degree
Stands in attainder of eternal shame.
Suggestions are to other as to me;
But I believe, although I seem so loath,
I am the last that will last keep his oath.
But is there no quick recreation granted?
FERDINAND: Ay, that there is. Our court, you know, is haunted
With a refined traveller of Spain;
A man in all the world's new fashion planted,
That hath a mint of phrases in his brain;
One whom the music of his own vain tongue
Doth ravish like enchanting harmony;
A man of complements, whom right and wrong
Have chose as umpire of their mutiny.
This child of fancy, that Armado hight,
For interim to our studies shall relate
In high-born words the worth of many a knight
From tawny Spain lost in the world's debate.
How you delight, my lords, I know not, I;
But, I protest, I love to hear him lie
And I will use him for my minstrelsy.
BEROWNE: Armado is a most illustrious wight,
A man of fire-new words, fashion's own knight.
LONGAVILLE: Costard the swain and he shall be our sport;
And so to study, three years is but short.
Enter DULL with a letter, and COSTARD
DULL: Which is the duke's own person?
BEROWNE: This, fellow. What wouldst?
DULL: I myself reprehend his own person, for I am his grace's farborough; but I would see his own person in flesh and blood.
BEROWNE: This is he.
DULL: Signior Arme—Arme—commends you. There's villainy abroad: this letter will tell you more.

COSTARD: Sir, the contempts thereof are as touching me.

FERDINAND: A letter from the magnificent Armado.

BEROWNE: How low soever the matter, I hope in God for high words.

LONGAVILLE: A high hope for a low heaven. God grant us patience!

BEROWNE: To hear? or forbear laughing?

LONGAVILLE: To hear meekly, sir, and to laugh moderately; or to forbear both.

BEROWNE: Well, sir, be it as the style shall give us cause to climb in the merriness.

COSTARD: The matter is to me, sir, as concerning Jaquenetta. The manner of it is, I was taken with the manner.

BEROWNE: In what manner?

COSTARD: In manner and form following, sir; all those three: I was seen with her in the manor-house, sitting with her upon the form, and taken following her into the park; which, put together, is in manner and form following. Now, sir, for the manner—it is the manner of a man to speak to a woman. For the form—in some form.

BEROWNE: For the following, sir?

COSTARD: As it shall follow in my correction: and God defend the right!

FERDINAND: Will you hear this letter with attention?

BEROWNE: As we would hear an oracle.

COSTARD: Such is the simplicity of man to hearken after the flesh.

FERDINAND: [*Reads*] 'Great deputy, the welkin's vicegerent and sole dominator of Navarre, my soul's earth's god, and body's fostering patron.'

COSTARD: Not a word of Costard yet.

FERDINAND: [*Reads*] 'So it is,'—

COSTARD: It may be so; but if he say it is so, he is, in telling true, but so.

FERDINAND: Peace!

COSTARD: Be to me and every man that dares not fight!

FERDINAND: No words!

COSTARD: Of other men's secrets, I beseech you.

FERDINAND: [*Reads*] 'So it is, besieged with sable-coloured melancholy, I did commend the black-oppressing humour to the most wholesome physic of thy health-giving air; and, as I am a gentleman, betook myself to walk. The time when. About the sixth hour; when beasts most graze, birds best peck, and men sit down to that nourishment which is called supper. So much for the time when. Now for the ground which; which, I mean, I walked upon; it is y-cleped thy park. Then for the place where; where, I mean, I did encounter that obscene and preposterous event, that draweth from my snow-white pen the ebon-coloured ink, which here thou viewest, beholdest, surveyest, or seest. But to the place where; it standeth north-north-east and by east from the west corner of thy curious-knotted garden. There did I see that low-spirited swain, that base minnow of thy mirth,'—

COSTARD: Me?

FERDINAND: 'that unlettered small-knowing soul,'

COSTARD: Me?

FERDINAND: 'that shallow vassal,'—

COSTARD: Still me?

FERDINAND: 'which, as I remember, hight Costard,'

COSTARD: O, me!

FERDINAND: 'sorted and consorted, contrary to thy established proclaimed edict and continent canon, which with,—O, with—but with this I passion to say wherewith,—

COSTARD: With a wench.

FERDINAND: 'with a child of our grandmother Eve, a female; or, for thy more sweet understanding, a woman. Him I, as my ever-esteemed duty pricks me on, have sent to thee, to receive the meed of punishment, by thy sweet grace's officer, Anthony Dull; a man of good repute, carriage, bearing, and estimation.'

DULL: Me, an't shall please you; I am Anthony Dull.

FERDINAND: 'For Jaquenetta—so is the weaker vessel called which I apprehended with the aforesaid swain—I keep her as a vessel of the law's fury; and shall, at the least of thy sweet notice, bring her to trial. Thine, in all compliments of devoted and heart-burning heat of duty. DON ADRIANO DE ARMADO.'

BEROWNE: This is not so well as I looked for, but the best that ever I heard.

FERDINAND: Ay, the best for the worst. But, sirrah, what say you to this?

COSTARD: Sir, I confess the wench.

FERDINAND: Did you hear the proclamation?

COSTARD: I do confess much of the hearing it but little of the marking of it.

FERDINAND: It was proclaimed a year's imprisonment, to be taken with a wench.

COSTARD: I was taken with none, sir; I was taken with a damsel.

FERDINAND: Well, it was proclaimed 'damsel.'

COSTARD: This was no damsel, neither, sir; she was a virgin.

FERDINAND: It is so varied, too; for it was proclaimed 'virgin.'

COSTARD: If it were, I deny her virginity; I was taken with a maid.

FERDINAND: This maid will not serve your turn, sir.

COSTARD: This maid will serve my turn, sir.

FERDINAND: Sir, I will pronounce your sentence: you shall fast a week with bran and water.

COSTARD: I had rather pray a month with mutton and porridge.

FERDINAND: And Don Armado shall be your keeper.
My Lord Berowne, see him deliver'd o'er;
And go we, lords, to put in practise that
Which each to other hath so strongly sworn.

Exeunt FERDINAND, LONGAVILLE, and DUMAIN

BEROWNE: I'll lay my head to any good man's hat,
These oaths and laws will prove an idle scorn.
Sirrah, come on.

COSTARD: I suffer for the truth, sir; for true it is, I was taken with Jaquenetta, and Jaquenetta is a true girl; and therefore welcome the sour cup of prosperity! Affliction may one day smile again; and till then, sit thee down, sorrow!

Exeunt

SCENE II—*The park*

Enter DON ADRIANO DE ARMADO and MOTH

DON ADRIANO DE ARMADO: Boy, what sign is it when a man of great spirit grows melancholy?

MOTH: A great sign, sir, that he will look sad.

DON ADRIANO DE ARMADO: Why, sadness is one and the self-same thing, dear imp.

MOTH: No, no; O Lord, sir, no.

DON ADRIANO DE ARMADO: How canst thou part sadness and melancholy, my tender juvenal?

MOTH: By a familiar demonstration of the working, my tough senior.

DON ADRIANO DE ARMADO: Why tough senior? why tough senior?

MOTH: Why tender juvenal? why tender juvenal?

DON ADRIANO DE ARMADO: I spoke it, tender juvenal, as a congruent epitheton appertaining to thy young days, which we may nominate tender.

MOTH: And I, tough senior, as an appertinent title to your old time, which we may name tough.

DON ADRIANO DE ARMADO: Pretty and apt.

MOTH: How mean you, sir? I pretty, and my saying apt? or I apt, and my saying pretty?

DON ADRIANO DE ARMADO: Thou pretty, because little.

MOTH: Little pretty, because little. Wherefore apt?

DON ADRIANO DE ARMADO: And therefore apt, because quick.

MOTH: Speak you this in my praise, master?

DON ADRIANO DE ARMADO: In thy condign praise.

MOTH: I will praise an eel with the same praise.

DON ADRIANO DE ARMADO: What, that an eel is ingenious?

MOTH: That an eel is quick.

DON ADRIANO DE ARMADO: I do say thou art quick in answers; thou heatest my blood.

MOTH: I am answered, sir.

DON ADRIANO DE ARMADO: I love not to be crossed.

MOTH: [*Aside*] He speaks the mere contrary; crosses love not him.

DON ADRIANO DE ARMADO: I have promised to study three years with the duke.

MOTH: You may do it in an hour, sir.

DON ADRIANO DE ARMADO: Impossible.

MOTH: How many is one thrice told?

DON ADRIANO DE ARMADO: I am ill at reckoning; it fitteth the spirit of a tapster.

MOTH: You are a gentleman and a gamester, sir.

DON ADRIANO DE ARMADO: I confess both; they are both the varnish of a complete man.

MOTH: Then, I am sure, you know how much the gross sum of deuce-ace amounts to.

DON ADRIANO DE ARMADO: It doth amount to one more than two.

MOTH: Which the base vulgar do call three.

DON ADRIANO DE ARMADO: True.

MOTH: Why, sir, is this such a piece of study? Now here is three studied, ere ye'll thrice wink; and how easy it is to put 'years' to the word 'three,' and study three years in two words, the dancing horse will tell you.

DON ADRIANO DE ARMADO: A most fine figure!

MOTH: [*Aside*] To prove you a cipher.

DON ADRIANO DE ARMADO: I will hereupon confess I am in love. And as it is base for a soldier to love, so am I in love with a base wench. If drawing my sword against the humour of affection would deliver me from the reprobate thought of it, I would take Desire prisoner, and ransom him to any French courtier for a new-devised courtesy. I think scorn to sigh; methinks I should outswear Cupid. Comfort, me, boy; what great men have been in love?

MOTH: Hercules, master.

DON ADRIANO DE ARMADO: Most sweet Hercules! More authority, dear boy, name more; and, sweet my child, let them be men of good repute and carriage.

MOTH: Samson, master; he was a man of good carriage, great carriage, for he carried the town-gates on his back like a porter; and he was in love.

DON ADRIANO DE ARMADO: O well-knit Samson! strong-jointed Samson! I do excel thee in my rapier as much as thou didst me in carrying gates. I am in love too. Who was Samson's love, my dear Moth?

MOTH: A woman, master.

DON ADRIANO DE ARMADO: Of what complexion?

MOTH: Of all the four, or the three, or the two, or one of the four.

DON ADRIANO DE ARMADO: Tell me precisely of what complexion.

MOTH: Of the sea-water green, sir.

DON ADRIANO DE ARMADO: Is that one of the four complexions?

MOTH: As I have read, sir; and the best of them too.

DON ADRIANO DE ARMADO: Green indeed is the colour of lovers; but to have a love of that colour, methinks Samson had small reason for it. He surely affected her for her wit.

MOTH: It was so, sir; for she had a green wit.

DON ADRIANO DE ARMADO: My love is most immaculate white and red.

MOTH: Most maculate thoughts, master, are masked under such colours.

DON ADRIANO DE ARMADO: Define, define, well-educated infant.

MOTH: My father's wit and my mother's tongue, assist me!

DON ADRIANO DE ARMADO: Sweet invocation of a child; most pretty and pathetical!

MOTH: If she be made of white and red,
Her faults will ne'er be known,
For blushing cheeks by faults are bred
And fears by pale white shown.
Then if she fear, or be to blame,
By this you shall not know,
For still her cheeks possess the same
Which native she doth owe.

A dangerous rhyme, master, against the reason of white and red.

DON ADRIANO DE ARMADO: Is there not a ballad, boy, of the King and the Beggar?

MOTH: The world was very guilty of such a ballad some three ages since; but I think now 'tis not to be found; or, if it were, it would neither serve for the writing nor the tune.

DON ADRIANO DE ARMADO: I will have that subject newly writ o'er, that I may example my digression by some mighty precedent. Boy, I do love that country girl that I took in the park with the rational hind Costard: she deserves well.

MOTH: [*Aside*] To be whipped; and yet a better love than my master.

DON ADRIANO DE ARMADO: Sing, boy; my spirit grows heavy in love.

MOTH: And that's great marvel, loving a light wench.

DON ADRIANO DE ARMADO: I say, sing.

MOTH: Forbear till this company be past.

Enter DULL, COSTARD, and JAQUENETTA

DULL: Sir, the duke's pleasure is, that you keep Costard safe; and you must suffer him to take no delight nor no penance; but a' must fast three days a week. For this damsel, I must keep her at the park; she is allowed for the day-woman. Fare you well.

DON ADRIANO DE ARMADO: I do betray myself with blushing. Maid!

JAQUENETTA: Man?

DON ADRIANO DE ARMADO: I will visit thee at the lodge.

JAQUENETTA: That's hereby.

DON ADRIANO DE ARMADO: I know where it is situate.

JAQUENETTA: Lord, how wise you are!

DON ADRIANO DE ARMADO: I will tell thee wonders.

JAQUENETTA: With that face?

DON ADRIANO DE ARMADO: I love thee.

JAQUENETTA: So I heard you say.

DON ADRIANO DE ARMADO: And so, farewell.

JAQUENETTA: Fair weather after you!

DULL: Come, Jaquenetta, away.

Exeunt DULL and JAQUENETTA

DON ADRIANO DE ARMADO: Villain, thou shalt fast for thy offences ere thou be pardoned.

COSTARD: Well, sir, I hope, when I do it, I shall do it on a full stomach.

DON ADRIANO DE ARMADO: Thou shalt be heavily punished.

COSTARD: I am more bound to you than your fellows, for they are but lightly rewarded.

DON ADRIANO DE ARMADO: Take away this villain; shut him up.

MOTH: Come, you transgressing slave; away.

COSTARD: Let me not be pent up, sir; I will fast, being loose.

MOTH: No, sir; that were fast and loose. Thou shalt to prison.

COSTARD: Well, if ever I do see the merry days of desolation that I have seen, some shall see.

MOTH: What shall some see?

COSTARD: Nay, nothing, Master Moth, but what they look upon. It is not for prisoners to be too silent in their words; and therefore I will say nothing. I thank God I have as little patience as another man; and therefore I can be quiet.

Exeunt MOTH and COSTARD

DON ADRIANO DE ARMADO: I do affect the very ground, which is base, where her shoe, which is baser, guided by her foot, which is basest, doth tread. I shall be forsworn, which is a great argument of falsehood, if I love. And how can that be true love which is falsely attempted? Love is a familiar; Love is a devil. There is no evil angel but Love. Yet was Samson so tempted, and he had an excellent strength; yet was Solomon so seduced, and he had a very good wit. Cupid's butt-shaft is too hard for Hercules' club; and therefore too much odds for a Spaniard's rapier. The first and second cause will not serve my turn; the passado he respects not, the duello he regards not; his disgrace is to be called boy; but his glory is to subdue men. Adieu, valour! rust rapier; be still, drum; for your manager is in love; yea, he loveth. Assist me, some extemporal god of rhyme, for I am sure I shall turn sonnet. Devise, wit; write, pen; for I am for whole volumes in folio.

Exit

ACT II

SCENE I—*The park*

Enter the PRINCESS of France, ROSALINE, MARIA, KATHARINE, BOYET, Lords, and other Attendants

BOYET: Now, madam, summon up your dearest spirits.
Consider who the king your father sends,
To whom he sends, and what's his embassy:
Yourself, held precious in the world's esteem,
To parley with the sole inheritor
Of all perfections that a man may owe,
Matchless Navarre; the plea of no less weight
Than Aquitaine, a dowry for a queen.
Be now as prodigal of all dear grace
As Nature was in making graces dear
When she did starve the general world beside
And prodigally gave them all to you.

PRINCESS: Good Lord Boyet, my beauty, though but mean,
Needs not the painted flourish of your praise.
Beauty is bought by judgement of the eye,
Not utter'd by base sale of chapmen's tongues;
I am less proud to hear you tell my worth
Than you much willing to be counted wise
In spending your wit in the praise of mine.
But now to task the tasker: good Boyet,
You are not ignorant, all-telling fame
Doth noise abroad, Navarre hath made a vow,
Till painful study shall outwear three years,
No woman may approach his silent court.
Therefore to's seemeth it a needful course,
Before we enter his forbidden gates,
To know his pleasure; and in that behalf,
Bold of your worthiness, we single you
As our best-moving fair solicitor.
Tell him, the daughter of the King of France,
On serious business, craving quick dispatch,
Importunes personal conference with his grace.
Haste, signify so much; while we attend,
Like humble-visaged suitors, his high will.

BOYET: Proud of employment, willingly I go.

PRINCESS: All pride is willing pride, and yours is so.

Exit BOYET

Who are the votaries, my loving lords,
That are vow-fellows with this virtuous duke?

FIRST LORD: Lord Longaville is one.

PRINCESS: Know you the man?

MARIA: I know him, madam; at a marriage-feast,
Between Lord Perigort and the beauteous heir
Of Jaques Falconbridge, solemnized
In Normandy, saw I this Longaville.
A man of sovereign parts, peerless esteemed,
Well fitted in arts, glorious in arms;
Nothing becomes him ill that he would well.
The only soil of his fair virtue's gloss,
If virtue's gloss will stain with any soil,
Is a sharp wit matched with too blunt a will;
Whose edge hath power to cut, whose will still wills
It should none spare that come within his power.

PRINCESS: Some merry mocking lord, belike; is't so?

MARIA: They say so most that most his humours know.

PRINCESS: Such short-lived wits do wither as they grow.
Who are the rest?

KATHARINE: The young Dumain, a well-accomplished youth,
Of all that virtue love for virtue loved;
Most power to do most harm, least knowing ill;
For he hath wit to make an ill shape good,
And shape to win grace though he had no wit.
I saw him at the Duke Alencon's once;
And much too little of that good I saw
Is my report to his great worthiness.

ROSALINE: Another of these students at that time

Was there with him, if I have heard a truth.
BEROWNE they call him; but a merrier man,
Within the limit of becoming mirth,
I never spent an hour's talk withal.
His eye begets occasion for his wit;
For every object that the one doth catch
The other turns to a mirth-moving jest,
Which his fair tongue, conceit's expositor,
Delivers in such apt and gracious words
That aged ears play truant at his tales
And younger hearings are quite ravished;
So sweet and voluble is his discourse.

PRINCESS: God bless my ladies! are they all in love,
That every one her own hath garnished
With such bedecking ornaments of praise?

FIRST LORD: Here comes Boyet.

Re-enter BOYET

PRINCESS: Now, what admittance, lord?

BOYET: Navarre had notice of your fair approach;
And he and his competitors in oath
Were all address'd to meet you, gentle lady,
Before I came. Marry, thus much I have learnt:
He rather means to lodge you in the field,
Like one that comes here to besiege his court,
Than seek a dispensation for his oath,
To let you enter his unpeopled house.
Here comes Navarre.

Enter FERDINAND, LONGAVILLE, DUMAIN, BEROWNE, and Attendants

FERDINAND: Fair Princess, welcome to the court of Navarre.

PRINCESS: 'Fair' I give you back again; and 'welcome' I have not yet. The roof of this court is too high to be yours; and welcome to the wide fields too base to be mine.

FERDINAND: You shall be welcome, madam, to my court.

PRINCESS: I will be welcome, then; conduct me thither.

FERDINAND: Hear me, dear lady: I have sworn an oath.

PRINCESS: Our Lady help my lord! He'll be forsworn.

FERDINAND: Not for the world, fair madam, by my will.

PRINCESS: Why, will shall break it; will and nothing else.

FERDINAND: Your ladyship is ignorant what it is.

PRINCESS: Were my lord so, his ignorance were wise,
Where now his knowledge must prove ignorance.
I hear your grace hath sworn out house-keeping.
'Tis deadly sin to keep that oath, my lord,
And sin to break it.
But pardon me. I am too sudden-bold;
To teach a teacher ill beseemeth me.
Vouchsafe to read the purpose of my coming,
And suddenly resolve me in my suit.

Giving a paper

FERDINAND: Madam, I will, if suddenly I may.

PRINCESS: You will the sooner, that I were away;
For you'll prove perjured if you make me stay.

BEROWNE: Did not I dance with you in Brabant once?

ROSALINE: Did not I dance with you in Brabant once?

BEROWNE: I know you did.

ROSALINE: How needless was it then to ask the question!

BEROWNE: You must not be so quick.

ROSALINE: 'Tis long of you that spur me with such questions.

BEROWNE: Your wit's too hot, it speeds too fast, 'twill tire.

ROSALINE: Not till it leave the rider in the mire.

BEROWNE: What time o' day?

ROSALINE: The hour that fools should ask.

BEROWNE: Now fair befall your mask!

ROSALINE: Fair fall the face it covers!

BEROWNE: And send you many lovers!

ROSALINE: Amen, so you be none.

BEROWNE: Nay, then will I be gone.

FERDINAND: Madam, your father here doth intimate
The payment of a hundred thousand crowns;
Being but the one half of an entire sum
Disbursed by my father in his wars.
But say that he or we, as neither have,
Received that sum, yet there remains unpaid
A hundred thousand more; in surety of the which,
One part of Aquitaine is bound to us,
Although not valued to the money's worth.

If then the king your father will restore
But that one half which is unsatisfied,
We will give up our right in Aquitaine,
And hold fair friendship with his majesty.
But that, it seems, he little purposeth,
For here he doth demand to have repaid
A hundred thousand crowns; and not demands,
On payment of a hundred thousand crowns,
To have his title live in Aquitaine;
Which we much rather had depart withal
And have the money by our father lent
Than Aquitaine so gelded as it is.
Dear Princess, were not his requests so far
From reason's yielding, your fair self should make
A yielding 'gainst some reason in my breast
And go well satisfied to France again.

PRINCESS: You do the king my father too much wrong
And wrong the reputation of your name,
In so unseeming to confess receipt
Of that which hath so faithfully been paid.

FERDINAND: I do protest I never heard of it;
And if you prove it, I'll repay it back
Or yield up Aquitaine.

PRINCESS: We arrest your word.
Boyet, you can produce acquittances
For such a sum from special officers
Of Charles his father.

FERDINAND: Satisfy me so.

BOYET: So please your grace, the packet is not come
Where that and other specialties are bound;
To-morrow you shall have a sight of them.

FERDINAND: It shall suffice me; at which interview
All liberal reason I will yield unto.
Meantime receive such welcome at my hand
As honour without breach of honour may
Make tender of to thy true worthiness.
You may not come, fair princess, in my gates;
But here without you shall be so received
As you shall deem yourself lodged in my heart,
Though so denied fair harbour in my house.
Your own good thoughts excuse me, and farewell.
To-morrow shall we visit you again.

PRINCESS: Sweet health and fair desires consort your grace!

FERDINAND: Thy own wish wish I thee in every place!

Exit

BEROWNE: Lady, I will commend you to mine own heart.

ROSALINE: Pray you, do my commendations; I would be glad to see it.

BEROWNE: I would you heard it groan.

ROSALINE: Is the fool sick?

BEROWNE: Sick at the heart.

ROSALINE: Alack, let it blood.

BEROWNE: Would that do it good?

ROSALINE: My physic says 'ay.'

BEROWNE: Will you prick't with your eye?

ROSALINE: No point, with my knife.

BEROWNE: Now, God save thy life!

ROSALINE: And yours from long living!

BEROWNE: I cannot stay thanksgiving.

Retiring

DUMAIN: Sir, I pray you, a word: what lady is that same?

BOYET: The heir of Alencon, Katharine her name.

DUMAIN: A gallant lady. Monsieur, fare you well.

Exit

LONGAVILLE: I beseech you a word: what is she in the white?

BOYET: A woman sometimes, an you saw her in the light.

LONGAVILLE: Perchance light in the light. I desire her name.

BOYET: She hath but one for herself; to desire that were a shame.

LONGAVILLE: Pray you, sir, whose daughter?

BOYET: Her mother's, I have heard.

LONGAVILLE: God's blessing on your beard!

BOYET: Good sir, be not offended.
She is an heir of Falconbridge.

LONGAVILLE: Nay, my choler is ended.
She is a most sweet lady.

BOYET: Not unlike, sir, that may be.

Exit LONGAVILLE

BEROWNE: What's her name in the cap?

BOYET: Rosaline, by good hap.

BEROWNE: Is she wedded or no?

BOYET: To her will, sir, or so.

BEROWNE: You are welcome, sir: adieu.

BOYET: Farewell to me, sir, and welcome to you.

Exit BEROWNE

MARIA: That last is BEROWNE, the merry madcap lord;
Not a word with him but a jest.
BOYET: And every jest but a word.
PRINCESS: It was well done of you to take him at his word.
BOYET: I was as willing to grapple as he was to board.
KATHARINE: Two hot sheeps, marry.
BOYET: And wherefore not ships?
No sheep, sweet lamb, unless we feed on your lips.
KATHARINE: You sheep, and I pasture—shall that finish the jest?
BOYET: So you grant pasture for me.

Offering to kiss her

KATHARINE: Not so, gentle beast;
My lips are no common, though several they be.
BOYET: Belonging to whom?
KATHARINE: To my fortunes and me.
PRINCESS: Good wits will be jangling; but, gentles, agree;
This civil war of wits were much better used
On Navarre and his book-men; for here 'tis abused.
BOYET: If my observation, which very seldom lies,
By the heart's still rhetoric disclosed with eyes,
Deceive me not now, Navarre is infected.
PRINCESS: With what?
BOYET: With that which we lovers entitle affected.
PRINCESS: Your reason?
BOYET: Why, all his behaviors did make their retire
To the court of his eye, peeping thorough desire.
His heart, like an agate, with your print impress'd,
Proud with his form, in his eye pride express'd;
His tongue, all impatient to speak and not see,
Did stumble with haste in his eyesight to be;
All senses to that sense did make their repair,
To feel only looking on fairest of fair.
Methought all his senses were lock'd in his eye,
As jewels in crystal for some prince to buy;
Who, tendering their own worth from where they were glass'd,
Did point you to buy them, along as you pass'd.
His face's own margent did quote such amazes
That all eyes saw his eyes enchanted with gazes.
I'll give you Aquitaine and all that is his,
An you give him for my sake but one loving kiss.
PRINCESS: Come to our pavilion. Boyet is disposed.
BOYET: But to speak that in words which his eye hath disclosed.
I only have made a mouth of his eye,
By adding a tongue which I know will not lie.
MARIA: Thou art an old love-monger and speakest skilfully.
KATHARINE: He is Cupid's grandfather and learns news of him.
ROSALINE: Then was Venus like her mother, for her father is but grim.
BOYET: Do you hear, my mad wenches?
MARIA: No.
BOYET: What then, do you see?
MARIA: Ay, our way to be gone.
BOYET: You are too hard for me.

Exeunt

Act III
Scene I—*The park*

Enter DON ADRIANO DE ARMADO and MOTH

DON ADRIANO DE ARMADO: Warble, child; make passionate my sense of hearing.

MOTH: Concolinel.

Singing

DON ADRIANO DE ARMADO: Sweet air! Go, tenderness of years; take this key, give enlargement to the swain, bring him festinately hither; I must employ him in a letter to my love.

MOTH: Master, will you win your love with a French brawl?

DON ADRIANO DE ARMADO: How meanest thou? brawling in French?

MOTH: No, my complete master; but to jig off a tune at the tongue's end, canary to it with your feet, humour it with turning up your eyelids, sigh a note and sing a note, sometime through the throat, as if you swallowed love with singing love, sometime through the nose, as if you snuffed up love by smelling love; with your hat penthouse-like o'er the shop of your eyes; with your arms crossed on your thin-belly doublet like a rabbit on a spit; or your hands in your pocket like a man after the old painting; and keep not too long in one tune, but a snip and away. These are complements, these are humours; these betray nice wenches, that would be betrayed without these; and make them men of note—do you note me?—that most are affected to these.

DON ADRIANO DE ARMADO: How hast thou purchased this experience?

MOTH: By my penny of observation.

DON ADRIANO DE ARMADO: But O—but O—

MOTH: 'The hobby-horse is forgot.'

DON ADRIANO DE ARMADO: Callest thou my love 'hobby-horse'?

MOTH: No, master; the hobby-horse is but a colt, and your love perhaps a hackney. But have you forgot your love?

DON ADRIANO DE ARMADO: Almost I had.

MOTH: Negligent student! learn her by heart.

DON ADRIANO DE ARMADO: By heart and in heart, boy.

MOTH: And out of heart, master; all those three I will prove.

DON ADRIANO DE ARMADO: What wilt thou prove?

MOTH: A man, if I live; and this, by, in, and without, upon the instant. By heart you love her, because your heart cannot come by her; in heart you love her, because your heart is in love with her; and out of heart you love her, being out of heart that you cannot enjoy her.

DON ADRIANO DE ARMADO: I am all these three.

MOTH: And three times as much more, and yet nothing at all.

DON ADRIANO DE ARMADO: Fetch hither the swain; he must carry me a letter.

MOTH: A message well sympathized; a horse to be ambassador for an ass.

DON ADRIANO DE ARMADO: Ha, ha! what sayest thou?

MOTH: Marry, sir, you must send the ass upon the horse, for he is very slow-gaited. But I go.

DON ADRIANO DE ARMADO: The way is but short: away!

MOTH: As swift as lead, sir.

DON ADRIANO DE ARMADO: The meaning, pretty ingenious?

Is not lead a metal heavy, dull, and slow?

MOTH: Minime, honest master; or rather, master, no.

DON ADRIANO DE ARMADO: I say lead is slow.

MOTH: You are too swift, sir, to say so:

Is that lead slow which is fired from a gun?

DON ADRIANO DE ARMADO: Sweet smoke of rhetoric!

He reputes me a cannon; and the bullet, that's he;
I shoot thee at the swain.

MOTH: Thump then and I flee.

Exit

DON ADRIANO DE ARMADO: A most acute juvenal; voluble and free of grace!

By thy favour, sweet welkin, I must sigh in thy face;

Most rude melancholy, valour gives thee place.

My herald is return'd.

Re-enter MOTH with COSTARD

MOTH: A wonder, master! here's a costard broken in a shin.

DON ADRIANO DE ARMADO: Some enigma, some riddle; come, thy l'envoy; begin.

COSTARD: No enigma, no riddle, no l'envoy; no salve in the mail, sir. O, sir, plantain, a plain plantain! No l'envoy, no l'envoy; no salve, sir, but a plantain!

DON ADRIANO DE ARMADO: By virtue, thou enforcest laughter; thy silly thought my spleen; the heaving of my lungs provokes me to ridiculous smiling. O, pardon me, my stars! Doth the inconsiderate take salve for l'envoy, and the word l'envoy for a salve?

MOTH: Do the wise think them other? is not l'envoy a salve?

DON ADRIANO DE ARMADO: No, page; it is an epilogue or discourse, to make plain

Some obscure precedence that hath tofore been sain.

I will example it:

The fox, the ape, and the humble-bee,

Were still at odds, being but three.

There's the moral. Now the l'envoy.

MOTH: I will add the l'envoy. Say the moral again.

DON ADRIANO DE ARMADO: The fox, the ape, and the humble-bee,

Were still at odds, being but three.

MOTH: Until the goose came out of door,

And stay'd the odds by adding four.

Now will I begin your moral, and do you follow with my l'envoy.

The fox, the ape, and the humble-bee,

Were still at odds, being but three.

DON ADRIANO DE ARMADO: Until the goose came out of door,

Staying the odds by adding four.

MOTH: A good l'envoy, ending in the goose; would you desire more?

COSTARD: The boy hath sold him a bargain, a goose, that's flat.

Sir, your pennyworth is good, an your goose be fat.

To sell a bargain well is as cunning as fast and loose;

Let me see: a fat l'envoy; ay, that's a fat goose.

DON ADRIANO DE ARMADO: Come hither, come hither. How did this argument begin?

MOTH: By saying that a costard was broken in a shin.

Then call'd you for the l'envoy.

COSTARD: True, and I for a plantain. Thus came your argument in;

Then the boy's fat l'envoy, the goose that you bought;

And he ended the market.

DON ADRIANO DE ARMADO: But tell me: how was there a costard broken in a shin?

MOTH: I will tell you sensibly.

COSTARD: Thou hast no feeling of it, Moth; I will speak that l'envoy.

I Costard, running out, that was safely within,

Fell over the threshold and broke my shin.

DON ADRIANO DE ARMADO: We will talk no more of this matter.

COSTARD: Till there be more matter in the shin.

DON ADRIANO DE ARMADO: Sirrah Costard, I will enfranchise thee.

COSTARD: O, marry me to one Frances! I smell some l'envoy, some goose, in this.

DON ADRIANO DE ARMADO: By my sweet soul, I mean setting thee at liberty, enfreedoming thy person; thou wert immured, restrained, captivated, bound.

COSTARD: True, true; and now you will be my purgation and let me loose.

DON ADRIANO DE ARMADO: I give thee thy liberty, set thee from durance; and, in lieu thereof, impose on thee nothing but this: bear this significant (*Giving a letter*) to the country maid Jaquenetta; there is remuneration; for the best ward of mine honour is rewarding my dependents. Moth, follow.

Exit

MOTH: Like the sequel, I. Signior Costard, adieu.

COSTARD: My sweet ounce of man's flesh! my incony Jew!

Exit MOTH

Now will I look to his remuneration. Remuneration! O, that's the Latin word for three farthings. Three farthings—remuneration.—'What's the price of this inkle?'—One penny.'—'No, I'll give you a remuneration.' Why, it carries it. Remuneration! why, it is a fairer name than French crown. I will never buy and sell out of this word.

Enter BEROWNE

BEROWNE: O, my good knave Costard! exceedingly well met.

COSTARD: Pray you, sir, how much carnation ribbon may a man buy for a remuneration?

BEROWNE: What is a remuneration?

COSTARD: Marry, sir, halfpenny farthing.

BEROWNE: Why, then, three-farthing worth of silk.

COSTARD: I thank your worship. God be wi' you!

BEROWNE: Stay, slave; I must employ thee.
As thou wilt win my favour, good my knave,
Do one thing for me that I shall entreat.

COSTARD: When would you have it done, sir?

BEROWNE: This afternoon.

COSTARD: Well, I will do it, sir; fare you well.

BEROWNE: Thou knowest not what it is.

COSTARD: I shall know, sir, when I have done it.

BEROWNE: Why, villain, thou must know first.

COSTARD: I will come to your worship to-morrow morning.

BEROWNE: It must be done this afternoon.
Hark, slave, it is but this:
The princess comes to hunt here in the park,
And in her train there is a gentle lady;
When tongues speak sweetly, then they name her name,
And Rosaline they call her. Ask for her;
And to her white hand see thou do commend
This seal'd-up counsel. There's thy guerdon; go.

Giving him a shilling

COSTARD: Gardon, O sweet gardon! better than remuneration, a'leven-pence farthing better; most sweet gardon! I will do it sir, in print. Gardon! Remuneration!

Exit

BEROWNE: And I, forsooth, in love! I, that have been love's whip;
A very beadle to a humorous sigh;
A critic, nay, a night-watch constable;
A domineering pedant o'er the boy;
Than whom no mortal so magnificent!
This whimpled, whining, purblind, wayward boy;
This senior-junior, giant-dwarf, Dan Cupid;
Regent of love-rhymes, lord of folded arms,
The anointed sovereign of sighs and groans,
Liege of all loiterers and malcontents,
Dread prince of plackets, king of codpieces,
Sole imperator and great general
Of trotting paritors. O my little heart!
And I to be a corporal of his field,
And wear his colours like a tumbler's hoop!
What, I! I love! I sue! I seek a wife!
A woman, that is like a German clock,
Still a-repairing, ever out of frame,
And never going aright, being a watch,
But being watch'd that it may still go right!
Nay, to be perjured, which is worst of all;
And, among three, to love the worst of all;
A wightly wanton with a velvet brow,
With two pitch-balls stuck in her face for eyes;
Ay, and by heaven, one that will do the deed
Though Argus were her eunuch and her guard.
And I to sigh for her! to watch for her!
To pray for her! Go to; it is a plague
That Cupid will impose for my neglect
Of his almighty dreadful little might.
Well, I will love, write, sigh, pray, sue and groan:
Some men must love my lady and some Joan.

Exit

ACT IV

SCENE I—*The park*

Enter the PRINCESS, and her train, a Forester, BOYET, ROSALINE, MARIA, and KATHARINE

PRINCESS: Was that the King, that spurred his horse so hard
Against the steep uprising of the hill?

BOYET: I know not; but I think it was not he.

PRINCESS: Whoe'er a' was, a' show'd a mounting mind.
Well, lords, to-day we shall have our dispatch;
On Saturday we will return to France.
Then, forester, my friend, where is the bush
That we must stand and play the murderer in?

FORESTER: Hereby, upon the edge of yonder coppice;
A stand where you may make the fairest shoot.

PRINCESS: I thank my beauty, I am fair that shoot,
And thereupon thou speak'st the fairest shoot.

FORESTER: Pardon me, madam, for I meant not so.

PRINCESS: What, what? first praise me and again say no?
O short-lived pride! Not fair? alack for woe!

FORESTER: Yes, madam, fair.

PRINCESS: Nay, never paint me now;
Where fair is not, praise cannot mend the brow.
Here, good my glass, take this for telling true:

Giving him money

Fair payment for foul words is more than due.

FORESTER: Nothing but fair is that which you inherit.

PRINCESS: See see, my beauty will be saved by merit!
O heresy in fair, fit for these days!
A giving hand, though foul, shall have fair praise.
But come, the bow. Now mercy goes to kill,
And shooting well is then accounted ill.
Thus will I save my credit in the shoot:
Not wounding, pity would not let me do't;
If wounding, then it was to show my skill,
That more for praise than purpose meant to kill.
And out of question so it is sometimes:
Glory grows guilty of detested crimes,
When, for fame's sake, for praise, an outward part,
We bend to that the working of the heart;
As I for praise alone now seek to spill
The poor deer's blood, that my heart means no ill.

BOYET: Do not curst wives hold that self-sovereignty
Only for praise sake, when they strive to be
Lords o'er their lords?

PRINCESS: Only for praise; and praise we may afford
To any lady that subdues a lord.

BOYET: Here comes a member of the commonwealth.

Enter COSTARD

COSTARD: God dig-you-den all! Pray you, which is the head lady?

PRINCESS: Thou shalt know her, fellow, by the rest that have no heads.

COSTARD: Which is the greatest lady, the highest?

PRINCESS: The thickest and the tallest.

COSTARD: The thickest and the tallest! it is so; truth is truth.
An your waist, mistress, were as slender as my wit,
One o' these maids' girdles for your waist should be fit.
Are not you the chief woman? you are the thickest here.

PRINCESS: What's your will, sir? What's your will?

COSTARD: I have a letter from Monsieur BEROWNE to one Lady Rosaline.

PRINCESS: O, thy letter, thy letter! he's a good friend of mine.
Stand aside, good bearer. Boyet, you can carve;
Break up this capon.

BOYET: I am bound to serve.

This letter is mistook, it importeth none here;

It is writ to Jaquenetta.

PRINCESS: We will read it, I swear.

Break the neck of the wax, and every one give ear.

BOYET: [*Reads*] 'By heaven, that thou art fair, is most infallible; true, that thou art beauteous; truth itself, that thou art lovely. More fairer than fair, beautiful

than beauteous, truer than truth itself, have commiseration on thy heroical vassal. The magnanimous and most illustrate king Cophetua set eye upon the pernicious and indubitate beggar Zenelophon; and he it was that might rightly say, Veni, vidi, vici; which to annothanize in the vulgar,—O base and obscure vulgar!—videlicet, He came, saw, and overcame. He came, one; saw two; overcame, three. Who came? the king. Why did he come? to see. Why did he see? to overcome. To whom came he? to the beggar. What saw he? the beggar. Who overcame he? the beggar. The conclusion is victory; on whose side? the king's. The captive is enriched; on whose side? The beggar's. The catastrophe is a nuptial; on whose side? the king's. No, on both in one, or one in both. I am the king; for so stands the comparison; thou the beggar; for so witnesseth thy lowliness. Shall I command thy love? I may. Shall I enforce thy love? I could. Shall I entreat thy love? I will. What shalt thou exchange for rags? robes; for tittles? titles; for thyself? me. Thus, expecting thy reply, I profane my lips on thy foot, my eyes on thy picture, and my heart on thy every part. Thine, in the dearest design of industry,

DON ADRIANO DE ARMADO: Thus dost thou hear the Nemean lion roar

'Gainst thee, thou lamb, that standest as his prey.

Submissive fall his princely feet before,

And he from forage will incline to play.

But if thou strive, poor soul, what art thou then?

Food for his rage, repasture for his den.

PRINCESS: What plume of feathers is he that indited this letter?

What vane? what weathercock? Did you ever hear better?

BOYET: I am much deceived but I remember the style.

PRINCESS: Else your memory is bad, going o'er it erewhile.

BOYET: This Armado is a Spaniard, that keeps here in court;

A phantasime, a Monarcho, and one that makes sport

To the prince and his bookmates.

PRINCESS: Thou fellow, a word.

Who gave thee this letter?

COSTARD: I told you: my lord.

PRINCESS: To whom shouldst thou give it?

COSTARD: From my lord to my lady.

PRINCESS: From which lord to which lady?

COSTARD: From my lord BEROWNE, a good master of mine,

To a lady of France that he call'd Rosaline.

PRINCESS: Thou hast mistaken his letter. Come, lords, away. [*To Rosaline*] Here, sweet, put up this; 'twill be thine another day.

Exeunt PRINCESS and train

BOYET: Who is the shooter? who is the shooter?

ROSALINE: Shall I teach you to know?

BOYET: Ay, my continent of beauty.

ROSALINE: Why, she that bears the bow.

Finely put off!

BOYET: My lady goes to kill horns; but, if thou marry,

Hang me by the neck, if horns that year miscarry.

Finely put on!

ROSALINE: Well, then, I am the shooter.

BOYET: And who is your deer?

ROSALINE: If we choose by the horns, yourself come not near.

Finely put on, indeed!

MARIA: You still wrangle with her, Boyet, and she strikes at the brow.

BOYET: But she herself is hit lower. Have I hit her now?

ROSALINE: Shall I come upon thee with an old saying, that was a man when King Pepin of France was a little boy, as touching the hit it?

BOYET: So I may answer thee with one as old, that was a woman when Queen Guinover of Britain was a little wench, as touching the hit it.

ROSALINE: [*Singing*] Thou canst not hit it, hit it, hit it,

Thou canst not hit it, my good man.

BOYET: An I cannot, cannot, cannot,

An I cannot, another can.

Exeunt ROSALINE and KATHARINE

COSTARD: By my troth, most pleasant. How both did fit it!

MARIA: A mark marvellous well shot, for they both did hit it.

BOYET: A mark! O, mark but that mark! A mark, says my lady!

Let the mark have a prick in't, to mete at, if it may be.

MARIA: Wide o' the bow hand! I' faith, your hand is out.

COSTARD: Indeed, a' must shoot nearer, or he'll ne'er hit the clout.

BOYET: An if my hand be out, then belike your hand is in.

COSTARD: Then will she get the upshoot by cleaving the pin.

MARIA: Come, come, you talk greasily; your lips grow foul.

COSTARD: She's too hard for you at pricks, sir; challenge her to bowl.

BOYET: I fear too much rubbing. Good night, my good owl.

Exeunt BOYET and MARIA

COSTARD: By my soul, a swain! a most simple clown!

Lord, Lord, how the ladies and I have put him down!

O' my troth, most sweet jests! most incony vulgar wit!

When it comes so smoothly off, so obscenely, as it were, so fit.

Armado o' th' one side—O, a most dainty man!

To see him walk before a lady and to bear her fan!

To see him kiss his hand, and how most sweetly a' will swear!

And his page o' t' other side, that handful of wit!

Ah, heavens, it is a most pathetical nit! Sola, sola!

Exit COSTARD

SCENE II—*The park*

Enter HOLOFERNES, SIR NATHANIEL, and DULL

SIR NATHANIEL: Very reverend sport, truly; and done in the testimony of a good conscience.

HOLOFERNES: The deer was, as you know, sanguis, in blood; ripe as the pomewater, who now hangeth like a jewel in the ear of caelo, the sky, the welkin, the heaven; and anon falleth like a crab on the face of terra, the soil, the land, the earth.

SIR NATHANIEL: Truly, Master Holofernes, the epithets are sweetly varied, like a scholar at the least; but, sir, I assure ye, it was a buck of the first head.

HOLOFERNES: Sir Nathaniel, haud credo.

DULL: 'Twas not a haud credo; 'twas a pricket.

HOLOFERNES: Most barbarous intimation! yet a kind of insinuation, as it were, in via, in way, of explication; facere, as it were, replication, or rather, ostentare, to show, as it were, his inclination, after his undressed, unpolished, uneducated, unpruned, untrained, or rather, unlettered, or ratherest, unconfirmed fashion, to insert again my haud credo for a deer.

DULL: I said the deer was not a haud credo; 'twas a pricket.

HOLOFERNES: Twice-sod simplicity, his coctus!

O thou monster Ignorance, how deformed dost thou look!

SIR NATHANIEL: Sir, he hath never fed of the dainties that are bred in a book; he hath not eat paper, as it were; he hath not drunk ink; his intellect is not replenished; he is only an animal, only sensible in the duller parts;

And such barren plants are set before us, that we thankful should be,

Which we of taste and feeling are, for those parts that do fructify in us more than he.

For as it would ill become me to be vain, indiscreet, or a fool,

So were there a patch set on learning, to see him in a school.

But omne bene, say I; being of an old father's mind,

Many can brook the weather that love not the wind.

DULL: You two are book-men: can you tell me by your wit

What was a month old at Cain's birth, that's not five weeks old as yet?

HOLOFERNES: Dictynna, goodman Dull; Dictynna, goodman Dull.

DULL: What is Dictynna?

SIR NATHANIEL: A title to Phoebe, to Luna, to the moon.

HOLOFERNES: The moon was a month old when Adam was no more,

And raught not to five weeks when he came to five-score.

The allusion holds in the exchange.

DULL: 'Tis true indeed; the collusion holds in the exchange.

HOLOFERNES: God comfort thy capacity! I say, the allusion holds in the exchange.

DULL: And I say, the pollusion holds in the exchange; for the moon is never but a month old; and I say beside that, 'twas a pricket that the princess killed.

HOLOFERNES: Sir Nathaniel, will you hear an extemporal epitaph on the death of the deer? And, to humour the ignorant, call I the deer the princess killed a pricket.

SIR NATHANIEL: Perge, good Master Holofernes, perge; so it shall please you to abrogate scurrility.

HOLOFERNES: I will something affect the letter, for it argues facility.

The preyful princess pierced and prick'd a pretty pleasing pricket.

Some say a sore; but not a sore, till now made sore with shooting.

The dogs did yell; put L to sore, then sorel jumps from thicket;

Or pricket sore, or else sorel; the people fall a-hooting.

If sore be sore, then L to sore makes fifty sores one sorel.

Of one sore I an hundred make by adding but one more L.

SIR NATHANIEL: A rare talent!

DULL: [*Aside*] If a talent be a claw, look how he claws him with a talent.

HOLOFERNES: This is a gift that I have, simple, simple; a foolish extravagant spirit, full of forms, figures, shapes, objects, ideas, apprehensions, motions, revolutions. These are begot in the ventricle of memory, nourished in the womb of pia mater, and delivered upon the mellowing of occasion. But the gift is good in those in whom it is acute, and I am thankful for it.

SIR NATHANIEL: Sir, I praise the Lord for you; and so may my parishioners; for their sons are well tutored by you, and their daughters profit very greatly under you. You are a good member of the commonwealth.

HOLOFERNES: Mehercle, if their sons be ingenuous, they shall want no instruction; if their daughters be capable, I will put it to them; but vir sapit qui pauca loquitur. A soul feminine saluteth us.

Enter JAQUENETTA and COSTARD

JAQUENETTA: God give you good morrow, master Parson.

HOLOFERNES: Master Parson, quasi pers-on. And if one should be pierced, which is the one?

COSTARD: Marry, master schoolmaster, he that is likest to a hogshead.

HOLOFERNES: Piercing a hogshead! a good lustre of conceit in a tuft of earth; fire enough for a flint, pearl enough for a swine: 'tis pretty; it is well.

JAQUENETTA: Good master Parson, be so good as read me this letter; it was given me by Costard, and sent me from Don Armado. I beseech you, read it.

HOLOFERNES: Fauste, precor gelida quando pecus omne sub umbra Ruminat—and so forth. Ah, good old Mantuan! I may speak of thee as the traveller doth of Venice: Venetia, Venetia, Chi non ti vede non ti pretia. Old Mantuan, old Mantuan! who understandeth thee not, loves thee not. Ut, re, sol, la, mi, fa. Under pardon, sir, what are the contents? or rather, as Horace says in his—What, my soul, verses?

SIR NATHANIEL: Ay, sir, and very learned.

HOLOFERNES: Let me hear a staff, a stanze, a verse; lege, domine.

SIR NATHANIEL: [*Reads*] If love make me forsworn, how shall I swear to love?

Ah, never faith could hold, if not to beauty vow'd!

Though to myself forsworn, to thee I'll faithful prove;

Those thoughts to me were oaks, to thee like osiers bow'd.

Study his bias leaves and makes his book thine eyes,

Where all those pleasures live that art would comprehend.

If knowledge be the mark, to know thee shall suffice;

Well learned is that tongue that well can thee commend,

All ignorant that soul that sees thee without wonder;

Which is to me some praise that I thy parts admire.

Thy eye Jove's lightning bears, thy voice his dreadful thunder,

Which not to anger bent, is music and sweet fire.

Celestial as thou art, O, pardon, love, this wrong,

That sings heaven's praise with such an earthly tongue.

HOLOFERNES: You find not the apostraphas, and so miss the accent: let me supervise the canzonet. Here are only numbers ratified; but, for the elegancy, facility, and golden cadence of poesy, caret. Ovidius Naso was the man: and why, indeed, Naso, but for smelling out the odouriferous flowers of fancy, the jerks of invention? Imitari is nothing: so doth the hound his master, the ape his keeper, the tired horse his rider. But, damosella virgin, was this directed to you?

JAQUENETTA: Ay, sir, from one Monsieur BEROWNE, one of the strange queen's lords.

HOLOFERNES: I will overglance the superscript: 'To the snow-white hand of the most beauteous Lady Rosaline.' I will look again on the intellect of the letter, for the nomination of the party writing to the person written unto: 'Your ladyship's in all desired employment, BEROWNE.' Sir Nathaniel, this BEROWNE is one of the votaries with the king; and here he hath framed a letter to a sequent of the stranger queen's, which accidentally, or by the way of progression, hath miscarried. Trip and go, my sweet; deliver this paper into the royal hand of the king; it may concern much. Stay not thy compliment; I forgive thy duty; adieu.

JAQUENETTA: Good Costard, go with me. Sir, God save your life!

COSTARD: Have with thee, my girl.

Exeunt COSTARD and JAQUENETTA

SIR NATHANIEL: Sir, you have done this in the fear of God, very religiously; and, as a certain father saith—

HOLOFERNES: Sir tell me not of the father; I do fear colourable colours. But to return to the verses: did they please you, Sir Nathaniel?

SIR NATHANIEL: Marvellous well for the pen.

HOLOFERNES: I do dine to-day at the father's of a certain pupil of mine; where, if, before repast, it shall please you to gratify the table with a grace, I will, on my privilege I have with the parents of the foresaid child or pupil, undertake your ben venuto; where I will prove those verses to be very unlearned, neither savouring of poetry, wit, nor invention. I beseech your society.

SIR NATHANIEL: And thank you too; for society, saith the text, is the happiness of life.

HOLOFERNES: And, certes, the text most infallibly concludes it. [*To Dull*] Sir, I do invite you too; you shall not say me nay: pauca verba. Away! the gentles are at their game, and we will to our recreation.

Exeunt

SCENE III—*The park*

Enter BEROWNE, with a paper

BEROWNE: The king he is hunting the deer; I am coursing myself. They have pitched a toil; I am toiling in a pitch—pitch that defiles. Defile! a foul word. Well, set thee down, sorrow! for so they say the fool said, and so say I, and I am the fool. Well proved, wit! By the Lord, this love is as mad as Ajax: it kills sheep; it kills me, I a sheep. Well proved again o' my side! I will not love; if I do, hang me; I' faith, I will not. O, but her eye,—by this light, but for her eye, I would not love her; yes, for her two eyes. Well, I do nothing in the world but lie, and lie in my throat. By heaven, I do love; and it hath taught me to rhyme and to be melancholy; and here is part of my rhyme, and here my melancholy. Well, she hath one o' my sonnets already; the clown bore it, the fool sent it, and the lady hath it; sweet clown, sweeter fool, sweetest lady! By the world, I would not care a pin, if the other three were in. Here comes one with a paper; God give him grace to groan!

Stands aside

Enter FERDINAND, with a paper

FERDINAND: Ay me!

BEROWNE: [*Aside*] Shot, by heaven! Proceed, sweet Cupid; thou hast thumped him with thy bird-bolt under the left pap. In faith, secrets!

FERDINAND: [*Reads*]

So sweet a kiss the golden sun gives not

To those fresh morning drops upon the rose,

As thy eye-beams, when their fresh rays have smote

The night of dew that on my cheeks down flows;

Nor shines the silver moon one half so bright

Through the transparent bosom of the deep,
As doth thy face through tears of mine give light;
Thou shinest in every tear that I do weep;
No drop but as a coach doth carry thee;
So ridest thou triumphing in my woe.
Do but behold the tears that swell in me,
And they thy glory through my grief will show.
But do not love thyself; then thou wilt keep
My tears for glasses, and still make me weep.
O queen of queens! how far dost thou excel,
No thought can think, nor tongue of mortal tell.
How shall she know my griefs? I'll drop the paper—
Sweet leaves, shade folly. Who is he comes here?

Steps aside

What, Longaville! and reading! listen, ear.

BEROWNE: Now, in thy likeness, one more fool appear!

Enter LONGAVILLE, with a paper

LONGAVILLE: Ay me, I am forsworn!

BEROWNE: Why, he comes in like a perjure, wearing papers.

FERDINAND: In love, I hope; sweet fellowship in shame!

BEROWNE: One drunkard loves another of the name.

LONGAVILLE: Am I the first that have been perjured so?

BEROWNE: I could put thee in comfort. Not by two that I know;
Thou makest the triumviry, the corner-cap of society,
The shape of Love's Tyburn that hangs up simplicity.

LONGAVILLE: I fear these stubborn lines lack power to move.
O sweet Maria, empress of my love!
These numbers will I tear, and write in prose.

BEROWNE: O, rhymes are guards on wanton Cupid's hose: Disfigure not his slop.

LONGAVILLE: This same shall go.

Reads

Did not the heavenly rhetoric of thine eye,
'Gainst whom the world cannot hold argument,
Persuade my heart to this false perjury?
Vows for thee broke deserve not punishment.
A woman I forswore; but I will prove,
Thou being a goddess, I forswore not thee:
My vow was earthly, thou a heavenly love;
Thy grace being gain'd cures all disgrace in me.
Vows are but breath, and breath a vapour is;
Then thou, fair sun, which on my earth dost shine,
Exhalest this vapour-vow; in thee it is.
If broken then, it is no fault of mine;
If by me broke, what fool is not so wise
To lose an oath to win a paradise?

BEROWNE: This is the liver-vein, which makes flesh a deity,
A green goose a goddess: pure, pure idolatry.
God amend us, God amend! We are much out o' the way.

LONGAVILLE: By whom shall I send this?—Company! stay.

Steps aside

BEROWNE: All hid, all hid; an old infant play.
Like a demigod here sit I in the sky.
And wretched fools' secrets heedfully o'ereye.
More sacks to the mill! O heavens, I have my wish!

Enter DUMAIN, with a paper

Dumain transform'd! Four woodcocks in a dish!

DUMAIN: O most divine Kate!

BEROWNE: O most profane coxcomb!

DUMAIN: By heaven, the wonder in a mortal eye!

BEROWNE: By earth, she is not, corporal, there you lie.

DUMAIN: Her amber hair for foul hath amber quoted.

BEROWNE: An amber-colour'd raven was well noted.

DUMAIN: As upright as the cedar.

BEROWNE: Stoop, I say;
Her shoulder is with child.

DUMAIN: As fair as day.

BEROWNE: Ay, as some days; but then no sun must shine.

DUMAIN: O that I had my wish!

LONGAVILLE: And I had mine!

FERDINAND: And I mine too, good Lord!

BEROWNE: Amen, so I had mine! Is not that a good word?

DUMAIN: I would forget her; but a fever she
Reigns in my blood and will remember'd be.
BEROWNE: A fever in your blood! why, then incision
Would let her out in saucers: sweet misprision!
DUMAIN: Once more I'll read the ode that I have writ.
BEROWNE: Once more I'll mark how love can vary wit.
DUMAIN: [*Reads*]
On a day—alack the day!—
Love, whose month is ever May,
Spied a blossom passing fair
Playing in the wanton air.
Through the velvet leaves the wind,
All unseen, can passage find;
That the lover, sick to death,
Wish himself the heaven's breath.
Air, quoth he, thy cheeks may blow;
Air, would I might triumph so!
But, alack, my hand is sworn
Ne'er to pluck thee from thy thorn;
Vow, alack, for youth unmeet,
Youth so apt to pluck a sweet!
Do not call it sin in me,
That I am forsworn for thee;
Thou for whom Jove would swear
Juno but an Ethiope were;
And deny himself for Jove,
Turning mortal for thy love.
This will I send, and something else more plain,
That shall express my true love's fasting pain.
O, would the king, Berowne, and Longaville,
Were lovers too! Ill, to example ill,
Would from my forehead wipe a perjured note;
For none offend where all alike do dote.
LONGAVILLE: [*Advancing*] Dumain, thy love is far from charity.
You may look pale, but I should blush, I know,
To be o'erheard and taken napping so.
FERDINAND: [*Advancing*] Come, sir, you blush; as his your case is such.
You chide at him, offending twice as much:
You do not love Maria; Longaville
Did never sonnet for her sake compile,
Nor never lay his wreathed arms athwart
His loving bosom to keep down his heart.
I have been closely shrouded in this bush
And mark'd you both and for you both did blush.
I heard your guilty rhymes, observed your fashion,
Saw sighs reek from you, noted well your passion.
Ay me! says one; O Jove! the other cries;
One, her hairs were gold, crystal the other's eyes.
[*To Longaville*] You would for paradise break faith, and troth;
[*To Dumain*] And Jove, for your love would infringe an oath.
What will Berowne say when that he shall hear
Faith so infringed, which such zeal did swear?
How will he scorn! how will he spend his wit!
How will he triumph, leap and laugh at it!
For all the wealth that ever I did see,
I would not have him know so much by me.
BEROWNE: [*Deseending*] Now step I forth to whip hypocrisy.
Ah, good my liege, I pray thee, pardon me!
Good heart, what grace hast thou, thus to reprove
These worms for loving, that art most in love?
Your eyes do make no coaches; in your tears
There is no certain princess that appears;
You'll not be perjured, 'tis a hateful thing;
Tush, none but minstrels like of sonneting!
But are you not ashamed? nay, are you not,
All three of you, to be thus much o'ershot?
You found his mote; the king your mote did see;
But I a beam do find in each of three.
O, what a scene of foolery have I seen,
Of sighs, of groans, of sorrow and of teen!
O me, with what strict patience have I sat,
To see a king transformed to a gnat!
To see great Hercules whipping a gig,
And profound Solomon to tune a jig,
And Nestor play at push-pin with the boys,
And critic Timon laugh at idle toys!
Where lies thy grief, O, tell me, good Dumain?
And gentle Longaville, where lies thy pain?
And where my liege's? All about the breast. A caudle, ho!
FERDINAND: Too bitter is thy jest.
Are we betray'd thus to thy over-view?
BEROWNE: Not you to me, but I betray'd by you.

I, that am honest; I, that hold it sin
To break the vow I am engaged in;
I am betray'd, by keeping company
With men like men of inconstancy.
When shall you see me write a thing in rhyme?
Or groan for love? or spend a minute's time
In pruning me? When shall you hear that I
Will praise a hand, a foot, a face, an eye,
A gait, a state, a brow, a breast, a waist,
A leg, a limb?

FERDINAND: Soft! whither away so fast?
A true man or a thief that gallops so?

BEROWNE: I post from love; good lover, let me go.

Enter JAQUENETTA and COSTARD

JAQUENETTA: God bless the king!

FERDINAND: What present hast thou there?

COSTARD: Some certain treason.

FERDINAND: What makes treason here?

COSTARD: Nay, it makes nothing, sir.

FERDINAND: If it mar nothing neither,
The treason and you go in peace away together.

JAQUENETTA: I beseech your grace, let this letter be read;
Our person misdoubts it; 'twas treason, he said.

FERDINAND: Berowne, read it over.

Berowne reads the letter

Where hadst thou it?

JAQUENETTA: Of Costard.

FERDINAND: Where hadst thou it?

COSTARD: Of Dun Adramadio, Dun Adramadio.

Berowne tears the letter

FERDINAND: How now! what is in you? why dost thou tear it?

BEROWNE: A toy, my liege, a toy! Your grace needs not fear it.

LONGAVILLE: It did move him to passion, and therefore let's hear it.

DUMAIN: It is Berowne's writing, and here is his name.

Gathering up the pieces

BEROWNE: [*To Costard*] Ah, you whoreson loggerhead! you were born to do me shame.
Guilty, my lord, guilty! I confess, I confess.

FERDINAND: What?

BEROWNE: That you three fools lack'd me fool to make up the mess;
He, he, and you, and you, my liege, and I,
Are pick-purses in love, and we deserve to die.
O, dismiss this audience, and I shall tell you more.

DUMAIN: Now the number is even.

BEROWNE: True, true; we are four.
Will these turtles be gone?

FERDINAND: Hence, sirs; away!

COSTARD: Walk aside the true folk, and let the traitors stay.

Exeunt COSTARD and JAQUENETTA

BEROWNE: Sweet lords, sweet lovers, O, let us embrace!
As true we are as flesh and blood can be.
The sea will ebb and flow, heaven show his face;
Young blood doth not obey an old decree.
We cannot cross the cause why we were born;
Therefore of all hands must we be forsworn.

FERDINAND: What, did these rent lines show some love of thine?

BEROWNE: Did they, quoth you? Who sees the heavenly Rosaline,
That, like a rude and savage man of Inde,
At the first opening of the gorgeous east,
Bows not his vassal head and strucken blind
Kisses the base ground with obedient breast?
What peremptory eagle-sighted eye
Dares look upon the heaven of her brow,
That is not blinded by her majesty?

FERDINAND: What zeal, what fury hath inspired thee now?
My love, her mistress, is a gracious moon;
She an attending star, scarce seen a light.

BEROWNE: My eyes are then no eyes, nor I Berowne.
O, but for my love, day would turn to night!
Of all complexions the cull'd sovereignty
Do meet, as at a fair, in her fair cheek,
Where several worthies make one dignity,
Where nothing wants that want itself doth seek.
Lend me the flourish of all gentle tongues—
Fie, painted rhetoric! O, she needs it not!
To things of sale a seller's praise belongs,
She passes praise; then praise too short doth blot.
A wither'd hermit, five-score winters worn,
Might shake off fifty, looking in her eye.
Beauty doth varnish age, as if new-born,
And gives the crutch the cradle's infancy.

O, 'tis the sun that maketh all things shine.
FERDINAND: By heaven, thy love is black as ebony.
BEROWNE: Is ebony like her? O wood divine!
A wife of such wood were felicity.
O, who can give an oath? where is a book?
That I may swear beauty doth beauty lack,
If that she learn not of her eye to look.
No face is fair that is not full so black.
FERDINAND: O paradox! Black is the badge of hell,
The hue of dungeons and the school of night;
And beauty's crest becomes the heavens well.
BEROWNE: Devils soonest tempt, resembling spirits of light.
O, if in black my lady's brows be deck'd,
It mourns that painting and usurping hair
Should ravish doters with a false aspect;
And therefore is she born to make black fair.
Her favour turns the fashion of the days,
For native blood is counted painting now;
And therefore red, that would avoid dispraise,
Paints itself black, to imitate her brow.
DUMAIN: To look like her are chimney-sweepers black.
LONGAVILLE: And since her time are colliers counted bright.
FERDINAND: And Ethiopes of their sweet complexion crack.
DUMAIN: Dark needs no candles now, for dark is light.
BEROWNE: Your mistresses dare never come in rain,
For fear their colours should be wash'd away.
FERDINAND: 'Twere good, yours did; for, sir, to tell you plain,
I'll find a fairer face not wash'd to-day.
BEROWNE: I'll prove her fair, or talk till doomsday here.
FERDINAND: No devil will fright thee then so much as she.
DUMAIN: I never knew man hold vile stuff so dear.
LONGAVILLE: Look, here's thy love: my foot and her face see.
BEROWNE: O, if the streets were paved with thine eyes,
Her feet were much too dainty for such tread!
DUMAIN: O, vile! then, as she goes, what upward lies
The street should see as she walk'd overhead.
FERDINAND: But what of this? Are we not all in love?
BEROWNE: Nothing so sure; and thereby all forsworn.
FERDINAND: Then leave this chat; and, good Berowne, now prove
Our loving lawful, and our faith not torn.
DUMAIN: Ay, marry, there; some flattery for this evil.
LONGAVILLE: O, some authority how to proceed;
Some tricks, some quillets, how to cheat the devil.
DUMAIN: Some salve for perjury.
BEROWNE: 'Tis more than need.
Have at you, then, affection's men at arms.
Consider what you first did swear unto,
To fast, to study, and to see no woman;
Flat treason 'gainst the kingly state of youth.
Say, can you fast? your stomachs are too young;
And abstinence engenders maladies.
And where that you have vow'd to study, lords,
In that each of you have forsworn his book,
Can you still dream and pore and thereon look?
For when would you, my lord, or you, or you,
Have found the ground of study's excellence
Without the beauty of a woman's face?
From women's eyes this doctrine I derive;
They are the ground, the books, the academes
From whence doth spring the true Promethean fire
Why, universal plodding poisons up
The nimble spirits in the arteries,
As motion and long-during action tires
The sinewy vigour of the traveller.
Now, for not looking on a woman's face,
You have in that forsworn the use of eyes
And study too, the causer of your vow;
For where is any author in the world
Teaches such beauty as a woman's eye?
Learning is but an adjunct to ourself
And where we are our learning likewise is;
Then when ourselves we see in ladies' eyes,
Do we not likewise see our learning there?
O, we have made a vow to study, lords,
And in that vow we have forsworn our books.
For when would you, my liege, or you, or you,
In leaden contemplation have found out
Such fiery numbers as the prompting eyes

Of beauty's tutors have enrich'd you with?
Other slow arts entirely keep the brain;
And therefore, finding barren practisers,
Scarce show a harvest of their heavy toil;
But love, first learned in a lady's eyes,
Lives not alone immured in the brain;
But, with the motion of all elements,
Courses as swift as thought in every power,
And gives to every power a double power,
Above their functions and their offices.
It adds a precious seeing to the eye:
A lover's eyes will gaze an eagle blind.
A lover's ear will hear the lowest sound,
When the suspicious head of theft is stopp'd.
Love's feeling is more soft and sensible
Than are the tender horns of cockl'd snails;
Love's tongue proves dainty Bacchus gross in taste.
For valour, is not Love a Hercules,
Still climbing trees in the Hesperides?
Subtle as Sphinx; as sweet and musical
As bright Apollo's lute, strung with his hair.
And when Love speaks, the voice of all the gods
Makes heaven drowsy with the harmony.
Never durst poet touch a pen to write
Until his ink were temper'd with Love's sighs;
O, then his lines would ravish savage ears
And plant in tyrants mild humility.
From women's eyes this doctrine I derive.
They sparkle still the right Promethean fire;
They are the books, the arts, the academes,
That show, contain and nourish all the world,
Else none at all in ought proves excellent.
Then fools you were these women to forswear,
Or keeping what is sworn, you will prove fools.
For wisdom's sake, a word that all men love,
Or for love's sake, a word that loves all men,
Or for men's sake, the authors of these women,
Or women's sake, by whom we men are men—
Let us once lose our oaths to find ourselves,
Or else we lose ourselves to keep our oaths.
It is religion to be thus forsworn;
For charity itself fulfills the law,
And who can sever love from charity?

FERDINAND: Saint Cupid, then! and, soldiers, to the field!

BEROWNE: Advance your standards, and upon them, lords;
Pell-mell, down with them! but be first advised,
In conflict that you get the sun of them.

LONGAVILLE: Now to plain-dealing; lay these glozes by.
Shall we resolve to woo these girls of France?

FERDINAND: And win them too; therefore let us devise
Some entertainment for them in their tents.

BEROWNE: First, from the park let us conduct them thither;
Then homeward every man attach the hand
Of his fair mistress. In the afternoon
We will with some strange pastime solace them,
Such as the shortness of the time can shape;
For revels, dances, masks and merry hours
Forerun fair Love, strewing her way with flowers.

FERDINAND: Away, away! no time shall be omitted
That will betime, and may by us be fitted.

BEROWNE: Allons! allons! Sow'd cockle reap'd no corn;
And justice always whirls in equal measure.
Light wenches may prove plagues to men forsworn;
If so, our copper buys no better treasure.

Exeunt

Act V

Scene I—*The park*

Enter HOLOFERNES, SIR NATHANIEL, and DULL

HOLOFERNES: Satis quod sufficit.

SIR NATHANIEL: I praise God for you, sir. Your reasons at dinner have been sharp and sententious; pleasant without scurrility, witty without affection, audacious without impudency, learned without opinion, and strange without heresy. I did converse this quondam day with a companion of the king's, who is intituled, nominated, or called, Don Adriano de Armado.

HOLOFERNES: Novi hominem tanquam te. His humour is lofty, his discourse peremptory, his tongue filed, his eye ambitious, his gait majestical, and his general behavior vain, ridiculous, and thrasonical. He is too picked, too spruce, too affected, too odd, as it were, too peregrinate, as I may call it.

SIR NATHANIEL: A most singular and choice epithet.

Draws out his table-book

HOLOFERNES: He draweth out the thread of his verbosity finer than the staple of his argument. I abhor such fanatical phantasimes, such insociable and point-devise companions; such rackers of orthography, as to speak dout, fine, when he should say doubt; det, when he should pronounce debt—d, e, b, t, not d, e, t: he clepeth a calf, cauf; half, hauf; neighbour vocatur nebor; neigh abbreviated ne. This is abhominable—which he would call abominable. It insinuateth me of insanie: anne intelligis, domine? to make frantic, lunatic.

SIR NATHANIEL: Laus Deo, bene intelligo.

HOLOFERNES: Bon, bon, fort bon, Priscian! a little scratch'd, 'twill serve.

SIR NATHANIEL: Videsne quis venit?

HOLOFERNES: Video, et gaudeo.

Enter DON ADRIANO DE ARMADO, MOTH, and COSTARD

DON ADRIANO DE ARMADO: [*To Moth*] Chirrah!

HOLOFERNES: Quare chirrah, not sirrah?

DON ADRIANO DE ARMADO: Men of peace, well encountered.

HOLOFERNES: Most military sir, salutation.

MOTH: [*Aside to Costard*] They have been at a great feast of languages, and stolen the scraps.

COSTARD: O, they have lived long on the alms-basket of words. I marvel thy master hath not eaten thee for a word; for thou art not so long by the head as honorificabilitudinitatibus; thou art easier swallowed than a flap-dragon.

MOTH: Peace! the peal begins.

DON ADRIANO DE ARMADO: [*To Holofernes*] Monsieur, are you not lettered?

MOTH: Yes, yes; he teaches boys the hornbook. What is a, b, spelt backward, with the horn on his head?

HOLOFERNES: Ba, pueritia, with a horn added.

MOTH: Ba, most silly sheep with a horn. You hear his learning.

HOLOFERNES: Quis, quis, thou consonant?

MOTH: The third of the five vowels, if you repeat them; or the fifth, if I.

HOLOFERNES: I will repeat them: a, e, I,—

MOTH: The sheep; the other two concludes it: o, U.

DON ADRIANO DE ARMADO: Now, by the salt wave of the Mediterraneum, a sweet touch, a quick venue of wit! snip, snap, quick and home. It rejoiceth my intellect. True wit!

MOTH: Offered by a child to an old man; which is wit-old.

HOLOFERNES: What is the figure? what is the figure?

MOTH: Horns.

HOLOFERNES: Thou disputes like an infant; go, whip thy gig.

MOTH: Lend me your horn to make one, and I will whip about your infamy circum circa—a gig of a cuckold's horn.

COSTARD: An I had but one penny in the world, thou shouldst have it to buy gingerbread. Hold, there is the very remuneration I had of thy master, thou halfpenny purse of wit, thou pigeon-egg of discretion. O, an the heavens were so pleased that thou wert but my bastard, what a joyful father wouldst thou make me! Go to; thou hast it ad dunghill, at the fingers' ends, as they say.

HOLOFERNES: O, I smell false Latin; dunghill for unguem.

DON ADRIANO DE ARMADO: Arts-man, preambulate, we will be singled from the barbarous. Do you not educate youth at the charge house on the top of the mountain?

HOLOFERNES: Or mons, the hill.

DON ADRIANO DE ARMADO: At your sweet pleasure, for the mountain.

HOLOFERNES: I do, sans question.

DON ADRIANO DE ARMADO: Sir, it is the king's most sweet pleasure and affection to congratulate the princess at her pavilion in the posteriors of this day, which the rude multitude call the afternoon.

HOLOFERNES: The posterior of the day, most generous sir, is liable, congruent and measurable for the afternoon. The word is well culled, chose, sweet and apt, I do assure you, sir, I do assure.

DON ADRIANO DE ARMADO: Sir, the king is a noble gentleman, and my familiar, I do assure ye, very good friend. For what is inward between us, let it pass. I do beseech thee, remember thy courtesy; I beseech thee, apparel thy head. And among other important and most serious designs, and of great import indeed, too, but let that pass;. for I must tell thee, it will please his grace, by the world, sometime to lean upon my poor shoulder, and with his royal finger, thus, dally with my excrement, with my mustachio; but, sweet heart, let that pass. By the world, I recount no fable: some certain special honours it pleaseth his greatness to impart to Armado, a soldier, a man of travel, that hath seen the world; but let that pass. The very all of all is—but, sweet heart, I do implore secrecy—that the king would have me present the princess, sweet chuck, with some delightful ostentation, or show, or pageant, or antique, or firework. Now, understanding that the curate and your sweet self are good at such eruptions and sudden breaking out of mirth, as it were, I have acquainted you withal, to the end to crave your assistance.

HOLOFERNES: Sir, you shall present before her the Nine Worthies. Sir, as concerning some entertainment of time, some show in the posterior of this day, to be rendered by our assistants, at the king's command, and this most gallant, illustrate, and learned gentleman, before the princess; I say none so fit as to present the Nine Worthies.

SIR NATHANIEL: Where will you find men worthy enough to present them?

HOLOFERNES: Joshua, yourself; myself, Alexander and this gallant gentleman, Judas Maccabaeus; this swain, because of his great limb or joint, shall pass Pompey the Great; the page, Hercules.

DON ADRIANO DE ARMADO: Pardon, sir; error: he is not quantity enough for that Worthy's thumb; he is not so big as the end of his club.

HOLOFERNES: Shall I have audience? he shall present Hercules in minority: his enter and exit shall be strangling a snake; and I will have an apology for that purpose.

MOTH: An excellent device! so, if any of the audience hiss, you may cry 'Well done, Hercules! now thou crushest the snake!' that is the way to make an offence gracious, though few have the grace to do it.

DON ADRIANO DE ARMADO: For the rest of the Worthies?—

HOLOFERNES: I will play three myself.

MOTH: Thrice-worthy gentleman!

DON ADRIANO DE ARMADO: Shall I tell you a thing?

HOLOFERNES: We attend.

DON ADRIANO DE ARMADO: We will have, if this fadge not, an antique. I beseech you, follow.

HOLOFERNES: Via, goodman Dull! thou hast spoken no word all this while.

DULL: Nor understood none neither, sir.

HOLOFERNES: Allons! we will employ thee.

DULL: I'll make one in a dance, or so; or I will play
On the tabour to the Worthies, and let them dance the hay.

HOLOFERNES: Most dull, honest Dull! To our sport, away!

Exeunt

SCENE II—*The park*

Enter the PRINCESS, KATHARINE, ROSALINE, and MARIA

PRINCESS: Sweet hearts, we shall be rich ere we depart,
If fairings come thus plentifully in.

A lady wall'd about with diamonds!
Look you what I have from the loving king.

ROSALINE: Madame, came nothing else along with that?

PRINCESS: Nothing but this! yes, as much love in rhyme
As would be cramm'd up in a sheet of paper,
Writ o' both sides the leaf, margent and all,
That he was fain to seal on Cupid's name.

ROSALINE: That was the way to make his godhead wax,
For he hath been five thousand years a boy.

KATHARINE: Ay, and a shrewd unhappy gallows too.

ROSALINE: You'll ne'er be friends with him: a' kill'd your sister.

KATHARINE: He made her melancholy, sad, and heavy;
And so she died. Had she been light, like you,
Of such a merry, nimble, stirring spirit,
She might ha' been a grandam ere she died.
And so may you; for a light heart lives long.

ROSALINE: What's your dark meaning, mouse, of this light word?

KATHARINE: A light condition in a beauty dark.

ROSALINE: We need more light to find your meaning out.

KATHARINE: You'll mar the light by taking it in snuff;
Therefore I'll darkly end the argument.

ROSALINE: Look what you do, you do it still i' the dark.

KATHARINE: So do not you, for you are a light wench.

ROSALINE: Indeed I weigh not you, and therefore light.

KATHARINE: You weigh me not? O, that's you care not for me.

ROSALINE: Great reason; for 'past cure is still past care.'

PRINCESS: Well bandied both; a set of wit well play'd.
But Rosaline, you have a favour too:
Who sent it? and what is it?

ROSALINE: I would you knew.
An if my face were but as fair as yours,
My favour were as great; be witness this.
Nay, I have verses too, I thank Berowne;
The numbers true; and, were the numbering too,
I were the fairest goddess on the ground.
I am compared to twenty thousand fairs.
O, he hath drawn my picture in his letter!

PRINCESS: Any thing like?

ROSALINE: Much in the letters; nothing in the praise.

PRINCESS: Beauteous as ink; a good conclusion.

KATHARINE: Fair as a text B in a copy-book.

ROSALINE: Ware pencils, ho! let me not die your debtor,
My red dominical, my golden letter:
O, that your face were not so full of O's!

KATHARINE: A pox of that jest! and I beshrew all shrows.

PRINCESS: But, Katharine, what was sent to you from fair Dumain?

KATHARINE: Madam, this glove.

PRINCESS: Did he not send you twain?

KATHARINE: Yes, madam, and moreover
Some thousand verses of a faithful lover,
A huge translation of hypocrisy,
Vilely compiled, profound simplicity.

MARIA: This and these pearls to me sent Longaville;
The letter is too long by half a mile.

PRINCESS: I think no less. Dost thou not wish in heart
The chain were longer and the letter short?

MARIA: Ay, or I would these hands might never part.

PRINCESS: We are wise girls to mock our lovers so.

ROSALINE: They are worse fools to purchase mocking so.
That same Berowne I'll torture ere I go.
O that I knew he were but in by the week!
How I would make him fawn and beg and seek
And wait the season and observe the times
And spend his prodigal wits in bootless rhymes
And shape his service wholly to my hests
And make him proud to make me proud that jests!
So perttaunt-like would I o'ersway his state
That he should be my fool and I his fate.

PRINCESS: None are so surely caught, when they are catch'd,
As wit turn'd fool; folly, in wisdom hatch'd,
Hath wisdom's warrant and the help of school
And wit's own grace to grace a learned fool.

ROSALINE: The blood of youth burns not with such excess
As gravity's revolt to wantonness.
MARIA: Folly in fools bears not so strong a note
As foolery in the wise, when wit doth dote;
Since all the power thereof it doth apply
To prove, by wit, worth in simplicity.
PRINCESS: Here comes Boyet, and mirth is in his face.

Enter BOYET

BOYET: O, I am stabb'd with laughter! Where's her grace?
PRINCESS: Thy news Boyet?
BOYET: Prepare, madam, prepare!
Arm, wenches, arm! encounters mounted are
Against your peace. Love doth approach disguised,
Armed in arguments; you'll be surprised.
Muster your wits; stand in your own defence;
Or hide your heads like cowards, and fly hence.
PRINCESS: Saint Denis to Saint Cupid! What are they
That charge their breath against us? say, scout, say.
BOYET: Under the cool shade of a sycamore
I thought to close mine eyes some half an hour;
When, lo! to interrupt my purposed rest,
Toward that shade I might behold addrest
The king and his companions; warily
I stole into a neighbour thicket by,
And overheard what you shall overhear,
That, by and by, disguised they will be here.
Their herald is a pretty knavish page,
That well by heart hath conn'd his embassage.
Action and accent did they teach him there:
'Thus must thou speak,' and 'thus thy body bear,'
And ever and anon they made a doubt
Presence majestical would put him out,
'For,' quoth the king, 'an angel shalt thou see;
Yet fear not thou, but speak audaciously.'
The boy replied, 'An angel is not evil;
I should have fear'd her had she been a devil.'
With that, all laugh'd and clapp'd him on the shoulder,
Making the bold wag by their praises bolder:
One rubb'd his elbow thus, and fleer'd and swore
A better speech was never spoke before;
Another, with his finger and his thumb,
Cried, 'Via! we will do't, come what will come;'
The third he caper'd, and cried, 'All goes well.'
The fourth turn'd on the toe, and down he fell.
With that, they all did tumble on the ground,
With such a zealous laughter, so profound,
That in this spleen ridiculous appears,
To cheque their folly, passion's solemn tears.
PRINCESS: But what, but what, come they to visit us?
BOYET: They do, they do; and are apparell'd thus.
Like Muscovites or Russians, as I guess.
Their purpose is to parle, to court and dance;
And every one his love-feat will advance
Unto his several mistress, which they'll know
By favours several which they did bestow.
PRINCESS: And will they so? the gallants shall be task'd;
For, ladies, we shall every one be mask'd;
And not a man of them shall have the grace,
Despite of suit, to see a lady's face.
Hold, Rosaline, this favour thou shalt wear,
And then the king will court thee for his dear;
Hold, take thou this, my sweet, and give me thine,
So shall BEROWNE take me for Rosaline.
And change your favours too; so shall your loves
Woo contrary, deceived by these removes.
ROSALINE: Come on, then; wear the favours most in sight.
KATHARINE: But in this changing what is your intent?
PRINCESS: The effect of my intent is to cross theirs.
They do it but in mocking merriment;
And mock for mock is only my intent.
Their several counsels they unbosom shall
To loves mistook, and so be mock'd withal
Upon the next occasion that we meet,
With visages displayed, to talk and greet.
ROSALINE: But shall we dance, if they desire to't?
PRINCESS: No, to the death, we will not move a foot;
Nor to their penn'd speech render we no grace,
But while 'tis spoke each turn away her face.
BOYET: Why, that contempt will kill the speaker's heart,
And quite divorce his memory from his part.
PRINCESS: Therefore I do it; and I make no doubt
The rest will ne'er come in, if he be out.

There's no such sport as sport by sport o'erthrown,
To make theirs ours and ours none but our own;
So shall we stay, mocking intended game,
And they, well mock'd, depart away with shame.

Trumpets sound within

BOYET: The trumpet sounds: be mask'd; the maskers come.

The Ladies mask

Enter Blackamoors with music; MOTH; FERDINAND, BEROWNE, LONGAVILLE, and DUMAIN, in Russian habits, and masked

MOTH: All hail, the richest beauties on the earth!

BOYET: Beauties no richer than rich taffeta.

MOTH: A holy parcel of the fairest dames.

The Ladies turn their backs to him

That ever turn'd their—backs—to mortal views!

BEROWNE: [*Aside to Moth*] Their eyes, villain, their eyes!

MOTH: That ever turn'd their eyes to mortal views!—Out—

BOYET: True; out indeed.

MOTH: Out of your favours, heavenly spirits, vouchsafe
Not to behold—

BEROWNE: [*Aside to Moth*] Once to behold, rogue.

MOTH: Once to behold with your sun-beamed eyes —with your sun-beamed eyes—

BOYET: They will not answer to that epithet;
You were best call it 'daughter-beamed eyes.'

MOTH: They do not mark me, and that brings me out.

BEROWNE: Is this your perfectness? be gone, you rogue!

Exit MOTH

ROSALINE: What would these strangers? know their minds, Boyet.
If they do speak our language, 'tis our will
That some plain man recount their purposes
Know what they would.

BOYET: What would you with the princess?

BEROWNE: Nothing but peace and gentle visitation.

ROSALINE: What would they, say they?

BOYET: Nothing but peace and gentle visitation.

ROSALINE: Why, that they have; and bid them so be gone.

BOYET: She says, you have it, and you may be gone.

FERDINAND: Say to her, we have measured many miles
To tread a measure with her on this grass.

BOYET: They say, that they have measured many a mile
To tread a measure with you on this grass.

ROSALINE: It is not so. Ask them how many inches
Is in one mile? If they have measured many,
The measure then of one is easily told.

BOYET: If to come hither you have measured miles,
And many miles, the princess bids you tell
How many inches doth fill up one mile.

BEROWNE: Tell her, we measure them by weary steps.

BOYET: She hears herself.

ROSALINE: How many weary steps,
Of many weary miles you have o'ergone,
Are number'd in the travel of one mile?

BEROWNE: We number nothing that we spend for you;
Our duty is so rich, so infinite,
That we may do it still without accompt.
Vouchsafe to show the sunshine of your face,
That we, like savages, may worship it.

ROSALINE: My face is but a moon, and clouded too.

FERDINAND: Blessed are clouds, to do as such clouds do!
Vouchsafe, bright moon, and these thy stars, to shine,
Those clouds removed, upon our watery eyne.

ROSALINE: O vain petitioner! beg a greater matter;
Thou now request'st but moonshine in the water.

FERDINAND: Then, in our measure do but vouchsafe one change.
Thou bid'st me beg: this begging is not strange.

ROSALINE: Play, music, then! Nay, you must do it soon.
Not yet! no dance! Thus change I like the moon.

FERDINAND: Will you not dance? How come you thus estranged?

ROSALINE: You took the moon at full, but now she's changed.

FERDINAND: Yet still she is the moon, and I the man.

The music plays; vouchsafe some motion to it.

ROSALINE: Our ears vouchsafe it.

FERDINAND: But your legs should do it.

ROSALINE: Since you are strangers and come here by chance,

We'll not be nice; take hands. We will not dance.

FERDINAND: Why take we hands, then?

ROSALINE: Only to part friends.

Curtsy, sweet hearts; and so the measure ends.

FERDINAND: More measure of this measure; be not nice.

ROSALINE: We can afford no more at such a price.

FERDINAND: Prize you yourselves: what buys your company?

ROSALINE: Your absence only.

FERDINAND: That can never be.

ROSALINE: Then cannot we be bought; and so, adieu;

Twice to your visor, and half once to you.

FERDINAND: If you deny to dance, let's hold more chat.

ROSALINE: In private, then.

FERDINAND: I am best pleased with that.

They converse apart

BEROWNE: White-handed mistress, one sweet word with thee.

PRINCESS: Honey, and milk, and sugar; there is three.

BEROWNE: Nay then, two treys, and if you grow so nice,

Metheglin, wort, and malmsey; well run, dice!

There's half-a-dozen sweets.

PRINCESS: Seventh sweet, adieu!

Since you can cog, I'll play no more with you.

BEROWNE: One word in secret.

PRINCESS: Let it not be sweet.

BEROWNE: Thou grievest my gall.

PRINCESS: Gall! bitter.

BEROWNE: Therefore meet.

They converse apart

DUMAIN: Will you vouchsafe with me to change a word?

MARIA: Name it.

DUMAIN: Fair lady—

MARIA: Say you so? Fair lord—

Take that for your fair lady.

DUMAIN: Please it you,

As much in private, and I'll bid adieu.

They converse apart

KATHARINE: What, was your vizard made without a tongue?

LONGAVILLE: I know the reason, lady, why you ask.

KATHARINE: O for your reason! quickly, sir; I long.

LONGAVILLE: You have a double tongue within your mask,

And would afford my speechless vizard half.

KATHARINE: Veal, quoth the Dutchman. Is not 'veal' a calf?

LONGAVILLE: A calf, fair lady!

KATHARINE: No, a fair lord calf.

LONGAVILLE: Let's part the word.

KATHARINE: No, I'll not be your half

Take all, and wean it; it may prove an ox.

LONGAVILLE: Look, how you butt yourself in these sharp mocks!

Will you give horns, chaste lady? do not so.

KATHARINE: Then die a calf, before your horns do grow.

LONGAVILLE: One word in private with you, ere I die.

KATHARINE: Bleat softly then; the butcher hears you cry.

They converse apart

BOYET: The tongues of mocking wenches are as keen

As is the razor's edge invisible,

Cutting a smaller hair than may be seen,

Above the sense of sense; so sensible

Seemeth their conference; their conceits have wings

Fleeter than arrows, bullets, wind, thought, swifter things.

ROSALINE: Not one word more, my maids; break off, break off.

BEROWNE: By heaven, all dry-beaten with pure scoff!

FERDINAND: Farewell, mad wenches; you have simple wits.

PRINCESS: Twenty adieus, my frozen Muscovits.

Exeunt FERDINAND, Lords, and Blackamoors

Are these the breed of wits so wonder'd at?

BOYET: Tapers they are, with your sweet breaths puff'd out.

ROSALINE: Well-liking wits they have; gross, gross; fat, fat.

PRINCESS: O poverty in wit, kingly-poor flout!
Will they not, think you, hang themselves tonight?
Or ever, but in vizards, show their faces?
This pert BEROWNE was out of countenance quite.

ROSALINE: O, they were all in lamentable cases!
The king was weeping-ripe for a good word.

PRINCESS: BEROWNE did swear himself out of all suit.

MARIA: Dumain was at my service, and his sword.
No point, quoth I; my servant straight was mute.

KATHARINE: Lord Longaville said, I came o'er his heart;
And trow you what he called me?

PRINCESS: Qualm, perhaps.

KATHARINE: Yes, in good faith.

PRINCESS: Go, sickness as thou art!

ROSALINE: Well, better wits have worn plain statute-caps.
But will you hear? The king is my love sworn.

PRINCESS: And quick BEROWNE hath plighted faith to me.

KATHARINE: And Longaville was for my service born.

MARIA: Dumain is mine, as sure as bark on tree.

BOYET: Madam, and pretty mistresses, give ear:
Immediately they will again be here
In their own shapes; for it can never be
They will digest this harsh indignity.

PRINCESS: Will they return?

BOYET: They will, they will, God knows,
And leap for joy, though they are lame with blows;
Therefore change favours; and, when they repair,
Blow like sweet roses in this summer air.

PRINCESS: How blow? how blow? speak to be understood.

BOYET: Fair ladies mask'd are roses in their bud;
Dismask'd, their damask sweet commixture shown,
Are angels vailing clouds, or roses blown.

PRINCESS: Avaunt, perplexity! What shall we do,
If they return in their own shapes to woo?

ROSALINE: Good madam, if by me you'll be advised,
Let's, mock them still, as well known as disguised.
Let us complain to them what fools were here,
Disguised like Muscovites, in shapeless gear;
And wonder what they were and to what end
Their shallow shows and prologue vilely penn'd
And their rough carriage so ridiculous,
Should be presented at our tent to us.

BOYET: Ladies, withdraw; the gallants are at hand.

PRINCESS: Whip to our tents, as roes run o'er land.

Exeunt PRINCESS, ROSALINE, KATHARINE, and MARIA

Re-enter FERDINAND, BEROWNE, LONGAVILLE, and DUMAIN, in their proper habits

FERDINAND: Fair sir, God save you! Where's the princess?

BOYET: Gone to her tent. Please it your majesty
Command me any service to her thither?

FERDINAND: That she vouchsafe me audience for one word.

BOYET: I will; and so will she, I know, my lord.

Exit

BEROWNE: This fellow pecks up wit as pigeons pease,
And utters it again when God doth please.
He is wit's pedler, and retails his wares
At wakes and wassails, meetings, markets, fairs;
And we that sell by gross, the Lord doth know,
Have not the grace to grace it with such show.
This gallant pins the wenches on his sleeve;
Had he been Adam, he had tempted Eve.
A' can carve too, and lisp: why, this is he
That kiss'd his hand away in courtesy;
This is the ape of form, monsieur the nice,
That, when he plays at tables, chides the dice
In honourable terms; nay, he can sing
A mean most meanly; and in ushering
Mend him who can. The ladies call him sweet;
The stairs, as he treads on them, kiss his feet.
This is the flower that smiles on every one,
To show his teeth as white as whale's bone;
And consciences, that will not die in debt,
Pay him the due of honey-tongued Boyet.

FERDINAND: A blister on his sweet tongue, with my heart,
That put Armado's page out of his part!

BEROWNE: See where it comes! Behavior, what wert thou
Till this madman show'd thee? and what art thou now?

Re-enter the PRINCESS, ushered by BOYET, ROSALINE, MARIA, and KATHARINE

FERDINAND: All hail, sweet madam, and fair time of day!
PRINCESS: 'Fair' in 'all hail' is foul, as I conceive.
FERDINAND: Construe my speeches better, if you may.
PRINCESS: Then wish me better; I will give you leave.
FERDINAND: We came to visit you, and purpose now
To lead you to our court; vouchsafe it then.
PRINCESS: This field shall hold me; and so hold your vow:
Nor God, nor I, delights in perjured men.
FERDINAND: Rebuke me not for that which you provoke.
The virtue of your eye must break my oath.
PRINCESS: You nickname virtue: vice you should have spoke:
For virtue's office never breaks men's troth.
Now by my maiden honour, yet as pure
As the unsullied lily, I protest,
A world of torments though I should endure,
I would not yield to be your house's guest;
So much I hate a breaking cause to be
Of heavenly oaths, vow'd with integrity.
FERDINAND: O, you have lived in desolation here,
Unseen, unvisited, much to our shame.
PRINCESS: Not so, my lord; it is not so, I swear;
We have had pastimes here and pleasant game;
A mess of Russians left us but of late.
FERDINAND: How, madam! Russians!
PRINCESS: Ay, in truth, my lord;
Trim gallants, full of courtship and of state.
ROSALINE: Madam, speak true. It is not so, my lord.
My lady, to the manner of the days,
In courtesy gives undeserving praise.
We four indeed confronted were with four
In Russian habit; here they stay'd an hour,
And talk'd apace; and in that hour, my lord,
They did not bless us with one happy word.
I dare not call them fools; but this I think,
When they are thirsty, fools would fain have drink.
BEROWNE: This jest is dry to me. Fair gentle sweet,
Your wit makes wise things foolish; when we greet,
With eyes best seeing, heaven's fiery eye,
By light we lose light; your capacity
Is of that nature that to your huge store
Wise things seem foolish and rich things but poor.
ROSALINE: This proves you wise and rich, for in my eye—
BEROWNE: I am a fool, and full of poverty.
ROSALINE: But that you take what doth to you belong,
It were a fault to snatch words from my tongue.
BEROWNE: O, I am yours, and all that I possess!
ROSALINE: All the fool mine?
BEROWNE: I cannot give you less.
ROSALINE: Which of the vizards was it that you wore?
BEROWNE: Where? when? what vizard? Why demand you this?
ROSALINE: There, then, that vizard; that superfluous case
That hid the worse and show'd the better face.
FERDINAND: We are descried; they'll mock us now downright.
DUMAIN: Let us confess and turn it to a jest.
PRINCESS: Amazed, my lord? Why looks your highness sad?
ROSALINE: Help, hold his brows! he'll swoon! Why look you pale?
Sea-sick, I think, coming from Muscovy.
BEROWNE: Thus pour the stars down plagues for perjury.
Can any face of brass hold longer out?
Here stand I, lady, dart thy skill at me;
Bruise me with scorn, confound me with a flout;
Thrust thy sharp wit quite through my ignorance;
Cut me to pieces with thy keen conceit;
And I will wish thee never more to dance,
Nor never more in Russian habit wait.
O, never will I trust to speeches penn'd,
Nor to the motion of a schoolboy's tongue,
Nor never come in vizard to my friend,
Nor woo in rhyme, like a blind harper's song!
Taffeta phrases, silken terms precise,
Three-piled hyperboles, spruce affectation,

Figures pedantical; these summer-flies
Have blown me full of maggot ostentation.
I do forswear them; and I here protest,
By this white glove—how white the hand, God knows!—
Henceforth my wooing mind shall be express'd
In russet yeas and honest kersey noes.
And, to begin, wench,—so God help me, law!—
My love to thee is sound, sans crack or flaw.
ROSALINE: Sans sans, I pray you.
BEROWNE: Yet I have a trick
Of the old rage; bear with me, I am sick;
I'll leave it by degrees. Soft, let us see—
Write, 'Lord have mercy on us' on those three;
They are infected; in their hearts it lies;
They have the plague, and caught it of your eyes;
These lords are visited; you are not free,
For the Lord's tokens on you do I see.
PRINCESS: No, they are free that gave these tokens to us.
BEROWNE: Our states are forfeit: seek not to undo us.
ROSALINE: It is not so; for how can this be true,
That you stand forfeit, being those that sue?
BEROWNE: Peace! for I will not have to do with you.
ROSALINE: Nor shall not, if I do as I intend.
BEROWNE: Speak for yourselves; my wit is at an end.
FERDINAND: Teach us, sweet madam, for our rude transgression
Some fair excuse.
PRINCESS: The fairest is confession.
Were not you here but even now disguised?
FERDINAND: Madam, I was.
PRINCESS: And were you well advised?
FERDINAND: I was, fair madam.
PRINCESS: When you then were here,
What did you whisper in your lady's ear?
FERDINAND: That more than all the world I did respect her.
PRINCESS: When she shall challenge this, you will reject her.
FERDINAND: Upon mine honour, no.
PRINCESS: Peace, peace! Forbear;
Your oath once broke, you force not to forswear.
FERDINAND: Despise me, when I break this oath of mine.
PRINCESS: I will; and therefore keep it. Rosaline,
What did the Russian whisper in your ear?
ROSALINE: Madam, he swore that he did hold me dear
As precious eyesight, and did value me
Above this world; adding thereto moreover
That he would wed me, or else die my lover.
PRINCESS: God give thee joy of him! the noble lord
Most honourably doth unhold his word.
FERDINAND: What mean you, madam? by my life, my troth,
I never swore this lady such an oath.
ROSALINE: By heaven, you did; and to confirm it plain,
You gave me this; but take it, sir, again.
FERDINAND: My faith and this the princess I did give;
I knew her by this jewel on her sleeve.
PRINCESS: Pardon me, sir, this jewel did she wear;
And Lord Berowne, I thank him, is my dear.
What, will you have me, or your pearl again?
BEROWNE: Neither of either; I remit both twain.
I see the trick on't: here was a consent,
Knowing aforehand of our merriment,
To dash it like a Christmas comedy.
Some carry-tale, some please-man, some slight zany,
Some mumble-news, some trencher-knight, some Dick,
That smiles his cheek in years and knows the trick
To make my lady laugh when she's disposed,
Told our intents before; which once disclosed,
The ladies did change favours; and then we,
Following the signs, woo'd but the sign of she.
Now, to our perjury to add more terror,
We are again forsworn, in will and error.
Much upon this it is; [*To Boyet*] and might not you
Forestall our sport, to make us thus untrue?
Do not you know my lady's foot by the squier,
And laugh upon the apple of her eye?
And stand between her back, sir, and the fire,
Holding a trencher, jesting merrily?
You put our page out. Go, you are allow'd;
Die when you will, a smock shall be your shroud.
You leer upon me, do you? there's an eye

Wounds like a leaden sword.

BOYET: Full merrily

Hath this brave manage, this career, been run.

BEROWNE: Lo, he is tilting straight! Peace! I have done.

Enter COSTARD

Welcome, pure wit! thou partest a fair fray.

COSTARD: O Lord, sir, they would know

Whether the three Worthies shall come in or no.

BEROWNE: What, are there but three?

COSTARD: No, sir; but it is vara fine,

For every one pursents three.

BEROWNE: And three times thrice is nine.

COSTARD: Not so, sir; under correction, sir; I hope it is not so.

You cannot beg us, sir, I can assure you, sir we know what we know:

I hope, sir, three times thrice, sir—

BEROWNE: Is not nine.

COSTARD: Under correction, sir, we know whereuntil it doth amount.

BEROWNE: By Jove, I always took three threes for nine.

COSTARD: O Lord, sir, it were pity you should get your living by reckoning, sir.

BEROWNE: How much is it?

COSTARD: O Lord, sir, the parties themselves, the actors, sir, will show whereuntil it doth amount. For mine own part, I am, as they say, but to parfect one man in one poor man, Pompion the Great, sir.

BEROWNE: Art thou one of the Worthies?

COSTARD: It pleased them to think me worthy of Pompion the Great; for mine own part, I know not the degree of the Worthy, but I am to stand for him.

BEROWNE: Go, bid them prepare.

COSTARD: We will turn it finely off, sir; we will take some care.

Exit

FERDINAND: Berowne, they will shame us; let them not approach.

BEROWNE: We are shame-proof, my lord, and 'tis some policy

To have one show worse than the king's and his company.

FERDINAND: I say they shall not come.

PRINCESS: Nay, my good lord, let me o'errule you now.

That sport best pleases that doth least know how;

Where zeal strives to content, and the contents

Dies in the zeal of that which it presents.

Their form confounded makes most form in mirth,

When great things labouring perish in their birth.

BEROWNE: A right description of our sport, my lord.

Enter DON ADRIANO DE ARMADO

DON ADRIANO DE ARMADO: Anointed, I implore so much expense of thy royal sweet breath as will utter a brace of words.

Converses apart with FERDINAND, and delivers him a paper

PRINCESS: Doth this man serve God?

BEROWNE: Why ask you?

PRINCESS: He speaks not like a man of God's making.

DON ADRIANO DE ARMADO: That is all one, my fair, sweet, honey monarch; for, I protest, the schoolmaster is exceeding fantastical; too, too vain, too too vain; but we will put it, as they say, to fortuna de la guerra. I wish you the peace of mind, most royal couplement!

Exit

FERDINAND: Here is like to be a good presence of Worthies.

He presents Hector of Troy; the swain, Pompey the Great; the parish curate, Alexander; Armado's page, Hercules; the pedant, Judas Maccabaeus.

And if these four Worthies in their first show thrive,

These four will change habits, and present the other five.

BEROWNE: There is five in the first show.

FERDINAND: You are deceived; 'tis not so.

BEROWNE: The pedant, the braggart, the hedge-priest, the fool and the boy;

Abate throw at novum, and the whole world again

Cannot pick out five such, take each one in his vein.

FERDINAND: The ship is under sail, and here she comes amain.

Enter COSTARD, for Pompey

COSTARD: I Pompey am—

BOYET: You lie, you are not he.

COSTARD: I Pompey am—

BOYET: With libbard's head on knee.

BEROWNE: Well said, old mocker; I must needs be friends with thee.

COSTARD: I Pompey am, Pompey surnamed the Big—

DUMAIN: The Great.

COSTARD: It is, 'Great,' sir:—

Pompey surnamed the Great;

That oft in field, with targe and shield, did make my foe to sweat;

And travelling along this coast, I here am come by chance,

And lay my arms before the legs of this sweet lass of France,

If your ladyship would say, 'Thanks, Pompey,' I had done.

PRINCESS: Great thanks, great Pompey.

COSTARD: 'Tis not so much worth; but I hope I was perfect: I made a little fault in 'Great.'

BEROWNE: My hat to a halfpenny, Pompey proves the best Worthy.

Enter SIR NATHANIEL, for Alexander

SIR NATHANIEL: When in the world I lived, I was the world's commander;

By east, west, north, and south, I spread my conquering might.

My scutcheon plain declares that I am Alisander,—

BOYET: Your nose says, no, you are not for it stands too right.

BEROWNE: Your nose smells 'no' in this, most tender-smelling knight.

PRINCESS: The conqueror is dismay'd. Proceed, good Alexander.

SIR NATHANIEL: When in the world I lived, I was the world's commander—

BOYET: Most true, 'tis right; you were so, Alisander.

BEROWNE: Pompey the Great—

COSTARD: Your servant, and Costard.

BEROWNE: Take away the conqueror, take away Alisander.

COSTARD: [*To Sir Nathaniel*] O, sir, you have overthrown Alisander the conqueror! You will be scraped out of the painted cloth for this. Your lion, that holds his poll-axe sitting on a close-stool, will be given to Ajax. He will be the ninth Worthy. A conqueror, and afeard to speak! run away for shame, Alisander. (*Sir Nathaniel retires*)

There, an't shall please you; a foolish mild man; an honest man, look you, and soon dashed. He is a marvellous good neighbour, faith, and a very good bowler; but, for Alisander,—alas, you see how 'tis,—a little o'erparted. But there are Worthies a-coming will speak their mind in some other sort.

Enter HOLOFERNES, for Judas; and MOTH, for Hercules

HOLOFERNES: Great Hercules is presented by this imp,

Whose club kill'd Cerberus, that three-headed canis;

And when he was a babe, a child, a shrimp,
Thus did he strangle serpents in his manus.
Quoniam he seemeth in minority,
Ergo I come with this apology.
Keep some state in thy exit, and vanish.

MOTH retires

Judas I am,—

DUMAIN: A Judas!

HOLOFERNES: Not Iscariot, sir.

Judas I am, ycliped Maccabaeus.

DUMAIN: Judas Maccabaeus clipt is plain Judas.

BEROWNE: A kissing traitor. How art thou proved Judas?

HOLOFERNES: Judas I am—

DUMAIN: The more shame for you, Judas.

HOLOFERNES: What mean you, sir?

BOYET: To make Judas hang himself.

HOLOFERNES: Begin, sir; you are my elder.

BEROWNE: Well followed: Judas was hanged on an elder.

HOLOFERNES: I will not be put out of countenance.

BEROWNE: Because thou hast no face.

HOLOFERNES: What is this?

BOYET: A cittern-head.

DUMAIN: The head of a bodkin.

BEROWNE: A Death's face in a ring.

LONGAVILLE: The face of an old Roman coin, scarce seen.

BOYET: The pommel of Caesar's falchion.

DUMAIN: The carved-bone face on a flask.

BEROWNE: Saint George's half-cheek in a brooch.

DUMAIN: Ay, and in a brooch of lead.

BEROWNE: Ay, and worn in the cap of a tooth-drawer.

And now forward; for we have put thee in countenance.

HOLOFERNES: You have put me out of countenance.

BEROWNE: False; we have given thee faces.

HOLOFERNES: But you have out-faced them all.

BEROWNE: An thou wert a lion, we would do so.

BOYET: Therefore, as he is an ass, let him go.

And so adieu, sweet Jude! nay, why dost thou stay?

DUMAIN: For the latter end of his name.

BEROWNE: For the ass to the Jude; give it him—Judas, away!

HOLOFERNES: This is not generous, not gentle, not humble.

BOYET: A light for Monsieur Judas! it grows dark, he may stumble.

HOLOFERNES retires

PRINCESS: Alas, poor Maccabaeus, how hath he been baited!

Enter DON ADRIANO DE ARMADO, for Hector

BEROWNE: Hide thy head, Achilles; here comes Hector in arms.

DUMAIN: Though my mocks come home by me, I will now be merry.

FERDINAND: Hector was but a Troyan in respect of this.

BOYET: But is this Hector?

FERDINAND: I think Hector was not so clean-timbered.

LONGAVILLE: His leg is too big for Hector's.

DUMAIN: More calf, certain.

BOYET: No; he is best endued in the small.

BEROWNE: This cannot be Hector.

DUMAIN: He's a god or a painter; for he makes faces.

DON ADRIANO DE ARMADO: The armipotent Mars, of lances the almighty, Gave Hector a gift—

DUMAIN: A gilt nutmeg.

BEROWNE: A lemon.

LONGAVILLE: Stuck with cloves.

DUMAIN: No, cloven.

DON ADRIANO DE ARMADO: Peace!

The armipotent Mars, of lances the almighty
Gave Hector a gift, the heir of Ilion;
A man so breathed, that certain he would fight; ye,
From morn till night, out of his pavilion.
I am that flower—

DUMAIN: That mint.

LONGAVILLE: That columbine.

DON ADRIANO DE ARMADO: Sweet Lord Longaville, rein thy tongue.

LONGAVILLE: I must rather give it the rein, for it runs against Hector.

DUMAIN: Ay, and Hector's a greyhound.

DON ADRIANO DE ARMADO: The sweet war-man is dead and rotten; sweet chucks, beat not the bones of the buried; when he breathed, he was a man. But I will forward with my device. (*To the Princess*) Sweet royalty, bestow on me the sense of hearing.

PRINCESS: Speak, brave Hector: we are much delighted.

DON ADRIANO DE ARMADO: I do adore thy sweet grace's slipper.

BOYET: [*Aside to Dumain*] Loves her by the foot—

DUMAIN: [*Aside to Boyet*] He may not by the yard.

DON ADRIANO DE ARMADO: This Hector far surmounted Hannibal—

COSTARD: The party is gone, fellow Hector, she is gone; she is two months on her way.

DON ADRIANO DE ARMADO: What meanest thou?

COSTARD: Faith, unless you play the honest Troyan, the poor wench is cast away. She's quick; the child brags in her belly already; 'tis yours.

DON ADRIANO DE ARMADO: Dost thou infamonize me among potentates? thou shalt die.

COSTARD: Then shall Hector be whipped for Jaquenetta that is quick by him and hanged for Pompey that is dead by him.

DUMAIN: Most rare Pompey!

BOYET: Renowned Pompey!

BEROWNE: Greater than great, great, great, great Pompey!

Pompey the Huge!

DUMAIN: Hector trembles.

BEROWNE: Pompey is moved. More Ates, more Ates! stir them on! stir them on!

DUMAIN: Hector will challenge him.

BEROWNE: Ay, if a' have no man's blood in's belly than will sup a flea.

DON ADRIANO DE ARMADO: By the north pole, I do challenge thee.

COSTARD: I will not fight with a pole, like a northern man; I'll slash; I'll do it by the sword. I bepray you, let me borrow my arms again.
DUMAIN: Room for the incensed Worthies!
COSTARD: I'll do it in my shirt.
DUMAIN: Most resolute Pompey!
MOTH: Master, let me take you a buttonhole lower.
Do you not see Pompey is uncasing for the combat?
What mean you? You will lose your reputation.
DON ADRIANO DE ARMADO: Gentlemen and soldiers, pardon me; I will not combat in my shirt.
DUMAIN: You may not deny it: Pompey hath made the challenge.
DON ADRIANO DE ARMADO: Sweet bloods, I both may and will.
BEROWNE: What reason have you for't?
DON ADRIANO DE ARMADO: The naked truth of it is, I have no shirt; I go woolward for penance.
BOYET: True, and it was enjoined him in Rome for want of linen; since when, I'll be sworn, he wore none but a dishclout of Jaquenetta's, and that a' wears next his heart for a favour.

Enter MERCADE

MERCADE: God save you, madam!
PRINCESS: Welcome, Mercade;
But that thou interrupt'st our merriment.
MERCADE: I am sorry, madam; for the news I bring
Is heavy in my tongue. The king your father—
PRINCESS: Dead, for my life!
MERCADE: Even so; my tale is told.
BEROWNE: Worthies, away! the scene begins to cloud.
DON ADRIANO DE ARMADO: For mine own part, I breathe free breath. I have seen the day of wrong through the little hole of discretion, and I will right myself like a soldier.

Exeunt Worthies

FERDINAND: How fares your majesty?
PRINCESS: Boyet, prepare; I will away tonight.
FERDINAND: Madam, not so; I do beseech you, stay.
PRINCESS: Prepare, I say. I thank you, gracious lords,
For all your fair endeavors; and entreat,
Out of a new-sad soul, that you vouchsafe
In your rich wisdom to excuse or hide
The liberal opposition of our spirits,
If over-boldly we have borne ourselves
In the converse of breath: your gentleness
Was guilty of it. Farewell worthy lord!
A heavy heart bears not a nimble tongue.
Excuse me so, coming too short of thanks
For my great suit so easily obtain'd.
FERDINAND: The extreme parts of time extremely forms
All causes to the purpose of his speed,
And often at his very loose decides
That which long process could not arbitrate.
And though the mourning brow of progeny
Forbid the smiling courtesy of love
The holy suit which fain it would convince,
Yet, since love's argument was first on foot,
Let not the cloud of sorrow justle it
From what it purposed; since, to wail friends lost
Is not by much so wholesome-profitable
As to rejoice at friends but newly found.
PRINCESS: I understand you not; my griefs are double.
BEROWNE: Honest plain words best pierce the ear of grief;
And by these badges understand the king.
For your fair sakes have we neglected time,
Play'd foul play with our oaths; your beauty, ladies,
Hath much deform'd us, fashioning our humours
Even to the opposed end of our intents;
And what in us hath seem'd ridiculous,
As love is full of unbefitting strains,
All wanton as a child, skipping and vain,
Form'd by the eye and therefore, like the eye,
Full of strange shapes, of habits and of forms,
Varying in subjects as the eye doth roll
To every varied object in his glance;
Which parti-coated presence of loose love
Put on by us, if, in your heavenly eyes,
Have misbecomed our oaths and gravities,
Those heavenly eyes, that look into these faults,
Suggested us to make. Therefore, ladies,
Our love being yours, the error that love makes
Is likewise yours. We to ourselves prove false,
By being once false for ever to be true
To those that make us both—fair ladies, you;
And even that falsehood, in itself a sin,
Thus purifies itself and turns to grace.

PRINCESS: We have received your letters full of love;
Your favours, the ambassadors of love;
And, in our maiden council, rated them
At courtship, pleasant jest and courtesy,
As bombast and as lining to the time;
But more devout than this in our respects
Have we not been; and therefore met your loves
In their own fashion, like a merriment.
DUMAIN: Our letters, madam, show'd much more than jest.
LONGAVILLE: So did our looks.
ROSALINE: We did not quote them so.
FERDINAND: Now, at the latest minute of the hour,
Grant us your loves.
PRINCESS: A time, methinks, too short
To make a world-without-end bargain in.
No, no, my lord, your grace is perjured much,
Full of dear guiltiness; and therefore this,
If for my love, as there is no such cause,
You will do aught, this shall you do for me:
Your oath I will not trust; but go with speed
To some forlorn and naked hermitage,
Remote from all the pleasures of the world;
There stay until the twelve celestial signs
Have brought about the annual reckoning.
If this austere insociable life
Change not your offer made in heat of blood;
If frosts and fasts, hard lodging and thin weeds
Nip not the gaudy blossoms of your love,
But that it bear this trial and last love;
Then, at the expiration of the year,
Come challenge me, challenge me by these deserts;
And, by this virgin palm now kissing thine
I will be thine; and till that instant shut
My woeful self up in a mourning house,
Raining the tears of lamentation
For the remembrance of my father's death.
If this thou do deny, let our hands part,
Neither entitled in the other's heart.
FERDINAND: If this, or more than this, I would deny,
To flatter up these powers of mine with rest,
The sudden hand of death close up mine eye!
Hence ever then my heart is in thy breast.
BEROWNE: *And what to me, my love? and what to me?*
ROSALINE: *You must be purged too, your sins are racked;*
You are attaint with faults and perjury;
Therefore, if you my favour mean to get,
A twelvemonth shall you spand, and never rest
But seek the weary beds of people sick.
DUMAIN: But what to me, my love? but what to me? A wife?
KATHARINE: A beard, fair health, and honesty;
With threefold love I wish you all these three.
DUMAIN: O, shall I say, I thank you, gentle wife?
KATHARINE: Not so, my lord; a twelvemonth and a day
I'll mark no words that smooth-faced wooers say.
Come when the King doth to my lady come;
Then, if I have much love, I'll give you some.
DUMAIN: I'll serve thee true and faithfully till then.
KATHARINE: Yet swear not, lest ye be forsworn again.
LONGAVILLE: What says Maria?
MARIA: At the twelvemonth's end
I'll change my black gown for a faithful friend.
LONGAVILLE: I'll stay with patience; but the time is long.
MARIA: The liker you; few taller are so young.
BEROWNE: Studies my lady? Mistress, look on me;
Behold the window of my heart, mine eye,
What humble suit attends thy answer there.
Impose some service on me for thy love.
ROSALINE: Oft have I heard of you, my Lord Berowne,
Before I saw you; and the world's large tongue
Proclaims you for a man replete with mocks,
Full of comparisons and wounding flouts,
Which you on all estates will execute
That lie within the mercy of your wit.
To weed this wormwood from your fruitful brain,
And therewithal to win me, if you please,
Without the which I am not to be won,
You shall this twelvemonth term from day to day
Visit the speechless sick and still converse
With groaning wretches; and your task shall be,
With all the fierce endeavor of your wit
To enforce the pained impotent to smile.
BEROWNE: To move wild laughter in the throat of death?

It cannot be; it is impossible:
Mirth cannot move a soul in agony.

ROSALINE: Why, that's the way to choke a gibing spirit,
Whose influence is begot of that loose grace
Which shallow laughing hearers give to fools.
A jest's prosperity lies in the ear
Of him that hears it, never in the tongue
Of him that makes it: then, if sickly ears,
Deaf'd with the clamours of their own dear groans,
Will hear your idle scorns, continue then,
And I will have you and that fault withal.
But if they will not, throw away that spirit,
And I shall find you empty of that fault,
Right joyful of your reformation.

BEROWNE: A twelvemonth! well; befall what will befall,
I'll jest a twelvemonth in an hospital.

PRINCESS: [*To Ferdinand*] Ay, sweet my lord; and so I take my leave.

FERDINAND: No, madam; we will bring you on your way.

BEROWNE: Our wooing doth not end like an old play;
Jack hath not Jill. These ladies' courtesy
Might well have made our sport a comedy.

FERDINAND: Come, sir, it wants a twelvemonth and a day,
And then 'twill end.

BEROWNE: That's too long for a play.

Re-enter DON ADRIANO DE ARMADO

DON ADRIANO DE ARMADO: Sweet majesty, vouchsafe me—

PRINCESS: Was not that Hector?

DUMAIN: The worthy knight of Troy.

DON ADRIANO DE ARMADO: I will kiss thy royal finger, and take leave. I am a votary; I have vowed to Jaquenetta to hold the plough for her sweet love three years. But, most esteemed greatness, will you hear the dialogue that the two learned men have compiled in praise of the owl and the cuckoo? It should have followed in the end of our show.

FERDINAND: Call them forth quickly; we will do so.

DON ADRIANO DE ARMADO: Holla! approach.

Re-enter HOLOFERNES, SIR NATHANIEL, MOTH, COSTARD, and others

This side is Hiems, Winter, this Ver, the Spring; the one maintained by the owl, the other by the cuckoo. Ver, begin.

Spring

When daisies pied and violets blue
And lady-smocks all silver-white
And cuckoo-buds of yellow hue
Do paint the meadows with delight,
The cuckoo then, on every tree,
Mocks married men; for thus sings he,
Cuckoo;
Cuckoo, cuckoo: O word of fear,
Unpleasing to a married ear!
When shepherds pipe on oaten straws
And merry larks are ploughmen's clocks,
When turtles tread, and rooks, and daws,
And maidens bleach their summer smocks
The cuckoo then, on every tree,
Mocks married men; for thus sings he, Cuckoo;
Cuckoo, cuckoo: O word of fear,
Unpleasing to a married ear!

Winter

When icicles hang by the wall
And Dick the shepherd blows his nail
And Tom bears logs into the hall
And milk comes frozen home in pail,
When blood is nipp'd and ways be foul,
Then nightly sings the staring owl, Tu-whit;
Tu-who, a merry note,
While greasy Joan doth keel the pot.
When all aloud the wind doth blow
And coughing drowns the parson's saw
And birds sit brooding in the snow
And Marian's nose looks red and raw,
When roasted crabs hiss in the bowl,
Then nightly sings the staring owl, Tu-whit;
Tu-who, a merry note,
While greasy Joan doth keel the pot.

DON ADRIANO DE ARMADO: The words of Mercury are harsh after the songs of Apollo. You that way: we this way.

Exeunt

MEASURE FOR MEASURE

DRAMATIS PERSONÆ

VINCENTIO, *the Duke*
ANGELO, *the Deputy*
ESCALUS, *an ancient Lord*
CLAUDIO, *a young gentleman*
LUCIO, *a fantastic*
Two other like gentlemen
VARRIUS, *a gentleman, servant to the Duke*
PROVOST
THOMAS,
PETER, *two friars*
A JUSTICE
ELBOW, *a simple constable*
FROTH, *a foolish gentleman*
POMPEY, *a clown and servant to Mistress Overdone*
ABHORSON, *an executioner*
BARNARDINE, *a dissolute prisoner*
ISABELLA, *sister to Claudio*
MARIANA, *betrothed to Angelo*
JULIET, *beloved of Claudio*
FRANCISCA, *a nun*
MISTRESS OVERDONE, *a bawd*
Lords, Officers, Citizens, Boy, and Attendants

THE SCENE: *Vienna*

ACT I

SCENE I—*The Duke's palace*

Enter DUKE VINCENTIO, ESCALUS, Lords and Attendants

DUKE VINCENTIO: Escalus!

ESCALUS: My lord.

DUKE VINCENTIO: Of government the properties to unfold
Would seem in me to affect speech and discourse,
Since I am put to know that your own science
Exceeds, in that, the lists of all advice
My strength can give you: then no more remains
But that to your sufficiency as your Worth is able,
And let them work. The nature of our people,
Our city's institutions, and the terms
For common justice, you're as pregnant in
As art and practice hath enriched any
That we remember. There is our commission,
From which we would not have you warp. Call hither,
I say, bid come before us Angelo.

Exit an Attendant

What figure of us think you he will bear?
For you must know, we have with special soul
Elected him our absence to supply,
Lent him our terror, dress'd him with our love,
And given his deputation all the organs
Of our own power. What think you of it?

ESCALUS: If any in Vienna be of worth
To undergo such ample grace and honour,
It is Lord Angelo.

Enter ANGELO

DUKE VINCENTIO: Look where he comes.

ANGELO: Always obedient to your grace's will,
I come to know your pleasure.

DUKE VINCENTIO: Angelo,
There is a kind of character in thy life,
That to the observer doth thy history
Fully unfold. Thyself and thy belongings
Are not thine own so proper as to waste
Thyself upon thy virtues, they on thee.
Heaven doth with us as we with torches do,
Not light them for themselves; for if our virtues
Did not go forth of us, 'twere all alike
As if we had them not. Spirits are not finely touch'd
But to fine issues; nor Nature never lends
The smallest scruple of her excellence
But, like a thrifty goddess, she determines
Herself the glory of a creditor,
Both thanks and use. But I do bend my speech
To one that can my part in him advertise.
Hold therefore, Angelo—
In our remove be thou at full ourself;
Mortality and mercy in Vienna
Live in thy tongue and heart. Old Escalus,
Though first in question, is thy secondary.
Take thy commission.

ANGELO: Now, good my lord,
Let there be some more test made of my metal,
Before so noble and so great a figure
Be stamp'd upon it.

DUKE VINCENTIO: No more evasion!
We have with a leaven'd and prepared choice
Proceeded to you; therefore take your honours.
Our haste from hence is of so quick condition
That it prefers itself and leaves unquestion'd
Matters of needful value. We shall write to you,
As time and our concernings shall importune,
How it goes with us, and do look to know
What doth befall you here. So, fare you well.
To the hopeful execution do I leave you
Of your commissions.

ANGELO: Yet give leave, my lord,
That we may bring you something on the way.

DUKE VINCENTIO: My haste may not admit it;
Nor need you, on mine honour, have to do
With any scruple; your scope is as mine own,
So to enforce or qualify the laws
As to your soul seems good. Give me your hand:
I'll privily away. I love the people,
But do not like to stage me to their eyes:
Through it do well, I do not relish well
Their loud applause and Aves vehement;
Nor do I think the man of safe discretion
That does affect it. Once more, fare you well.

ANGELO: The heavens give safety to your purposes!

ESCALUS: Lead forth and bring you back in happiness!

DUKE: I thank you. Fare you well.

Exit

ESCALUS: I shall desire you, sir, to give me leave
To have free speech with you; and it concerns me
To look into the bottom of my place:
A power I have, but of what strength and nature
I am not yet instructed.

ANGELO: 'Tis so with me. Let us withdraw together,
And we may soon our satisfaction have
Touching that point.

ESCALUS: I'll wait upon your honour.

Exeunt

SCENE II—*A street*

Enter LUCIO and two other Gentlemen

LUCIO: If the Duke with the other dukes come not to composition with the King of Hungary, why then all the dukes fall upon the king.

FIRST GENTLEMAN: Heaven grant us its peace, but not the King of Hungary's !

SECOND GENTLEMAN: Amen.

LUCIO: Thou concludest like the sanctimonious pirate, that went to sea with the Ten Commandments, but scraped one out of the table.

SECOND GENTLEMAN: 'Thou shalt not steal'?

LUCIO: Ay, that he razed.

FIRST GENTLEMAN: Why, 'twas a commandment to command the captain and all the rest from their functions: they put forth to steal. There's not a soldier of us all, that, in the thanksgiving before meat, do relish the petition well that prays for peace.

SECOND GENTLEMAN: I never heard any soldier dislike it.

LUCIO: I believe thee; for I think thou never wast where grace was said.

SECOND GENTLEMAN: No? A dozen times at least.

FIRST GENTLEMAN: What, in metre?

LUCIO: In any proportion or in any language.

FIRST GENTLEMAN: I think, or in any religion.

LUCIO: Ay, why not? Grace is grace, despite of all controversy; as, for example, thou thyself art a wicked villain, despite of all grace.

FIRST GENTLEMAN: Well, there went but a pair of shears between us.

LUCIO: I grant; as there may between the lists and the velvet. Thou art the list.

FIRST GENTLEMAN: And thou the velvet; thou art good velvet; thou 'rt a three-piled piece, I warrant thee. I had as lief be a list of an English kersey as be piled, as thou art piled, for a French velvet. Do I speak
feelingly now?

LUCIO: I think thou dost; and, indeed, with most painful feeling of thy speech. I will, out of thine own confession, learn to begin thy health; but, whilst I live, forget to drink after thee.

FIRST GENTLEMAN: I think I have done myself wrong, have I not?

SECOND GENTLEMAN: Yes, that thou hast, whether thou art tainted or free.

LUCIO: Behold, behold, where Madam Mitigation comes! I have purchased as many diseases under her roof as come to—

SECOND GENTLEMAN: To what, I pray?

FIRST GENTLEMAN: Judge.

SECOND GENTLEMAN: To three thousand dolours a year.

FIRST GENTLEMAN: Ay, and more.

LUCIO: A French crown more.

FIRST GENTLEMAN: Thou art always figuring diseases in me, but thou art full of error; I am sound.

LUCIO: Nay, not as one would say, healthy; but so sound as things that are hollow: thy bones are hollow; impiety has made a feast of thee.

Enter MISTRESS OVERDONE

FIRST GENTLEMAN: How now! which of your hips has the most profound sciatica?

MISTRESS OVERDONE: Well, well! there's one yonder arrested and carried to prison was worth five thousand of you all.

FIRST GENTLEMAN: Who's that, I pray thee?

MISTRESS OVERDONE: Marry, sir, that's Claudio, Signior Claudio.

FIRST GENTLEMAN: Claudio to prison? 'tis not so.

MISTRESS OVERDONE: Nay, but I know 'tis so: I saw him arrested; saw him carried away; and, which is more, within these three days his head to be chopped off.

LUCIO: But, after all this fooling, I would not have it so. Art thou sure of this?

MISTRESS OVERDONE: I am too sure of it: and it is for getting Madam Julietta with child.

LUCIO: Believe me, this may be; he promised to meet me two hours since, and he was ever precise in promise-keeping.

SECOND GENTLEMAN: Besides, you know, it draws something near to the speech we had to such a purpose.

FIRST GENTLEMAN: But, most of all, agreeing with the proclamation.

LUCIO: Away; let's go learn the truth of it.

Exeunt LUCIO and Gentlemen

MISTRESS OVERDONE: Thus, what with the war, what with the sweat, what with the gallows, and what with poverty, I am custom-shrunk.

Enter POMPEY

How now! what's the news with you?

POMPEY: Yonder man is carried to prison.

MISTRESS OVERDONE: Well; what has he done?

POMPEY: A woman.

MISTRESS OVERDONE: But what's his offence?

POMPEY: Groping for trouts in a peculiar river.

MISTRESS OVERDONE: What, is there a maid with child by him?

POMPEY: No, but there's a woman with maid by him. You have not heard of the proclamation, have you?

MISTRESS OVERDONE: What proclamation, man?

POMPEY: All houses in the suburbs of Vienna must be plucked down.

MISTRESS OVERDONE: And what shall become of those in the city?

POMPEY: They shall stand for seed: they had gone down too, but that a wise burgher put in for them.

MISTRESS OVERDONE: But shall all our houses of resort in the suburbs be pulled down?

POMPEY: To the ground, mistress.

MISTRESS OVERDONE: Why, here's a change indeed in the commonwealth! What shall become of me?

POMPEY: Come; fear you not: good counsellors lack no clients. Though you change your place, you need not change your trade; I'll be your tapster still. Courage! there will be pity taken on you; you that have worn your eyes almost out in the service, you will be considered.

MISTRESS OVERDONE: What's to do here, Thomas tapster? let's withdraw.

POMPEY: Here comes Signior Claudio, led by the provost to prison; and there's Madam Juliet.

Exeunt

Enter Provost, CLAUDIO, JULIET, and Officers

CLAUDIO: Fellow, why dost thou show me thus to the world?
Bear me to prison, where I am committed.

PROVOST: I do it not in evil disposition,
But from Lord Angelo by special charge.

CLAUDIO: Thus can the demigod Authority
Make us pay down for our offence by weight
The words of heaven; on whom it will, it will;
On whom it will not, so; yet still 'tis just.

Re-enter LUCIO and two Gentlemen

LUCIO: Why, how now, Claudio! whence comes this restraint?

CLAUDIO: From too much liberty, my Lucio, liberty;
As surfeit is the father of much fast,
So every scope by the immoderate use
Turns to restraint. Our natures do pursue,
Like rats that ravin down their proper bane,
A thirsty evil; and when we drink we die.

LUCIO: If could speak so wisely under an arrest, I would send for certain of my creditors; and yet, to say the truth, I had as lief have the foppery of freedom as the morality of imprisonment. What's thy offence, Claudio?

CLAUDIO: What but to speak of would offend again.

LUCIO: What, is't murder?

CLAUDIO: No.

LUCIO: Lechery?

CLAUDIO: Call it so.

Provost: Away, sir; you must go.

CLAUDIO: One word, good friend. Lucio, a word with you.

LUCIO: A hundred, if they'll do you any good.
Is lechery so look'd after?

CLAUDIO: Thus stands it with me: upon a true contract
I got possession of Julietta's bed.
You know the lady; she is fast my wife,
Save that we do the denunciation lack
Of outward order; this we came not to,
Only for propagation of a dower
Remaining in the coffer of her friends.
From whom we thought it meet to hide our love
Till time had made them for us. But it chances
The stealth of our most mutual entertainment,
With character too gross is writ on Juliet.

LUCIO: With child, perhaps?

CLAUDIO: Unhappily, even so.
And the new deputy now for the duke—
Whether it be the fault and glimpse of newness,
Or whether that the body public be
A horse whereon the governor doth ride,
Who, newly in the seat, that it may know
He can command, lets it straight feel the spur;
Whether the tyranny be in his place,
Or in his emmence that fills it up,
I stagger in:—but this new governor
Awakes me all the enrolled penalties
Which have, like unscour'd armour, hung by the wall
So long that nineteen zodiacs have gone round
And none of them been worn; and, for a name,
Now puts the drowsy and neglected act
Freshly on me. 'Tis surely for a name.

LUCIO: I warrant it is: and thy head stands so tickle on thy shoulders that a milkmaid, if she be in love, may sigh it off. Send after the Duke, and appeal to him.

CLAUDIO: I have done so, but he's not to be found.
I prithee, Lucio, do me this kind service:
This day my sister should the cloister enter
And there receive her approbation;
Acquaint her with the danger of my state;

Implore her, in my voice, that she make friends
To the strict deputy; bid herself assay him.
I have great hope in that; for in her youth
There is a prone and speechless dialect,
Such as move men; beside, she hath prosperous art
When she will play with reason and discourse,
And well she can persuade.

LUCIO: I pray she may; as well for the encouragement of the like, which else would stand under grievous imposition, as for the enjoying of thy life, who I would be sorry should be thus foolishly lost at a game of tick-tack. I'll to her.

CLAUDIO: I thank you, good friend Lucio.

LUCIO: Within two hours.

CLAUDIO: Come, officer, away!

Exeunt

SCENE III—*A monastery*

Enter DUKE VINCENTIO and FRIAR THOMAS

DUKE VINCENTIO: No, holy father; throw away that thought;
Believe not that the dribbling dart of love
Can pierce a complete bosom. Why I desire thee
To give me secret harbour, hath a purpose
More grave and wrinkled than the aims and ends
Of burning youth.

FRIAR THOMAS: May your grace speak of it?

DUKE VINCENTIO: My holy sir, none better knows than you
How I have ever loved the life removed,
And held in idle price to haunt assemblies
Where youth, and cost, and witless bravery keeps.
I have deliver'd to Lord Angelo,
A man of stricture and firm abstinence,
My absolute power and place here in Vienna,
And he supposes me travell'd to Poland;
For so I have strew'd it in the common ear,
And so it is received. Now, pious sir,
You will demand of me why I do this?

FRIAR THOMAS: Gladly, my lord.

DUKE VINCENTIO: We have strict statutes and most biting laws,
The needful bits and curbs to headstrong weeds,
Which for this nineteen years we have let slip;
Even like an o'ergrown lion in a cave,
That goes not out to prey. Now, as fond fathers,
Having bound up the threatening twigs of birch,
Only to stick it in their children's sight
For terror, not to use, in time the rod
Becomes more mock'd than fear'd; so our decrees,
Dead to infliction, to themselves are dead;
And liberty plucks justice by the nose;
The baby beats the nurse, and quite athwart
Goes all decorum.

FRIAR THOMAS: It rested in your grace
To unloose this tied-up justice when you pleased;
And it in you more dreadful would have seem'd
Than in Lord Angelo.

DUKE VINCENTIO: I do fear, too dreadful.
Sith 'twas my fault to give the people scope,
'Twould be my tyranny to strike and gall them
For what I bid them do; for we bid this be done,
When evil deeds have their permissive pass
And not the punishment. Therefore indeed, my father,
I have on Angelo imposed the office;
Who may, in the ambush of my name, strike home,
And yet my nature never in the fight
To do in slander. And to behold his sway,
I will, as 'twere a brother of your order,
Visit both prince and people. Therefore, I prithee,
Supply me with the habit and instruct me
How I may formally in person bear me
Like a true friar. More reasons for this action
At our more leisure shall I render you;
Only, this one: Lord Angelo is precise;
Stands at a guard with envy; scarce confesses
That his blood flows, or that his appetite
Is more to bread than stone. Hence shall we see,
If power change purpose, what our seemers be.

Exeunt

SCENE IV—*A nunnery*

Enter ISABELLA and FRANCISCA

ISABELLA: And have you nuns no farther privileges?

FRANCISCA: Are not these large enough?

ISABELLA: Yes, truly; I speak not as desiring more;
But rather wishing a more strict restraint

Upon the sisterhood, the votarists of Saint Clare.

LUCIO: [*Within*] Ho! Peace be in this place!

ISABELLA: Who's that which calls?

FRANCISCA: It is a man's voice. Gentle Isabella,
Turn you the key, and know his business of him;
You may, I may not; you are yet unsworn;
When you have vow'd, you must not speak with men
But in the presence of the prioress:
Then, if you speak, you must not show your face,
Or, if you show your face, you must not speak.
He calls again; I pray you answer him.

Exit FRANCISCA

ISABELLA: Peace and prosperity! Who is't that calls

Enter LUCIO

LUCIO: Hail, virgin, if you be, as those cheek-roses
Proclaim you are no less. Can you so stead me
As bring me to the sight of Isabella,
A novice of this place and the fair sister
To her unhappy brother Claudio?

ISABELLA: Why her 'unhappy brother'? Let me ask,
The rather, for I now must make you know
I am that Isabella and his sister.

LUCIO: Gentle and fair, your brother kindly greets you.
Not to be weary with you, he's in prison.

ISABELLA: Woe me! For what?

LUCIO: For that which, if myself might be his judge,
He should receive his punishment in thanks:
He hath got his friend with child.

ISABELLA: Sir, make me not your story.

LUCIO: It is true.
I would not—though 'tis my familiar sin
With maids to seem the lapwing and to jest,
Tongue far from heart—play with all virgins so:
I hold you as a thing ensky'd and sainted,
By your renouncement an immortal spirit,
And to be talk'd with in sincerity,
As with a saint.

ISABELLA: You do blaspheme the good in mocking me.

LUCIO: Do not believe it. Fewness and truth, 'tis thus:
Your brother and his lover have embraced.
As those that feed grow full, as blossoming time
That from the seedness the bare fallow brings
To teeming foison, even so her plenteous womb
Expresseth his full tilth and husbandry.

ISABELLA: Some one with child by him? My cousin Juliet?

LUCIO: Is she your cousin?

ISABELLA: Adoptedly; as school-maids change their names
By vain though apt affection.

LUCIO: She it is.

ISABELLA: O, let him marry her!

LUCIO: This is the point.
The duke is very strangely gone from hence;
Bore many gentlemen, myself being one,
In hand and hope of action; but we do learn,
By those that know the very nerves of state,
His givings-out were of an infinite distance
From his true-meant design. Upon his place,
And with full line of his authority,
Governs Lord Angelo; a man whose blood
Is very snow-broth; one who never feels
The wanton stings and motions of the sense,
But doth rebate and blunt his natural edge
With profits of the mind, study and fast.
He—to give fear to use and liberty,
Which have for long run by the hideous law,
As mice by lions—hath pick'd out an act,
Under whose heavy sense your brother's life
Falls into forfeit; he arrests him on it;
And follows close the rigour of the statute,
To make him an example. All hope is gone,
Unless you have the grace by your fair prayer
To soften Angelo. And that's my pith of business
'Twixt you and your poor brother.

ISABELLA: Doth he so seek his life?

LUCIO: Has censured him
Already; and, as I hear, the provost hath
A warrant for his execution.

ISABELLA: Alas! what poor ability's in me
To do him good?

LUCIO: Assay the power you have.

ISABELLA: My power? Alas, I doubt—

LUCIO: Our doubts are traitors,
And make us lose the good we oft might win

By fearing to attempt. Go to Lord Angelo,
And let him learn to know, when maidens sue,
Men give like gods; but when they weep and kneel,
All their petitions are as freely theirs
As they themselves would owe them.

ISABELLA: I'll see what I can do.

LUCIO: But speedily.

ISABELLA: I will about it straight;
No longer staying but to give the Mother
Notice of my affair. I humbly thank you.
Commend me to my brother: soon at night
I'll send him certain word of my success.

LUCIO: I take my leave of you.

ISABELLA: Good sir, adieu.

Exeunt

ACT II

SCENE I—*A hall in Angelo's house*

Enter ANGELO, ESCALUS, and a Justice, Provost, Officers, and other Attendants, behind

ANGELO: We must not make a scarecrow of the law,
Setting it up to fear the birds of prey,
And let it keep one shape, till custom make it
Their perch and not their terror.

ESCALUS: Ay, but yet
Let us be keen, and rather cut a little
Than fall, and bruise to death. Alas! this gentleman,
Whom I would save, had a most noble father!
Let but your honour know,
Whom I believe to be most strait in virtue,
That, in the working of your own affections,
Had time cohered with place or place with wishing,
Or that the resolute acting of our blood
Could have attain'd the effect of your own purpose,
Whether you had not sometime in your life
Err'd in this point which now you censure him,
And pull'd the law upon you.

ANGELO: 'Tis one thing to be tempted, Escalus,
Another thing to fall. I not deny
The jury, passing on the prisoner's life,
May in the sworn twelve have a thief or two
Guiltier than him they try. What's open made to justice,
That justice seizes. What know the laws
That thieves do pass on thieves? 'Tis very pregnant,
The jewel that we find, we stoop and take, 't
Because we see it; but what we do not see
We tread upon, and never think of it.
You may not so extenuate his offence
For I have had such faults; but rather tell me,
When I, that censure him, do so offend,
Let mine own judgment pattern out my death,
And nothing come in partial. Sir, he must die.

ESCALUS: Be it as your wisdom will.

ANGELO: Where is the provost?

Provost: Here, if it like your honour.

ANGELO: See that Claudio
Be executed by nine to-morrow morning;
Bring him his confessor, let him be prepared;
For that's the utmost of his pilgrimage.

Exit Provost

ESCALUS: [*Aside*] Well, heaven forgive him! and forgive us all!
Some rise by sin, and some by virtue fall;
Some run from breaks of ice, and answer none,
And some condemned for a fault alone.

Enter ELBOW, and Officers with FROTH and POMPEY

ELBOW: Come, bring them away; if these be good people in a commonweal that do nothing but use their abuses in common houses, I know no law; bring them away.

ANGELO: How now, sir! What's your name, and what's the matter?

ELBOW: If it Please your honour, I am the poor duke's constable, and my name is Elbow; I do lean upon justice, sir, and do bring in here before your good honour two notorious benefactors.

ANGELO: Benefactors? Well—what benefactors are they? Are they not malefactors?

ELBOW: If it? please your honour, I know not well what they are; but precise villains they are, that I am sure of; and void of all profanation in the world that good Christians ought to have.

ESCALUS: This comes off well; here's a wise officer.

ANGELO: Go to; what quality are they of? Elbow is your name? Why dost thou not speak, Elbow?

POMPEY: He cannot, sir; he's out at elbow.

ANGELO: What are you, sir?

ELBOW: He, sir? A tapster, sir; parcel-bawd; one that serves a bad woman; whose house, sir, was, as they say, plucked down in the suburbs; and now she professes a hot-house, which, I think, is a very ill house too.

ESCALUS: How know you that?

ELBOW: My wife, sir, whom I detest before heaven and your honour—

ESCALUS: How! thy wife?

ELBOW: Ay, sir; whom, I thank heaven, is an honest woman—

ESCALUS: Dost thou detest her therefore?

ELBOW: I say, sir, I will detest myself also, as well as she, that this house, if it be not a bawd's house, it is pity of her life, for it is a naughty house.

ESCALUS: How dost thou know that, constable?

ELBOW: Marry, sir, by my wife; who, if she had been a woman cardinally given, might have been accused in fornication, adultery, and all uncleanliness there.

ESCALUS: By the woman's means?

ELBOW: Ay, sir, by Mistress Overdone's means; but as she spit in his face, so she defied him.

POMPEY: Sir, if it please your honour, this is not so.

ELBOW: Prove it before these varlets here, thou honourable man; prove it.

ESCALUS: Do you hear how he misplaces?

POMPEY: Sir, she came in great with child; and longing, saving your honour's reverence, for stewed prunes. Sir, we had but two in the house, which at that very distant time stood, as it were, in a fruit-dish, a dish of some three-pence; your honours have seen such dishes; they are not China dishes, but very good dishes.

ESCALUS: Go to, go to; no matter for the dish, sir.

POMPEY: No, indeed, sir, not of a pin; you are therein in the right; but to the point. As I say, this Mistress Elbow, being, as I say, with child, and being great-bellied, and longing, as I said, for prunes; and having but two in the dish, as I said, Master Froth here, this very man, having eaten the rest, as I said, and, as I say, paying for them very honestly; for, as you know, Master Froth, I could not give you three-pence again.

FROTH: No, indeed.

POMPEY: Very well; you being then, if you be remembered, cracking the stones of the foresaid prunes—

FROTH: Ay, so I did indeed.

POMPEY: Why, very well; I telling you then, if you be remembered, that such a one and such a one were past cure of the thing you wot of, unless they kept very good diet, as I told you—

FROTH: All this is true.

POMPEY: Why, very well, then—

ESCALUS: Come, you are a tedious fool. To the purpose: what was done to Elbow's wife that he hath cause to complain of? Come me to what was done to her.

POMPEY: Sir, your honour cannot come to that yet.

ESCALUS: No, sir, nor I mean it not.

POMPEY: Sir, but you shall come to it, by your honour's leave. And, I beseech you, look into Master Froth here, sir; a man of four-score pound a year; whose father died at Hallowmas—was't not at Hallowmas, Master Froth?

FROTH: All-hallond eve.

POMPEY: Why, very well; I hope here be truths. He, sir, sitting, as I say, in a lower chair, sir; 'twas in the Bunch of Grapes, where, indeed, you have a delight to sit, have you not?

FROTH: I have so; because it is an open room and good for winter.

POMPEY: Why, very well then; I hope here be truths.

ANGELO: This will last out a night in Russia,
When nights are longest there; I'll take my leave.
And leave you to the hearing of the cause;
Hoping you'll find good cause to whip them all.

ESCALUS: I think no less. Good morrow to your lordship.

Exit ANGELO

Now, sir, come on; what was done to Elbow's wife, once more?

POMPEY: Once, sir? There was nothing done to her once.

ELBOW: I beseech you, sir, ask him what this man did to my wife.

POMPEY: I beseech your honour, ask me.

ESCALUS: Well, sir; what did this gentleman to her?

POMPEY: I beseech you, sir, look in this gentleman's face. Good Master Froth, look upon his honour; 'tis for a good purpose. Doth your honour mark his face?

ESCALUS: Ay, sir, very well.

POMPEY: Nay; I beseech you, mark it well.

ESCALUS: Well, I do so.

POMPEY: Doth your honour see any harm in his face?

ESCALUS: Why, no.

POMPEY: I'll be supposed upon a book, his face is the worst thing about him. Good, then; if his face be the worst thing about him, how could Master Froth do the constable's wife any harm? I would know that of your honour.

ESCALUS: He's in the right. Constable, what say you to it?

ELBOW: First, an it like you, the house is a respected house; next, this is a respected fellow; and his mistress is a respected woman.

POMPEY: By this hand, sir, his wife is a more respected person than any of us all.

ELBOW: Varlet, thou liest; thou liest, wicked varlet; the time is yet to come that she was ever respected with man, woman, or child.

POMPEY: Sir, she was respected with him before he married with her.

ESCALUS: Which is the wiser here. Justice or Iniquity? Is this true?

ELBOW: O thou caitiff! O thou varlet! O thou wicked Hannibal! I respected with her before I was married to her! If ever I was respected with her, or she with me, let not your worship think me the poor Duke's officer. Prove this, thou wicked Hannibal, or I'll have mine action of battery on thee.

ESCALUS: If he took you a box o' the ear, you might have your action of slander too.

ELBOW: Marry, I thank your good worship for it. What is't your worship's pleasure I shall do with this wicked caitiff?

ESCALUS: Truly, officer, because he hath some offences in him that thou wouldst discover if thou couldst, let him continue in his courses till thou knowest what they are.

ELBOW: Marry, I thank your worship for it. Thou seest, thou wicked varlet, now, what's come upon thee: thou art to continue now, thou varlet; thou art to continue.

ESCALUS: Where were you born, friend?

FROTH: Here in Vienna, sir.

ESCALUS: Are you of fourscore pounds a year?

FROTH: Yes, an't please you, sir.

ESCALUS: So. What trade are you of, sir?

POMPEY: Tapster; a poor widow's tapster.

ESCALUS: Your mistress' name?

POMPEY: Mistress Overdone.

ESCALUS: Hath she had any more than one husband?

POMPEY: Nine, sir; Overdone by the last.

ESCALUS: Nine! Come hither to me, Master Froth. Master Froth, I would not have you acquainted with tapsters: they will draw you, Master Froth, and you will hang them. Get you gone, and let me hear no more of you.

FROTH: I thank your worship. For mine own part, I never come into any room in a taphouse, but I am drawn in.

ESCALUS: Well, no more of it, Master Froth: farewell.

Exit FROTH

Come you hither to me, Master tapster. What's your name, Master tapster?

POMPEY: Pompey.

ESCALUS: What else?

POMPEY: Bum, sir.

ESCALUS: Troth, and your bum is the greatest thing about you; so that, in the beastliest sense you are Pompey the Great. Pompey, you are partly a bawd, Pompey, howsoever you colour it in being a tapster. Are you not? Come, tell me true; it shall be the better for you.

POMPEY: Truly, sir, I am a poor fellow that would live.

ESCALUS: How would you live, Pompey—by being a bawd? What do you think of the trade, Pompey? Is it a lawful trade?

POMPEY: If the law would allow it, sir.

ESCALUS: But the law will not allow it, Pompey; nor it shall not be allowed in Vienna.

POMPEY: Does your worship mean to geld and splay all the youth of the city?

ESCALUS: No, Pompey.

POMPEY: Truly, sir, in my poor opinion, they will to't then. If your worship will take order for the drabs and the knaves, you need not to fear the bawds.

ESCALUS: There is pretty orders beginning, I can tell you: it is but heading and hanging.

POMPEY: If you head and hang all that offend that way but for ten year together, you'll be glad to give out a commission for more heads; if this law hold in Vienna ten year, I'll rent the fairest house in it after three-pence a bay: if you live to see this come to pass, say Pompey told you so.

ESCALUS: Thank you, good Pompey; and, in requital of your prophecy, hark you: I advise you, let me not find you before me again upon any complaint whatsoever—no, not for dwelling where you do; if I do, Pompey, I shall beat you to your tent, and prove a shrewd Caesar to you; in plain dealing, Pompey, I shall have you whipt. So, for this time, Pompey, fare you well.

POMPEY: I thank your worship for your good counsel; [*Aside*] but I shall follow it as the flesh and fortune shall better determine.

Whip me? No, no; let carman whip his jade;
The valiant heart is not whipt out of his trade.

Exit

ESCALUS: Come hither to me, Master Elbow; come hither, Master constable. How long have you been in this place of constable?

ELBOW: Seven year and a half, sir.

ESCALUS: I thought, by your readiness in the office, you had continued in it some time. You say, seven years together?

ELBOW: And a half, sir.

ESCALUS: Alas, it hath been great pains to you. They do you wrong to put you so oft upon't. Are there not men in your ward sufficient to serve it?

ELBOW: Faith, sir, few of any wit in such matters; as they are chosen, they are glad to choose me for them; I do it for some piece of money, and go through with all.

ESCALUS: Look you, bring me in the names of some six or seven, the most sufficient of your parish.

ELBOW: To your worship's house, sir?

ESCALUS: To my house. Fare you well.

Exit ELBOW

What's o'clock, think you?

JUSTICE: Eleven, sir.

ESCALUS: I pray you home to dinner with me.

JUSTICE: I humbly thank you.

ESCALUS: It grieves me for the death of Claudio;
But there's no remedy.

JUSTICE: Lord Angelo is severe.

ESCALUS: It is but needful:
Mercy is not itself that oft looks so;
Pardon is still the nurse of second woe.
But yet, poor Claudio! There is no remedy.
Come, sir.

Exeunt

SCENE II—*Another room in Angelo's house*

Enter Provost and a Servant

SERVANT: He's hearing of a cause; he will come straight.
I'll tell him of you.

PROVOST: Pray you, do.

Exit Servant

I'll know
His pleasure; may be he will relent. Alas,
He hath but as offended in a dream!
All sects, all ages, smack of this vice; and he
To die for't!

Enter ANGELO

ANGELO: Now, what's the matter. Provost?

PROVOST: Is it your will Claudio shall die tomorrow?

ANGELO: Did not I tell thee yea? Hadst thou not order?
Why dost thou ask again?

PROVOST: Lest I might be too rash;
Under your good correction, I have seen,
When, after execution, judgment hath
Repented o'er his doom.

ANGELO: Go to; let that be mine.
Do you your office, or give up your place,
And you shall well be spared.

PROVOST: I crave your honour's pardon.
What shall be done, sir, with the groaning Juliet?
She's very near her hour.

ANGELO: Dispose of her
To some more fitter place, and that with speed.

Re-enter Servant

SERVANT: Here is the sister of the man condemn'd
Desires access to you.

ANGELO: Hath he a sister?

PROVOST: Ay, my good lord; a very virtuous maid,
And to be shortly of a sisterhood,
If not already.

ANGELO: Well, let her be admitted.

Exit Servant

See you the fornicatress be removed;
Let have needful, but not lavish means;
There shall be order for't.

Enter ISABELLA and LUCIO

PROVOST: [*Going*] God save your honour!
ANGELO: Stay a little while.
(*To Isabella*) You're welcome; what's your will?
ISABELLA: I am a woeful suitor to your honour,
Please but your honour hear me.
ANGELO: Well; what's your suit?
ISABELLA: There is a vice that most I do abhor,
And most desire should meet the blow of justice;
For which I would not plead, but that I must;
For which I must not plead, but that I am
At war 'twixt will and will not.
ANGELO: Well; the matter?
ISABELLA: I have a brother is condemn'd to die;
I do beseech you, let it be his fault,
And not my brother.
PROVOST: [*Aside*] Heaven give thee moving graces!
ANGELO: Condemn the fault and not the actor of it!
Why, every fault's condemn'd ere it be done:
Mine were the very cipher of a function,
To fine the faults whose fine stands in record,
And let go by the actor.
ISABELLA: O just but severe law!
I had a brother, then. Heaven keep your honour!
LUCIO: [*Aside to Isabella*] Give't not o'er so: to him again, entreat him;
Kneel down before him, hang upon his gown:
You are too cold; if you should need a pin,
You could not with more tame a tongue desire it.
To him, I say.
ISABELLA: Must he needs die?
ANGELO: Maiden, no remedy.
ISABELLA: Yes; I do think that you might pardon him,
And neither heaven nor man grieve at the mercy.
ANGELO: I will not do't.
ISABELLA: But can you, if you would?
ANGELO: Look, what I will not, that I cannot do.
ISABELLA: But might you do't, and do the world no wrong,
If so your heart were touch'd with that remorse
As mine is to him?
ANGELO: He's sentenced; 'tis too late.
LUCIO: [*Aside to Isabella*] You are too cold.
ISABELLA: Too late? why, no; I, that do speak a word.
May call it back again. Well, believe this,
No ceremony that to great ones longs,
Not the king's crown, nor the deputed sword,
The marshal's truncheon, nor the judge's robe,
Become them with one half so good a grace
As mercy does.
If he had been as you and you as he,
You would have slip'd like him; but he, like you,
Would not have been so stern.
ANGELO: Pray you, be gone.
ISABELLA: I would to heaven I had your potency,
And you were Isabel! Should it then be thus?
No; I would tell what 'twere to be a judge,
And what a prisoner.
LUCIO: [*Aside to Isabella*] Ay, touch him; there's the vein.
ANGELO: Your brother is a forfeit of the law,
And you but waste your words.
ISABELLA: Alas, alas!
Why, all the souls that were were forfeit once;
And He that might the vantage best have took
Found out the remedy. How would you be,
If He, which is the top of judgment, should
But judge you as you are? O, think on that;
And mercy then will breathe within your lips,
Like man new made.
ANGELO: Be you content, fair maid;
It is the law, not I condemn your brother:
Were he my kinsman, brother, or my son,
It should be thus with him. He must die tomorrow.
ISABELLA: To-morrow! O, that's sudden! Spare him, spare him.
He's not prepared for death. Even for our kitchens
We kill the fowl of season; shall we serve heaven
With less respect than we do minister
To our gross selves? Good, good my lord, bethink you;
Who is it that hath died for this offence?
There's many have committed it.
LUCIO: [*Aside to Isabella*] Ay, well said.
ANGELO: The law hath not been dead, though it hath slept,
Those many had not dared to do that evil,
If the first that did the edict infringe
Had answer'd for his deed: now 'tis awake

Takes note of what is done; and, like a prophet,
Looks in a glass, that shows what future evils,
Either new, or by remissness new-conceived,
And so in progress to be hatch'd and born,
Are now to have no successive degrees,
But, ere they live, to end.

ISABELLA: Yet show some pity.

ANGELO: I show it most of all when I show justice;
For then I pity those I do not know,
Which a dismiss'd offence would after gall;
And do him right that, answering one foul wrong,
Lives not to act another. Be satisfied;
Your brother dies to-morrow; be content.

ISABELLA: So you must be the first that gives this sentence,
And he, that suffer's. O, it is excellent
To have a giant's strength! But it is tyrannous
To use it like a giant.

LUCIO: [*Aside to Isabella*] That's well said.

ISABELLA: Could great men thunder
As Jove himself does, Jove would ne'er be quiet,
For every pelting, petty officer
Would use his heaven for thunder;
Nothing but thunder. Merciful Heaven,
Thou rather with thy sharp and sulphurous bolt
Splits the unwedgeable and gnarled oak
Than the soft myrtle: but man, proud man,
Dressed in a little brief authority,
Most ignorant of what he's most assured,
His glassy essence, like an angry ape,
Plays such fantastic tricks before high heaven
As makes the angels weep; who, with our spleens,
Would all themselves laugh mortal.

LUCIO: [*Aside to Isabella*] O, to him, to him, wench! He will relent;
He's coming; I perceive 't.

PROVOST: [*Aside*] Pray heaven she win him.

ISABELLA: We cannot weigh our brother with ourself:
Great men may jest with saints; 'tis wit in them,
But in the less foul profanation.

LUCIO (*To Isabella*): Thou'rt i' the right, girl; more o' that.

ISABELLA: That in the captain's but a choleric word,
Which in the soldier is flat blasphemy.

LUCIO: [*Aside to Isabella*] Art avised o' that? More on't.

ANGELO: Why do you put these sayings upon me?

ISABELLA: Because authority, though it err like others,
Hath yet a kind of medicine in itself,
That skins the vice o' the top. Go to your bosom;
Knock there, and ask your heart what it doth know
That's like my brother's fault: if it confess
A natural guiltiness such as is his,
Let it not sound a thought upon your tongue
Against my brother's life.

ANGELO: [*Aside*] She speaks, and 'tis
Such sense that my sense breeds with it. Fare you well.

ISABELLA: Gentle my lord, turn back.

ANGELO: I will bethink me: come again tomorrow.

ISABELLA: Hark how I'll bribe you: good my lord, turn back.

ANGELO: How! bribe me?

ISABELLA: Ay, with such gifts that heaven shall share with you.

LUCIO: [*Aside to Isabella*] You had marr'd all else.

ISABELLA: Not with fond sicles of the tested gold,
Or stones whose rates are either rich or poor
As fancy values them; but with true prayers
That shall be up at heaven and enter there
Ere sun-rise, prayers from preserved souls,
From fasting maids whose minds are dedicate
To nothing temporal.

ANGELO: Well; come to me to-morrow.

LUCIO: [*Aside to Isabella*] Go to; 'tis well; away!

ISABELLA: Heaven keep your honour safe!

ANGELO: [*Aside*] Amen;
For I am that way going to temptation,
Where prayers cross.

ISABELLA: At what hour to-morrow
Shall I attend your lordship?

ANGELO: At any time 'fore noon.

ISABELLA: Save your honour!

Exeunt ISABELLA, LUCIO, and Provost

ANGELO: From thee, even from thy virtue!
What's this, what's this? Is this her fault or mine?
The tempter or the tempted, who sins most?

Ha!
Not she; nor doth she tempt; but it is I
That, lying by the violet in the sun,
Do as the carrion does, not as the flower,
Corrupt with virtuous season. Can it be
That modesty may more betray our sense
Than woman's lightness? Having waste ground enough,
Shall we desire to raze the sanctuary
And pitch our evils there? O, fie, fie, fie!
What dost thou, or what art thou, Angelo?
Dost thou desire her foully for those things
That make her good? O, let her brother live!
Thieves for their robbery have authority
When judges steal themselves. What, do I love her,
That I desire to hear her speak again,
And feast upon her eyes? What is't I dream on?
O cunning enemy, that, to catch a saint,
With saints dost bait thy hook! Most dangerous
Is that temptation that doth goad us on
To sin in loving virtue. Never could the strumpet,
With all her double vigour, art and nature,
Once stir my temper; but this virtuous maid
Subdues me quite. Even till now,
When men were fond, I smiled and wonder'd how.

Exit

SCENE III—*A prison*

Enter, severally, DUKE VINCENTIO disguised as a Friar, and Provost

DUKE VINCENTIO: Hail to you, provost! so I think you are.

PROVOST: I am the Provost. What's your will, good friar?

DUKE VINCENTIO: Bound by my charity and my blest order,
I come to visit the afflicted spirits
Here in the prison. Do me the common right
To let me see them and to make me know
The nature of their crimes, that I may minister
To them accordingly.

PROVOST: I would do more than that, if more were needful.

Enter JULIET

Look, here comes one; a gentlewoman of mine,
Who, falling in the flaws of her own youth,
Hath blister'd her report: she is with child;
And he that got it, sentenced—a young man
More fit to do another such offence
Than die for this.

DUKE VINCENTIO: When must he die?

PROVOST: As I do think, to-morrow.
[*To Juliet*] I have provided for you: stay awhile,
And you shall be conducted.

DUKE VINCENTIO: Repent you, fair one, of the sin you carry?

JULIET: I do; and bear the shame most patiently.

DUKE VINCENTIO: I'll teach you how you shall arraign your conscience,
And try your penitence, if it be sound,
Or hollowly put on.

JULIET: I'll gladly learn.

DUKE VINCENTIO: Love you the man that wrong'd you?

JULIET: Yes, as I love the woman that wrong'd him.

DUKE VINCENTIO: So then it seems your most offenceful act
Was mutually committed?

JULIET: Mutually.

DUKE VINCENTIO: Then was your sin of heavier kind than his.

JULIET: I do confess it, and repent it, father.

DUKE VINCENTIO: 'Tis meet so, daughter: but lest you do repent,
As that the sin hath brought you to this shame,
Which sorrow is always toward ourselves, not heaven,
Showing we would not spare heaven as we love it,
But as we stand in fear—

JULIET: I do repent me, as it is an evil,
And take the shame with joy.

DUKE VINCENTIO: There rest.
Your partner, as I hear, must die tomorrow,
And I am going with instruction to him.
Grace go with you, Benedicite!

Exit

JULIET: Must die to-morrow! O injurious love,
That respites me a life, whose very comfort
Is still a dying horror!

PROVOST: 'Tis pity of him.

Exeunt

SCENE IV—*Angelo's house*

Enter ANGELO

ANGELO: When I would pray and think, I think and pray
To several subjects. Heaven hath my empty words;
Whilst my invention, hearing not my tongue,
Anchors on Isabel: Heaven in my mouth,
As if I did but only chew his name;
And in my heart the strong and swelling evil
Of my conception. The state, whereon I studied
Is like a good thing, being often read,
Grown sere and tedious; yea, my gravity,
Wherein—let no man hear me—I take pride,
Could I with boot change for an idle plume
Which the air beats for vain. O place, O form,
How often dost thou with thy case, thy habit,
Wrench awe from fools and tie the wiser souls
To thy false seeming! Blood, thou art blood
Let's write 'good angel' on the devil's horn:
'Tis not the devil's crest.

Enter a Servant

How now! who's there?

SERVANT: One Isabel, a sister, desires access to you.

ANGELO: Teach her the way.

Exit Servant

O heavens!
Why does my blood thus muster to my heart,
Making both it unable for itself,
And dispossessing all my other parts
Of necessary fitness?
So play the foolish throngs with one that swoons;
Come all to help him, and so stop the air
By which he should revive: and even so
The general, subject to a well-wish'd king,
Quit their own part, and in obsequious fondness
Crowd to his presence, where their untaught love
Must needs appear offence.

Enter ISABELLA

How now, fair maid?

ISABELLA: I am come to know your pleasure.

ANGELO: That you might know it would much better please me
Than to demand what 'tis. Your brother cannot live.

ISABELLA: Even so. Heaven keep your honour!

ANGELO: Yet may he live awhile; and, it may be,
As long as you or I: yet he must die.

ISABELLA: Under your sentence?

ANGELO: Yea.

ISABELLA: When, I beseech you? that in his reprieve,
Longer or shorter, he may be so fitted
That his soul sicken not.

ANGELO: Ha! fie, these filthy vices! It were as good
To pardon him that hath from nature stolen
A man already made, as to remit
Their saucy sweetness that do coin heaven's image
In stamps that are forbid: 'tis all as easy
Falsely to take away a life true made
As to put metal in restrained means
To make a false one.

ISABELLA: 'Tis set down so in heaven, but not in earth.

ANGELO: Say you so? then I shall pose you quickly.
Which had you rather, that the most just law
Now took your brother's life; or, to redeem him,
Give up your body to such sweet uncleanness
As she that he hath stain'd?

ISABELLA: Sir, believe this,
I had rather give my body than my soul.

ANGELO: I talk not of your soul: our compell'd sins
Stand more for number than for accompt.

ISABELLA: How say you?

ANGELO: Nay, I'll not warrant that; for I can speak
Against the thing I say. Answer to this:
I, now the voice of the recorded law,
Pronounce a sentence on your brother's life;
Might there not be a charity in sin
To save this brother's life?

ISABELLA: Please you to do't,
I'll take it as a peril to my soul,
It is no sin at all, but charity.

ANGELO: Pleased you to do't at peril of your soul,
Were equal poise of sin and charity.

ISABELLA: That I do beg his life, if it be sin,
Heaven let me bear it! you granting of my suit,
If that be sin, I'll make it my morn prayer

To have it added to the faults of mine,
And nothing of your answer.
ANGELO: Nay, but hear me.
Your sense pursues not mine; either you are ignorant,
Or seem so craftily; and that's not good.
ISABELLA: Let me be ignorant, and in nothing good,
But graciously to know I am no better.
ANGELO: Thus wisdom wishes to appear most bright
When it doth tax itself; as these black masks
Proclaim an enshielded beauty ten times louder
Than beauty could, display'd. But mark me;
To be received plain, I'll speak more gross:
Your brother is to die.
ISABELLA: So.
ANGELO: And his offence is so, as it appears,
Accountant to the law upon that pain.
ISABELLA: True.
ANGELO: Admit no other way to save his life,
As I subscribe not that, nor any other,
But in the loss of question, that you, his sister,
Finding yourself desired of such a person,
Whose credit with the judge, or own great place,
Could fetch your brother from the manacles
Of the all-building law; and that there were
No earthly mean to save him, but that either
You must lay down the treasures of your body
To this supposed, or else to let him suffer;
What would you do?
ISABELLA: As much for my poor brother as myself:
That is, were I under the terms of death,
The impression of keen whips I'ld wear as rubies,
And strip myself to death, as to a bed
That longing have been sick for, ere I'ld yield
My body up to shame.
ANGELO: Then must your brother die.
ISABELLA: And 'twere the cheaper way:
Better it were a brother died at once,
Than that a sister, by redeeming him,
Should die for ever.
ANGELO: Were not you, then, as cruel as the sentence
That you have slander'd so?
ISABELLA: Ignomy in ransom and free pardon
Are of two houses: lawful mercy
Is nothing kin to foul redemption.
ANGELO: You seem'd of late to make the law a tyrant;
And rather proved the sliding of your brother
A merriment than a vice.
ISABELLA: O, pardon me, my lord! It oft falls out,
To have what we would have, we speak not what we mean:
I something do excuse the thing I hate,
For his advantage that I dearly love.
ANGELO: We are all frail.
ISABELLA: Else let my brother die,
If not a fedary, but only he
Owe and succeed thy weakness.
ANGELO: Nay, women are frail too.
ISABELLA: Ay, as the glasses where they view themselves;
Which are as easy broke as they make forms.
Women! Help Heaven! Men their creation mar
In profiting by them. Nay, call us ten times frail;
For we are soft as our complexions are,
And credulous to false prints.
ANGELO: I think it well:
And from this testimony of your own sex,--
Since I suppose we are made to be no stronger
Than faults may shake our frames, let me be bold;
I do arrest your words. Be that you are,
That is, a woman; if you be more, you're none;
If you be one, as you are well express'd
By all external warrants, show it now,
By putting on the destined livery.
ISABELLA: I have no tongue but one: gentle my lord,
Let me entreat you speak the former language.
ANGELO: Plainly conceive, I love you.
ISABELLA: My brother did love Juliet,
And you tell me that he shall die for it.
ANGELO: He shall not, Isabel, if you give me love.
ISABELLA: I know your virtue hath a licence in't,
Which seems a little fouler than it is,
To pluck on others.
ANGELO: Believe me, on mine honour,
My words express my purpose.
ISABELLA: Ha! little honour to be much believed,
And most pernicious purpose! Seeming, seeming!

I will proclaim thee, Angelo; look for't.
Sign me a present pardon for my brother,
Or with an outstretch'd throat I'll tell the world aloud
What man thou art.

ANGELO: Who will believe thee, Isabel?
My unsoil'd name, the austereness of my life,
My vouch against you, and my place i' the state,
Will so your accusation overweigh,
That you shall stifle in your own report
And smell of calumny. I have begun,
And now I give my sensual race the rein:
Fit thy consent to my sharp appetite;
Lay by all nicety and prolixious blushes,
That banish what they sue for; redeem thy brother
By yielding up thy body to my will;
Or else he must not only die the death,
But thy unkindness shall his death draw out
To lingering sufferance. Answer me tomorrow,
Or, by the affection that now guides me most,
I'll prove a tyrant to him. As for you,
Say what you can, my false o'erweighs your true.

Exit

ISABELLA: To whom should I complain? Did I tell this,
Who would believe me? O perilous mouths,
That bear in them one and the self-same tongue
Either of condemnation or approof,
Bidding the law make court'sy to their will;
Hooking both right and wrong to the appetite,
To follow as it draws! I'll to my brother.
Though he hath fallen by prompture of the blood,
Yet hath he in him such a mind of honour.
That, had he twenty heads to tender down
On twenty bloody blocks, he'd yield them up,
Before his sister should her body stoop
To such abhorr'd pollution.
Then, Isabel, live chaste, and, brother, die:
More than our brother is our chastity.
I'll tell him yet of Angelo's request,
And fit his mind to death, for his soul's rest.

Exit

Act III

Scene I—*The prison*

Enter DUKE VINCENTIO disguised as before, CLAUDIO, and Provost

DUKE VINCENTIO: So then you hope of pardon from Lord Angelo?

CLAUDIO: The miserable have no other medicine
But only hope:
I've hope to live, and am prepared to die.

DUKE VINCENTIO: Be absolute for death; either death or life
Shall thereby be the sweeter. Reason thus with life.
If I do lose thee, I do lose a thing
That none but fools would keep. A breath thou art,
Servile to all the skyey influences,
That dost this habitation, where thou keep'st,
Hourly afflict: merely, thou art death's fool;
For him thou labour'st by thy flight to shun
And yet run'st toward him still. Thou art not noble;
For all the accommodations that thou bear'st
Are nursed by baseness. Thou 'rt by no means valiant;
For thou dost fear the soft and tender fork
Of a poor worm. Thy best of rest is sleep,
And that thou oft provokest; yet grossly fear'st
Thy death, which is no more. Thou art not thyself;
For thou exists on many a thousand grains
That issue out of dust. Happy thou art not;
For what thou hast not, still thou strivest to get,
And what thou hast, forget'st. Thou art not certain;
For thy complexion shifts to strange effects,
After the moon. If thou art rich, thou'rt poor;
For, like an ass whose back with ingots bows,
Thou bear'st thy heavy riches but a journey,
And death unloads thee. Friend hast thou none;
For thine own bowels, which do call thee sire,
The mere effusion of thy proper loins,
Do curse the gout, serpigo, and the rheum,
For ending thee no sooner. Thou hast nor youth nor age,
But, as it were, an after-dinner's sleep,
Dreaming on both; for all thy blessed youth
Becomes as aged, and doth beg the alms
Of palsied eld; and when thou art old and rich,
Thou hast neither heat, affection, limb, nor beauty,
To make thy riches pleasant. What's yet in this
That bears the name of life? Yet in this life
Lie hid moe thousand deaths; yet death we fear,
That makes these odds all even.

CLAUDIO: I humbly thank you.
To sue to live, I find I seek to die;
And, seeking death, find life. Let it come on.

ISABELLA: [*Within*] What, ho! Peace here; grace and good company!

PROVOST: Who's there? Come in; the wish deserves a welcome.

DUKE VINCENTIO: Dear sir, ere long I'll visit you again.

CLAUDIO: Most holy sir, I thank you.

Enter ISABELLA

ISABELLA: My business is a word or two with Claudio.

PROVOST: And very welcome. Look, signior, here's your sister.

DUKE VINCENTIO: Provost, a word with you.

PROVOST: As many as you please.

DUKE VINCENTIO: Bring me to hear them speak, where I may be concealed.

Exeunt DUKE VINCENTIO and Provost

CLAUDIO: Now, sister, what's the comfort?

ISABELLA: Why,
As all comforts are; most good, most good, indeed.

Lord Angelo, having affairs to heaven,
Intends you for his swift ambassador,
Where you shall be an everlasting leiger.
Therefore your best appointment make with speed;
To-morrow you set on.

CLAUDIO: Is there no remedy?

ISABELLA: None, but such remedy as, to save a head,
To cleave a heart in twain.

CLAUDIO: But is there any?

ISABELLA: Yes, brother, you may live:
There is a devilish mercy in the judge,
If you'll implore it, that will free your life,
But fetter you till death.

CLAUDIO: Perpetual durance?

ISABELLA: Ay, just; perpetual durance, a restraint,
Though all the world's vastidity you had,
To a determined scope.

CLAUDIO: But in what nature?

ISABELLA: In such a one as, you consenting to't,
Would bark your honour from that trunk you bear,
And leave you naked.

CLAUDIO: Let me know the point.

ISABELLA: O, I do fear thee, Claudio; and I quake,
Lest thou a feverous life shouldst entertain,
And six or seven winters more respect
Than a perpetual honour. Darest thou die?
The sense of death is most in apprehension;
And the poor beetle, that we tread upon,
In corporal sufferance finds a pang as great
As when a giant dies.

CLAUDIO: Why give you me this shame?
Think you I can a resolution fetch
From flowery tenderness? If I must die,
I will encounter darkness as a bride,
And hug it in mine arms.

ISABELLA: There spake my brother; there my father's grave
Did utter forth a voice. Yes, thou must die:
Thou art too noble to conserve a life
In base appliances. This outward-sainted deputy,
Whose settled visage and deliberate word
Nips youth i' the head and follies doth enew
As falcon doth the fowl, is yet a devil;
His filth within being cast, he would appear
A pond as deep as hell.

CLAUDIO: The precise Angelo!

ISABELLA: O, 'tis the cunning livery of hell,
The damned'st body to invest and cover
In precise guards! Dost thou think, Claudio?
If I would yield him my virginity,
Thou mightst be freed.

CLAUDIO: O heavens! it cannot be.

ISABELLA: Yes, he would give't thee, from this rank offence,
So to offend him still. This night's the time
That I should do what I abhor to name,
Or else thou diest to-morrow.

CLAUDIO: Thou shalt not do't.

ISABELLA: O, were it but my life,
I'ld throw it down for your deliverance
As frankly as a pin.

CLAUDIO: Thanks, dear Isabel.

ISABELLA: Be ready, Claudio, for your death tomorrow.

CLAUDIO: Yes. Has he affections in him,
That thus can make him bite the law by the nose,
When he would force it? Sure, it is no sin,
Or of the deadly seven, it is the least.

ISABELLA: Which is the least?

CLAUDIO: If it were damnable, he being so wise,
Why would he for the momentary trick
Be perdurably fined? O Isabel!

ISABELLA: What says my brother?

CLAUDIO: Death is a fearful thing.

ISABELLA: And shamed life a hateful.

CLAUDIO: Ay, but to die, and go we know not where;
To lie in cold obstruction and to rot;
This sensible warm motion to become
A kneaded clod; and the delighted spirit
To bathe in fiery floods, or to reside
In thrilling region of thick-ribbed ice;
To be imprison'd in the viewless winds,
And blown with restless violence round about
The pendent world; or to be worse than worst
Of those that lawless and incertain thought
Imagine howling: 'tis too horrible!
The weariest and most loathed worldly life
That age, ache, penury and imprisonment

Can lay on nature is a paradise
To what we fear of death.

ISABELLA: Alas, alas!

CLAUDIO: Sweet sister, let me live.
What sin you do to save a brother's life,
Nature dispenses with the deed so far
That it becomes a virtue.

ISABELLA: O you beast!
O faithless coward! O dishonest wretch!
Wilt thou be made a man out of my vice?
Is't not a kind of incest, to take life
From thine own sister's shame? What should I think?
Heaven shield my mother play'd my father fair!
For such a warped slip of wilderness
Ne'er issued from his blood. Take my defiance!
Die, perish! Might but my bending down
Reprieve thee from thy fate, it should proceed:
I'll pray a thousand prayers for thy death,
No word to save thee.

CLAUDIO: Nay, hear me, Isabel.

ISABELLA: O, fie, fie, fie!
Thy sin's not accidental, but a trade.
Mercy to thee would prove itself a bawd:
'Tis best thou diest quickly.

CLAUDIO: O hear me, Isabella!

Re-enter DUKE VINCENTIO

DUKE VINCENTIO: Vouchsafe a word, young sister, but one word.

ISABELLA: What is your will?

DUKE VINCENTIO: Might you dispense with your leisure, I would by and by have some speech with you; the satisfaction I would require is likewise your own benefit.

ISABELLA: I have no superfluous leisure; my stay must be stolen out of other affairs; but I will attend you awhile.

Walks apart

DUKE VINCENTIO: Son, I have overheard what hath passed between you and your sister. Angelo had never the purpose to corrupt her; only he hath made an essay of her virtue to practise his judgment with the disposition of natures. She, having the truth of honour in her, hath made him that gracious denial which he is most glad to receive. I am confessor to Angelo, and I know this to be true; therefore prepare yourself to death. Do not satisfy your resolution with hopes that are fallible; tomorrow you must die; go to your knees and make ready.

CLAUDIO: Let me ask my sister pardon. I am so out of love with life that I will sue to be rid of it.

DUKE VINCENTIO: Hold you there: farewell.

Exit CLAUDIO

Provost, a word with you.

Re-enter PROVOST

PROVOST: What's your will, father?

DUKE VINCENTIO: That now you are come, you will be gone. Leave me a while with the maid: my mind promises with my habit no loss shall touch her by my company.

PROVOST: In good time.

Exit Provost. ISABELLA comes forward

DUKE VINCENTIO: The hand that hath made you fair hath made you good; the goodness that is cheap in beauty makes beauty brief in goodness; but grace, being the soul of your complexion, shall keep the body of it ever fair. The assault that Angelo hath made to you, fortune hath conveyed to my understanding; and, but that frailty hath examples for his falling, I should wonder at Angelo. How will you do to content this substitute, and to save your brother?

ISABELLA: I am now going to resolve him: I had rather my brother die by the law than my son should be unlawfully born. But, O, how much is the good Duke deceived in Angelo! If ever he return and I can speak to him, I will open my lips in vain, or discover his government.

DUKE VINCENTIO: That shall not be much amiss; yet, as the matter now stands, he will avoid your accusation; he made trial of you only. Therefore fasten your ear on my advisings: to the love I have in doing good a remedy presents itself. I do make myself believe that you may most uprighteously do a poor wronged lady a merited benefit; redeem your brother from the angry law; do no stain to your own gracious person; and much please the absent Duke, if peradventure he shall ever return to have hearing of this business.

ISABELLA: Let me hear you speak farther. I have spirit to do anything that appears not foul in the truth of my spirit.

DUKE VINCENTIO: Virtue is bold, and goodness never fearful. Have you not heard speak of Mariana, the sister of Frederick the great soldier who miscarried at sea?

ISABELLA: I have heard of the lady, and good words went with her name.

DUKE VINCENTIO: She should this Angelo have married; was affianced to her by oath, and the nuptial appointed: between which time of the contract and limit of the solemnity, her brother Frederick was wrecked at sea, having in that perished vessel the dowry of his sister. But mark how heavily this befell to the poor gentlewoman: there she lost a noble and renowned brother, in his love toward her ever most kind and natural; with him, the portion and sinew of her fortune, her marriage-dowry; with both, her combinate husband, this well-seeming Angelo.

ISABELLA: Can this be so? did Angelo so leave her?

DUKE VINCENTIO: Left her in her tears, and dried not one of them with his comfort; swallowed his vows whole, pretending in her discoveries of dishonor; in few, bestowed her on her own lamentation, which she yet wears for his sake; and he, a marble to her tears, is washed with them, but relents not.

ISABELLA: What a merit were it in death to take this poor maid from the world! What corruption in this life, that it will let this man live! But how out of this can she avail ?

DUKE VINCENTIO: It is a rupture that you may easily heal; and the cure of it not only saves your brother, but keeps you from dishonour in doing it.

ISABELLA: Show me how, good father.

DUKE VINCENTIO: This forenamed maid hath yet in her the continuance of her first affection; his unjust unkindness, that in all reason should have quenched her love, hath, like an impediment in the current, made it more violent and unruly. Go you to Angelo; answer his requiring with a plausible obedience; agree with his demands to the point; only refer yourself to this advantage: first, that your stay with him may not be long; that the time may have all shadow and silence in it; and the place answer to convenience. This being granted in course—-and now follows all—we shall advise this wronged maid to stead up your appointment, go in your place. If the encounter acknowledge itself hereafter, it may compel him to her recompense; and here, by this, is your brother saved, your honour untainted, the poor Mariana advantaged, and the corrupt deputy scaled. The maid will I frame and make fit for his attempt. If you think well to carry this as you may, the doubleness of the benefit defends the deceit from reproof. What think you of it?

ISABELLA: The image of it gives me content already; and I trust it will grow to a most prosperous perfection.

DUKE VINCENTIO: It lies much in your holding up. Haste you speedily to Angelo; if for this night he entreat you to his bed, give him promise of satisfaction. I will presently to Saint Luke's: there, at the moated grange, resides this dejected Mariana. At that place call upon me; and dispatch with Angelo, that it may be quickly.

ISABELLA: I thank you for this comfort. Fare you well, good father.

Exeunt severally

SCENE II—*The street before the prison*

Enter, on one side, DUKE VINCENTIO disguised as before; on the other, ELBOW, and Officers with POMPEY

ELBOW: Nay, if there be no remedy for it, but that you will needs buy and sell men and women like beasts, we shall have all the world drink brown and white bastard.

DUKE VINCENTIO: O heavens! what stuff is here?

POMPEY: 'Twas never merry world since, of two usuries, the merriest was put down, and the worser allowed by order of law a furred gown to keep him warm; and furred with fox and lamb-skins too, to signify, that craft, being richer than innocency, stands for the facing.

ELBOW: Come your way, sir. Bless you, good father friar.

DUKE VINCENTIO: And you, good brother father. What offence hath this man made you, sir?

ELBOW: Marry, sir, he hath offended the law; and, sir, we take him to be a thief too, sir; for we have found upon him, sir, a strange picklock, which we have sent to the deputy.

DUKE VINCENTIO: Fie, sirrah! a bawd, a wicked bawd!

The evil that thou causest to be done,
That is thy means to live. Do thou but think
What 'tis to cram a maw or clothe a back
From such a filthy vice; say to thyself,
From their abominable and beastly touches
I drink, I eat, array myself, and live.

Canst thou believe thy living is a life,
So stinkingly depending? Go mend, go mend.

POMPEY: Indeed, it does stink in some sort, sir; but yet, sir, I would prove—

DUKE VINCENTIO: Nay, if the devil have given thee proofs for sin,
Thou wilt prove his. Take him to prison, officer;
Correction and instruction must both work
Ere this rude beast will profit.

ELBOW: He must before the deputy, sir; he has given him warning. The deputy cannot abide a whoremaster; if he be a whoremonger, and comes before him, he were as good go a mile on his errand.

DUKE VINCENTIO: That we were all, as some would seem to be,
From our faults, as his faults from seeming, free!

ELBOW: His neck will come to your waist—a cord, sir.

Enter LUCIO

POMPEY: I spy comfort; I cry bail. Here's a gentleman and a friend of mine.

LUCIO: How now, noble Pompey! What, at the wheels of Caesar? art thou led in triumph? What, is there none of Pygmalion's images, newly made woman, to be had now, for putting the hand in the pocket and extracting it clutch'd? What reply, ha? What sayest thou to this tune, matter and method? Is't not drowned i' the last rain, ha? What sayest thou, trot? Is the world as it was, man? Which is the way? Is it sad, and few words? or how? The trick of it?

DUKE VINCENTIO: Still thus, and thus; still worse!

LUCIO: How doth my dear morsel, thy mistress? Procures she still, ha?

POMPEY: Troth, sir, she hath eaten up all her beef, and she is herself in the tub.

LUCIO: Why, 'tis good; it is the right of it; it must be so; ever your fresh whore and your powdered bawd: an unshunned consequence; it must be so. Art going to prison, Pompey?

POMPEY: Yes, faith, sir.

LUCIO: Why, 'tis not amiss, Pompey. Farewell; go, say I sent thee thither. For debt, Pompey—or how?

ELBOW: For being a bawd, for being a bawd.

LUCIO: Well, then, imprison him: if imprisonment be the due of a bawd, why, 'tis his right: bawd is he doubtless, and of antiquity too; bawd-born. Farewell, good Pompey. Commend me to the prison, Pompey: you will turn good husband now, Pompey; you will keep the house.

POMPEY: I hope, sir, your good worship will be my bail.

LUCIO: No, indeed, will I not, Pompey; it is not the wear. I will pray, Pompey, to increase your bondage. If you take it not patiently, why, your mettle is the more. Adieu, trusty Pompey. Bless you, friar.

DUKE VINCENTIO: And you.

LUCIO: Does Bridget paint still, Pompey, ha?

ELBOW: Come your ways, sir; come.

POMPEY: You will not bail me then, sir?

LUCIO: Then, Pompey, nor now. What news abroad, friar? what news?

ELBOW: Come your ways, sir; come.

LUCIO: Go to kennel, Pompey; go.

Exeunt ELBOW, POMPEY and Officers

What news, friar, of the Duke?

DUKE VINCENTIO: I know none. Can you tell me of any?

LUCIO: Some say he is with the Emperor of Russia; other some, he is in Rome; but where is he, think you?

DUKE VINCENTIO: I know not where; but wheresoever, I wish him well.

LUCIO: It was a mad fantastical trick of him to steal from the state, and usurp the beggary he was never born to. Lord Angelo dukes it well in his absence; he puts transgression to 't.

DUKE VINCENTIO: He does well in't.

LUCIO: A little more lenity to lechery would do no harm in him. Something too crabbed that way, friar.

DUKE VINCENTIO: It is too general a vice, and severity must cure it.

LUCIO: Yes, in good sooth, the vice is of a great kindred; it is well allied; but it is impossible to extirp it quite, friar, till eating and drinking be put down. They say this Angelo was not made by man and woman after this downright way of creation: is it true, think you?

DUKE VINCENTIO: How should he be made, then?

LUCIO: Some report a sea-maid spawned him; some, that he was begot between two stock-fishes. But it is certain that when he makes water his urine is congealed ice; that I know to be true: and he is a motion generative; that's infallible.

DUKE VINCENTIO: You are pleasant, sir, and speak apace.

LUCIO: Why, what a ruthless thing is this in him, for the rebellion of a codpiece to take away the life of a man! Would the Duke that is absent have done this? Ere he would have hanged a man for the getting a hundred bastards, he would have paid for the nursing a thousand: he had some feeling of the sport; he knew the service, and that instructed him to mercy.

DUKE VINCENTIO: I never heard the absent Duke much detected for women; he was not inclined that way.

LUCIO: O, sir, you are deceived.

DUKE VINCENTIO: 'Tis not possible.

LUCIO: Who, not the Duke? Yes, your beggar of fifty; and his use was to put a ducat in her clack-dish: the Duke had crotchets in him. He would be drunk too; that let me inform you.

DUKE VINCENTIO: You do him wrong, surely.

LUCIO: Sir, I was an inward of his. A shy fellow was the duke: and I believe I know the cause of his withdrawing.

DUKE VINCENTIO: What, I prithee, might be the cause?

LUCIO: No, pardon; 'tis a secret must be locked within the teeth and the lips; but this I can let you understand, the greater file of the subject held the duke to be wise.

DUKE VINCENTIO: Wise! why, no question but he was.

LUCIO: A very superficial, ignorant, unweighing fellow.

DUKE VINCENTIO: Either this is the envy in you, folly, or mistaking; the very stream of his life and the business he hath helmed must, upon a warranted need, give him a better proclamation. Let him be but testimonied in his own bringings-forth, and he shall appear to the envious a scholar, a statesman and a soldier. Therefore you speak unskillfully; or if your knowledge be more, it is much darkened in your malice.

LUCIO: Sir, I know him, and I love him.

DUKE VINCENTIO: Love talks with better knowledge, and knowledge with dearer love.

LUCIO: Come, sir, I know what I know.

DUKE VINCENTIO: I can hardly believe that, since you know not what you speak. But, if ever the Duke return, as our prayers are he may, let me desire you to make your answer before him. If it be honest you have spoke, you have courage to maintain it; I am bound to call upon you; and, I pray you, your name?

LUCIO: Sir, my name is Lucio; well known to the Duke.

DUKE VINCENTIO: He shall know you better, sir, if I may live to report you.

LUCIO: I fear you not.

DUKE VINCENTIO: O, you hope the Duke will return no more; or you imagine me too unhurtful an opposite. But, indeed, I can do you little harm; you'll forswear this again.

LUCIO: I'll be hanged first: thou art deceived in me, friar. But no more of this. Canst thou tell if Claudio die to-morrow or no?

DUKE VINCENTIO: Why should he die, sir?

LUCIO: Why? For filling a bottle with a tundish. I would the duke we talk of were returned again. This ungenitured agent will unpeople the province with continency; sparrows must not build in his house-eaves, because they are lecherous. The Duke yet would have dark deeds darkly answered; he would never bring them to light: would he were returned! Marry, this Claudio is condemned for untrussing. Farewell, good friar; I prithee, pray for me. The Duke, I say to thee again, would eat mutton on Fridays. He's not past it yet, and I say to thee, he would mouth with a beggar, though she smelt brown bread and garlic: say that I said so. Farewell.

Exit

DUKE VINCENTIO: No might nor greatness in mortality
Can censure scape; back-wounding calumny
The whitest virtue strikes. What king so strong
Can tie the gall up in the slanderous tongue?
But who comes here?

Enter ESCALUS, Provost, and Officers with MISTRESS OVERDONE

ESCALUS: Go; away with her to prison.

MISTRESS OVERDONE: Good my lord, be good to me; your honour is accounted a merciful man; good my lord.

ESCALUS: Double and treble admonition, and still forfeit in the same kind! This would make mercy swear and play the tyrant.

PROVOST: A bawd of eleven years' continuance, may it please your honour.

MISTRESS OVERDONE: My lord, this is one Lucio's information against me. Mistress Kate Keepdown was with child by him in the Duke's time; he promised her marriage: his child is a year and a quarter old, come Philip and Jacob; I have kept it myself; and see how he goes about to abuse me.

ESCALUS: That fellow is a fellow of much licence: let him be called before us. Away with her to prison! Go to; no more words. (*Exeunt Officers with Mistress Overdone*) Provost, my brother Angelo will not be altered; Claudio must die to-morrow. Let him be furnished with divines, and have all charitable preparation. if my brother wrought by my pity, it should not be so with him.

Provost: So please you, this friar hath been with him, and advised him for the entertainment of death.

ESCALUS: Good even, good father.

DUKE VINCENTIO: Bliss and goodness on you!

ESCALUS: Of whence are you?

DUKE VINCENTIO: Not of this country, though my chance is now

To use it for my time. I am a brother
Of gracious order, late come from the See
In special business from his Holiness.

ESCALUS: What news abroad i' the world?

DUKE VINCENTIO: None, but that there is so great a fever on goodness, that the dissolution of it must cure it. Novelty is only in request; and as it is as dangerous to be aged in any kind of course, as it is virtuous to be constant in any undertaking. There is scarce truth enough alive to make societies secure; but security enough to make fellowships accurst. Much upon this riddle runs the wisdom of the world. This news is old enough, yet it is every day's news. I pray you, sir, of what disposition was the Duke?

ESCALUS: One that, above all other strifes, contended especially to know himself.

DUKE VINCENTIO: What pleasure was he given to?

ESCALUS: Rather rejoicing to see another merry, than merry at anything which professed to make him rejoice: a gentleman of all temperance. But leave we him to his events, with a prayer they may prove prosperous; and let me desire to know how you find Claudio prepared. I am made to understand that you have lent him visitation.

DUKE VINCENTIO: He professes to have received no sinister measure from his judge, but most willingly humbles himself to the determination of justice. Yet had he framed to himself, by the instruction of his frailty, many deceiving promises of life; which I by my good leisure have discredited to him, and now is he resolved to die.

ESCALUS: You have paid the heavens your function, and the prisoner the very debt of your calling. I have laboured for the poor gentleman to the extremest shore of my modesty; but my brother justice have I found so severe, that he hath forced me to tell him he is indeed Justice.

DUKE VINCENTIO: If his own life answer the straitness of his proceeding, it shall become him well; wherein if he chance to fail, he hath sentenced himself.

ESCALUS: I am going to visit the prisoner. Fare you well.

DUKE VINCENTIO: Peace be with you!

Exeunt ESCALUS and Provost

He who the sword of heaven will bear
Should be as holy as severe;
Pattern in himself to know,
Grace to stand, and virtue go;
More nor less to others paying
Than by self-offences weighing.
Shame to him whose cruel striking
Kills for faults of his own liking!
Twice treble shame on Angelo,
To weed my vice and let his grow!
O, what may man within him hide,
Though angel on the outward side!
How may likeness made in crimes,
Make a practice on the times,
To draw with idle spiders' strings
Most ponderous and substantial things!
Craft against vice I must apply:
With Angelo to-night shall lie
His old betrothed but despised;
So disguise shall, by the disguised,
Pay with falsehood false exacting,
And perform an old contracting.

Exit

Act IV

Scene I—*The moated grange at Saint Luke's*

Enter MARIANA and a Boy

Boy sings

Take, O, take those lips away,
That so sweetly were forsworn;
And those eyes, the break of day,
Lights that do mislead the morn:
But my kisses bring again, bring again;
Seals of love, but sealed in vain, sealed in vain.

MARIANA: Break off thy song, and haste thee quick away;
Here comes a man of comfort, whose advice
Hath often still'd my brawling discontent.

Exit Boy

Enter DUKE VINCENTIO, disguised as before

I cry you mercy, sir; and well could wish
You had not found me here so musical.
Let me excuse me, and believe me so,
My mirth it much displeased, but pleased my woe.

DUKE VINCENTIO: 'Tis good; though music oft hath such a charm
To make bad good, and good provoke to harm.
I pray, you tell me, hath anybody inquired
for me here to-day? Much upon this time have
I promised here to meet.

MARIANA: You have not been inquired after;
I have sat here all day.

Enter ISABELLA

DUKE VINCENTIO: I do constantly believe you. The time is come even now. I shall crave your forbearance a little. May be I will call upon you anon, for some advantage to yourself.

MARIANA: I am always bound to you.

Exit

DUKE VINCENTIO: Very well met, and well come.
What is the news from this good deputy?

ISABELLA: He hath a garden circummured with brick,
Whose western side is with a vineyard back'd;
And to that vineyard is a planched gate,
That makes his opening with this bigger key;
This other doth command a little door
Which from the vineyard to the garden leads;
There have I made my promise
Upon the heavy middle of the night
To call upon him.

DUKE VINCENTIO: But shall you on your knowledge find this way?

ISABELLA: I have ta'en a due and wary note upon't;
With whispering and most guilty diligence,
In action all of precept, he did show me
The way twice o'er.

DUKE VINCENTIO: Are there no other tokens
Between you greed concerning her observance?

ISABELLA: No, none, but only a repair i' the dark;
And that I have possess'd him my most stay
Can be but brief; for I have made him know
I have a servant comes with me along,
That stays upon me, whose persuasion is
I come about my brother.

DUKE VINCENTIO: 'Tis well borne up.
I have not yet made known to Mariana
A word of this. What, ho, within! come forth.

Re-enter MARIANA

I pray you, be acquainted with this maid;
She comes to do you good.

ISABELLA: I do desire the like.

DUKE VINCENTIO: Do you persuade yourself that I respect you?

MARIANA: Good friar, I know you do, and have found it.

DUKE VINCENTIO: Take, then, this your companion by the hand,
Who hath a story ready for your ear.
I shall attend your leisure; but make haste;
The vaporous night approaches.

MARIANA: Will't please you walk aside?

Exeunt MARIANA and ISABELLA

DUKE VINCENTIO: O place and greatness! Millions of false eyes

Are stuck upon thee. Volumes of report
Run with these false and most contrarious quest
Upon thy doings. Thousand escapes of wit
Make thee the father of their idle dream
And rack thee in their fancies.

Re-enter MARIANA and ISABELLA

Welcome, how agreed?

ISABELLA: She'll take the enterprise upon her, father,
If you advise it.

DUKE VINCENTIO: It is not my consent,
But my entreaty too.

ISABELLA: Little have you to say
When you depart from him, but, soft and low,
'Remember now my brother.'

MARIANA: Fear me not.

DUKE VINCENTIO: Nor, gentle daughter, fear you not at all.

He is your husband on a pre-contract.
To bring you thus together, 'tis no sin,
Sith that the justice of your title to him
Doth flourish the deceit. Come, let us go;
Our corn's to reap, for yet our tithe's to sow.

Exeunt

SCENE II—*The prison*

Enter PROVOST and POMPEY

PROVOST: Come hither, sirrah. Can you cut off a man's head?

POMPEY: If the man be a bachelor, sir, I can; but if he be a married man, he's his wife's head, and I can never cut off a woman's head.

PROVOST: Come, sir, leave me your snatches, and yield me a direct answer. To-morrow morning are to die Claudio and Barnardine. Here is in our prison a common executioner, who in his office lacks a helper: if you will take it on you to assist him, it shall redeem you from your gyves; if not, you shall have your full time of imprisonment and your deliverance with an unpitied whipping, for you have been a notorious bawd.

POMPEY: Sir, I have been an unlawful bawd time out of mind; but yet I will be content to be a lawful hangman. I would be glad to receive some instruction from my fellow partner.

PROVOST: What, ho! Abhorson! Where's Abhorson, there?

Enter ABHORSON

ABHORSON: Do you call, sir?

PROVOST: Sirrah, here's a fellow will help you to-morrow in your execution. If you think it meet, compound with him by the year, and let him abide here with you; if not, use him for the present and dismiss him. He cannot plead his estimation with you; he hath been a bawd.

ABHORSON: A bawd, sir? fie upon him! he will discredit our mystery.

PROVOST: Go to, sir; you weigh equally; a feather will turn the scale.

Exit

POMPEY: Pray, sir, by your good favour—for surely, sir, a good favour you have, but that you have a hanging look,—do you call, sir, your occupation a mystery?

ABHORSON: Ay, sir; a mystery

POMPEY: Painting, sir, I have heard say, is a mystery; and your whores, sir, being members of my occupation, using painting, do prove my occupation a mystery: but what mystery there should be in hanging, if I should be hanged, I cannot imagine.

ABHORSON: Sir, it is a mystery.

POMPEY: Proof?

ABHORSON: Every true man's apparel fits your thief: if it be too little for your thief, your true man thinks it big enough; if it be too big for your thief, your thief thinks it little enough: so every true man's apparel fits your thief.

Re-enter PROVOST

PROVOST: Are you agreed?

POMPEY: Sir, I will serve him; for I do find your hangman is a more penitent trade than your bawd; he doth oftener ask forgiveness.

PROVOST: You, sirrah, provide your block and your axe to-morrow four o'clock.

ABHORSON: Come on, bawd; I will instruct thee in my trade; follow.

POMPEY: I do desire to learn, sir; and I hope, if you have occasion to use me for your own turn, you shall find me yare; for truly, sir, for your kindness I owe you a good turn.

PROVOST: Call hither Barnardine and Claudio.

Exeunt POMPEY and ABHORSON

The one has my pity; not a jot the other,
Being a murderer, though he were my brother.

Enter CLAUDIO

Look, here's the warrant, Claudio, for thy death;
'Tis now dead midnight, and by eight to-morrow
Thou must be made immortal. Where's Barnardine?

CLAUDIO: As fast lock'd up in sleep as guiltless labour
When it lies starkly in the traveller's bones.
He will not wake.

PROVOST: Who can do good on him?
Well, go, prepare yourself. (*Knocking within*) But, hark, what noise?
Heaven give your spirits comfort!

Exit CLAUDIO

(*Knocking continues*) By and by.
I hope it is some pardon or reprieve
For the most gentle Claudio.

Enter DUKE VINCENTIO disguised as before

Welcome father.

DUKE VINCENTIO: The best and wholesomest spirits of the night
Envelope you, good Provost! Who call'd here of late?

PROVOST: None, since the curfew rung.

DUKE VINCENTIO: Not Isabel?

PROVOST: No.

DUKE VINCENTIO: They will, then, ere't be long.

PROVOST: What comfort is for Claudio?

DUKE VINCENTIO: There's some in hope.

PROVOST: It is a bitter deputy.

DUKE VINCENTIO: Not so, not so; his life is parallel'd
Even with the stroke and line of his great justice;
He doth with holy abstinence subdue
That in himself which he spurs on his power
To qualify in others. Were he meal'd with that
Which he corrects, then were he tyrannous;
But this being so, he's just. (*Knocking within*)
Now are they come.

Exit PROVOST

This is a gentle provost; seldom when
The steeled gaoler is the friend of men.

Knocking within

How now! what noise? That spirit's possessed with haste
That wounds the unsisting postern with these strokes.

Re-enter PROVOST

PROVOST: There he must stay until the officer
Arise to let him in; he is call'd up.

DUKE VINCENTIO: Have you no countermand for Claudio yet,
But he must die to-morrow?

PROVOST: None, sir, none.

DUKE VINCENTIO: As near the dawning, provost, as it is,
You shall hear more ere morning.

PROVOST: Happily
You something know; yet I believe there comes
No countermand; no such example have we.
Besides, upon the very siege of justice
Lord Angelo hath to the public ear
Profess'd the contrary.

Enter a Messenger

This is his lordship's man.

DUKE VINCENTIO: And here comes Claudio's pardon.

MESSENGER: [*Giving a paper*] My lord hath sent you this note; and by me this further charge, that you swerve not from the smallest article of it, neither in time, matter, or other circumstance. Good morrow; for, as I take it, it is almost day.

PROVOST: I shall obey him.

Exit Messenger

DUKE VINCENTIO: [*Aside*] This is his pardon, purchased by such sin
For which the pardoner himself is in.
Hence hath offence his quick celerity,
When it is born in high authority.
When vice makes mercy, mercy's so extended,
That for the fault's love is the offender friended.
Now, sir, what news?

PROVOST: I told you. Lord Angelo, belike thinking me remiss in mine office, awakens me with this unwonted putting-on; methinks strangely, for he hath not used it before.

DUKE VINCENTIO: Pray you, let's hear.

PROVOST: [*Reads*]

'Whatsoever you may hear to the contrary, let Claudio be executed by four of the clock; and in the afternoon Barnardine: for my better satisfaction, let me have Claudio's head sent me by five. Let this be duly performed; with a thought that more depends on it than we must yet deliver. Thus fail not to do your office, as you will answer it at your peril.'

What say you to this, sir?

DUKE VINCENTIO: What is that Barnardine who is to be executed in the afternoon?

PROVOST: A Bohemian born, but here nursed up and bred; one that is a prisoner nine years old.

DUKE VINCENTIO: How came it that the absent Duke had not either delivered him to his liberty or executed him? I have heard it was ever his manner to do so.

PROVOST: His friends still wrought reprieves for him; and, indeed, his fact, till now in the government of Lord Angelo, came not to an undoubtful proof.

DUKE VINCENTIO: It is now apparent?

PROVOST: Most manifest, and not denied by himself.

DUKE VINCENTIO: Hath he born himself penitently in prison? How seems he to be touched?

PROVOST: A man that apprehends death no more dreadfully but as a drunken sleep; careless, reckless, and fearless of what's past, present, or to come; insensible of mortality, and desperately mortal.

DUKE VINCENTIO: He wants advice.

PROVOST: He will hear none. He hath evermore had the liberty of the prison; give him leave to escape hence, he would not; drunk many times a day, if not many days entirely drunk. We have very oft awaked him, as if to carry him to execution, and showed him a seeming warrant for it: it hath not moved him at all.

DUKE VINCENTIO: More of him anon. There is written in your brow, Provost, honesty and constancy: if I read it not truly, my ancient skill beguiles me; but, in the boldness of my cunning, I will lay myself in hazard. Claudio, whom here you have warrant to execute, is no greater forfeit to the law than Angelo who hath sentenced him. To make you understand this in a manifested effect, I crave but four days' respite; for the which you are to do me both a present and a dangerous courtesy.

PROVOST: Pray, sir, in what?

DUKE VINCENTIO: In the delaying death.

PROVOST: A lack, how may I do it, having the hour limited, and an express command, under penalty, to deliver his head in the view of Angelo? I may make my case as Claudio's, to cross this in the smallest.

DUKE VINCENTIO: By the vow of mine order I warrant you, if my instructions may be your guide. Let this Barnardine be this morning executed, and his head born to Angelo.

PROVOST: Angelo hath seen them both, and will discover the favour.

DUKE VINCENTIO: O, death's a great disguiser; and you may add to it. Shave the head, and tie the beard; and say it was the desire of the penitent to be so bared before his death. You know the course is common. If any thing fall to you upon this, more than thanks and good fortune, by the saint whom I profess, I will plead against it with my life.

PROVOST: Pardon me, good father; it is against my oath.

DUKE VINCENTIO: Were you sworn to the Duke, or to the deputy?

PROVOST: To him, and to his substitutes.

DUKE VINCENTIO: You will think you have made no offence, if the Duke avouch the justice of your dealing?

PROVOST: But what likelihood is in that?

DUKE VINCENTIO: Not a resemblance, but a certainty. Yet since I see you fearful, that neither my coat, integrity, nor persuasion can with ease attempt you, I will go further than I meant, to pluck all fears out of you. Look you, sir, here is the hand and seal of the Duke. You know the character, I doubt not; and the signet is not strange to you.

PROVOST: I know them both.

DUKE VINCENTIO: The contents of this is the return of the Duke. You shall anon over-read it at your pleasure; where you shall find, within these two days he will be here. This is a thing that Angelo knows not; for he this very day receives letters of strange tenor; perchance of the Duke's death; perchance entering into some monastery; but, by chance, nothing of what is writ. Look, the unfolding star calls up the shepherd. Put not yourself into amazement how these things should be: all difficulties are but easy when they are known. Call your executioner, and off with Barnardine's head. I will give him a present shrift and advise him for a better place. Yet you are amazed; but this shall absolutely resolve you. Come away; it is almost clear dawn.

Exeunt

SCENE III—*The prison*

Enter POMPEY

POMPEY: I am as well acquainted here as I was in our house of profession; one would think it were Mistress Overdone's own house, for here be many of her old customers. First, here's young Master Rash; he's in for a commodity of brown paper and old ginger, nine score and seventeen pounds; of which he made five marks, ready money: marry, then ginger was not much in request, for the old women were all dead. Then is there here one Master Caper, at the suit of Master Three-pile the mercer, for some four suits of peach-coloured satin, which now peaches him a beggar. Then have we here young Dizy, and young Master Deepvow, and Master Copperspur, and Master Starvelackey the rapier and dagger man, and young Dropheir that killed lusty Pudding, and Master Forthlight the tilter, and brave Master Shootie the great traveller, and wild Half-can that stabbed Pots, and, I think, forty more—all great doers in our trade, and are now 'for the Lord's sake'.

Enter ABHORSON

ABHORSON: Sirrah, bring Barnardine hither.

POMPEY: Master Barnardine! You must rise and be hanged. Master Barnardine!

ABHORSON: What, ho, Barnardine!

BARNARDINE: [*Within*] A pox o' your throats! Who makes that noise there? What are you?

POMPEY: Your friends, sir; the hangman. You must be so good, sir, to rise and be put to death.

BARNARDINE: [*Within*] Away, you rogue, away; I am sleepy.

ABHORSON: Tell him he must awake, and that quickly too.

POMPEY: Pray, Master Barnardine, awake till you are executed, and sleep afterwards.

ABHORSON: Go in to him, and fetch him out.

POMPEY: He is coming, sir, he is coming; I hear his straw rustle.

ABHORSON: Is the axe upon the block, sirrah?

POMPEY: Very ready, sir.

Enter BARNARDINE

BARNARDINE: How now, Abhorson? what's the news with you?

ABHORSON: Truly, sir, I would desire you to clap into your prayers; for, look you, the warrant's come.

BARNARDINE: You rogue, I have been drinking all night; I am not fitted for 't.

POMPEY: O, the better, sir! For he that drinks all night, and is hanged betimes in the morning, may sleep the sounder all the next day.

ABHORSON: Look you, sir; here comes your ghostly father. Do we jest now, think you?

Enter DUKE VINCENTIO disguised as before

DUKE VINCENTIO: Sir, induced by my charity, and hearing how hastily you are to depart, I am come to advise you, comfort you and pray with you.

BARNARDINE: Friar, not I; I have been drinking hard all night, and I will have more time to prepare me, or they shall beat out my brains with billets. I will not consent to die this day, that's certain.

DUKE VINCENTIO: O, sir, you must; and therefore I beseech you

Look forward on the journey you shall go.

BARNARDINE: I swear I will not die to-day for any man's persuasion.

DUKE VINCENTIO: But hear you.

BARNARDINE: Not a word: if you have any thing to say to me, come to my ward; for thence will not I to-day.

Exit

DUKE VINCENTIO: Unfit to live or die. O gravel heart!

After him, fellows; bring him to the block.

Exeunt ABHORSON and POMPEY

Re-enter Provost

PROVOST: Now, sir, how do you find the prisoner?

DUKE VINCENTIO: A creature unprepared, unmeet for death;

And to transport him in the mind he is
Were damnable.

PROVOST: Here in the prison, father,

There died this morning of a cruel fever
One Ragozine, a most notorious pirate,
A man of Claudio's years; his beard and head
Just of his colour. What if we do omit
This reprobate till he were well inclined,
And satisfy the deputy with the visage
Of Ragozine, more like to Claudio?

DUKE VINCENTIO: O, 'tis an accident that heaven provides!

Dispatch it presently; the hour draws on
Prefix'd by Angelo. See this be done,

And sent according to command; whiles I
Persuade this rude wretch willingly to die.

PROVOST: This shall be done, good father, presently.
But Barnardine must die this afternoon;
And how shall we continue Claudio,
To save me from the danger that might come
If he were known alive?

DUKE VINCENTIO: Let this be done.
Put them in secret holds, both Barnardine and Claudio.
Ere twice the sun hath made his journal greeting
To the under generation, you shall find
Your safety manifested.

PROVOST: I am your free dependant.

DUKE VINCENTIO: Quick, dispatch, and send the head to Angelo.

Exit PROVOST

Now will I write letters to Angelo—
The provost, he shall bear them, whose contents
Shall witness to him I am near at home,
And that, by great injunctions, I am bound
To enter publicly. Him I'll desire
To meet me at the consecrated fount
A league below the city; and from thence,
By cold gradation and well-balanced form,
We shall proceed with Angelo.

Re-enter PROVOST

PROVOST: Here is the head; I'll carry it myself.

DUKE VINCENTIO: Convenient is it. Make a swift return;
For I would commune with you of such things
That want no ear but yours.

PROVOST: I'll make all speed.

Exit

ISABELLA: [*Within*] Peace, ho, be here!

DUKE VINCENTIO: The tongue of Isabel. She's come to know
If yet her brother's pardon be come hither;
But I will keep her ignorant of her good,
To make her heavenly comforts of despair,
When it is least expected.

Enter ISABELLA

ISABELLA: Ho, by your leave!

DUKE VINCENTIO: Good morning to you, fair and gracious daughter.

ISABELLA: The better, given me by so holy a man.
Hath yet the deputy sent my brother's pardon?

DUKE VINCENTIO: He hath released him, Isabel, from the world:
His head is off and sent to Angelo.

ISABELLA: Nay, but it is not so.

DUKE VINCENTIO: It is no other. Show your wisdom, daughter, in your close patience.

ISABELLA: O, I will to him and pluck out his eyes!

DUKE VINCENTIO: You shall not be admitted to his sight.

ISABELLA: Unhappy Claudio! Wretched Isabel!
Injurious world! Most damned Angelo!

DUKE VINCENTIO: This nor hurts him nor profits you a jot;
Forbear it therefore; give your cause to heaven.
Mark what I say, which you shall find
By every syllable a faithful verity.
The Duke comes home to-morrow; nay, dry your eyes;
One of our convent, and his confessor,
Gives me this instance. Already he hath carried
Notice to Escalus and Angelo,
Who do prepare to meet him at the gates,
There to give up their power. If you can, pace your wisdom
In that good path that I would wish it go,
And you shall have your bosom on this wretch,
Grace of the Duke, revenges to your heart,
And general honour.

ISABELLA: I am directed by you.

DUKE VINCENTIO: This letter, then, to Friar Peter give;
'Tis that he sent me of the duke's return.
Say, by this token, I desire his company
At Mariana's house to-night. Her cause and yours
I'll perfect him withal, and he shall bring you
Before the duke, and to the head of Angelo
Accuse him home and home. For my poor self,
I am combined by a sacred vow
And shall be absent. Wend you with this letter.
Command these fretting waters from your eyes
With a light heart; trust not my holy order,
If I pervert your course. Who's here?

Enter LUCIO

LUCIO: Good even. Friar, where's the provost?

DUKE VINCENTIO: Not within, sir.

LUCIO: O pretty Isabella, I am pale at mine heart to see thine eyes so red: thou must be patient. I am fain to dine and sup with water and bran; I dare not for my head fill my belly; one fruitful meal would set me to't. But they say the Duke will be here to-morrow. By my troth, Isabel, I loved thy brother. if the old fantastical duke of dark corners had been at home, he had lived.

Exit ISABELLA

DUKE VINCENTIO: Sir, the Duke is marvellous little beholding to your reports; but the best is, he lives not in them.

LUCIO: Friar, thou knowest not the duke so well as I do: he's a better woodman than thou takest him for.

DUKE VINCENTIO: Well, you'll answer this one day. Fare ye well.

LUCIO: Nay, tarry; I'll go along with thee
I can tell thee pretty tales of the Duke.

DUKE VINCENTIO: You have told me too many of him already, sir, if they be true; if not true, none were enough.

LUCIO: I was once before him for getting a wench with child.

DUKE VINCENTIO: Did you such a thing?

LUCIO: Yes, marry, did I but I was fain to forswear it; they would else have married me to the rotten medlar.

DUKE VINCENTIO: Sir, your company is fairer than honest. Rest you well.

LUCIO: By my troth, I'll go with thee to the lane's end: if bawdy talk offend you, we'll have very little of it. Nay, friar, I am a kind of burr; I shall stick.

Exeunt

SCENE IV—*Angelo's house*

Enter ANGELO and ESCALUS

ESCALUS: Every letter he hath writ hath disvouched other.

ANGELO: In most uneven and distracted manner. His actions show much like to madness: pray heaven his wisdom be not tainted! And why meet him at the gates, and redeliver our authorities there

ESCALUS: I guess not.

ANGELO: And why should we proclaim it in an hour before his entering, that if any crave redress of injustice, they should exhibit their petitions in the street?

ESCALUS: He shows his reason for that: to have a dispatch of complaints, and to deliver us from devices hereafter, which shall then have no power to stand against us.

ANGELO: Well, I beseech you, let it be proclaimed Betimes i' the morn; I'll call you at your house. Give notice to such men of sort and suit as are to meet him.

ESCALUS: I shall, sir. Fare you well.

ANGELO: Good night.

Exit ESCALUS

This deed unshapes me quite, makes me unpregnant
And dull to all proceedings. A deflower'd maid!
And by an eminent body that enforced
The law against it! But that her tender shame
Will not proclaim against her maiden loss,
How might she tongue me! Yet reason dares her no;
For my authority bears of a credent bulk,
That no particular scandal once can touch
But it confounds the breather. He should have lived,
Save that riotous youth, with dangerous sense,
Might in the times to come have ta'en revenge,
By so receiving a dishonour'd life
With ransom of such shame. Would yet he had lived!
A lack, when once our grace we have forgot,
Nothing goes right; we would, and we would not.

Exit

SCENE V—*Fields without the town*

Enter DUKE VINCENTIO in his own habit, and FRIAR PETER

DUKE VINCENTIO: These letters at fit time deliver me.

Giving letters

The provost knows our purpose and our plot.
The matter being afoot, keep your instruction,
And hold you ever to our special drift;
Though sometimes you do blench from this to that,
As cause doth minister. Go call at Flavius' house,

And tell him where I stay: give the like notice
To Valentinus, Rowland, and to Crassus,
And bid them bring the trumpets to the gate;
But send me Flavius first.

FRIAR PETER: It shall be speeded well.

Exit FRIAR

Enter VARRIUS

DUKE VINCENTIO: I thank thee, Varrius; thou hast made good haste.
Come, we will walk. There's other of our friends
Will greet us here anon, my gentle Varrius.

Exeunt

SCENE VI—*Street near the city gate*

Enter ISABELLA and MARIANA

ISABELLA: To speak so indirectly I am loath:
I would say the truth; but to accuse him so,
That is your part: yet I am advised to do it;
He says, to veil full purpose.

MARIANA: Be ruled by him.

ISABELLA: Besides, he tells me that, if peradventure
He speak against me on the adverse side,
I should not think it strange; for 'tis a physic
That's bitter to sweet end.

MARIANA: I would Friar Peter—

ISABELLA: O, peace! the friar is come.

Enter FRIAR PETER

FRIAR PETER: Come, I have found you out a stand most fit,
Where you may have such vantage on the Duke,
He shall not pass you. Twice have the trumpets sounded;
The generous and gravest citizens
Have hent the gates, and very near upon
The Duke is entering: therefore, hence, away!

Exeunt

Act V

Scene I—*The city gate*

MARIANA veiled, ISABELLA, and FRIAR PETER, at their stand. Enter DUKE VINCENTIO, VARRIUS, Lords, ANGELO, ESCALUS, LUCIO, Provost, Officers, and Citizens, at several doors

DUKE VINCENTIO: My very worthy cousin, fairly met!
Our old and faithful friend, we are glad to see you.

ANGELO: Happy return be to your royal

ESCALUS: Grace!

DUKE VINCENTIO: Many and hearty thankings to you both.
We have made inquiry of you; and we hear
Such goodness of your justice, that our soul
Cannot but yield you forth to public thanks,
Forerunning more requital.

ANGELO: You make my bonds still greater.

DUKE VINCENTIO: O, your desert speaks loud; and I should wrong it,
To lock it in the wards of covert bosom,
When it deserves, with characters of brass,
A forted residence 'gainst the tooth of time
And razure of oblivion. Give me your hand,
And let the subject see, to make them know
That outward courtesies would fain proclaim
Favours that keep within. Come, Escalus,
You must walk by us on our other hand;
And good supporters are you.

FRIAR PETER and ISABELLA come forward

FRIAR PETER: Now is your time; speak loud and kneel before him.

ISABELLA: Justice, O royal Duke! Vail your regard
Upon a wrong'd, I would fain have said, a maid!
O worthy prince, dishonour not your eye
By throwing it on any other object
Till you have heard me in my true complaint
And given me justice, justice, justice, justice!

DUKE VINCENTIO: Relate your wrongs. In what? by whom? be brief.
Here is Lord Angelo shall give you justice;
Reveal yourself to him.

ISABELLA: O worthy Duke,
You bid me seek redemption of the devil:
Hear me yourself; for that which I must speak
Must either punish me, not being believed,
Or wring redress from you. Hear me, O hear me, here!

ANGELO: My lord, her wits, I fear me, are not firm;
She hath been a suitor to me for her brother
Cut off by course of justice—

ISABELLA: By course of justice!

ANGELO: And she will speak most bitterly and strange.

ISABELLA: Most strange, but yet most truly, will I speak.
That Angelo's forsworn; is it not strange?
That Angelo's a murderer; is 't not strange?
That Angelo is an adulterous thief,
An hypocrite, a virgin-violator;
Is it not strange and strange?

DUKE VINCENTIO: Nay, it is ten times strange.

ISABELLA: It is not truer he is Angelo
Than this is all as true as it is strange;
Nay, it is ten times true; for truth is truth
To the end of reckoning.

DUKE VINCENTIO: Away with her! Poor soul,
She speaks this in the infirmity of sense.

ISABELLA: O prince, I conjure thee, as thou believest
There is another comfort than this world,
That thou neglect me not, with that opinion
That I am touch'd with madness! Make not impossible
That which but seems unlike: 'tis not impossible
But one, the wicked'st caitiff on the ground,

May seem as shy, as grave, as just, as absolute
As Angelo; even so may Angelo,
In all his dressings, characts, titles, forms,
Be an arch-villain; Believe it, royal Prince:
If he be less, he's nothing; but he's more,
Had I more name for badness.

DUKE VINCENTIO: By mine honesty,
If she be mad, as I believe no other,
Her madness hath the oddest frame of sense,
Such a dependency of thing on thing,
As e'er I heard in madness.

ISABELLA: O gracious Duke,
Harp not on that, nor do not banish reason
For inequality; but let your reason serve
To make the truth appear where it seems hid,
And hide the false seems true.

DUKE VINCENTIO: Many that are not mad
Have, sure, more lack of reason. What would you say?

ISABELLA: I am the sister of one Claudio,
Condemn'd upon the act of fornication
To lose his head; condemn'd by Angelo:
I, in probation of a sisterhood,
Was sent to by my brother; one Lucio
As then the messenger—

LUCIO: That's I, an't like your Grace.
I came to her from Claudio, and desired her
To try her gracious fortune with Lord Angelo
For her poor brother's pardon.

ISABELLA: That's he, indeed.

DUKE VINCENTIO: You were not bid to speak.

LUCIO: No, my good lord;
Nor wish'd to hold my peace.

DUKE VINCENTIO: I wish you now, then;
Pray you, take note of it: and when you have
A business for yourself, pray heaven you then
Be perfect.

LUCIO: I warrant your honour.

DUKE VINCENTIO: The warrants for yourself; take heed to't.

ISABELLA: This gentleman told somewhat of my tale.

LUCIO: Right.

DUKE VINCENTIO: It may be right; but you are i' the wrong
To speak before your time. Proceed.

ISABELLA: I went
To this pernicious caitiff deputy.

DUKE VINCENTIO: That's somewhat madly spoken.

ISABELLA: Pardon it;
The phrase is to the matter.

DUKE VINCENTIO: Mended again. The matter—proceed.

ISABELLA: In brief—to set the needless process by,
How I persuaded, how I pray'd, and kneel'd,
How he refell'd me, and how I replied,
For this was of much length, the vile conclusion
I now begin with grief and shame to utter:
He would not, but by gift of my chaste body
To his concupiscible intemperate lust,
Release my brother; and, after much debatement,
My sisterly remorse confutes mine honour,
And I did yield to him. But the next morn betimes,
His purpose surfeiting, he sends a warrant
For my poor brother's head.

DUKE VINCENTIO: This is most likely!

ISABELLA: O, that it were as like as it is true!

DUKE VINCENTIO: By heaven, fond wretch, thou know'st not what thou speak'st,
Or else thou art suborn'd against his honour
In hateful practice. First, his integrity
Stands without blemish. Next, it imports no reason
That with such vehemency he should pursue
Faults proper to himself: if he had so offended,
He would have weigh'd thy brother by himself
And not have cut him off. Some one hath set you on:
Confess the truth, and say by whose advice
Thou camest here to complain.

ISABELLA: And is this all?
Then, O you blessed ministers above,
Keep me in patience, and with ripen'd time
Unfold the evil which is here wrapt up
In countenance! Heaven shield your grace from woe,
As I, thus wrong'd, hence unbelieved go!

DUKE VINCENTIO: I know you'ld fain be gone. An officer!
To prison with her! Shall we thus permit
A blasting and a scandalous breath to fall

On him so near us? This needs must be a practise.
Who knew of Your intent and coming hither?
ISABELLA: One that I would were here, Friar Lodowick.
DUKE VINCENTIO: A ghostly father, belike. Who knows that Lodowick?
LUCIO: My lord, I know him; 'tis a meddling friar.
I do not like the man: had he been lay, my lord
For certain words he spake against your Grace
In your retirement, I had swinged him soundly.
DUKE VINCENTIO: Words against me? This is a good friar, belike!
And to set on this wretched woman here
Against our substitute! Let this friar be found.
LUCIO: But yesternight, my lord, she and that friar,
I saw them at the prison: a saucy friar,
A very scurvy fellow.
FRIAR PETER: Blessed be your royal Grace!
I have stood by, my lord, and I have heard
Your royal ear abused. First, hath this woman
Most wrongfully accused your substitute;
Who is as free from touch or soil with her
As she from one ungot.
DUKE VINCENTIO: We did believe no less.
Know you that Friar Lodowick that she speaks of?
FRIAR PETER: I know him for a man divine and holy;
Not scurvy, nor a temporary meddler,
As he's reported by this gentleman;
And, on my trust, a man that never yet
Did, as he vouches, misreport your Grace.
LUCIO: My lord, most villanously; believe it.
FRIAR PETER: Well, he in time may come to clear himself;
But at this instant he is sick my lord,
Of a strange fever. Upon his mere request—
Being come to knowledge that there was complaint
Intended 'gainst Lord Angelo, came I hither
To speak, as from his mouth, what he doth know
Is true and false; and what he with his oath
And all probation will make up full clear,
Whensoever he's convented. First, for this woman.
To justify this worthy nobleman,
So vulgarly and personally accused—
Her shall you hear disproved to her eyes,
Till she herself confess it.
DUKE VINCENTIO: Good friar, let's hear it.

ISABELLA is carried off guarded; and MARIANA comes forward

Do you not smile at this, Lord Angelo?
O heaven, the vanity of wretched fools!
Give us some seats. Come, cousin Angelo;
In this I'll be impartial; be you judge
Of your own cause. Is this the witness, friar?
First, let her show her face, and after speak.
MARIANA: Pardon, my lord; I will not show my face
Until my husband bid me.
DUKE VINCENTIO: What, are you married?
MARIANA: No, my lord.
DUKE VINCENTIO: Are you a maid?
MARIANA: No, my lord.
DUKE VINCENTIO: A widow, then?
MARIANA: Neither, my lord.
DUKE VINCENTIO: Why, you are nothing then: neither maid, widow, nor wife?
LUCIO: My lord, she may be a punk; for many of them are neither maid, widow, nor wife.
DUKE VINCENTIO: Silence that fellow: I would he had some cause
To prattle for himself.
LUCIO: Well, my lord.
MARIANA: My lord; I do confess I ne'er was married;
And I confess besides I am no maid.
I have known my husband; yet my husband
Knows not that ever he knew me.
LUCIO: He was drunk then, my lord: it can be no better.
DUKE VINCENTIO: For the benefit of silence, would thou wert so too!
LUCIO: Well, my lord.
DUKE VINCENTIO: This is no witness for Lord Angelo.
MARIANA: Now I come to't my lord:
She that accuses him of fornication,
In self-same manner doth accuse my husband,
And charges him my lord, with such a time
When I'll depose I had him in mine arms
With all the effect of love.
ANGELO: Charges she more than me?
MARIANA: Not that I know.

DUKE VINCENTIO: No? you say your husband.
MARIANA: Why, just, my lord, and that is Angelo,
Who thinks he knows that he ne'er knew my body,
But knows he thinks that he knows Isabel's.
ANGELO: This is a strange abuse. Let's see thy face.
MARIANA: My husband bids me; now I will unmask. (*Unveiling*)
This is that face, thou cruel Angelo,
Which once thou sworest was worth the looking on;
This is the hand which, with a vow'd contract,
Was fast belock'd in thine; this is the body
That took away the match from Isabel,
And did supply thee at thy garden-house
In her imagined person.
DUKE VINCENTIO: Know you this woman?
LUCIO: Carnally, she says.
DUKE VINCENTIO: Sirrah, no more!
LUCIO: Enough, my lord.
ANGELO: My lord, I must confess I know this woman;
And five years since there was some speech of marriage
Betwixt myself and her; which was broke off,
Partly for that her promised proportions
Came short of composition, but in chief
For that her reputation was disvalued
In levity: since which time of five years
I never spake with her, saw her, nor heard from her,
Upon my faith and honour.
MARIANA: Noble Prince,
As there comes light from heaven and words from breath,
As there is sense in truth and truth in virtue,
I am affianced this man's wife as strongly
As words could make up vows: and, my good lord,
But Tuesday night last gone in's garden-house
He knew me as a wife. As this is true,
Let me in safety raise me from my knees,
Or else for ever be confixed here,
A marble monument!
ANGELO: I did but smile till now:
Now, good my lord, give me the scope of justice
My patience here is touch'd. I do perceive
These poor informal women are no more
But instruments of some more mightier member
That sets them on: let me have way, my lord,
To find this practice out.
DUKE VINCENTIO: Ay, with my heart
And punish them to your height of pleasure.
Thou foolish friar, and thou pernicious woman,
Compact with her that's gone, think'st thou thy oaths,
Though they would swear down each particular saint,
Were testimonies against his worth and credit
That's seal'd in approbation? You, Lord Escalus,
Sit with my cousin; lend him your kind pains
To find out this abuse, whence 'tis derived.
There is another friar that set them on;
Let him be sent for.
FRIAR PETER: Would he were here, my lord! For he indeed
Hath set the women on to this complaint:
Your provost knows the place where he abides
And he may fetch him.
DUKE VINCENTIO: Go do it instantly.

Exit Provost

And you, my noble and well-warranted cousin,
Whom it concerns to hear this matter forth,
Do with your injuries as seems you best,
In any chastisement: I for a while will leave you;
But stir not you till you have well determined
Upon these slanderers.
ESCALUS: My lord, we'll do it throughly.

Exit DUKE

Signior Lucio, did not you say you knew that
Friar Lodowick to be a dishonest person?
LUCIO: 'Cucullus non facit monachum:' honest in nothing but in his clothes; and one that hath spoke most villanous speeches of the Duke.
ESCALUS: We shall entreat you to abide here till he come and enforce them against him: we shall find this friar a notable fellow.
LUCIO: As any in Vienna, on my word.
ESCALUS: Call that same Isabel here once again; I would speak with her.

Exit an Attendant

Pray you, my lord, give me leave to question; you shall see how I'll handle her.
LUCIO: Not better than he, by her own report.

ESCALUS: Say you?

LUCIO: Marry, sir, I think, if you handled her privately, she would sooner confess: perchance, publicly, she'll be ashamed.

ESCALUS: I will go darkly to work with her.

LUCIO: That's the way; for women are light at midnight.

Re-enter Officers with ISABELLA; and Provost with the DUKE VINCENTIO in his friar's habit

ESCALUS: Come on, mistress: here's a gentlewoman denies all that you have said.

LUCIO: My lord, here comes the rascal I spoke of; here with the Provost.

ESCALUS: In very good time: speak not you to him till we call upon you.

LUCIO: Mum.

ESCALUS: Come, sir: did you set these women on to slander Lord Angelo? they have confessed you did.

DUKE VINCENTIO: 'Tis false.

ESCALUS: How! know you where you are?

DUKE VINCENTIO: Respect to your great place! and let the devil
Be sometime honour'd for his burning throne!
Where is the Duke? 'tis he should hear me speak.

ESCALUS: The Duke's in us; and we will hear you speak:
Look you speak justly.

DUKE VINCENTIO: Boldly, at least. But, O, poor souls,
Come you to seek the lamb here of the fox?
Good night to your redress! Is the Duke gone?
Then is your cause gone too. The Duke's unjust,
Thus to retort your manifest appeal,
And put your trial in the villain's mouth
Which here you come to accuse.

LUCIO: This is the rascal; this is he I spoke of.

ESCALUS: Why, thou unreverend and unhallow'd friar,
Is't not enough thou hast suborn'd these women
To accuse this worthy man, but, in foul mouth,
And in the witness of his proper ear,
To call him villain? and then to glance from him
To the Duke himself, to tax him with injustice?
Take him hence; to the rack with him! We'll touse you
Joint by joint, but we will know his purpose.
What 'unjust'!

DUKE VINCENTIO: Be not so hot; the Duke
Dare no more stretch this finger of mine than he
Dare rack his own: his subject am I not,
Nor here provincial. My business in this state
Made me a looker on here in Vienna,
Where I have seen corruption boil and bubble
Till it o'er-run the stew; laws for all faults,
But faults so countenanced, that the strong statutes
Stand like the forfeits in a barber's shop,
As much in mock as mark.

ESCALUS: Slander to the state! Away with him to prison!

ANGELO: What can you vouch against him, Signior Lucio?
Is this the man that you did tell us of?

LUCIO: 'Tis he, my lord. Come hither, goodman baldpate: do you know me?

DUKE VINCENTIO: I remember you, sir, by the sound of your voice: I met you at the prison, in the absence of the Duke.

LUCIO: O, did you so? And do you remember what you said of the Duke?

DUKE VINCENTIO: Most notedly, sir.

LUCIO: Do you so, sir? And was the Duke a fleshmonger, a fool, and a coward, as you then reported him to be?

DUKE VINCENTIO: You must, sir, change persons with me, ere you make that my report: you, indeed, spoke so of him; and much more, much worse.

LUCIO: O thou damnable fellow! Did not I pluck thee by the nose for thy speeches?

DUKE VINCENTIO: I protest I love the Duke as I love myself.

ANGELO: Hark, how the villain would close now, after his treasonable abuses!

ESCALUS: Such a fellow is not to be talked withal.
Away with him to prison! Where is the provost?
Away with him to prison! lay bolts enough upon him: let him speak no more. Away with those giglots too, and with the other confederate companion!

The Provost lays hands on the Duke

DUKE VINCENTIO: [*To Provost*] Stay, sir; stay awhile.

ANGELO: What, resists he? Help him, Lucio.

LUCIO: Come, sir; come, sir; come, sir; foh, sir! Why, you bald-pated, lying rascal, you must be hooded, must you? Show your knave's visage, with a pox to you! show your sheep-biting face, and be hanged an hour! Will't not off?

Pulls off the friar's hood, and discovers DUKE VINCENTIO

DUKE VINCENTIO: Thou art the first knave that e'er madest a duke.
First, Provost, let me bail these gentle three. [*To Lucio*] Sneak not away, sir; for the friar and you
Must have a word anon. Lay hold on him.

LUCIO: This may prove worse than hanging.

DUKE VINCENTIO: [*To Escalus*] What you have spoke I pardon; sit you down:
We'll borrow place of him. [*To Angelo*] Sir, by your leave.
Hast thou or word, or wit, or impudence,
That yet can do thee office? If thou hast,
Rely upon it till my tale be heard,
And hold no longer out.

ANGELO: O my dread lord,
I should be guiltier than my guiltiness,
To think I can be undiscernible,
When I perceive your grace, like power divine,
Hath look'd upon my passes. Then, good Prince,
No longer session hold upon my shame,
But let my trial be mine own confession:
Immediate sentence then and sequent death
Is all the grace I beg.

DUKE VINCENTIO: Come hither, Mariana.
Say, wast thou e'er contracted to this woman?

ANGELO: I was, my lord.

DUKE VINCENTIO: Go take her hence, and marry her instantly.
Do you the office, friar; which consummate,
Return him here again. Go with him, provost.

Exeunt ANGELO, MARIANA, FRIAR PETER and Provost

ESCALUS: My lord, I am more amazed at his dishonor
Than at the strangeness of it.

DUKE VINCENTIO: Come hither, Isabel.
Your friar is now your prince: as I was then
Advertising and holy to your business,
Not changing heart with habit, I am still
Attorney'd at your service.

ISABELLA: O, give me pardon,
That I, your vassal, have employ'd and pain'd
Your unknown sovereignty!

DUKE VINCENTIO: You are pardon'd, Isabel:
And now, dear maid, be you as free to us.
Your brother's death, I know, sits at your heart;
And you may marvel why I obscured myself,
Labouring to save his life, and would not rather
Make rash remonstrance of my hidden power
Than let him so be lost. O most kind maid,
It was the swift celerity of his death,
Which I did think with slower foot came on,
That brain'd my purpose. But, peace be with him!
That life is better life, past fearing death,
Than that which lives to fear: make it your comfort,
So happy is your brother.

ISABELLA: I do, my lord.

Re-enter ANGELO, MARIANA, FRIAR PETER, and Provost

DUKE VINCENTIO: For this new-married man approaching here,
Whose salt imagination yet hath wrong'd
Your well defended honour, you must pardon
For Mariana's sake; but as he adjudged your brother—
Being criminal, in double violation
Of sacred chastity and of promise-breach
Thereon dependent, for your brother's life—
The very mercy of the law cries out
Most audible, even from his proper tongue,
'An Angelo for Claudio, death for death!'
Haste still pays haste, and leisure answers leisure;
Like doth quit like, and Measure still For Measure.
Then, Angelo, thy fault's thus manifested;
Which, though thou wouldst deny, denies thee vantage.
We do condemn thee to the very block
Where Claudio stoop'd to death, and with like haste.
Away with him!

MARIANA: O my most gracious lord,
I hope you will not mock me with a husband.

DUKE VINCENTIO: It is your husband mock'd you with a husband.
Consenting to the safeguard of your honour,
I thought your marriage fit; else imputation,

For that he knew you, might reproach your life
And choke your good to come; for his possessions,
Although by confiscation they are ours,
We do instate and widow you withal,
To buy you a better husband.

MARIANA: O my dear lord,
I crave no other, nor no better man.

DUKE VINCENTIO: Never crave him; we are definitive.

MARIANA: Gentle my liege—

Kneeling

DUKE VINCENTIO: You do but lose your labour.
Away with him to death! (*To Lucio*) Now, sir, to you.

MARIANA: O my good lord! Sweet Isabel, take my part;
Lend me your knees, and all my life to come
I'll lend you all my life to do you service.

DUKE VINCENTIO: Against all sense you do importune her:
Should she kneel down in mercy of this fact,
Her brother's ghost his paved bed would break,
And take her hence in horror.

MARIANA: Isabel,
Sweet Isabel, do yet but kneel by me;
Hold up your hands, say nothing; I'll speak all.
They say, best men are moulded out of faults;
And, for the most, become much more the better
For being a little bad: so may my husband.
O Isabel, will you not lend a knee?

DUKE VINCENTIO: He dies for Claudio's death.

ISABELLA: Most bounteous sir,

Kneeling

Look, if it please you, on this man condemn'd,
As if my brother lived: I partly think
A due sincerity govern'd his deeds,
Till he did look on me: since it is so,
Let him not die. My brother had but justice,
In that he did the thing for which he died:
For Angelo,
His act did not o'ertake his bad intent,
And must be buried but as an intent
That perish'd by the way: thoughts are no subjects;
Intents but merely thoughts.

MARIANA: Merely, my lord.

DUKE VINCENTIO: Your suit's unprofitable; stand up, I say.
I have bethought me of another fault.
Provost, how came it Claudio was beheaded
At an unusual hour?

PROVOST: It was commanded so.

DUKE VINCENTIO: Had you a special warrant for the deed?

PROVOST: No, my good lord; it was by private message.

DUKE VINCENTIO: For which I do discharge you of your office:
Give up your keys.

PROVOST: Pardon me, noble lord:
I thought it was a fault, but knew it not;
Yet did repent me, after more advice;
For testimony whereof, one in the prison,
That should by private order else have died,
I have reserved alive.

DUKE VINCENTIO: What's he?

PROVOST: His name is Barnardine.

DUKE VINCENTIO: I would thou hadst done so by Claudio.
Go fetch him hither; let me look upon him.

Exit PROVOST

ESCALUS: I am sorry one so learned and so wise
As you, Lord Angelo, have still appear'd,
Should slip so grossly, both in the heat of blood.
And lack of temper'd judgment afterward.

ANGELO: I am sorry that such sorrow I procure:
And so deep sticks it in my penitent heart
That I crave death more willingly than mercy;
'Tis my deserving, and I do entreat it.

Re-enter PROVOST, with BARNARDINE, CLAUDIO (muffled), and JULIET

DUKE VINCENTIO: Which is that Barnardine?

PROVOST: This, my lord.

DUKE VINCENTIO: There was a friar told me of this man.
Sirrah, thou art said to have a stubborn soul.
That apprehends no further than this world,
And squarest thy life according. Thou'rt condemn'd:
But, for those earthly faults, I quit them all;
And pray thee take this mercy to provide
For better times to come. Friar, advise him;

I leave him to your hand. What muffled fellow's that?

PROVOST: This is another prisoner that I saved.

Who should have died when Claudio lost his head;

As like almost to Claudio as himself.

Unmuffles CLAUDIO

DUKE VINCENTIO: [*To Isabella*] If he be like your brother, for his sake

Is he pardon'd; and, for your lovely sake,
Give me your hand and say you will be mine.
He is my brother too: but fitter time for that.
By this Lord Angelo perceives he's safe;
Methinks I see a quickening in his eye.
Well, Angelo, your evil quits you well:
Look that you love your wife; her worth worth yours.
I find an apt remission in myself;
And yet here's one in place I cannot pardon.
[*To Lucio*] You, sirrah, that knew me for a fool, a coward,
One all of luxury, an ass, a madman;
Wherein have I so deserved of you,
That you extol me thus?

LUCIO: Faith, my lord. I spoke it but according to the trick. If you will hang me for it, you may; but I had rather it would please you I might be whipt.

DUKE VINCENTIO: Whipt first, sir, and hanged after.

Proclaim it, Provost, round about the city.
Is any woman wrong'd by this lewd fellow,
As I have heard him swear himself there's one
Whom he begot with child, let her appear,
And he shall marry her: the nuptial finish'd,
Let him be whipt and hang'd.

LUCIO: I beseech your highness, do not marry me to a whore. Your highness said even now, I made you a duke: good my lord, do not recompense me in making me a cuckold.

DUKE VINCENTIO: Upon mine honour, thou shalt marry her.

Thy slanders I forgive; and therewithal
Remit thy other forfeits. Take him to prison;
And see our pleasure herein executed.

LUCIO: Marrying a punk, my lord, is pressing to death, whipping, and hanging.

DUKE VINCENTIO: Slandering a prince deserves it.

Exit Officers with LUCIO

She, Claudio, that you wrong'd, look you restore.
Joy to you, Mariana! Love her, Angelo;
I have confess'd her and I know her virtue.
Thanks, good friend Escalus, for thy much goodness;
There's more behind that is more gratulate.
Thanks, Provost, for thy care and secrecy:
We shall employ thee in a worthier place.
Forgive him, Angelo, that brought you home
The head of Ragozine for Claudio's:
The offence pardons itself. Dear Isabel,
I have a motion much imports your good;
Whereto if you'll a willing ear incline,
What's mine is yours and what is yours is mine.
So, bring us to our palace; where we'll show
What's yet behind, that's meet you all should know.

Exeunt

The Merry Wives Of Windsor

DRAMATIS PERSONÆ

SIR JOHN FALSTAFF
FENTON, *a young gentleman*
SHALLOW, *a country Justice*
SLENDER, *cousin to Shallow*
FORD, PAGE, *gentlemen of Windsor*
WILLIAM PAGE, *a boy, son to Page*
SIR HUGH EVANS, *a Welsh parson*
DOCTOR CAIUS, *a French physician*
HOST *of the Garter Inn*
BARDOLPH, PISTOL, NYM, *followers of Falstaff*
ROBIN, *page to Falstaff*
SIMPLE, *servant to Slender*
RUGBY, *servant to Doctor Caius*
MISTRESS FORD
MISTRESS PAGE
MISTRESS ANNE PAGE, *her daughter*
MISTRESS QUICKLY, *servant to Doctor Caius*
Servants to Page, Ford, & c

THE SCENE: *Windsor, and the neighbourhood*

Act I

Scene I—*Windsor: Before Page's house*

Enter SHALLOW, SLENDER, and SIR HUGH EVANS

SHALLOW: Sir Hugh, persuade me not; I will make a Star-chamber matter of it; if he were twenty Sir John Falstaffs, he shall not abuse Robert Shallow, esquire.

SLENDER: In the county of Gloucester, justice of peace and Coram.'

SHALLOW: Ay, cousin Slender, and 'Custalourum.

SLENDER: Ay, and 'Rato-lorum' too; and a gentleman born, Master Parson; who writes himself 'Armigero,' in any bill, warrant, quittance, or obligation, 'Armigero.'

SHALLOW: Ay, that I do; and have done any time these three hundred years.

SLENDER: All his successors gone before him hath done't; and all his ancestors that come after him may: they may give the dozen white luces in their coat.

SHALLOW: It is an old coat.

SIR HUGH EVANS: The dozen white louses do become an old coat well; it agrees well, passant; it is a familiar beast to man, and signifies love.

SHALLOW: The luce is the fresh fish; the salt fish is an old coat.

SLENDER: I may quarter, coz.

SHALLOW: You may, by marrying.

SIR HUGH EVANS: It is marring indeed, if he quarter it.

SHALLOW: Not a whit.

SIR HUGH EVANS: Yes, py'r lady; if he has a quarter of your coat, there is but three skirts for yourself, in my simple conjectures; but that is all one. If Sir John Falstaff have committed disparagements unto you, I am of the church, and will be glad to do my benevolence to make atonements and compremises between you.

SHALLOW: The council shall bear it; it is a riot.

SIR HUGH EVANS: It is not meet the council hear a riot; there is no fear of Got in a riot; the council, look you, shall desire to hear the fear of Got, and not to hear a riot; take your vizaments in that.

SHALLOW: Ha! o' my life, if I were young again, the sword should end it.

SIR HUGH EVANS: It is petter that friends is the sword, and end it: and there is also another device in my prain, which peradventure prings goot discretions with it: there is Anne Page, which is daughter to Master Thomas Page, which is pretty virginity.

SLENDER: Mistress Anne Page? She has brown hair, and speaks small like a woman.

SIR HUGH EVANS: It is that fery person for all the orld, as just as you will desire; and seven hundred pounds of moneys, and gold and silver, is her grandsire upon his death's-bed—Got deliver to a joyful resurrections!—give, when she is able to overtake seventeen years old: it were a goot motion if we leave our pribbles and prabbles, and desire a marriage between Master Abraham and Mistress Anne Page.

SLENDER: Did her grandsire leave her seven hundred pound?

SIR HUGH EVANS: Ay, and her father is make her a petter penny.

SLENDER: I know the young gentlewoman; she has good gifts.

SIR HUGH EVANS: Seven hundred pounds and possibilities is goot gifts.

SHALLOW: Well, let us see honest Master Page. Is Falstaff there?

SIR HUGH EVANS: Shall I tell you a lie? I do despise a liar as I do despise one that is false, or as I despise one that is not true. The knight, Sir John, is there; and, I beseech you, be ruled by your well-willers. I will peat the door for Master Page. (*Knocks*) What, hoa! Got pless your house here!

PAGE: [*Within*] Who's there?

Enter PAGE

SIR HUGH EVANS: Here is Got's plessing, and your friend, and Justice Shallow; and here young Master Slender, that peradventures shall tell you another tale, if matters grow to your likings.

PAGE: I am glad to see your worships well. I thank you for my venison, Master Shallow.

SHALLOW: Master Page, I am glad to see you; much good do it your good heart! I wished your venison better; it was ill killed. How doth good Mistress Page?—and I thank you always with my heart, la! with my heart.

PAGE: Sir, I thank you.

SHALLOW: Sir, I thank you; by yea and no, I do.

PAGE: I am glad to see you, good Master Slender.

SLENDER: How does your fallow greyhound, sir? I heard say he was outrun on Cotsall.

PAGE: It could not be judged, sir.

SLENDER: You'll not confess, you'll not confess.

SHALLOW: That he will not. 'Tis your fault, 'tis your fault; 'tis a good dog.

PAGE: A cur, sir.

SHALLOW: Sir, he's a good dog, and a fair dog: can there be more said? he is good and fair. Is Sir John Falstaff here?

PAGE: Sir, he is within; and I would I could do a good office between you.

SIR HUGH EVANS: It is spoke as a Christians ought to speak.

SHALLOW: He hath wronged me, Master Page.

PAGE: Sir, he doth in some sort confess it.

SHALLOW: If it be confessed, it is not redress'd: is not that so, Master Page? He hath wronged me; indeed he hath, at a word, he hath, believe me; Robert Shallow, esquire, saith, he is wronged.

PAGE: Here comes Sir John.

Enter FALSTAFF, BARDOLPH, NYM, and PISTOL

FALSTAFF: Now, Master Shallow, you'll complain of me to the king?

SHALLOW: Knight, you have beaten my men, killed my deer, and broke open my lodge.

FALSTAFF: But not kissed your keeper's daughter?

SHALLOW: Tut, a pin! this shall be answered.

FALSTAFF: I will answer it straight; I have done all this. That is now answered.

SHALLOW: The council shall know this.

FALSTAFF: 'Twere better for you if it were known in counsel: you'll be laughed at.

SIR HUGH EVANS: Pauca verba, Sir John; goot worts.

FALSTAFF: Good worts! good cabbage. Slender, I broke your head; what matter have you against me?

SLENDER: Marry, sir, I have matter in my head against you; and against your cony-catching rascals, Bardolph, Nym, and Pistol. They carried me to a tavern and made me drunk, and afterward pick'd my pocket

BARDOLPH: You Banbury cheese!

SLENDER: Ay, it is no matter.

PISTOL: How now, Mephostophilus!

SLENDER: Ay, it is no matter.

NYM: Slice, I say! pauca, pauca; slice! that's my humour.

SLENDER: Where's Simple, my man? Can you tell, cousin?

SIR HUGH EVANS: Peace, I pray you. Now let us understand. There is three umpires in this matter, as I understand: that is, Master Page, fidelicet Master Page; and there is myself, fidelicet myself; and the three party is, lastly and finally, mine host of the Garter.

PAGE: We three, to hear it and end it between them.

SIR HUGH EVANS: Fery goot: I will make a prief of it in my note-book; and we will afterwards ork upon the cause with as great discreetly as we can.

FALSTAFF: Pistol!

PISTOL: He hears with ears.

SIR HUGH EVANS: The tevil and his tam! what phrase is this, 'He hears with ear'? why, it is affectations.

FALSTAFF: Pistol, did you pick Master Slender's purse?

SLENDER: Ay, by these gloves, did he, or I would I might never come in mine own great chamber again else, of seven groats in mill-sixpences, and two Edward shovel-boards, that cost me two shilling and two pence apiece of Yead Miller, by these gloves.

FALSTAFF: Is this true, Pistol?

SIR HUGH EVANS: No; it is false, if it is a pick-purse.

PISTOL: Ha, thou mountain-foreigner! Sir John and Master mine,

I combat challenge of this latten bilbo.

Word of denial in thy labras here!

Word of denial: froth and scum, thou liest!

SLENDER: By these gloves, then, 'twas he.

NYM: Be avised, sir, and pass good humours; I will say 'marry trap' with you, if you run the nuthook's humour on me; that is the very note of it.

SLENDER: By this hat, then, he in the red face had it; for though I cannot remember what I did when you made me drunk, yet I am not altogether an ass.

FALSTAFF: What say you, Scarlet and John?

BARDOLPH: Why, sir, for my part I say the gentleman had drunk himself out of his five sentences.

SIR HUGH EVANS: It is his five senses; fie, what the ignorance is!

BARDOLPH: And being fap, sir, was, as they say, cashiered; and so conclusions passed the careers.

SLENDER: Ay, you spake in Latin then too; but 'tis no matter; I'll ne'er be drunk whilst I live again, but in honest, civil, godly company, for this trick: if I be drunk, I'll be drunk with those that have the fear of God, and not with drunken knaves.

SIR HUGH EVANS: So Got udge me, that is a virtuous mind.

FALSTAFF: You hear all these matters denied, gentlemen; you hear it.

Enter MISTRESS ANNE PAGE, with wine; MISTRESS FORD and MISTRESS PAGE, following

PAGE: Nay, daughter, carry the wine in; we'll drink within.

Exit ANNE PAGE

SLENDER: O heaven! this is Mistress Anne Page.

PAGE: How now, Mistress Ford!

FALSTAFF: Mistress Ford, by my troth, you are very well met; by your leave, good mistress.

Kisses her

PAGE: Wife, bid these gentlemen welcome. Come, we have a hot venison pasty to dinner; come, gentlemen, I hope we shall drink down all unkindness.

Exeunt all except SHALLOW, SLENDER, and SIR HUGH EVANS

SLENDER: I had rather than forty shillings I had my Book of Songs and Sonnets here.

Enter SIMPLE

How now, Simple! where have you been? I must wait on myself, must I? You have not the Book of Riddles about you, have you?

SIMPLE: Book of Riddles! Why, did you not lend it to Alice Shortcake upon All-hallowmas last, a fortnight afore Michaelmas?

SHALLOW: Come, coz; come, coz; we stay for you. A word with you, coz; marry, this, coz: there is, as 'twere, a tender, a kind of tender, made afar off by Sir Hugh here. Do you understand me?

SLENDER: Ay, sir, you shall find me reasonable; if it be so, I shall do that that is reason.

SHALLOW: Nay, but understand me.

SLENDER: So I do, sir.

SIR HUGH EVANS: Give ear to his motions, Master Slender, I will description the matter to you, if you be capacity of it.

SLENDER: Nay, I will do as my cousin Shallow says; I pray you, pardon me; he's a justice of peace in his country, simple though I stand here.

SIR HUGH EVANS: But that is not the question: the question is concerning your marriage.

SHALLOW: Ay, there's the point, sir.

SIR HUGH EVANS: Marry, is it; the very point of it; to Mistress Anne Page.

SLENDER: Why, if it be so, I will marry her upon any reasonable demands.

SIR HUGH EVANS: But can you affection the 'oman? Let us command to know that of your mouth or of your lips; for divers philosophers hold that the lips is parcel of the mouth. Therefore, precisely, can you carry your goodwill to the maid?

SHALLOW: Cousin Abraham Slender, can you love her?

SLENDER: I hope, sir, I will do as it shall become one that would do reason.

SIR HUGH EVANS: Nay, Got's lords and his ladies! you must speak possitable, if you can carry her your desires towards her.

SHALLOW: That you must. Will you, upon good dowry, marry her?

SLENDER: I will do a greater thing than that, upon your request, cousin, in any reason.

SHALLOW: Nay, conceive me, conceive me, sweet coz; what I do is to pleasure you, coz. Can you love the maid?

SLENDER: I will marry her, sir, at your request; but if there be no great love in the beginning, yet heaven may decrease it upon better acquaintance, when we are married and have more occasion to know one another. I hope, upon familiarity will grow more contempt: but if you say, 'Marry her,' I will marry her; that I am freely dissolved, and dissolutely.

SIR HUGH EVANS: It is a fery discretion answer; save the fall is in the ort 'dissolutely': the ort is, according to our meaning, 'resolutely;' his meaning is good.

SHALLOW: Ay, I think my cousin meant well.

SLENDER: Ay, or else I would I might be hanged, la!

SHALLOW: Here comes fair Mistress Anne.

Re-enter ANNE PAGE

Would I were young for your sake, Mistress Anne!

ANNE PAGE: The dinner is on the table; my father desires your worships' company.

SHALLOW: I will wait on him, fair Mistress Anne.

SIR HUGH EVANS: Od's plessed will ! I will not be absence at the grace.

Exeunt SHALLOW and SIR HUGH EVANS

ANNE PAGE: Will't please your worship to come in, sir?

SLENDER: No, I thank you, forsooth, heartily; I am very well.

ANNE PAGE: The dinner attends you, sir.

SLENDER: I am not a-hungry, I thank you, forsooth. Go, sirrah, for all you are my man, go wait upon my cousin Shallow. (*Exit Simple*) A justice of peace sometimes may be beholding to his friend for a man. I keep but three men and a boy yet, till my mother be dead: but what though? Yet I live like a poor gentleman born.

ANNE PAGE: I may not go in without your worship; they will not sit till you come.

SLENDER: I' faith, I'll eat nothing; I thank you as much as though I did.

ANNE PAGE: I pray you, sir, walk in.

SLENDER: I had rather walk here, I thank you. I bruised my shin th' other day with playing at sword and dagger with a master of fence; three veneys for a dish of stewed prunes—and, I with my ward defending my bead, he hot my shin and, by my troth, I cannot abide the smell of hot meat since. Why do your dogs bark so? Be there bears i' the town?

ANNE PAGE: I think there are, sir; I heard them talked of.

SLENDER: I love the sport well but I shall as soon quarrel at it as any man in England. You are afraid, if you see the bear loose, are you not?

ANNE PAGE: Ay, indeed, sir.

SLENDER: That's meat and drink to me, now. I have seen Sackerson loose twenty times, and have taken him by the chain; but, I warrant you, the women have so cried and shrieked at it, that it passed; but women, indeed, cannot abide 'em; they are very ill-favored rough things.

Re-enter PAGE

PAGE: Come, gentle Master Slender, come; we stay for you.

SLENDER: I'll eat nothing, I thank you, sir.

PAGE: By cock and pie, you shall not choose, sir! Come, come.

SLENDER: Nay, pray you, lead the way.

PAGE: Come on, sir.

SLENDER: Mistress Anne, yourself shall go first.

ANNE PAGE: Not I, sir; pray you, keep on.

SLENDER: Truly, I will not go first; truly, la! I will not do you that wrong.

ANNE: I pray you, Sir.

SLENDER: I'll rather be unmannerly than troublesome. You do yourself wrong, indeed, la!

Exeunt

SCENE II—*Before Page's house*

Enter SIR HUGH EVANS and SIMPLE

SIR HUGH EVANS: Go your ways, and ask of Doctor Caius' house which is the way; and there dwells one Mistress Quickly, which is in the manner of his nurse, or his dry nurse, or his cook, or his laundry, his washer, and his wringer.

SIMPLE: Well, sir.

SIR HUGH EVANS: Nay, it is petter yet. Give her this letter; for it is a oman that altogether 's acquaintance with Mistress Anne Page; and the letter is, to desire and require her to solicit your master's desires to Mistress Anne Page. I pray you, be gone: I will make an end of my dinner; there's pippins and cheese to come.

Exeunt

SCENE III—*Garter Inn*

Enter FALSTAFF, Host, BARDOLPH, NYM, PISTOL, and ROBIN

FALSTAFF: Mine host of the Garter!

HOST: What says my bully-rook? Speak scholarly and wisely.

FALSTAFF: Truly, mine host, I must turn away some of my followers.

HOST: Discard, bully Hercules; cashier; let them wag; trot, trot.

FALSTAFF: I sit at ten pounds a week.

HOST: Thou'rt an emperor, Caesar, Keiser, and Pheazar. I will entertain Bardolph; he shall draw, he shall tap: said I well, bully Hector?

FALSTAFF: Do so, good mine host.

HOST: I have spoke; let him follow. (*To Bardolph*) Let me see thee froth and lime: I am at a word; follow.

Exit Host

FALSTAFF: Bardolph, follow him. A tapster is a good trade: an old cloak makes a new jerkin; a withered serving-man a fresh tapster. Go; adieu.

BARDOLPH: It is a life that I have desired; I will thrive.

PISTOL: O base Hungarian wight! wilt thou the spigot wield?

Exit BARDOLPH

NYM: He was gotten in drink: is not the humour conceited?

FALSTAFF: I am glad I am so acquit of this tinderbox: his thefts were too open; his filching was like an unskilful singer; he kept not time.

NYM: The good humour is to steal at a minute's rest.

PISTOL: 'Convey,' the wise it call. 'Steal' foh! a fico for the phrase!

FALSTAFF: Well, sirs, I am almost out at heels.

PISTOL: Why, then, let kibes ensue.

FALSTAFF: There is no remedy; I must cony-catch; I must shift.

PISTOL: Young ravens must have food.

FALSTAFF: Which of you know Ford of this town?

PISTOL: I ken the wight: he is of substance good.

FALSTAFF: My honest lads, I will tell you what I am about.

PISTOL: Two yards, and more.

FALSTAFF: No quips now, Pistol! Indeed, I am in the waist two yards about; but I am now about no waste; I am about thrift. Briefly, I do mean to make love to Ford's wife; I spy entertainment in her; she discourses, she carves, she gives the leer of invitation: I can construe the action of her familiar style; and the hardest voice of her behavior, to be Englished rightly, is, 'I am Sir John Falstaff's'.

PISTOL: He hath studied her will, and translated her will, out of honesty into English.

NYM: The anchor is deep; will that humour pass?

FALSTAFF: Now, the report goes she has all the rule of her husband's purse: he hath a legion of angels.

PISTOL: As many devils entertain; and 'To her, boy,' say I.

NYM: The humour rises; it is good; humour me the angels.

FALSTAFF: I have writ me here a letter to her: and here another to Page's wife, who even now gave me good eyes too, examined my parts with most judicious oeillades; sometimes the beam of her view gilded my foot, sometimes my portly belly.

PISTOL: Then did the sun on dunghill shine.

NYM: I thank thee for that humour.

FALSTAFF: O, she did so course o'er my exteriors with such a greedy intention, that the appetite of her eye did seem to scorch me up like a burning-glass! Here's another letter to her: she bears the purse too; she is a region in Guiana, all gold and bounty. I will be cheaters to them both, and they shall be exchequers to me; they shall be my East and West Indies, and I will trade to them both. Go bear thou this letter to Mistress Page; and thou this to Mistress Ford: we will thrive, lads, we will thrive.

PISTOL: Shall I Sir Pandarus of Troy become,
And by my side wear steel? then, Lucifer take all!

NYM: I will run no base humour: here, take the humour-letter: I will keep the havior of reputation.

FALSTAFF: [*To Robin*] Hold, sirrah, bear you these letters tightly;
Sail like my pinnace to these golden shores.
Rogues, hence, avaunt! vanish like hailstones, go;
Trudge, plod away i' the hoof; seek shelter, pack!
Falstaff will learn the humour of the age,
French thrift, you rogues; myself and skirted page.

Exeunt FALSTAFF and ROBIN

PISTOL: Let vultures gripe thy guts! for gourd and fullam holds,
And high and low beguiles the rich and poor;
Tester I'll have in pouch when thou shalt lack,
Base Phrygian Turk!

NYM: I have operations in my head which be humours of revenge.

PISTOL: Wilt thou revenge?

NYM: By welkin and her star!

PISTOL: With wit or steel?

NYM: With both the humours, I.
I will discuss the humour of this love to Page.

PISTOL: And I to Ford shall eke unfold
How Falstaff, varlet vile,
His dove will prove, his gold will hold,
And his soft couch defile.

NYM: My humour shall not cool: I will incense Page to deal with poison; I will possess him with yellowness, for the revolt of mine is dangerous: that is my true humour.

PISTOL: Thou art the Mars of malecontents: I second thee; troop on.

Exeunt

SCENE IV—*Doctor Caius' house*

Enter MISTRESS QUICKLY, SIMPLE, and RUGBY

MISTRESS QUICKLY: What, John Rugby! I pray thee, go to the casement, and see if you can see my master, Master Doctor Caius, coming. If he do, i' faith, and find anybody in the house, here will be an old abusing of God's patience and the king's English.

RUGBY: I'll go watch.

MISTRESS QUICKLY: Go; and we'll have a posset for't soon at night, in faith, at the latter end of a sea-coal fire.

Exit RUGBY

An honest, willing, kind fellow, as ever servant shall come in house withal, and, I warrant you, no tell-tale nor no breed-bate: his worst fault is, that he is given to prayer; he is something peevish that way: but nobody but has his fault; but let that pass. Peter Simple, you say your name is?

SIMPLE: Ay, for fault of a better.

MISTRESS QUICKLY: And Master Slender's your master?

SIMPLE: Ay, forsooth.

MISTRESS QUICKLY: Does he not wear a great round beard, like a glover's paring-knife?

SIMPLE: No, forsooth; he hath but a little wee face, with a little yellow beard, a Cain-coloured beard.

MISTRESS QUICKLY: A softly-sprighted man, is he not?

SIMPLE: Ay, forsooth; but he is as tall a man of his hands as any is between this and his head; he hath fought with a warrener.

MISTRESS QUICKLY: How say you? O, I should remember him: does he not hold up his head, as it were, and strut in his gait?

SIMPLE: Yes, indeed, does he.

MISTRESS QUICKLY: Well, heaven send Anne Page no worse fortune! Tell Master Parson Evans I will do what I can for your master: Anne is a good girl, and I wish—

Re-enter RUGBY

RUGBY: Out, alas! here comes my master.

MISTRESS QUICKLY: We shall all be shent. Run in here, good young man; go into this closet: he will not stay long. (*Shuts SIMPLE in the closet*) What, John Rugby! John! what, John, I say! Go, John, go inquire for my master; I doubt he be not well, that he comes not home. (*Singing*) And down, down, adown-a, etc.

Enter DOCTOR CAIUS

DOCTOR CAIUS: Vat is you sing? I do not like des toys. Pray you, go and vetch me in my closet un boitier vert, a box, a green-a box: do intend vat I speak? a green-a box.

MISTRESS QUICKLY: Ay, forsooth; I'll fetch it you. (*Aside*) I am glad he went not in himself: if he had found the young man, he would have been horn-mad.

DOCTOR CAIUS: Fe, fe, fe, fe! ma foi, il fait fort chaud. Je m'en vais a la cour—la grande affaire.

MISTRESS QUICKLY: Is it this, sir?

DOCTOR CAIUS: Oui; mette le au mon pocket: depeche, quickly. Vere is dat knave Rugby?

MISTRESS QUICKLY: What, John Rugby! John!

RUGBY: Here, sir!

DOCTOR CAIUS: You are John Rugby, and you are Jack Rugby. Come, take-a your rapier, and come after my heel to the court.

RUGBY: 'Tis ready, sir, here in the porch.

DOCTOR CAIUS: By my trot, I tarry too long. Od's me! Qu'ai-j'oublie! Dere is some simples in my closet, dat I vill not for the varld I shall leave behind.

MISTRESS QUICKLY: Ay me, he'll find the young man these, and be mad!

DOCTOR CAIUS: O diable, diable! vat is in my closet? Villain! larron! (*Pulling SIMPLE out*) Rugby, my rapier!

MISTRESS QUICKLY: Good master, be content.

DOCTOR CAIUS: Wherefore shall I be content-a?

MISTRESS QUICKLY: The young man is an honest man.

DOCTOR CAIUS: What shall de honest man do in my closet? dere is no honest man dat shall come in my closet.

MISTRESS QUICKLY: I beseech you, be not so phlegmatic. Hear the truth of it: he came of an errand to me from Parson Hugh.

DOCTOR CAIUS: Vell?

SIMPLE: Ay, forsooth; to desire her to—

MISTRESS QUICKLY: Peace, I pray you.

DOCTOR CAIUS: Peace-a your tongue. Speak-a your tale.

SIMPLE: To desire this honest gentlewoman, your maid, to speak a good word to Mistress Anne Page for my master in the way of marriage.

MISTRESS QUICKLY: This is all, indeed, la! but I'll ne'er put my finger in the fire, and need not.

DOCTOR CAIUS: Sir Hugh send-a you? Rugby, baille me some paper. Tarry you a little-a while.

Writes

MISTRESS QUICKLY: [*Aside to SIMPLE*] I am glad he is so quiet; if he had been thoroughly moved, you should have heard him so loud and so melancholy. But notwithstanding, man, I'll do you your master what good I can: and the very yea and the no is, the French doctor, my master—I may call him my master, look you, for I keep his house; and I wash, wring, brew, bake, scour, dress meat and drink, make the beds and do all myself—

SIMPLE: [*Aside to MISTRESS QUICKLY*] 'Tis a great charge to come under one body's hand.

MISTRESS QUICKLY: [*Aside to SIMPLE*] Are you avised o' that? You shall find it a great charge: and to be up early and down late; but notwithstanding—to tell you in your ear; I would have no words of it—my master himself is in love with Mistress Anne Page; but notwithstanding that, I know Anne's mind—that's neither here nor there.

DOCTOR CAIUS: You jack'nape, give-a this letter to Sir Hugh; by gar, it is a shallenge; I will cut his troat in de park; and I will teach a scurvy jack-a-nape priest to meddle or make. You may be gone; it is not good you tarry here. By gar, I will cut all his two stones; by gar, he shall not have a stone to throw at his dog.

Exit SIMPLE

MISTRESS QUICKLY: Alas, he speaks but for his friend.

DOCTOR CAIUS: It is no matter-a ver dat: do not you tell-a me dat I shall have Anne Page for myself? By gar, I vill kill de Jack priest; and I have appointed mine host of de Jarteer to measure our weapon. By gar, I will myself have Anne Page.

MISTRESS QUICKLY: Sir, the maid loves you, and all shall be well. We must give folks leave to prate: what, the good-jer!

DOCTOR CAIUS: Rugby, come to the court with me. By gar, if I have not Anne Page, I shall turn your head out of my door. Follow my heels, Rugby.

Exeunt DOCTOR CAIUS and RUGBY

MISTRESS QUICKLY: You shall have—An fool's-head of your own. No, I know Anne's mind for that: never a woman in Windsor knows more of Anne's mind than I do; nor can do more than I do with her, I thank heaven.

FENTON: [*Within*] Who's within there? ho!

MISTRESS QUICKLY: Who's there, I trow! Come near the house, I pray you.

Enter FENTON

FENTON: How now, good woman? how dost thou?

MISTRESS QUICKLY: The better that it pleases your good worship to ask.

FENTON: What news? how does pretty Mistress Anne?

MISTRESS QUICKLY: In truth, sir, and she is pretty, and honest, and gentle; and one that is your friend, I can tell you that by the way; I praise heaven for it.

FENTON: Shall I do any good, thinkest thou? shall I not lose my suit?

MISTRESS QUICKLY: Troth, sir, all is in His hands above: but notwithstanding, Master Fenton, I'll be sworn on a book, she loves you. Have not your worship a wart above your eye?

FENTON: Yes, marry, have I; what of that?

MISTRESS QUICKLY: Well, thereby hangs a tale; good faith, it is such another Nan; but, I detest, an honest maid as ever broke bread: we had an hour's talk of that wart. I shall never laugh but in that maid's company! But indeed she is given too much to allicholy and musing; but for you—well, go to.

FENTON: Well, I shall see her to-day. Hold, there's money for thee; let me have thy voice in my behalf: if thou seest her before me, commend me.

MISTRESS QUICKLY: Will I? i'faith, that we will; and I will tell your worship more of the wart the next time we have confidence; and of other wooers.

FENTON: Well, farewell; I am in great haste now.

MISTRESS QUICKLY: Farewell to your worship.

Exit FENTON

Truly, an honest gentleman; but Anne loves him not; for I know Anne's mind as well as another does. Out upon't! what have I forgot?

Exit

Act II

Scene I—*Before Page's house*

Enter MISTRESS PAGE, with a letter

MISTRESS PAGE: What, have I scaped love-letters in the holiday-time of my beauty, and am I now a subject for them? Let me see.

Reads

'Ask me no reason why I love you; for though Love use Reason for his physician, he admits him not for his counsellor. You are not young, no more am I; go to then, there's sympathy: you are merry, so am I; ha, ha! then there's more sympathy: you love sack, and so do I; would you desire better sympathy? Let it suffice thee, Mistress Page—at the least, if the love of soldier can suffice—that I love thee. I will not say, pity me; 'tis not a soldier-like phrase: but I say, love me. By me,

Thine own true knight,
By day or night,
Or any kind of light,
With all his might
For thee to fight,

JOHN FALSTAFF'

What a Herod of Jewry is this! O wicked world! One that is well-nigh worn to pieces with age to show himself a young gallant! What an unweighed behavior hath this Flemish drunkard picked—with the devil's name!—out of my conversation, that he dares in this manner assay me? Why, he hath not been thrice in my company! What should I say to him? I was then frugal of my mirth. Heaven forgive me! Why, I'll exhibit a bill in the parliament for the putting down of men. How shall I be revenged on him? for revenged I will be, as sure as his guts are made of puddings.

Enter MISTRESS FORD

MISTRESS FORD: Mistress Page! trust me, I was going to your house.

MISTRESS PAGE: And, trust me, I was coming to you. You look very ill.

MISTRESS FORD: Nay, I'll ne'er believe that; I have to show to the contrary.

MISTRESS PAGE: Faith, but you do, in my mind.

MISTRESS FORD: Well, I do then; yet I say I could show you to the contrary. O Mistress Page, give me some counsel!

MISTRESS PAGE: What's the matter, woman?

MISTRESS FORD: O woman, if it were not for one trifling respect, I could come to such honour!

MISTRESS PAGE: Hang the trifle, woman! take the honour. What is it? dispense with trifles; what is it?

MISTRESS FORD: If I would but go to hell for an eternal moment or so, I could be knighted.

MISTRESS PAGE: What? thou liest! Sir Alice Ford!

These knights will hack; and so thou shouldst not alter the article of thy gentry.

MISTRESS FORD: We burn daylight: here, read, read; perceive how I might be knighted. I shall think the worse of fat men, as long as I have an eye to make difference of men's liking: and yet he would not swear; praised women's modesty; and gave such orderly and well-behaved reproof to all uncomeliness, that I would have sworn his disposition would have gone to the truth of his words; but they do no more adhere and keep place together than the Hundredth Psalm to the tune of 'Greensleeves.' What tempest, I trow, threw this whale, with so many tuns of oil in his belly, ashore at Windsor? How shall I be revenged on him? I think the best way were to entertain him with hope, till the wicked fire of lust have melted him in his own grease. Did you ever hear the like?

MISTRESS PAGE: Letter for letter, but that the name of Page and Ford differs! To thy great comfort in this mystery of ill opinions, here's the twin-brother of thy letter: but let thine inherit first; for, I protest, mine never shall. I warrant he hath a thousand of these letters, writ with blank space for different names—sure, more,—and these are of the second edition: he will print them, out of doubt; for he cares not what he puts into the press, when he would put us two. I had rather be a giantess, and lie under Mount Pelion. Well, I will find you twenty lascivious turtles ere one chaste man.

MISTRESS FORD: Why, this is the very same; the very hand, the very words. What doth he think of us?

MISTRESS PAGE: Nay, I know not; it makes me almost ready to wrangle with mine own honesty. I'll entertain myself like one that I am not acquainted withal; for, sure, unless he know some strain in me, that I know not myself, he would never have boarded me in this fury.

MISTRESS FORD: 'Boarding,' call you it? I'll be sure to keep him above deck.

MISTRESS PAGE: So will I if he come under my hatches, I'll never to sea again. Let's be revenged on him; let's appoint him a meeting; give him a show of comfort in his suit and lead him on with a fine-baited delay, till he hath pawned his horses to mine host of the Garter.

MISTRESS FORD: Nay, I will consent to act any villany against him, that may not sully the chariness of our honesty. O, that my husband saw this letter! It would give eternal food to his jealousy.

MISTRESS PAGE: Why, look where he comes; and my good man too: he's as far from jealousy as I am from giving him cause; and that I hope, is an unmeasurable distance.

MISTRESS FORD: You are the happier woman.

MISTRESS PAGE: Let's consult together against this greasy knight. Come hither.

They retire

Enter FORD with PISTOL, and PAGE with NYM

FORD: Well, I hope it be not so.

PISTOL: Hope is a curtal dog in some affairs:
Sir John affects thy wife.

FORD: Why, sir, my wife is not young.

PISTOL: He wooes both high and low, both rich and poor,
Both young and old, one with another, Ford;
He loves the gallimaufry: Ford, perpend.

FORD: Love my wife!

PISTOL: With liver burning hot. Prevent, or go thou,
Like Sir Actaeon he, with Ringwood at thy heels:
O, odious is the name!

FORD: What name, sir?

PISTOL: The horn, I say. Farewell.
Take heed, have open eye, for thieves do foot by night;
Take heed, ere summer comes or cuckoo-birds do sing.
Away, Sir Corporal Nym!
Believe it, Page; he speaks sense.

Exit Pistol

FORD: [*Aside*] I will be patient; I will find out this.

NYM: [*To PAGE*] And this is true; I like not the humour of lying. He hath wronged me in some humours; I should have borne the humoured letter to her; but I have a sword and it shall bite upon my necessity. He loves your wife; there's the short and the long.
My name is Corporal Nym; I speak and I avouch;
'tis true: my name is Nym and Falstaff loves your wife.
Adieu. I love not the humour of bread and cheese, and there's the humour of it. Adieu.

Exit Nym

PAGE: 'The humour of it,' quoth a'! here's a fellow frights English out of his wits.

FORD: I will seek out Falstaff.

PAGE: I never heard such a drawling, affecting rogue.

FORD: If I do find it: well.

PAGE: I will not believe such a Cataian, though the priest o' the town commended him for a true man.

FORD: 'Twas a good sensible fellow, well.

PAGE: How now, Meg!

MISTRESS PAGE and MISTRESS FORD come forward

MISTRESS PAGE: Whither go you, George? Hark you.

MISTRESS FORD: How now, sweet Frank! why art thou melancholy?

FORD: I melancholy! I am not melancholy. Get you home, go.

MISTRESS FORD: 'Faith, thou hast some crotchets in thy head now. Will you go, Mistress Page?

MISTRESS PAGE: Have with you. You'll come to dinner, George? (*Aside to MISTRESS FORD*) Look who comes yonder, she shall be our messenger to this paltry knight.

MISTRESS FORD: [*Aside to MISTRESS PAGE*] Trust me, I thought on her; she'll fit it.

Enter MISTRESS QUICKLY

MISTRESS PAGE: You are come to see my daughter Anne?

MISTRESS QUICKLY: Ay, forsooth; and, I pray, how does good Mistress Anne?

MISTRESS PAGE: Go in with us and see; we have an hour's talk with you.

Exeunt MISTRESS PAGE, MISTRESS FORD, and MISTRESS QUICKLY

PAGE: How now, Master Ford!

FORD: You heard what this knave told me, did you not?

PAGE: Yes: and you heard what the other told me?

FORD: Do you think there is truth in them?

PAGE: Hang 'em, slaves! I do not think the knight would offer it; but these that accuse him in his intent towards our wives are a yoke of his discarded men; very rogues, now they be out of service.

FORD: Were they his men?

PAGE: Marry, were they.

FORD: I like it never the better for that. Does he lie at the Garter?

PAGE: Ay, marry, does he. If he should intend this voyage towards my wife, I would turn her loose to him; and what he gets more of her than sharp words, let it lie on my head.

FORD: I do not misdoubt my wife; but I would be loath to turn them together. A man may be too confident. I would have nothing lie on my head. I cannot be thus satisfied.

PAGE: Look where my ranting host of the Garter comes: there is either liquor in his pate or money in his purse when he looks so merrily.

Enter Host

How now, mine host!

HOST: How now, bully-rook! thou'rt a gentleman. (*To Shallow following*) Cavaleiro-justice, I say!

Enter SHALLOW

SHALLOW: I follow, mine host, I follow. Good even and twenty, good Master Page! Master Page, will you go with us? we have sport in hand.

HOST: Tell him, cavaleiro-justice; tell him, bully-rook.

SHALLOW: Sir, there is a fray to be fought between Sir Hugh the Welsh priest and Caius the French doctor.

FORD: Good mine host o' the Garter, a word with you.

They go aside

HOST: What sayest thou, my bully-rook?

SHALLOW: [To PAGE] Will you go with us to behold it? My merry host hath had the measuring of their weapons; and, I think, hath appointed them contrary places; for, believe me, I hear the parson is no jester. Hark, I will tell you what our sport shall be.

They converse apart

HOST: Hast thou no suit against my knight, my guest-cavaleire?

FORD: None, I protest; but I'll give you a pottle of burnt sack to give me recourse to him and tell him my name is Brook: only for a jest.

HOST: My hand, bully; thou shalt have egress and regress—said I well?—and thy name shall be Brook. It is a merry knight. Will you go, Mynheers?

SHALLOW: Have with you, mine host.

PAGE: I have heard the Frenchman hath good skill in his rapier.

SHALLOW: Tut, sir, I could have told you more. In these times you stand on distance, your passes, stoccadoes, and I know not what: 'tis the heart, Master Page; 'tis here, 'tis here. I have seen the time, with my long sword I would have made you four tall fellows skip like rats.

HOST: Here, boys, here, here! shall we wag?

PAGE: Have with you. I would rather hear them scold than fight.

Exeunt Host, SHALLOW, and PAGE

FORD: Though Page be a secure fool, and stands so firmly on his wife's frailty, yet I cannot put off my opinion so easily: she was in his company at Page's house; and what they made there, I know not. Well, I will look further into't: and I have a disguise to sound Falstaff. If I find her honest, I lose not my labour; if she be otherwise, 'tis labour well bestowed.

Exit

SCENE II—*A room in the Garter Inn*

Enter FALSTAFF and PISTOL

FALSTAFF: I will not lend thee a penny.

PISTOL: I will retort the sum in equipage.

FALSTAFF: Not a penny.

PISTOL: Why, then the world's mine oyster.
Which I with sword will open.

FALSTAFF: Not a penny. I have been content, sir, you should lay my countenance to pawn; I have grated upon my good friends for three reprieves for you and your coach-fellow Nym; or else you had looked through the grate, like a geminy of baboons. I am damned in hell for swearing to gentlemen my friends, you were good soldiers and tall fellows; and when Mistres Bridget lost the handle of her fan, I took't upon mine honour thou hadst it not.

PISTOL: Didst not thou share? hadst thou not fifteen pence?

FALSTAFF: Reason, you rogue, reason: thinkest thou I'll endanger my soul gratis? At a word, hang no more about me, I am no gibbet for you. Go. A short knife and a throng! To your manor of Pickt-hatch! Go. You'll not bear a letter for me, you rogue! You stand upon your honour! Why, thou unconfinable baseness, it is as much as I can do to keep the terms of my honour precise. I, I, I myself sometimes, leaving the fear of God on the left hand and hiding mine honour in my necessity, am fain to shuffle, to hedge and to lurch; and yet you, rogue, will ensconce your rags, your cat-a-mountain looks, your red-lattice phrases, and your bold-beating oaths, under the shelter of your honour! You will not do it, you!

PISTOL: I do relent: what would thou more of man?

Enter ROBIN

ROBIN: Sir, here's a woman would speak with you.

FALSTAFF: Let her approach.

Enter MISTRESS QUICKLY

MISTRESS QUICKLY: Give your worship good morrow.

FALSTAFF: Good morrow, good wife.

MISTRESS QUICKLY: Not so, an't please your worship.

FALSTAFF: Good maid, then.

MISTRESS QUICKLY: I'll be sworn,
As my mother was, the first hour I was born.

FALSTAFF: I do believe the swearer. What with me?

MISTRESS QUICKLY: Shall I vouchsafe your worship a word or two?

FALSTAFF: Two thousand, fair woman; and I'll vouchsafe thee the hearing.

MISTRESS QUICKLY: There is one Mistress Ford, sir—I pray, come a little nearer this ways—I myself dwell with master Doctor Caius—

FALSTAFF: Well, on: Mistress Ford, you say—

MISTRESS QUICKLY: Your worship says very true I pray your worship, come a little nearer this ways.

FALSTAFF: I warrant thee, nobody hears; mine own people, mine own people.

MISTRESS QUICKLY: Are they so? God bless them and make them his servants!

FALSTAFF: Well, Mistress Ford; what of her?

MISTRESS QUICKLY: Why, sir, she's a good creature. Lord Lord! Your worship's a wanton! Well, heaven forgive you and all of us, I pray!

FALSTAFF: Mistress Ford; come, Mistress Ford—

MISTRESS QUICKLY: Marry, this is the short and the long of it; you have brought her into such a canaries as 'tis wonderful. The best courtier of them all, when the court lay at Windsor, could never have brought her to such a canary. Yet there has been knights, and lords, and gentlemen, with their coaches, I warrant you, coach after coach, letter after letter, gift after gift; smelling so sweetly, all musk, and so rushling, I warrant you, in silk and gold; and in such alligant terms; and in such wine and sugar of the best and the fairest, that would have won any woman's heart; and, I warrant you, they could never get an eye-wink of her. I had myself twenty angels given me this morning; but I defy all angels, in any such sort, as they say, but in the way of honesty; and, I warrant you, they could never get her so much as sip on a cup with the proudest of them all: and yet there has been earls, nay, which is more, pensioners; but, I warrant you, all is one with her.

FALSTAFF: But what says she to me? Be brief, my good she-Mercury.

MISTRESS QUICKLY: Marry, she hath received your letter, for the which she thanks you a thousand times; and she gives you to notify that her husband will be absence from his house between ten and eleven.

FALSTAFF: Ten and eleven?

MISTRESS QUICKLY: Ay, forsooth; and then you may come and see the picture, she says, that you wot of. Master Ford, her husband, will be from home. Alas! the sweet woman leads an ill life with him: he's a very jealousy man; she leads a very frampold life with him, good heart.

FALSTAFF: Ten and eleven. Woman, commend me to her; I will not fail her.

MISTRESS QUICKLY: Why, you say well. But I have another messenger to your worship. Mistress Page hath her hearty commendations to you too: and let me tell you in your ear, she's as fartuous a civil modest wife, and one, I tell you, that will not miss you morning nor evening prayer, as any is in Windsor, whoe'er be the other: and she bade me tell your worship that her husband is seldom from home; but she hopes there will come a time. I never knew a woman so dote upon a man; surely I think you have charms, la! yes, in truth.

FALSTAFF: Not I, I assure thee: setting the attractions of my good parts aside I have no other charms.

MISTRESS QUICKLY: Blessing on your heart for't!

FALSTAFF: But, I pray thee, tell me this: has Ford's wife and Page's wife acquainted each other how they love me?

MISTRESS QUICKLY: That were a jest indeed! they have not so little grace, I hope: that were a trick indeed! But Mistress Page would desire you to send her your little page, of all loves. Her husband has a marvellous infection to the little page; and truly Master Page is an honest man. Never a wife in Windsor leads a better life than she does: do what she will, say what she will, take all, pay all, go to bed when she list, rise when she list, all is as she will: and truly she deserves it; for if there be a kind woman in Windsor, she is one. You must send her your page; no remedy.

FALSTAFF: Why, I will.

MISTRESS QUICKLY: Nay, but do so, then: and, look you, he may come and go between you both; and in any case have a nay-word, that you may know one another's mind, and the boy never need to understand any thing; for 'tis not good that children should know any wickedness: old folks, you know, have discretion, as they say, and know the world.

FALSTAFF: Fare thee well: commend me to them both: there's my purse; I am yet thy debtor. Boy, go along with this woman.

Exeunt MISTRESS QUICKLY and ROBIN

This news distracts me!

PISTOL: This punk is one of Cupid's carriers:
Clap on more sails; pursue; up with your fights:
Give fire: she is my prize, or ocean whelm them all!

Exit Pistol

FALSTAFF: Sayest thou so, old Jack; go thy ways; I'll make more of thy old body than I have done. Will they yet look after thee? Wilt thou, after the expense of so much money, be now a gainer? Good body, I thank thee. Let them say 'tis grossly done; so it be fairly done, no matter.

Enter BARDOLPH

BARDOLPH: Sir John, there's one Master Brook below would fain speak with you, and be acquainted with you; and hath sent your worship a morning's draught of sack.

FALSTAFF: Brook is his name?

BARDOLPH: Ay, sir.

FALSTAFF: Call him in.

Exit BARDOLPH

Such Brooks are welcome to me, that o'erflow such liquor. Ah, ha! Mistress Ford and Mistress Page, have I encompassed you? go to; via!

Re-enter BARDOLPH, with FORD disguised

FORD: Bless you, sir!

FALSTAFF: And you, sir! Would you speak with me?

FORD: I make bold to press with so little preparation upon you.

FALSTAFF: You're welcome. What's your will? Give us leave, drawer.

Exit BARDOLPH

FORD: Sir, I am a gentleman that have spent much; my name is Brook.

FALSTAFF: Good Master Brook, I desire more acquaintance of you.

FORD: Good Sir John, I sue for yours: not to charge you; for I must let you understand I think myself in better plight for a lender than you are: the which hath something embolden'd me to this unseasoned intrusion; for they say, if money go before, all ways do lie open.

FALSTAFF: Money is a good soldier, sir, and will on.

FORD: Troth, and I have a bag of money here troubles me; if you will help to bear it, Sir John, take all, or half, for easing me of the carriage.

FALSTAFF: Sir, I know not how I may deserve to be your porter.

FORD: I will tell you, sir, if you will give me the hearing.

FALSTAFF: Speak, good Master Brook: I shall be glad to be your servant.

FORD: Sir, I hear you are a scholar—I will be brief with you—and you have been a man long known to me, though I had never so good means, as desire, to make myself acquainted with you. I shall discover a thing to you, wherein I must very much lay open mine own imperfection: but, good Sir John, as you have one eye upon my follies, as you hear them unfolded, turn another into the register of your own; that I may pass with a reproof the easier, sith you yourself know how easy it is to be such an offender.

FALSTAFF: Very well, sir; proceed.

FORD: There is a gentlewoman in this town; her husband's name is Ford.

FALSTAFF: Well, sir.

FORD: I have long loved her, and, I protest to you, bestowed much on her; followed her with a doting observance; engrossed opportunities to meet her; fee'd every slight occasion that could but niggardly give me sight of her; not only bought many presents to give her, but have given largely to many to know what she would have given; briefly, I have pursued her as love hath pursued me; which hath been on the wing of all occasions. But whatsoever I have merited, either in my mind or, in my means, meed, I am sure, I have received none; unless experience be a jewel that I have purchased at an infinite rate, and that hath taught me to say this: 'Love like a shadow flies when substance love pursues; Pursuing that that flies, and flying what pursues.'

FALSTAFF: Have you received no promise of satisfaction at her hands?

FORD: Never.

FALSTAFF: Have you importuned her to such a purpose?

FORD: Never.

FALSTAFF: Of what quality was your love, then?

FORD: Like a fair house built on another man's ground; so that I have lost my edifice by mistaking the place where I erected it.

FALSTAFF: To what purpose have you unfolded this to me?

FORD: When I have told you that, I have told you all. Some say, that though she appear honest to me, yet in other places she enlargeth her mirth so far that there is shrewd construction made of her. Now, Sir John, here is the heart of my purpose: you are a gentleman of excellent breeding, admirable discourse, of great admittance, authentic in your place and person, generally allowed for your many war-like, court-like, and learned preparations.

FALSTAFF: O, sir!

FORD: Believe it, for you know it. There is money; spend it, spend it; spend more; spend all I have; only give me so much of your time in exchange of it, as to lay an amiable siege to the honesty of this Ford's wife: use your art of wooing; win her to consent to you; if any man may, you may as soon as any.

FALSTAFF: Would it apply well to the vehemency of your affection, that I should win what you would enjoy? Methinks you prescribe to yourself very preposterously.

FORD: O, understand my drift. She dwells so securely on the excellency of her honour, that the folly of my soul dares not present itself: she is too bright to be looked against. Now, could I come to her with any detection in my hand, my desires had instance and argument to commend themselves: I could drive her then from the ward of her purity, her reputation, her marriage-vow, and a thousand other her defences, which now are too too strongly embattled against me. What say you to't, Sir John?

FALSTAFF: Master Brook, I will first make bold with your money; next, give me your hand; and last, as I am a gentleman, you shall, if you will, enjoy Ford's wife.

FORD: O good sir!

FALSTAFF: I say you shall.

FORD: Want no money, Sir John; you shall want none.

FALSTAFF: Want no Mistress Ford, Master Brook; you shall want none. I shall be with her, I may tell you, by her own appointment; even as you came in to me, her assistant or go-between parted from me: I say I shall be with her between ten and eleven; for at that time the jealous rascally knave her husband will be forth. Come you to me at night; you shall know how I speed.

FORD: I am blest in your acquaintance. Do you know Ford, sir?

FALSTAFF: Hang him, poor cuckoldly knave! I know him not; yet I wrong him to call him poor; they say the jealous wittolly knave hath masses of money; for the which his wife seems to me well-favored. I will use her as the key of the cuckoldly rogue's coffer; and there's my harvest-home.

FORD: I would you knew Ford, sir, that you might avoid him if you saw him.

FALSTAFF: Hang him, mechanical salt-butter rogue! I will stare him out of his wits; I will awe him with my cudgel: it shall hang like a meteor o'er the cuckold's horns. Master Brook, thou shalt know I will predominate over the peasant, and thou shalt lie with his wife. Come to me soon at night. Ford's a knave, and I will aggravate his style; thou, Master Brook, shalt know him for knave and cuckold. Come to me soon at night.

Exit

FORD: What a damned Epicurean rascal is this! My heart is ready to crack with impatience. Who says this is improvident jealousy? My wife hath sent to him; the hour is fixed; the match is made. Would any man have thought this? See the hell of having a false woman! My bed shall be abused, my coffers ransacked, my reputation gnawn at; and I shall not only receive this villanous wrong, but stand under the adoption of abominable terms, and by him that does me this wrong. Terms! names! Amaimon sounds well; Lucifer, well; Barbason, well; yet they are devils' additions, the names of fiends: but Cuckold! Wittol!--Cuckold! the devil himself hath not such a name. Page is an ass, a secure ass: he will trust his wife; he will not be jealous. I will rather trust a Fleming with my butter, Parson Hugh the Welshman with my cheese, an Irishman with my aqua-vitae bottle, or a thief to walk my ambling gelding, than my wife with herself. Then she plots, then she ruminates, then she devises; and what they think in their hearts they may effect, they will break their hearts but they will effect. God be praised for my jealousy! Eleven o'clock the hour. I will prevent this, detect my wife, be revenged on Falstaff, and laugh at Page. I will about it; better three hours too soon than a minute too late. Fie, fie, fie! cuckold! cuckold! cuckold!

Exit

SCENE III—*A field near Windsor*

Enter DOCTOR CAIUS and RUGBY

DOCTOR CAIUS: Jack Rugby!

RUGBY: Sir?

DOCTOR CAIUS: Vat is de clock, Jack?

RUGBY: 'Tis past the hour, sir, that Sir Hugh promised to meet.

DOCTOR CAIUS: By gar, he has save his soul, dat he is no come; he has pray his Pible well, dat he is no come: by gar, Jack Rugby, he is dead already, if he be come.

RUGBY: He is wise, sir; he knew your worship would kill him, if he came.

DOCTOR CAIUS: By gar, de herring is no dead so as I vill kill him.

Take your rapier, Jack; I vill tell you how I vill kill him.

RUGBY: Alas, sir, I cannot fence.

DOCTOR CAIUS: Villany, take your rapier.

RUGBY: Forbear; here's company.

Enter Host, SHALLOW, SLENDER, and PAGE

HOST: Bless thee, bully doctor!

SHALLOW: Save you, Master Doctor Caius!

PAGE: Now, good master doctor!

SLENDER: Give you good morrow, sir.

DOCTOR CAIUS: Vat be all you, one, two, tree, four, come for?

HOST: To see thee fight, to see thee foin, to see thee traverse; to see thee here, to see thee there; to see thee pass thy punto, thy stock, thy reverse, thy distance, thy montant. Is he dead, my Ethiopian? is he dead, my Francisco? Ha, bully! What says my AEsculapius? my Galen? my heart of elder? Ha! is he dead, bully stale? is he dead?

DOCTOR CAIUS: By gar, he is de coward Jack priest of de vorld; he is not show his face.

HOST: Thou art a Castalion-King-Urinal. Hector of Greece, my boy!

DOCTOR CAIUS: I pray you, bear vitness that me have stay six or seven, two, tree hours for him, and he is no come.

SHALLOW: He is the wiser man, Master Doctor: he is a curer of souls, and you a curer of bodies; if you should fight, you go against the hair of your professions. Is it not true, Master Page?

PAGE: Master Shallow, you have yourself been a great fighter, though now a man of peace.

SHALLOW: Bodykins, Master Page, though I now be old and of the peace, if I see a sword out, my finger itches to make one. Though we are justices and doctors and churchmen, Master Page, we have some salt of our youth in us; we are the sons of women, Master Page.

PAGE: 'Tis true, Master Shallow.

SHALLOW: It will be found so, Master Page. Master Doctor Caius, I am come to fetch you home. I am sworn of the peace; you have showed yourself a wise physician, and Sir Hugh hath shown himself a wise and patient churchman. You must go with me, Master Doctor.

HOST: Pardon, Guest Justice. A word, Mounseur Mockwater.

DOCTOR CAIUS: Mock-vater! Vat is dat?

HOST: Mock-water, in our English tongue, is valour, bully.

DOCTOR CAIUS: By gar, then, I have as mush mock-vater as de Englishman. Scurvy jack-dog priest! By gar, me vill cut his ears.

HOST: He will clapper-claw thee tightly, bully.

DOCTOR CAIUS: Clapper-de-claw! Vat is dat?

HOST: That is, he will make thee amends.

DOCTOR CAIUS: By gar, me do look he shall clapper-de-claw me; for, by gar, me vill have it.

HOST: And I will provoke him to't, or let him wag.

DOCTOR CAIUS: Me tank you for dat.

HOST: And, moreover, bully—but first, (*Aside to the others*) Master Guest, and Master Page, and eke Cavaleiro Slender, go you through the town to Frogmore.

Aside to them

PAGE: Sir Hugh is there, is he?

HOST: He is there: see what humour he is in; and I will bring the doctor about by the fields. Will it do well?

SHALLOW: We will do it.

PAGE, SHALLOW AND SLENDER: Adieu, good Master Doctor.

Exeunt PAGE, SHALLOW, and SLENDER

DOCTOR CAIUS: By gar, me vill kill de priest; for he speak for a jack-an-ape to Anne Page.

HOST: Let him die: sheathe thy impatience, throw cold water on thy choler: go about the fields with me through Frogmore: I will bring thee where Mistress Anne Page is, at a farm-house a-feasting; and thou shalt woo her. Cried game? Said I well?

DOCTOR CAIUS: By gar, me dank you for dat: by gar, I love you; and I shall procure-a you de good guest, de earl, de knight, de lords, de gentlemen, my patients.

HOST: For the which I will be thy adversary toward Anne Page. Said I well?

DOCTOR CAIUS: By gar, 'tis good; vell said.

HOST: Let us wag, then.

DOCTOR CAIUS: Come at my heels, Jack Rugby.

Exeunt

Act III

Scene I—*A field near Frogmore*

Enter SIR HUGH EVANS and SIMPLE

SIR HUGH EVANS: I pray you now, good master Slender's serving-man, and friend Simple by your name, which way have you looked for Master Caius, that calls himself Doctor of Physic?

SIMPLE: Marry, sir, the pittie-ward, the park-ward, every way; old Windsor way, and every way but the town way.

SIR HUGH EVANS: I most fehemently desire you you will also look that way.

SIMPLE: I will, sir.

Exit

SIR HUGH EVANS: Pless my soul, how full of chollors I am, and trempling of mind! I shall be glad if he have deceived me. How melancholies I am! I will knog his urinals about his knave's costard when I have good opportunities for the ork. Pless my soul!

Sings

To shallow rivers, to whose falls
Melodious birds sings madrigals;
There will we make our peds of roses,
And a thousand fragrant posies.
To shallow—
Mercy on me! I have a great dispositions to cry.

Sings

Melodious birds sing madrigals—
When as I sat in Pabylon—
And a thousand vagram posies.
To shallow etc.

Re-enter SIMPLE

SIMPLE: Yonder he is coming, this way, Sir Hugh.

SIR HUGH EVANS: He's welcome.

Sings

To shallow rivers, to whose falls—
Heaven prosper the right! What weapons is he?

SIMPLE: No weapons, sir. There comes my master, Master Shallow, and another gentleman, from Frogmore, over the stile, this way.

SIR HUGH EVANS: Pray you, give me my gown; or else keep it in your arms.

[Takes out a book]

Enter PAGE, SHALLOW, and SLENDER

SHALLOW: How now, master Parson! Good morrow, good Sir Hugh. Keep a gamester from the dice, and a good student from his book, and it is wonderful.

SLENDER: [*Aside*] Ah, sweet Anne Page!

PAGE: Save you, good Sir Hugh!

SIR HUGH EVANS: 'Pless you from his mercy sake, all of you!

SHALLOW: What, the sword and the word! Do you study them both, Master Parson?

PAGE: And youthful still! in your doublet and hose this raw rheumatic day!

SIR HUGH EVANS: There is reasons and causes for it.

PAGE: We are come to you to do a good office, Master Parson.

SIR HUGH EVANS: Fery well; what is it?

PAGE: Yonder is a most reverend gentleman, who, belike having received wrong by some person, is at most odds with his own gravity and patience that ever you saw.

SHALLOW: I have lived fourscore years and upward; I never heard a man of his place, gravity and learning, so wide of his own respect.

SIR HUGH EVANS: What is he?

PAGE: I think you know him; Master Doctor Caius, the renowned French physician.

SIR HUGH EVANS: Got's will, and his passion of my heart! I had as lief you would tell me of a mess of porridge.

PAGE: Why?

SIR HUGH EVANS: He has no more knowledge in Hibocrates and Galen,—and he is a knave besides;

a cowardly knave as you would desires to be acquainted withal.

PAGE: I warrant you, he's the man should fight with him.

SLENDER: [*Aside*] O sweet Anne Page!

SHALLOW: It appears so by his weapons. Keep them asunder: here comes Doctor Caius.

Enter Host, DOCTOR CAIUS, and RUGBY

PAGE: Nay, good Master Parson, keep in your weapon.

SHALLOW: So do you, Good Master Doctor.

HOST: Disarm them, and let them question; let them keep their limbs whole and hack our English.

DOCTOR CAIUS: I pray you, let-a me speak a word with your ear. Vherefore vill you not meet-a me?

SIR HUGH EVANS: [*Aside to Doctor Caius*] Pray you, use your patience; in good time.

DOCTOR CAIUS: By gar, you are de coward, de Jack dog, John ape.

SIR HUGH EVANS: [*Aside to Doctor Caius*] Pray you let us not be laughing-stocks to other men's humours; I desire you in friendship, and I will one way or other make you amends. (*Aloud*) I will knog your urinals about your knave's cockscomb for missing your meetings and appointments.

DOCTOR CAIUS: Diable! Jack Rugby—mine host de Jarteer—have I not stay for him to kill him? Have I not, at de place I did appoint?

SIR HUGH EVANS: As I am a Christians soul now, look you, this is the place appointed: I'll be judgement by mine host of the Garter.

HOST: Peace, I say, Gallia and Gaul, French and Welsh, soul-curer and body-curer!

DOCTOR CAIUS: Ay, dat is very good; excellent.

HOST: Peace, I say! hear mine host of the Garter. Am I politic? am I subtle? am I a Machiavel? Shall I lose my doctor? no; he gives me the potions and the motions. Shall I lose my parson, my priest, my Sir Hugh? no; he gives me the proverbs and the no verbs. Give me thy hand, terrestrial; so. Give me thy hand, celestial; so. Boys of art, I have deceived you both; I have directed you to wrong places: your hearts are mighty, your skins are whole, and let burnt sack be the issue. Come, lay their swords to pawn. Follow me, lads of peace; follow, follow, follow.

SHALLOW: Trust me, a mad host. Follow, gentlemen, follow.

SLENDER: [*Aside*] O sweet Anne Page!

Exeunt SHALLOW, SLENDER, PAGE, and Host

DOCTOR CAIUS: Ha, do I perceive dat? have you make-a de sot of us, ha, ha?

SIR HUGH EVANS: This is well; he has made us his vlouting-stog. I desire you that we may be friends; and let us knog our prains together to be revenge on this same scall, scurvy cogging companion, the host of the Garter.

DOCTOR CAIUS: By gar, with all my heart. He promise to bring me where is Anne Page; by gar, he deceive me too.

SIR HUGH EVANS: Well, I will smite his noddles. Pray you, follow.

Exeunt

Scene II—*A street in Windsor*

Enter MISTRESS PAGE and ROBIN

MISTRESS PAGE: Nay, keep your way, little gallant; you were wont to be a follower, but now you are a leader. Whether had you rather lead mine eyes, or eye your master's heels?

ROBIN: I had rather, forsooth, go before you like a man than follow him like a dwarf.

MISTRESS PAGE: O, you are a flattering boy; now I see you'll be a courtier.

Enter FORD

FORD: Well met, Mistress Page. Whither go you?

MISTRESS PAGE: Truly, sir, to see your wife. Is she at home?

FORD: Ay; and as idle as she may hang together, for want of company. I think, if your husbands were dead, you two would marry.

MISTRESS PAGE: Be sure of that—two other husbands.

FORD: Where had you this pretty weather-cock?

MISTRESS PAGE: I cannot tell what the dickens his name is my husband had him of. What do you call your knight's name, sirrah?

ROBIN: Sir John Falstaff.

FORD: Sir John Falstaff!

MISTRESS PAGE: He, he; I can never hit on's name. There is such a league between my good man and he! Is your wife at home indeed?

FORD: Indeed she is.

MISTRESS PAGE: By your leave, sir: I am sick till I see her.

Exeunt MISTRESS PAGE and ROBIN

FORD: Has Page any brains? hath he any eyes? hath he any thinking? Sure, they sleep; he hath no use of them. Why, this boy will carry a letter twenty mile, as easy as a cannon will shoot point-blank twelve score. He pieces out his wife's inclination; he gives her folly motion and advantage; and now she's going to my wife, and Falstaff's boy with her. A man may hear this shower sing in the wind. And Falstaff's boy with her! Good plots, they are laid; and our revolted wives share damnation together. Well; I will take him, then torture my wife, pluck the borrowed veil of modesty from the so seeming Mistress Page, divulge Page himself for a secure and wilful Actaeon; and to these violent proceedings all my neighbours shall cry aim. (*Clock heard*) The clock gives me my cue, and my assurance bids me search: there I shall find Falstaff: I shall be rather praised for this than mocked; for it is as positive as the earth is firm that Falstaff is there: I will go.

Enter PAGE, SHALLOW, SLENDER, Host, SIR HUGH EVANS, DOCTOR CAIUS, and RUGBY

SHALLOW, PAGE &C: Well met, Master Ford.

FORD: Trust me, a good knot: I have good cheer at home; and I pray you all go with me.

SHALLOW: I must excuse myself, Master Ford.

SLENDER: And so must I, sir; we have appointed to dine with Mistress Anne, and I would not break with her for more money than I'll speak of.

SHALLOW: We have lingered about a match between Anne Page and my cousin Slender, and this day we shall have our answer.

SLENDER: I hope I have your good will, father Page.

PAGE: You have, Master Slender; I stand wholly for you: but my wife, master doctor, is for you altogether.

DOCTOR CAIUS: Ay, be-gar; and de maid is love-a me: my nursh-a Quickly tell me so mush.

Host: What say you to young Master Fenton? He capers, he dances, he has eyes of youth, he writes verses, he speaks holiday, he smells April and May: he will carry't, he will carry't; 'tis in his buttons; he will carry't.

PAGE: Not by my consent, I promise you. The gentleman is of no having: he kept company with the wild prince and Poins; he is of too high a region; he knows too much. No, he shall not knit a knot in his fortunes with the finger of my substance: if he take her, let him take her simply; the wealth I have waits on my consent, and my consent goes not that way.

FORD: I beseech you heartily, some of you go home with me to dinner: besides your cheer, you shall have sport; I will show you a monster. Master doctor, you shall go; so shall you, Master Page; and you, Sir Hugh.

SHALLOW: Well, fare you well; we shall have the freer wooing at Master Page's.

Exeunt SHALLOW, and SLENDER

DOCTOR CAIUS: Go home, John Rugby; I come anon.

Exit RUGBY

HOST: Farewell, my hearts: I will to my honest knight Falstaff, and drink canary with him.

Exit

FORD: [*Aside*] I think I shall drink in pipe wine first with him; I'll make him dance. Will you go, gentles?

ALL: Have with you to see this monster.

Exeunt

SCENE III—*Ford's house*

Enter MISTRESS FORD and MISTRESS PAGE

MISTRESS FORD: What, John! What, Robert!

MISTRESS PAGE: Quickly, quickly! is the buck-basket—

MISTRESS FORD: I warrant. What, Robin, I say!

Enter Servants with a basket

MISTRESS PAGE: Come, come, come.

MISTRESS FORD: Here, set it down.

MISTRESS PAGE: Give your men the charge; we must be brief.

MISTRESS FORD: Marry, as I told you before, John and Robert, be ready here hard by in the brew-house: and when I suddenly call you, come forth, and without any pause or staggering, take this basket on your shoulders: that done, trudge with it in all haste, and carry it among the whitsters in Datchet-mead, and there empty it in the muddy ditch close by the Thames side.

MISTRESS PAGE: You will do it?

MISTRESS FORD: I ha' told them over and over; they lack no direction. Be gone, and come when you are called.

Exeunt Servants

MISTRESS PAGE: Here comes little Robin.

Enter ROBIN

MISTRESS FORD: How now, my eyas-musket! what news with you?

ROBIN: My master, Sir John, is come in at your back-door, Mistress Ford, and requests your company.

MISTRESS PAGE: You little Jack-a-Lent, have you been true to us?

ROBIN: Ay, I'll be sworn. My master knows not of your being here and hath threatened to put me into everlasting liberty if I tell you of it; for he swears he'll turn me away.

MISTRESS PAGE: Thou'rt a good boy: this secrecy of thine shall be a tailor to thee and shall make thee a new doublet and hose. I'll go hide me.

MISTRESS FORD: Do so. Go tell thy master I am alone.

Exit ROBIN

Mistress Page, remember you your cue.

MISTRESS PAGE: I warrant thee; if I do not act it, hiss me.

Exit MISTRESS PAGE

MISTRESS FORD: Go to, then: we'll use this unwholesome humidity, this gross watery pumpion; we'll teach him to know turtles from jays.

Enter FALSTAFF

FALSTAFF: Have I caught thee, my heavenly jewel? Why, now let me die, for I have lived long enough: this is the period of my ambition: O this blessed hour!

MISTRESS FORD: O sweet Sir John!

FALSTAFF: Mistress Ford, I cannot cog, I cannot prate, Mistress Ford. Now shall I sin in my wish: I would thy husband were dead: I'll speak it before the best lord; I would make thee my lady.

MISTRESS FORD: I your lady, Sir John! Alas, I should be a pitiful lady!

FALSTAFF: Let the court of France show me such another. I see how thine eye would emulate the diamond: thou hast the right arched beauty of the brow that becomes the ship-tire, the tire-valiant, or any tire of Venetian admittance.

MISTRESS FORD: A plain kerchief, Sir John: my brows become nothing else; nor that well neither.

FALSTAFF: By the Lord, thou art a traitor to say so: thou wouldst make an absolute courtier; and the firm fixture of thy foot would give an excellent motion to thy gait in a semi-circled farthingale. I see what thou wert, if Fortune thy foe were not, Nature thy friend. Come, thou canst not hide it.

MISTRESS FORD: Believe me, there is no such thing in me.

FALSTAFF: What made me love thee? Let that persuade thee there's something extraordinary in thee. Come, I cannot cog and say thou art this and that, like a many of these lisping hawthorn-buds, that come like women in men's apparel, and smell like Bucklersbury in simple time; I cannot: but I love thee; none but thee; and thou deservest it.

MISTRESS FORD: Do not betray me, sir. I fear you love Mistress Page.

FALSTAFF: Thou mightst as well say I love to walk by the Counter-gate, which is as hateful to me as the reek of a lime-kiln.

MISTRESS FORD: Well, heaven knows how I love you; and you shall one day find it.

FALSTAFF: Keep in that mind; I'll deserve it.

MISTRESS FORD: Nay, I must tell you, so you do; or else I could not be in that mind.

ROBIN: [*Within*] Mistress Ford, Mistress Ford! here's Mistress Page at the door, sweating and blowing and looking wildly, and would needs speak with you presently.

FALSTAFF: She shall not see me: I will ensconce me behind the arras.

MISTRESS FORD: Pray you, do so: she's a very tattling woman.

Falstaff hides himself

Re-enter MISTRESS PAGE and ROBIN

What's the matter? How now!

MISTRESS PAGE: O Mistress Ford, what have you done? You're shamed, you're overthrown, you're undone for ever!

MISTRESS FORD: What's the matter, good Mistress Page?

MISTRESS PAGE: O well-a-day, Mistress Ford! having an honest man to your husband, to give him such cause of suspicion!

MISTRESS FORD: What cause of suspicion?

MISTRESS PAGE: What cause of suspicion! Out upon you, how am I mistook in you!

MISTRESS FORD: Why, alas, what's the matter?

MISTRESS PAGE: Your husband's coming hither, woman, with all the officers in Windsor, to search for a gentleman that he says is here now in the house by your consent, to take an ill advantage of his assence. You are undone.

MISTRESS FORD: 'Tis not so, I hope.

MISTRESS PAGE: Pray heaven it be not so, that you have such a man here! but 'tis most certain your husband's coming, with half Windsor at his heels, to search for such a one. I come before to tell you. If you know yourself clear, why, I am glad of it; but if you have a friend here convey, convey him out. Be not amazed; call all your senses to you; defend your reputation, or bid farewell to your good life for ever.

MISTRESS FORD: What shall I do? There is a gentleman my dear friend; and I fear not mine own shame so much as his peril: I had rather than a thousand pound he were out of the house.

MISTRESS PAGE: For shame! never stand 'you had rather' and 'you had rather': your husband's here at hand, bethink you of some conveyance: in the house you cannot hide him. O, how have you deceived me! Look, here is a basket: if he be of any reasonable stature, he may creep in here; and throw foul linen upon him, as if it were going to bucking: or—it is whiting-time—send him by your two men to Datchet-mead.

MISTRESS FORD: He's too big to go in there. What shall I do?

FALSTAFF: [*Coming forward*] Let me see't, let me see't, O, let me see't! I'll in, I'll in. Follow your friend's counsel. I'll in.

MISTRESS PAGE: What, Sir John Falstaff! (*Aside to Falstaff*) Are these your letters, knight?

FALSTAFF: (*Aside to Mistress Page*)I love thee and none but thee; help me away. Let me creep in here. I'll never—

Gets into the basket; they cover him with foul linen

MISTRESS PAGE: Help to cover your master, boy. Call your men, Mistress Ford. You dissembling knight!

MISTRESS FORD: What, John! Robert! John!

Exit ROBIN

Re-enter Servants

Go take up these clothes here quickly. Where's the cowl-staff? look, how you drumble! Carry them to the laundress in Datchet Mead; quickly, come.

Enter FORD, PAGE, DOCTOR CAIUS, and SIR HUGH EVANS

FORD: Pray you, come near: if I suspect without cause, why then make sport at me; then let me be your jest; I deserve it. How now! whither bear you this?

SERVANT: To the laundress, forsooth.

MISTRESS FORD: Why, what have you to do whither they bear it? You were best meddle with buck-washing.

FORD: Buck! I would I could wash myself of the buck! Buck, buck, buck! Ay, buck; I warrant you, buck; and of the season too, it shall appear.

Exeunt Servants with the basket

Gentlemen, I have dreamed to-night; I'll tell you my dream. Here, here, here be my keys: ascend my chambers; search, seek, find out: I'll warrant we'll unkennel the fox. Let me stop this way first. (*Locking the door*) So, now uncape.

PAGE: Good Master Ford, be contented: you wrong yourself too much.

FORD: True, Master Page. Up, gentlemen: you shall see sport anon: follow me, gentlemen.

Exit

SIR HUGH EVANS: This is fery fantastical humours and jealousies.

DOCTOR CAIUS: By gar, 'tis no the fashion of France; it is not jealous in France.

PAGE: Nay, follow him, gentlemen; see the issue of his search.

Exeunt PAGE, DOCTOR CAIUS, and SIR HUGH EVANS

MISTRESS PAGE: Is there not a double excellency in this?

MISTRESS FORD: I know not which pleases me better, that my husband is deceived, or Sir John.

MISTRESS PAGE: What a taking was he in when your husband asked who was in the basket!

MISTRESS FORD: I am half afraid he will have need of washing; so throwing him into the water will do him a benefit.

MISTRESS PAGE: Hang him, dishonest rascal! I would all of the same strain were in the same distress.

MISTRESS FORD: I think my husband hath some special suspicion of Falstaff's being here; for I never saw him so gross in his jealousy till now.

MISTRESS PAGE: I will lay a plot to try that; and we will yet have more tricks with Falstaff: his dissolute disease will scarce obey this medicine.

MISTRESS FORD: Shall we send that foolish carrion, Mistress Quickly, to him, and excuse his throwing into the water; and give him another hope, to betray him to another punishment?

MISTRESS PAGE: We will do it: let him be sent for to-morrow, eight o'clock, to have amends.

Re-enter FORD, PAGE, DOCTOR CAIUS, and SIR HUGH EVANS

FORD: I cannot find him: may be the knave bragged of that he could not compass.

MISTRESS PAGE: [*Aside to Mistress Ford*] Heard you that?

MISTRESS FORD: You use me well, Master Ford, do you?

FORD: Ay, I do so.

MISTRESS FORD: Heaven make you better than your thoughts!

FORD: Amen!

MISTRESS PAGE: You do yourself mighty wrong, Master Ford.

FORD: Ay, ay; I must bear it.

SIR HUGH EVANS: If there be any pody in the house, and in the chambers, and in the coffers, and in the presses, heaven forgive my sins at the day of judgment!

DOCTOR CAIUS: By gar, nor I too: there is no bodies.

PAGE: Fie, fie, Master Ford! are you not ashamed? What spirit, what devil suggests this imagination? I would not ha' your distemper in this kind for the wealth of Windsor Castle.

FORD: 'Tis my fault, Master Page: I suffer for it.

SIR HUGH EVANS: You suffer for a pad conscience: your wife is as honest a 'omans as I will desires among five thousand, and five hundred too.

DOCTOR CAIUS: By gar, I see 'tis an honest woman.

FORD: Well, I promised you a dinner. Come, come, walk in the Park: I pray you, pardon me; I will hereafter make known to you why I have done this. Come, wife; come, Mistress Page. I pray you, pardon me; pray heartily, pardon me.

PAGE: Let's go in, gentlemen; but, trust me, we'll mock him. I do invite you to-morrow morning to my house to breakfast: after, we'll a-birding together; I have a fine hawk for the bush. Shall it be so?

FORD: Any thing.

SIR HUGH EVANS: If there is one, I shall make two in the company.

DOCTOR CAIUS: If there be one or two, I shall make-a the turd.

FORD: Pray you, go, Master Page.

SIR HUGH EVANS: I pray you now, remembrance tomorrow on the lousy knave, mine host.

DOCTOR CAIUS: Dat is good; by gar, with all my heart.

SIR HUGH EVANS: A lousy knave, to have his gibes and his mockeries!

Exeunt

SCENE IV—*Before Page's house*

Enter FENTON and ANNE PAGE

FENTON: I see I cannot get thy father's love;
Therefore no more turn me to him, sweet Nan.

ANNE PAGE: Alas, how then?

FENTON: Why, thou must be thyself.
He doth object I am too great of birth;
And that, my state being gall'd with my expense,
I seek to heal it only by his wealth.
Besides these, other bars he lays before me,
My riots past, my wild societies;
And tells me 'tis a thing impossible
I should love thee but as a property.

ANNE PAGE: May be he tells you true.

FENTON: No, heaven so speed me in my time to come!
Albeit I will confess thy father's wealth
Was the first motive that I woo'd thee, Anne:
Yet, wooing thee, I found thee of more value
Than stamps in gold or sums in sealed bags;
And 'tis the very riches of thyself
That now I aim at.

ANNE PAGE: Gentle Master Fenton,
Yet seek my father's love; still seek it, sir:
If opportunity and humblest suit
Cannot attain it, why, then—hark you hither!

They converse apart

Enter SHALLOW, SLENDER, and MISTRESS QUICKLY

SHALLOW: Break their talk, Mistress Quickly: my kinsman shall speak for himself.

SLENDER: I'll make a shaft or a bolt on't: 'slid, 'tis but venturing.

SHALLOW: Be not dismayed.

SLENDER: No, she shall not dismay me: I care not for that, but that I am afeard.

MISTRESS QUICKLY: Hark ye; Master Slender would speak a word with you.

ANNE PAGE: I come to him. [*Aside*] This is my father's choice.

O, what a world of vile ill-favor'd faults

Looks handsome in three hundred pounds a-year!

MISTRESS QUICKLY: And how does good Master Fenton? Pray you, a word with you.

SHALLOW: She's coming; to her, coz. O boy, thou hadst a father!

SLENDER: I had a father, Mistress Anne; my uncle can tell you good jests of him. Pray you, uncle, tell Mistress Anne the jest, how my father stole two geese out of a pen, good uncle.

SHALLOW: Mistress Anne, my cousin loves you.

SLENDER: Ay, that I do; as well as I love any woman in Gloucestershire.

SHALLOW: He will maintain you like a gentlewoman.

SLENDER: Ay, that I will, come cut and long-tail, under the degree of a squire.

SHALLOW: He will make you a hundred and fifty pounds jointure.

ANNE PAGE: Good Master Shallow, let him woo for himself.

SHALLOW: Marry, I thank you for it; I thank you for that good comfort. She calls you, coz: I'll leave you.

ANNE PAGE: Now, Master Slender—

SLENDER: Now, good Mistress Anne—

ANNE PAGE: What is your will?

SLENDER: My will! 'od's heartlings, that's a pretty jest indeed! I ne'er made my will yet, I thank heaven; I am not such a sickly creature, I give heaven praise.

ANNE PAGE: I mean, Master Slender, what would you with me?

SLENDER: Truly, for mine own part, I would little or nothing with you. Your father and my uncle hath made motions: if it be my luck, so; if not, happy man be his dole! They can tell you how things go better than I can: you may ask your father; here he comes.

Enter PAGE and MISTRESS PAGE

PAGE: Now, Master Slender: Love him, daughter Anne—

Why, how now! what does Master Fenton here?

You wrong me, sir, thus still to haunt my house:

I told you, sir, my daughter is disposed of.

FENTON: Nay, Master Page, be not impatient.

MISTRESS PAGE: Good Master Fenton, come not to my child.

PAGE: She is no match for you.

FENTON: Sir, will you hear me?

PAGE: No, good Master Fenton.

Come, Master Shallow; come, son Slender, in.

Knowing my mind, you wrong me, Master Fenton.

Exeunt PAGE, SHALLOW, and SLENDER

MISTRESS QUICKLY: Speak to Mistress Page.

FENTON: Good Mistress Page, for that I love your daughter

In such a righteous fashion as I do,

Perforce, against all checks, rebukes and manners,

I must advance the colours of my love

And not retire: let me have your good will.

ANNE PAGE: Good mother, do not marry me to yond fool.

MISTRESS PAGE: I mean it not; I seek you a better husband.

MISTRESS QUICKLY: That's my master, master doctor.

ANNE PAGE: Alas, I had rather be set quick i' the earth

And bowl'd to death with turnips!

MISTRESS PAGE: Come, trouble not yourself. Good Master Fenton,

I will not be your friend nor enemy;

My daughter will I question how she loves you,

And as I find her, so am I affected.

Till then farewell, sir: she must needs go in;

Her father will be angry.

FENTON: Farewell, gentle mistress: farewell, Nan.

Exeunt MISTRESS PAGE and ANNE PAGE

MISTRESS QUICKLY: This is my doing, now: 'Nay,' said I, 'will you cast away your child on a fool, and a physician? Look on Master Fenton:' This is my doing.

FENTON: I thank thee; and I pray thee, once to-night

Give my sweet Nan this ring. There's for thy pains.

MISTRESS QUICKLY: Now heaven send thee good fortune!

Exit FENTON

A kind heart he hath; a woman would run through fire and water for such a kind heart. But yet I would my master had Mistress Anne; or I would Master Slender had her; or, in sooth, I would Master Fenton had her; I will do what I can for them all three; for so I have promised, and I'll be as good as my word; but speciously for Master Fenton. Well, I must of another errand to Sir John

Falstaff from my two mistresses: what a beast am I to slack it!

Exit

SCENE V—*The Garter Inn*

Enter FALSTAFF and BARDOLPH

FALSTAFF: Bardolph, I say!

BARDOLPH: Here, sir.

FALSTAFF: Go fetch me a quart of sack; put a toast in't.

Exit BARDOLPH

Have I lived to be carried in a basket, like a barrow of butcher's offal, and to be thrown in the Thames? Well, if I be served such another trick, I'll have my brains ta'en out and buttered, and give them to a dog for a new-year's gift. The rogues slighted me into the river with as little remorse as they would have drowned a blind bitch's puppies, fifteen i' the litter: and you may know by my size that I have a kind of alacrity in sinking; if the bottom were as deep as hell, I should down. I had been drowned, but that the shore was shelvy and shallow—a death that I abhor; for the water swells a man; and what a thing should I have been when I had been swelled! I should have been a mountain of mummy.

Re-enter BARDOLPH with sack

BARDOLPH: Here's Mistress Quickly, sir, to speak with you.

FALSTAFF: Let me pour in some sack to the Thames water; for my belly's as cold as if I had swallowed snowballs for pills to cool the reins. Call her in.

BARDOLPH: Come in, woman!

Enter MISTRESS QUICKLY

MISTRESS QUICKLY: By your leave; I cry you mercy: give your worship good morrow.

FALSTAFF: Take away these chalices. Go brew me a pottle of sack finely.

BARDOLPH: With eggs, sir?

FALSTAFF: Simple of itself; I'll no pullet-sperm in my brewage.

Exit BARDOLPH

How now!

MISTRESS QUICKLY: Marry, sir, I come to your worship from Mistress Ford.

FALSTAFF: Mistress Ford! I have had ford enough; I was thrown into the ford; I have my belly full of ford.

MISTRESS QUICKLY: Alas the day! good heart, that was not her fault: she does so take on with her men; they mistook their erection.

FALSTAFF: So did I mine, to build upon a foolish woman's promise.

MISTRESS QUICKLY: Well, she laments, sir, for it, that it would yearn your heart to see it. Her husband goes this morning a-birding; she desires you once more to come to her between eight and nine: I must carry her word quickly: she'll make you amends, I warrant you.

FALSTAFF: Well, I will visit her: tell her so; and bid her think what a man is: let her consider his frailty, and then judge of my merit.

MISTRESS QUICKLY: I will tell her.

FALSTAFF: Do so. Between nine and ten, sayest thou?

MISTRESS QUICKLY: Eight and nine, sir.

FALSTAFF: Well, be gone: I will not miss her.

MISTRESS QUICKLY: Peace be with you, sir.

Exit

FALSTAFF: I marvel I hear not of Master Brook; he sent me word to stay within: I like his money well. O, here he comes.

Enter FORD

FORD: Bless you, sir!

FALSTAFF: Now, master Brook, you come to know what hath passed between me and Ford's wife?

FORD: That, indeed, Sir John, is my business.

FALSTAFF: Master Brook, I will not lie to you: I was at her house the hour she appointed me.

FORD: And sped you, sir?

FALSTAFF: Very ill-favoredly, Master Brook.

FORD: How so, sir? Did she change her determination?

FALSTAFF: No, Master Brook; but the peaking Cornuto her husband, Master Brook, dwelling in a continual 'larum of jealousy, comes me in the instant of our encounter, after we had embraced, kissed, protested, and, as it were, spoke the prologue of our comedy; and at his heels a rabble of his companions, thither provoked and instigated by his distemper, and, forsooth, to search his house for his wife's love.

FORD: What, while you were there?

FALSTAFF: While I was there.

FORD: And did he search for you, and could not find you?

FALSTAFF: You shall hear. As good luck would have it, comes in one Mistress Page; gives intelligence of Ford's approach; and, in her invention and Ford's wife's distraction, they conveyed me into a buck-basket.

FORD: A buck-basket!

FALSTAFF: By the Lord, a buck-basket! Rammed me in with foul shirts and smocks, socks, foul stockings, greasy napkins; that, Master Brook, there was the rankest compound of villanous smell that ever offended nostril.

FORD: And how long lay you there?

FALSTAFF: Nay, you shall hear, Master Brook, what I have suffered to bring this woman to evil for your good. Being thus crammed in the basket, a couple of Ford's knaves, his hinds, were called forth by their mistress to carry me in the name of foul clothes to Datchet-lane: they took me on their shoulders; met the jealous knave their master in the door, who asked them once or twice what they had in their basket: I quaked for fear, lest the lunatic knave would have searched it; but fate, ordaining he should be a cuckold, held his hand. Well, on went he for a search, and away went I for foul clothes. But mark the sequel, Master Brook: I suffered the pangs of three several deaths: first, an intolerable fright, to be detected with a jealous rotten bell-wether; next, to be compassed, like a good bilbo, in the circumference of a peck, hilt to point, heel to head; and then, to be stopped in, like a strong distillation, with stinking clothes that fretted in their own grease. Think of that—a man of my kidney. Think of that—that am as subject to heat as butter; a man of continual dissolution and thaw: it was a miracle to scape suffocation. And in the height of this bath, when I was more than half stewed in grease, like a Dutch dish, to be thrown into the Thames, and cooled, glowing hot, in that surge, like a horse-shoe; think of that—hissing hot. Think of that, Master Brook.

FORD: In good sadness, Sir, I am sorry that for my sake you have suffered all this. My suit then is desperate; you'll undertake her no more?

FALSTAFF: Master Brook, I will be thrown into Etna, as I have been into Thames, ere I will leave her thus. Her husband is this morning gone a-birding; I have received from her another embassy of meeting; 'twixt eight and nine is the hour, Master Brook.

FORD: 'Tis past eight already, sir.

FALSTAFF: Is it? I will then address me to my appointment. Come to me at your convenient leisure, and you shall know how I speed; and the conclusion shall be crowned with your enjoying her. Adieu. You shall have her, Master Brook; Master Brook, you shall cuckold Ford.

Exit

FORD: Hum! ha! is this a vision? is this a dream? do I sleep? Master Ford awake! awake, Master Ford! there's a hole made in your best coat, Master Ford. This 'tis to be married! this 'tis to have linen and buck-baskets! Well, I will proclaim myself what I am: I will now take the lecher; he is at my house; he cannot 'scape me; 'tis impossible he should; he cannot creep into a halfpenny purse, nor into a pepper-box. But, lest the devil that guides him should aid him, I will search impossible places. Though what I am I cannot avoid, yet to be what I would not shall not make me tame: if I have horns to make one mad, let the proverb go with me: I'll be horn-mad.

Exit

Act IV

Scene I—*Windsor: A street*

Enter MISTRESS PAGE, MISTRESS Quickly, and WILLIAM PAGE

MISTRESS PAGE: Is he at Master Ford's already, think'st thou?

MISTRESS QUICKLY: Sure he is by this, or will be presently: but, truly, he is very courageous mad about his throwing into the water. Mistress Ford desires you to come suddenly.

MISTRESS PAGE: I'll be with her by and by; I'll but bring my young man here to school. Look, where his master comes; 'tis a playing-day, I see.

Enter SIR HUGH EVANS

How now, Sir Hugh! no school to-day?

SIR HUGH EVANS: No; Master Slender is let the boys leave to play.

MISTRESS QUICKLY: Blessing of his heart!

MISTRESS PAGE: Sir Hugh, my husband says my son profits nothing in the world at his book. I pray you, ask him some questions in his accidence.

SIR HUGH EVANS: Come hither, William; hold up your head; come.

MISTRESS PAGE: Come on, sirrah; hold up your head; answer your master, be not afraid.

SIR HUGH EVANS: William, how many numbers is in nouns?

WILLIAM PAGE: Two.

MISTRESS QUICKLY: Truly, I thought there had been one number more, because they say, ''Od's nouns'.

SIR HUGH EVANS: Peace your tattlings! What is 'fair', William?

WILLIAM PAGE: Pulcher.

MISTRESS QUICKLY: Polecats! there are fairer things than polecats, sure.

SIR HUGH EVANS: You are a very simplicity oman; I pray you peace. What is 'lapis', William?

WILLIAM PAGE: A stone.

SIR HUGH EVANS: And what is 'a stone', William?

WILLIAM PAGE: A pebble.

SIR HUGH EVANS: No, it is 'lapis'; I pray you, remember in your prain.

WILLIAM PAGE: Lapis.

SIR HUGH EVANS: That is a good William. What is he, William, that does lend articles?

WILLIAM PAGE: Articles are borrowed of the pronoun, and be thus declined, Singulariter, nominativo, hic, haec, hoc.

SIR HUGH EVANS: Nominativo, hig, hag, hog; pray you, mark: genitivo, hujus. Well, what is your accusative case?

WILLIAM PAGE: Accusativo, hinc.

SIR HUGH EVANS: I pray you, have your remembrance, child, accusative, hung, hang, hog.

MISTRESS QUICKLY: 'Hang-hog' is Latin for bacon, I warrant you.

SIR HUGH EVANS: Leave your prabbles, oman. What is the focative case, William?

WILLIAM PAGE: O—vocativo, O.

SIR HUGH EVANS: Remember, William; focative is caret.

MISTRESS QUICKLY: And that's a good root.

SIR HUGH EVANS: 'Oman, forbear.

MISTRESS PAGE: Peace!

SIR HUGH EVANS: What is your genitive case plural, William?

WILLIAM PAGE: Genitive case!

SIR HUGH EVANS: Ay.

WILLIAM PAGE: Genitive—horum, harum, horum.

MISTRESS QUICKLY: Vengeance of Jenny's case! fie on her! never name her, child, if she be a whore.

SIR HUGH EVANS: For shame, oman.

MISTRESS QUICKLY: You do ill to teach the child such words: he teaches him to hick and to hack, which they'll do fast enough of themselves, and to call 'horum:' fie upon you!

SIR HUGH EVANS: Oman, art thou lunatics? Hast thou no understandings for thy cases and the numbers of the genders? Thou art as foolish Christian creatures as I would desires.

MISTRESS PAGE: Prithee, hold thy peace.

SIR HUGH EVANS: Show me now, William, some declensions of your pronouns.

WILLIAM PAGE: Forsooth, I have forgot.

SIR HUGH EVANS: It is qui, quae, quod: if you forget your 'quies,' your 'quaes,' and your 'quods,' you must be preeches. Go your ways, and play; go.

MISTRESS PAGE: He is a better scholar than I thought he was.

SIR HUGH EVANS: He is a good sprag memory. Farewell, Mistress Page.

MISTRESS PAGE: Adieu, good Sir Hugh.

Exit SIR HUGH EVANS

Get you home, boy. Come, we stay too long.

Exeunt

SCENE II—*Ford's house*

Enter FALSTAFF and MISTRESS FORD

FALSTAFF: Mistress Ford, your sorrow hath eaten up my sufferance. I see you are obsequious in your love, and I profess requital to a hair's breadth; not only, Mistress Ford, in the simple office of love, but in all the accoutrement, complement and ceremony of it. But are you sure of your husband now?

MISTRESS FORD: He's a-birding, sweet Sir John.

MISTRESS PAGE: [*Within*] What, ho, gossip Ford! what, ho!

MISTRESS FORD: Step into the chamber, Sir John.

Exit FALSTAFF

Enter MISTRESS PAGE

MISTRESS PAGE: How now, sweetheart! who's at home besides yourself?

MISTRESS FORD: Why, none but mine own people.

MISTRESS PAGE: Indeed!

MISTRESS FORD: No, certainly. (*Aside to her*) Speak louder.

MISTRESS PAGE: Truly, I am so glad you have nobody here.

MISTRESS FORD: Why?

MISTRESS PAGE: Why, woman, your husband is in his old lunes again: he so takes on yonder with my husband; so rails against all married mankind; so curses all Eve's daughters, of what complexion soever; and so buffets himself on the forehead, crying, 'Peer out, peer out!' that any madness I ever yet beheld seemed but tameness, civility and patience, to this his distemper he is in now: I am glad the fat knight is not here.

MISTRESS FORD: Why, does he talk of him?

MISTRESS PAGE: Of none but him; and swears he was carried out, the last time he searched for him, in a basket; protests to my husband he is now here, and hath drawn him and the rest of their company from their sport, to make another experiment of his suspicion: but I am glad the knight is not here; now he shall see his own foolery.

MISTRESS FORD: How near is he, Mistress Page?

MISTRESS PAGE: Hard by; at street end; he will be here anon.

MISTRESS FORD: I am undone! The knight is here.

MISTRESS PAGE: Why then you are utterly shamed, and he's but a dead man. What a woman are you! Away with him, away with him! better shame than murder.

FORD: Which way should he go? How should I bestow him? Shall I put him into the basket again?

Re-enter FALSTAFF

FALSTAFF: No, I'll come no more i' the basket. May I not go out ere he come?

MISTRESS PAGE: Alas, three of Master Ford's brothers watch the door with pistols, that none shall issue out; otherwise you might slip away ere he came. But what make you here?

FALSTAFF: What shall I do? I'll creep up into the chimney.

MISTRESS FORD: There they always use to discharge their birding-pieces. Creep into the kiln-hole.

FALSTAFF: Where is it?

MISTRESS FORD: He will seek there, on my word. Neither press, coffer, chest, trunk, well, vault, but he hath an abstract for the remembrance of such places, and goes to them by his note: there is no hiding you in the house.

FALSTAFF: I'll go out then.

MISTRESS PAGE: If you go out in your own semblance, you die, Sir John. Unless you go out disguised.

MISTRESS FORD: How might we disguise him?

MISTRESS PAGE: Alas the day, I know not! There is no woman's gown big enough for him otherwise he might put on a hat, a muffler and a kerchief, and so escape.

FALSTAFF: Good hearts, devise something: any extremity rather than a mischief.

MISTRESS FORD: My maid's aunt, the fat woman of Brentford, has a gown above.

MISTRESS PAGE: On my word, it will serve him; she's as big as he is: and there's her thrummed hat and her muffler too. Run up, Sir John.

MISTRESS FORD: Go, go, sweet Sir John: Mistress Page and I will look some linen for your head.

MISTRESS PAGE: Quick, quick! we'll come dress you straight: put on the gown the while.

Exit FALSTAFF

MISTRESS FORD: I would my husband would meet him in this shape; he cannot abide the old woman of Brentford; he swears she's a witch; forbade her my house and hath threatened to beat her.

MISTRESS PAGE: Heaven guide him to thy husband's cudgel, and the devil guide his cudgel afterwards!

MISTRESS FORD: But is my husband coming?

MISTRESS PAGE: Ah, in good sadness, is he; and talks of the basket too, howsoever he hath had intelligence.

MISTRESS FORD: We'll try that; for I'll appoint my men to carry the basket again, to meet him at the door with it, as they did last time.

MISTRESS PAGE: Nay, but he'll be here presently; let's go dress him like the witch of Brentford.

MISTRESS FORD: I'll first direct my men what they shall do with the basket. Go up; I'll bring linen for him straight.

Exit

MISTRESS PAGE: Hang him, dishonest varlet! we cannot misuse him enough.

We'll leave a proof, by that which we will do,
Wives may be merry, and yet honest too.
We do not act that often jest and laugh;
'Tis old, but true, Still swine eat all the draff.

Exit

Re-enter MISTRESS FORD with two Servants

MISTRESS FORD: Go, sirs, take the basket again on your shoulders: your master is hard at door; if he bid you set it down, obey him; quickly, dispatch.

Exit

FIRST SERVANT: Come, come, take it up.

SECOND SERVANT: Pray heaven it be not full of knight again.

FIRST SERVANT: I hope not; I had as lief bear so much lead.

Enter FORD, PAGE, SHALLOW, DOCTOR CAIUS, and SIR HUGH EVANS

FORD: Ay, but if it prove true, Master Page, have you any way then to unfool me again? Set down the basket, villain! Somebody call my wife. Youth in a basket! O you panderly rascals! there's a knot, a ging, a pack, a conspiracy against me: now shall the devil be shamed. What, wife, I say! Come, come forth! Behold what honest clothes you send forth to bleaching!

PAGE: Why, this passes, Master Ford; you are not to go loose any longer; you must be pinioned.

SIR HUGH EVANS: Why, this is lunatics. This is mad as a mad dog!

SHALLOW: Indeed, Master Ford, this is not well, indeed.

FORD: So say I too, sir.

Re-enter MISTRESS FORD

Come hither, Mistress Ford; Mistress Ford the honestwoman, the modest wife, the virtuous creature, that hath the jealous fool to her husband! I suspect without cause, mistress, do I?

MISTRESS FORD: Heaven be my witness you do, if you suspect me in any dishonesty.

FORD: Well said, brazen-face! hold it out. Come forth, sirrah!

Pulling clothes out of the basket

PAGE: This passes!

MISTRESS FORD: Are you not ashamed? Let the clothes alone.

FORD: I shall find you anon.

SIR HUGH EVANS: 'Tis unreasonable! Will you take up your wife's clothes? Come away.

FORD: Empty the basket, I say!

MISTRESS FORD: Why, man, why?

FORD: Master Page, as I am a man, there was one conveyed out of my house yesterday in this basket: why may not he be there again? In my house I am sure he is: my intelligence is true; my jealousy is reasonable. Pluck me out all the linen.

MISTRESS FORD: If you find a man there, he shall die a flea's death.

PAGE: Here's no man.

SHALLOW: By my fidelity, this is not well, Master Ford; this wrongs you.

SIR HUGH EVANS: Master Ford, you must pray, and not follow the imaginations of your own heart: this is jealousies.

FORD: Well, he's not here I seek for.

PAGE: No, nor nowhere else but in your brain.

FORD: Help to search my house this one time. If I find not what I seek, show no colour for my extremity; let me for ever be your table-sport; let them say of me, 'As jealous as Ford, that searched a hollow walnut for his wife's leman'. Satisfy me once more; once more search with me.

MISTRESS FORD: What, ho, Mistress Page! Come you and the old woman down; my husband will come into the chamber.

FORD: Old woman! what old woman's that?

MISTRESS FORD: Nay, it is my maid's aunt of Brentford.

FORD: A witch, a quean, an old cozening quean! Have I not forbid her my house? She comes of errands, does she? We are simple men; we do not know what's brought to pass under the profession of fortune-telling. She works by charms, by spells, by the figure, and such daubery as this is, beyond our element we know nothing. Come down, you witch, you hag, you; come down, I say.

MISTRESS FORD: Nay, good, sweet husband! Good gentlemen, let him not strike the old woman.

Re-enter FALSTAFF in woman's clothes, and MISTRESS PAGE

MISTRESS PAGE: Come, Mother Prat; come, give me your hand.

FORD: I'll prat her. [*Beating him*] Out of my door, you witch, you hag, you baggage, you polecat, you runyon! out, out! I'll conjure you, I'll fortune-tell you.

Exit FALSTAFF

MISTRESS PAGE: Are you not ashamed? I think you have killed the poor woman.

MISTRESS FORD: Nay, he will do it. 'Tis a goodly credit for you.

FORD: Hang her, witch!

SIR HUGH EVANS: By yea and no, I think the 'oman is a witch indeed: I like not when a 'oman has a great peard; I spy a great peard under his muffler.

FORD: Will you follow, gentlemen? I beseech you, follow; see but the issue of my jealousy; if I cry out thus upon no trail, never trust me when I open again.

PAGE: Let's obey his humour a little further. Come, gentlemen.

Exeunt FORD, PAGE, SHALLOW, DOCTOR CAIUS, and SIR HUGH EVANS

MISTRESS PAGE: Trust me, he beat him most pitifully.

MISTRESS FORD: Nay, by the mass, that he did not; he beat him most unpitifully, methought.

MISTRESS PAGE: I'll have the cudgel hallowed and hung o'er the altar; it hath done meritorious service.

MISTRESS FORD: What think you? May we, with the warrant of womanhood and the witness of a good conscience, pursue him with any further revenge?

MISTRESS PAGE: The spirit of wantonness is, sure, scared out of him; if the devil have him not in fee-simple, with fine and recovery, he will never, I think, in the way of waste, attempt us again.

MISTRESS FORD: Shall we tell our husbands how we have served him?

MISTRESS PAGE: Yes, by all means; if it be but to scrape the figures out of your husband's brains. If they can find in their hearts the poor unvirtuous fat knight shall be any further afflicted, we two will still be the ministers.

MISTRESS FORD: I'll warrant they'll have him publicly shamed; and methinks there would be no period to the jest, should he not be publicly shamed.

MISTRESS PAGE: Come, to the forge with it then; shape it. I would not have things cool.

Exeunt

SCENE III—*Garter Inn*

Enter Host and BARDOLPH

BARDOLPH: Sir, the Germans desire to have three of your horses; the duke himself will be to-morrow at court, and they are going to meet him.

HOST: What duke should that be comes so secretly? I hear not of him in the court. Let me speak with the gentlemen; they speak English?

BARDOLPH: Ay, sir; I'll call them to you.

HOST: They shall have my horses; but I'll make them pay; I'll sauce them: they have had my house a week at command; I have turned away my other guests: they must come off; I'll sauce them. Come.

Exeunt

SCENE IV—*Ford's house*

Enter PAGE, FORD, MISTRESS PAGE, MISTRESS FORD, and SIR HUGH EVANS

SIR HUGH EVANS: 'Tis one of the best discretions of a 'oman as ever I did look upon.

PAGE: And did he send you both these letters at an instant?

MISTRESS PAGE: Within a quarter of an hour.
FORD: Pardon me, wife. Henceforth do what thou wilt;
I rather will suspect the sun with cold
Than thee with wantonness: now doth thy honour stand
In him that was of late an heretic,
As firm as faith.
PAGE: 'Tis well, 'tis well; no more.
Be not as extreme in submission
As in offence.
But let our plot go forward: let our wives
Yet once again, to make us public sport,
Appoint a meeting with this old fat fellow,
Where we may take him and disgrace him for it.
FORD: There is no better way than that they spoke of.
PAGE: How? to send him word they'll meet him in the park at midnight? Fie, fie! he'll never come.
SIR HUGH EVANS: You say he has been thrown in the rivers and has been grievously peaten as an old 'oman: methinks there should be terrors in him that he should not come; methinks his flesh is punished, he shall have no desires.
PAGE: So think I too.
MISTRESS FORD: Devise but how you'll use him when he comes,
And let us two devise to bring him thither.
MISTRESS PAGE: There is an old tale goes that Herne the hunter,
Sometime a keeper here in Windsor forest,
Doth all the winter-time, at still midnight,
Walk round about an oak, with great ragg'd horns;
And there he blasts the tree and takes the cattle
And makes milch-kine yield blood and shakes a chain
In a most hideous and dreadful manner.
You have heard of such a spirit, and well you know
The superstitious idle-headed eld
Received and did deliver to our age
This tale of Herne the hunter for a truth.
PAGE: Why, yet there want not many that do fear
In deep of night to walk by this Herne's oak:
But what of this?
MISTRESS FORD: Marry, this is our device:
That Falstaff at that oak shall meet with us.
Disguis'd like Heone, with huge horns on his head.
PAGE: Well, let it not be doubted but he'll come:
And in this shape when you have brought him thither,
What shall be done with him? what is your plot?
MISTRESS PAGE: That likewise have we thought upon, and thus:
Nan Page my daughter and my little son
And three or four more of their growth we'll dress
Like urchins, ouphes and fairies, green and white,
With rounds of waxen tapers on their heads,
And rattles in their hands; upon a sudden,
As Falstaff, she and I, are newly met,
Let them from forth a sawpit rush at once
With some diffused song; upon their sight,
We two in great amazedness will fly:
Then let them all encircle him about
And, fairy-like, to-pinch the unclean knight,
And ask him why, that hour of fairy revel,
In their so sacred paths he dares to tread
In shape profane.
MISTRESS FORD: And till he tell the truth,
Let the supposed fairies pinch him sound
And burn him with their tapers.
MISTRESS PAGE: The truth being known,
We'll all present ourselves, dis-horn the spirit,
And mock him home to Windsor.
FORD: The children must
Be practised well to this, or they'll ne'er do't.
SIR HUGH EVANS: I will teach the children their behaviors; and I will be like a jack-an-apes also, to burn the knight with my taber.
FORD: That will be excellent. I'll go buy them vizards.
MISTRESS PAGE: My Nan shall be the queen of all the fairies, Finely attired in a robe of white.
PAGE: That silk will I go buy. (*Aside*)
And in that time
Shall Master Slender steal my Nan away
And marry her at Eton. Go send to Falstaff straight.
FORD: Nay I'll to him again in name of Brook
He'll tell me all his purpose: sure, he'll come.
MISTRESS PAGE: Fear not you that. Go get us properties
And tricking for our fairies.

SIR HUGH EVANS: Let us about it: it is admirable pleasures and fery honest knaveries.

Exeunt PAGE, FORD, and SIR HUGH EVANS

MISTRESS PAGE: Go, Mistress Ford,
Send quickly to Sir John, to know his mind.

Exit MISTRESS FORD

I'll to the doctor: he hath my good will,
And none but he, to marry with Nan Page.
That Slender, though well landed, is an idiot;
And he my husband best of all affects.
The doctor is well money'd, and his friends
Potent at court: he, none but he, shall have her,
Though twenty thousand worthier come to crave her.

Exit

SCENE V—*The Garter Inn*

Enter Host and SIMPLE

HOST: What wouldst thou have, boor? What, thick-skin? speak, breathe, discuss; brief, short, quick, snap.

SIMPLE: Marry, sir, I come to speak with Sir John Falstaff from Master Slender.

HOST: There's his chamber, his house, his castle, his standing-bed and truckle-bed; 'tis painted about with the story of the Prodigal, fresh and new.

Go knock and call; hell speak like an Anthropophaginian unto thee: knock, I say.

SIMPLE: There's an old woman, a fat woman, gone up into his chamber: I'll be so bold as stay, sir, till she come down; I come to speak with her, indeed.

HOST: Ha! a fat woman! the knight may be robbed. I'll call. Bully knight! bully Sir John! speak from thy lungs military: art thou there? it is thine host, thine Ephesian, calls.

FALSTAFF: [*Above*] How now, mine host!

HOST: Here's a Bohemian-Tartar tarries the coming down of thy fat woman. Let her descend, bully, let her descend; my chambers are honourable: fie! privacy? fie!

Enter FALSTAFF

FALSTAFF: There was, mine host, an old fat woman even now with me; but she's gone.

SIMPLE: Pray you, sir, was't not the wise woman of Brentford?

FALSTAFF: Ay, marry, was it, mussel-shell: what would you with her?

SIMPLE: My master, sir, Master Slender, sent to her, seeing her go through the streets, to know, sir, whether one Nym, sir, that beguiled him of a chain, had the chain or no.

FALSTAFF: I spake with the old woman about it.

SIMPLE: And what says she, I pray, sir?

FALSTAFF: Marry, she says that the very same man that beguiled Master Slender of his chain cozened him of it.

SIMPLE: I would I could have spoken with the woman herself; I had other things to have spoken with her too from him.

FALSTAFF: What are they? let us know.

HOST: Ay, come; quick.

SIMPLE: I may not conceal them, sir.

FALSTAFF: Conceal them, or thou diest.

SIMPLE: Why, sir, they were nothing but about Mistress Anne Page; to know if it were my master's fortune to have her or no.

FALSTAFF: 'Tis, 'tis his fortune.

SIMPLE: What, sir?

FALSTAFF: To have her, or no. Go; say the woman told me so.

SIMPLE: May I be bold to say so, sir?

FALSTAFF: Ay, sir; like who more bold.

SIMPLE: I thank your worship: I shall make my master glad with these tidings.

Exit Simple

HOST: Thou art clerkly, thou art clerkly, Sir John.
Was there a wise woman with thee?

FALSTAFF: Ay, that there was, mine host; one that hath taught me more wit than ever I learned before in my life; and I paid nothing for it neither, but was paid for my learning.

Enter BARDOLPH

BARDOLPH: Out, alas, sir, cozenage, mere cozenage!

HOST: Where be my horses? speak well of them, varletto.

BARDOLPH: Run away with the cozeners; for so soon as I came beyond Eton, they threw me off from behind one of them, in a slough of mire; and set spurs and away, like three German devils, three Doctor Faustuses.

HOST: They are gone but to meet the duke, villain; do not say they be fled; Germans are honest men.

Enter SIR HUGH EVANS

SIR HUGH EVANS: Where is mine host?

HOST: What is the matter, sir?

SIR HUGH EVANS: Have a care of your entertainments: there is a friend of mine come to town tells me there is three cozen-germans that has cozened all the hosts of Readins, of Maidenhead, of Colebrook, of horses and money. I tell you for good will, look you: you are wise and full of gibes and vlouting-stocks, and 'tis not convenient you should be cozened. Fare you well.

Exit

Enter DOCTOR CAIUS

DOCTOR CAIUS: Vere is mine host de Jarteer?

HOST: Here, Master Doctor, in perplexity and doubtful dilemma.

DOCTOR CAIUS: I cannot tell vat is dat: but it is tell-a me dat you make grand preparation for a duke de Jamany: by my trot, dere is no duke dat the court is know to come. I tell you for good vill. adieu. *[Exit*

HOST: Hue and cry, villain, go! Assist me, knight. I am undone! Fly, run, hue and cry, villain! I am undone!

Exeunt Host and BARDOLPH

FALSTAFF: I would all the world might be cozened; for I have been cozened and beaten too. If it should come to the ear of the court, how I have been transformed and how my transformation hath been washed and cudgelled, they would melt me out of my fat drop by drop and liquor fishermen's boots with me; I warrant they would whip me with their fine wits till I were as crest-fallen as a dried pear. I never prospered since I forswore myself at primero. Well, if my wind were but long enough to say my prayers, I would repent.

Enter MISTRESS QUICKLY

Now, whence come you?

MISTRESS QUICKLY: From the two parties, forsooth.

FALSTAFF: The devil take one party and his dam the other! And so they shall be both bestowed. I have suffered more for their sakes, more than the villanous inconstancy of man's disposition is able to bear.

MISTRESS QUICKLY: And have not they suffered? Yes, I warrant; speciously one of them; Mistress Ford, good heart, is beaten black and blue, that you cannot see a white spot about her.

FALSTAFF: What tellest thou me of black and blue? I was beaten myself into all the colours of the rainbow; and I was like to be apprehended for the witch of Brentford: but that my admirable dexterity of wit, my counterfeiting the action of an old woman, delivered me, the knave constable had set me i' the stocks, i' the common stocks, for a witch.

MISTRESS QUICKLY: Sir, let me speak with you in your chamber: you shall hear how things go; and, I warrant, to your content. Here is a letter will say somewhat. Good hearts, what ado here is to bring you together! Sure, one of you does not serve heaven well, that you are so crossed.

FALSTAFF: Come up into my chamber.

Exeunt

SCENE VI—*The Garter Inn*

Enter FENTON and Host

HOST: Master Fenton, talk not to me; my mind is heavy: I will give over all.

FENTON: Yet hear me speak. Assist me in my purpose,
And, as I am a gentleman, I'll give thee
A hundred pound in gold more than your loss.

HOST: I will hear you, Master Fenton; and I will at the least keep your counsel.

FENTON: From time to time I have acquainted you
With the dear love I bear to fair Anne Page;
Who mutually hath answer'd my affection,
So far forth as herself might be her chooser,
Even to my wish. I have a letter from her
Of such contents as you will wonder at;
The mirth whereof so larded with my matter,
That neither singly can be manifested,
Without the show of both; fat Falstaff
Hath a great scene: the image of the jest
I'll show you here at large. Hark, good mine host.
To-night at Herne's oak, just 'twixt twelve and one,
Must my sweet Nan present the Fairy Queen;
The purpose why, is here: in which disguise,
While other jests are something rank on foot,
Her father hath commanded her to slip
Away with Slender and with him at Eton
Immediately to marry: she hath consented: Now, sir,
Her mother, ever strong against that match
And firm for Doctor Caius, hath appointed
That he shall likewise shuffle her away,
While other sports are tasking of their minds,
And at the deanery, where a priest attends,

Straight marry her: to this her mother's plot
She seemingly obedient likewise hath
Made promise to the doctor. Now, thus it rests:
Her father means she shall be all in white,
And in that habit, when Slender sees his time
To take her by the hand and bid her go,
She shall go with him: her mother hath intended,
The better to denote her to the doctor,
For they must all be mask'd and vizarded,
That quaint in green she shall be loose enrobed,
With ribands pendent, flaring 'bout her head;
And when the doctor spies his vantage ripe,
To pinch her by the hand, and, on that token,
The maid hath given consent to go with him.

HOST: Which means she to deceive, father or mother?

FENTON: Both, my good host, to go along with me:
And here it rests, that you'll procure the vicar
To stay for me at church 'twixt twelve and one,
And, in the lawful name of marrying,
To give our hearts united ceremony.

Host: Well, husband your device; I'll to the vicar:
Bring you the maid, you shall not lack a priest.

FENTON: So shall I evermore be bound to thee;
Besides, I'll make a present recompense.

Exeunt

ACT V

SCENE I—*A room in the Garter Inn*

Enter FALSTAFF and MISTRESS QUICKLY

FALSTAFF: Prithee, no more prattling; go. I'll hold. This is the third time; I hope good luck lies in odd numbers. Away go. They say there is divinity in odd numbers, either in nativity, chance, or death. Away!

MISTRESS QUICKLY: I'll provide you a chain; and I'll do what I can to get you a pair of horns.

FALSTAFF: Away, I say; time wears: hold up your head, and mince.

Exit MISTRESS QUICKLY

Enter FORD disguised

How now, Master Brook! Master Brook, the matter will be known to-night, or never. Be you in the Park about midnight, at Herne's oak, and you shall see wonders.

FORD: Went you not to her yesterday, sir, as you told me you had appointed?

FALSTAFF: I went to her, Master Brook, as you see, like a poor old man: but I came from her, Master Brook, like a poor old woman. That same knave Ford, her husband, hath the finest mad devil of jealousy in him, Master Brook, that ever governed frenzy. I will tell you: he beat me grievously, in the shape of a woman; for in the shape of man, Master Brook, I fear not Goliath with a weaver's beam; because I know also life is a shuttle. I am in haste; go along with me: I'll tell you all, Master Brook. Since I plucked geese, played truant and whipped top, I knew not what 'twas to be beaten till lately. Follow me: I'll tell you strange things of this knave Ford, on whom to-night I will be revenged, and I will deliver his wife into your hand. Follow. Strange things in hand, Master Brook! Follow.

Exeunt

SCENE II—*Windsor Park*

Enter PAGE, SHALLOW, and SLENDER

PAGE: Come, come; we'll couch i' the castle-ditch till we see the light of our fairies. Remember, son Slender, my daughter.

SLENDER: Ay, forsooth; I have spoke with her and we have a nay-word how to know one another. I come to her in white, and cry 'mum'; she cries 'budget'; and by that we know one another.

SHALLOW: That's good too: but what needs either your 'mum' or her 'budget'? The white will decipher her well enough. It hath struck ten o'clock.

PAGE: The night is dark; light and spirits will become it well. Heaven prosper our sport! No man means evil but the devil, and we shall know him by his horns. Let's away; follow me.

Exeunt

SCENE III—*A street leading to the Park*

Enter MISTRESS PAGE, MISTRESS FORD, and DOCTOR CAIUS

MISTRESS PAGE: Master doctor, my daughter is in green: when you see your time, take her by the band, away with her to the deanery, and dispatch it quickly. Go before into the Park: we two must go together.

DOCTOR CAIUS: I know vat I have to do. Adieu.

MISTRESS PAGE: Fare you well, sir.

Exit DOCTOR CAIUS

My husband will not rejoice so much at the abuse of Falstaff as he will chafe at the doctor's marrying my daughter: but 'tis no matter; better a little chiding than a great deal of heart-break.

MISTRESS FORD: Where is Nan now and her troop of fairies, and the Welsh devil Hugh?

MISTRESS PAGE: They are all couched in a pit hard by Herne's oak, with obscured lights; which, at the very instant of Falstaff's and our meeting, they will at once display to the night.

MISTRESS FORD: That cannot choose but amaze him.

MISTRESS PAGE: If he be not amazed, he will be mocked; if he be amazed, he will every way be mocked.

MISTRESS FORD: We'll betray him finely.

MISTRESS PAGE: Against such lewdsters and their lechery

Those that betray them do no treachery.

MISTRESS FORD: The hour draws on. To the oak, to the oak!

Exeunt

SCENE IV—*Windsor Park*

Enter SIR HUGH EVANS, disguised, with others as Fairies

SIR HUGH EVANS: Trib, trib, fairies; come; and remember your parts: be pold, I pray you; follow me into the pit; and when I give the watch-'ords, do as I pid you: come, come; trib, trib.

Exeunt

SCENE V—*Another part of the Park*

Enter FALSTAFF disguised as Herne

FALSTAFF: The Windsor bell hath struck twelve; the minute draws on. Now, the hot-blooded gods assist me! Remember, Jove, thou wast a bull for thy Europa; love set on thy horns. O powerful love! that, in some respects, makes a beast a man, in some other, a man a beast. You were also, Jupiter, a swan for the love of Leda. O omnipotent Love! how near the god drew to the complexion of a goose! A fault done first in the form of a beast. O Jove, a beastly fault! And then another fault in the semblance of a fowl; think on 't, Jove; a foul fault! When gods have hot backs, what shall poor men do? For me, I am here a Windsor stag; and the fattest, I think, i' the forest. Send me a cool rut-time, Jove, or who can blame me to piss my tallow? Who comes here? My doe?

Enter MISTRESS FORD and MISTRESS PAGE

MISTRESS FORD: Sir John! art thou there, my deer? my male deer?

FALSTAFF: My doe with the black scut! Let the sky rain potatoes; let it thunder to the tune of Green Sleeves, hail kissing-comfits and snow eringoes; let there come a tempest of provocation, I will shelter me here.

Embracing her

MISTRESS FORD: Mistress Page is come with me, sweetheart.

FALSTAFF: Divide me like a bribe buck, each a haunch; I will keep my sides to myself, my shoulders for the fellow of this walk, and my horns I bequeath your husbands. Am I a woodman, ha? Speak I like Herne the hunter? Why, now is Cupid a child of conscience; he makes restitution. As I am a true spirit, welcome!

Noise within

MISTRESS PAGE: Alas, what noise?

MISTRESS FORD: Heaven forgive our sins!

FALSTAFF: What should this be?

MISTRESS FORD & MISTRESS PAGE: Away, away!

They run off

FALSTAFF: I think the devil will not have me damned, lest the oil that's in me should set hell on fire; he would never else cross me thus.

Enter SIR HUGH EVANS, disguised as before; PISTOL, as Hobgoblin; MISTRESS QUICKLY, ANNE PAGE, and others, as Fairies, with tapers

FAIRY QUEEN: Fairies, black, grey, green, and white,

You moonshine revellers and shades of night,
You orphan heirs of fixed destiny,
Attend your office and your quality.
Crier Hobgoblin, make the fairy oyes.

PISTOL: Elves, list your names; silence, you airy toys.

Cricket, to Windsor chimneys shalt thou leap:
Where fires thou find'st unraked and hearths unswept,
There pinch the maids as blue as bilberry:
Our radiant queen hates sluts and sluttery.

FALSTAFF: They are fairies; he that speaks to them shall die: I'll wink and couch: no man their works must eye.

Lies down upon his face

SIR HUGH EVANS: Where's Pede? Go you, and where you find a maid

That, ere she sleep, has thrice her prayers said,
Raise up the organs of her fantasy;
Sleep she as sound as careless infancy:
But those as sleep and think not on their sins,
Pinch them, arms, legs, backs, shoulders, sides and shins.

FAIRY QUEEN: About, about;

Search Windsor Castle, elves, within and out:

Strew good luck, ouphes, on every sacred room:
That it may stand till the perpetual doom,
In state as wholesome as in state 'tis fit,
Worthy the owner, and the owner it.
The several chairs of order look you scour
With juice of balm and every precious flower:
Each fair instalment, coat, and several crest,
With loyal blazon, evermore be blest!
And nightly, meadow-fairies, look you sing,
Like to the Garter's compass, in a ring:
The expressure that it bears, green let it be,
More fertile-fresh than all the field to see;
And 'Honi soit qui mal y pense' write
In emerald tufts, flowers purple, blue and white;
Let sapphire, pearl and rich embroidery,
Buckled below fair knighthood's bending knee:
Fairies use flowers for their charactery.
Away; disperse: but till 'tis one o'clock,
Our dance of custom round about the oak
Of Herne the hunter, let us not forget.

SIR HUGH EVANS: Pray you, lock hand in hand; yourselves in order set
And twenty glow-worms shall our lanterns be,
To guide our measure round about the tree.
But, stay; I smell a man of middle-earth.

FALSTAFF: Heavens defend me from that Welsh fairy, lest he transform me to a piece of cheese!

PISTOL: Vile worm, thou wast o'erlook'd even in thy birth.

MISTRESS QUICKLY: With trial-fire touch me his finger-end:
If he be chaste, the flame will back descend
And turn him to no pain; but if he start,
It is the flesh of a corrupted heart.

PISTOL: A trial, come.

SIR HUGH EVANS: Come, will this wood take fire?

They burn him with their tapers

FALSTAFF: Oh, Oh, Oh!

MISTRESS QUICKLY: Corrupt, corrupt, and tainted in desire!
About him, fairies; sing a scornful rhyme;
And, as you trip, still pinch him to your time.

Song.

Fie on sinful fantasy!
Fie on lust and luxury!
Lust is but a bloody fire,
Kindled with unchaste desire,
Fed in heart, whose flames aspire
As thoughts do blow them, higher and higher.
Pinch him, fairies, mutually;
Pinch him for his villany;
Pinch him, and burn him, and turn him about,
Till candles and starlight and moonshine be out.

During this song they pinch FALSTAFF. DOCTOR CAIUS comes one way, and steals away a fairy in green; SLENDER another way, and takes off a fairy in white; and FENTON comes and steals away ANN PAGE. A noise of hunting is heard within. All the Fairies run away. FALSTAFF pulls off his buck's head, and rises

Enter PAGE, FORD, MISTRESS PAGE, MISTRESS FORD and SIR HUGH EVANS

PAGE: Nay, do not fly; I think we have watch'd you now
Will none but Herne the hunter serve your turn?

MISTRESS PAGE: I pray you, come, hold up the jest no higher
Now, good Sir John, how like you Windsor wives?
See you these, husband? Do not these fair yokes
Become the forest better than the town?

FORD: Now, sir, who's a cuckold now? Master Brook, Falstaff's a knave, a cuckoldly knave; here are his horns, Master Brook; and, Master Brook, he hath enjoyed nothing of Ford's but his buck-basket, his cudgel, and twenty pounds of money, which must be paid to Master Brook; his horses are arrested for it, Master Brook.

MISTRESS FORD: Sir John, we have had ill luck; we could never meet. I will never take you for my love again; but I will always count you my deer.

FALSTAFF: I do begin to perceive that I am made an ass.

FORD: Ay, and an ox too; both the proofs are extant.

FALSTAFF: And these are not fairies; I was three or four times in the thought they were not fairies; and yet the guiltiness of my mind, the sudden surprise of my powers, drove the grossness of the foppery into a received belief, in despite of the teeth of all rhyme and reason, that they were fairies. See now how wit may be made a Jack-a-Lent, when 'tis upon ill employment!

SIR HUGH EVANS: Sir John Falstaff, serve Got, and leave your desires, and fairies will not pinse you.

FORD: Well said, fairy Hugh.

SIR HUGH EVANS: And leave your jealousies too, I pray you.

FORD: I will never mistrust my wife again till thou art able to woo her in good English.

FALSTAFF: Have I laid my brain in the sun and dried it, that it wants matter to prevent so gross o'er reaching as this? Am I ridden with a Welsh goat too? Shall I have a coxcomb of frize? 'Tis time I were choked with a piece of toasted cheese.

SIR HUGH EVANS: Seese is not good to give putter; your belly is all putter.

FALSTAFF: 'Seese' and 'putter'! have I lived to stand at the taunt of one that makes fritters of English? This is enough to be the decay of lust and late-walking through the realm.

MISTRESS PAGE: Why Sir John, do you think, though we would have the virtue out of our hearts by the head and shoulders and have given ourselves without scruple to hell, that ever the devil could have made you our delight?

FORD: What, a hodge-pudding? a bag of flax?

MISTRESS PAGE: A puffed man?

PAGE: Old, cold, withered and of intolerable entrails?

FORD: And one that is as slanderous as Satan?

PAGE: And as poor as Job?

FORD: And as wicked as his wife?

SIR HUGH EVANS: And given to fornications, and to taverns and sack and wine and metheglins, and to drinkings and swearings and starings, pribbles and prabbles?

FALSTAFF: Well, I am your theme; you have the start of me; I am dejected; I am not able to answer the Welsh flannel; ignorance itself is a plummet o'er me: use me as you will.

FORD: Marry, sir, we'll bring you to Windsor, to one Master Brook, that you have cozened of money, to whom you should have been a pander: over and above that you have suffered, I think to repay that money will be a biting affliction.

PAGE: Yet be cheerful, knight; thou shalt eat a posset to-night at my house; where I will desire thee to laugh at my wife, that now laughs at thee: tell her Master Slender hath married her daughter.

MISTRESS PAGE: [*Aside*] Doctors doubt that; if Anne Page be my daughter, she is, by this, Doctor Caius' wife.

Enter SLENDER

SLENDER: Whoa ho! ho, father Page!

PAGE: Son, how now! how now, son! have you dispatched?

SLENDER: Dispatched! I'll make the best in Gloucestershire know on't; would I were hanged, la, else.

PAGE: Of what, son?

SLENDER: I came yonder at Eton to marry Mistress Anne Page, and she's a great lubberly boy. If it had not been i' the church, I would have swinged him, or he should have swinged me. If I did not think it had been Anne Page, would I might never stir!--and 'tis a postmaster's boy.

PAGE: Upon my life, then, you took the wrong.

SLENDER: What need you tell me that? I think so, when I took a boy for a girl. If I had been married to him, for all he was in woman's apparel, I would not have had him.

PAGE: Why, this is your own folly. Did not I tell you how you should know my daughter by her garments?

SLENDER: I went to her in white, and cried 'mum' and she cried 'budget' as Anne and I had appointed; and yet it was not Anne, but a postmaster's boy.

MISTRESS PAGE: Good George, be not angry: I knew of your purpose; turned my daughter into green; and, indeed, she is now with the doctor at the deanery, and there married.

Enter DOCTOR CAIUS

DOCTOR CAIUS: Vere is Mistress Page? By gar, I am cozened: I ha' married un garcon, a boy; un paysan, by gar, a boy; it is not Anne Page: by gar, I am cozened.

MISTRESS PAGE: Why, did you take her in green?

DOCTOR CAIUS: Ay, be gar, and 'tis a boy: be gar, I'll raise all Windsor.

Exit DOCTOR CAIUS

FORD: This is strange. Who hath got the right Anne?

PAGE: My heart misgives me: here comes Master Fenton.

Enter FENTON and ANNE PAGE

How now, Master Fenton!

ANNE PAGE: Pardon, good father! good my mother, pardon!

PAGE: Now, mistress, how chance you went not with Master Slender?

MISTRESS PAGE: Why went you not with master doctor, maid?

FENTON: You do amaze her: hear the truth of it.
You would have married her most shamefully,
Where there was no proportion held in love.
The truth is, she and I, long since contracted,
Are now so sure that nothing can dissolve us.
The offence is holy that she hath committed;
And this deceit loses the name of craft,
Of disobedience, or unduteous title,
Since therein she doth evitate and shun
A thousand irreligious cursed hours,
Which forced marriage would have brought upon her.

FORD: Stand not amazed; here is no remedy:
In love the heavens themselves do guide the state;
Money buys lands, and wives are sold by fate.

FALSTAFF: I am glad, though you have ta'en a special stand to strike at me, that your arrow hath glanced.

PAGE: Well, what remedy? Fenton, heaven give thee joy!
What cannot be eschew'd must be embraced.

FALSTAFF: When night-dogs run, all sorts of deer are chased.

MISTRESS PAGE: Well, I will muse no further. Master Fenton,
Heaven give you many, many merry days!
Good husband, let us every one go home,
And laugh this sport o'er by a country fire;
Sir John and all.

FORD: Let it be so. Sir John,
To Master Brook you yet shall hold your word
For he tonight shall lie with Mistress Ford.

Exeunt

THE MERCHANT OF VENICE

DRAMATIS PERSONÆ

THE DUKE OF VENICE
THE PRINCE OF MOROCCO, PRINCE OF ARRAGON, *suitors to Portia*
ANTONIO, *a merchant of Venice*
BASSANIO, his friend, *suitios to Portia*
GRATIANO, SOLANIO
SALERIO, *friends to Antonio and Bassanio*
LORENZO, *in love with Jessica*
SHYLOCK, *a rich Jew*
TUBAL, *a Jew, his friend*
LAUNCELOT GOBBO, *a clown, servant to Shylock*
OLD GOBBO, *father to Launcelot*
LEONARDO, *servant to Bassanio*
BALTHASAR, STEPHANO, *servants to Portia*
PORTIA, *a rich heiress*
NERISSA, *her waiting-maid*
JESSICA, *daughter to Shylock*
Magnificoes of Venice, Officers of the Court of Justice, Gaoler, Servants *and other* Attendants

THE SCENE: *Venice, and Portia's house at Belmont*

ACT I

SCENE I—*Venice: A street*

Enter ANTONIO, SALERIO, and SOLANIO

ANTONIO: In sooth, I know not why I am so sad:
It wearies me; you say it wearies you;
But how I caught it, found it, or came by it,
What stuff 'tis made of, whereof it is born,
I am to learn;
And such a want-wit sadness makes of me,
That I have much ado to know myself.
SALERIO: Your mind is tossing on the ocean;
There, where your argosies with portly sail,
Like signiors and rich burghers on the flood,
Or, as it were, the pageants of the sea,
Do overpeer the petty traffickers,
That curtsy to them, do them reverence,
As they fly by them with their woven wings.
SOLANIO: Believe me, sir, had I such venture forth,
The better part of my affections would
Be with my hopes abroad. I should be still
Plucking the grass, to know where sits the wind,
Peering in maps for ports and piers and roads;
And every object that might make me fear
Misfortune to my ventures, out of doubt
Would make me sad.
SALERIO: My wind cooling my broth
Would blow me to an ague, when I thought
What harm a wind too great might do at sea.
I should not see the sandy hour-glass run,
But I should think of shallows and of flats,
And see my wealthy Andrew dock'd in sand,
Vailing her high-top lower than her ribs

To kiss her burial. Should I go to church
And see the holy edifice of stone,
And not bethink me straight of dangerous rocks,
Which touching but my gentle vessel's side,
Would scatter all her spices on the stream,
Enrobe the roaring waters with my silks,
And, in a word, but even now worth this,
And now worth nothing? Shall I have the thought
To think on this, and shall I lack the thought
That such a thing bechanced would make me sad?
But tell not me; I know, Antonio
Is sad to think upon his merchandise.

ANTONIO: Believe me, no: I thank my fortune for it,
My ventures are not in one bottom trusted,
Nor to one place; nor is my whole estate
Upon the fortune of this present year:
Therefore my merchandise makes me not sad.

SALERIO: Why, then you are in love.

ANTONIO: Fie, fie!

SALERIO: Not in love neither? Then let us say you are sad,
Because you are not merry; and 'twere as easy
For you to laugh and leap and say you are merry,
Because you are not sad. Now, by two-headed Janus,
Nature hath framed strange fellows in her time:
Some that will evermore peep through their eyes
And laugh like parrots at a bag-piper,
And other of such vinegar aspect
That they'll not show their teeth in way of smile,
Though Nestor swear the jest be laughable.

Enter BASSANIO, LORENZO, and GRATIANO

Here comes Bassanio, your most noble kinsman,
Gratiano and Lorenzo. Fare ye well:
We leave you now with better company.

SALERIO: I would have stay'd till I had made you merry,
If worthier friends had not prevented me.

ANTONIO: Your worth is very dear in my regard.
I take it, your own business calls on you
And you embrace the occasion to depart.

SALERIO: Good morrow, my good lords.

BASSANIO: Good signiors both, when shall we laugh? say, when?
You grow exceeding strange: must it be so?

SALERIO: We'll make our leisures to attend on yours.

Exeunt SALERIO and SOLANIO

LORENZO: My Lord Bassanio, since you have found Antonio,
We two will leave you: but at dinner-time,
I pray you, have in mind where we must meet.

BASSANIO: I will not fail you.

GRATIANO: You look not well, Signior Antonio;
You have too much respect upon the world:
They lose it that do buy it with much care:
Believe me, you are marvellously changed.

ANTONIO: I hold the world but as the world, Gratiano;
A stage where every man must play a part,
And mine a sad one.

GRATIANO: Let me play the fool.
With mirth and laughter let old wrinkles come,
And let my liver rather heat with wine
Than my heart cool with mortifying groans.
Why should a man, whose blood is warm within,
Sit like his grandsire cut in alabaster?
Sleep when he wakes and creep into the jaundice
By being peevish? I tell thee what, Antonio—
I love thee, and it is my love that speaks—
There are a sort of men whose visages
Do cream and mantle like a standing pond,
And do a wilful stillness entertain,
With purpose to be dress'd in an opinion
Of wisdom, gravity, profound conceit,
As who should say 'I am Sir Oracle,
And when I ope my lips let no dog bark!'
O my Antonio, I do know of these
That therefore only are reputed wise
For saying nothing; when, I am very sure,
If they should speak, would almost damn those ears,
Which, hearing them, would call their brothers fools.
I'll tell thee more of this another time:
But fish not, with this melancholy bait,
For this fool gudgeon, this opinion.
Come, good Lorenzo. Fare ye well awhile:
I'll end my exhortation after dinner.

LORENZO: Well, we will leave you then till dinner-time.
I must be one of these same dumb wise men,
For Gratiano never lets me speak.
GRATIANO: Well, keep me company but two years moe,
Thou shalt not know the sound of thine own tongue.
ANTONIO: Fare you well; I'll grow a talker for this gear.
GRATIANO: Thanks, i' faith, for silence is only commendable
In a neat's tongue dried and a maid not vendible.
Exeunt GRATIANO and LORENZO
ANTONIO: Is that anything now?
BASSANIO: Gratiano speaks an infinite deal of nothing, more than any man in all Venice. His reasons are as two grains of wheat hid in two bushels of chaff: you shall seek all day ere you find them, and when you have them, they are not worth the search.
ANTONIO: Well, tell me now what lady is the same
To whom you swore a secret pilgrimage,
That you to-day promised to tell me of?
BASSANIO: 'Tis not unknown to you, Antonio,
How much I have disabled mine estate,
By something showing a more swelling port
Than my faint means would grant continuance;
Nor do I now make moan to be abridged
From such a noble rate; but my chief care
Is to come fairly off from the great debts
Wherein my time something too prodigal
Hath left me gaged. To you, Antonio,
I owe the most, in money and in love,
And from your love I have a warranty
To unburden all my plots and purposes
How to get clear of all the debts I owe.
ANTONIO: I pray you, good Bassanio, let me know it;
And if it stand, as you yourself still do,
Within the eye of honour, be assured,
My purse, my person, my extremest means,
Lie all unlock'd to your occasions.
BASSANIO: In my school-days, when I had lost one shaft,
I shot his fellow of the self-same flight
The self-same way with more advised watch,
To find the other forth, and by adventuring both
I oft found both: I urge this childhood proof,
Because what follows is pure innocence.
I owe you much, and, like a wilful youth,
That which I owe is lost; but if you please
To shoot another arrow that self way
Which you did shoot the first, I do not doubt,
As I will watch the aim, or to find both
Or bring your latter hazard back again
And thankfully rest debtor for the first.
ANTONIO: You know me well, and herein spend but time
To wind about my love with circumstance;
And out of doubt you do me now more wrong
In making question of my uttermost
Than if you had made waste of all I have:
Then do but say to me what I should do
That in your knowledge may by me be done,
And I am prest unto it: therefore, speak.
BASSANIO: In Belmont is a lady richly left;
And she is fair, and, fairer than that word,
Of wondrous virtues: sometimes from her eyes
I did receive fair speechless messages:
Her name is Portia, nothing undervalued
To Cato's daughter, Brutus' Portia:
Nor is the wide world ignorant of her worth,
For the four winds blow in from every coast
Renowned suitors, and her sunny locks
Hang on her temples like a golden fleece;
Which makes her seat of Belmont Colchos' strond,
And many Jasons come in quest of her.
O my Antonio, had I but the means
To hold a rival place with one of them,
I have a mind presages me such thrift,
That I should questionless be fortunate!
ANTONIO: Thou know'st that all my fortunes are at sea;
Neither have I money nor commodity
To raise a present sum: therefore go forth;
Try what my credit can in Venice do:
That shall be rack'd, even to the uttermost,
To furnish thee to Belmont, to fair Portia.
Go, presently inquire, and so will I,
Where money is, and I no question make
To have it of my trust or for my sake.
Exeunt

Scene II—*Belmont: A room in Portia's house*

Enter PORTIA and NERISSA

PORTIA: By my troth, Nerissa, my little body is aweary of this great world.

NERISSA: You would be, sweet madam, if your miseries were in the same abundance as your good fortunes are; and yet, for aught I see, they are as sick that surfeit with too much as they that starve with nothing. It is no mean happiness therefore, to be seated in the mean: superfluity comes sooner by white hairs, but competency lives longer.

PORTIA: Good sentences and well pronounced.

NERISSA: They would be better, if well followed.

PORTIA: If to do were as easy as to know what were good to do, chapels had been churches and poor men's cottages princes' palaces. It is a good divine that follows his own instructions: I can easier teach twenty what were good to be done, than be one of the twenty to follow mine own teaching. The brain may devise laws for the blood, but a hot temper leaps o'er a cold decree: such a hare is madness the youth, to skip o'er the meshes of good counsel the cripple. But this reasoning is not in the fashion to choose me a husband. O me, the word 'choose'! I may neither choose whom I would nor refuse whom I dislike; so is the will of a living daughter curbed by the will of a dead father. Is it not hard, Nerissa, that I cannot choose one nor refuse none?

NERISSA: Your father was ever virtuous; and holy men at their death have good inspirations; therefore the lottery, that he hath devised in these three chests of gold, silver and lead, whereof who chooses his meaning chooses you, will, no doubt, never be chosen by any rightly but one who you shall rightly love. But what warmth is there in your affection towards any of these princely suitors that are already come?

PORTIA: I pray thee, over-name them; and as thou namest them, I will describe them; and, according to my description, level at my affection.

NERISSA: First, there is the Neapolitan prince.

PORTIA: Ay, that's a colt indeed, for he doth nothing but talk of his horse; and he makes it a great appropriation to his own good parts, that he can shoe him himself. I am much afeard my lady his mother played false with a smith.

NERISSA: Then there is the County Palatine.

PORTIA: He doth nothing but frown, as who should say 'An you will not have me, choose'. he hears merry tales and smiles not: I fear he will prove the weeping philosopher when he grows old, being so full of unmannerly sadness in his youth. I had rather be married to a death's-head with a bone in his mouth than to either of these. God defend me from these two!

NERISSA: How say you by the French lord, Monsieur Le Bon?

PORTIA: God made him, and therefore let him pass for a man. In truth, I know it is a sin to be a mocker: but, he! why, he hath a horse better than the Neapolitan's, a better bad habit of frowning than the Count Palatine; he is every man in no man; if a throstle sing, he falls straight a-capering; he will fence with his own shadow; if I should marry him, I should marry twenty husbands. If he would despise me I would forgive him, for if he love me to madness, I shall never requite him.

NERISSA: What say you, then, to Falconbridge, the young baron of England?

PORTIA: You know I say nothing to him, for he understands not me, nor I him: he hath neither Latin, French, nor Italian, and you will come into the court and swear that I have a poor pennyworth in the English. He is a proper man's picture, but, alas, who can converse with a dumb-show? How oddly he is suited! I think he bought his doublet in Italy, his round hose in France, his bonnet in Germany and his behavior everywhere.

NERISSA: What think you of the Scottish lord, his neighbour?

PORTIA: That he hath a neighbourly charity in him, for he borrowed a box of the ear of the Englishman and swore he would pay him again when he was able: I think the Frenchman became his surety and sealed under for another.

NERISSA: How like you the young German, the Duke of Saxony's nephew?

PORTIA: Very vilely in the morning, when he is sober, and most vilely in the afternoon, when he is drunk: when he is best, he is a little worse than a man, and when he is worst, he is little better than a beast: and the worst fall that ever fell, I hope I shall make shift to go without him.

NERISSA: If he should offer to choose, and choose the right casket, you should refuse to perform your father's will, if you should refuse to accept him.

PORTIA: Therefore, for fear of the worst, I pray thee, set a deep glass of rhenish wine on the contrary casket, for if the devil be within and that temptation without, I know he will choose it. I will do anything, Nerissa, ere I'll be married to a sponge.

NERISSA: You need not fear, lady, the having any of these lords: they have acquainted me with their determinations; which is, indeed, to return to their home and to trouble you with no more suit, unless you may be won by some other sort than your father's imposition depending on the caskets.

PORTIA: If I live to be as old as Sibylla, I will die as chaste as Diana, unless I be obtained by the manner of my father's will. I am glad this parcel of wooers are so reasonable, for there is not one among them but I dote on his very absence, and I pray God grant them a fair departure.

NERISSA: Do you not remember, lady, in your father's time, a Venetian, a scholar and a soldier, that came hither in company of the Marquis of Montferrat?

PORTIA: Yes, yes, it was Bassanio; as I think, so was he called.

NERISSA: True, madam: he, of all the men that ever my foolish eyes looked upon, was the best deserving a fair lady.

PORTIA: I remember him well, and I remember him worthy of thy praise.

Enter a Serving-man

How now! what news?

SERVANT: The four strangers seek for you, madam, to take their leave; and there is a forerunner come from a fifth, the Prince of Morocco, who brings word the prince his master will be here to-night.

PORTIA: If I could bid the fifth welcome with so good a heart as I can bid the other four farewell, I should be glad of his approach; if he have the condition of a saint and the complexion of a devil, I had rather he should shrive me than wive me. Come, Nerissa. Sirrah, go before. Whiles we shut the gates upon one wooer, another knocks at the door.

Exeunt

SCENE III—*Venice: A public place*

Enter BASSANIO and SHYLOCK

SHYLOCK: Three thousand ducats; well.

BASSANIO: Ay, sir, for three months.

SHYLOCK: For three months; well.

BASSANIO: For the which, as I told you, Antonio shall be bound.

SHYLOCK: Antonio shall become bound; well.

BASSANIO: May you stead me? will you pleasure me? shall I know your answer?

SHYLOCK: Three thousand ducats for three months and Antonio bound.

BASSANIO: Your answer to that.

SHYLOCK: Antonio is a good man.

BASSANIO: Have you heard any imputation to the contrary?

SHYLOCK: Oh, no, no, no, no; my meaning in saying he is a good man is to have you understand me that he is sufficient. Yet his means are in supposition: he hath an argosy bound to Tripolis, another to the Indies; I understand moreover, upon the Rialto, he hath a third at Mexico, a fourth for England, and other ventures he hath, squandered abroad. But ships are but boards, sailors but men: there be land-rats and water-rats, water-thieves and land-thieves, I mean pirates, and then there is the peril of waters, winds and rocks. The man is, notwithstanding, sufficient. Three thousand ducats; I think I may take his bond.

BASSANIO: Be assured you may.

SHYLOCK: I will be assured I may; and, that I may be assured, I will bethink me. May I speak with Antonio?

BASSANIO: If it please you to dine with us.

SHYLOCK: Yes, to smell pork; to eat of the habitation which your prophet the Nazarite conjured the devil into. I will buy with you, sell with you, talk with you, walk with you, and so following, but I will not eat with you, drink with you, nor pray with you. What news on the Rialto? Who is he comes here?

Enter ANTONIO

BASSANIO: This is Signior Antonio.

SHYLOCK: [*Aside*] How like a fawning publican he looks!

I hate him for he is a Christian,
But more for that in low simplicity
He lends out money gratis and brings down
The rate of usance here with us in Venice.
If I can catch him once upon the hip,
I will feed fat the ancient grudge I bear him.
He hates our sacred nation, and he rails,

Even there where merchants most do congregate,
On me, my bargains and my well-won thrift,
Which he calls interest. Cursed be my tribe,
If I forgive him!

BASSANIO: Shylock, do you hear?

SHYLOCK: I am debating of my present store,
And, by the near guess of my memory,
I cannot instantly raise up the gross
Of full three thousand ducats. What of that?
Tubal, a wealthy Hebrew of my tribe,
Will furnish me. But soft! how many months
Do you desire?
(To ANTONIO) Rest you fair, good signior
Your worship was the last man in our mouths.

ANTONIO: Shylock, albeit I neither lend nor borrow
By taking nor by giving of excess,
Yet, to supply the ripe wants of my friend,
I'll break a custom. *(To BASSANIO)* Is he yet possess'd
How much ye would?

SHYLOCK: Ay, ay, three thousand ducats.

ANTONIO: And for three months.

SHYLOCK: I had forgot; three months; you told me so.
Well then, your bond; and let me see; but hear you;
Methought you said you neither lend nor borrow
Upon advantage.

ANTONIO: I do never use it.

SHYLOCK: When Jacob grazed his uncle Laban's sheep—
This Jacob from our holy Abram was,
As his wise mother wrought in his behalf,
The third possessor; ay, he was the third—

ANTONIO: And what of him? did he take interest?

SHYLOCK: No, not take interest, not, as you would say,
Directly interest: mark what Jacob did.
When Laban and himself were compromised
That all the eanlings which were streak'd and pied
Should fall as Jacob's hire, the ewes, being rank,
In the end of autumn turned to the rams,
And, when the work of generation was
Between these woolly breeders in the act,
The skilful shepherd peel'd me certain wands,
And, in the doing of the deed of kind,
He stuck them up before the fulsome ewes,
Who then conceiving did in eaning time
Fall parti-colour'd lambs, and those were Jacob's.
This was a way to thrive, and he was blest:
And thrift is blessing, if men steal it not.

ANTONIO: This was a venture, sir, that Jacob served for;
A thing not in his power to bring to pass,
But sway'd and fashion'd by the hand of heaven.
Was this inserted to make interest good?
Or is your gold and silver ewes and rams?

SHYLOCK: I cannot tell; I make it breed as fast.
But note me, signior.

ANTONIO: Mark you this, Bassanio,
The devil can cite Scripture for his purpose.
An evil soul producing holy witness
Is like a villain with a smiling cheek,
A goodly apple rotten at the heart:
O, what a goodly outside falsehood hath!

SHYLOCK: Three thousand ducats; 'tis a good round sum.
Three months from twelve; then, let me see; the rate—

ANTONIO: Well, Shylock, shall we be beholding to you?

SHYLOCK: Signior Antonio, many a time and oft
In the Rialto you have rated me
About my moneys and my usances:
Still have I borne it with a patient shrug,
For sufferance is the badge of all our tribe.
You call me misbeliever, cut-throat dog,
And spit upon my Jewish gaberdine,
And all for use of that which is mine own.
Well then, it now appears you need my help:
Go to, then; you come to me, and you say
'Shylock, we would have moneys'. you say so;
You, that did void your rheum upon my beard
And foot me as you spurn a stranger cur
Over your threshold: moneys is your suit
What should I say to you? Should I not say
'Hath a dog money? is it possible
A cur can lend three thousand ducats?' Or
Shall I bend low and in a bondman's key,
With bated breath and whispering humbleness,

Say this;
'Fair sir, you spit on me on Wednesday last;
You spurn'd me such a day; another time
You call'd me dog; and for these courtesies
I'll lend you thus much moneys'?

ANTONIO: I am as like to call thee so again,
To spit on thee again, to spurn thee too.
If thou wilt lend this money, lend it not
As to thy friends; for when did friendship take
A breed for barren metal of his friend?
But lend it rather to thine enemy,
Who, if he break, thou mayst with better face
Exact the penalty.

SHYLOCK: Why, look you, how you storm!
I would be friends with you and have your love,
Forget the shames that you have stain'd me with,
Supply your present wants and take no doit
Of usance for my moneys, and you'll not hear me:
This is kind I offer.

BASSANIO: This were kindness.

SHYLOCK: This kindness will I show.
Go with me to a notary, seal me there
Your single bond; and, in a merry sport,
If you repay me not on such a day,
In such a place, such sum or sums as are
Express'd in the condition, let the forfeit
Be nominated for an equal pound
Of your fair flesh, to be cut off and taken
In what part of your body pleaseth me.

ANTONIO: Content, i' faith: I'll seal to such a bond
And say there is much kindness in the Jew.

BASSANIO: You shall not seal to such a bond for me;
I'll rather dwell in my necessity.

ANTONIO: Why, fear not, man; I will not forfeit it:
Within these two months, that's a month before
This bond expires, I do expect return
Of thrice three times the value of this bond.

SHYLOCK: O father Abram, what these Christians are,
Whose own hard dealings teaches them suspect
The thoughts of others! Pray you, tell me this;
If he should break his day, what should I gain
By the exaction of the forfeiture?
A pound of man's flesh taken from a man
Is not so estimable, profitable neither,
As flesh of muttons, beefs, or goats. I say,
To buy his favour, I extend this friendship:
If he will take it, so; if not, adieu;
And, for my love, I pray you wrong me not.

ANTONIO: Yes Shylock, I will seal unto this bond.

SHYLOCK: Then meet me forthwith at the notary's;
Give him direction for this merry bond,
And I will go and purse the ducats straight,
See to my house, left in the fearful guard
Of an unthrifty knave, and presently
I will be with you.

ANTONIO: Hie thee, gentle Jew.

Exit Shylock

The Hebrew will turn Christian: he grows kind.

BASSANIO: I like not fair terms and a villain's mind.

ANTONIO: Come on: in this there can be no dismay;
My ships come home a month before the day.

Exeunt

Act II

Scene I—*Belmont: A room in Portia's house*

Flourish of cornets. Enter the PRINCE of MOROCCO and his train; PORTIA, NERISSA, and others attending

MOROCCO: Mislike me not for my complexion,
The shadow'd livery of the burnish'd sun,
To whom I am a neighbour and near bred.
Bring me the fairest creature northward born,
Where Phoebus' fire scarce thaws the icicles,
And let us make incision for your love,
To prove whose blood is reddest, his or mine.
I tell thee, lady, this aspect of mine
Hath fear'd the valiant; by my love I swear
The best-regarded virgins of our clime
Have loved it too: I would not change this hue,
Except to steal your thoughts, my gentle queen.

PORTIA: In terms of choice I am not solely led
By nice direction of a maiden's eyes;
Besides, the lottery of my destiny
Bars me the right of voluntary choosing:
But if my father had not scanted me
And hedged me by his wit, to yield myself
His wife who wins me by that means I told you,
Yourself, renowned prince, then stood as fair
As any comer I have look'd on yet
For my affection.

MOROCCO: Even for that I thank you:
Therefore, I pray you, lead me to the caskets
To try my fortune. By this scimitar
That slew the Sophy and a Persian prince
That won three fields of Sultan Solyman,
I would outstare the sternest eyes that look,
Outbrave the heart most daring on the earth,
Pluck the young sucking cubs from the she-bear,
Yea, mock the lion when he roars for prey,
To win thee, lady. But, alas the while!
If Hercules and Lichas play at dice
Which is the better man, the greater throw
May turn by fortune from the weaker hand:
So is Alcides beaten by his page;
And so may I, blind fortune leading me,
Miss that which one unworthier may attain,
And die with grieving.

PORTIA: You must take your chance,
And either not attempt to choose at all
Or swear before you choose, if you choose wrong
Never to speak to lady afterward
In way of marriage; therefore be advised.

MOROCCO: Nor will not. Come, bring me unto my chance.

PORTIA: First, forward to the temple: after dinner
Your hazard shall be made.

MOROCCO: Good fortune then!
To make me blest or cursed'st among men.

Cornets, and exeunt

Scene II—*Venice. A street*

Enter LAUNCELOT

LAUNCELOT: Certainly my conscience will serve me to run from this Jew my master. The fiend is at mine elbow and tempts me, saying to me 'Gobbo, Launcelot Gobbo, good Launcelot,' or 'good Gobbo,' or 'good Launcelot Gobbo, use your legs, take the start, run away'. My conscience says 'No; take heed, honest Launcelot; take heed, honest Gobbo', or, as aforesaid, 'honest Launcelot Gobbo; do not run; scorn running with thy heels'. Well, the most courageous fiend bids me pack: 'Via!' says the fiend; 'away!' says the fiend; 'for the heavens, rouse up a brave mind,' says the fiend, 'and run.' Well, my conscience, hanging about the neck of my heart, says very wisely to me 'My honest friend Launcelot, being an honest man's son,' or rather 'an honest woman's son'; for, indeed, my father did something smack, something grow to, he had a kind of taste; well, my conscience says 'Launcelot, budge not.' 'Budge,' says the fiend. 'Budge not', says my conscience. 'Conscience', say I, 'you counsel well'; 'Fiend,' say I, 'you counsel well': to be ruled by my conscience, I should stay with the Jew my master, who, God bless the mark, is a kind of devil; and, to run away from the Jew, I should be ruled by the fiend, who, saving your reverence, is the devil himself. Certainly the Jew is the very devil incarnal; and, in my conscience, my conscience is but a kind of hard conscience, to offer to counsel me to stay with the Jew. The fiend gives the more friendly counsel: I will run, fiend; my heels are at your command; I will run.

Enter Old GOBBO, with a basket

GOBBO: Master young man, you, I pray you, which is the way to master Jew's?

LAUNCELOT: [*Aside*] O heavens, this is my true-begotten father! who, being more than sand-blind, high-gravel blind, knows me not: I will try confusions with him.

GOBBO: Master young gentleman, I pray you, which is the way to master Jew's?

LAUNCELOT: Turn up on your right hand at the next turning, but, at the next turning of all, on your left; marry, at the very next turning, turn of no hand, but turn down indirectly to the Jew's house.

GOBBO: By God's sonties, 'twill be a hard way to hit. Can you tell me whether one Launcelot, that dwells with him, dwell with him or no?

LAUNCELOT: Talk you of young Master Launcelot? (*Aside*) Mark me now; now will I raise the waters. Talk you of young Master Launcelot?

GOBBO: No master, sir, but a poor man's son; his father, though I say it, is an honest exceeding poor man and, God be thanked, well to live.

LAUNCELOT: Well, let his father be what a' will, we talk of young Master Launcelot.

GOBBO: Your worship's friend and Launcelot, sir.

LAUNCELOT: But I pray you, ergo, old man, ergo, I beseech you, talk you of young Master Launcelot?

GOBBO: Of Launcelot, an't please your mastership.

LAUNCELOT: Ergo, Master Launcelot. Talk not of Master Launcelot, father; for the young gentleman, according to Fates and Destinies and such odd sayings, the Sisters Three and such branches of learning, is indeed deceased, or, as you would say in plain terms, gone to heaven.

GOBBO: Marry, God forbid! the boy was the very staff of my age, my very prop.

LAUNCELOT: Do I look like a cudgel or a hovel-post, a staff or a prop? Do you know me, father?

GOBBO: Alack the day, I know you not, young gentleman: but, I pray you, tell me, is my boy, God rest his soul, alive or dead?

LAUNCELOT: Do you not know me, father?

GOBBO: Alack, sir, I am sand-blind; I know you not.

LAUNCELOT: Nay, indeed, if you had your eyes, you might fail of the knowing me: it is a wise father that knows his own child. Well, old man, I will tell you news of your son: give me your blessing: truth will come to light; murder cannot be hid long; a man's son may, but at the length truth will out.

GOBBO: Pray you, sir, stand up: I am sure you are not Launcelot, my boy.

LAUNCELOT: Pray you, let's have no more fooling about it, but give me your blessing: I am Launcelot, your boy that was, your son that is, your child that shall be.

GOBBO: I cannot think you are my son.

LAUNCELOT: I know not what I shall think of that; but I am Launcelot, the Jew's man, and I am sure Margery your wife is my mother.

GOBBO: Her name is Margery, indeed: I'll be sworn, if thou be Launcelot, thou art mine own flesh and blood. Lord worshipped might he be! what a beard hast thou got! thou hast got more hair on thy chin than Dobbin my fill-horse has on his tail.

LAUNCELOT: It should seem, then, that Dobbin's tail grows backward: I am sure he had more hair of his tail than I have of my face when I last saw him.

GOBBO: Lord, how art thou changed! How dost thou and thy master agree? I have brought him a present. How 'gree you now?

LAUNCELOT: Well, well: but, for mine own part, as I have set up my rest to run away, so I will not rest till I have run some ground. My master's a very Jew: give him a present! give him a halter. I am famished in his service; you may tell every finger I have with my ribs. Father, I am glad you are come: give me your present to one Master Bassanio, who, indeed, gives rare new liveries: if I serve not him, I will run as far as God has any ground. O rare fortune! here comes the man: to him, father; for I am a Jew, if I serve the Jew any longer.

Enter BASSANIO, with LEONARDO and other followers

BASSANIO: You may do so; but let it be so hasted that supper be ready at the farthest by five of the clock. See these letters delivered; put the liveries to making, and desire Gratiano to come anon to my lodging.

Exit a Servant

LAUNCELOT: To him, father.

GOBBO: God bless your worship!

BASSANIO: Gramercy! wouldst thou aught with me?

GOBBO: Here's my son, sir, a poor boy—

LAUNCELOT: Not a poor boy, sir, but the rich Jew's man; that would, sir, as my father shall specify—

GOBBO: He hath a great infection, sir, as one would say, to serve—

LAUNCELOT: Indeed, the short and the long is, I serve the Jew, and have a desire, as my father shall specify—

GOBBO: His master and he, saving your worship's reverence, are scarce cater-cousins—

LAUNCELOT: To be brief, the very truth is that the Jew, having done me wrong, doth cause me, as my father, being, I hope, an old man, shall frutify unto you—

GOBBO: I have here a dish of doves that I would bestow upon your worship, and my suit is—

LAUNCELOT: In very brief, the suit is impertinent to myself, as your worship shall know by this honest old man; and, though I say it, though old man, yet poor man, my father.

BASSANIO: One speak for both. What would you?

LAUNCELOT: Serve you, sir.

GOBBO: That is the very defect of the matter, sir.

BASSANIO: I know thee well; thou hast obtain'd thy suit.

Shylock thy master spoke with me this day,
And hath preferr'd thee, if it be preferment
To leave a rich Jew's service, to become
The follower of so poor a gentleman.

LAUNCELOT: The old proverb is very well parted between my master Shylock and you, sir: you have the grace of God, sir, and he hath enough.

BASSANIO: Thou speak'st it well. Go, father, with thy son.

Take leave of thy old master and inquire
My lodging out. (*To a Servant*) Give him a livery
More guarded than his fellows': see it done.

LAUNCELOT: Father, in. I cannot get a service, no; I have ne'er a tongue in my head. (*Looking on his palm*) Well, if any man in Italy have a fairer table which doth offer to swear upon a book, I shall have good fortune. Go to, here's a simple line of life: here's a small trifle of wives: alas, fifteen wives is nothing! Eleven widows and nine maids is a simple coming-in for one man: and then to 'scape drowning thrice, and to be in peril of my life with the edge of a feather-bed; here are simple scapes. Well, if Fortune be a woman, she's a good wench for this gear. Father, come; I'll take my leave of the Jew in the twinkling of an eye.

Exeunt Launcelot and Old Gobbo

BASSANIO: I pray thee, good Leonardo, think on this:

These things being bought and orderly bestow'd,
Return in haste, for I do feast to-night
My best-esteem'd acquaintance: hie thee, go.

LEONARDO: My best endeavours shall be done herein.

Enter GRATIANO

GRATIANO: Where is your master?

LEONARDO: Yonder, sir, he walks.

Exit

GRATIANO: Signior Bassanio!

BASSANIO: Gratiano!

GRATIANO: I have suit to you.

BASSANIO: You have obtain'd it.

GRATIANO: You must not deny me: I must go with you to Belmont.

BASSANIO: Why then you must. But hear thee, Gratiano;

Thou art too wild, too rude and bold of voice;
Parts that become thee happily enough
And in such eyes as ours appear not faults;
But where thou art not known, why, there they show
Something too liberal. Pray thee, take pain
To allay with some cold drops of modesty
Thy skipping spirit, lest through thy wild behavior
I be misconstrued in the place I go to,
And lose my hopes.

GRATIANO: Signior Bassanio, hear me:

If I do not put on a sober habit,
Talk with respect and swear but now and then,
Wear prayer-books in my pocket, look demurely,
Nay more, while grace is saying, hood mine eyes
Thus with my hat, and sigh and say 'amen,'
Use all the observance of civility,

Like one well studied in a sad ostent
To please his grandam, never trust me more.

BASSANIO: Well, we shall see your bearing.

GRATIANO: Nay, but I bar to-night: you shall not gauge me
By what we do to-night.

BASSANIO: No, that were pity:
I would entreat you rather to put on
Your boldest suit of mirth, for we have friends
That purpose merriment. But fare you well:
I have some business.

GRATIANO: And I must to Lorenzo and the rest:
But we will visit you at supper-time.

Exeunt

SCENE III—*The same: A room in Shylock's house*

Enter JESSICA and LAUNCELOT

JESSICA: I am sorry thou wilt leave my father so.
Our house is hell, and thou, a merry devil,
Didst rob it of some taste of tediousness.
But fare thee well, there is a ducat for thee:
And, Launcelot, soon at supper shalt thou see
Lorenzo, who is thy new master's guest:
Give him this letter; do it secretly;
And so farewell: I would not have my father
See me in talk with thee.

LAUNCELOT: Adieu! tears exhibit my tongue. Most beautiful pagan, most sweet Jew! if a Christian do not play the knave and get thee, I am much deceived. But, adieu: these foolish drops do something drown my manly spirit: adieu.

JESSICA: Farewell, good Launcelot.

Exit LAUNCELOT

Alack, what heinous sin is it in me
To be ashamed to be my father's child!
But though I am a daughter to his blood,
I am not to his manners. O Lorenzo,
If thou keep promise, I shall end this strife,
Become a Christian and thy loving wife.

Exit

SCENE IV—*Venice: A street*

Enter GRATIANO, LORENZO, SALERIO, *and* SOLANIO

LORENZO: Nay, we will slink away in supper-time,
Disguise us at my lodging and return,
All in an hour.

GRATIANO: We have not made good preparation.

SALERIO: We have not spoke us yet of torch-bearers.

SOLANIO: 'Tis vile, unless it may be quaintly order'd,
And better in my mind not undertook.

LORENZO: 'Tis now but four o'clock: we have two hours
To furnish us.

Enter LAUNCELOT, with a letter

Friend Launcelot, what's the news?

LAUNCELOT: An it shall please you to break up this, it shall seem to signify.

LORENZO: I know the hand: in faith, 'tis a fair hand;
And whiter than the paper it writ on
Is the fair hand that writ.

GRATIANO: Love-news, in faith.

LAUNCELOT: By your leave, sir.

LORENZO: Whither goest thou?

LAUNCELOT: Marry, sir, to bid my old master the Jew to sup to-night with my new master the Christian.

LORENZO: Hold here, take this: tell gentle Jessica
I will not fail her; speak it privately.
Go, gentlemen,

Exit LAUNCELOT

Will you prepare you for this masque tonight?
I am provided of a torch-bearer.

SOLANIO: Ay, marry, I'll be gone about it straight.

SOLANIO: And so will I.

LORENZO: Meet me and Gratiano
At Gratiano's lodging some hour hence.

SALERIO: 'Tis good we do so.

Exeunt SALERIO and SOLANIO

GRATIANO: Was not that letter from fair Jessica ?

LORENZO: I must needs tell thee all. She hath directed
How I shall take her from her father's house,
What gold and jewels she is furnish'd with,
What page's suit she hath in readiness.
If e'er the Jew her father come to heaven,
It will be for his gentle daughter's sake:
And never dare misfortune cross her foot,
Unless she do it under this excuse,
That she is issue to a faithless Jew.
Come, go with me; peruse this as thou goest:
Fair Jessica shall be my torch-bearer.

Exeunt

SCENE V—*The same: Before Shylock's house*

Enter SHYLOCK and LAUNCELOT

SHYLOCK: Well, thou shalt see, thy eyes shall be thy judge,
The difference of old Shylock and Bassanio:—
What, Jessica!—thou shalt not gormandise,
As thou hast done with me—What, Jessica!—
And sleep and snore, and rend apparel out;--
Why, Jessica, I say !

LAUNCELOT: Why, Jessica!

SHYLOCK: Who bids thee call? I do not bid thee call.

LAUNCELOT: Your worship was wont to tell me
I could do nothing without bidding.

Enter JESSICA

JESSICA: Call you? what is your will?

SHYLOCK: I am bid forth to supper, Jessica:
There are my keys. But wherefore should I go?
I am not bid for love; they flatter me:
But yet I'll go in hate, to feed upon
The prodigal Christian. Jessica, my girl,
Look to my house. I am right loath to go:
There is some ill a-brewing towards my rest,
For I did dream of money-bags to-night.

LAUNCELOT: I beseech you, sir, go: my young master doth expect your reproach.

SHYLOCK: So do I his.

LAUNCELOT: And they have conspired together, I will not say you shall see a masque; but if you do, then it was not for nothing that my nose fell a-bleeding on Black-Monday last at six o'clock i' the morning, falling out that year on Ash-Wednesday was four year, in the afternoon.

SHYLOCK: What, are there masques? Hear you me, Jessica:
Lock up my doors; and when you hear the drum
And the vile squealing of the wry-neck'd fife,
Clamber not you up to the casements then,
Nor thrust your head into the public street
To gaze on Christian fools with varnish'd faces,
But stop my house's ears, I mean my casements:
Let not the sound of shallow foppery enter
My sober house. By Jacob's staff, I swear,
I have no mind of feasting forth to-night:
But I will go. Go you before me, sirrah;
Say I will come.

LAUNCELOT: I will go before, sir. Mistress, look out at window, for all this, There will come a Christian boy will be worth a Jewess' eye.

Exit

SHYLOCK: What says that fool of Hagar's offspring, ha?

JESSICA: His words were 'Farewell mistress'; nothing else.

SHYLOCK: The patch is kind enough, but a huge feeder;
Snail-slow in profit, and he sleeps by day
More than the wild-cat: drones hive not with me;
Therefore I part with him, and part with him
To one that would have him help to waste
His borrow'd purse. Well, Jessica, go in;
Perhaps I will return immediately:
Do as I bid you; shut doors after you:
Fast bind, fast find;
A proverb never stale in thrifty mind.

Exit

JESSICA: Farewell; and if my fortune be not crost,
I have a father, you a daughter, lost.

Exit

SCENE VI—*The same*

Enter GRATIANO and SALERIO, *masqued*

GRATIANO: This is the pent-house under which Lorenzo
Desired us to make stand.

SALERIO: His hour is almost past.

GRATIANO: And it is marvel he out-dwells his hour,
For lovers ever run before the clock.

SALERIO: O, ten times faster Venus' pigeons fly
To seal love's bonds new-made, than they are wont
To keep obliged faith unforfeited!

GRATIANO: That ever holds: who riseth from a feast
With that keen appetite that he sits down?
Where is the horse that doth untread again
His tedious measures with the unbated fire
That he did pace them first? All things that are,
Are with more spirit chased than enjoy'd.
How like a younker or a prodigal
The scarfed bark puts from her native bay,
Hugg'd and embraced by the strumpet wind!
How like the prodigal doth she return,
With over-weather'd ribs and ragged sails,
Lean, rent and beggar'd by the strumpet wind!

SALERIO: Here comes Lorenzo; more of this hereafter.

Enter LORENZO

LORENZO: Sweet friends, your patience for my long abode;
Not I, but my affairs, have made you wait:
When you shall please to play the thieves for wives,
I'll watch as long for you then. Approach;
Here dwells my father Jew. Ho! who's within?

Enter JESSICA, above, in boy's clothes

JESSICA: Who are you? Tell me, for more certainty,
Albeit I'll swear that I do know your tongue.

LORENZO: Lorenzo, and thy love.

JESSICA: Lorenzo, certain, and my love indeed,
For who love I so much? And now who knows
But you, Lorenzo, whether I am yours?

LORENZO: Heaven and thy thoughts are witness that thou art.

JESSICA: Here, catch this casket; it is worth the pains.
I am glad 'tis night, you do not look on me,
For I am much ashamed of my exchange;
But love is blind and lovers cannot see
The pretty follies that themselves commit;
For if they could, Cupid himself would blush
To see me thus transformed to a boy.

LORENZO: Descend, for you must be my torchbearer.

JESSICA: What! must I hold a candle to my shames?
They in themselves, good-sooth, are too too light.
Why, 'tis an office of discovery, love;
And I should be obscured.

LORENZO: So are you, sweet,
Even in the lovely garnish of a boy.
But come at once;
For the close night doth play the runaway,
And we are stay'd for at Bassanio's feast.

JESSICA: I will make fast the doors, and gild myself
With some more ducats, and be with you straight.

Exit above

GRATIANO: Now, by my hood, a gentile and no Jew.

LORENZO: Beshrew me but I love her heartily;
For she is wise, if I can judge of her,
And fair she is, if that mine eyes be true,
And true she is, as she hath proved herself,
And therefore, like herself, wise, fair and true,
Shall she be placed in my constant soul.

Enter JESSICA, below

What, art thou come? On, gentlemen; away!
Our masquing mates by this time for us stay.

Exit with JESSICA and SALERIO

Enter ANTONIO

ANTONIO: Who's there?

GRATIANO: Signior Antonio!

ANTONIO: Fie, fie, Gratiano! where are all the rest?
'Tis nine o'clock: our friends all stay for you.
No masque to-night; the wind is come about;
Bassanio presently will go aboard;
I have sent twenty out to seek for you.

GRATIANO: I am glad on't: I desire no more delight
Than to be under sail and gone to-night.

Exeunt

SCENE VII—*Belmont: A room in Portia's house*

Flourish of cornets. Enter PORTIA, with the PRINCE of MOROCCO, and their trains

PORTIA: Go draw aside the curtains and discover
The several caskets to this noble Prince.
Now make your choice.

MOROCCO: The first, of gold, who this inscription bears,
'Who chooseth me shall gain what many men desire;'
The second, silver, which this promise carries,
'Who chooseth me shall get as much as he deserves;'
This third, dull lead, with warning all as blunt,
'Who chooseth me must give and hazard all he hath.'
How shall I know if I do choose the right?

PORTIA: The one of them contains my picture, prince;
If you choose that, then I am yours withal.

MOROCCO: Some god direct my judgment! Let me see;
I will survey the inscriptions back again.
What says this leaden casket?
'Who chooseth me must give and hazard all he hath.'
Must give: for what? for lead? hazard for lead?

This casket threatens. Men that hazard all
Do it in hope of fair advantages:
A golden mind stoops not to shows of dross;
I'll then nor give nor hazard aught for lead.
What says the silver with her virgin hue?
'Who chooseth me shall get as much as he deserves.'
As much as he deserves! Pause there, Morocco,
And weigh thy value with an even hand.
If thou be'st rated by thy estimation,
Thou dost deserve enough; and yet enough
May not extend so far as to the lady;
And yet to be afeard of my deserving
Were but a weak disabling of myself.
As much as I deserve! Why, that's the lady:
I do in birth deserve her, and in fortunes,
In graces and in qualities of breeding;
But more than these, in love I do deserve.
What if I stray'd no farther, but chose here?
Let's see once more this saying graved in gold
'Who chooseth me shall gain what many men desire.'
Why, that's the lady; all the world desires her;
From the four corners of the earth they come,
To kiss this shrine, this mortal-breathing saint:
The Hyrcanian deserts and the vasty wilds
Of wide Arabia are as thoroughfares now
For princes to come view fair Portia.
The watery kingdom, whose ambitious head
Spits in the face of heaven, is no bar
To stop the foreign spirits, but they come,
As o'er a brook, to see fair Portia.
One of these three contains her heavenly picture.
Is't like that lead contains her? 'Twere damnation
To think so base a thought: it were too gross
To rib her cerecloth in the obscure grave.
Or shall I think in silver she's immured,
Being ten times undervalued to tried gold?
O sinful thought! Never so rich a gem
Was set in worse than gold. They have in England
A coin that bears the figure of an angel
Stamped in gold, but that's insculp'd upon;
But here an angel in a golden bed
Lies all within. Deliver me the key;
Here do I choose, and thrive I as I may!

PORTIA: There, take it, Prince; and if my form lie there,
Then I am yours.

He unlocks the golden casket

MOROCCO: O hell! what have we here?
A carrion Death, within whose empty eye
There is a written scroll! I'll read the writing.

Reads

All that glitters is not gold;
Often have you heard that told:
Many a man his life hath sold
But my outside to behold:
Gilded tombs do worms infold.
Had you been as wise as bold,
Young in limbs, in judgment old,
Your answer had not been inscroll'd:
Fare you well; your suit is cold.
Cold, indeed; and labour lost:
Then, farewell, heat, and welcome, frost!
Portia, adieu. I have too grieved a heart
To take a tedious leave; thus losers part.

Exit with his train. Flourish of cornets

PORTIA: A gentle riddance. Draw the curtains, go.
Let all of his complexion choose me so.

Exeunt

SCENE VIII—*Venice: A street*

Enter SALERIO *and* SOLANIO

SALERIO: Why, man, I saw Bassanio under sail;
With him is Gratiano gone along;
And in their ship I am sure Lorenzo is not.

SOLANIO: The villain Jew with outcries raised the Duke,
Who went with him to search Bassanio's ship.

SALERIO: He came too late, the ship was under sail:
But there the Duke was given to understand
That in a gondola were seen together
Lorenzo and his amorous Jessica:
Besides, Antonio certified the Duke
They were not with Bassanio in his ship.

SOLANIO: I never heard a passion so confused,
So strange, outrageous, and so variable,
As the dog Jew did utter in the streets.

'My daughter! O my ducats! O my daughter!
Fled with a Christian! O my Christian ducats!
Justice! the law! my ducats, and my daughter!
A sealed bag, two sealed bags of ducats,
Of double ducats, stolen from me by my daughter!
And jewels, two stones, two rich and precious stones,
Stolen by my daughter! Justice! find the girl;
She hath the stones upon her, and the ducats.'

SALERIO: Why, all the boys in Venice follow him,
Crying, his stones, his daughter, and his ducats.

SOLANIO: Let good Antonio look he keep his day,
Or he shall pay for this.

SALERIO: Marry, well remember'd.
I reason'd with a Frenchman yesterday,
Who told me, in the narrow seas that part
The French and English, there miscarried
A vessel of our country richly fraught.
I thought upon Antonio when he told me;
And wish'd in silence that it were not his.

SOLANIO: You were best to tell Antonio what you hear;
Yet do not suddenly, for it may grieve him.

SALERIO: A kinder gentleman treads not the earth.
I saw Bassanio and Antonio part.
Bassanio told him he would make some speed
Of his return: he answer'd, 'Do not so;
Slubber not business for my sake, Bassanio
But stay the very riping of the time;
And for the Jew's bond which he hath of me,
Let it not enter in your mind of love;
Be merry, and employ your chiefest thoughts
To courtship and such fair ostents of love
As shall conveniently become you there:'
And even there, his eye being big with tears,
Turning his face, he put his hand behind him,
And with affection wondrous sensible
He wrung Bassanio's hand; and so they parted.

SOLANIO: I think he only loves the world for him.
I pray thee, let us go and find him out
And quicken his embraced heaviness
With some delight or other.

SALERIO: Do we so.

Exeunt

SCENE IX—*Belmont: A room in Portia's house*

Enter NERISSA with a Servitor

NERISSA: Quick, quick, I pray thee; draw the curtain straight:
The Prince of Arragon hath ta'en his oath,
And comes to his election presently.

Flourish of cornets. Enter the PRINCE OF ARRAGON, PORTIA, and their trains

PORTIA: Behold, there stand the caskets, noble Prince:
If you choose that wherein I am contain'd,
Straight shall our nuptial rites be solemnized;
But if you fail, without more speech, my lord,
You must be gone from hence immediately.

ARRAGON: I am enjoin'd by oath to observe three things:
First, never to unfold to any one
Which casket 'twas I chose; next, if I fail
Of the right casket, never in my life
To woo a maid in way of marriage; Lastly,
If I do fail in fortune of my choice,
Immediately to leave you and be gone.

PORTIA: To these injunctions every one doth swear
That comes to hazard for my worthless self.

ARRAGON: And so have I address'd me. Fortune now
To my heart's hope! Gold; silver; and base lead.
'Who chooseth me must give and hazard all he hath.'
You shall look fairer, ere I give or hazard.
What says the golden chest? Ha! let me see:
'Who chooseth me shall gain what many men desire.'
What many men desire! that 'many' may be meant
By the fool multitude, that choose by show,
Not learning more than the fond eye doth teach;
Which pries not to the interior, but, like the martlet,
Builds in the weather on the outward wall,
Even in the force and road of casualty.
I will not choose what many men desire,
Because I will not jump with common spirits
And rank me with the barbarous multitudes.
Why, then to thee, thou silver treasure-house;
Tell me once more what title thou dost bear:

'Who chooseth me shall get as much as he deserves:'

And well said too; for who shall go about
To cozen fortune and be honourable
Without the stamp of merit? Let none presume
To wear an undeserved dignity.
O, that estates, degrees and offices
Were not derived corruptly, and that clear honour
Were purchased by the merit of the wearer!
How many then should cover that stand bare!
How many be commanded that command!
How much low peasantry would then be glean'd
From the true seed of honour! and how much honour
Pick'd from the chaff and ruin of the times,
To be new-varnish'd! Well, but to my choice.
'Who chooseth me shall get as much as he deserves.'
I will assume desert. Give me a key for this,
And instantly unlock my fortunes here.

He opens the silver casket

PORTIA: [*Aside*] Too long a pause for that which you find there.

ARRAGON: What's here? the portrait of a blinking idiot,
Presenting me a schedule! I will read it.
How much unlike art thou to Portia!
How much unlike my hopes and my deservings!
'Who chooseth me shall have as much as he deserves.'
Did I deserve no more than a fool's head?
Is that my prize? are my deserts no better?

PORTIA: To offend, and judge, are distinct offices
And of opposed natures.

ARRAGON: What is here?

Reads

The fire seven times tried this:
Seven times tried that judgment is,
That did never choose amiss.
Some there be that shadows kiss;
Such have but a shadow's bliss.
There be fools alive, iwis,
Silver'd o'er; and so was this.
Take what wife you will to bed,
I will ever be your head:
So be gone: you are sped.
Still more fool I shall appear
By the time I linger here
With one fool's head I came to woo,
But I go away with two.
Sweet, adieu. I'll keep my oath,
Patiently to bear my wroth.

Exeunt Arragon and train

PORTIA: Thus hath the candle singed the moth.
O, these deliberate fools! when they do choose,
They have the wisdom by their wit to lose.

NERISSA: The ancient saying is no heresy,
Hanging and wiving goes by destiny.

PORTIA: Come, draw the curtain, Nerissa.

Enter a Servant

SERVANT: Where is my lady?

PORTIA: Here; what would my lord?

SERVANT: Madam, there is alighted at your gate
A young Venetian, one that comes before
To signify the approaching of his lord;
From whom he bringeth sensible regreets,
To wit, besides commends and courteous breath,
Gifts of rich value. Yet I have not seen
So likely an ambassador of love.
A day in April never came so sweet,
To show how costly summer was at hand,
As this fore-spurrer comes before his lord.

PORTIA: No more, I pray thee: I am half afeard
Thou wilt say anon he is some kin to thee,
Thou spend'st such high-day wit in praising him.
Come, come, Nerissa; for I long to see
Quick Cupid's post that comes so mannerly.

NERISSA: Bassanio, Lord Love, if thy will it be!

Exeunt

ACT III

SCENE I—*Venice: A street*

Enter SALANIO and SALERIO

SOLANIO: Now, what news on the Rialto?

SALERIO: Why, yet it lives there uncheck'd that Antonio hath a ship of rich lading wrecked on the narrow seas; the Goodwins, I think they call the place; a very dangerous flat and fatal, where the carcasses of many a tall ship lie buried, as they say, if my gossip Report be an honest woman of her word.

SOLANIO: I would she were as lying a gossip in that as ever knapped ginger or made her neighbours believe she wept for the death of a third husband. But it is true, without any slips of prolixity or crossing the plain highway of talk, that the good Antonio, the honest Antonio—O that I had a title good enough to keep his name company!—

SALERIO: Come, the full stop.

SOLANIO: Ha! what sayest thou? Why, the end is, he hath lost a ship.

SALERIO: I would it might prove the end of his losses.

SOLANIO: Let me say 'amen' betimes, lest the devil cross my prayer, for here he comes in the likeness of a Jew.

Enter SHYLOCK

How now, Shylock! what news among the merchants?

SHYLOCK: You knew, none so well, none so well as you, of my daughter's flight.

SALERIO: That's certain: I, for my part, knew the tailor that made the wings she flew withal.

SOLANIO: And Shylock, for his own part, knew the bird was fledge; and then it is the complexion of them all to leave the dam.

SHYLOCK: She is damned for it.

SOLANIO: That's certain, if the devil may be her judge.

SHYLOCK: My own flesh and blood to rebel!

SOLANIO: Out upon it, old carrion! rebels it at these years?

SHYLOCK: I say, my daughter is my flesh and my blood.

SALERIO: There is more difference between thy flesh and hers than between jet and ivory; more between your bloods than there is between red wine and rhenish. But tell us, do you hear whether Antonio have had any loss at sea or no?

SHYLOCK: There I have another bad match: a bankrupt, a prodigal, who dare scarce show his head on the Rialto; a beggar, that was used to come so smug upon the mart; let him look to his bond: he was wont to call me usurer; let him look to his bond: he was wont to lend money for a Christian courtesy; let him look to his bond.

SALERIO: Why, I am sure, if he forfeit, thou wilt not take his flesh: what's that good for?

SHYLOCK: To bait fish withal: if it will feed nothing else, it will feed my revenge. He hath disgraced me, and hindered me half a million; laughed at my losses, mocked at my gains, scorned my nation, thwarted my bargains, cooled my friends, heated mine enemies; and what's his reason? I am a Jew. Hath not a Jew eyes? Hath not a Jew hands, organs, dimensions, senses, affections, passions, fed with the same food, hurt with the same weapons, subject to the same diseases, healed by the same means, warmed and cooled by the same winter and summer, as a Christian is? If you prick us, do we not bleed? if you tickle us, do we not laugh? if you poison us, do we not die? and if you wrong us, shall we not revenge? If we are like you in the rest, we will resemble you in that. If a Jew wrong a Christian, what is his humility? Revenge. If a Christian wrong a Jew, what should his sufferance be by Christian example? Why, revenge. The villany you teach me, I will execute, and it shall go hard but I will better the instruction.

Enter a Servant

SERVANT: Gentlemen, my master Antonio is at his house and desires to speak with you both.

SALERIO: We have been up and down to seek him.

Enter TUBAL

SOLANIO: Here comes another of the tribe: a third cannot be matched, unless the devil himself turn Jew.

Exeunt SOLANIO, SALERIO, and Servant

SHYLOCK: How now, Tubal! what news from Genoa? hast thou found my daughter?

TUBAL: I often came where I did hear of her, but cannot find her.

SHYLOCK: Why there, there, there, there! a diamond gone, cost me two thousand ducats in Frankfort! The curse never fell upon our nation till now; I never felt it till now: two thousand ducats in that; and other precious, precious jewels. I would my daughter were dead at my foot, and the jewels in her ear! would she were hearsed at my foot, and the ducats in her coffin! No news of them? Why, so: and I know not what's spent in the search: why, thou loss upon loss! the thief gone with so much, and so much to find the thief; and no satisfaction, no revenge; nor no in luck stirring but what lights on my shoulders; no sighs but of my breathing; no tears but of my shedding.

TUBAL: Yes, other men have ill luck too: Antonio, as I heard in Genoa—

SHYLOCK: What, what, what? ill luck, ill luck?

TUBAL: Hath an argosy cast away, coming from Tripolis.

SHYLOCK: I thank God, I thank God. Is't true, is't true?

TUBAL: I spoke with some of the sailors that escaped the wreck.

SHYLOCK: I thank thee, good Tubal. Good news, good news! ha, ha!—heard in Genoa?

TUBAL: Your daughter spent in Genoa, as I heard, one night fourscore ducats.

SHYLOCK: Thou stickest a dagger in me: I shall never see my gold again: fourscore ducats at a sitting! fourscore ducats!

TUBAL: There came divers of Antonio's creditors in my company to Venice, that swear he cannot choose but break.

SHYLOCK: I am very glad of it; I'll plague him; I'll torture him; I am glad of it.

TUBAL: One of them showed me a ring that he had of your daughter for a monkey.

SHYLOCK: Out upon her! Thou torturest me, Tubal: it was my turquoise; I had it of Leah when I was a bachelor: I would not have given it for a wilderness of monkeys.

TUBAL: But Antonio is certainly undone.

SHYLOCK: Nay, that's true, that's very true. Go, Tubal, fee me an officer; bespeak him a fortnight before. I will have the heart of him, if he forfeit; for, were he out of Venice, I can make what merchandise I will. Go, go, Tubal, and meet me at our synagogue; go, good Tubal; at our synagogue, Tubal.

Exeunt

SCENE II—*Belmont: A room in Portia's house*

Enter BASSANIO, PORTIA, GRATIANO, NERISSA, and Attendants

PORTIA: I pray you, tarry; pause a day or two
Before you hazard; for, in choosing wrong,
I lose your company; therefore forbear awhile.
There's something tells me, but it is not love,
I would not lose you; and you know yourself,
Hate counsels not in such a quality.
But lest you should not understand me well—
And yet a maiden hath no tongue but thought—
I would detain you here some month or two
Before you venture for me. I could teach you
How to choose right, but I am then forsworn;
So will I never be: so may you miss me;
But if you do, you'll make me wish a sin,
That I had been forsworn. Beshrew your eyes,
They have o'erlook'd me and divided me;
One half of me is yours, the other half yours,
Mine own, I would say; but if mine, then yours,
And so all yours. O, these naughty times
Puts bars between the owners and their rights!
And so, though yours, not yours. Prove it so,
Let fortune go to hell for it, not I.
I speak too long; but 'tis to peize the time,
To eke it and to draw it out in length,
To stay you from election.

BASSANIO: Let me choose
For as I am, I live upon the rack.

PORTIA: Upon the rack, Bassanio! then confess
What treason there is mingled with your love.

BASSANIO: None but that ugly treason of mistrust,
Which makes me fear the enjoying of my love:
There may as well be amity and life

'Tween snow and fire, as treason and my love.
PORTIA: Ay, but I fear you speak upon the rack,
Where men enforced do speak anything.
BASSANIO: Promise me life, and I'll confess the truth.
PORTIA: Well then, confess and live.
BASSANIO: 'Confess' and 'love'
Had been the very sum of my confession.
O happy torment, when my torturer
Doth teach me answers for deliverance!
But let me to my fortune and the caskets.
PORTIA: Away, then! I am lock'd in one of them.
If you do love me, you will find me out.
Nerissa and the rest, stand all aloof.
Let music sound while he doth make his choice;
Then, if he lose, he makes a swan-like end,
Fading in music: that the comparison
May stand more proper, my eye shall be the stream
And watery death-bed for him. He may win;
And what is music then? Then music is
Even as the flourish when true subjects bow
To a new-crowned monarch: such it is
As are those dulcet sounds in break of day
That creep into the dreaming bridegroom's ear,
And summon him to marriage. Now he goes,
With no less presence, but with much more love,
Than young Alcides, when he did redeem
The virgin tribute paid by howling Troy
To the sea-monster. I stand for sacrifice
The rest aloof are the Dardanian wives,
With bleared visages, come forth to view
The issue of the exploit. Go, Hercules!
Live thou, I live: with much, much more dismay
I view the fight than thou that makest the fray.
A Song whilst BASSANIO comments on the caskets to himself

Song.

Tell me where is fancy bred,
Or in the heart, or in the head?
How begot, how nourished?
Reply, reply.
It is engender'd in the eyes,
With gazing fed; and fancy dies
In the cradle where it lies.
Let us all ring fancy's knell
I'll begin it—Ding, dong, bell.
ALL: Ding, dong, bell.
BASSANIO: So may the outward shows be least themselves;
The world is still deceived with ornament.
In law, what plea so tainted and corrupt,
But, being seasoned with a gracious voice,
Obscures the show of evil? In religion,
What damned error, but some sober brow
Will bless it and approve it with a text,
Hiding the grossness with fair ornament?
There is no vice so simple but assumes
Some mark of virtue on his outward parts.
How many cowards, whose hearts are all as false
As stairs of sand, wear yet upon their chins
The beards of Hercules and frowning Mars;
Who, inward search'd, have livers white as milk;
And these assume but valour's excrement
To render them redoubted! Look on beauty,
And you shall see 'tis purchased by the weight;
Which therein works a miracle in nature,
Making them lightest that wear most of it;
So are those crisped snaky golden locks
Which make such wanton gambols with the wind,
Upon supposed fairness, often known
To be the dowry of a second head,
The skull that bred them in the sepulchre.
Thus ornament is but the guiled shore
To a most dangerous sea; the beauteous scarf
Veiling an Indian beauty; in a word,
The seeming truth which cunning times put on
To entrap the wisest. Therefore, thou gaudy gold,
Hard food for Midas, I will none of thee;
Nor none of thee, thou pale and common drudge
'Tween man and man; but thou, thou meagre lead,
Which rather threatenest than dost promise aught,
Thy paleness moves me more than eloquence;
And here choose I; joy be the consequence!
PORTIA: [*Aside*] How all the other passions fleet to air,
As doubtful thoughts, and rash-embraced despair,
And shuddering fear, and green-eyed jealousy!
O love, Be moderate; allay thy ecstasy,
In measure rein thy joy; scant this excess.
I feel too much thy blessing: make it less,
For fear I surfeit.

BASSANIO: What find I here?

Opening the leaden casket

Fair Portia's counterfeit! What demi-god
Hath come so near creation? Move these eyes?
Or whether, riding on the balls of mine,
Seem they in motion? Here are sever'd lips,
Parted with sugar breath: so sweet a bar
Should sunder such sweet friends. Here in her hairs
The painter plays the spider and hath woven
A golden mesh to entrap the hearts of men,
Faster than gnats in cobwebs; but her eyes—
How could he see to do them? having made one,
Methinks it should have power to steal both his
And leave itself unfurnish'd. Yet look, how far
The substance of my praise doth wrong this shadow
In underprizing it, so far this shadow
Doth limp behind the substance. Here's the scroll,
The continent and summary of my fortune.

Reads

You that choose not by the view,
Chance as fair and choose as true!
Since this fortune falls to you,
Be content and seek no new,
If you be well pleased with this
And hold your fortune for your bliss,
Turn you where your lady is
And claim her with a loving kiss.
A gentle scroll. Fair lady, by your leave;
I come by note, to give and to receive.
Like one of two contending in a prize,
That thinks he hath done well in people's eyes,
Hearing applause and universal shout,
Giddy in spirit, still gazing in a doubt
Whether these pearls of praise be his or no;
So, thrice fair lady, stand I, even so;
As doubtful whether what I see be true,
Until confirm'd, sign'd, ratified by you.

PORTIA: You see me, Lord Bassanio, where I stand,
Such as I am: though for myself alone
I would not be ambitious in my wish,
To wish myself much better; yet, for you
I would be trebled twenty times myself;
A thousand times more fair, ten thousand times more rich;
That only to stand high in your account,
I might in virtue, beauties, livings, friends,
Exceed account; but the full sum of me
Is sum of something, which, to term in gross,
Is an unlesson'd girl, unschool'd, unpractised;
Happy in this, she is not yet so old
But she may learn; happier than this,
She is not bred so dull but she can learn;
Happiest of all is that her gentle spirit
Commits itself to yours to be directed,
As from her lord, her governor, her king.
Myself and what is mine to you and yours
Is now converted: but now I was the lord
Of this fair mansion, master of my servants,
Queen o'er myself; and even now, but now,
This house, these servants and this same myself
Are yours, my lord: I give them with this ring;
Which when you part from, lose, or give away,
Let it presage the ruin of your love
And be my vantage to exclaim on you.

BASSANIO: Madam, you have bereft me of all words,
Only my blood speaks to you in my veins;
And there is such confusion in my powers,
As after some oration fairly spoke
By a beloved prince, there doth appear
Among the buzzing pleased multitude;
Where every something, being blent together,
Turns to a wild of nothing, save of joy,
Express'd and not express'd. But when this ring
Parts from this finger, then parts life from hence;
O, then be bold to say Bassanio's dead!

NERISSA: My lord and lady, it is now our time,
That have stood by and seen our wishes prosper,
To cry 'Good Joy'. Good joy, my lord and lady!

GRATIANO: My lord Bassanio and my gentle lady,
I wish you all the joy that you can wish;
For I am sure you can wish none from me;
And when your honours mean to solemnize
The bargain of your faith, I do beseech you,
Even at that time I may be married too.

BASSANIO: With all my heart, so thou canst get a wife.

GRATIANO: I thank your lordship, you have got me one.
My eyes, my lord, can look as swift as yours:
You saw the mistress, I beheld the maid;
You loved, I loved; for intermission.
No more pertains to me, my lord, than you.
Your fortune stood upon the casket there,
And so did mine too, as the matter falls;
For wooing here until I sweat again,
And sweating until my very roof was dry
With oaths of love, at last, if promise last,
I got a promise of this fair one here
To have her love, provided that your fortune
Achieved her mistress.

PORTIA: Is this true, Nerissa ?

NERISSA: Madam, it is, so you stand pleased withal.

BASSANIO: And do you, Gratiano, mean good faith?

GRATIANO: Yes, faith, my lord.

BASSANIO: Our feast shall be much honour'd in your marriage.

GRATIANO: We'll play with them the first boy for a thousand ducats.

NERISSA: What, and stake down?

GRATIANO: No; we shall ne'er win at that sport, and stake down.
But who comes here? Lorenzo and his infidel?
What, and my old Venetian friend Salerio?

Enter LORENZO, JESSICA, and SALERIO, a Messenger from Venice

BASSANIO: Lorenzo and Salerio, welcome hither;
If that the youth of my new interest here
Have power to bid you welcome. By your leave,
I bid my very friends and countrymen,
Sweet Portia, welcome.

PORTIA: So do I, my lord;
They are entirely welcome.

LORENZO: I thank your honour. For my part, my lord,
My purpose was not to have seen you here;
But meeting with Salerio by the way,
He did entreat me, past all saying nay,
To come with him along.

SALERIO: I did, my lord;
And I have reason for it. Signior Antonio
Commends him to you.

Gives Bassanio a letter

BASSANIO: Ere I ope his letter,
I pray you, tell me how my good friend doth.

SALERIO: Not sick, my lord, unless it be in mind;
Nor well, unless in mind: his letter there
Will show you his estate.

Bassanio opens the letter.

GRATIANO: Nerissa, cheer yond stranger; bid her welcome.
Your hand, Salerio: what's the news from Venice?
How doth that royal merchant, good Antonio?
I know he will be glad of our success;
We are the Jasons, we have won the fleece.

SALERIO: I would you had won the fleece that he hath lost.

PORTIA: There are some shrewd contents in yond same paper,
That steals the colour from Bassanio's cheek:
Some dear friend dead; else nothing in the world
Could turn so much the constitution
Of any constant man. What, worse and worse!
With leave, Bassanio: I am half yourself,
And I must freely have the half of anything
That this same paper brings you.

BASSANIO: O sweet Portia,
Here are a few of the unpleasant'st words
That ever blotted paper! Gentle lady,
When I did first impart my love to you,
I freely told you, all the wealth I had
Ran in my veins, I was a gentleman;
And then I told you true: and yet, dear lady,
Rating myself at nothing, you shall see
How much I was a braggart. When I told you
My state was nothing, I should then have told you
That I was worse than nothing; for indeed,
I have engaged myself to a dear friend,
Engaged my friend to his mere enemy,
To feed my means. Here is a letter, lady;
The paper as the body of my friend,
And every word in it a gaping wound,
Issuing life-blood. But is it true, Salerio?
Hath all his ventures fail'd ? What, not one hit?
From Tripolis, from Mexico and England,
From Lisbon, Barbary and India,
And not one vessel 'scape the dreadful touch
Of merchant-marring rocks?

SALERIO: Not one, my lord.

Besides, it should appear, that if he had
The present money to discharge the Jew,
He would not take it. Never did I know
A creature, that did bear the shape of man,
So keen and greedy to confound a man:
He plies the Duke at morning and at night,
And doth impeach the freedom of the state,
If they deny him justice. Twenty merchants,
The Duke himself, and the magnificoes
Of greatest port, have all persuaded with him;
But none can drive him from the envious plea
Of forfeiture, of justice and his bond.

JESSICA: When I was with him I have heard him swear
To Tubal and to Chus, his countrymen,
That he would rather have Antonio's flesh
Than twenty times the value of the sum
That he did owe him: and I know, my lord,
If law, authority and power deny not,
It will go hard with poor Antonio.

PORTIA: Is it your dear friend that is thus in trouble?

BASSANIO: The dearest friend to me, the kindest man,
The best-condition'd and unwearied spirit
In doing courtesies, and one in whom
The ancient Roman honour more appears
Than any that draws breath in Italy.

PORTIA: What sum owes he the Jew?

BASSANIO: For me three thousand ducats.

PORTIA: What, no more?
Pay him six thousand, and deface the bond;
Double six thousand, and then treble that,
Before a friend of this description
Shall lose a hair through Bassanio's fault.
First go with me to church and call me wife,
And then away to Venice to your friend;
For never shall you lie by Portia's side
With an unquiet soul. You shall have gold
To pay the petty debt twenty times over.
When it is paid, bring your true friend along.
My maid Nerissa and myself meantime
Will live as maids and widows. Come, away!
For you shall hence upon your wedding-day.
Bid your friends welcome, show a merry cheer;
Since you are dear bought, I will love you dear.
But let me hear the letter of your friend.

BASSANIO: [*Reads*] Sweet Bassanio, my ships have all miscarried, my creditors grow cruel, my estate is very low, my bond to the Jew is forfeit; and since in paying it, it is impossible I should live, all debts are cleared between you and I, if I might but see you at my death. Notwithstanding, use your pleasure; if your love do not persuade you to come, let not my letter.

PORTIA: O love, dispatch all business, and be gone!

BASSANIO: Since I have your good leave to go away,
I will make haste; but, till I come again,
No bed shall e'er be guilty of my stay,
Nor rest be interposer 'twixt us twain.

Exeunt

SCENE III—*Venice: A street*

Enter SHYLOCK, SOLANIO, ANTONIO, and Gaoler

SHYLOCK: Gaoler, look to him. Tell not me of mercy—
This is the fool that lent out money gratis.
Gaoler, look to him.

ANTONIO: Hear me yet, good Shylock.

SHYLOCK: I'll have my bond; speak not against my bond.
I have sworn an oath that I will have my bond.
Thou call'dst me dog before thou hadst a cause;
But, since I am a dog, beware my fangs;
The Duke shall grant me justice. I do wonder,
Thou naughty gaoler, that thou art so fond
To come abroad with him at his request.

ANTONIO: I pray thee, hear me speak.

SHYLOCK: I'll have my bond; I will not hear thee speak;
I'll have my bond; and therefore speak no more.
I'll not be made a soft and dull-eyed fool,
To shake the head, relent, and sigh, and yield
To Christian intercessors. Follow not;
I'll have no speaking: I will have my bond.

Exit

SOLANIO: It is the most impenetrable cur
That ever kept with men.

ANTONIO: Let him alone;
I'll follow him no more with bootless prayers.
He seeks my life; his reason well I know:
I oft deliver'd from his forfeitures
Many that have at times made moan to me;
Therefore he hates me.

SOLANIO: I am sure the Duke

Will never grant this forfeiture to hold.

ANTONIO: The Duke cannot deny the course of law;
For the commodity that strangers have
With us in Venice, if it be denied,
Will much impeach the justice of his state;
Since that the trade and profit of the city
Consisteth of all nations. Therefore, go:
These griefs and losses have so bated me,
That I shall hardly spare a pound of flesh
To-morrow to my bloody creditor.
Well, gaoler, on. Pray God, Bassanio come
To see me pay his debt, and then I care not!

Exeunt

SCENE IV—*Belmont: A room in Portia's house*

Enter PORTIA, NERISSA, LORENZO, JESSICA, and BALTHASAR

LORENZO: Madam, although I speak it in your presence,
You have a noble and a true conceit
Of godlike amity; which appears most strongly
In bearing thus the absence of your lord.
But if you knew to whom you show this honour,
How true a gentleman you send relief,
How dear a lover of my lord your husband,
I know you would be prouder of the work
Than customary bounty can enforce you.

PORTIA: I never did repent for doing good,
Nor shall not now; for in companions
That do converse and waste the time together,
Whose souls do bear an equal yoke of love,
There must be needs a like proportion
Of lineaments, of manners and of spirit;
Which makes me think that this Antonio,
Being the bosom lover of my lord,
Must needs be like my lord. If it be so,
How little is the cost I have bestow'd
In purchasing the semblance of my soul
From out the state of hellish misery!
This comes too near the praising of myself;
Therefore no more of it; hear other things.
Lorenzo, I commit into your hands
The husbandry and manage of my house
Until my lord's return; for mine own part,
I have toward heaven breathed a secret vow
To live in prayer and contemplation,
Only attended by Nerissa here,
Until her husband and my lord's return.
There is a monastery two miles off;
And there will we abide. I do desire you
Not to deny this imposition;
The which my love and some necessity
Now lays upon you.

LORENZO: Madam, with all my heart;
I shall obey you in all fair commands.

PORTIA: My people do already know my mind,
And will acknowledge you and Jessica
In place of Lord Bassanio and myself.
So fare you well, till we shall meet again.

LORENZO: Fair thoughts and happy hours attend on you!

JESSICA: I wish your ladyship all heart's content.

PORTIA: I thank you for your wish, and am well pleased
To wish it back on you: fare you well Jessica.

Exeunt JESSICA and LORENZO

Now, Balthasar,
As I have ever found thee honest-true,
So let me find thee still. Take this same letter,
And use thou all the endeavour of a man
In speed to Padua; see thou render this
Into my cousin's hand, Doctor Bellario;
And, look, what notes and garments he doth give thee,
Bring them, I pray thee, with imagined speed
Unto the tranect, to the common ferry
Which trades to Venice. Waste no time in words,
But get thee gone; I shall be there before thee.

BALTHASAR: Madam, I go with all convenient speed.

Exit

PORTIA: Come on, Nerissa; I have work in hand
That you yet know not of: we'll see our husbands
Before they think of us.

NERISSA: Shall they see us?

PORTIA: They shall, Nerissa; but in such a habit,
That they shall think we are accomplished
With that we lack. I'll hold thee any wager,
When we are both accoutred like young men,
I'll prove the prettier fellow of the two,

And wear my dagger with the braver grace,
And speak between the change of man and boy
With a reed voice, and turn two mincing steps
Into a manly stride, and speak of frays
Like a fine bragging youth, and tell quaint lies,
How honourable ladies sought my love,
Which I denying, they fell sick and died:
I could not do withal; then I'll repent,
And wish for all that, that I had not killed them;
And twenty of these puny lies I'll tell,
That men shall swear I have discontinued school
Above a twelvemonth. I have within my mind
A thousand raw tricks of these bragging Jacks,
Which I will practise.

NERISSA: Why, shall we turn to men ?

PORTIA: Fie, what a question's that,
If thou wert near a lewd interpreter!
But come, I'll tell thee all my whole device
When I am in my coach, which stays for us
At the park gate; and therefore haste away,
For we must measure twenty miles to-day.

Exeunt

SCENE V—*The same: A garden*

Enter LAUNCELOT and JESSICA

LAUNCELOT: Yes, truly; for, look you, the sins of the father are to be laid upon the children; therefore, I promise ye, I fear you. I was always plain with you, and so now I speak my agitation of the matter: therefore be of good cheer, for truly I think you are damned. There is but one hope in it that can do you any good; and that is but a kind of bastard hope neither.

JESSICA: And what hope is that, I pray thee ?

LAUNCELOT: Marry, you may partly hope that your father got you not, that you are not the Jew's daughter.

JESSICA: That were a kind of bastard hope, indeed; so the sins of my mother should be visited upon me.

LAUNCELOT: Truly then I fear you are damned both by father and mother; thus when I shun Scylla, your father, I fall into Charybdis, your mother; well, you are gone both ways.

JESSICA: I shall be saved by my husband; he hath made me a Christian.

LAUNCELOT: Truly, the more to blame he: we were Christians enow before; e'en as many as could well live, one by another. This making of Christians will raise the price of hogs: if we grow all to be pork-eaters, we shall not shortly have a rasher on the coals for money.

Enter LORENZO

JESSICA: I'll tell my husband, Launcelot, what you say: here he comes.

LORENZO: I shall grow jealous of you shortly, Launcelot, if you thus get my wife into corners.

JESSICA: Nay, you need not fear us, Lorenzo: Launcelot and I are out. He tells me flatly, there is no mercy for me in heaven, because I am a Jew's daughter: and he says, you are no good member of the commonwealth, for in converting Jews to Christians, you raise the price of pork.

LORENZO: I shall answer that better to the commonwealth than you can the getting up of the negro's belly: the Moor is with child by you, Launcelot.

LAUNCELOT: It is much that the Moor should be more than reason: but if she be less than an honest woman, she is indeed more than I took her for.

LORENZO: How every fool can play upon the word! I think the best grace of wit will shortly turn into silence, and discourse grow commendable in none only but parrots. Go in, sirrah; bid them prepare for dinner.

LAUNCELOT: That is done, sir; they have all stomachs.

LORENZO: Goodly Lord, what a wit-snapper are you! then bid them prepare dinner.

LAUNCELOT: That is done too, sir; only 'cover' is the word.

LORENZO: Will you cover then, sir ?

LAUNCELOT: Not so, sir, neither; I know my duty.

LORENZO: Yet more quarrelling with occasion! Wilt thou show the whole wealth of thy wit in an instant? I pray thee, understand a plain man in his plain meaning: go to thy fellows; bid them cover the table, serve in the meat, and we will come in to dinner.

LAUNCELOT: For the table, sir, it shall be served in; for the meat, sir, it shall be covered; for your coming in to dinner, sir, why, let it be as humours and conceits shall govern.

Exit

LORENZO: O dear discretion, how his words are suited!
The fool hath planted in his memory
An army of good words; and I do know

A many fools, that stand in better place,
Garnish'd like him, that for a tricksy word
Defy the matter. How cheerest thou, Jessica?
And now, good sweet, say thy opinion,
How dost thou like the Lord Bassanio's wife?

JESSICA: Past all expressing. It is very meet
The Lord Bassanio live an upright life;
For, having such a blessing in his lady,
He finds the joys of heaven here on earth;
And if on earth he do not mean it, then
In reason he should never come to heaven
Why, if two gods should play some heavenly match
And on the wager lay two earthly women,
And Portia one, there must be something else
Pawn'd with the other, for the poor rude world
Hath not her fellow.

LORENZO: Even such a husband
Hast thou of me as she is for a wife.

JESSICA: Nay, but ask my opinion too of that.

LORENZO: I will anon: first, let us go to dinner.

JESSICA: Nay, let me praise you while I have a stomach.

LORENZO: No, pray thee, let it serve for table-talk;
Then, howso'er thou speak'st, 'mong other things
I shall digest it.

JESSICA: Well, I'll set you forth.

Exeunt

Act IV

Scene I—*Venice: A court of justice*

Enter the DUKE, the Magnificoes, ANTONIO, BASSANIO, GRATIANO, SALERIO, and Others

DUKE: What, is Antonio here?
ANTONIO: Ready, so please your grace.
DUKE: I am sorry for thee; thou art come to answer
A stony adversary, an inhuman wretch,
Uncapable of pity, void and empty
From any dram of mercy.
ANTONIO: I have heard
Your grace hath ta'en great pains to qualify
His rigorous course; but since he stands obdurate
And that no lawful means can carry me
Out of his envy's reach, I do oppose
My patience to his fury, and am arm'd
To suffer, with a quietness of spirit
The very tyranny and rage of his.
DUKE: Go one, and call the Jew into the court.
SALERIO: He is ready at the door; he comes, my lord.

Enter SHYLOCK

DUKE: Make room, and let him stand before our face.
Shylock, the world thinks, and I think so too,
That thou but leadest this fashion of thy malice
To the last hour of act; and then, 'tis thought
Thou'lt show thy mercy and remorse more strange
Than is thy strange apparent cruelty;
And where thou now exacts the penalty,
Which is a pound of this poor merchant's flesh,
Thou wilt not only loose the forfeiture,
But, touch'd with human gentleness and love,
Forgive a moiety of the principal,
Glancing an eye of pity on his losses,
That have of late so huddled on his back—
Enow to press a royal merchant down,
And pluck commiseration of his state
From brassy bosoms and rough hearts of flint,
From stubborn Turks and Tartars, never train'd
To offices of tender courtesy.
We all expect a gentle answer, Jew.
SHYLOCK: I have possess'd your grace of what I purpose,
And by our holy Sabbath have I sworn
To have the due and forfeit of my bond.
If you deny it, let the danger light
Upon your charter and your city's freedom.
You'll ask me, why I rather choose to have
A weight of carrion flesh than to receive
Three thousand ducats, I'll not answer that.
But say it is my humour—is it answer'd?
What if my house be troubled with a rat,
And I be pleased to give ten thousand ducats
To have it baned? What, are you answer'd yet?
Some men there are love not a gaping pig;
Some that are mad if they behold a cat;
And others, when the bagpipe sings i' the nose,
Cannot contain their urine; for affection,
Mistress of passion, sways it to the mood
Of what it likes or loathes. Now, for your answer:
As there is no firm reason to be render'd
Why he cannot abide a gaping pig;
Why he, a harmless necessary cat;
Why he, a woollen bagpipe; but of force
Must yield to such inevitable shame
As to offend, himself being offended;
So can I give no reason, nor I will not,
More than a lodged hate and a certain loathing
I bear Antonio, that I follow thus
A losing suit against him. Are you answer'd?
BASSANIO: This is no answer, thou unfeeling man,
To excuse the current of thy cruelty.
SHYLOCK: I am not bound to please thee with my answers.

BASSANIO: Do all men kill the things they do not love?

SHYLOCK: Hates any man the thing he would not kill?

BASSANIO: Every offence is not a hate at first.

SHYLOCK: What, wouldst thou have a serpent sting thee twice?

ANTONIO: I pray you, think you question with the Jew.

You may as well go stand upon the beach
And bid the main flood bate his usual height;
You may as well use question with the wolf,
Why he hath made the ewe bleat for the lamb;
You may as well forbid the mountain pines
To wag their high tops and to make no noise,
When they are fretten with the gusts of heaven;
You may as well do anything most hard
As seek to soften that—than which what's harder?—
His Jewish heart. Therefore, I do beseech you,
Make no more offers, use no farther means,
But with all brief and plain conveniency
Let me have judgment and the Jew his will.

BASSANIO: For thy three thousand ducats here is six.

SHYLOCK: If every ducat in six thousand ducats
Were in six parts, and every part a ducat,
I would not draw them; I would have my bond.

DUKE: How shalt thou hope for mercy, rendering none?

SHYLOCK: What judgment shall I dread, doing no wrong?
You have among you many a purchased slave,
Which, like your asses and your dogs and mules,
You use in abject and in slavish parts,
Because you bought them; shall I say to you
'Let them be free, marry them to your heirs—
Why sweat they under burdens?—let their beds
Be made as soft as yours, and let their palates
Be season'd with such viands? You will answer
'The slaves are ours'. So do I answer you:
The pound of flesh which I demand of him
Is dearly bought, 'tis mine, and I will have it.
If you deny me, fie upon your law!
There is no force in the decrees of Venice.
I stand for judgment; answer; shall I have it?

DUKE: Upon my power I may dismiss this court,
Unless Bellario, a learned doctor,
Whom I have sent for to determine this,
Come here to-day.

SALERIO: My lord, here stays without
A messenger with letters from the doctor,
New come from Padua.

DUKE: Bring us the letter; call the messenger.

BASSANIO: Good cheer, Antonio! What, man, courage yet!
The Jew shall have my flesh, blood, bones and all,
Ere thou shalt lose for me one drop of blood.

ANTONIO: I am a tainted wether of the flock,
Meetest for death; the weakest kind of fruit
Drops earliest to the ground, and so let me.
You cannot better be employ'd, Bassanio,
Than to live still and write mine epitaph.

Enter NERISSA, dressed like a lawyer's clerk

DUKE: Came you from Padua, from Bellario?

NERISSA: From both, my lord. Bellario greets your grace.

Presenting a letter

BASSANIO: Why dost thou whet thy knife so earnestly?

SHYLOCK: To cut the forfeiture from that bankrupt there.

GRATIANO: Not on thy sole, but on thy soul, harsh Jew,
Thou makest thy knife keen; but no metal can,
No, not the hangman's axe, bear half the keenness
Of thy sharp envy. Can no prayers pierce thee?

SHYLOCK: No, none that thou hast wit enough to make.

GRATIANO: O, be thou damn'd, inexecrable dog!
And for thy life let justice be accused.
Thou almost makest me waver in my faith,
To hold opinion with Pythagoras
That souls of animals infuse themselves
Into the trunks of men. Thy currish spirit
Govern'd a wolf who, hang'd for human slaughter,
Even from the gallows did his fell soul fleet,
And, whilst thou lay'st in thy unhallow'd dam,
Infused itself in thee; for thy desires
Are wolfish, bloody, starved and ravenous.

SHYLOCK: Till thou canst rail the seal from off my bond,
Thou but offend'st thy lungs to speak so loud;

Repair thy wit, good youth, or it will fall
To cureless ruin. I stand here for law.
DUKE: This letter from Bellario doth commend
A young and learned doctor to our court.
Where is he?
NERISSA: He attendeth here hard by
To know your answer, whether you'll admit him.
DUKE: With all my heart. Some three or four of you
Go give him courteous conduct to this place.
Meantime the court shall hear Bellario's letter.
CLERK: [*Reads*] 'Your grace shall understand that at the receipt of your letter I am very sick; but in the instant that your messenger came, in loving visitation was with me a young doctor of Rome—his name is Balthazar. I acquainted him with the cause in controversy between the Jew and Antonio the merchant; we turned o'er many books together; he is furnished with my opinion which, bettered with his own learning—the greatness whereof I cannot enough commend—comes with him at my importunity to fill up your grace's request in my stead. I beseech you, let his lack of years be no impediment to let him lack a reverend estimation; for I never knew so young a body with so old a head. I leave him to your gracious acceptance, whose trial shall better publish his commendation,

Enter PORTIA, dressed like a Doctor of Laws

DUKE: You hear the learn'd Bellario, what he writes: And here, I take it, is the doctor come.
Give me your hand, come you from old Bellario?
PORTIA: I did, my lord.
DUKE: You are welcome; take your place.
Are you acquainted with the difference
That holds this present question in the court?
PORTIA: I am informed thoroughly of the cause.
Which is the merchant here, and which the Jew?
DUKE: Antonio and old Shylock, both stand forth.
PORTIA: Is your name Shylock?
SHYLOCK: Shylock is my name.
PORTIA: Of a strange nature is the suit you follow;
Yet in such rule that the Venetian law
Cannot impugn you as you do proceed.
You stand within his danger, do you not?
ANTONIO: Ay, so he says.
PORTIA: Do you confess the bond?
ANTONIO: I do.
PORTIA: Then must the Jew be merciful.
SHYLOCK: On what compulsion must I? tell me that.
PORTIA: The quality of mercy is not strain'd;
It droppeth as the gentle rain from heaven
Upon the place beneath. It is twice blest:
It blesseth him that gives and him that takes.
'Tis mightiest in the mightiest: it becomes
The throned monarch better than his crown;
His sceptre shows the force of temporal power,
The attribute to awe and majesty,
Wherein doth sit the dread and fear of kings;
But mercy is above this sceptred sway,
It is enthroned in the hearts of kings,
It is an attribute to God himself;
And earthly power doth then show likest God's
When mercy seasons justice. Therefore, Jew,
Though justice be thy plea, consider this—
That in the course of justice none of us
Should see salvation; we do pray for mercy,
And that same prayer doth teach us all to render
The deeds of mercy. I have spoke thus much
To mitigate the justice of thy plea,
Which if thou follow, this strict court of Venice
Must needs give sentence 'gainst the merchant there.
SHYLOCK: My deeds upon my head! I crave the law,
The penalty and forfeit of my bond.
PORTIA: Is he not able to discharge the money?
BASSANIO: Yes; here I tender it for him in the court;
Yea, twice the sum; if that will not suffice,
I will be bound to pay it ten times o'er
On forfeit of my hands, my head, my heart;
If this will not suffice, it must appear
That malice bears down truth. And I beseech you,
Wrest once the law to your authority;
To do a great right, do a little wrong,
And curb this cruel devil of his will.
PORTIA: It must not be; there is no power in Venice
Can alter a decree established;
'Twill be recorded for a precedent,
And many an error by the same example,
Will rush into the state; it cannot be.
SHYLOCK: A Daniel come to judgment! yea, a Daniel!
O wise young judge, how I do honour thee!
PORTIA: I pray you, let me look upon the bond.
SHYLOCK: Here 'tis, most reverend Doctor; here it is.

PORTIA: Shylock, there's thrice thy money offer'd thee.

SHYLOCK: An oath, an oath! I have an oath in heaven.
Shall I lay perjury upon my soul?
No, not for Venice.

PORTIA: Why, this bond is forfeit;
And lawfully by this the Jew may claim
A pound of flesh, to be by him cut off
Nearest the merchant's heart. Be merciful.
Take thrice thy money; bid me tear the bond.

SHYLOCK: When it is paid according to the tenour.
It doth appear you are a worthy judge;
You know the law; your exposition
Hath been most sound; I charge you by the law,
Whereof you are a well-deserving pillar,
Proceed to judgment. By my soul I swear
There is no power in the tongue of man
To alter me: I stay here on my bond.

ANTONIO: Most heartily I do beseech the court
To give the judgment.

PORTIA: Why then, thus it is:
You must prepare your bosom for his knife.

SHYLOCK: O noble judge! O excellent young man!

PORTIA: For the intent and purpose of the law
Hath full relation to the penalty,
Which here appeareth due upon the bond.

SHYLOCK: 'Tis very true. O wise and upright judge,
How much more elder art thou than thy looks!

PORTIA: Therefore lay bare your bosom.

SHYLOCK: Ay, his breast—
So says the bond; doth it not, noble judge?
'Nearest his heart', those are the very words.

PORTIA: It is so. Are there balance here to weigh
The flesh?

SHYLOCK: I have them ready.

PORTIA: Have by some surgeon, Shylock, on your charge,
To stop his wounds, lest he do bleed to death.

SHYLOCK: Is it so nominated in the bond?

PORTIA: It is not so express'd, but what of that?
'Twere good you do so much for charity.

SHYLOCK: I cannot find it; 'tis not in the bond.

PORTIA: You, merchant, have you any thing to say?

ANTONIO: But little: I am arm'd and well prepared.
Give me your hand, Bassanio; fare you well.
Grieve not that I am fallen to this for you,
For herein Fortune shows herself more kind
Than is her custom. It is still her use
To let the wretched man outlive his wealth,
To view with hollow eye and wrinkled brow
An age of poverty; from which lingering penance
Of such misery doth she cut me off.
Commend me to your honourable wife;
Tell her the process of Antonio's end;
Say how I loved you, speak me fair in death;
And, when the tale is told, bid her be judge
Whether Bassanio had not once a love.
Repent but you that you shall lose your friend,
And he repents not that he pays your debt;
For if the Jew do cut but deep enough,
I'll pay it presently with all my heart.

BASSANIO: Antonio, I am married to a wife
Which is as dear to me as life itself;
But life itself, my wife, and all the world,
Are not with me esteem'd above thy life;
I would lose all, ay, sacrifice them all
Here to this devil, to deliver you.

PORTIA: Your wife would give you little thanks for that,
If she were by to hear you make the offer

GRATIANO: I have a wife, whom, I protest I love;
I would she were in heaven, so she could
Entreat some power to change this currish Jew.

NERISSA: 'Tis well you offer it behind her back;
The wish would make else an unquiet house.

SHYLOCK: (*Aside*) These be the Christian husbands. I have a daughter—
Would any of the stock of Barrabas
Had been her husband rather than a Christian—
We trifle time; I pray thee, pursue sentence.

PORTIA: A pound of that same merchant's flesh is thine.
The court awards it and the law doth give it.

SHYLOCK: Most rightful judge!

PORTIA: And you must cut this flesh from off his breast.
The law allows it and the court awards it.

SHYLOCK: Most learned judge! A sentence! Come, prepare.

PORTIA: Tarry a little; there is something else.
This bond doth give thee here no jot of blood.
The words expressly are 'a pound of flesh'.
Take then thy bond, take thou thy pound of flesh;

But, in the cutting it, if thou dost shed
One drop of Christian blood, thy lands and goods
Are, by the laws of Venice, confiscate
Unto the state of Venice.

GRATIANO: O upright judge! Mark, Jew. O learned judge!

SHYLOCK: Is that the law?

PORTIA: Thyself shalt see the act;
For, as thou urgest justice, be assured
Thou shalt have justice, more than thou desirest.

GRATIANO: O learned judge! Mark, Jew. A learned judge!

SHYLOCK: I take this offer, then: pay the bond thrice,
And let the Christian go.

BASSANIO: Here is the money.

PORTIA: Soft!
The Jew shall have all justice; soft! No haste.
He shall have nothing but the penalty.

GRATIANO: O Jew! an upright judge, a learned judge!

PORTIA: Therefore, prepare thee to cut off the flesh.
Shed thou no blood, nor cut thou less nor more
But just a pound of flesh; if thou tak'st more
Or less than a just pound—be it but so much
As makes it light or heavy in the substance,
Or the division of the twentieth part
Of one poor scruple; nay, if the scale do turn
But in the estimation of a hair—
Thou diest, and all thy goods are confiscate.

GRATIANO: A second Daniel, a Daniel, Jew!
Now, infidel, I have you on the hip.

PORTIA: Why doth the Jew pause? Take thy forfeiture.

SHYLOCK: Give me my principal, and let me go.

BASSANIO: I have it ready for thee; here it is.

PORTIA: He hath refused it in the open court;
He shall have merely justice and his bond.

GRATIANO: A Daniel still say I, a second Daniel!
I thank thee, Jew, for teaching me that word.

SHYLOCK: Shall I not have barely my principal?

PORTIA: Thou shalt have nothing but the forfeiture
To be so taken at thy peril, Jew.

SHYLOCK: Why, then the devil give him good of it!
I'll stay no longer question.

PORTIA: Tarry, Jew.
The law hath yet another hold on you.
It is enacted in the laws of Venice,
If it be proved against an alien
That by direct or indirect attempts
He seek the life of any citizen,
The party 'gainst the which he doth contrive
Shall seize one half his goods; the other half
Comes to the privy coffer of the state;
And the offender's life lies in the mercy
Of the duke only, 'gainst all other voice.
In which predicament, I say, thou stand'st;
For it appears, by manifest proceeding
That indirectly and directly too,
Thou hast contrived against the very life
Of the defendant; and thou hast incurr'd
The danger formerly by me rehearsed.
Down therefore and beg mercy of the Duke.

GRATIANO: Beg that thou mayst have leave to hang thyself;
And yet, thy wealth being forfeit to the state,
Thou hast not left the value of a cord;
Therefore thou must be hang'd at the state's charge.

DUKE: That thou shalt see the difference of our spirits,
I pardon thee thy life before thou ask it.
For half thy wealth, it is Antonio's;
The other half comes to the general state,
Which humbleness may drive unto a fine.

PORTIA: Ay, for the state, not for Antonio.

SHYLOCK: Nay, take my life and all, pardon not that.
You take my house when you do take the prop
That doth sustain my house; you take my life
When you do take the means whereby I live.

PORTIA: What mercy can you render him, Antonio?

GRATIANO: A halter gratis; nothing else, for God's sake.

ANTONIO: So please my lord the Duke and all the court
To quit the fine for one half of his goods,
I am content; so he will let me have
The other half in use, to render it
Upon his death, unto the gentleman
That lately stole his daughter—
Two things provided more: that, for this favour,
He presently become a Christian;
The other, that he do record a gift,
Here in the court, of all he dies possess'd,
Unto his son Lorenzo and his daughter.

DUKE: He shall do this, or else I do recant
The pardon that I late pronounced here.
PORTIA: Art thou contented, Jew? What dost thou say?
SHYLOCK: I am content.
PORTIA: Clerk, draw a deed of gift.
SHYLOCK: I pray you, give me leave to go from hence;
I am not well; send the deed after me
And I will sign it.
DUKE: Get thee gone, but do it.
GRATIANO: In christening shalt thou have two god-fathers:
Had I been judge, thou shouldst have had ten more,
To bring thee to the gallows, not the font.

Exit SHYLOCK

DUKE: Sir, I entreat you home with me to dinner.
PORTIA: I humbly do desire your grace of pardon:
I must away this night toward Padua,
And it is meet I presently set forth.
DUKE: I am sorry that your leisure serves you not.
Antonio, gratify this gentleman,
For in my mind you are much bound to him.

Exeunt Duke, Magnificoes, and Train

BASSANIO: Most worthy gentleman, I and my friend
Have by your wisdom been this day acquitted
Of grievous penalties; in lieu whereof
Three thousand ducats, due unto the Jew,
We freely cope your courteous pains withal.
ANTONIO: And stand indebted, over and above,
In love and service to you evermore.
PORTIA: He is well paid that is well satisfied;
And I, delivering you, am satisfied
And therein do account myself well paid.
My mind was never yet more mercenary.
I pray you, know me when we meet again;
I wish you well, and so I take my leave.
BASSANIO: Dear sir, of force I must attempt you further;
Take some remembrance of us, as a tribute,
Not as a fee. Grant me two things, I pray you,
Not to deny me, and to pardon me.
PORTIA: You press me far, and therefore I will yield.

To ANTONIO

Give me your gloves, I'll wear them for your sake.

To BASSANIO

And, for your love, I'll take this ring from you.
Do not draw back your hand: I'll take no more,
And you in love shall not deny me this.
BASSANIO: This ring, good sir—alas, it is a trifle;
I will not shame myself to give you this.
PORTIA: I will have nothing else but only this;
And now, methinks I have a mind to it.
BASSANIO: There's more depends on this than on the value.
The dearest ring in Venice will I give you,
And find it out by proclamation;
Only for this, I pray you, pardon me.
PORTIA: I see, sir, you are liberal in offers;
You taught me first to beg; and now, methinks,
You teach me how a beggar should be answer'd.
BASSANIO: Good sir, this ring was given me by my wife;
And when she put it on, she made me vow
That I should neither sell, nor give, nor lose it.
PORTIA: That 'scuse serves many men to save their' gifts.
An if your wife be not a mad-woman,
And know how well I have deserved the ring,
She would not hold out enemy for ever.
For giving it to me. Well, peace be with you!

Exeunt Portia and Nerissa

ANTONIO: My Lord Bassanio, let him have the ring.
Let his deservings and my love withal,
Be valued against your wife's commandment.
BASSANIO: Go, Gratiano, run and overtake him;
Give him the ring, and bring him, if thou canst,
Unto Antonio's house: away, make haste.

Exit GRATIANO

Come, you and I will thither presently;
And in the morning early will we both
Fly toward Belmont. Come, Antonio.

Exeunt

SCENE II—*Venice: A street*

Enter PORTIA and NERISSA

PORTIA: Inquire the Jew's house out, give him this deed,
And let him sign it; we'll away to-night,
And be a day before our husbands home.
This deed will be well welcome to Lorenzo.

Enter GRATIANO

GRATIANO: Fair sir, you are well o'erta'en.
My Lord Bassanio upon more advice
Hath sent you here this ring, and doth entreat
Your company at dinner.
PORTIA: That cannot be.
His ring I do accept most thankfully,
And so, I pray you, tell him. Furthermore,
I pray you, show my youth old Shylock's house.
GRATIANO: That will I do.
NERISSA: Sir, I would speak with you.
Aside to PORTIA
I'll see if I can get my husband's ring,
Which I did make him swear to keep for ever.
PORTIA: [*To NERISSA*] Thou mayst, I warrant.
We shall have old swearing
That they did give the rings away to men;
But we'll outface them, and outswear them too.
Aloud
Away, make haste: thou knowist where I will tarry.
NERISSA: Come, good sir, will you show me to this house?
Exeunt

Act V

Scene I—*Belmont: The garden before Portia's house*

Enter LORENZO and JESSICA

LORENZO: The moon shines bright. In such a night as this,
When the sweet wind did gently kiss the trees,
And they did make no noise—in such a night,
Troilus methinks mounted the Troyan walls,
And sigh'd his soul toward the Grecian tents,
Where Cressid lay that night.

JESSICA: In such a night
Did Thisby fearfully o'ertrip the dew,
And saw the lion's shadow ere himself,
And ran dismay'd away.

LORENZO: In such a night
Stood Dido with a willow in her hand
Upon the wild sea-banks and waft her love
To come again to Carthage.

JESSICA: In such a night
Medea gather'd the enchanted herbs
That did renew old Æson.

LORENZO: In such a night
Did Jessica steal from the wealthy Jew
And with an unthrift love did run from Venice
As far as Belmont.

JESSICA: In such a night
Did young Lorenzo swear he loved her well,
Stealing her soul with many vows of faith,
And ne'er a true one.

LORENZO: In such a night
Did pretty Jessica, like a little shrew,
Slander her love, and he forgave it her.

JESSICA: I would out-night you, did no body come;
But, hark, I hear the footing of a man.

Enter STEPHANO

LORENZO: Who comes so fast in silence of the night?

STEPHANO: A friend.

LORENZO: A friend! What friend? Your name, I pray you, friend?

STEPHANO: Stephano is my name, and I bring word
My mistress will before the break of day
Be here at Belmont; she doth stray about
By holy crosses, where she kneels and prays
For happy wedlock hours.

LORENZO: Who comes with her?

STEPHANO: None but a holy hermit and her maid.
I pray you, is my master yet return'd?

LORENZO: He is not, nor we have not heard from him.
But go we in, I pray thee, Jessica,
And ceremoniously let us prepare
Some welcome for the mistress of the house.

Enter LAUNCELOT

LAUNCELOT: Sola, sola! wo ha, ho! sola, sola!

LORENZO: Who calls?

LAUNCELOT: Sola! Did you see Master Lorenzo?
Master Lorenzo! Sola, sola!

LORENZO: Leave holloaing, man. Here!

LAUNCELOT: Sola! Where? where?

LORENZO: Here.

LAUNCELOT: Tell him there's a post come from my master, with his horn full of good news; my master will be here ere morning.

Exit

LORENZO: Sweet soul, let's in, and there expect their coming.
And yet no matter—why should we go in?
My friend Stephano, signify, I pray you,
Within the house, your mistress is at hand;
And bring your music forth into the air.

Exit STEPHANO

How sweet the moonlight sleeps upon this bank!
Here will we sit and let the sounds of music
Creep in our ears; soft stillness and the night
Become the touches of sweet harmony.
Sit, Jessica. Look how the floor of heaven

Is thick inlaid with patines of bright gold;
There's not the smallest orb which thou behold'st
But in his motion like an angel sings,
Still quiring to the young-eyed cherubins;
Such harmony is in immortal souls;
But whilst this muddy vesture of decay
Doth grossly close it in, we cannot hear it.

Enter Musicians

Come, ho, and wake Diana with a hymn;
With sweetest touches pierce your mistress' ear,
And draw her home with music.

Music

JESSICA: I am never merry when I hear sweet music.

LORENZO: The reason is, your spirits are attentive;
For do but note a wild and wanton herd,
Or race of youthful and unhandled colts,
Fetching mad bounds, bellowing and neighing loud,
Which is the hot condition of their blood—
If they but hear perchance a trumpet sound,
Or any air of music touch their ears,
You shall perceive them make a mutual stand,
Their savage eyes turn'd to a modest gaze
By the sweet power of music. Therefore the poet
Did feign that Orpheus drew trees, stones, and floods;
Since nought so stockish, hard, and full of rage,
But music for the time doth change his nature.
The man that hath no music in himself,
Nor is not moved with concord of sweet sounds,
Is fit for treasons, stratagems, and spoils;
The motions of his spirit are dull as night,
And his affections dark as Erebus.
Let no such man be trusted. Mark the music.

Enter PORTIA and NERISSA

PORTIA: That light we see is burning in my hall.
How far that little candle throws his beams!
So shines a good deed in a naughty world.

NERISSA: When the moon shone, we did not see the candle.

PORTIA: So doth the greater glory dim the less:
A substitute shines brightly as a king
Unto the king be by, and then his state
Empties itself, as doth an inland brook
Into the main of waters. Music! hark!

NERISSA: It is your music, madam, of the house.

PORTIA: Nothing is good, I see, without respect;
Methinks it sounds much sweeter than by day.

NERISSA: Silence bestows that virtue on it, madam.

PORTIA: The crow doth sing as sweetly as the lark,
When neither is attended, and I think
The nightingale, if she should sing by day,
When every goose is cackling, would be thought
No better a musician than the wren.
How many things by season season'd are
To their right praise and true perfection!
Peace, ho! the moon sleeps with Endymion,
And would not be awaked.

Music ceases

LORENZO: That is the voice,
Or I am much deceived, of Portia.

PORTIA: He knows me as the blind man knows the cuckoo,
By the bad voice.

LORENZO: Dear lady, welcome home.

PORTIA: We have been praying for our husbands' welfare,
Which speed, we hope, the better for our words.
Are they return'd?

LORENZO: Madam, they are not yet;
But there is come a messenger before,
To signify their coming.

PORTIA: Go in, Nerissa;
Give order to my servants that they take
No note at all of our being absent hence;
Nor you, Lorenzo; Jessica, nor you.

A tucket sounds

LORENZO: Your husband is at hand; I hear his trumpet.
We are no tell-tales, madam; fear you not.

PORTIA: This night methinks is but the daylight sick;
It looks a little paler; 'tis a day
Such as the day is when the sun is hid.

Enter BASSANIO, ANTONIO, GRATIANO, and their followers

BASSANIO: We should hold day with the Antipodes,
If you would walk in absence of the sun.

PORTIA: Let me give light, but let me not be light;
For a light wife doth make a heavy husband,
And never be Bassanio so for me;
But God sort all! You are welcome home, my lord.

BASSANIO: I thank you, madam. Give welcome to my friend.
 This is the man, this is Antonio,
 To whom I am so infinitely bound.
PORTIA: You should in all sense be much bound to him.
 For, as I hear, he was much bound for you.
ANTONIO: No more than I am well acquitted of.
PORTIA: Sir, you are very welcome to our house.
 It must appear in other ways than words,
 Therefore I scant this breathing courtesy.
GRATIANO: [*To NERISSA*] By yonder moon I swear you do me wrong;
 In faith, I gave it to the judge's clerk.
 Would he were gelt that had it, for my part,
 Since you do take it, love, so much at heart.
PORTIA: A quarrel, ho, already! What's the matter?
GRATIANO: About a hoop of gold, a paltry ring
 That she did give me, whose posy was
 For all the world like cutler's poetry
 Upon a knife, 'Love me, and leave me not'.
NERISSA: What talk you of the posy or the value?
 You swore to me, when I did give it you,
 That you would wear it till your hour of death,
 And that it should lie with you in your grave;
 Though not for me, yet for your vehement oaths,
 You should have been respective and have kept it.
 Gave it a judge's clerk! no, God's my judge,
 The clerk will ne'er wear hair on's face that had it.
GRATIANO: He will, an if he live to be a man.
NERISSA: Ay, if a woman live to be a man.
GRATIANO: Now, by this hand I gave it to a youth,
 A kind of boy, a little scrubbed boy,
 No higher than thyself; the judge's clerk,
 A prating boy that begg'd it as a fee;
 I could not for my heart deny it him.
PORTIA: You were to blame, I must be plain with you,
 To part so slightly with your wife's first gift,
 A thing stuck on with oaths upon your finger
 And so riveted with faith unto your flesh.
 I gave my love a ring, and made him swear
 Never to part with it, and here he stands;
 I dare be sworn for him he would not leave it
 Nor pluck it from his finger, for the wealth
 That the world masters. Now, in faith, Gratiano,
 You give your wife too unkind a cause of grief;
 An 'twere to me, I should be mad at it.
BASSANIO: [*Aside*] Why, I were best to cut my left hand off.
 And swear I lost the ring defending it.
GRATIANO: My Lord Bassanio gave his ring away
 Unto the judge that begg'd it and indeed
 Deserved it too; and then the boy, his clerk,
 That took some pains in writing, he begg'd mine;
 And neither man nor master would take aught
 But the two rings.
PORTIA: What ring gave you, my lord?
 Not that, I hope, which you received of me.
BASSANIO: If I could add a lie unto a fault,
 I would deny it; but you see my finger
 Hath not the ring upon it; it is gone.
PORTIA: Even so void is your false heart of truth;
 By heaven, I will ne'er come in your bed
 Until I see the ring.
NERISSA: Nor I in yours
 Till I again see mine.
BASSANIO: Sweet Portia,
 If you did know to whom I gave the ring,
 If you did know for whom I gave the ring,
 And would conceive for what I gave the ring,
 And how unwillingly I left the ring,
 When nought would be accepted but the ring,
 You would abate the strength of your displeasure.
PORTIA: If you had known the virtue of the ring,
 Or half her worthiness that gave the ring,
 Or your own honour to contain the ring,
 You would not then have parted with the ring.
 What man is there so much unreasonable,
 If you had pleased to have defended it
 With any terms of zeal, wanted the modesty
 To urge the thing held as a ceremony?
 Nerissa teaches me what to believe:
 I'll die for't but some woman had the ring.
BASSANIO: No, by my honour, madam, by my soul,
 No woman had it, but a civil doctor,
 Which did refuse three thousand ducats of me,
 And begg'd the ring; the which I did deny him,
 And suffer'd him to go displeased away—
 Even he that had held up the very life
 Of my dear friend. What should I say, sweet lady?
 I was enforced to send it after him;
 I was beset with shame and courtesy;
 My honour would not let ingratitude
 So much besmear it. Pardon me, good lady;

For by these blessed candles of the night,
Had you been there, I think you would have begg'd
The ring of me to give the worthy doctor.

PORTIA: Let not that doctor e'er come near my house;
Since he hath got the jewel that I loved,
And that which you did swear to keep for me,
I will become as liberal as you;
I'll not deny him any thing I have,
No, not my body nor my husband's bed.
Know him I shall, I am well sure of it.
Lie not a night from home; watch me like Argus:
If you do not, if I be left alone,
Now, by mine honour, which is yet mine own,
I'll have that doctor for my bedfellow.

NERISSA: And I his clerk; therefore be well advised
How you do leave me to mine own protection.

GRATIANO: Well, do you so; let not me take him then;
For, if I do, I'll mar the young clerk's pen.

ANTONIO: I am the unhappy subject of these quarrels.

PORTIA: Sir, grieve not you; you are welcome notwithstanding.

BASSANIO: Portia, forgive me this enforced wrong;
And, in the hearing of these many friends
I swear to thee, even by thine own fair eyes,
Wherein I see myself—

PORTIA: Mark you but that!
In both my eyes he doubly sees himself;
In each eye one; swear by your double self,
And there's an oath of credit.

BASSANIO: Nay, but hear me.
Pardon this fault, and by my soul I swear
I never more will break an oath with thee.

ANTONIO: I once did lend my body for his wealth;
Which, but for him that had your husband's ring,
Had quite miscarried; I dare be bound again,
My soul upon the forfeit, that your lord
Will never more break faith advisedly.

PORTIA: Then you shall be his surety. Give him this,
And bid him keep it better than the other.

ANTONIO: Here, Lord Bassanio; swear to keep this ring.

BASSANIO: By heaven, it is the same I gave the doctor!

PORTIA: I had it of him. Pardon me, Bassanio;
For, by this ring, the doctor lay with me.

NERISSA: And pardon me, my gentle Gratiano;
For that same scrubbed boy, the doctor's clerk,
In lieu of this last night did lie with me.

GRATIANO: Why, this is like the mending of highways
In summer, where the ways are fair enough.
What, are we cuckolds ere we have deserved it?

PORTIA: Speak not so grossly. You are all amazed.
Here is a letter; read it at your leisure;
It comes from Padua, from Bellario;
There you shall find that Portia was the doctor,
Nerissa there her clerk. Lorenzo here
Shall witness I set forth as soon as you,
And even but now return'd; I have not yet
Enter'd my house. Antonio, you are welcome;
And I have better news in store for you
Than you expect. Unseal this letter soon;
There you shall find three of your argosies
Are richly come to harbour suddenly.
You shall not know by what strange accident
I chanced on this letter.

ANTONIO: I am dumb.

BASSANIO: Were you the doctor, and I knew you not?

GRATIANO: Were you the clerk that is to make me cuckold?

NERISSA: Ay, but the clerk that never means to do it,
Unless he live until he be a man.

BASSANIO: Sweet doctor, you shall be my bed-fellow;
When I am absent, then lie with my wife.

ANTONIO: Sweet lady, you have given me life and living;
For here I read for certain that my ships
Are safely come to road.

PORTIA: How now, Lorenzo!
My clerk hath some good comforts too for you.

NERISSA: Ay, and I'll give them him without a fee.
There do I give to you and Jessica,
From the rich Jew, a special deed of gift,
After his death, of all he dies possess'd of.

LORENZO: Fair ladies, you drop manna in the way
Of starved people.

PORTIA: It is almost morning,
And yet I am sure you are not satisfied
Of these events at full. Let us go in,
And charge us there upon inter'gatories,
And we will answer all things faithfully.

GRATIANO: Let it be so. The first inter'gatory
That my Nerissa shall be sworn on is,
Whether till the next night she had rather stay,
Or go to bed now, being two hours to day.
But were the day come, I should wish it dark,
That I were couching with the doctor's clerk.
Well, while I live I'll fear no other thing
So sore as keeping safe Nerissa's ring.

Exeunt

A Midsummer Night's Dream

DRAMATIS PERSONÆ

THESEUS, *Duke of Athens*
EGEUS, *father to Hermia*
LYSANDER, DEMETRIUS, *in love with Hermia*
PHILOSTRATE, *Master of the Revels to Theseus*
QUINCE, *a carpenter*
SNUG, *a joiner*
BOTTOM, *a weaver*
FLUTE, *a bellows-mender*
SNOUT, *a tinker*
STARVELING, *a tailor*
HIPPOLYTA, *Queen of the Amazons, betrothed to Theseus*
HERMIA, *daughter to Egeus, in love with Lysander*
HELENA, *in love with Demetrius*
OBERON, *King of the Fairies*
TITANIA, *Queen of the Fairies*
PUCK, or ROBIN GOODFELLOW
PEASEBLOSSOM, COBWEB,
MOTH, MUSTARDSEED, *fairies*
PROLOGUE, PYRAMUS, THISBY, WALL, MOONSHINE, LION, QUINCE, BOTTOM, FLUTE, SNOUT, STARVELING, SNUG,

Other Fairies *attending their King and Queen*. Attendants *on Theseus and Hippolyta*

THE SCENE: *Athens and a wood near it*

Act I

Scene I—*Athens: The palace of Theseus*

Enter THESEUS, HIPPOLYTA, PHILOSTRATE, and Attendants

THESEUS: Now, fair Hippolyta, our nuptial hour
Draws on apace; four happy days bring in
Another moon: but, O, methinks, how slow
This old moon wanes! She lingers my desires,
Like to a step-dame or a dowager
Long withering out a young man's revenue.

HIPPOLYTA: Four days will quickly steep themselves in night;
Four nights will quickly dream away the time;
And then the moon, like to a silver bow
New-bent in heaven, shall behold the night
Of our solemnities.

THESEUS: Go, Philostrate,
Stir up the Athenian youth to merriments;
Awake the pert and nimble spirit of mirth;
Turn melancholy forth to funerals;
The pale companion is not for our pomp.

Exit PHILOSTRATE

Hippolyta, I woo'd thee with my sword,
And won thy love, doing thee injuries;
But I will wed thee in another key,
With pomp, with triumph and with revelling.

Enter EGEUS, and his daughter HERMIA, LYSANDER, and DEMETRIUS

EGEUS: Happy be Theseus, our renowned Duke!

THESEUS: Thanks, good Egeus; what's the news with thee?

EGEUS: Full of vexation come I, with complaint
Against my child, my daughter Hermia.
Stand forth, Demetrius. My noble lord,
This man hath my consent to marry her.
Stand forth, Lysander: and my gracious Duke,
This man hath bewitch'd the bosom of my child;
Thou, thou, Lysander, thou hast given her rhymes,
And interchanged love-tokens with my child;
Thou hast by moonlight at her window sung,
With feigning voice, verses of feigning love,
And stolen the impression of her fantasy
With bracelets of thy hair, rings, gawds, conceits,
Knacks, trifles, nosegays, sweetmeats—messengers
Of strong prevailment in unharden'd youth;
With cunning hast thou filch'd my daughter's heart,
Turn'd her obedience, which is due to me,
To stubborn harshness. And, my gracious Duke,
Be it so she; will not here before your grace
Consent to marry with Demetrius,
I beg the ancient privilege of Athens:
As she is mine, I may dispose of her;
Which shall be either to this gentleman
Or to her death, according to our law
Immediately provided in that case.

THESEUS: What say you, Hermia? Be advised, fair maid.
To you your father should be as a god;
One that composed your beauties, yea, and one
To whom you are but as a form in wax,
By him imprinted and within his power
To leave the figure, or disfigure it.
Demetrius is a worthy gentleman.

HERMIA: So is Lysander.

THESEUS: In himself he is;
But in this kind, wanting your father's voice,
The other must be held the worthier.

HERMIA: I would my father look'd but with my eyes.

THESEUS: Rather your eyes must with his judgment look.

HERMIA: I do entreat your grace to pardon me.
I know not by what power I am made bold,
Nor how it may concern my modesty,
In such a presence here to plead my thoughts;
But I beseech your Grace that I may know
The worst that may befall me in this case,
If I refuse to wed Demetrius.

THESEUS: Either to die the death or to abjure
For ever the society of men.
Therefore, fair Hermia, question your desires;
Know of your youth, examine well your blood,
Whether, if you yield not to your father's choice,
You can endure the livery of a nun,
For aye to be in shady cloister mew'd,
To live a barren sister all your life,
Chanting faint hymns to the cold fruitless moon.
Thrice-blessed they that master so their blood
To undergo such maiden pilgrimage;
But earthlier happy is the rose distill'd,
Than that which withering on the virgin thorn
Grows, lives and dies in single blessedness.

HERMIA: So will I grow, so live, so die, my lord,
Ere I will my virgin patent up
Unto his lordship, whose unwished yoke
My soul consents not to give sovereignty.

THESEUS: Take time to pause; and by the next new moon—
The sealing-day betwixt my love and me
For everlasting bond of fellowship—
Upon that day either prepare to die
For disobedience to your father's will,
Or else to wed Demetrius, as he would;
Or on Diana's altar to protest
For aye austerity and single life.

DEMETRIUS: Relent, sweet Hermia; and, Lysander, yield
Thy crazed title to my certain right.

LYSANDER: You have her father's love, Demetrius;
Let me have Hermia's; do you marry him.

EGEUS: Scornful Lysander, true, he hath my love,
And what is mine my love shall render him;
And she is mine, and all my right of her
I do estate unto Demetrius.

LYSANDER: I am, my lord, as well derived as he,
As well possess'd; my love is more than his;
My fortunes every way as fairly rank'd,
If not with vantage, as Demetrius';
And, which is more than all these boasts can be,
I am beloved of beauteous Hermia.
Why should not I then prosecute my right?
Demetrius, I'll avouch it to his head,
Made love to Nedar's daughter, Helena,
And won her soul; and she, sweet lady, dotes,
Devoutly dotes, dotes in idolatry,
Upon this spotted and inconstant man.
THESEUS: I must confess that I have heard so much,
And with Demetrius thought to have spoke thereof;
But, being over-full of self-affairs,
My mind did lose it. But, Demetrius, come;
And come, Egeus; you shall go with me,
I have some private schooling for you both.
For you, fair Hermia, look you arm yourself
To fit your fancies to your father's will;
Or else the law of Athens yields you up—
Which by no means we may extenuate—
To death, or to a vow of single life.
Come, my Hippolyta; what cheer, my love?
Demetrius, and Egeus, go along;
I must employ you in some business
Against our nuptial, and confer with you
Of something nearly that concerns yourselves.
EGEUS: With duty and desire we follow you.

Exeunt all but LYSANDER and HERMIA

LYSANDER: How now, my love! Why is your cheek so pale?
How chance the roses there do fade so fast?
HERMIA: Belike for want of rain, which I could well
Beteem them from the tempest of my eyes.
LYSANDER: Ay me! for aught that I could ever read,
Could ever hear by tale or history,
The course of true love never did run smooth;
But, either it was different in blood—
HERMIA: O cross! too high to be enthrall'd to low.
LYSANDER: Or else misgraffed in respect of years—
HERMIA: O spite! too old to be engaged to young.
LYSANDER: Or else it stood upon the choice of friends—
HERMIA: O hell! to choose love by another's eyes.
LYSANDER: Or, if there were a sympathy in choice,
War, death, or sickness did lay siege to it,
Making it momentary as a sound,
Swift as a shadow, short as any dream;
Brief as the lightning in the collied night,
That, in a spleen, unfolds both heaven and earth,
And ere a man hath power to say 'Behold!'
The jaws of darkness do devour it up;
So quick bright things come to confusion.
HERMIA: If then true lovers have been ever cross'd,
It stands as an edict in destiny.
Then let us teach our trial patience,
Because it is a customary cross,
As due to love as thoughts and dreams and sighs,
Wishes and tears, poor fancy's followers.
LYSANDER: A good persuasion; therefore, hear me, Hermia:
I have a widow aunt, a dowager
Of great revenue, and she hath no child—
From Athens is her house remote seven leagues—
And she respects me as her only son.
There, gentle Hermia, may I marry thee;
And to that place the sharp Athenian law
Cannot pursue us. If thou lovest me then,
Steal forth thy father's house to-morrow night;
And in the wood, a league without the town,
Where I did meet thee once with Helena,
To do observance to a morn of May,
There will I stay for thee.
HERMIA: My good Lysander!
I swear to thee by Cupid's strongest bow,
By his best arrow with the golden head,
By the simplicity of Venus' doves,
By that which knitteth souls and prospers loves,
And by that fire which burn'd the Carthage Queen,
When the false Troyan under sail was seen,
By all the vows that ever men have broke,
In number more than ever women spoke,
In that same place thou hast appointed me,
To-morrow truly will I meet with thee.
LYSANDER: Keep promise, love. Look, here comes Helena.

Enter HELENA

HERMIA: God speed fair Helena! Whither away?
HELENA: Call you me fair? That fair again unsay.
Demetrius loves your fair. O happy fair!

Your eyes are lode-stars; and your tongue's sweet air
More tuneable than lark to shepherd's ear,
When wheat is green, when hawthorn buds appear.
Sickness is catching; O, were favour so,
Yours would I catch, fair Hermia, ere I go!
My ear should catch your voice, my eye your eye,
My tongue should catch your tongue's sweet melody.
Were the world mine, Demetrius being bated,
The rest I'd give to be to you translated.
O, teach me how you look, and with what art
You sway the motion of Demetrius' heart!

HERMIA: I frown upon him, yet he loves me still.

HELENA: O that your frowns would teach my smiles such skill!

HERMIA: I give him curses, yet he gives me love.

HELENA: O that my prayers could such affection move!

HERMIA: The more I hate, the more he follows me.

HELENA: The more I love, the more he hateth me.

HERMIA: His folly, Helena, is no fault of mine.

HELENA: None, but your beauty; would that fault were mine!

HERMIA: Take comfort: he no more shall see my face;
Lysander and myself will fly this place.
Before the time I did Lysander see,
Seem'd Athens as a paradise to me.
O, then, what graces in my love do dwell,
That he hath turn'd a heaven unto a hell!

LYSANDER: Helen, to you our minds we will unfold:
To-morrow night, when Phoebe doth behold
Her silver visage in the watery glass,
Decking with liquid pearl the bladed grass,
A time that lovers' flights doth still conceal,
Through Athens' gates have we devised to steal.

HERMIA: And in the wood, where often you and I
Upon faint primrose beds were wont to lie,
Emptying our bosoms of their counsel sweet,
There my Lysander and myself shall meet;
And thence from Athens turn away our eyes,
To seek new friends and stranger companies.
Farewell, sweet playfellow; pray thou for us;
And good luck grant thee thy Demetrius!
Keep word, Lysander; we must starve our sight
From lovers' food till morrow deep midnight.

LYSANDER: I will, my Hermia.

Exit HERMIA

Helena, adieu;
As you on him, Demetrius dote on you!

Exit LYSANDER

HELENA: How happy some o'er other some can be!
Through Athens I am thought as fair as she.
But what of that? Demetrius thinks not so;
He will not know what all but he do know.
And as he errs, doting on Hermia's eyes,
So I, admiring of his qualities.
Things base and vile, holding no quantity,
Love can transpose to form and dignity.
Love looks not with the eyes, but with the mind;
And therefore is wing'd Cupid painted blind.
Nor hath Love's mind of any judgement taste;
Wings and no eyes figure unheedy haste;
And therefore is Love said to be a child,
Because in choice he is so oft beguiled.
As waggish boys in game themselves forswear,
So the boy Love is perjured every where;
For ere Demetrius look'd on Hermia's eyne,
He hail'd down oaths that he was only mine;
And when this hail some heat from Hermia felt,
So he dissolved, and showers of oaths did melt.
I will go tell him of fair Hermia's flight;
Then to the wood will he to-morrow night
Pursue her; and for this intelligence
If I have thanks, it is a dear expense.
But herein mean I to enrich my pain,
To have his sight thither and back again.

Exit

SCENE II—*Athens: Quince's house*

Enter QUINCE, SNUG, BOTTOM, FLUTE, SNOUT, and STARVELING

QUINCE: Is all our company here?

BOTTOM: You were best to call them generally, man by man, according to the scrip.

QUINCE: Here is the scroll of every man's name, which is thought fit, through all Athens, to play in our interlude before the Duke and the Duchess, on his wedding-day at night.

BOTTOM: First, good Peter Quince, say what the play treats on, then read the names of the actors, and so grow to a point.

QUINCE: Marry, our play is, 'The most Lamentable Comedy, and most Cruel Death of Pyramus and Thisby'.

BOTTOM: A very good piece of work, I assure you, and a merry. Now, good Peter Quince, call forth your actors by the scroll. Masters, spread yourselves.

QUINCE: Answer, as I call you. Nick Bottom, the weaver.

BOTTOM: Ready. Name what part I am for, and proceed.

QUINCE: You, Nick Bottom, are set down for Pyramus.

BOTTOM: What is Pyramus? A lover, or a tyrant?

QUINCE: A lover, that kills himself most gallant for love.

BOTTOM: That will ask some tears in the true performing of it. If I do it, let the audience look to their eyes; I will move storms, I will condole in some measure. To the rest—yet my chief humour is for a tyrant. I could play Ercles rarely, or a part to tear a cat in, to make all split.

'The raging rocks
And shivering shocks
Shall break the locks
Of prison gates;
And Phibbus' car
Shall shine from far,
And make and mar
The foolish Fates.'

This was lofty! Now name the rest of the players.

This is Ercles' vein, a tyrant's vein: a lover is more condoling.

QUINCE: Francis Flute, the bellows-mender.

FLUTE: Here, Peter Quince.

QUINCE: Flute, you must take Thisby on you.

FLUTE: What is Thisby? A wandering knight?

QUINCE: It is the lady that Pyramus must love.

FLUTE: Nay, faith, let me not play a woman; I have a beard coming.

QUINCE: That's all one; you shall play it in a mask, and you may speak as small as you will.

BOTTOM: An I may hide my face, let me play Thisby too, I'll speak in a monstrous little voice. 'Thisne, Thisne;' 'Ah, Pyramus, lover dear! Thy Thisby dear, and lady dear!'

QUINCE: No, no; you must play Pyramus, and, Flute, you Thisby.

BOTTOM: Well, proceed.

QUINCE: Robin Starveling, the tailor.

STARVELING: Here, Peter Quince.

QUINCE: Robin Starveling, you must play Thisby's mother. Tom Snout, the tinker.

SNOUT: Here, Peter Quince.

QUINCE: You, Pyramus' father; myself, Thisby's father; Snug, the joiner; you, the lion's part. And, I hope, here is a play fitted.

SNUG: Have you the lion's part written? Pray you, if it be, give it me, for I am slow of study.

QUINCE: You may do it extempore, for it is nothing but roaring.

BOTTOM: Let me play the lion too. I will roar, that I will do any man's heart good to hear me; I will roar, that I will make the Duke say 'Let him roar again, let him roar again'.

QUINCE: An you should do it too terribly, you would fright the Duchess and the ladies, that they would shriek; and that were enough to hang us all.

ALL: That would hang us, every mother's son.

BOTTOM: I grant you, friends, if that you should fright the ladies out of their wits, they would have no more discretion but to hang us; but I will aggravate my voice so that I will roar you as gently as any sucking dove; I will roar you an, 'twere any nightingale.

QUINCE: You can play no part but Pyramus; for Pyramus is a sweet-faced man; a proper man, as one shall see in a summer's day; a most lovely gentleman-like man; therefore you must needs play Pyramus.

BOTTOM: Well, I will undertake it. What beard were I best to play it in?

QUINCE: Why, what you will.

BOTTOM: I will discharge it in either your straw-colour beard, your orange-tawny beard, your purple-in-grain beard, or your French-crown-colour beard, your perfect yellow.

QUINCE: Some of your French crowns have no hair at all, and then you will play bare-faced. But, masters, here are your parts, and I am to entreat you, request you and desire you, to con them by to-morrow night; and meet me in the palace wood, a mile without the town, by moonlight; there will we rehearse, for if we meet in the city, we shall be dogged with company, and our devices known. In the meantime I will draw a bill of properties, such as our play wants. I pray you, fail me not.

BOTTOM: We will meet; and there we may rehearse most obscenely and courageously. Take pains; be perfect; adieu.

QUINCE: At the Duke's oak we meet.

BOTTOM: Enough; hold or cut bow-strings.

Exeunt

ACT II

SCENE I—*A wood near Athens*

Enter, from opposite sides, a Fairy, and PUCK

PUCK: How now, spirit! whither wander you?

Fairy: Over hill, over dale,
Thorough bush, thorough brier,
Over park, over pale,
Thorough flood, thorough fire,
I do wander everywhere,
Swifter than the moon's sphere;
And I serve the fairy Queen,
To dew her orbs upon the green.
The cowslips tall her pensioners be;
In their gold coats spots you see;
Those be rubies, fairy favours,
In those freckles live their savours.
I must go seek some dewdrops here,
And hang a pearl in every cowslip's ear.
Farewell, thou lob of spirits; I'll be gone.
Our Queen and all her elves come here anon.

PUCK: The king doth keep his revels here to-night;
Take heed the Queen come not within his sight;
For Oberon is passing fell and wrath,
Because that she as her attendant hath
A lovely boy, stolen from an Indian king.
She never had so sweet a changeling;
And jealous Oberon would have the child
Knight of his train, to trace the forests wild;
But she perforce withholds the loved boy,
Crowns him with flowers and makes him all her joy.
And now they never meet in grove or green,
By fountain clear, or spangled starlight sheen,
But, they do square, that all their elves for fear
Creep into acorn cups and hide them there.

FAIRY: Either I mistake your shape and making quite,
Or else you are that shrewd and knavish sprite
Call'd Robin Goodfellow. Are not you he
That frights the maidens of the villagery;
Skim milk, and sometimes labour in the quern,
And bootless make the breathless housewife churn;
And sometime make the drink to bear no barm;
Mislead night-wanderers, laughing at their harm?
Those that Hobgoblin call you and sweet Puck,
You do their work, and they shall have good luck.
Are not you he?

PUCK: Thou speak'st aright:
I am that merry wanderer of the night.
I jest to Oberon, and make him smile
When I a fat and bean-fed horse beguile,
Neighing in likeness of a filly foal;
And sometime lurk I in a gossip's bowl,
In very likeness of a roasted crab,
And when she drinks, against her lips I bob,
And on her wither'd dewlap pour the ale.
The wisest aunt, telling the saddest tale,
Sometime for three-foot stool mistaketh me;
Then slip I from her bum, down topples she,
And 'tailor' cries, and falls into a cough;
And then the whole quire hold their hips and laugh,
And waxen in their mirth and neeze, and swear
A merrier hour was never wasted there.
But, room, fairy, here comes Oberon.

FAIRY: And here my mistress. Would that he were gone!

Enter, from one side, OBERON, with his train; from the other, TITANIA, with hers

OBERON: Ill met by moonlight, proud Titania.

TITANIA: What, jealous Oberon! Fairies, skip hence;
I have forsworn his bed and company.

OBERON: Tarry, rash wanton; am not I thy lord?

TITANIA: Then I must be thy lady; but I know
When thou hast stolen away from fairy land,
And in the shape of Corin sat all day,
Playing on pipes of corn, and versing love

To amorous Phillida. Why art thou here,
Come from the farthest Steep of India,
But that, forsooth, the bouncing Amazon,
Your buskin'd mistress and your warrior love,
To Theseus must be wedded, and you come
To give their bed joy and prosperity?

OBERON: How canst thou, thus for shame, Titania,
Glance at my credit with Hippolyta,
Knowing I know thy love to Theseus?
Didst thou not lead him through the glimmering night
From Perigouna, whom he ravished?
And make him with fair AEgle break his faith,
With Ariadne and Antiopa?

TITANIA: These are the forgeries of jealousy;
And never, since the middle summer's spring,
Met we on hill, in dale, forest or mead,
By paved fountain or by rushy brook,
Or in the beached margent of the sea,
To dance our ringlets to the whistling wind,
But with thy brawls thou hast disturb'd our sport.
Therefore the winds, piping to us in vain,
As in revenge, have suck'd up from the sea
Contagious fogs; which falling in the land,
Have every pelting river made so proud
That they have overborne their continents.
The ox hath therefore stretch'd his yoke in vain,
The ploughman lost his sweat, and the green corn
Hath rotted ere his youth attain'd a beard;
The fold stands empty in the drowned field,
And crows are fatted with the murrion flock;
The nine men's morris is fill'd up with mud,
And the quaint mazes in the wanton green
For lack of tread, are undistinguishable.
The human mortals want their winter here;
No night is now with hymn or carol blest;
Therefore the moon, the governess of floods,
Pale in her anger, washes all the air,
That rheumatic diseases do abound.
And thorough this distemperature we see
The seasons alter: hoary-headed frosts
Far in the fresh lap of the crimson rose;
And on old Hiems' thin and icy crown
An odorous chaplet of sweet summer buds
Is, as in mockery, set. The spring, the summer,
The childing autumn, angry winter, change
Their wonted liveries; and the mazed world,
By their increase, now knows not which is which.
And this same progeny of evils comes
From our debate, from our dissension;
We are their parents and original.

OBERON: Do you amend it then; it lies in you.
Why should Titania cross her Oberon?
I do but beg a little changeling boy,
To be my henchman.

TITANIA: Set your heart at rest;
The fairy land buys not the child of me.
His mother was a votaress of my order;
And, in the spiced Indian air, by night,
Full often hath she gossip'd by my side;
And sat with me on Neptune's yellow sands,
Marking the embarked traders on the flood;
When we have laugh'd to see the sails conceive
And grow big-bellied with the wanton wind;
Which she, with pretty and with swimming gait
Following—her womb then rich with my young squire—
Would imitate, and sail upon the land,
To fetch me trifles, and return again,
As from a voyage, rich with merchandise.
But she, being mortal, of that boy did die;
And for her sake do I rear up her boy;
And for her sake I will not part with him.

OBERON: How long within this wood intend you stay?

TITANIA: Perchance till after Theseus' wedding-day.
If you will patiently dance in our round,
And see our moonlight revels, go with us;
If not, shun me, and I will spare your haunts.

OBERON: Give me that boy, and I will go with thee.

TITANIA: Not for thy fairy kingdom. Fairies, away.
We shall chide downright, if I longer stay.

Exit TITANIA with her train

OBERON: Well, go thy way; thou shalt not from this grove
Till I torment thee for this injury.
My gentle Puck, come hither. Thou rememberest
Since once I sat upon a promontory,
And heard a mermaid on a dolphin's back
Uttering such dulcet and harmonious breath
That the rude sea grew civil at her song,
And certain stars shot madly from their spheres
To hear the sea-maid's music.

PUCK: I remember.

OBERON: That very time I saw, but thou couldst not,
Flying between the cold moon and the earth,
Cupid all arm'd; a certain aim he took
At a fair vestal throned by the west,
And loosed his love-shaft smartly from his bow,
As it should pierce a hundred thousand hearts;
But I might see young Cupid's fiery shaft
Quench'd in the chaste beams of the watery moon,
And the imperial votaress passed on,
In maiden meditation, fancy-free.
Yet mark'd I where the bolt of Cupid fell.
It fell upon a little western flower,
Before milk-white, now purple with love's wound,
And maidens call it Love-in-idleness.
Fetch me that flower; the herb I shew'd thee once.
The juice of it on sleeping eye-lids laid
Will make or man or woman madly dote
Upon the next live creature that it sees.
Fetch me this herb; and be thou here again
Ere the leviathan can swim a league.

PUCK: I'll put a girdle round about the earth
In forty minutes.

Exit PUCK

OBERON: Having once this juice,
I'll watch Titania when she is asleep,
And drop the liquor of it in her eyes;
The next thing then she waking looks upon,
Be it on lion, bear, or wolf, or bull,
On meddling monkey, or on busy ape,
She shall pursue it with the soul of love.
And ere I take this charm from off her sight,
As I can take it with another herb,
I'll make her render up her page to me.
But who comes here? I am invisible;
And I will overhear their conference.

Enter DEMETRIUS, HELENA, following him

DEMETRIUS: I love thee not, therefore pursue me not.
Where is Lysander and fair Hermia?
The one I'll slay, the other slayeth me.
Thou told'st me they were stolen unto this wood;
And here am I, and wode within this wood,
Because I cannot meet my Hermia.
Hence, get thee gone, and follow me no more.

HELENA: You draw me, you hard-hearted adamant;
But yet you draw not iron, for my heart
Is true as steel. Leave you your power to draw,
And I shall have no power to follow you.

DEMETRIUS: Do I entice you? do I speak you fair?
Or, rather, do I not in plainest truth
Tell you, I do not, nor I cannot love you?

HELENA: And even for that do I love you the more.
I am your spaniel; and, Demetrius,
The more you beat me, I will fawn on you.
Use me but as your spaniel, spurn me, strike me,
Neglect me, lose me; only give me leave,
Unworthy as I am, to follow you.
What worser place can I beg in your love,
And yet a place of high respect with me,
Than to be used as you use your dog?

DEMETRIUS: Tempt not too much the hatred of my spirit;
For I am sick when I do look on thee.

HELENA: And I am sick when I look not on you.

DEMETRIUS: You do impeach your modesty too much
To leave the city and commit yourself
Into the hands of one that loves you not;
To trust the opportunity of night,
And the ill counsel of a desert place,
With the rich worth of your virginity.

HELENA: Your virtue is my privilege for that:
It is not night when I do see your face,
Therefore I think I am not in the night;
Nor doth this wood lack worlds of company,
For you, in my respect are all the world.
Then how can it be said I am alone
When all the world is here to look on me?

DEMETRIUS: I'll run from thee and hide me in the brakes,
And leave thee to the mercy of wild beasts.

HELENA: The wildest hath not such a heart as you.
Run when you will, the story shall be changed:
Apollo flies, and Daphne holds the chase;
The dove pursues the griffin; the mild hind
Makes speed to catch the tiger—bootless speed,
When cowardice pursues and valour flies.

DEMETRIUS: I will not stay thy questions; let me go;
Or, if thou follow me, do not believe
But I shall do thee mischief in the wood.

HELENA: Ay, in the temple, in the town, the field,
You do me mischief. Fie, Demetrius!
Your wrongs do set a scandal on my sex.
We cannot fight for love, as men may do;
We should be wood and were not made to woo.

Exit DEMETRIUS

I'll follow thee and make a heaven of hell,
To die upon the hand I love so well.

Exit Helena

OBERON: Fare thee well, nymph: ere he do leave this grove,
Thou shalt fly him, and he shall seek thy love.

Re-enter PUCK

Hast thou the flower there? Welcome, wanderer.

PUCK: Ay, there it is.

OBERON: I pray thee, give it me.
I know a bank where the wild thyme blows,
Where oxlips and the nodding violet grows,
Quite over-canopied with luscious woodbine,
With sweet musk-roses and with eglantine;
There sleeps Titania sometime of the night,
Lull'd in these flowers with dances and delight;
And there the snake throws her enamell'd skin,
Weed wide enough to wrap a fairy in;
And with the juice of this I'll streak her eyes,
And make her full of hateful fantasies.
Take thou some of it, and seek through this grove:
A sweet Athenian lady is in love
With a disdainful youth; anoint his eyes;
But do it when the next thing he espies
May be the lady. Thou shalt know the man
By the Athenian garments he hath on.
Effect it with some care, that he may prove
More fond on her than she upon her love.
And look thou meet me ere the first cock crow.

PUCK: Fear not, my lord, your servant shall do so.

Exeunt

SCENE II—*Another part of the wood*

Enter TITANIA, with her Train

TITANIA: Come, now a roundel and a fairy song;
Then, for the third part of a minute, hence:
Some to kill cankers in the musk-rose buds,
Some war with rere-mice for their leathern wings,
To make my small elves coats, and some keep back
The clamorous owl that nightly hoots and wonders
At our quaint spirits. Sing me now asleep;
Then to your offices and let me rest.

The Fairies sing

1 *Fairy*: You spotted snakes with double tongue,
Thorny hedgehogs, be not seen;
Newts and blind-worms, do no wrong,
Come not near our fairy Queen.
Chorus: Philomel, with melody
Sing in our sweet lullaby.
Lulla, lulla, lullaby, lulla, lulla, lullaby.
Never harm,
Nor spell nor charm,
Come our lovely lady nigh.
So, good night, with lullaby.
2 *Fairy*: Weaving spiders, come not here;
Hence, you long-legg'd spinners, hence.
Beetles black, approach not near;
Worm nor snail, do no offence.
Chorus: Philomel, with melody, etc.

TITANIA sleeps

1 *Fairy*: Hence, away; now all is well.
One aloof stand sentinel.

Exeunt Fairies

Enter OBERON and squeezes the flower on TITANIA's eyelids

OBERON: What thou seest when thou dost wake,
Do it for thy true-love take,
Love and languish for his sake.
Be it ounce, or cat, or bear,
Pard, or boar with bristled hair,
In thy eye that shall appear
When thou wakest, it is thy dear.
Wake when some vile thing is near.

Exit

Enter LYSANDER and HERMIA

LYSANDER: Fair love, you faint with wandering in the wood;
And, to speak troth, I have forgot our way;
We'll rest us, Hermia, if you think it good,
And tarry for the comfort of the day.

HERMIA: Be it so, Lysander: find you out a bed;
For I upon this bank will rest my head.

LYSANDER: One turf shall serve as pillow for us both;
One heart, one bed, two bosoms and one troth.

HERMIA: Nay, good Lysander; for my sake, my dear,
Lie further off yet, do not lie so near.

LYSANDER: O, take the sense, sweet, of my innocence!
Love takes the meaning in love's conference.
I mean, that my heart unto yours is knit,
So that but one heart we can make of it;
Two bosoms interchained with an oath;
So then two bosoms and a single troth.
Then by your side no bed-room me deny;
For lying so, Hermia, I do not lie.

HERMIA: Lysander riddles very prettily.
Now much beshrew my manners and my pride,
If Hermia meant to say Lysander lied!
But, gentle friend, for love and courtesy
Lie further off; in human modesty,
Such separation as may well be said
Becomes a virtuous bachelor and a maid,
So far be distant; and, good night, sweet friend.
Thy love ne'er alter till thy sweet life end!

LYSANDER: Amen, amen, to that fair prayer, say I;
And then end life when I end loyalty!
Here is my bed; sleep give thee all his rest!

HERMIA: With half that wish the wisher's eyes be press'd!

They sleep

Enter PUCK

PUCK: Through the forest have I gone.
But Athenian found I none,
On whose eyes I might approve
This flower's force in stirring love.
Night and silence—Who is here?
Weeds of Athens he doth wear:
This is he, my master said,
Despised the Athenian maid;
And here the maiden, sleeping sound,
On the dank and dirty ground.
Pretty soul! she durst not lie
Near this lack-love, this kill-courtesy.
Churl, upon thy eyes I throw
All the power this charm doth owe:
When thou wakest, let love forbid
Sleep his seat on thy eyelid.
So awake when I am gone;
For I must now to Oberon.

Exit

Enter DEMETRIUS and HELENA, running

HELENA: Stay, though thou kill me, sweet Demetrius.

DEMETRIUS: I charge thee, hence, and do not haunt me thus.

HELENA: O, wilt thou darkling leave me? Do not so.

DEMETRIUS: Stay, on thy peril; I alone will go.

Exit DEMETRIUS

HELENA: O, I am out of breath in this fond chase!
The more my prayer, the lesser is my grace.
Happy is Hermia, wheresoe'er she lies;
For she hath blessed and attractive eyes.
How came her eyes so bright? Not with salt tears;
If so, my eyes are oftener wash'd than hers.
No, no, I am as ugly as a bear;
For beasts that meet me run away for fear;
Therefore no marvel though Demetrius
Do, as a monster fly my presence thus.
What wicked and dissembling glass of mine
Made me compare with Hermia's sphery eyne?
But who is here? Lysander! on the ground!
Dead? or asleep? I see no blood, no wound.
Lysander, if you live, good sir, awake.

LYSANDER: [*Awaking*] And run through fire I will for thy sweet sake.
Transparent Helena! Nature shows art,
That through thy bosom makes me see thy heart.
Where is Demetrius? O, how fit a word
Is that vile name to perish on my sword!

HELENA: Do not say so, Lysander; say not so.
What though he love your Hermia? Lord, what though?
Yet Hermia still loves you; then be content.

LYSANDER: Content with Hermia! No; I do repent
The tedious minutes I with her have spent.
Not Hermia but Helena I love:
Who will not change a raven for a dove?
The will of man is by his reason sway'd;
And reason says you are the worthier maid.
Things growing are not ripe until their season;
So I, being young, till now ripe not to reason;
And touching now the point of human skill,
Reason becomes the marshal to my will,
And leads me to your eyes, where I o'erlook
Love's stories written in Love's richest book.

HELENA: Wherefore was I to this keen mockery born?
When at your hands did I deserve this scorn?
Is't not enough, is't not enough, young man,

That I did never, no, nor never can,
Deserve a sweet look from Demetrius' eye,
But you must flout my insufficiency?
Good troth, you do me wrong, good sooth, you do,
In such disdainful manner me to woo.
But fare you well; perforce I must confess
I thought you lord of more true gentleness.
O, that a lady, of one man refused
Should of another therefore be abused!

Exit

LYSANDER: She sees not Hermia. Hermia, sleep thou there;
And never mayst thou come Lysander near!
For, as a surfeit of the sweetest things
The deepest loathing to the stomach brings,
Or as tie heresies that men do leave
Are hated most of those they did deceive,
So thou, my surfeit and my heresy,
Of all be hated, but the most of me!
And, all my powers, address your love and might
To honour Helen and to be her knight!

Exit

HERMIA: [*Awaking*] Help me, Lysander, help me! do thy best
To pluck this crawling serpent from my breast.
Ay me, for pity! What a dream was here!
Lysander, look how I do quake with fear.
Methought a serpent eat my heart away,
And you sat smiling at his cruel prey.
Lysander! What, removed? Lysander! lord!
What, out of hearing gone? No sound, no word?
Alack, where are you speak, an if you hear;
Speak, of all loves! I swoon almost with fear.
No? Then I well perceive you all not nigh.
Either death or you I'll find immediately.

Exit

Act III

Scene I—*The wood: Titania lying asleep*

Enter QUINCE, SNUG, BOTTOM, FLUTE, SNOUT, and STARVELING

BOTTOM: Are we all met?

QUINCE: Pat, pat; and here's a marvellous convenient place for our rehearsal. This green plot shall be our stage, this hawthorn brake our tiring-house; and we will do it in action as we will do it before the Duke.

BOTTOM: Peter Quince!—

QUINCE: What sayest thou, bully Bottom?

BOTTOM: There are things in this comedy of Pyramus and Thisby that will never please. First, Pyramus must draw a sword to kill himself; which the ladies cannot abide. How answer you that?

SNOUT: By'r lakin, a parlous fear.

STARVELING: I believe we must leave the killing out, when all is done.

BOTTOM: Not a whit; I have a device to make all well. Write me a prologue; and let the prologue seem to say, we will do no harm with our swords, and that Pyramus is not killed indeed; and, for the more better assurance, tell them that I, Pyramus, am not Pyramus, but Bottom the weaver. This will put them out of fear.

QUINCE: Well, we will have such a prologue; and it shall be written in eight and six.

BOTTOM: No, make it two more; let it be written in eight and eight.

SNOUT: Will not the ladies be afeard of the lion?

STARVELING: I fear it, I promise you.

BOTTOM: Masters, you ought to consider with yourselves to bring in—God shield us!—a lion among ladies, is a most dreadful thing; for there is not a more fearful wild-fowl than your lion living; and we ought to look to't.

SNOUT: Therefore another prologue must tell he is not a lion.

BOTTOM: Nay, you must name his name, and half his face must be seen through the lion's neck; and he himself must speak through, saying thus, or to the same defect: 'Ladies,' or 'Fair ladies, I would wish you' or 'I would request you' or 'I would entreat you not to fear, not to tremble. My life for yours! If you think I come hither as a lion, it were pity of my life. I am no such thing; I am a man as other men are'. And there, indeed, let him name his name, and tell them plainly he is Snug the joiner.

QUINCE: Well, it shall be so. But there is two hard things—that is, to bring the moonlight into a chamber; for, you know, Pyramus and Thisby meet by moonlight.

SNOUT: Doth the moon shine that night we play our play?

BOTTOM: A calendar, a calendar! Look in the almanac; find out moonshine, find out moonshine.

QUINCE: Yes, it doth shine that night.

BOTTOM: Why, then may you leave a casement of the great chamber window, where we play, open, and the moon may shine in at the casement.

QUINCE: Ay; or else one must come in with a bush of thorns and a lantern, and say he comes to disfigure, or to present, the person of Moonshine. Then, there is another thing: we must have a wall in the great chamber; for Pyramus and Thisby says the story, did talk through the chink of a wall.

SNOUT: You can never bring in a wall. What say you, Bottom?

BOTTOM: Some man or other must present Wall; and let him have some plaster, or some loam, or some rough-cast about him, to signify wall; and let him hold his fingers thus, and through that cranny shall Pyramus and Thisby whisper.

QUINCE: If that may be, then all is well. Come, sit down, every mother's son, and rehearse your parts. Pyramus, you begin; when you have spoken your speech, enter into that brake; and so every one according to his cue.

Enter PUCK behind

PUCK: What hempen homespuns have we swaggering here,

So near the cradle of the Fairy Queen?
What, a play toward! I'll be an auditor;
An actor too, perhaps, if I see cause.

QUINCE: Speak, Pyramus. Thisby, stand forth.

BOTTOM: Thisby, the flowers of odious savours sweet—

QUINCE: 'Odious', odours!

BOTTOM: —odours savours sweet;
So hath thy breath, my dearest Thisby dear.
But hark, a voice! Stay thou but here awhile,
And by and by I will to thee appear.

Exit

PUCK: A stranger Pyramus than e'er played here!

Exit

FLUTE: Must I speak now?

QUINCE: Ay, marry, must you; for you must understand he goes but to see a noise that he heard, and is to come again.

FLUTE: Most radiant Pyramus, most lily-white of hue,
Of colour like the red rose on triumphant brier,
Most brisky juvenal and eke most lovely Jew,
As true as truest horse, that yet would never tire,
I'll meet thee, Pyramus, at Ninny's tomb.

QUINCE: 'Ninus' tomb,' man! Why, you must not speak that yet; that you answer to Pyramus. You speak all your part at once, cues and all. Pyramus enter: your cue is past; it is, 'never tire'.

FLUTE: O—As true as truest horse, that yet would never tire.

Re-enter PUCK, and BOTTOM with an ass's head

BOTTOM: If I were fair, Thisby, I were only thine.

QUINCE: O monstrous! O strange! We are haunted. Pray, masters! fly, masters! Help!

Exeunt QUINCE, SNUG, FLUTE, SNOUT, and STARVELING

PUCK: I'll follow you, I'll lead you about a round,
Through bog, through bush, through brake, through brier;
Sometime a horse I'll be, sometime a hound,
A hog, a headless bear, sometime a fire;
And neigh, and bark, and grunt, and roar, and burn,
Like horse, hound, hog, bear, fire, at every turn.

Exit

BOTTOM: Why do they run away? This is a knavery of them to make me afeard.

Re-enter SNOUT

SNOUT: O Bottom, thou art changed! What do I see on thee?

BOTTOM: What do you see? You see an asshead of your own, do you?

Exit SNOUT

Re-enter QUINCE

QUINCE: Bless thee, Bottom! bless thee! Thou art translated.

Exit

BOTTOM: I see their knavery: this is to make an ass of me; to fright me, if they could. But I will not stir from this place, do what they can; I will walk up and down here, and I will sing, that they shall hear I am not afraid.

Sings

The ousel cock, so black of hue,
With orange-tawny bill,
The throstle with his note so true,
The wren with little quill.

TITANIA: [*Awaking*] What angel wakes me from my flowery bed?

BOTTOM: [*Sings*]
The finch, the sparrow and the lark,
The plain-song cuckoo grey,
Whose note full many a man doth mark,
And dares not answer nay—
for, indeed, who would set his wit to so foolish a bird? Who would give a bird the lie, though he cry
'cuckoo' never so?

TITANIA: I pray thee, gentle mortal, sing again.
Mine ear is much enamour'd of thy note;
So is mine eye enthralled to thy shape;
And thy fair virtue's force perforce doth move me,
On the first view, to say, to swear, I love thee.

BOTTOM: Methinks, mistress, you should have little reason for that. And yet, to say the truth, reason and love keep little company together now-a-days. The more the pity that some honest neighbours will not make them friends. Nay, I can gleek upon occasion.

TITANIA: Thou art as wise as thou art beautiful.

BOTTOM: Not so, neither; but if I had wit enough to get out of this wood, I have enough to serve mine own turn.

TITANIA: Out of this wood do not desire to go;
Thou shalt remain here, whether thou wilt or no.
I am a spirit of no common rate;

The summer still doth tend upon my state;
And I do love thee; therefore, go with me.
I'll give thee fairies to attend on thee,
And they shall fetch thee jewels from the deep,
And sing, while thou on pressed flowers dost sleep;
And I will purge thy mortal grossness so
That thou shalt like an airy spirit go.
Peaseblossom! Cobweb! Moth! and Mustardseed!

Enter PEASEBLOSSOM, COBWEB, MOTH, and MUSTARDSEED

PEASEBLOSSOM: Ready.
COBWEB: And I.
MOTH: And I.
MUSTARDSEED: And I.
ALL: Where shall we go?
TITANIA: Be kind and courteous to this gentleman;
Hop in his walks and gambol in his eyes;
Feed him with apricocks and dewberries,
With purple grapes, green figs, and mulberries;
The honey-bags steal from the humble-bees,
And for night-tapers crop their waxen thighs,
And light them at the fiery glow-worm's eyes,
To have my love to bed and to arise;
And pluck the wings from Painted butterflies,
To fan the moonbeams from his sleeping eyes.
Nod to him, elves, and do him courtesies.
PEASEBLOSSOM: Hail, mortal!
COBWEB: Hail!
MOTH: Hail!
MUSTARDSEED: Hail!
BOTTOM: I cry your worship's mercy, heartily; I beseech your worship's name.
COBWEB: Cobweb.
BOTTOM: I shall desire you of more acquaintance, good Master Cobweb. If I cut my finger, I shall make bold with you. Your name, honest gentleman?
PEASEBLOSSOM: Peaseblossom.
BOTTOM: I pray you, commend me to Mistress Squash, your mother, and to Master Peascod, your father. Good Master Peaseblossom, I shall desire you of more acquaintance too. Your name, I beseech you, sir?
MUSTARDSEED: Mustardseed.
BOTTOM: Good Master Mustardseed, I know your patience well. That same cowardly, giant-like ox-beef hath devoured many a gentleman of your house. I promise you your kindred had made my eyes water ere now. I desire your more acquaintance, good Master Mustardseed.
TITANIA: Come, wait upon him; lead him to my bower.
The moon, methinks, looks with a watery eye;
And when she weeps, weeps every little flower,
Lamenting some enforced chastity.
Tie up my love's tongue bring him silently.

Exeunt

SCENE II—*Another part of the wood*

Enter OBERON

OBERON: I wonder if Titania be awaked;
Then, what it was that next came in her eye,
Which she must dote on in extremity.

Enter PUCK

Here comes my messenger.
How now, mad spirit!
What night-rule now about this haunted grove?
PUCK: My mistress with a monster is in love.
Near to her close and consecrated bower,
While she was in her dull and sleeping hour,
A crew of patches, rude mechanicals,
That work for bread upon Athenian stalls,
Were met together to rehearse a play
Intended for great Theseus' nuptial-day.
The shallowest thick-skin of that barren sort,
Who Pyramus presented, in their sport
Forsook his scene and enter'd in a brake;
When I did him at this advantage take,
An ass's nole I fixed on his head.
Anon his Thisby must be answered,
And forth my mimic comes. When they him spy,
As wild geese that the creeping fowler eye,
Or russet-pated choughs, many in sort,
Rising and cawing at the gun's report,
Sever themselves and madly sweep the sky,
So, at his sight, away his fellows fly;
And, at our stamp, here o'er and o'er one falls;
He murder cries and help from Athens calls.
Their sense thus weak, lost with their fears thus strong,
Made senseless things begin to do them wrong;
For briers and thorns at their apparel snatch;
Some sleeves, some hats, from yielders all things catch.

I led them on in this distracted fear,
And left sweet Pyramus translated there;
When in that moment, so it came to pass,
Titania waked, and straightway loved an ass.

OBERON: This falls out better than I could devise.
But hast thou yet latch'd the Athenian's eyes
With the love-juice, as I did bid thee do?

PUCK: I took him sleeping—that is finish'd too—
And the Athenian woman by his side;
That, when he waked, of force she must be eyed.

Enter HERMIA and DEMETRIUS

OBERON: Stand close; this is the same Athenian.

PUCK: This is the woman, but not this the man.

DEMETRIUS: O, why rebuke you him that loves you so?
Lay breath so bitter on your bitter foe.

HERMIA: Now I but chide; but I should use thee worse,
For thou, I fear, hast given me cause to curse.
If thou hast slain Lysander in his sleep,
Being o'er shoes in blood, plunge in the deep,
And kill me too.
The sun was not so true unto the day
As he to me. Would he have stolen away
From sleeping Hermia? I'll believe as soon
This whole earth may be bored and that the moon
May through the centre creep and so displease
Her brother's noontide with Antipodes.
It cannot be but thou hast murder'd him;
So should a murderer look, so dead, so grim.

DEMETRIUS: So should the murder'd look, and so should I,
Pierced through the heart with your stern cruelty;
Yet you, the murderer, look as bright, as clear,
As yonder Venus in her glimmering sphere.

HERMIA: What's this to my Lysander? Where is he?
Ah, good Demetrius, wilt thou give him me?

DEMETRIUS: I had rather give his carcass to my hounds.

HERMIA: Out, dog! out, cur! Thou drivest me past the bounds
Of maiden's patience. Hast thou slain him, then?
Henceforth be never number'd among men!
O, once tell true, tell true, even for my sake!
Durst thou have look'd upon him being awake,
And hast thou kill'd him sleeping? O brave touch!
Could not a worm, an adder, do so much?
An adder did it; for with doubler tongue
Than thine, thou serpent, never adder stung.

DEMETRIUS: You spend your passion on a misprised mood:
I am not guilty of Lysander's blood;
Nor is he dead, for aught that I can tell.

HERMIA: I pray thee, tell me then that he is well.

DEMETRIUS: An if I could, what should I get therefore?

HERMIA: A privilege never to see me more.
And from thy hated presence part I so;
See me no more, whether he be dead or no.

Exit

DEMETRIUS: There is no following her in this fierce vein;
Here, therefore, for a while I will remain.
So sorrow's heaviness doth heavier grow
For debt that bankrupt sleep doth sorrow owe;
Which now in some slight measure it will pay,
If for his tender here I make some stay.

Lies down and sleeps

OBERON: What hast thou done? Thou hast mistaken quite,
And laid the love-juice on some true-love's sight.
Of thy misprision must perforce ensue
Some true love turn'd and not a false turn'd true.

PUCK: Then fate o'er-rules, that, one man holding troth,
A million fail, confounding oath on oath.

OBERON: About the wood go swifter than the wind,
And Helena of Athens look thou find;
All fancy-sick she is and pale of cheer,
With sighs of love, that costs the fresh blood dear.
By some illusion see thou bring her here;
I'll charm his eyes against she do appear.

PUCK: I go, I go; look how I go,
Swifter than arrow from the Tartar's bow.

Exit

OBERON: Flower of this purple dye,
Hit with Cupid's archery,
Sink in apple of his eye.
When his love he doth espy,
Let her shine as gloriously

As the Venus of the sky.
When thou wakest, if she be by,
Beg of her for remedy.

Re-enter PUCK

PUCK: Captain of our fairy band,
Helena is here at hand;
And the youth, mistook by me,
Pleading for a lover's fee;
Shall we their fond pageant see?
Lord, what fools these mortals be!

OBERON: Stand aside. The noise they make
Will cause Demetrius to awake.

PUCK: Then will two at once woo one.
That must needs be sport alone;
And those things do best please me
That befal preposterously.

Enter LYSANDER and HELENA

LYSANDER: Why should you think that I should woo in scorn?
Scorn and derision never come in tears.
Look, when I vow, I weep; and vows so born,
In their nativity all truth appears.
How can these things in me seem scorn to you,
Bearing the badge of faith, to prove them true?

HELENA: You do advance your cunning more and more.
When truth kills truth, O devilish-holy fray!
These vows are Hermia's. Will you give her o'er?
Weigh oath with oath, and you will nothing weigh:
Your vows to her and me, put in two scales,
Will even weigh, and both as light as tales.

LYSANDER: I had no judgment when to her I swore.

HELENA: Nor none, in my mind, now you give her o'er.

LYSANDER: Demetrius loves her, and he loves not you.

DEMETRIUS: [*Awaking*] O Helen, goddess, nymph, perfect, divine!
To what, my love, shall I compare thine eyne?
Crystal is muddy. O, how ripe in show
Thy lips, those kissing cherries, tempting grow!
That pure congealed white, high Taurus' snow,
Fann'd with the eastern wind, turns to a crow
When thou hold'st up thy hand. O, let me kiss
This princess of pure white, this seal of bliss!

HELENA: O spite! O hell! I see you all are bent
To set against me for your merriment:
If you were civil and knew courtesy,
You would not do me thus much injury.
Can you not hate me, as I know you do,
But you must join in souls to mock me too?
If you were men, as men you are in show,
You would not use a gentle lady so:
To vow, and swear, and superpraise my parts,
When I am sure you hate me with your hearts.
You both are rivals, and love Hermia;
And now both rivals, to mock Helena:
A trim exploit, a manly enterprise,
To conjure tears up in a poor maid's eyes
With your derision! none of noble sort
Would so offend a virgin, and extort
A poor soul's patience, all to make you sport.

LYSANDER: You are unkind, Demetrius; be not so;
For you love Hermia. This you know I know;
And here, with all good will, with all my heart,
In Hermia's love I yield you up my part;
And yours of Helena to me bequeath,
Whom I do love and will do till my death.

HELENA: Never did mockers waste more idle breath.

DEMETRIUS: Lysander, keep thy Hermia; I will none.
If e'er I loved her, all that love is gone.
My heart to her but as guest-wise sojourn'd,
And now to Helen is it home return'd,
There to remain.

LYSANDER: Helen, it is not so.

DEMETRIUS: Disparage not the faith thou dost not know,
Lest, to thy peril, thou aby it dear.
Look, where thy love comes; yonder is thy dear.

Re-enter HERMIA

HERMIA: Dark night, that from the eye his function takes,
The ear more quick of apprehension makes;
Wherein it doth impair the seeing sense,
It pays the hearing double recompense.
Thou art not by mine eye, Lysander, found;
Mine ear, I thank it, brought me to thy sound
But why unkindly didst thou leave me so?

LYSANDER: Why should he stay, whom love doth press to go?

HERMIA: What love could press Lysander from my side?
LYSANDER: Lysander's love, that would not let him bide—
    Fair Helena, who more engilds the night
    Than all you fiery oes and eyes of light.
    Why seek'st thou me? could not this make thee know,
    The hate I bear thee made me leave thee so?
HERMIA: You speak not as you think; it cannot be.
HELENA: Lo, she is one of this confederacy!
    Now I perceive they have conjoin'd all three
    To fashion this false sport, in spite of me.
    Injurious Hermia! most ungrateful maid!
    Have you conspired, have you with these contrived
    To bait me with this foul derision?
    Is all the counsel that we two have shared,
    The sisters' vows, the hours that we have spent,
    When we have chid the hasty-footed time
    For parting us—O, is it all forgot?
    All school-days' friendship, childhood innocence?
    We, Hermia, like two artificial gods,
    Have with our needles created both one flower,
    Both on one sampler, sitting on one cushion,
    Both warbling of one song, both in one key,
    As if our hands, our sides, voices and minds,
    Had been incorporate. So we grow together,
    Like to a double cherry, seeming parted,
    But yet an union in partition;
    Two lovely berries moulded on one stem;
    So, with two seeming bodies, but one heart;
    Two of the first, like coats in heraldry,
    Due but to one and crowned with one crest.
    And will you rent our ancient love asunder,
    To join with men in scorning your poor friend?
    It is not friendly, 'tis not maidenly;
    Our sex, as well as I, may chide you for it,
    Though I alone do feel the injury.
HERMIA: I am amazed at your passionate words;
    I scorn you not; it seems that you scorn me.
HELENA: Have you not set Lysander, as in scorn,
    To follow me and praise my eyes and face?
    And made your other love, Demetrius,
    Who even but now did spurn me with his foot,
    To call me goddess, nymph, divine and rare,
    Precious, celestial? Wherefore speaks he this
    To her he hates? A wherefore doth Lysander
    Deny your love, so rich within his soul,
    And tender me, forsooth, affection,
    But by your setting on, by your consent?
    What thought I be not so in grace as you,
    So hung upon with love, so fortunate,
    But miserable most, to love unloved?
    This you should pity rather than despise.
HERMIA: I understand not what you mean by this.
HELENA: Ay, do—persever, counterfeit sad looks,
    Make mouths upon me when I turn my back;
    Wink each at other; hold the sweet jest up;
    This sport, well carried, shall be chronicled.
    If you have any pity, grace, or manners,
    You would not make me such an argument.
    But fare ye well; 'tis partly my own fault;
    Which death or absence soon shall remedy.
LYSANDER: Stay, gentle Helena; hear my excuse;
    My love, my life, my soul, fair Helena!
HELENA: O excellent!
HERMIA: Sweet, do not scorn her so.
DEMETRIUS: If she cannot entreat, I can compel.
LYSANDER: Thou canst compel no more than she entreat;
    Thy threats have no more strength than her weak prayers.
    Helen, I love thee; by my life, I do;
    I swear by that which I will lose for thee,
    To prove him false that says I love thee not.
DEMETRIUS: I say I love thee more than he can do.
LYSANDER: If thou say so, withdraw, and prove it too.
DEMETRIUS: Quick, come!
HERMIA: Lysander, whereto tends all this?
LYSANDER: Away, you Ethiope!
DEMETRIUS: No, no; he'll
    Seem to break loose—take on as you would follow,
    But yet come not. You are a tame man, go!
LYSANDER: Hang off, thou cat, thou burr! vile thing, let loose,
    Or I will shake thee from me like a serpent.
HERMIA: Why are you grown so rude? What change is this,
    Sweet love?
LYSANDER: Thy love! Out, tawny Tartar, out!
    Out, loathed medicine! O hated potion, hence!

HERMIA: Do you not jest?
HELENA: Yes, sooth; and so do you.
LYSANDER: Demetrius, I will keep my word with thee.
DEMETRIUS: I would I had your bond, for I perceive
A weak bond holds you; I'll not trust your word.
LYSANDER: What, should I hurt her, strike her, kill her dead?
Although I hate her, I'll not harm her so.
HERMIA: What, can you do me greater harm than hate?
Hate me! wherefore? O me! what news, my love?
Am not I Hermia? Are not you Lysander?
I am as fair now as I was erewhile.
Since night you loved me; yet since night you left me.
Why, then you left me—O, the gods forbid!—
In earnest, shall I say?
LYSANDER: Ay, by my life!
And never did desire to see thee more.
Therefore be out of hope, of question, of doubt;
Be certain, nothing truer; 'tis no jest
That I do hate thee and love Helena.
HERMIA: O me! you juggler! you canker-blossom!
You thief of love! What, have you come by night,
And stolen my love's heart from him?
HELENA: Fine, i' faith!
Have you no modesty, no maiden shame,
No touch of bashfulness? What! Will you tear
Impatient answers from my gentle tongue?
Fie, fie! you counterfeit, you puppet, you!
HERMIA: Puppet? why so? Ay, that way goes the game.
Now I perceive that she hath made compare
Between our statures; she hath urged her height;
And with her personage, her tall personage,
Her height, forsooth, she hath prevail'd with him.
And are you grown so high in his esteem
Because I am so dwarfish and so low?
How low am I, thou painted maypole? Speak.
How low am I? I am not yet so low
But that my nails can reach unto thine eyes.
HELENA: I pray you, though you mock me, gentlemen,
Let her not hurt me. I was never curst;
I have no gift at all in shrewishness;
I am a right maid for my cowardice;
Let her not strike me. You perhaps may think,
Because she is something lower than myself,
That I can match her.
HERMIA: Lower! hark, again.
HELENA: Good Hermia, do not be so bitter with me.
I evermore did love you, Hermia,
Did ever keep your counsels, never wrong'd you;
Save that, in love unto Demetrius,
I told him of your stealth unto this wood.
He follow'd you; for love I follow'd him;
But he hath chid me hence and threaten'd me
To strike me, spurn me, nay, to kill me too;
And now, so you will let me quiet go,
To Athens will I bear my folly back,
And follow you no further. Let me go.
You see how simple and how fond I am.
HERMIA: Why, get you gone! Who is't that hinders you?
HELENA: A foolish heart, that I leave here behind.
HERMIA: What, with Lysander?
HELENA: With Demetrius.
LYSANDER: Be not afraid; she shall not harm thee, Helena.
DEMETRIUS: No, sir, she shall not, though you take her part.
HELENA: O, when she's angry, she is keen and shrewd;
She was a vixen when she went to school;
And though she be but little, she is fierce.
HERMIA: 'Little' again! Nothing but 'low' and 'little'!
Why will you suffer her to flout me thus?
Let me come to her.
LYSANDER: Get you gone, you dwarf;
You minimus, of hindering knot-grass made;
You bead, you acorn.
DEMETRIUS: You are too officious
In her behalf that scorns your services.
Let her alone; speak not of Helena;
Take not her part; for, if thou dost intend
Never so little show of love to her,
Thou shalt aby it.
LYSANDER: Now she holds me not.
Now follow, if thou darest, to try whose right,
Of thine or mine, is most in Helena.
DEMETRIUS: Follow! Nay, I'll go with thee, cheek by jowl.

Exeunt LYSANDER and DEMETRIUS

HERMIA: You, mistress, all this coil is 'long of you.
Nay, go not back.
HELENA: I will not trust you, I;
Nor longer stay in your curst company.
Your hands than mine are quicker for a fray,
My legs are longer though, to run away.

Exit

HERMIA: I am amazed, and know not what to say.

Exit

OBERON: This is thy negligence. Still thou mistakest,
Or else committ'st thy knaveries wilfully.
PUCK: Believe me, king of shadows, I mistook.
Did not you tell me I should know the man
By the Athenian garment be had on?
And so far blameless proves my enterprise,
That I have 'nointed an Athenian's eyes;
And so far am I glad it so did sort,
As this their jangling I esteem a sport.
OBERON: Thou seest these lovers seek a place to fight.
Hie therefore, Robin, overcast the night;
The starry welkin cover thou anon
With drooping fog as black as Acheron,
And lead these testy rivals so astray
As one come not within another's way.
Like to Lysander sometime frame thy tongue,
Then stir Demetrius up with bitter wrong;
And sometime rail thou like Demetrius;
And from each other look thou lead them thus,
Till o'er their brows death-counterfeiting sleep
With leaden legs and batty wings doth creep.
Then crush this herb into Lysander's eye;
Whose liquor hath this virtuous property,
To take from thence all error with his might,
And make his eyeballs roll with wonted sight.
When they next wake, all this derision
Shall seem a dream and fruitless vision,
And back to Athens shall the lovers wend,
With league whose date till death shall never end.
Whiles I in this affair do thee employ,
I'll to my queen, and beg her Indian boy;
And then I will her charmed eye release
From monster's view, and all things shall be peace.
PUCK: My fairy lord, this must be done with haste,
For night's swift dragons cut the clouds full fast,
And yonder shines Aurora's harbinger;
At whose approach, ghosts, wandering here and there,
Troop home to churchyards. Damned spirits all,
That in crossways and floods have burial,
Already to their wormy beds are gone;
For fear lest day should look their shames upon,
They willfully themselves exiled from light,
And must for aye consort with black-brow'd night.
OBERON: But we are spirits of another sort:
I with the morning's love have oft made sport,
And, like a forester, the groves may tread,
Even till the eastern gate, all fiery-red,
Opening on Neptune with fair blessed beams,
Turns into yellow gold his salt green streams.
But, notwithstanding, haste; make no delay;
We may effect this business yet ere day.

Exit OBERON

PUCK: Up and down, up and down,
I will lead them up and down.
I am fear'd in field and town.
Goblin, lead them up and down.
Here comes one.

Re-enter LYSANDER

LYSANDER: Where art thou, proud Demetrius? speak thou now.
PUCK: Here, villain; drawn and ready. Where art thou?
LYSANDER: I will be with thee straight.
PUCK: Follow me, then,
To plainer ground.

Exit LYSANDER, as following the voice

Re-enter DEMETRIUS

DEMETRIUS: Lysander! speak again!
Thou runaway, thou coward, art thou fled?
Speak! In some bush? Where dost thou hide thy head?
PUCK: Thou coward, art thou bragging to the stars,
Telling the bushes that thou look'st for wars,
And wilt not come? Come, recreant; come, thou child;
I'll whip thee with a rod. He is defiled
That draws a sword on thee.
DEMETRIUS: Yea, art thou there?
PUCK: Follow my voice; we'll try no manhood here.

Exeunt

Re-enter LYSANDER

LYSANDER: He goes before me and still dares me on;
When I come where he calls, then he is gone.
The villain is much lighter-heel'd than I.
I follow'd fast, but faster he did fly;
That fallen am I in dark uneven way,
And here will rest me.

Lies down

Come, thou gentle day.
For if but once thou show me thy grey light,
I'll find Demetrius, and revenge this spite.

Sleeps

Re-enter PUCK and DEMETRIUS

PUCK: Ho, ho, ho! Coward, why comest thou not?

DEMETRIUS: Abide me, if thou darest; for well I wot
Thou runn'st before me, shifting every place,
And darest not stand, nor look me in the face.
Where art thou now?

PUCK: Come hither; I am here.

DEMETRIUS: Nay, then, thou mock'st me. Thou shalt buy this dear,
If ever I thy face by daylight see;
Now, go thy way. Faintness constraineth me
To measure out my length on this cold bed.
By day's approach look to be visited.

Lies down and sleeps

Re-enter HELENA

HELENA: O weary night, O long and tedious night,
Abate thy hour! Shine comforts from the east,
That I may back to Athens by daylight,
From these that my poor company detest.
And sleep, that sometimes shuts up sorrow's eye,
Steal me awhile from mine own company.

Sleeps

PUCK: Yet but three? Come one more;
Two of both kinds make up four.
Here she comes, curst and sad.
Cupid is a knavish lad,
Thus to make poor females mad.

Re-enter HERMIA

HERMIA: Never so weary, never so in woe,
Bedabbled with the dew and torn with briers,
I can no further crawl, no further go;
My legs can keep no pace with my desires.
Here will I rest me till the break of day.
Heavens shield Lysander, if they mean a fray!

Lies down and sleeps

PUCK: On the ground
Sleep sound;
I'll apply
To your eye,
Gentle lover, remedy.

Squeezing the juice on LYSANDER's eyes

When thou wakest,
Thou takest
True delight
In the sight
Of thy former lady's eye;
And the country proverb known,
That every man should take his own,
In your waking shall be shown.
Jack shall have Jill;
Nought shall go ill;
The man shall have his mare again, and all shall be well.

Exit

Act IV

Scene I—*The wood: Lysander, Demetrius, Helena, and Hermia, lying asleep*

Enter TITANIA and BOTTOM; PEASEBLOSSOM, COBWEB, MOTH, MUSTARDSEED, and other Fairies attending; OBERON behind unseen

TITANIA: Come, sit thee down upon this flowery bed,
While I thy amiable cheeks do coy,
And stick musk-roses in thy sleek smooth head,
And kiss thy fair large ears, my gentle joy.

BOTTOM: Where's Peaseblossom?

PEASEBLOSSOM: Ready.

BOTTOM: Scratch my head Peaseblossom. Where's Mounsieur Cobweb?

COBWEB: Ready.

BOTTOM: Mounsieur Cobweb, good mounsieur, get you your weapons in your hand, and kill me a red-hipped humble-bee on the top of a thistle; and, good mounsieur, bring me the honey-bag. Do not fret yourself too much in the action, mounsieur; and, good mounsieur, have a care the honey-bag break not; I would be loath to have you overflown with a honey-bag, signior. Where's Mounsieur Mustardseed?

MUSTARDSEED: Ready.

BOTTOM: Give me your neaf, Mounsieur Mustardseed. Pray you, leave your courtesy, good mounsieur.

MUSTARDSEED: What's your Will?

BOTTOM: Nothing, good mounsieur, but to help Cavalery Cobweb to scratch. I must to the barber's, monsieur; for methinks I am marvellous hairy about the face; and I am such a tender ass, if my hair do but tickle me, I must scratch.

TITANIA: What, wilt thou hear some music, my sweet love?

BOTTOM: I have a reasonable good ear in music.
Let's have the tongs and the bones.

TITANIA: Or say, sweet love, what thou desirest to eat.

BOTTOM: Truly, a peck of provender; I could munch your good dry oats. Methinks I have a great desire to a bottle of hay. Good hay, sweet hay, hath no fellow.

TITANIA: I have a venturous fairy that shall seek
The squirrel's hoard, and fetch thee new nuts.

BOTTOM: I had rather have a handful or two of dried peas. But, I pray you, let none of your people stir me; I have an exposition of sleep come upon me.

TITANIA: Sleep thou, and I will wind thee in my arms.
Fairies, begone, and be all ways away.

Exeunt Fairies

So doth the woodbine the sweet honeysuckle
Gently entwist; the female ivy so
Enrings the barky fingers of the elm.
O, how I love thee! how I dote on thee!

They sleep

Enter PUCK

OBERON: [*Advancing*] Welcome, good Robin.
See'st thou this sweet sight?
Her dotage now I do begin to pity;
For, meeting her of late behind the wood,
Seeking sweet favours from this hateful fool,
I did upbraid her and fall out with her.
For she his hairy temples then had rounded
With a coronet of fresh and fragrant flowers;
And that same dew, which sometime on the buds
Was wont to swell like round and orient pearls,
Stood now within the pretty flowerets' eyes
Like tears that did their own disgrace bewail.
When I had at my pleasure taunted her
And she in mild terms begg'd my patience,
I then did ask of her her changeling child;
Which straight she gave me, and her fairy sent
To bear him to my bower in fairy land.
And now I have the boy, I will undo
This hateful imperfection of her eyes.

And, gentle Puck, take this transformed scalp
From off the head of this Athenian swain;
That, he awaking when the other do,
May all to Athens back again repair
And think no more of this night's accidents
But as the fierce vexation of a dream.
But first I will release the fairy queen.
Be as thou wast wont to be;
See as thou wast wont to see.
Dian's bud o'er Cupid's flower
Hath such force and blessed power.
Now, my Titania; wake you, my sweet queen.

TITANIA: My Oberon! what visions have I seen!
Methought I was enamour'd of an ass.

OBERON: There lies your love.

TITANIA: How came these things to pass?
O, how mine eyes do loathe his visage now!

OBERON: Silence awhile. Robin, take off this head.
Titania, music call; and strike more dead
Than common sleep of all these five the sense.

TITANIA: Music, ho! music, such as charmeth sleep!
Music, still

PUCK: Now, when thou wakest, with thine own fool's eyes peep.

OBERON: Sound, music! Come, my queen, take hands with me,
And rock the ground whereon these sleepers be.
Now thou and I are new in amity,
And will to-morrow midnight solemnly
Dance in Duke Theseus' house triumphantly,
And bless it to all fair prosperity.
There shall the pairs of faithful lovers be
Wedded, with Theseus, all in jollity.

PUCK: Fairy king, attend, and mark;
I do hear the morning lark.

OBERON: Then, my queen, in silence sad,
Trip we after the night's shade.
We the globe can compass soon,
Swifter than the wandering moon.

TITANIA: Come, my lord, and in our flight
Tell me how it came this night
That I sleeping here was found
With these mortals on the ground.

Exeunt

Horns winded within

Enter THESEUS, HIPPOLYTA, EGEUS, and train

THESEUS: Go, one of you, find out the forester;
For now our observation is perform'd;
And since we have the vaward of the day,
My love shall hear the music of my hounds.
Uncouple in the western valley; let them go.
Dispatch, I say, and find the forester.

Exit an Attendant

We will, fair Queen, up to the mountain's top,
And mark the musical confusion
Of hounds and echo in conjunction.

HIPPOLYTA: I was with Hercules and Cadmus once,
When in a wood of Crete they bay'd the bear
With hounds of Sparta; never did I hear
Such gallant chiding, for, besides the groves,
The skies, the fountains, every region near
Seem'd all one mutual cry. I never heard
So musical a discord, such sweet thunder.

THESEUS: My hounds are bred out of the Spartan kind,
So flew'd, so sanded, and their heads are hung
With ears that sweep away the morning dew;
Crook-knee'd, and dew-lapp'd like Thessalian bulls;
Slow in pursuit, but match'd in mouth like bells,
Each under each. A cry more tuneable
Was never holla'd to, nor cheer'd with horn,
In Crete, in Sparta, nor in Thessaly.
Judge when you hear. But, soft! what nymphs are these?

EGEUS: My lord, this is my daughter here asleep;
And this, Lysander; this Demetrius is;
This Helena, old Nedar's Helena.
I wonder of their being here together.

THESEUS: No doubt they rose up early to observe
The rite of May, and hearing our intent,
Came here in grace our solemnity.
But speak, Egeus; is not this the day
That Hermia should give answer of her choice?

EGEUS: It is, my lord.

THESEUS: Go, bid the huntsmen wake them with their horns.

Horns and shout within. LYSANDER, DEMETRIUS, HELENA, and HERMIA wake and start up

Good morrow, friends. Saint Valentine is past:
Begin these wood-birds but to couple now?

LYSANDER: Pardon, my lord.

THESEUS: I pray you all, stand up.
I know you two are rival enemies;
How comes this gentle concord in the world,
That hatred is so far from jealousy,
To sleep by hate, and fear no enmity?

LYSANDER: My lord, I shall reply amazedly,
Half sleep, half waking; but as yet, I swear,
I cannot truly say how I came here;
But, as I think—-for truly would I speak,
And now do I bethink me, so it is—
I came with Hermia hither. Our intent
Was to be gone from Athens, where we might,
Without the peril of the Athenian law.

EGEUS: Enough, enough, my lord; you have enough;
I beg the law, the law, upon his head.
They would have stolen away; they would, Demetrius,
Thereby to have defeated you and me,
You of your wife and me of my consent,
Of my consent that she should be your wife.

DEMETRIUS: My lord, fair Helen told me of their stealth,
Of this their purpose hither to this wood;
And I in fury hither follow'd them,
Fair Helena in fancy following me.
But, my good lord, I wot not by what power—
But by some power it is—my love to Hermia,
Melted as the snow, seems to me now
As the remembrance of an idle gaud
Which in my childhood I did dote upon;
And all the faith, the virtue of my heart,
The object and the pleasure of mine eye,
Is only Helena. To her, my lord,
Was I betroth'd ere I saw Hermia.
But, like in sickness, did I loathe this food;
But, as in health, come to my natural taste,
Now I do wish it, love it, long for it,
And will for evermore be true to it.

THESEUS: Fair lovers, you are fortunately met;
Of this discourse we more will hear anon.
Egeus, I will overbear your will;
For in the temple by and by with us
These couples shall eternally be knit.
And, for the morning now is something worn,
Our purposed hunting shall be set aside.
Away with us to Athens; three and three,
We'll hold a feast in great solemnity.
Come, Hippolyta.

Exeunt THESEUS, HIPPOLYTA, EGEUS, and train

DEMETRIUS: These things seem small and undistinguishable,

HERMIA: Methinks I see these things with parted eye,
When every thing seems double.

HELENA: So methinks;
And I have found Demetrius like a jewel,
Mine own, and not mine own.

DEMETRIUS: Are you sure
That we are awake? It seems to me
That yet we sleep, we dream. Do not you think
The duke was here, and bid us follow him?

HERMIA: Yea; and my father.

HELENA: And Hippolyta.

LYSANDER: And he did bid us follow to the temple.

DEMETRIUS: Why, then, we are awake; let's follow him
And by the way let us recount our dreams.

Exeunt

BOTTOM: [*Awaking*]. When my cue comes, call me, and I will answer. My next is, 'Most fair Pyramus.' Heigh-ho! Peter Quince! Flute, the bellows-mender! Snout, the tinker! Starveling! God's my life, stolen hence, and left me asleep! I have had a most rare vision. I have had a dream, past the wit of man to say what dream it was. Man is but an ass, if he go about to expound this dream. Methought I was—there is no man can tell what. Methought I was—and methought I had,—but man is but a patched fool, if he will offer to say what methought I had. The eye of man hath not heard, the ear of man hath not seen, man's hand is not able to taste, his tongue to conceive, nor his heart to report, what my dream was. I will get Peter Quince to write a ballad of this dream. It shall be called Bottom's Dream, because it hath no bottom; and I will sing it in the latter end of a play, before the Duke. Peradventure, to make it the more gracious, I shall sing it at her death.

Exit

SCENE II—*Athens: Quince's house*

Enter QUINCE, FLUTE, SNOUT, and STARVELING

QUINCE: Have you sent to Bottom's house ? Is he come home yet?

STARVELING: He cannot be heard of. Out of doubt he is transported.

FLUTE: If he come not, then the play is marred; it goes not forward, doth it?

QUINCE: It is not possible. You have not a man in all Athens able to discharge Pyramus but he.

FLUTE: No, he hath simply the best wit of any handicraft man in Athens.

QUINCE: Yea and the best person too; and he is a very paramour for a sweet voice.

FLUTE: You must say 'paragon'. A paramour is, God bless us, a thing of naught.

Enter SNUG

SNUG: Masters, the Duke is coming from the temple, and there is two or three lords and ladies more married. If our sport had gone forward, we had all been made men.

FLUTE: O sweet bully Bottom! Thus hath he lost sixpence a day during his life; he could not have scaped sixpence a day. An the Duke had not given him sixpence a day for playing Pyramus, I'll be hanged; he would have deserved it: sixpence a day in Pyramus, or nothing.

Enter BOTTOM

BOTTOM: Where are these lads? where are these hearts?

QUINCE: Bottom! O most courageous day! O most happy hour!

BOTTOM: Masters, I am to discourse wonders; but ask me not what; for if I tell you, I am no true Athenian. I will tell you every thing, right as it fell out.

QUINCE: Let us hear, sweet Bottom.

BOTTOM: Not a word of me. All that I will tell you is, that the Duke hath dined. Get your apparel together, good strings to your beards, new ribbons to your pumps; meet presently at the palace; every man look o'er his part; for the short and the long is, our play is preferred. In any case, let Thisby have clean linen; and let not him that plays the lion pair his nails, for they shall hang out for the lion's claws. And, most dear actors, eat no onions nor garlic, for we are to utter sweet breath; and I do not doubt but to hear them say, it is a sweet comedy. No more words: away! go, away!

Exeunt

Act V

Scene I—*Athens: The palace of Theseus*

Enter THESEUS, HIPPOLYTA, PHILOSTRATE, Lords and Attendants

HIPPOLYTA: 'Tis strange my Theseus, that these lovers speak of.

THESEUS: More strange than true. I never may believe
These antique fables, nor these fairy toys.
Lovers and madmen have such seething brains,
Such shaping fantasies, that apprehend
More than cool reason ever comprehends.
The lunatic, the lover and the poet
Are of imagination all compact.
One sees more devils than vast hell can hold,
That is, the madman. The lover, all as frantic,
Sees Helen's beauty in a brow of Egypt.
The poet's eye, in fine frenzy rolling,
Doth glance from heaven to earth, from earth to heaven;
And as imagination bodies forth
The forms of things unknown, the poet's pen
Turns them to shapes and gives to airy nothing
A local habitation and a name.
Such tricks hath strong imagination,
That if it would but apprehend some joy,
It comprehends some bringer of that joy;
Or in the night, imagining some fear,
How easy is a bush supposed a bear!

HIPPOLYTA: But all the story of the night told over,
And all their minds transfigured so together,
More witnesseth than fancy's images
And grows to something of great constancy;
But, howsoever, strange and admirable.

THESEUS: Here come the lovers, full of joy and mirth.

Enter LYSANDER, DEMETRIUS, HERMIA, and HELENA

Joy, gentle friends! joy and fresh days of love
Accompany your hearts!

LYSANDER: More than to us
Wait in your royal walks, your board, your bed!

THESEUS: Come now; what masques, what dances shall we have,
To wear away this long age of three hours
Between our after-supper and bed-time?
Where is our usual manager of mirth?
What revels are in hand? Is there no play,
To ease the anguish of a torturing hour?
Call Philostrate.

PHILOSTRATE: Here, mighty Theseus.

THESEUS: Say, what abridgement have you for this evening?
What masque? what music? How shall we beguile
The lazy time, if not with some delight?

PHILOSTRATE: There is a brief how many sports are ripe;
Make choice of which your highness will see first.

Giving a paper

THESEUS: [*Reads*] 'The battle with the Centaurs, to be sung
By an Athenian eunuch to the harp.'
We'll none of that: that have I told my love,
In glory of my kinsman Hercules.

Reads

'The riot of the tipsy Bacchanals,
Tearing the Thracian singer in their rage.'
That is an old device; and it was play'd
When I from Thebes came last a conqueror.
'The thrice three Muses mourning for the death
Of Learning, late deceased in beggary.'
That is some satire, keen and critical,
Not sorting with a nuptial ceremony.
'A tedious brief scene of young Pyramus
And his love Thisby; very tragical mirth.'
Merry and tragical! tedious and brief!

That is, hot ice and wondrous strange snow.
How shall we find the concord of this discord?

PHILOSTRATE: A play there is, my lord, some ten words long,
Which is as brief as I have known a play;
But by ten words, my lord, it is too long,
Which makes it tedious; for in all the play
There is not one word apt, one player fitted.
And tragical, my noble lord, it is;
For Pyramus therein doth kill himself.
Which, when I saw rehearsed, I must confess,
Made mine eyes water; but more merry tears
The passion of loud laughter never shed.

THESEUS: What are they that do play it?

PHILOSTRATE: Hard-handed men that work in Athens here,
Which never labour'd in their minds till now,
And now have toil'd their unbreathed memories
With this same play, against your nuptial.

THESEUS: And we will hear it.

PHILOSTRATE: No, my noble lord;
It is not for you. I have heard it over,
And it is nothing, nothing in the world;
Unless you can find sport in their intents,
Extremely stretch'd and conn'd with cruel pain,
To do you service.

THESEUS: I will hear that play;
For never anything can be amiss,
When simpleness and duty tender it.
Go, bring them in; and take your places, ladies.

Exit PHILOSTRATE

HIPPOLYTA: I love not to see wretchedness o'er charged
And duty in his service perishing.

THESEUS: Why, gentle sweet, you shall see no such thing.

HIPPOLYTA: He says they can do nothing in this kind.

THESEUS: The kinder we, to give them thanks for nothing.
Our sport shall be to take what they mistake;
And what poor duty cannot do, noble respect
Takes it in might, not merit.
Where I have come, great clerks have purposed
To greet me with premeditated welcomes;
Where I have seen them shiver and look pale,
Make periods in the midst of sentences,
Throttle their practised accent in their fears
And in conclusion dumbly have broke off,
Not paying me a welcome. Trust me, sweet,
Out of this silence yet I pick'd a welcome;
And in the modesty of fearful duty
I read as much as from the rattling tongue
Of saucy and audacious eloquence.
Love, therefore, and tongue-tied simplicity
In least speak most, to my capacity.

Re-enter PHILOSTRATE

PHILOSTRATE: So please your grace, the Prologue is address'd.

THESEUS: Let him approach.

Flourish of trumpets

Enter QUINCE for the Prologue

PROLOGUE: If we offend, it is with our good will.
That you should think, we come not to offend,
But with good will. To show our simple skill,
That is the true beginning of our end.
Consider then we come but in despite.
We do not come as minding to contest you,
Our true intent is. All for your delight
We are not here. That you should here repent you,
The actors are at hand and by their show
You shall know all that you are like to know.

THESEUS: This fellow doth not stand upon points.

LYSANDER: He hath rid his prologue like a rough colt; he knows not the stop. A good moral, my lord: it is not enough to speak, but to speak true.

HIPPOLYTA: Indeed he hath played on his prologue like a child on a recorder; a sound, but not in government.

THESEUS: His speech, was like a tangled chain; nothing impaired, but all disordered. Who is next?

Enter PYRAMUS and THISBY, WALL, MOONSHINE, and LION

PROLOGUE: Gentles, perchance you wonder at this show;
But wonder on, till truth make all things plain.
This man is Pyramus, if you would know;
This beauteous lady Thisby is certain.
This man, with lime and rough-cast, doth present
Wall, that vile Wall which did these lovers sunder;
And through Wall's chink, poor souls, they are content
To whisper. At the which let no man wonder.

This man, with lanthorn, dog, and bush of thorn,
Presenteth Moonshine; for, if you will know,
By moonshine did these lovers think no scorn
To meet at Ninus' tomb, there, there to woo.
This grisly beast, which Lion hight by name,
The trusty Thisby, coming first by night,
Did scare away, or rather did affright;
And, as she fled, her mantle she did fall,
Which Lion vile with bloody mouth did stain.
Anon comes Pyramus, sweet youth and tall,
And finds his trusty Thisby's mantle slain;
Whereat, with blade, with bloody blameful blade,
He bravely broach'd is boiling bloody breast;
And Thisby, tarrying in mulberry shade,
His dagger drew, and died. For all the rest,
Let Lion, Moonshine, Wall, and lovers twain
At large discourse, while here they do remain.

Exeunt PROLOGUE, THISBY, LION, and MOONSHINE

THESEUS: I wonder if the lion be to speak.

DEMETRIUS: No wonder, my lord: one lion may, when many asses do.

Wall: In this same interlude it doth befall
That I, one Snout by name, present a wall;
And such a wall, as I would have you think,
That had in it a crannied hole or chink,
Through which the lovers, Pyramus and Thisby,
Did whisper often very secretly.
This loam, this rough-cast and this stone doth show
That I am that same wall; the truth is so;
And this the cranny is, right and sinister,
Through which the fearful lovers are to whisper.

THESEUS: Would you desire lime and hair to speak better?

DEMETRIUS: It is the wittiest partition that ever I heard discourse, my lord.

Enter PYRAMUS

THESEUS: Pyramus draws near the wall; silence!

PYRAMUS: O grim-look'd night! O night with hue so black!
O night, which ever art when day is not
O night, O night! alack, alack, alack,
I fear my Thisby's promise is forgot!
And thou, O wall, O sweet, O lovely wall,
That stand'st between her father's ground and mine!
Thou wall, O wall, O sweet and lovely wall,
Show me thy chink, to blink through with mine eyne!

Wall holds up his fingers

Thanks, courteous wall. Jove shield thee well for this!
But what see I? No Thisby do I see.
O wicked wall, through whom I see no bliss!
Cursed be thy stones for thus deceiving me!

THESEUS: The wall, methinks, being sensible, should curse again.

PYRAMUS: No, in truth, sir, he should not. 'Deceiving me' is Thisby's cue. She is to enter now, and I am to spy her through the wall. You shall see, it will fall pat as I told you. Yonder she comes.

Enter THISBY

THISBY: O wall, full often hast thou heard my moans,
For parting my fair Pyramus and me!
My cherry lips have often kiss'd thy stones,
Thy stones with lime and hair knit up in thee.

PYRAMUS: I see a voice; now will I to the chink,
To spy an I can hear my Thisby's face. Thisby!

THISBY: My love thou art, my love I think.

PYRAMUS: Think what thou wilt, I am thy lover's grace;
And, like Limander, am I trusty still.

THISBY: And I like Helen, till the Fates me kill.

PYRAMUS: Not Shafalus to Procrus was so true.

THISBY: As Shafalus to Procrus, I to you.

PYRAMUS: O kiss me through the hole of this vile wall!

THISBY: I kiss the wall's hole, not your lips at all.

PYRAMUS: Wilt thou at Ninny's tomb meet me straightway?

THISBY: 'Tide life, 'tide death, I come without delay.

Exeunt PYRAMUS and THISBY

WALL: Thus have I, Wall, my part discharged so;
And, being done, thus Wall away doth go.

Exit WALL

THESEUS: Now is the moon used between the two neighbours.

DEMETRIUS: No remedy, my lord, when walls are so wilful to hear without warning.

HIPPOLYTA: This is the silliest stuff that ever I heard.

THESEUS: The best in this kind are but shadows; and the worst are no worse, if imagination amend them.

HIPPOLYTA: It must be your imagination then, and not theirs.

THESEUS: If we imagine no worse of them than they of themselves, they may pass for excellent men. Here come two noble beasts in, a man and a lion.

Enter LION and MOONSHINE

LION: You, ladies, you, whose gentle hearts do fear
The smallest monstrous mouse that creeps on floor,
May now perchance both quake and tremble here,
When lion rough in wildest rage doth roar.
Then know that I, one Snug the joiner, am
A lion-fell, nor else no lion's dam;
For, if I should as lion come in strife
Into this place, 'twere pity on my life.

THESEUS: A very gentle beast, of a good conscience.

DEMETRIUS: The very best at a beast, my lord, that e'er I saw.

LYSANDER: This lion is a very fox for his valour.

THESEUS: True; and a goose for his discretion.

DEMETRIUS: Not so, my lord; for his valour cannot carry his discretion; and the fox carries the goose.

THESEUS: His discretion, I am sure, cannot carry his valour; for the goose carries not the fox. It is well. Leave it to his discretion, and let us listen to the moon.

Moonshine: This lanthorn doth the horned moon present—

DEMETRIUS: He should have worn the horns on his head.

THESEUS: He is no crescent, and his horns are invisible within the circumference.

Moonshine: This lanthorn doth the horned moon present;
Myself the man i' the moon do seem to be.

THESEUS: This is the greatest error of all the rest; the man should be put into the lanthorn. How is it else the man i' the moon?

DEMETRIUS: He dares not come there for the candle; for, you see, it is already in snuff.

HIPPOLYTA: I am aweary of this moon. Would he would change!

THESEUS: It appears, by his small light of discretion, that he is in the wane; but yet, in courtesy, in all reason, we must stay the time.

LYSANDER: Proceed, Moon.

Moonshine: All that I have to say, is, to tell you that the lanthorn is the moon; I, the man in the moon; this thorn-bush, my thorn-bush; and this dog, my dog.

DEMETRIUS: Why, all these should be in the lanthorn; for all these are in the moon. But, silence! here comes Thisby.

Enter THISBY

THISBY: This is old Ninny's tomb. Where is my love?

LION: [*Roaring*] Oh—

THISBY runs off

DEMETRIUS: Well roared, Lion.

THESEUS: Well run, Thisby.

HIPPOLYTA: Well shone, Moon. Truly, the moon shines with a good grace.

The Lion shakes Thisby's mantle, and exit

THESEUS: Well moused, Lion.

LYSANDER: And so the lion vanished.

DEMETRIUS: And then came Pyramus.

Enter PYRAMUS

PYRAMUS: Sweet Moon, I thank thee for thy sunny beams;
I thank thee, Moon, for shining now so bright;
For, by thy gracious, golden, glittering gleams,
I trust to take of truest Thisby sight.
But stay, O spite!
But mark, poor knight,
What dreadful dole is here!
Eyes, do you see?
How can it be?
O dainty duck! O dear!
Thy mantle good,
What, stain'd with blood!
Approach, ye Furies fell!
O Fates, come, come,
Cut thread and thrum;
Quail, crush, conclude, and quell!

THESEUS: This passion, and the death of a dear friend, would go near to make a man look sad.

HIPPOLYTA: Beshrew my heart, but I pity the man.

PYRAMUS: O wherefore, Nature, didst thou lions frame?

Since lion vile hath here deflower'd my dear;
Which is—no, no—which was the fairest dame
That lived, that loved, that liked, that look'd with cheer.
Come, tears, confound;
Out, sword, and wound
The pap of Pyramus;
Ay, that left pap,
Where heart doth hop.

STABS HIMSELF

Thus die I, thus, thus, thus.
Now am I dead,
Now am I fled;
My soul is in the sky.
Tongue, lose thy light;
Moon take thy flight.

Exit MOONSHINE

Now die, die, die, die, die.

Dies

DEMETRIUS: No die, but an ace, for him; for he is but one.

LYSANDER: Less than an ace, man; for he is dead; he is nothing.

THESEUS: With the help of a surgeon he might yet recover, and prove an ass.

HIPPOLYTA: How chance Moonshine is gone before Thisby comes back and finds her lover?

THESEUS: She will find him by starlight. Here she comes; and her passion ends the play.

Re-enter THISBY

HIPPOLYTA: Methinks she should not use a long one for such a Pyramus; I hope she will be brief.

DEMETRIUS: A mote will turn the balance, which Pyramus, which Thisby, is the better; he for a man, God warrant us; she for a woman, God bless us.

LYSANDER: She hath spied him already with those sweet eyes.

DEMETRIUS: And thus she means, videlicet:—

Thisby: Asleep, my love?
What, dead, my dove?
O Pyramus, arise!
Speak, speak. Quite dumb?
Dead, dead? A tomb
Must cover thy sweet eyes.
These My lips,
This cherry nose,
These yellow cowslip cheeks,
Are gone, are gone;
Lovers, make moan;
His eyes were green as leeks.
O Sisters Three,
Come, come to me,
With hands as pale as milk;
Lay them in gore,
Since you have shore
With shears his thread of silk.
Tongue, not a word.
Come, trusty sword;
Come, blade, my breast imbrue.

Stabs herself

And, farewell, friends;
Thus Thisby ends;
Adieu, adieu, adieu.

Dies

THESEUS: Moonshine and Lion are left to bury the dead.

DEMETRIUS: Ay, and Wall too.

BOTTOM: [*Starting up*] No, I assure you; the wall is down that parted their fathers. Will it please you to see the epilogue, or to hear a Bergomask dance between two of our company?

THESEUS: No epilogue, I pray you; for your play needs no excuse. Never excuse; for when the players are all dead, there needs none to be blamed. Marry, if he that writ it had played Pyramus and hanged himself in Thisby's garter, it would have been a fine tragedy. And so it is, truly; and very notably discharged. But come, your Bergomask; let your epilogue alone.

A dance

The iron tongue of midnight hath told twelve.
Lovers, to bed; 'tis almost fairy time.
I fear we shall out-sleep the coming morn
As much as we this night have overwatch'd.
This palpable-gross play hath well beguiled
The heavy gait of night. Sweet friends, to bed.
A fortnight hold we this solemnity,
In nightly revels and new jollity.

Exeunt

Enter PUCK

PUCK: Now the hungry lion roars,
And the wolf behowls the moon;
Whilst the heavy ploughman snores,
All with weary task fordone.

Now the wasted brands do glow,
Whilst the screech-owl, screeching loud,
Puts the wretch that lies in woe
In remembrance of a shroud.
Now it is the time of night
That the graves all gaping wide,
Every one lets forth his sprite,
In the church-way paths to glide.
And we fairies, that do run
By the triple Hecate's team,
From the presence of the sun,
Following darkness like a dream,
Now are frolic. Not a mouse
Shall disturb this hallow'd house.
I am sent with broom before,
To sweep the dust behind the door.

Enter OBERON and TITANIA with their train

OBERON: Through the house give glimmering light,
By the dead and drowsy fire;
Every elf and fairy sprite
Hop as light as bird from brier;
And this ditty, after me,
Sing, and dance it trippingly.

TITANIA: First, rehearse your song by rote
To each word a warbling note;
Hand in hand, with fairy grace,
Will we sing, and bless this place.

Song and dance

OBERON: Now, until the break of day,
Through this house each fairy stray.
To the best bride-bed will we,
Which by us shall blessed be;
And the issue there create
Ever shall be fortunate.
So shall all the couples three
Ever true in loving be;
And the blots of Nature's hand
Shall not in their issue stand;
Never mole, hare lip, nor scar,
Nor mark prodigious, such as are
Despised in nativity,
Shall upon their children be.
With this field-dew consecrate,
Every fairy take his gait;
And each several chamber bless,
Through this palace, with sweet peace;
And the owner of it blest
Ever shall in safety rest.
Trip away; make no stay;
Meet me all by break of day.

Exeunt OBERON, TITANIA, and train

PUCK: If we shadows have offended,
Think but this, and all is mended,
That you have but slumber'd here
While these visions did appear.
And this weak and idle theme,
No more yielding but a dream,
Gentles, do not reprehend.
If you pardon, we will mend.
And, as I am an honest Puck,
If we have unearned luck
Now to scape the serpent's tongue,
We will make amends ere long;
Else the Puck a liar call;
So, good night unto you all.
Give me your hands, if we be friends,
And Robin shall restore amends.

Exit

Much Ado About Nothing

DRAMATIS PERSONÆ

DON PEDRO, *Prince of Arragon*
DON JOHN, *his bastard brother*
CLAUDIO, *a young lord of Florence*
BENEDICK, *a young lord of Padua*
LEONATO, *Governor of Messina*
ANTONIO, *his brother*
BALTHASAR, *attendant on Don Pedro*
BORACHIO, CONRADE, *followers of Don John*
DOGBERRY, *a constable*
VERGES, *a headborough*
FRIAR FRANCIS
A Sexton
A Boy
HERO, *daughter to Leonato*
BEATRICE, *niece to Leonato*
MARGARET, URSULA, *gentlewomen attending on Hero*
Messengers, Watch, Attendants,

THE SCENE: *Messina*

Act I

Scene I—*Before Leonato's house*

Enter LEONATO, HERO, and BEATRICE, with a Messenger

LEONATO: I learn in this letter that Don Pedro of Arragon comes this night to Messina.

MESSENGER: He is very near by this; he was not three leagues off when I left him.

LEONATO: How many gentlemen have you lost in this action?

MESSENGER: But few of any sort, and none of name.

LEONATO: A victory is twice itself when the achiever brings home full numbers. I find here that Don Pedro hath bestowed much honour on a young Florentine called Claudio.

MESSENGER: Much deserved on his part, and equally remembered by Don Pedro. He hath borne himself beyond the promise of his age, doing, in the figure of a lamb, the feats of a lion; he hath, indeed, better bettered expectation than you must expect of me to tell you how.

LEONATO: He hath an uncle here in Messina will be very much glad of it.

MESSENGER: I have already delivered him letters, and there appears much joy in him; even so much that joy could not show itself modest enough without a badge of bitterness.

LEONATO: Did he break out into tears?

MESSENGER: In great measure.

LEONATO: A kind overflow of kindness. There are no faces truer than those that are so washed. How much better is it to weep at joy than to joy at weeping!

BEATRICE: I pray you, is Signior Mountanto returned from the wars or no?

MESSENGER: I know none of that name, lady; there was none such in the army of any sort.

LEONATO: What is he that you ask for, niece?

HERO: My cousin means Signior Benedick of Padua.

MESSENGER: O, he's returned, and as pleasant as ever he was.

BEATRICE: He set up his bills here in Messina, and challenged Cupid at the flight; and my uncle's fool, reading the challenge, subscribed for Cupid, and challenged him at the bird-bolt. I pray you, how many hath he killed and eaten in these wars? But how many hath he killed? For, indeed, I promised to eat all of his killing.

LEONATO: Faith, niece, you tax Signior Benedick too much; but he'll be meet with you, I doubt it not.

MESSENGER: He hath done good service, lady, in these wars.

BEATRICE: You had musty victual, and he hath holp to eat it. He is a very valiant trencherman; he hath an excellent stomach.

MESSENGER: And a good soldier too, lady.

BEATRICE: And a good soldier to a lady; but what is he to a lord?

MESSENGER: A lord to a lord, a man to a man; stuffed with all honourable virtues.

BEATRICE: It is so, indeed; he is no less than a stuffed man; but for the stuffing,—well, we are all mortal.

LEONATO: You must not, sir, mistake my niece. There is a kind of merry war betwixt Signior Benedick and her; they never meet but there's a skirmish of wit between them.

BEATRICE: Alas! he gets nothing by that. In our last conflict four of his five wits went halting off, and now is the whole man governed with one; so that if he have wit enough to keep himself warm, let him bear it for a difference between himself and his horse; for it is all the wealth that he hath left, to be known a reasonable creature. Who is his companion now? He hath every month a new sworn brother.

MESSENGER: Is't possible?

BEATRICE: Very easily possible: he wears his faith but as the fashion of his hat; it ever changes with the next block.

MESSENGER: I see, lady, the gentleman is not in your books.

BEATRICE: No; an he were, I would burn my study. But, I pray you, who is his companion? Is there no young squarer now that will make a voyage with him to the devil?

MESSENGER: He is most in the company of the right noble Claudio.

BEATRICE: O Lord! he will hang upon him like a disease; he is sooner caught than the pestilence, and the taker runs presently mad. God help the noble Claudio! If he have caught the Benedick, it will cost him a thousand pound ere' a be cured.

MESSENGER: I will hold friends with you, lady.

BEATRICE: Do, good friend.

LEONATO: You will never run mad, niece.

BEATRICE: No, not till a hot January.

MESSENGER: Don Pedro is approached.

Enter DON PEDRO, DON JOHN, CLAUDIO, BENEDICK, BALTHASAR and JOHN the bastard

DON PEDRO: Good Signior Leonato, are you come to meet your trouble? The fashion of the world is to avoid cost, and you encounter it.

LEONATO: Never came trouble to my house in the likeness of your grace; for trouble being gone, comfort should remain; but when you depart from me, sorrow abides and happiness takes his leave.

DON PEDRO: You embrace your charge too willingly. I think this is your daughter.

LEONATO: Her mother hath many times told me so.

BENEDICK: Were you in doubt, sir, that you asked her?

LEONATO: Signior Benedick, no; for then were you a child.

DON PEDRO: You have it full, Benedick; we may guess by this what you are, being a man. Truly, the lady fathers herself. Be happy, lady; for you are like an honourable father.

BENEDICK: If Signior Leonato be her father, she would not have his head on her shoulders for all Messina, as like him as she is.

BEATRICE: I wonder that you will still be talking, Signior Benedick; nobody marks you.

BENEDICK: What, my dear Lady Disdain! are you yet living?

BEATRICE: Is it possible disdain should die while she hath such meet food to feed it as Signior Benedick? Courtesy itself must convert to disdain, if you come in her presence.

BENEDICK: Then is courtesy a turncoat. But it is certain I am loved of all ladies, only you excepted; and I would I could find in my heart that I had not a hard heart; for, truly, I love none.

BEATRICE: A dear happiness to women: they would else have been troubled with a pernicious suitor. I thank God and my cold blood, I am of your humour for that: I had rather hear my dog bark at a crow than a man swear he loves me.

BENEDICK: God keep your ladyship still in that mind! So some gentleman or other shall 'scape a predestinate scratched face.

BEATRICE: Scratching could not make it worse, an 'twere such a face as yours were.

BENEDICK: Well, you are a rare parrot-teacher.

BEATRICE: A bird of my tongue is better than a beast of yours.

BENEDICK: I would my horse had the speed of your tongue, and so good a continuer. But keep your way, i' God's name; I have done.

BEATRICE: You always end with a jade's trick; I know you of old.

DON PEDRO: That is the sum of all, Leonato. Signior Claudio and Signior Benedick, my dear friend Leonato hath invited you all. I tell him we shall stay here at the least a month; and he heartily prays some occasion may detain us longer. I dare swear he is no hypocrite, but prays from his heart.

LEONATO: If you swear, my lord, you shall not be forsworn. [*To Don John*] Let me bid you welcome, my lord: being reconciled to the prince your brother, I owe you all duty.

DON JOHN: I thank you; I am not of many words, but I thank you.

LEONATO: Please it your Grace lead on?

DON PEDRO: Your hand, Leonato; we will go together.

Exeunt all except BENEDICK and CLAUDIO

CLAUDIO: Benedick, didst thou note the daughter of Signior Leonato?

BENEDICK: I noted her not, but I looked on her.

CLAUDIO: Is she not a modest young lady?

BENEDICK: Do you question me, as an honest man should do, for my simple true judgment; or would you have me speak after my custom, as being a professed tyrant to their sex?

CLAUDIO: No, I pray thee speak in sober judgment.

BENEDICK: Why, i' faith, methinks she's too low for a high praise, too brown for a fair praise and too little for a great praise; only this commendation I can afford her, that were she other than she is, she were unhandsome; and being no other but as she is, I do not like her.

CLAUDIO: Thou thinkest I am in sport; I pray thee tell me truly how thou likest her.

BENEDICK: Would you buy her, that you inquire after her?

CLAUDIO: Can the world buy such a jewel?

BENEDICK: Yea, and a case to put it into. But speak you this with a sad brow? or do you play the flouting Jack, to tell us Cupid is a good hare-finder and Vulcan a rare carpenter? Come, in what key shall a man take you, to go in the song?

CLAUDIO: In mine eye she is the sweetest lady that ever I looked on.

BENEDICK: I can see yet without spectacles and I see no such matter; there's her cousin, an she were not possessed with a fury, exceeds her as much in beauty as the first of May doth the last of December. But I hope you have no intent to turn husband, have you?

CLAUDIO: I would scarce trust myself, though I had sworn the contrary, if Hero would be my wife.

BENEDICK: Is't come to this? In faith, hath not the world one man but he will wear his cap with suspicion? Shall I never see a bachelor of three-score again? Go to, i' faith; an thou wilt needs thrust thy neck into a yoke, wear the print of it and sigh away Sundays. Look Don Pedro is returned to seek you.

Re-enter DON PEDRO

DON PEDRO: What secret hath held you here, that you followed not to Leonato's?

BENEDICK: I would your grace would constrain me to tell.

DON PEDRO: I charge thee on thy allegiance.

BENEDICK: You hear, Count Claudio; I can be secret as a dumb man; I would have you think so; but, on my allegiance, mark you this, on my allegiance. He is in love. With who? now that is your grace's part. Mark how short his answer is—With Hero, Leonato's short daughter.

CLAUDIO: If this were so, so were it uttered.

BENEDICK: Like the old tale, my lord: 'it is not so, nor 'twas not so, but, indeed, God forbid it should be so.'

CLAUDIO: If my passion change not shortly, God forbid it should be otherwise.

DON PEDRO: Amen, if you love her; for the lady is very well worthy.

CLAUDIO: You speak this to fetch me in, my lord.

DON PEDRO: By my troth, I speak my thought.

CLAUDIO: And, in faith, my lord, I spoke mine.

BENEDICK: And, by my two faiths and troths, my lord, I spoke mine.

CLAUDIO: That I love her, I feel.

DON PEDRO: That she is worthy, I know.

BENEDICK: That I neither feel how she should be loved nor know how she should be worthy, is the opinion that fire cannot melt out of me; I will die in it at the stake.

DON PEDRO: Thou wast ever an obstinate heretic in the despite of beauty.

CLAUDIO: And never could maintain his part but in the force of his will.

BENEDICK: That a woman conceived me, I thank her; that she brought me up, I likewise give her most humble thanks; but that I will have a recheat winded in my forehead, or hang my bugle in an invisible baldrick, all women shall pardon me. Because I will not do them the wrong to mistrust any, I will do myself the right to trust none; and the fine is, for the which I may go the finer, I will live a bachelor.

DON PEDRO: I shall see thee, ere I die, look pale with love.

BENEDICK: With anger, with sickness, or with hunger, my lord, not with love. Prove that ever I lose more blood with love than I will get again with drinking, pick out mine eyes with a ballad-maker's pen and hang me up at the door of a brothel-house for the sign of blind Cupid.

DON PEDRO: Well, if ever thou dost fall from this faith, thou wilt prove a notable argument.

BENEDICK: If I do, hang me in a bottle like a cat and shoot at me; and he that hits me, let him be clapped on the shoulder, and called Adam.

DON PEDRO: Well, as time shall try. 'In time the savage bull doth bear the yoke.'

BENEDICK: The savage bull may; but if ever the sensible Benedick bear it, pluck off the bull's horns and set them in my forehead, and let me be vilely painted, and in such great letters as they write 'Here is good horse to hire,' let them signify under my sign 'Here you may see Benedick the married man.'

CLAUDIO: If this should ever happen, thou wouldst be horn-mad.

DON PEDRO: Nay, if Cupid have not spent all his quiver in Venice, thou wilt quake for this shortly.

BENEDICK: I look for an earthquake too, then.

DON PEDRO: Well, you will temporize with the hours. In the meantime, good Signior Benedick, repair to Leonato's; commend me to him and tell him I will not fail him at supper; for indeed he hath made great preparation.

BENEDICK: I have almost matter enough in me for such an embassage; and so I commit you—

CLAUDIO: To the tuition of God. From my house, if I had it—

DON PEDRO: The sixth of July: Your loving friend, Benedick.

BENEDICK: Nay, mock not, mock not. The body of your discourse is sometime guarded with fragments, and the guards are but slightly basted on neither; ere you flout old ends any further, examine your conscience; and so I leave you.

Exit

CLAUDIO: My liege, your highness now may do me good.

DON PEDRO: My love is thine to teach; teach it but how,
And thou shalt see how apt it is to learn
Any hard lesson that may do thee good.

CLAUDIO: Hath Leonato any son, my lord?

DON PEDRO: No child but Hero; she's his only heir.
Dost thou affect her, Claudio?

CLAUDIO: O, my lord,
When you went onward on this ended action,
I look'd upon her with a soldier's eye,
That liked, but had a rougher task in hand
Than to drive liking to the name of love;
But now I am return'd and that war-thoughts
Have left their places vacant, in their rooms
Come thronging soft and delicate desires,
All prompting me how fair young Hero is,
Saying, I liked her ere I went to wars.

DON PEDRO: Thou wilt be like a lover presently
And tire the hearer with a book of words.
If thou dost love fair Hero, cherish it,
And I will break with her and with her father,

And thou shalt have her. Was't not to this end
That thou began'st to twist so fine a story?

CLAUDIO: How sweetly you do minister to love,
That know love's grief by his complexion!
But lest my liking might too sudden seem,
I would have salved it with a longer treatise.

DON PEDRO: What need the bridge much broader than the flood?
The fairest grant is the necessity.
Look, what will serve is fit. 'Tis once, thou lovest,
And I will fit thee with the remedy.
I know we shall have revelling to-night;
I will assume thy part in some disguise
And tell fair Hero I am Claudio,
And in her bosom I'll unclasp my heart
And take her hearing prisoner with the force
And strong encounter of my amorous tale.
Then after to her father will I break;
And the conclusion is, she shall be thine.
In practise let us put it presently.

Exeunt

SCENE II—*Leonato's house*

Enter LEONATO and ANTONIO, meeting

LEONATO: How now, brother! Where is my cousin, your son? Hath he provided this music?

ANTONIO: He is very busy about it. But, brother, I can tell you strange news that you yet dreamt not of.

LEONATO: Are they good?

ANTONIO: As the event stamps them; but they have a good cover; they show well outward. The prince and Count Claudio, walking in a thick-pleached alley in mine orchard, were thus much overheard by a man of mine: the prince discovered to Claudio that he loved my niece your daughter and meant to acknowledge it this night in a dance; and if he found her accordant, he meant to take the present time by the top and instantly break with you of it.

LEONATO: Hath the fellow any wit that told you this?

ANTONIO: A good sharp fellow; I will send for him; and question him yourself.

LEONATO: No, no; we will hold it as a dream till it appear itself; but I will acquaint my daughter withal, that she may be the better prepared for an answer, if peradventure this be true. Go you and tell her of it.

Enter Attendants

Cousins, you know what you have to do. O, I cry you mercy, friend; go you with me, and I will use your skill. Good cousin, have a care this busy time.

Exeunt

SCENE III—*The same*

Enter DON JOHN and CONRADE

CONRADE: What the good-year, my lord! Why are you thus out of measure sad?

DON JOHN: There is no measure in the occasion that breeds; therefore the sadness is without limit.

CONRADE: You should hear reason.

DON JOHN: And when I have heard it, what blessing brings it?

CONRADE: If not a present remedy, at least a patient sufferance.

DON JOHN: I wonder that thou, being, as thou sayest thou art, born under Saturn, goest about to apply a moral medicine to a mortifying mischief. I cannot hide what I am; I must be sad when I have cause and smile at no man's jests, eat when I have stomach and wait for no man's leisure, sleep when I am drowsy, and tend on no man's business, laugh when I am merry, and claw no man in his humour.

CONRADE: Yea, but you must not make the full show of this till you may do it without controlment. You have of late stood out against your brother, and he hath ta'en you newly into his grace; where it is impossible you should take true root but by the fair weather that you make yourself: it is needful that you frame the season for your own harvest.

DON JOHN: I had rather be a canker in a hedge than a rose in his Grace; and it better fits my blood to be disdained of all than to fashion a carriage to rob love from any. In this, though I cannot be said to be a flattering honest man, it must not be denied but I am a plain-dealing villain. I am trusted with a muzzle and enfranchised with a clog; therefore I have decreed not to sing in my cage. If I had my mouth, I would bite; if I had my liberty, I would do my liking; in the meantime let me be that I am and seek not to alter me.

CONRADE: Can you make no use of your discontent?

DON JOHN: I make all use of it, for I use it only.
Who comes here?

Enter BORACHIO

What news, Borachio?

BORACHIO: I came yonder from a great supper. The prince your brother is royally entertained by Leonato; and I can give you intelligence of an intended marriage.

DON JOHN: Will it serve for any model to build mischief on? What is he for a fool that betroths himself to unquietness?

BORACHIO: Marry, it is your brother's right hand.

DON JOHN: Who? The most exquisite Claudio?

BORACHIO: Even he.

DON JOHN: A proper squire! And who, and who? which way looks he?

BORACHIO: Marry, on Hero, the daughter and heir of Leonato.

DON JOHN: A very forward March-chick! How came you to this?

BORACHIO: Being entertained for a perfumer, as I was smoking a musty room, comes me the prince and Claudio, hand in hand in sad conference. I whipt me behind the arras; and there heard it agreed upon that the prince should woo Hero for himself, and having obtained her, give her to Count Claudio.

DON JOHN: Come, come, let us thither; this may prove food to my displeasure; that young start-up hath all the glory of my overthrow. If I can cross him any way, I bless myself every way. You are both sure, and will assist me?

CONRADE: To the death, my lord.

DON JOHN: Let us to the great supper; their cheer is the greater that I am subdued. Would the cook were of my mind! Shall we go prove what's to be done?

BORACHIO: We'll wait upon your lordship.

Exeunt

ACT II

SCENE I—*A hall in Leonato's house*

Enter leonato, antonio, hero, beatrice, and Others

LEONATO: Was not Count John here at supper?

ANTONIO: I saw him not.

BEATRICE: How tartly that gentleman looks! I never can see him but I am heart-burned an hour after.

HERO: He is of a very melancholy disposition.

BEATRICE: He were an excellent man that were made just in the midway between him and Benedick: the one is too like an image and says nothing, and the other too like my lady's eldest son, evermore tattling.

LEONATO: Then half Signior Benedick's tongue in Count John's mouth, and half Count John's melancholy in Signior Benedick's face—

BEATRICE: With a good leg and a good foot, uncle, and money enough in his purse, such a man would win any woman in the world, if a' could get her good-will.

LEONATO: By my troth, niece, thou wilt never get thee a husband if thou be so shrewd of thy tongue.

ANTONIO: In faith, she's too curst.

BEATRICE: Too curst is more than curst. I shall lessen God's sending that way; for it is said, 'God sends a curst cow short horns;' but to a cow too curst he sends none.

LEONATO: So, by being too curst, God will send you no horns.

BEATRICE: Just, if he send me no husband; for the which blessing I am at him upon my knees every morning and evening. Lord, I could not endure a husband with a beard on his face; I had rather lie in the woollen.

LEONATO: You may light on a husband that hath no beard.

BEATRICE: What should I do with him? Dress him in my apparel, and make him my waiting gentlewoman? He that hath a beard is more than a youth, and he that hath no beard is less than a man; and he that is more than a youth is not for me, and he that is less than a man, I am not for him; therefore, I will even take sixpence in earnest of the bear-ward, and lead his apes into hell.

LEONATO: Well, then, go you into hell?

BEATRICE: No, but to the gate; and there will the devil meet me, like an old cuckold, with horns on his head, and say 'Get you to heaven, Beatrice, get you to heaven; here's no place for you maids'. So deliver I up my apes, and away to Saint Peter for the heavens; he shows me where the bachelors sit, and there live we as merry as the day is long.

ANTONIO: [*To Hero*] Well, niece, I trust you will be ruled by your father.

BEATRICE: Yes, faith; it is my cousin's duty to make curtsy and say 'Father, as it please you.' But yet for all that, cousin, let him be a handsome fellow, or else make another curtsy and say 'Father, as it please me.'

LEONATO: Well, niece, I hope to see you one day fitted with a husband.

BEATRICE: Not till God make men of some other metal than earth. Would it not grieve a woman to be overmastered with a pierce of valiant dust, to make an account of her life to a clod of wayward marl? No, uncle, I'll none: Adam's sons are my brethren; and, truly, I hold it a sin to match in my kindred.

LEONATO: Daughter, remember what I told you: if the prince do solicit you in that kind, you know your answer.

BEATRICE: The fault will be in the music, cousin, if you be not wooed in good time. If the prince be too important, tell him there is measure in every thing and so dance out the answer. For, hear me, Hero: wooing, wedding, and repenting, is as a Scotch jig, a measure, and a cinque pace; the first suit is hot and hasty, like a Scotch jig, and full as fantastical; the wedding, mannerly-modest, as a measure, full of state and ancientry; and then comes repentance and, with his bad legs, falls into the cinquepace faster and faster, till he sink into his grave.

LEONATO: Cousin, you apprehend passing shrewdly.

BEATRICE: I have a good eye, uncle; I can see a church by daylight.

LEONATO: The revellers are entering, brother; make good room.

All put on their masks

Enter DON PEDRO, CLAUDIO, BENEDICK, BALTHASAR, DON JOHN, BORACHIO, MARGARET, URSULA and others, masked

DON PEDRO: Lady, will you walk about with your friend?

HERO: So you walk softly and look sweetly and say nothing, I am yours for the walk; and especially when I walk away.

DON PEDRO: With me in your company?

HERO: I may say so, when I please.

DON PEDRO: And when please you to say so?

HERO: When I like your favour; for God defend the lute should be like the case!

DON PEDRO: My visor is Philemon's roof; within the house is Jove.

HERO: Why, then, your visor should be thatched.

DON PEDRO: Speak low, if you speak love.

Drawing her aside

BALTHASAR: Well, I would you did like me.

MARGARET: So would not I, for your own sake; for I have many ill-qualities.

BALTHASAR: Which is one?

MARGARET: I say my prayers aloud.

BALTHASAR: I love you the better; the hearers may cry, Amen.

MARGARET: God match me with a good dancer!

BALTHASAR: Amen.

MARGARET: And God keep him out of my sight when the dance is done! Answer, clerk.

BALTHASAR: No more words; the clerk is answered.

URSULA: I know you well enough; you are Signior Antonio.

ANTONIO: At a word, I am not.

URSULA: I know you by the waggling of your head.

ANTONIO: To tell you true, I counterfeit him.

URSULA: You could never do him so ill-well, unless you were the very man. Here's his dry hand up and down; you are he, you are he.

ANTONIO: At a word, I am not.

URSULA: Come, come, do you think I do not know you by your excellent wit? Can virtue hide itself? Go to, mum, you are he; graces will appear, and there's an end.

BEATRICE: Will you not tell me who told you so?

BENEDICK: No, you shall pardon me.

BEATRICE: Nor will you not tell me who you are?

BENEDICK: Not now.

BEATRICE: That I was disdainful, and that I had my good wit out of the 'Hundred Merry Tales'—well this was Signior Benedick that said so.

BENEDICK: What's he?

BEATRICE: I am sure you know him well enough.

BENEDICK: Not I, believe me.

BEATRICE: Did he never make you laugh?

BENEDICK: I pray you, what is he?

BEATRICE: Why, he is the Prince's jester, a very dull fool; only his gift is in devising impossible slanders; none but libertines delight in him, and the commendation is not in his wit but in his villany; for he both pleases men and angers them, and then they laugh at him and beat him. I am sure he is in the fleet; I would he had boarded me.

BENEDICK: When I know the gentleman, I'll tell him what you say.

BEATRICE: Do, do; he'll but break a comparison or two on me; which, peradventure, not marked, or not laughed at, strikes him into melancholy; and then there's a partridge wing saved, for the fool will eat no supper that night.

Music

We must follow the leaders.

BENEDICK: In every good thing.

BEATRICE: Nay, if they lead to any ill, I will leave them at the next turning.

Dance. Then exeunt all except DON JOHN, BORACHIO, and CLAUDIO

DON JOHN: Sure, my brother is amorous on Hero, and hath withdrawn her father to break with him about it. The ladies follow her, and but one visor remains.

BORACHIO: And that is Claudio; I know him by his bearing.

DON JOHN: Are not you Signior Benedick?

CLAUDIO: You know me well; I am he.

DON JOHN: Signior, you are very near my brother in his love; he is enamoured on Hero; I pray you, dissuade him from her; she is no equal for his birth. You may do the part of an honest man in it.

CLAUDIO: How know you he loves her?

DON JOHN: I heard him swear his affection.

BORACHIO: So did I too; and he swore he would marry her to-night.

DON JOHN: Come, let us to the banquet.

Exeunt DON JOHN and BORACHIO

CLAUDIO: Thus answer I in the name of Benedick,
But hear these ill news with the ears of Claudio.
'Tis certain so; the prince wooes for himself.
Friendship is constant in all other things
Save in the office and affairs of love;
Therefore, all hearts in love use their own tongues.
Let every eye negotiate for itself
And trust no agent; for beauty is a witch
Against whose charms faith melteth into blood.
This is an accident of hourly proof,
Which I mistrusted not. Farewell, therefore, Hero!

Re-enter BENEDICK

BENEDICK: Count Claudio?

CLAUDIO: Yea, the same.

BENEDICK: Come, will you go with me?

CLAUDIO: Whither?

BENEDICK: Even to the next willow, about your own business, county. What fashion will you wear the garland of? About your neck, like an usurer's chain, or under your arm, like a lieutenant's scarf? You must wear it one way, for the prince hath got your Hero.

CLAUDIO: I wish him joy of her.

BENEDICK: Why, that's spoken like an honest drovier; so they sell bullocks. But did you think the prince would have served you thus?

CLAUDIO: I pray you, leave me.

BENEDICK: Ho! now you strike like the blind man; 'twas the boy that stole your meat, and you'll beat the post.

CLAUDIO: If it will not be, I'll leave you.

Exit

BENEDICK: Alas, poor hurt fowl! Now will he creep into sedges. But that my Lady Beatrice should know me, and not know me! The prince's fool! Ha? It may be I go under that title because I am merry. Yea, but so I am apt to do myself wrong; I am not so reputed; it is the base, though bitter, disposition of Beatrice that puts the world into her person and so gives me out. Well, I'll be revenged as I may.

Re-enter DON PEDRO

DON PEDRO: Now, signior, where's the count? did you see him?

BENEDICK: Troth, my lord, I have played the part of Lady Fame. I found him here as melancholy as a lodge in a warren; I told him, and I think I told him true, that your grace had got the good will of this young lady; and I offered him my company to a willow-tree, either to make him a garland, as being forsaken, or to bind him up a rod, as being worthy to be whipped.

DON PEDRO: To be whipped! What's his fault?

BENEDICK: The flat transgression of a schoolboy, who, being overjoyed with finding a birds' nest, shows it his companion, and he steals it.

DON PEDRO: Wilt thou make a trust a transgression? The transgression is in the stealer.

BENEDICK: Yet it had not been amiss the rod had been made, and the garland too; for the garland he might have worn himself, and the rod he might have bestowed on you, who, as I take it, have stolen his birds' nest.

DON PEDRO: I will but teach them to sing, and restore them to the owner.

BENEDICK: If their singing answer your saying, by my faith, you say honestly.

DON PEDRO: The Lady Beatrice hath a quarrel to you; the gentleman that danced with her told her she is much wronged by you.

BENEDICK: O, she misused me past the endurance of a block! an oak but with one green leaf on it would have answered her; my very visor began to assume life and scold with her. She told me, not thinking I had been myself, that I was the prince's jester, that I was duller than a great thaw; huddling jest upon jest with such impossible conveyance upon me that I stood like a man at a mark, with a whole army shooting at me. She speaks poniards, and every word stabs; if her breath were as terrible as her terminations, there were no living near her; she would infect to the north star. I would not marry her, though she were endowed with all that Adam bad left him before he transgressed; she would have made Hercules have turned spit, yea, and have cleft his club to make the fire too. Come, talk not of her; you shall find her the infernal Ate in good apparel. I would to God some scholar would conjure her; for certainly, while she is here, a man may live as quiet in hell as in a sanctuary; and people sin upon purpose, because they would go thither; so, indeed, all disquiet, horror and perturbation, follows her.

DON PEDRO: Look, here she comes.

Enter CLAUDIO, BEATRICE, HERO, and LEONATO

BENEDICK: Will your grace command me any service to the world's end? I will go on the slightest errand now to the Antipodes that you can devise to send me on; I will fetch you a tooth-picker now from the furthest inch of Asia, bring you the length of Prester John's foot, fetch you a hair off the great Cham's beard, do you any embassage to the Pigmies, rather than hold three words' conference with this harpy. You have no employment for me?

DON PEDRO: None, but to desire your good company.

BENEDICK: O God, sir, here's a dish I love not; I cannot endure my Lady Tongue.

Exit

DON PEDRO: Come, lady, come; you have lost the heart of Signior Benedick.

BEATRICE: Indeed, my lord, he lent it me awhile; and I gave him use for it, a double heart for his single one; marry, once before he won it of me with false dice, therefore your grace may well say I have lost it.

DON PEDRO: You have put him down, lady, you have put him down.

BEATRICE: So I would not he should do me, my lord, lest I should prove the mother of fools. I have brought Count Claudio, whom you sent me to seek.

DON PEDRO: Why, how now, count! wherefore are you sad?

CLAUDIO: Not sad, my lord.

DON PEDRO: How then, sick?

CLAUDIO: Neither, my lord.

BEATRICE: The count is neither sad, nor sick, nor merry, nor well; but civil count, civil as an orange, and something of that jealous complexion.

DON PEDRO: I' faith, lady, I think your blazon to be true; though, I'll be sworn, if he be so, his conceit is false. Here, Claudio, I have wooed in thy name, and fair Hero is won. I have broke with her father, and his good will obtained. Name the day of marriage, and God give thee joy!

LEONATO: Count, take of me my daughter, and with her my fortunes; his grace hath made the match, and an grace say Amen to it.

BEATRICE: Speak, count, 'tis your cue.

CLAUDIO: Silence is the perfectest herald of joy: I were but little happy, if I could say how much. Lady, as you are mine, I am yours; I give away myself for you and dote upon the exchange.

BEATRICE: Speak, cousin; or, if you cannot, stop his mouth with a kiss, and let not him speak neither.

DON PEDRO: In faith, lady, you have a merry heart.

BEATRICE: Yea, my lord; I thank it, poor fool, it keeps on the windy side of care. My cousin tells him in his ear that he is in her heart.

CLAUDIO: And so she doth, cousin.

BEATRICE: Good Lord, for alliance! Thus goes every one to the world but I, and I am sunburnt; I may sit in a corner and cry heigh-ho for a husband!

DON PEDRO: Lady Beatrice, I will get you one.

BEATRICE: I would rather have one of your father's getting. Hath your grace ne'er a brother like you? Your father got excellent husbands, if a maid could come by them.

DON PEDRO: Will you have me, lady?

BEATRICE: No, my lord, unless I might have another for working-days; your grace is too costly to wear every day. But, I beseech your grace, pardon me; I was born to speak all mirth and no matter.

DON PEDRO: Your silence most offends me, and to be merry best becomes you; for, out of question, you were born in a merry hour.

BEATRICE: No, sure, my lord, my mother cried; but then there was a star danced, and under that was I born. Cousins, God give you joy!

LEONATO: Niece, will you look to those things I told you of?

BEATRICE: I cry your mercy, uncle. By your grace's pardon.

Exit

DON PEDRO: By my troth, a pleasant-spirited lady.

LEONATO: There's little of the melancholy element in her, my lord; she is never sad but when she sleeps, and not ever sad then; for I have heard my daughter say, she hath often dreamed of unhappiness and waked herself with laughing.

DON PEDRO: She cannot endure to hear tell of a husband.

LEONATO: O, by no means; she mocks all her wooers out of suit.

DON PEDRO: She were an excellent wife for Benedick.

LEONATO: O Lord, my lord, if they were but a week married, they would talk themselves mad.

DON PEDRO: County Claudio, when mean you to go to church?

CLAUDIO: To-morrow, my lord. Time goes on crutches till love have all his rites.

LEONATO: Not till Monday, my dear son, which is hence a just seven-night; and a time too brief, too, to have all things answer my mind.

DON PEDRO: Come, you shake the head at so long a breathing; but, I warrant thee, Claudio, the time shall not go dully by us. I will in the interim undertake one of Hercules' labours; which is, to bring Signior Benedick and the Lady Beatrice into a mountain of affection the one with the other. I would fain have it a match, and I doubt not but to fashion it, if you three will but minister such assistance as I shall give you direction.

LEONATO: My lord, I am for you, though it cost me ten nights' watchings.

CLAUDIO: And I, my lord.

DON PEDRO: And you too, gentle Hero?

HERO: I will do any modest office, my lord, to help my cousin to a good husband.

DON PEDRO: And Benedick is not the unhopefullest husband that I know. Thus far can I praise him; he is of a noble strain, of approved valour and confirmed honesty. I will teach you how to humour your cousin, that she shall fall in love with Benedick; and I, with your two helps, will so practise on Benedick that, in despite of his quick wit and his queasy stomach, he shall fall in love with Beatrice. If we can do this, Cupid is no longer an archer; his glory shall be ours, for we are the only love-gods. Go in with me, and I will tell you my drift.

Exeunt

SCENE II—*The same*

Enter DON JOHN and BORACHIO

DON JOHN: It is so; the Count Claudio shall marry the daughter of Leonato.

BORACHIO: Yea, my lord; but I can cross it.

DON JOHN: Any bar, any cross, any impediment will be medicinable to me. I am sick in displeasure to him, and whatsoever comes athwart his affection ranges evenly with mine. How canst thou cross this marriage?

BORACHIO: Not honestly, my lord; but so covertly that no dishonesty shall appear in me.

DON JOHN: Show me briefly how.

BORACHIO: I think I told your lordship a year since, how much I am in the favour of Margaret, the waiting gentlewoman to Hero.

DON JOHN: I remember.

BORACHIO: I can, at any unseasonable instant of the night, appoint her to look out at her lady's chamber window.

DON JOHN: What life is in that, to be the death of this marriage?

BORACHIO: The poison of that lies in you to temper. Go you to the prince your brother; spare not to tell him that he hath wronged his honour in marrying the renowned Claudio—whose estimation do you mightily hold up—to a contaminated stale, such a one as Hero.

DON JOHN: What proof shall I make of that?

BORACHIO: Proof enough to misuse the prince, to vex Claudio, to undo Hero and kill Leonato. Look you for any other issue?

DON JOHN: Only to despite them, I will endeavour any thing.

BORACHIO: Go, then; find me a meet hour to draw Don Pedro and the Count Claudio alone; tell them that you know that Hero loves me; intend a kind of zeal both to the prince and Claudio—as in love of your brother's honour, who hath made this match, and his friend's reputation, who is thus like to be cozened with the semblance of a maid—that you have discovered thus. They will scarcely believe this without trial; offer them instances; which shall bear no less likelihood than to see me at her chamber-window, hear me call Margaret Hero, hear Margaret term me Claudio; and bring them to see this the very night before the intended wedding—for in the meantime I will so fashion the matter that Hero shall be absent—and there shall appear such seeming truth of Hero's disloyalty that jealousy shall be called assurance and all the preparation overthrown.

DON JOHN: Grow this to what adverse issue it can, I will put it in practise. Be cunning in the working this, and thy fee is a thousand ducats.

BORACHIO: Be you constant in the accusation, and my cunning shall not shame me.

DON JOHN: I will presently go learn their day of marriage.

Exeunt

SCENE III—*Leonato's orchard*

Enter Benedick

BENEDICK: Boy!

Enter Boy

BOY: [*Within*] Signior?

BENEDICK: In my chamber-window lies a book: bring it hither to me in the orchard.

BOY: [*Above, at chamber window*] I am here already, sir.

BENEDICK: I know that; but I would have thee hence, and here again.

Exit Boy

I do much wonder that one man, seeing how much another man is a fool when he dedicates his behaviors to love, will, after he hath laughed at such shallow follies in others, become the argument of his own scorn by failing in love; and such a man is Claudio. I have known when there was no music with him but the drum and the fife; and now had he rather hear the tabour and the pipe; I have known when he would have walked ten mile afoot to see a good armour; and now will he lie ten nights awake, carving the fashion of a new doublet. He was wont to speak plain and to the purpose, like an honest man and a soldier; and now is he turned orthography; his words are a very fantastical banquet, just so many strange dishes. May I be so converted and see with these eyes? I cannot tell; I think not. I will not be sworn but love may transform me to an oyster; but I'll take my oath on it, till he have made an oyster of me he shall never make me such a fool. One woman is fair, yet I am well; another is wise, yet I am well; another virtuous, yet I am well; but till all graces be in one woman, one woman shall not come in my grace. Rich she shall be, that's certain; wise, or I'll none; virtuous, or I'll never cheapen her; fair, or I'll never look on her; mild, or come not near me; noble, or not I for an angel; of good discourse, an excellent musician, and her hair shall be of what colour it please God. Ha! the Prince and Monsieur Love! I will hide me in the arbour.

Withdraws

Enter DON PEDRO, CLAUDIO, and LEONATO

DON PEDRO: Come, shall we hear this music?

CLAUDIO: Yea, my good lord. How still the evening is,
As hush'd on purpose to grace harmony!

DON PEDRO: See you where Benedick hath hid himself?

CLAUDIO: O, very well, my lord; the music ended,
We'll fit the kid-fox with a pennyworth.

Enter BALTHASAR with Music

DON PEDRO: Come, Balthasar, we'll hear that song again.

BALTHASAR: O, good my lord, tax not so bad a voice
To slander music any more than once.

DON PEDRO: It is the witness still of excellency
To put a strange face on his own perfection.
I pray thee, sing, and let me woo no more.

BALTHASAR: Because you talk of wooing, I will sing;
Since many a wooer doth commence his suit
To her he thinks not worthy, yet he wooes,
Yet will he swear he loves.

DON PEDRO: Now, pray thee, come;
Or, if thou wilt hold longer argument,
Do it in notes.

BALTHASAR: Note this before my notes;
There's not a note of mine that's worth the noting.

DON PEDRO: Why, these are very crotchets that he speaks; Note, notes, forsooth, and nothing.

Air

BENEDICK: Now, divine air! now is his soul ravished! Is it not strange that sheeps' guts should hale souls out of men's bodies? Well, a horn for my money, when all's done.

The Song

BALTHASAR: Sigh no more, ladies, sigh no more,
Men were deceivers ever,
One foot in sea and one on shore,
To one thing constant never.
Then sigh not so, but let them go,
And be you blithe and bonny,
Converting all your sounds of woe
Into Hey nonny, nonny.
Sing no more ditties, sing no moe,
Of dumps so dull and heavy;
The fraud of men was ever so,
Since summer first was leafy.
Then sigh not so, & c.

DON PEDRO: By my troth, a good song.

BALTHASAR: And an ill singer, my lord.

DON PEDRO: Ha, no, no, faith; thou singest well enough for a shift.

BENEDICK: An he had been a dog that should have howled thus, they would have hanged him; and I pray God his bad voice bode no mischief. I had as lief have heard the night-raven, come what plague could have come after it.

DON PEDRO: Yea, marry, dost thou hear, Balthasar? I pray thee, get us some excellent music; for to-morrow night we would have it at the Lady Hero's chamber-window.

BALTHASAR: The best I can, my lord.

DON PEDRO: Do so; farewell.

Exit BALTHASAR

Come hither, Leonato. What was it you told me of to-day, that your niece Beatrice was in love with Signior Benedick?

CLAUDIO: O, ay; stalk on, stalk on; the fowl sits. I did never think that lady would have loved any man.

LEONATO: No, nor I neither; but most wonderful that she should so dote on Signior Benedick, whom she hath in all outward behaviors seemed ever to abhor.

BENEDICK: Is't possible? Sits the wind in that corner?

LEONATO: By my troth, my lord, I cannot tell what to think of it but that she loves him with an enraged affection: it is past the infinite of thought.

DON PEDRO: May be she doth but counterfeit.

CLAUDIO: Faith, like enough.

LEONATO: O God, counterfeit! There was never counterfeit of passion came so near the life of passion as she discovers it.

DON PEDRO: Why, what effects of passion shows she?

CLAUDIO: Bait the hook well; this fish will bite.

LEONATO: What effects, my lord? She will sit you, you heard my daughter tell you how.

CLAUDIO: She did, indeed.

DON PEDRO: How, how, I pray you? You amaze me: I would have I thought her spirit had been invincible against all assaults of affection.

LEONATO: I would have sworn it had, my lord; especially against Benedick.

BENEDICK: I should think this a gull, but that the white-bearded fellow speaks it; knavery cannot, sure, hide himself in such reverence.

CLAUDIO: He hath ta'en the infection; hold it up.

DON PEDRO: Hath she made her affection known to Benedick?

LEONATO: No; and swears she never will; that's her torment.

CLAUDIO: 'Tis true, indeed; so your daughter says. 'Shall I,' says she, 'that have so oft encountered him with scorn, write to him that I love him?'

LEONATO: This says she now when she is beginning to write to him; for she'll be up twenty times a night, and there will she sit in her smock till she have writ a sheet of paper. My daughter tells us all.

CLAUDIO: Now you talk of a sheet of paper, I remember a pretty jest your daughter told us of.

LEONATO: O, when she had writ it and was reading it over, she found Benedick and Beatrice between the sheet?

CLAUDIO: That.

LEONATO: O, she tore the letter into a thousand halfpence; railed at herself, that she should be so immodest to write to one that she knew would flout her; 'I measure him,' says she, 'by my own spirit; for I should flout him, if he writ to me; yea, though I love him, I should.'

CLAUDIO: Then down upon her knees she falls, weeps, sobs, beats her heart, tears her hair, prays, curses; 'O sweet Benedick! God give me patience!'

LEONATO: She doth indeed; my daughter says so; and the ecstasy hath so much overborne her that my daughter is sometime afeared she will do a desperate outrage to herself. It is very true.

DON PEDRO: It were good that Benedick knew of it by some other, if she will not discover it.

CLAUDIO: To what end? He would make but a sport of it and torment the poor lady worse.

DON PEDRO: An he should, it were an alms to hang him. She's an excellent sweet lady; and, out of all suspicion, she is virtuous.

CLAUDIO: And she is exceeding wise.

DON PEDRO: In everything but in loving Benedick.

LEONATO: O, my lord, wisdom and blood combating in so tender a body, we have ten proofs to one that blood hath the victory. I am sorry for her, as I have just cause, being her uncle and her guardian.

DON PEDRO: I would she had bestowed this dotage on me; I would have daffed all other respects and made her half myself. I pray you, tell Benedick of it, and hear what a' will say.

LEONATO: Were it good, think you?

CLAUDIO: Hero thinks surely she will die; for she says she will die, if he love her not, and she will die, ere she make her love known; and she will die if he woo her, rather than she will bate one breath of her accustomed crossness.

DON PEDRO: She doth well; if she should make tender of her love, 'tis very possible he'll scorn it; for the man, as you know all, hath a contemptible spirit.

CLAUDIO: He is a very proper man.

DON PEDRO: He hath, indeed, a good outward happiness.

CLAUDIO: Before God and in my mind, very wise!

DON PEDRO: He doth, indeed, show some sparks that are like wit.

CLAUDIO: And I take him to be valiant.

DON PEDRO: As Hector, I assure you; and in the managing of quarrels you may say he is wise, for either he avoids them with great discretion, or undertakes them with a most Christian-like fear.

LEONATO: If he do fear God, 'a must necessarily keep peace; if he break the peace, he ought to enter into a quarrel with fear and trembling.

DON PEDRO: And so will he do; for the man doth fear God, howsoever it seems not in him by some large jests he will make. Well I am sorry for your niece. Shall we go seek Benedick, and tell him of her love?

CLAUDIO: Never tell him, my lord; let her wear it out with good counsel.

LEONATO: Nay, that's impossible; she may wear her heart out first.

DON PEDRO: Well, we will hear further of it by your daughter; let it cool the while. I love Benedick well; and I could wish he would modestly examine himself, to see how much he is unworthy so good a lady.

LEONATO: My lord, will you walk? Dinner is ready.

CLAUDIO: If he do not dote on her upon this, I will never trust my expectation.

DON PEDRO: Let there be the same net spread for her; and that must your daughter and her gentlewomen carry. The sport will be when they hold one an opinion of another's dotage, and no such matter; that's the scene that I would see, which will be merely a dumb-show. Let us send her to call him in to dinner.

Exeunt DON PEDRO, CLAUDIO, and LEONATO

BENEDICK: [*Coming forward*] This can be no trick: the conference was sadly borne. They have the truth of this from Hero. They seem to pity the lady; it seems her affections have their full bent. Love me! why, it must be requited. I hear how I am censured: they say I will bear myself proudly, if I perceive the love come from her; they say too that she will rather die than give any sign of affection. I did never think to marry. I must not seem proud; happy are they that hear their detractions and can put them to mending. They say the lady is fair; 'tis a truth, I can bear them witness; and virtuous; 'tis so, I cannot reprove it; and wise, but for loving me; by my troth, it is no addition to her wit, nor no great argument of her folly, for I will be horribly in love with her. I may chance have some odd quirks and remnants of wit broken on me, because I have railed so long against marriage; but doth not the appetite alter? A man loves the meat in his youth that he cannot endure in his age. Shall quips and sentences and these paper bullets of the brain awe a man from the career of his humour? No, the world must be peopled. When I said I would die a bachelor, I did not think I should live till I were married. Here comes Beatrice. By this day! she's a fair lady; I do spy some marks of love in her.

Enter BEATRICE

BEATRICE: Against my will I am sent to bid you come in to dinner.

BENEDICK: Fair Beatrice, I thank you for your pains.

BEATRICE: I took no more pains for those thanks than you take pains to thank me; if it had been painful, I would not have come.

BENEDICK: You take pleasure then in the message?

BEATRICE: Yea, just so much as you may take upon a knife's point, and choke a daw withal. You have no stomach, signior; fare you well.

Exit

BENEDICK: Ha! 'Against my will I am sent to bid you come in to dinner;' there's a double meaning in that 'I took no more pains for those thanks than you took pains to thank me.'—that's as much as to say, Any pains that I take for you is as easy as thanks. If I do not take pity of her, I am a villain; if I do not love her, I am a Jew. I will go get her picture.

Exit

ACT III

SCENE I—*Leonato's garden*

Enter HERO, MARGARET, and URSULA

HERO: Good Margaret, run thee to the parlor;
There shalt thou find my cousin Beatrice
Proposing with the Prince and Claudio.
Whisper her ear, and tell her I and Ursula
Walk in the orchard, and our whole discourse
Is all of her; say that thou overheard'st us;
And bid her steal into the pleached bower,
Where honeysuckles, ripen'd by the sun,
Forbid the sun to enter—like favourites,
Made proud by princes, that advance their pride
Against that power that bred it. There will she hide her,
To listen our purpose. This is thy office;
Bear thee well in it, and leave us alone.

MARGARET: I'll make her come, I warrant you, presently.

Exit

HERO: Now, Ursula, when Beatrice doth come,
As we do trace this alley up and down,
Our talk must only be of Benedick.
When I do name him, let it be thy part
To praise him more than ever man did merit;
My talk to thee must be how Benedick
Is sick in love with Beatrice. Of this matter
Is little Cupid's crafty arrow made,
That only wounds by hearsay.

Enter BEATRICE, behind

Now begin;
For look where Beatrice, like a lapwing, runs
Close by the ground, to hear our conference.

URSULA: The pleasant'st angling is to see the fish
Cut with her golden oars the silver stream,
And greedily devour the treacherous bait.
So angle we for Beatrice; who even now
Is couched in the woodbine coverture.
Fear you not my part of the dialogue.

HERO: Then go we near her, that her ear lose nothing
Of the false sweet bait that we lay for it.

Approaching the bower

No, truly, Ursula, she is too disdainful;
I know her spirits are as coy and wild
As haggerds of the rock.

URSULA: But are you sure
That Benedick loves Beatrice so entirely?

HERO: So says the prince and my new-trothed lord.

URSULA: And did they bid you tell her of it, madam?

HERO: They did entreat me to acquaint her of it;
But I persuaded them, if they loved Benedick,
To wish him wrestle with affection,
And never to let Beatrice know of it.

URSULA: Why did you so? Doth not the gentleman
Deserve as full as fortunate a bed
As ever Beatrice shall couch upon?

HERO: O god of love! I know he doth deserve
As much as may be yielded to a man;
But Nature never framed a woman's heart
Of prouder stuff than that of Beatrice.
Disdain and scorn ride sparkling in her eyes,
Misprising what they look on, and her wit
Values itself so highly that to her
All matter else seems weak. She cannot love,
Nor take no shape nor project of affection,
She is so self-endeared.

URSULA: Sure, I think so;
And therefore certainly it were not good
She knew his love, lest she make sport at it.

HERO: Why, you speak truth. I never yet saw man,
How wise, how noble, young, how rarely featured,
But she would spell him backward. If fair-faced,
She would swear the gentleman should be her sister;

If black, why, Nature, drawing of an antique,
Made a foul blot; if tall, a lance ill-headed;
If low, an agate very vilely cut;
If speaking, why, a vane blown with all winds;
If silent, why, a block moved with none.
So turns she every man the wrong side out
And never gives to truth and virtue that
Which simpleness and merit purchaseth.

URSULA: Sure, sure, such carping is not commendable.

HERO: No, not to be so odd and from all fashions
As Beatrice is, cannot be commendable;
sBut who dare tell her so? If I should speak,
She would mock me into air; O, she would laugh me
Out of myself, press me to death with wit.
Therefore let Benedick, like cover'd fire,
Consume away in sighs, waste inwardly.
It were a better death than die with mocks,
Which is as bad as die with tickling.

URSULA: Yet tell her of it; hear what she will say.

HERO: No; rather I will go to Benedick
And counsel him to fight against his passion.
And, truly, I'll devise some honest slanders
To stain my cousin with. One doth not know
How much an ill word may empoison liking.

URSULA: O, do not do your cousin such a wrong.
She cannot be so much without true judgment—
Having so swift and excellent a wit
As she is prized to have—as to refuse
So rare a gentleman as Signior Benedick.

HERO: He is the only man of Italy.
Always excepted my dear Claudio.

URSULA: I pray you, be not angry with me, madam,
Speaking my fancy: Signior Benedick,
For shape, for bearing, argument and valour,
Goes foremost in report through Italy.

HERO: Indeed, he hath an excellent good name.

URSULA: His excellence did earn it, ere he had it.
When are you married, madam?

HERO: Why, every day, to-morrow. Come, go in;
I'll show thee some attires, and have thy counsel
Which is the best to furnish me to-morrow.

URSULA: She's limed, I warrant you; we have caught her, madam.

HERO: If it proves so, then loving goes by haps:
Some Cupid kills with arrows, some with traps.

Exeunt HERO and URSULA

BEATRICE: [Coming forward] What fire is in mine ears? Can this be true?
Stand I condemn'd for pride and scorn so much?
Contempt, farewell! and maiden pride, adieu!
No glory lives behind the back of such.
And, Benedick, love on; I will requite thee,
Taming my wild heart to thy loving hand;
If thou dost love, my kindness shall incite thee
To bind our loves up in a holy band;
For others say thou dost deserve, and I
Believe it better than reportingly.

Exit

SCENE II—*Leonato's house*

Enter DON PEDRO, CLAUDIO, BENEDICK, and LEONATO

DON PEDRO: I do but stay till your marriage be consummate, and then go I toward Arragon.

CLAUDIO: I'll bring you thither, my lord, if you'll vouchsafe me.

DON PEDRO: Nay, that would be as great a soil in the new gloss of your marriage as to show a child his new coat and forbid him to wear it. I will only be bold with Benedick for his company; for, from the crown of his head to the sole of his foot, he is all mirth; he hath twice or thrice cut Cupid's bow string and the little hangman dare not shoot at him; he hath a heart as sound as a bell and his tongue is the clapper, for what his heart thinks his tongue speaks.

BENEDICK: Gallants, I am not as I have been.

LEONATO: So say I methinks you are sadder.

CLAUDIO: I hope he be in love.

DON PEDRO: Hang him, truant! there's no true drop of blood in him, to be truly touched with love; if he be sad, he wants money.

BENEDICK: I have the toothache.

DON PEDRO: Draw it.

BENEDICK: Hang it!

CLAUDIO: You must hang it first, and draw it afterwards.

DON PEDRO: What! sigh for the toothache?

LEONATO: Where is but a humour or a worm.

BENEDICK: Well, every one can master a grief but he that has it.

CLAUDIO: Yet, say I, he is in love.

DON PEDRO: There is no appearance of fancy in him, unless it be a fancy that he hath to strange disguises; as, to be a Dutchman today, a Frenchman to-morrow, or in the shape of two countries at once, as, a German from the waist downward, all slops, and a Spaniard from the hip upward, no doublet. Unless he have a fancy to this foolery, as it appears he hath, he is no fool for fancy, as you would have it appear he is.

CLAUDIO: If he be not in love with some woman, there is no believing old signs: a' brushes his hat o' mornings; what should that bode?

DON PEDRO: Hath any man seen him at the barber's?

CLAUDIO: No, but the barber's man hath been seen with him, and the old ornament of his cheek hath already stuffed tennis-balls.

LEONATO: Indeed, he looks younger than he did, by the loss of a beard.

DON PEDRO: Nay, a' rubs himself with civet. Can you smell him out by that?

CLAUDIO: That's as much as to say, the sweet youth's in love.

DON PEDRO: The greatest note of it is his melancholy.

CLAUDIO: And when was he wont to wash his face?

DON PEDRO: Yea, or to paint himself? for the which, I hear what they say of him.

CLAUDIO: Nay, but his jesting spirit; which is now crept into a lute-string and now governed by stops.

DON PEDRO: Indeed, that tells a heavy tale for him; conclude, conclude he is in love.

CLAUDIO: Nay, but I know who loves him.

DON PEDRO: That would I know too; I warrant, one that knows him not.

CLAUDIO: Yes, and his ill conditions; and, in despite of all, dies for him.

DON PEDRO: She shall be buried with her face upwards.

BENEDICK: Yet is this no charm for the toothache. Old signior, walk aside with me; I have studied eight or nine wise words to speak to you, which these hobby-horses must not hear.

Exeunt BENEDICK and LEONATO

DON PEDRO: For my life, to break with him about Beatrice.

CLAUDIO: 'Tis even so. Hero and Margaret have by this played their parts with Beatrice; and then the two bears will not bite one another when they meet.

Enter DON JOHN

DON JOHN: My lord and brother, God save you!

DON PEDRO: Good den, brother.

DON JOHN: If your leisure served, I would speak with you.

DON PEDRO: In private?

DON JOHN: If it please you; yet Count Claudio may hear; for what I would speak of concerns him.

DON PEDRO: What's the matter?

DON JOHN: [*To CLAUDIO*] Means your lordship to be married to-morrow?

DON PEDRO: You know he does.

DON JOHN: I know not that, when he knows what I know.

CLAUDIO: If there be any impediment, I pray you discover it.

DON JOHN: You may think I love you not; let that appear hereafter, and aim better at me by that I now will manifest. For my brother, I think he holds you well, and in dearness of heart hath holp to effect your ensuing marriage—surely suit ill spent and labour ill bestowed.

DON PEDRO: Why, what's the matter?

DON JOHN: I came hither to tell you; and, circumstances shortened, for she has been too long a talking of, the lady is disloyal.

CLAUDIO: Who, Hero?

DON PEDRO: Even she; Leonato's Hero, your Hero, every man's Hero.

CLAUDIO: Disloyal?

DON JOHN: The word is too good to paint out her wickedness; I could say she were worse; think you of a worse title, and I will fit her to it. Wonder not till further warrant; go but with me to-night, you shall see her chamber-window entered, even the night before her wedding-day. If you love her then, to-morrow wed her; but it would better fit your honour to change your mind.

CLAUDIO: May this be so?

DON PEDRO: I will not think it.

DON JOHN: If you dare not trust that you see, confess not that you know. If you will follow me, I will show you enough; and when you have seen more and heard more, proceed accordingly.

CLAUDIO: If I see anything to-night why I should not marry her to-morrow in the congregation, where I should wed, there will I shame her.

DON PEDRO: And, as I wooed for thee to obtain her, I will join with thee to disgrace her.

DON JOHN: I will disparage her no farther till you are my witnesses; bear it coldly but till midnight, and let the issue show itself.

DON PEDRO: O day untowardly turned!

CLAUDIO: O mischief strangely thwarting!

DON JOHN: O plague right well prevented! So will you say when you have seen the sequel.

Exeunt

SCENE III—*A street*

Enter DOGBERRY and VERGES with the Watchman

DOGBERRY: Are you good men and true?

VERGES: Yea, or else it were pity but they should suffer salvation, body and soul.

DOGBERRY: Nay, that were a punishment too good for them, if they should have any allegiance in them, being chosen for the prince's watch.

VERGES: Well, give them their charge, neighbour Dogberry.

DOGBERRY: First, who think you the most desertless man to be constable?

FIRST WATCHMAN: Hugh Otecake, sir, or George Seacole; for they can write and read.

DOGBERRY: Come hither, neighbour Seacole. God hath blessed you with a good name. To be a well-favoured man is the gift of fortune; but to write and read comes by nature.

SECOND WATCHMAN: Both which, master constable—

DOGBERRY: You have; I knew it would be your answer. Well, for your favour, sir, why, give God thanks, and make no boast of it; and for your writing and reading, let that appear when there is no need of such vanity. You are thought here to be the most senseless and fit man for the constable of the watch; therefore bear you the lantern. This is your charge: you shall comprehend all vagrom men; you are to bid any man stand, in the prince's name.

SECOND WATCHMAN: How if a' will not stand?

DOGBERRY: Why, then, take no note of him, but let him go; and presently call the rest of the watch together and thank God you are rid of a knave.

VERGES: If he will not stand when he is bidden, he is none of the prince's subjects.

DOGBERRY: True, and they are to meddle with none but the prince's subjects. You shall also make no noise in the streets; for, for the watch to babble and to talk is most tolerable and not to be endured.

SECOND WATCHMAN: We will rather sleep than talk: we know what belongs to a watch.

DOGBERRY: Why, you speak like an ancient and most quiet watchman; for I cannot see how sleeping should offend: only, have a care that your bills be not stolen. Well, you are to call at all the ale-houses, and bid those that are drunk get them to bed.

SECOND WATCHMAN: How if they will not?

DOGBERRY: Why, then, let them alone till they are sober: if they make you not then the better answer, you may say they are not the men you took them for.

SECOND WATCHMAN: Well, sir.

DOGBERRY: If you meet a thief, you may suspect him, by virtue of your office, to be no true man; and, for such kind of men, the less you meddle or make with them, why the more is for your honesty.

SECOND WATCHMAN: If we know him to be a thief, shall we not lay hands on him?

DOGBERRY: Truly, by your office, you may; but I think they that touch pitch will be defiled; the most peaceable way for you, if you do take a thief, is to let him show himself what he is and steal out of your company.

VERGES: You have been always called a merciful man, partner.

DOGBERRY: Truly, I would not hang a dog by my will, much more a man who hath any honesty in him.

VERGES: If you hear a child cry in the night, you must call to the nurse and bid her still it.

SECOND WATCHMAN: How if the nurse be asleep and will not hear us?

DOGBERRY: Why, then, depart in peace, and let the child wake her with crying; for the ewe that will not hear her lamb when it baes will never answer a calf when he bleats.

VERGES: 'Tis very true.

DOGBERRY: This is the end of the charge: you, constable, are to present the prince's own person; if you meet the prince in the night, you may stay him.

VERGES: Nay, by'r our lady, that I think a' cannot.

DOGBERRY: Five shillings to one on't, with any man that knows the statutes, he may stay him; marry, not without the prince be willing; for, indeed, the watch ought to offend no man; and it is an offence to stay a man against his will.

VERGES: By'r lady, I think it be so.

DOGBERRY: Ha, ha, ha! Well, masters, good night; an there be any matter of weight chances, call up me; keep your fellows' counsels and your own; and good night. Come, neighbour.

SECOND WATCHMAN: Well, masters, we hear our charge; let us go sit here upon the church-bench till two, and then all to bed.

DOGBERRY: One word more, honest neighbours. I pray you watch about Signior Leonato's door; for the wedding being there to-morrow, there is a great coil to-night. Adieu; be vigitant, I beseech you.

Exeunt DOGBERRY and VERGES

Enter BORACHIO and CONRADE

BORACHIO: What Conrade!

SECOND WATCHMAN: [*Aside*] Peace! stir not.

BORACHIO: Conrade, I say!

CONRADE: Here, man; I am at thy elbow.

BORACHIO: Mass, and my elbow itched; I thought there would a scab follow.

CONRADE: I will owe thee an answer for that; and now forward with thy tale.

BORACHIO: Stand thee close, then, under this pent-house, for it drizzles rain; and I will, like a true drunkard, utter all to thee.

SECOND WATCHMAN: [*Aside*] Some treason, masters; yet stand close.

BORACHIO: Therefore know I have earned of Don John a thousand ducats.

CONRADE: Is it possible that any villany should be so dear?

BORACHIO: Thou shouldst rather ask if it were possible any villany should be so rich; for when rich villains have need of poor ones, poor ones may make what price they will.

CONRADE: I wonder at it.

BORACHIO: That shows thou art unconfirmed. Thou knowest that the fashion of a doublet, or a hat, or a cloak, is nothing to a man.

CONRADE: Yes, it is apparel.

BORACHIO: I mean, the fashion.

CONRADE: Yes, the fashion is the fashion.

BORACHIO: Tush! I may as well say the fool's the fool. But seest thou not what a deformed thief this fashion is?

SECOND WATCHMAN: [*Aside*] I know that Deformed; a' has been a vile thief this seven year; a' goes up and down like a gentleman; I remember his name.

BORACHIO: Didst thou not hear somebody?

CONRADE: No; 'twas the vane on the house.

BORACHIO: Seest thou not, I say, what a deformed thief this fashion is? how giddily a' turns about all the hot bloods between fourteen and five-and-thirty? sometimes fashioning them like Pharaoh's soldiers in the reeky painting, sometime like god Bel's priests in the old church-window, sometime like the shaven Hercules in the smirched worm-eaten tapestry, where his codpiece seems as massy as his club?

CONRADE: All this I see; and I see that the fashion wears out more apparel than the man. But art not thou thyself giddy with the fashion too, that thou hast shifted out of thy tale into telling me of the fashion?

BORACHIO: Not so, neither; but know that I have to-night wooed Margaret, the Lady Hero's gentlewoman, by the name of Hero; she leans me out at her mistress' chamber-window, bids me a thousand times good night—I tell this tale vilely. I should first tell thee how the prince, Claudio and my master, planted and placed and possessed by my master Don John, saw afar off in the orchard this amiable encounter.

CONRADE: And thought they Margaret was Hero?

BORACHIO: Two of them did, the prince and Claudio; but the devil my master knew she was Margaret; and partly by his oaths, which first possessed them, partly by the dark night, which did deceive them, but chiefly by my villany, which did confirm any slander that Don John had made, away went Claudio enraged; swore he would meet her, as he was appointed, next morning at the temple, and there, before the whole congregation, shame her with what he saw o'er night and send her home again without a husband.

SECOND WATCHMAN: We charge you, in the prince's name, stand!

FIRST WATCHMAN: Call up the right master constable. We have here recovered the most dangerous piece of lechery that ever was known in the commonwealth.

SECOND WATCHMAN: And one Deformed is one of them; I know him; a' wears a lock.
CONRADE: Masters, masters!
SECOND WATCHMAN: You'll be made bring Deformed forth, I warrant you.
CONRADE: Masters—
FIRST WATCHMAN: Never speak, we charge you let us obey you to go with us.
BORACHIO: We are like to prove a goodly commodity, being taken up of these men's bills.
CONRADE: A commodity in question, I warrant you. Come, we'll obey you.

Exeunt

SCENE IV—*Hero's apartment*

Enter HERO, MARGARET, and URSULA

HERO: Good Ursula, wake my cousin Beatrice, and desire her to rise.
URSULA: I will, lady.
HERO: And bid her come hither.
URSULA: Well.

Exit URSULA

MARGARET: Troth, I think your other rabato were better.
HERO: No, pray thee, good Meg, I'll wear this.
MARGARET: By my troth's not so good; and I warrant your cousin will say so.
HERO: My cousin's a fool, and thou art another; I'll wear none but this.
MARGARET: I like the new tire within excellently, if the hair were a thought browner; and your gown's a most rare fashion, i' faith. I saw the Duchess of Milan's gown that they praise so.
HERO: O, that exceeds, they say.
MARGARET: By my troth's but a night-gown in respect of yours: cloth o' gold, and cuts, and laced with silver, set with pearls, down sleeves, side sleeves, and skirts, round underborne with a bluish tinsel; but for a fine, quaint, graceful and excellent fashion, yours is worth ten on 't.
HERO: God give me joy to wear it! for my heart is exceeding heavy.
MARGARET: 'Twill be heavier soon by the weight of a man.
HERO: Fie upon thee! art not ashamed?
MARGARET: Of what, lady, of speaking honourably? Is not marriage honourable in a beggar? Is not your lord honourable without marriage? I think you would have me say, 'saving your reverence, a husband;' and bad thinking do not wrest true speaking, I'll offend nobody. Is there any harm in 'the heavier for a husband'? None, I think, and it be the right husband and the right wife; otherwise 'tis light, and not heavy. Ask my Lady Beatrice else; here she comes.

Enter BEATRICE

HERO: Good morrow, coz.
BEATRICE: Good morrow, sweet Hero.
HERO: Why how now? do you speak in the sick tune?
BEATRICE: I am out of all other tune, methinks.
MARGARET: Clap's into 'Light o' love;' that goes without a burden. Do you sing it, and I'll dance it.
BEATRICE: Ye light o' love, with your heels! then, if your husband have stables enough, you'll see he shall lack no barns.
MARGARET: O illegitimate construction! I scorn that with my heels.
BEATRICE: 'Tis almost five o'clock, cousin; 'tis time you were ready. By my troth, I am exceeding ill. Heigh-ho!
MARGARET: For a hawk, a horse, or a husband?
BEATRICE: For the letter that begins them all, H.
MARGARET: Well, and you be not turned Turk, there's no more sailing by the star.
BEATRICE: What means the fool, trow?
MARGARET: Nothing I; but God send every one their heart's desire!
HERO: These gloves the count sent me; they are an excellent perfume.
BEATRICE: I am stuffed, cousin; I cannot smell.
MARGARET: A maid, and stuffed! there's goodly catching of cold.
BEATRICE: O, God help me! God help me! how long have you professed apprehension?
MARGARET: Even since you left it. Doth not my wit become me rarely?
BEATRICE: It is not seen enough, you should wear it in your cap. By my troth, I am sick.
MARGARET: Get you some of this distilled Carduus Benedictus, and lay it to your heart; it is the only thing for a qualm.
HERO: There thou prickest her with a thistle.
BEATRICE: Benedictus! why Benedictus? You have some moral in this Benedictus.
MARGARET: Moral! No, by my troth, I have no moral meaning; I meant, plain holy-thistle. You may think perchance that I think you are in love.

Nay, by'r lady, I am not such a fool to think what I list, nor I list not to think what I can, nor indeed I cannot think, if I would think my heart out of thinking, that you are in love or that you will be in love or that you can be in love. Yet Benedick was such another, and now is he become a man; he swore he would never marry, and yet now, in despite of his heart, he eats his meat without grudging. And how you may be converted I know not, but methinks you look with your eyes as other women do.

BEATRICE: What pace is this that thy tongue keeps?

MARGARET: Not a false gallop.

Re-enter URSULA

URSULA: Madam, withdraw; the prince, the count, Signior Benedick, Don John, and all the gallants of the town, are come to fetch you to church.

HERO: Help to dress me, good coz, good Meg, good Ursula.

Exeunt

SCENE V—*Leonato's house*

Enter LEONATO, with DOGBERRY and VERGES

LEONATO: What would you with me, honest neighbour?

DOGBERRY: Marry, sir, I would have some confidence with you that decerns you nearly.

LEONATO: Brief, I pray you; for you see it is a busy time with me.

DOGBERRY: Marry, this it is, sir.

VERGES: Yes, in truth it is, sir.

LEONATO: What is it, my good friends?

DOGBERRY: Goodman Verges, sir, speaks a little off the matter: an old man, sir, and his wits are not so blunt as, God help, I would desire they were; but, in faith, honest as the skin between his brows.

VERGES: Yes, I thank God I am as honest as any man living that is an old man and no honester than I.

DOGBERRY: Comparisons are odorous; palabras, neighbour Verges.

LEONATO: Neighbours, you are tedious.

DOGBERRY: It pleases your worship to say so, but we are the poor duke's officers; but truly, for mine own part, if I were as tedious as a king, I could find it in my heart to bestow it all of your worship.

LEONATO: All thy tediousness on me, ah?

DOGBERRY: Yea, an 'twere a thousand pound more than 'tis; for I hear as good exclamation on your worship as of any man in the city; and though I be but a poor man, I am glad to hear it.

VERGES: And so am I.

LEONATO: I would fain know what you have to say.

VERGES: Marry, sir, our watch to-night, excepting your worship's presence, ha' ta'en a couple of as arrant knaves as any in Messina.

DOGBERRY: A good old man, sir; he will be talking; as they say, when the age is in, the wit is out. God help us! it is a world to see. Well said, i' faith, neighbour Verges; well, God's a good man; an two men ride of a horse, one must ride behind. An honest soul, i' faith, sir; by my troth he is, as ever broke bread; but God is to be worshipped; all men are not alike; alas, good neighbour!

LEONATO: Indeed, neighbour, he comes too short of you.

DOGBERRY: Gifts that God gives.

LEONATO: I must leave you.

DOGBERRY: One word, sir: our watch, sir, have indeed comprehended two aspicious persons, and we would have them this morning examined before your worship.

LEONATO: Take their examination yourself and bring it me; I am now in great haste, as it may appear unto you.

DOGBERRY: It shall be suffigance.

LEONATO: Drink some wine ere you go; fare you well.

Enter a Messenger

MESSENGER: My lord, they stay for you to give your daughter to her husband.

LEONATO: I'll wait upon them; I am ready.

Exeunt LEONATO and Messenger

DOGBERRY: Go, good partner, go, get you to Francis Seacole; bid him bring his pen and inkhorn to the gaol; we are now to examination these men.

VERGES: And we must do it wisely.

DOGBERRY: We will spare for no wit, I warrant you; here's that shall drive some of them to a non-come; only get the learned writer to set down our excommunication and meet me at the gaol.

Exeunt

ACT IV

SCENE I—*A church*

Enter DON PEDRO, DON JOHN, LEONATO, FRIAR FRANCIS, CLAUDIO, BENEDICK, HERO, BEATRICE, and Attendants

LEONATO: Come, Friar Francis, be brief; only to the plain form of marriage, and you shall recount their particular duties afterwards.

FRIAR FRANCIS: You come hither, my lord, to marry this lady.

CLAUDIO: No.

LEONATO: To be married to her, friar, you come to marry her.

FRIAR FRANCIS: Lady, you come hither to be married to this count.

HERO: I do.

FRIAR FRANCIS: If either of you know any inward impediment why you should not be conjoined, charge you, on your souls, to utter it.

CLAUDIO: Know you any, Hero?

HERO: None, my lord.

FRIAR FRANCIS: Know you any, count?

LEONATO: I dare make his answer, none.

CLAUDIO: O, what men dare do! what men may do! What men daily do, not knowing what they do!

BENEDICK: How now! interjections? Why, then, some be of laughing, as, ah, ha, he!

CLAUDIO: Stand thee by, friar. Father, by your leave:
Will you with free and unconstrained soul
Give me this maid, your daughter?

LEONATO: As freely, son, as God did give her me.

CLAUDIO: And what have I to give you back, whose worth
May counterpoise this rich and precious gift?

DON PEDRO: Nothing, unless you render her again.

CLAUDIO: Sweet prince, you learn me noble thankfulness.
There, Leonato, take her back again;
Give not this rotten orange to your friend;
She's but the sign and semblance of her honour.
Behold how like a maid she blushes here!
O, what authority and show of truth
Can cunning sin cover itself withal!
Comes not that blood as modest evidence
To witness simple virtue? Would you not swear,
All you that see her, that she were a maid,
By these exterior shows? But she is none:
She knows the heat of a luxurious bed;
Her blush is guiltiness, not modesty.

LEONATO: What do you mean, my lord?

CLAUDIO: Not to be married,
Not to knit my soul to an approved wanton.

LEONATO: Dear my lord, if you, in your own proof,
Have vanquish'd the resistance of her youth,
And made defeat of her virginity—

CLAUDIO: I know what you would say. If I have known her,
You will say she did embrace me as a husband,
And so extenuate the 'forehand sin.
No, Leonato,
I never tempted her with word too large;
But, as a brother to his sister, show'd
Bashful sincerity and comely love.

HERO: And seem'd I ever otherwise to you?

CLAUDIO: Out on thee! Seeming! I will write against it.
You seem to me as Dian in her orb,
As chaste as is the bud ere it be blown;
But you are more intemperate in your blood
Than Venus, or those pamper'd animals
That rage in savage sensuality.

HERO: Is my lord well, that he doth speak so wide?

LEONATO: Sweet prince, why speak not you?

DON PEDRO: What should I speak?
I stand dishonour'd, that have gone about
To link my dear friend to a common stale.

LEONATO: Are these things spoken, or do I but dream?

DON JOHN: Sir, they are spoken, and these things are true.

BENEDICK: This looks not like a nuptial.

HERO: True! O God!

CLAUDIO: Leonato, stand I here?
Is this the prince? is this the prince's brother?
Is this face Hero's? Are our eyes our own?

LEONATO: All this is so; but what of this, my lord?

CLAUDIO: Let me but move one question to your daughter;
And, by that fatherly and kindly power
That you have in her, bid her answer truly.

LEONATO: I charge thee do so, as thou art my child.

HERO: O, God defend me! how am I beset!
What kind of catechising call you this?

CLAUDIO: To make you answer truly to your name.

HERO: Is it not Hero? Who can blot that name
With any just reproach?

CLAUDIO: Marry, that can Hero;
Hero itself can blot out Hero's virtue.
What man was he talk'd with you yesternight
Out at your window betwixt twelve and one?
Now, if you are a maid, answer to this.

HERO: I talk'd with no man at that hour, my lord.

DON PEDRO: Why, then are you no maiden. Leonato,
I am sorry you must hear: upon mine honour,
Myself, my brother and this grieved count
Did see her, hear her, at that hour last night
Talk with a ruffian at her chamber-window
Who hath indeed, most like a liberal villain,
Confess'd the vile encounters they have had
A thousand times in secret.

DON JOHN: Fie, fie! they are not to be named, my lord,
Not to be spoke of;
There is not chastity enough in language
Without offence to utter them. Thus, pretty lady,
I am sorry for thy much misgovernment.

CLAUDIO: O Hero, what a Hero hadst thou been,
If half thy outward graces had been placed
About thy thoughts and counsels of thy heart!
But fare thee well, most foul, most fair! farewell,
Thou pure impiety and impious purity!
For thee I'll lock up all the gates of love,
And on my eyelids shall conjecture hang,
To turn all beauty into thoughts of harm,
And never shall it more be gracious.

LEONATO: Hath no man's dagger here a point for me?

HERO swoons

BEATRICE: Why, how now, cousin! wherefore sink you down?

DON JOHN: Come, let us go. These things, come thus to light,
Smother her spirits up.

Exeunt DON PEDRO, DON JOHN, and CLAUDIO

BENEDICK: How doth the lady?

BEATRICE: Dead, I think. Help, uncle!
Hero! why, Hero! Uncle! Signior Benedick! Friar!

LEONATO: O Fate! take not away thy heavy hand.
Death is the fairest cover for her shame
That may be wish'd for.

BEATRICE: How now, cousin Hero!

FRIAR FRANCIS: Have comfort, lady.

LEONATO: Dost thou look up?

FRIAR FRANCIS: Yea, wherefore should she not?

LEONATO: Wherefore! Why, doth not every earthly thing
Cry shame upon her? Could she here deny
The story that is printed in her blood?
Do not live, Hero; do not ope thine eyes;
For, did I think thou wouldst not quickly die,
Thought I thy spirits were stronger than thy shames,
Myself would, on the rearward of reproaches,
Strike at thy life. Grieved I, I had but one?
Chid I for that at frugal nature's frame?
O, one too much by thee! Why had I one?
Why ever wast thou lovely in my eyes?
Why had I not with charitable hand
Took up a beggar's issue at my gates,
Who smirch'd thus and mired with infamy,
I might have said 'No part of it is mine;
This shame derives itself from unknown loins'?
But mine and mine I loved and mine I praised
And mine that I was proud on, mine so much
That I myself was to myself not mine,
Valuing of her—why, she, O, she is fallen
Into a pit of ink, that the wide sea
Hath drops too few to wash her clean again
And salt too little which may season give
To her foul-tainted flesh!

BENEDICK: Sir, sir, be patient.
For my part, I am so attired in wonder,
I know not what to say.
BEATRICE: O, on my soul, my cousin is belied!
BENEDICK: Lady, were you her bedfellow last night?
BEATRICE: No, truly not; although, until last night,
I have this twelvemonth been her bedfellow.
LEONATO: Confirm'd, confirm'd! O, that is stronger made
Which was before barr'd up with ribs of iron!
Would the two princes lie, and Claudio lie,
Who loved her so, that, speaking of her foulness,
Wash'd it with tears? Hence from her! let her die.
FRIAR FRANCIS: Hear me a little; for I have only been
Silent so long and given way unto
This course of fortune.
By noting of the lady I have mark'd
A thousand blushing apparitions
To start into her face, a thousand innocent shames
In angel whiteness beat away those blushes;
And in her eye there hath appear'd a fire,
To burn the errors that these princes hold
Against her maiden truth. Call me a fool;
Trust not my reading nor my observations,
Which with experimental seal doth warrant
The tenor of my book; trust not my age,
My reverence, calling, nor divinity,
If this sweet lady lie not guiltless here
Under some biting error.
LEONATO: Friar, it cannot be.
Thou seest that all the grace that she hath left
Is that she will not add to her damnation
A sin of perjury; she not denies it.
Why seek'st thou then to cover with excuse
That which appears in proper nakedness?
FRIAR FRANCIS: Lady, what man is he you are accused of?
HERO: They know that do accuse me; I know none.
If I know more of any man alive
Than that which maiden modesty doth warrant,
Let all my sins lack mercy! O my father,
Prove you that any man with me conversed
At hours unmeet, or that I yesternight
Maintain'd the change of words with any creature,
Refuse me, hate me, torture me to death!
FRIAR FRANCIS: There is some strange misprision in the princes.
BENEDICK: Two of them have the very bent of honour;
And if their wisdoms be misled in this,
The practise of it lives in John the bastard,
Whose spirits toil in frame of villanies.
LEONATO: I know not. If they speak but truth of her,
These hands shall tear her; if they wrong her honour,
The proudest of them shall well hear of it.
Time hath not yet so dried this blood of mine,
Nor age so eat up my invention,
Nor fortune made such havoc of my means,
Nor my bad life reft me so much of friends,
But they shall find, awaked in such a kind,
Both strength of limb and policy of mind,
Ability in means and choice of friends,
To quit me of them throughly.
FRIAR FRANCIS: Pause awhile,
And let my counsel sway you in this case.
Your daughter here the princes left for dead;
Let her awhile be secretly kept in,
And publish it that she is dead indeed;
Maintain a mourning ostentation
And on your family's old monument
Hang mournful epitaphs and do all rites
That appertain unto a burial.
LEONATO: What shall become of this? What will this do?
FRIAR FRANCIS: Marry, this well carried shall on her behalf
Change slander to remorse; that is some good.
But not for that dream I on this strange course,
But on this travail look for greater birth.
She dying, as it must so be maintain'd,
Upon the instant that she was accused,
Shall be lamented, pitied and excused
Of every hearer; for it so falls out
That what we have we prize not to the wort
Whiles we enjoy it, but being lack'd and lost,
Why, then we rack the value, then we find
The virtue that possession would not show us
Whiles it was ours. So will it fare with Claudio.
When he shall hear she died upon his words,

The idea of her life shall sweetly creep
Into his study of imagination,
And every lovely organ of her life
Shall come apparell'd in more precious habit,
More moving-delicate and full of life,
Into the eye and prospect of his soul,
Than when she lived indeed; then shall he mourn,
If ever love had interest in his liver,
And wish he had not so accused her,
No, though he thought his accusation true.
Let this be so, and doubt not but success
Will fashion the event in better shape
Than I can lay it down in likelihood.
But if all aim but this be levell'd false,
The supposition of the lady's death
Will quench the wonder of her infamy.
And if it sort not well, you may conceal her,
As best befits her wounded reputation,
In some reclusive and religious life,
Out of all eyes, tongues, minds and injuries.

BENEDICK: Signior Leonato, let the friar advise you;
And though you know my inwardness and love
Is very much unto the prince and Claudio,
Yet, by mine honour, I will deal in this
As secretly and justly as your soul
Should with your body.

LEONATO: Being that I flow in grief,
The smallest twine may lead me.

FRIAR FRANCIS: 'Tis well consented: presently away;
For to strange sores strangely they strain the cure.
Come, lady, die to live; this wedding-day
Perhaps is but prolong'd; have patience and endure.

Exeunt all but BENEDICK and BEATRICE

BENEDICK: Lady Beatrice, have you wept all this while?

BEATRICE: Yea, and I will weep a while longer.

BENEDICK: I will not desire that.

BEATRICE: You have no reason; I do it freely.

BENEDICK: Surely I do believe your fair cousin is wronged.

BEATRICE: Ah, how much might the man deserve of me that would right her!

BENEDICK: Is there any way to show such friendship?

BEATRICE: A very even way, but no such friend.

BENEDICK: May a man do it?

BEATRICE: It is a man's office, but not yours.

BENEDICK: I do love nothing in the world so well as you. Is not that strange?

BEATRICE: As strange as the thing I know not. It were as possible for me to say I loved nothing so well as you; but believe me not; and yet I lie not; I confess nothing, nor I deny nothing. I am sorry for my cousin.

BENEDICK: By my sword, Beatrice, thou lovest me.

BEATRICE: Do not swear, and eat it.

BENEDICK: I will swear by it that you love me; and I will make him eat it that says I love not you.

BEATRICE: Will you not eat your word?

BENEDICK: With no sauce that can be devised to it. I protest I love thee.

BEATRICE: Why, then, God forgive me!

BENEDICK: What offence, sweet Beatrice?

BEATRICE: You have stayed me in a happy hour; I was about to protest I loved you.

BENEDICK: And do it with all thy heart.

BEATRICE: I love you with so much of my heart that none is left to protest.

BENEDICK: Come, bid me do any thing for thee.

BEATRICE: Kill Claudio.

BENEDICK: Ha! not for the wide world.

BEATRICE: You kill me to deny it. Farewell.

BENEDICK: Tarry, sweet Beatrice.

BEATRICE: I am gone, though I am here; there is no love in you; nay, I pray you, let me go.

BENEDICK: Beatrice—

BEATRICE: In faith, I will go.

BENEDICK: We'll be friends first.

BEATRICE: You dare easier be friends with me than fight with mine enemy.

BENEDICK: Is Claudio thine enemy?

BEATRICE: Is he not approved in the height a villain, that hath slandered, scorned, dishonoured my kinswoman? O that I were a man! What, bear her in hand until they come to take hands; and then, with public accusation, uncovered slander, unmitigated rancour—O God, that I were a man! I would eat his heart in the market-place.

BENEDICK: Hear me, Beatrice.

BEATRICE: Talk with a man out at a window! A proper saying!

BENEDICK: Nay, but, Beatrice—

BEATRICE: Sweet Hero! She is wronged, she is slandered, she is undone.

BENEDICK: Beat—

BEATRICE: Princes and counties! Surely, a princely testimony, a goodly count, Count Comfect; a sweet gallant, surely! O that I were a man for his sake! or that I had any friend would be a man for my sake! But manhood is melted into courtesies, valour into compliment, and men are only turned into tongue, and trim ones too. He is now as valiant as Hercules that only tells a lie and swears it. I cannot be a man with wishing, therefore I will die a woman with grieving.

BENEDICK: Tarry, good Beatrice. By this hand, I love thee.

BEATRICE: Use it for my love some other way than swearing by it.

BENEDICK: Think you in your soul the Count Claudio hath wronged Hero?

BEATRICE: Yea, as sure as I have a thought or a soul.

BENEDICK: Enough, I am engaged; I will challenge him. I will kiss your hand, and so I leave you. By this hand, Claudio shall render me a dear account. As you hear of me, so think of me. Go, comfort your cousin; I must say she is dead; and so, farewell.

Exeunt

SCENE II—*A prison*

Enter DOGBERRY, VERGES, and Sexton, in gowns; and the Watchman with CONRADE and BORACHIO

DOGBERRY: Is our whole dissembly appeared?

VERGES: O, a stool and a cushion for the sexton.

SEXTON: Which be the malefactors?

DOGBERRY: Marry, that am I and my partner.

VERGES: Nay, that's certain; we have the exhibition to examine.

SEXTON: But which are the offenders that are to be examined? Let them come before master constable.

DOGBERRY: Yea, marry, let them come before me. What is your name, friend?

BORACHIO: Borachio.

DOGBERRY: Pray, write down, Borachio. Yours, sirrah?

CONRADE: I am a gentleman, sir, and my name is Conrade.

DOGBERRY: Write down, master gentleman Conrade. Masters, do you serve God?

CONRADE BORACHIO: Yea, sir, we hope.

DOGBERRY: Write down, that they hope they serve God; and write God first; for God defend but God should go before such villains! Masters, it is proved already that you are little better than false knaves; and it will go near to be thought so shortly. How answer you for yourselves?

CONRADE: Marry, sir, we say we are none.

DOGBERRY: A marvellous witty fellow, I assure you; but I will go about with him. Come you hither, sirrah; a word in your ear: sir, I say to you, it is thought you are false knaves.

BORACHIO: Sir, I say to you we are none.

DOGBERRY: Well, stand aside. Fore God, they are both in a tale. Have you writ down, that they are none?

SEXTON: Master constable, you go not the way to examine; you must call forth the watch that are their accusers.

DOGBERRY: Yea, marry, that's the eftest way. Let the watch come forth. Masters, I charge you, in the prince's name, accuse these men.

FIRST WATCHMAN: This man said, sir, that Don John, the prince's brother, was a villain.

DOGBERRY: Write down Prince John a villain. Why, this is flat perjury, to call a prince's brother villain.

BORACHIO: Master constable—

DOGBERRY: Pray thee, fellow, peace; I do not like thy look, I promise thee.

SEXTON: What heard you him say else?

SECOND WATCHMAN: Marry, that he had received a thousand ducats of Don John for accusing the Lady Hero wrongfully.

DOGBERRY: Flat burglary as ever was committed.

VERGES: Yea, by mass, that it is.

SEXTON: What else, fellow?

FIRST WATCHMAN: And that Count Claudio did mean, upon his words, to disgrace Hero before the whole assembly, and not marry her.

DOGBERRY: O villain! thou wilt be condemned into everlasting redemption for this.

SEXTON: What else?

SECOND WATCHMAN: This is all.

SEXTON: And this is more, masters, than you can deny. Prince John is this morning secretly stolen away; Hero was in this manner accused, in this very manner refused, and upon the grief of this suddenly died. Master constable, let these men be bound, and brought to Leonato's; I will go before and show him their examination.

Exit

DOGBERRY: Come, let them be opinioned.

VERGES: Let them be in the hands.

CONRADE: Off, coxcomb!

DOGBERRY: God's my life, where's the sexton? Let him write down the prince's officer coxcomb. Come, bind them. Thou naughty varlet!

CONRADE: Away! you are an ass, you are an ass.

DOGBERRY: Dost thou not suspect my place? Dost thou not suspect my years? O that he were here to write me down an ass! But, masters, remember that I am an ass; though it be not written down, yet forget not that I am an ass. No, thou villain, thou art full of piety, as shall be proved upon thee by good witness. I am a wise fellow, and, which is more, an officer, and, which is more, a householder, and, which is more, as pretty a piece of flesh as any is in Messina, and one that knows the law, go to; and a rich fellow enough, go to; and a fellow that hath had losses, and one that hath two gowns and every thing handsome about him. Bring him away. O that I had been writ down an ass!

Exeunt

Act V

Scene I—*Leonato's house*

Enter LEONATO and ANTONIO

ANTONIO: If you go on thus, you will kill yourself,
And 'tis not wisdom thus to second grief
Against yourself.
LEONATO: I pray thee, cease thy counsel,
Which falls into mine ears as profitless
As water in a sieve. Give not me counsel;
Nor let no comforter delight mine ear
But such a one whose wrongs do suit with mine.
Bring me a father that so loved his child,
Whose joy of her is overwhelm'd like mine,
And bid him speak of patience;
Measure his woe the length and breadth of mine
And let it answer every strain for strain,
As thus for thus and such a grief for such,
In every lineament, branch, shape, and form.
If such a one will smile and stroke his beard,
Bid sorrow wag, cry 'hem!' when he should groan,
Patch grief with proverbs, make misfortune drunk
With candle-wasters; bring him yet to me,
And I of him will gather patience.
But there is no such man; for, brother, men
Can counsel and speak comfort to that grief
Which they themselves not feel; but, tasting it,
Their counsel turns to passion, which before
Would give preceptial medicine to rage,
Fetter strong madness in a silken thread,
Charm ache with air and agony with words.
No, no; 'tis all men's office to speak patience
To those that wring under the load of sorrow,
But no man's virtue nor sufficiency
To be so moral when he shall endure
The like himself. Therefore give me no counsel;
My griefs cry louder than advertisement.
ANTONIO: Therein do men from children nothing differ.
LEONATO: I pray thee, peace. I will be flesh and blood;
For there was never yet philosopher
That could endure the toothache patiently,
However they have writ the style of gods
And made a push at chance and sufferance.
ANTONIO: Yet bend not all the harm upon yourself;
Make those that do offend you suffer too.
LEONATO: There thou speak'st reason; nay, I will do so.
My soul doth tell me Hero is belied;
And that shall Claudio know; so shall the prince
And all of them that thus dishonour her.
ANTONIO: Here comes the prince and Claudio hastily.

Enter DON PEDRO and CLAUDIO

DON PEDRO: Good den, good den.
CLAUDIO: Good day to both of you.
LEONATO: Hear you, my lords—
DON PEDRO: We have some haste, Leonato.
LEONATO: Some haste, my lord! well, fare you well, my lord.
Are you so hasty now? Well, all is one.
DON PEDRO: Nay, do not quarrel with us, good old man.
ANTONIO: If he could right himself with quarreling,
Some of us would lie low.
CLAUDIO: Who wrongs him?
LEONATO: Marry, thou dost wrong me; thou dissembler, thou!
Nay, never lay thy hand upon thy sword;
I fear thee not.
CLAUDIO: Marry, beshrew my hand,
If it should give your age such cause of fear:
In faith, my hand meant nothing to my sword.
LEONATO: Tush, tush, man; never fleer and jest at me;
I speak not like a dotard nor a fool,
As under privilege of age to brag
What I have done being young, or what would do
Were I not old. Know, Claudio, to thy head,

Thou hast so wrong'd mine innocent child and me
That I am forced to lay my reverence by
And, with grey hairs and bruise of many days,
Do challenge thee to trial of a man.
I say thou hast belied mine innocent child;
Thy slander hath gone through and through her heart,
And she lies buried with her ancestors;
O, in a tomb where never scandal slept,
Save this of hers, framed by thy villainy.

CLAUDIO: My villany?

LEONATO: Thine, Claudio; thine, I say.

DON PEDRO: You say not right, old man.

LEONATO: My lord, my lord,
I'll prove it on his body, if he dare,
Despite his nice fence and his active practise,
His May of youth and bloom of lustihood.

CLAUDIO: Away! I will not have to do with you.

LEONATO: Canst thou so daff me? Thou hast kill'd my child;
If thou kill'st me, boy, thou shalt kill a man.

ANTONIO: He shall kill two of us, and men indeed;
But that's no matter; let him kill one first;
Win me and wear me; let him answer me.
Come, follow me, boy; come, sir boy, come, follow me;
Sir boy, I'll whip you from your foining fence;
Nay, as I am a gentleman, I will.

LEONATO: Brother—

ANTONIO: Content yourself. God knows I loved my niece;
And she is dead, slander'd to death by villains,
That dare as well answer a man indeed
As I dare take a serpent by the tongue.
Boys, apes, braggarts, Jacks, milksops!

LEONATO: Brother Antony—

ANTONIO: Hold you content. What, man! I know them, yea,
And what they weigh, even to the utmost scruple—
Scrambling, out-facing, fashion-monging boys,
That lie and cog and flout, deprave and slander,
Go anticly, show outward hideousness,
And speak off half a dozen dangerous words,
How they might hurt their enemies, if they durst;
And this is all.

LEONATO: But, brother Antony—

ANTONIO: Come, 'tis no matter;
Do not you meddle; let me deal in this.

DON PEDRO: Gentlemen both, we will not wake your patience.
My heart is sorry for your daughter's death;
But, on my honour, she was charged with nothing
But what was true and very full of proof.

LEONATO: My lord, my lord—

DON PEDRO: I will not hear you.

LEONATO: No? Come, brother; away. I will be heard.

ANTONIO: And shall, or some of us will smart for it.

Exeunt LEONATO and ANTONIO

DON PEDRO: See, see; here comes the man we went to seek.

Enter BENEDICK

CLAUDIO: Now, signior, what news?

BENEDICK: Good day, my lord.

DON PEDRO: Welcome, signior; you are almost come to part almost a fray.

CLAUDIO: We had like to have had our two noses snapped off with two old men without teeth.

DON PEDRO: Leonato and his brother. What thinkest thou? Had we fought, I doubt we should have been too young for them.

BENEDICK: In a false quarrel there is no true valour. I came to seek you both.

CLAUDIO: We have been up and down to seek thee; for we are high-proof melancholy and would fain have it beaten away. Wilt thou use thy wit?

BENEDICK: It is in my scabbard; shall I draw it?

DON PEDRO: Dost thou wear thy wit by thy side?

CLAUDIO: Never any did so, though very many have been beside their wit. I will bid thee draw, as we do the minstrels; draw, to pleasure us.

DON PEDRO: As I am an honest man, he looks pale. Art thou sick, or angry?

CLAUDIO: What, courage, man! What though care killed a cat, thou hast mettle enough in thee to kill care.

BENEDICK: Sir, I shall meet your wit in the career, and you charge it against me. I pray you choose another subject.

CLAUDIO: Nay, then, give him another staff; this last was broke cross.

DON PEDRO: By this light, he changes more and more; I think he be angry indeed.

CLAUDIO: If he be, he knows how to turn his girdle.

BENEDICK: Shall I speak a word in your ear?

CLAUDIO: God bless me from a challenge!

BENEDICK: [*Aside to Claudio*] You are a villain; I jest not; I will make it good how you dare, with what you dare, and when you dare. Do me right, or I will protest your cowardice. You have killed a sweet lady, and her death shall fall heavy on you. Let me hear from you.

CLAUDIO: Well, I will meet you, so I may have good cheer.

DON PEDRO: What, a feast, a feast?

CLAUDIO: I' faith, I thank him; he hath bid me to a calf's head and a capon; the which if I do not carve most curiously, say my knife's naught. Shall I not find a woodcock too?

BENEDICK: Sir, your wit ambles well; it goes easily.

DON PEDRO: I'll tell thee how Beatrice praised thy wit the other day. I said, thou hadst a fine wit. 'True,' said she, 'a fine little one.' 'No,' said I, 'a great wit.' 'Right,' says she, 'a great gross one.' 'Nay,' said I, 'a good wit.' 'Just,' said she, 'it hurts nobody.' 'Nay,' said I, 'the gentleman is wise.' 'Certain,' said she, 'a wise gentleman.' 'Nay,' said I, 'he hath the tongues.' 'That I believe,' said she, 'for he swore a thing to me on Monday night, which he forswore on Tuesday morning; there's a double tongue; there's two tongues.' Thus did she, an hour together, transshape thy particular virtues; yet at last she concluded with a sigh, thou wast the properest man in Italy.

CLAUDIO: For the which she wept heartily and said she cared not.

DON PEDRO: Yea, that she did; but yet, for all that, an if she did not hate him deadly, she would love him dearly. The old man's daughter told us all.

CLAUDIO: All, all; and, moreover, God saw him when he was hid in the garden.

DON PEDRO: But when shall we set the savage bull's horns on the sensible Benedick's head?

CLAUDIO: Yea, and text underneath, 'Here dwells Benedick the married man'?

BENEDICK: Fare you well, boy; you know my mind; I will leave you now to your gossip-like humour: you break jests as braggarts do their blades, which God be thanked, hurt not. My lord, for your many courtesies I thank you. I must discontinue your company. Your brother the bastard is fled from Messina. You have among you killed a sweet and innocent lady. For my Lord Lackbeard there, he and I shall meet; and, till then, peace be with him.

Exit

DON PEDRO: He is in earnest.

CLAUDIO: In most profound earnest; and, I'll warrant you, for the love of Beatrice.

DON PEDRO: And hath challenged thee.

CLAUDIO: Most sincerely.

DON PEDRO: What a pretty thing man is when he goes in his doublet and hose and leaves off his wit!

CLAUDIO: He is then a giant to an ape; but then is an ape a doctor to such a man.

DON PEDRO: But, soft you, let me be; pluck up, my heart, and be sad. Did he not say, my brother was fled?

Enter DOGBERRY, VERGES, and the Watchman with CONRADE and BORACHIO

DOGBERRY: Come you, sir; if justice cannot tame you, she shall ne'er weigh more reasons in her balance; nay, an you be a cursing hypocrite once, you must be looked to.

DON PEDRO: How now? two of my brother's men bound! Borachio one!

CLAUDIO: Hearken after their offence, my lord.

DON PEDRO: Officers, what offence have these men done?

DOGBERRY: Marry, sir, they have committed false report; moreover, they have spoken untruths; secondarily, they are slanders; sixth and lastly, they have belied a lady; thirdly, they have verified unjust things; and, to conclude, they are lying knaves.

DON PEDRO: First, I ask thee what they have done; thirdly, I ask thee what's their offence; sixth and lastly, why they are committed; and, to conclude, what you lay to their charge.

CLAUDIO: Rightly reasoned, and in his own division; and, by my troth, there's one meaning well suited.

DON PEDRO: Who have you offended, masters, that you are thus bound to your answer? this learned constable is too cunning to be understood. What's your offence?

BORACHIO: Sweet prince, let me go no farther to mine answer; do you hear me, and let this count kill me. I have deceived even your very eyes. What your wisdoms could not discover, these shallow fools have brought to light; who in the night overheard me confessing to this man how Don John your brother incensed me to slander the Lady

Hero, how you were brought into the orchard and saw me court Margaret in Hero's garments, how you disgraced her, when you should marry her. My villany they have upon record; which I had rather seal with my death than repeat over to my shame. The lady is dead upon mine and my master's false accusation; and, briefly, I desire nothing but the reward of a villain.

DON PEDRO: Runs not this speech like iron through your blood?

CLAUDIO: I have drunk poison whiles he utter'd it.

DON PEDRO: But did my brother set thee on to this?

BORACHIO: Yea, and paid me richly for the practise of it.

DON PEDRO: He is composed and framed of treachery,
And fled he is upon this villany.

CLAUDIO: Sweet Hero! now thy image doth appear
In the rare semblance that I loved it first.

DOGBERRY: Come, bring away the plaintiffs; by this time our sexton hath reformed Signior Leonato of the matter. And, masters, do not forget to specify, when time and place shall serve, that I am an ass.

VERGES: Here, here comes master Signior Leonato, and the Sexton too.

Re-enter LEONATO and ANTONIO, with the Sexton

LEONATO: Which is the villain? Let me see his eyes,
That, when I note another man like him,
I may avoid him. Which of these is he?

BORACHIO: If you would know your wronger, look on me.

LEONATO: Art thou the slave that with thy breath hast kill'd
Mine innocent child?

BORACHIO: Yea, even I alone.

LEONATO: No, not so, villain; thou beliest thyself;
Here stand a pair of honourable men;
A third is fled, that had a hand in it.
I thank you, princes, for my daughter's death;
Record it with your high and worthy deeds;
'Twas bravely done, if you bethink you of it.

CLAUDIO: I know not how to pray your patience;
Yet I must speak. Choose your revenge yourself;
Impose me to what penance your invention
Can lay upon my sin; yet sinn'd I not
But in mistaking.

DON PEDRO: By my soul, nor I;
And yet, to satisfy this good old man,
I would bend under any heavy weight
That he'll enjoin me to.

LEONATO: I cannot bid you bid my daughter live;
That were impossible; but, I pray you both,
Possess the people in Messina here
How innocent she died; and if your love
Can labour ought in sad invention,
Hang her an epitaph upon her tomb
And sing it to her bones, sing it to-night.
To-morrow morning come you to my house,
And since you could not be my son-in-law,
Be yet my nephew. My brother hath a daughter,
Almost the copy of my child that's dead,
And she alone is heir to both of us.
Give her the right you should have given her cousin,
And so dies my revenge.

CLAUDIO: O noble sir,
Your over-kindness doth wring tears from me!
I do embrace your offer; and dispose
For henceforth of poor Claudio.

LEONATO: To-morrow then I will expect your coming;
To-night I take my leave. This naughty man
Shall face to face be brought to Margaret,
Who I believe was pack'd in all this wrong,
Hired to it by your brother.

BORACHIO: No, by my soul, she was not,
Nor knew not what she did when she spoke to me,
But always hath been just and virtuous
In anything that I do know by her.

DOGBERRY: Moreover, sir, which indeed is not under white and black, this plaintiff here, the offender, did call me ass; I beseech you, let it be remembered in his punishment. And also, the watch heard them talk of one Deformed; they say be wears a key in his ear and a lock hanging by it, and borrows money in God's name, the which he hath used so long and never paid that now men grow hard-hearted and will lend nothing for God's sake. Pray you, examine him upon that point.

LEONATO: I thank thee for thy care and honest pains.

DOGBERRY: Your worship speaks like a most thankful and reverend youth; and I praise God for you.

LEONATO: There's for thy pains.

DOGBERRY: God save the foundation!

LEONATO: Go, I discharge thee of thy prisoner, and I thank thee.

DOGBERRY: I leave an arrant knave with your worship; which I beseech your worship to correct yourself, for the example of others. God keep your worship! I wish your worship well; God restore you to health! I humbly give you leave to depart; and if a merry meeting may be wished, God prohibit it! Come, neighbour.

Exeunt DOGBERRY and VERGES

LEONATO: Until to-morrow morning, lords, farewell.

ANTONIO: Farewell, my lords; we look for you to-morrow.

DON PEDRO: We will not fail.

CLAUDIO: To-night I'll mourn with Hero.

LEONATO: [*To the Watch*] Bring you these fellows on.
We'll talk with Margaret,
How her acquaintance grew with this lewd fellow.

Exeunt, severally

SCENE II—*Leonato's garden*

Enter BENEDICK and MARGARET, meeting

BENEDICK: Pray thee, sweet Mistress Margaret, deserve well at my hands by helping me to the speech of Beatrice.

MARGARET: Will you then write me a sonnet in praise of my beauty?

BENEDICK: In so high a style, Margaret, that no man living shall come over it; for, in most comely truth, thou deservest it.

MARGARET: To have no man come over me! Why, shall I always keep below stairs?

BENEDICK: Thy wit is as quick as the greyhound's mouth; it catches.

MARGARET: And yours as blunt as the fencer's foils, which hit, but hurt not.

BENEDICK: A most manly wit, Margaret; it will not hurt a woman; and so, I pray thee, call Beatrice. I give thee the bucklers.

MARGARET: Give us the swords; we have bucklers of our own.

BENEDICK: If you use them, Margaret, you must put in the pikes with a vice; and they are dangerous weapons for maids.

MARGARET: Well, I will call Beatrice to you, who I think hath legs.

BENEDICK: And therefore will come.

Exit MARGARET

Sings

The god of love,
That sits above,
And knows me, and knows me,
How pitiful I deserve—

I mean in singing; but in loving, Leander the good swimmer, Troilus the first employer of panders, and a whole bookful of these quondam carpet-mangers, whose names yet run smoothly in the even road of a blank verse, why, they were never so truly turned over and over as my poor self in love. Marry, I cannot show it in rhyme; I have tried; I can find out no rhyme to 'lady' but 'baby,' an innocent rhyme; for 'scorn,' 'horn,' a hard rhyme; for, 'school,' 'fool,' a babbling rhyme; very ominous endings. No, I was not born under a rhyming planet, nor I cannot woo in festival terms.

Enter BEATRICE

Sweet Beatrice, wouldst thou come when I called thee?

BEATRICE: Yea, signior, and depart when you bid me.

BENEDICK: O, stay but till then!

BEATRICE: 'Then' is spoken; fare you well now: and yet, ere I go, let me go with that I came; which is, with knowing what hath passed between you and Claudio.

BENEDICK: Only foul words; and thereupon I will kiss thee.

BEATRICE: Foul words is but foul wind, and foul wind is but foul breath, and foul breath is noisome; therefore I will depart unkissed.

BENEDICK: Thou hast frighted the word out of his right sense, so forcible is thy wit. But I must tell thee plainly, Claudio undergoes my challenge; and either I must shortly hear from him, or I will subscribe him a coward. And, I pray thee now, tell me for which of my bad parts didst thou first fall in love with me?

BEATRICE: For them all together; which maintained so politic a state of evil that they will not admit any good part to intermingle with them.

But for which of my good parts did you first suffer love for me?

BENEDICK: Suffer love! a good epithet! I do suffer love indeed, for I love thee against my will.

BEATRICE: In spite of your heart, I think; alas, poor heart! If you spite it for my sake, I will spite it for yours; for I will never love that which my friend hates.

BENEDICK: Thou and I are too wise to woo peaceably.

BEATRICE: It appears not in this confession: there's not one wise man among twenty that will praise himself.

BENEDICK: An old, an old instance, Beatrice, that lived in the lime of good neighbours. If a man do not erect in this age his own tomb ere he dies, he shall live no longer in monument than the bell rings and the widow weeps.

BEATRICE: And how long is that, think you?

BENEDICK: Question. Why, an hour in clamour and a quarter in rheum. Therefore is it most expedient for the wise, if Don Worm, his conscience, find no impediment to the contrary, to be the trumpet of his own virtues, as I am to myself. So much for praising myself, who, I myself will bear witness, is praiseworthy. And now tell me, how doth your cousin?

BEATRICE: Very ill.

BENEDICK: And how do you?

BEATRICE: Very ill too.

BENEDICK: Serve God, love me and mend. There will I leave you too, for here comes one in haste.

Enter URSULA

URSULA: Madam, you must come to your uncle. Yonder's old coil at home. It is proved my Lady Hero hath been falsely accused, the prince and Claudio mightily abused; and Don John is the author of all, who is fed and gone. Will you come presently?

BEATRICE: Will you go hear this news, signior?

BENEDICK: I will live in thy heart, die in thy lap, and be buried in thy eyes; and moreover I will go with thee to thy uncle's.

Exeunt

SCENE III—*A church*

Enter DON PEDRO, CLAUDIO, and three or four with tapers

CLAUDIO: Is this the monument of Leonato?

Lord: It is, my lord.

CLAUDIO: [*Reading out of a scroll*]
Done to death by slanderous tongues
Was the Hero that here lies;
Death, in guerdon of her wrongs,
Gives her fame which never dies.
So the life that died with shame
Lives in death with glorious fame.
Hang thou there upon the tomb,
Praising her when I am dumb.
Now, music, sound, and sing your solemn hymn.

Song

Pardon, goddess of the night,
Those that slew thy virgin knight;
For the which, with songs of woe,
Round about her tomb they go.
Midnight, assist our moan;
Help us to sigh and groan,
Heavily, heavily.
Graves, yawn and yield your dead,
Till death be uttered,
Heavily, heavily.

CLAUDIO: Now, unto thy bones good night!
Yearly will I do this rite.

DON PEDRO: Good morrow, masters; put your torches out;
The wolves have prey'd; and look, the gentle day,
Before the wheels of Phoebus, round about
Dapples the drowsy east with spots of grey.
Thanks to you all, and leave us. Fare you well.

CLAUDIO: Good morrow, masters; each his several way.

DON PEDRO: Come, let us hence, and put on other weeds;
And then to Leonato's we will go.

CLAUDIO: And Hymen now with luckier issue speed's
Than this for whom we render'd up this woe.

Exeunt

SCENE IV—*Leonato's house*

Enter LEONATO, ANTONIO, BENEDICK, BEATRICE, MARGARET, URSULA, FRIAR FRANCIS, and HERO

FRIAR FRANCIS: Did I not tell you she was innocent?

LEONATO: So are the prince and Claudio, who accused her

Upon the error that you heard debated.
But Margaret was in some fault for this,
Although against her will, as it appears
In the true course of all the question.

ANTONIO: Well, I am glad that all things sort so well.

BENEDICK: And so am I, being else by faith enforced
To call young Claudio to a reckoning for it.

LEONATO: Well, daughter, and you gentle-women all,
Withdraw into a chamber by yourselves,
And when I send for you, come hither mask'd.

Exeunt Ladies

The prince and Claudio promised by this hour
To visit me. You know your office, brother:
You must be father to your brother's daughter
And give her to young Claudio.

ANTONIO: Which I will do with confirm'd countenance.

BENEDICK: Friar, I must entreat your pains, I think.

FRIAR FRANCIS: To do what, signior?

BENEDICK: To bind me, or undo me; one of them.
Signior Leonato, truth it is, good signior,
Your niece regards me with an eye of favour.

LEONATO: That eye my daughter lent her. 'Tis most true.

BENEDICK: And I do with an eye of love requite her.

LEONATO: The sight whereof I think you had from me,
From Claudio and the prince. But what's your will?

BENEDICK: Your answer, sir, is enigmatical.
But, for my will, my will is your good will
May stand with ours, this day to be conjoin'd
In the state of honourable marriage;
In which, good friar, I shall desire your help.

LEONATO: My heart is with your liking.

FRIAR FRANCIS: And my help.
Here comes the prince and Claudio.

Enter DON PEDRO and CLAUDIO, and two or three others

DON PEDRO: Good morrow to this fair assembly.

LEONATO: Good morrow, prince; good morrow, Claudio;
We here attend you. Are you yet determined
To-day to marry with my brother's daughter?

CLAUDIO: I'll hold my mind, were she an Ethiope.

LEONATO: Call her forth, brother; here's the friar ready.

Exit ANTONIO

DON PEDRO: Good morrow, Benedick. Why, what's the matter,
That you have such a February face,
So full of frost, of storm and cloudiness?

CLAUDIO: I think he thinks upon the savage bull.
Tush, fear not, man; we'll tip thy horns with gold
And all Europa shall rejoice at thee,
As once Europa did at lusty Jove,
When he would play the noble beast in love.

BENEDICK: Bull Jove, sir, had an amiable low;
And some such strange bull leap'd your father's cow,
And got a calf in that same noble feat
Much like to you, for you have just his bleat.

CLAUDIO: For this I owe you. Here comes other reckonings.

Re-enter ANTONIO, with the Ladies masked

Which is the lady I must seize upon?

ANTONIO: This same is she, and I do give you her.

CLAUDIO: Why, then she's mine. Sweet, let me see your face.

LEONATO: No, that you shall not, till you take her hand
Before this friar and swear to marry her.

CLAUDIO: Give me your hand; before this holy friar,
I am your husband, if you like of me.

HERO: And when I lived, I was your other wife;

Unmasking

And when you loved, you were my other husband.

CLAUDIO: Another Hero!

HERO: Nothing certainer.
One Hero died defiled, but I do live,
And surely as I live, I am a maid.

DON PEDRO: The former Hero! Hero that is dead!

LEONATO: She died, my lord, but whiles her slander lived.

FRIAR FRANCIS: All this amazement can I qualify,
When after that the holy rites are ended,
I'll tell you largely of fair Hero's death.
Meantime let wonder seem familiar,
And to the chapel let us presently.

BENEDICK: Soft and fair, friar. Which is Beatrice?

BEATRICE: [*Unmasking*] I answer to that name. What is your will?

BENEDICK: Do not you love me?

BEATRICE: Why, no; no more than reason.

BENEDICK: Why, then your uncle and the prince and Claudio
Have been deceived; they swore you did.

BEATRICE: Do not you love me?

BENEDICK: Troth, no; no more than reason.

BEATRICE: Why, then my cousin Margaret and Ursula
Are much deceived; for they did swear you did.

BENEDICK: They swore that you were almost sick for me.

BEATRICE: They swore that you were well-nigh dead for me.

BENEDICK: 'Tis no such matter. Then you do not love me?

BEATRICE: No, truly, but in friendly recompense.

LEONATO: Come, cousin, I am sure you love the gentleman.

CLAUDIO: And I'll be sworn upon't that he loves her;
For here's a paper written in his hand,
A halting sonnet of his own pure brain,
Fashion'd to Beatrice.

HERO: And here's another
Writ in my cousin's hand, stolen from her pocket,
Containing her affection unto Benedick.

BENEDICK: A miracle! here's our own hands against our hearts. Come, I will have thee; but, by this light, I take thee for pity.

BEATRICE: I would not deny you; but, by this good day, I yield upon great persuasion; and partly to save your life, for I was told you were in a consumption.

BENEDICK: Peace! I will stop your mouth.

Kissing her

DON PEDRO: How dost thou, Benedick, the married man?

BENEDICK: I'll tell thee what, prince; a college of wit-crackers cannot flout me out of my humour. Dost thou think I care for a satire or an epigram? No: if a man will be beaten with brains, a' shall wear nothing handsome about him. In brief, since I do purpose to marry, I will think nothing to any purpose that the world can say against it; and therefore never flout at me for what I have said against it; for man is a giddy thing, and this is my conclusion. For thy part, Claudio, I did think to have beaten thee, but in that thou art like to be my kinsman, live unbruised and love my cousin.

CLAUDIO: I had well hoped thou wouldst have denied Beatrice, that I might have cudgelled thee out of thy single life, to make thee a double-dealer; which, out of question, thou wilt be, if my cousin do not look exceedingly narrowly to thee.

BENEDICK: Come, come, we are friends. Let's have a dance ere we are married, that we may lighten our own hearts and our wives' heels.

LEONATO: We'll have dancing afterward.

BENEDICK: First, of my word; therefore play, music. Prince, thou art sad; get thee a wife, get thee a wife. There is no staff more reverend than one tipped with horn.

Enter a Messenger

MESSENGER: My lord, your brother John is ta'en in flight,
And brought with armed men back to Messina.

BENEDICK: Think not on him till to-morrow.
I'll devise thee brave punishments for him.
Strike up, pipers.

Dance Exeunt

Pericles, Prince of Tyre

DRAMATIS PERSONÆ

GOWER, *as Chorus*
ANTIOCHUS, *King of Antioch*
PERICLES, *Prince of Tyre*
HELICANUS & ESCANES, *two lords of Tyre*
SIMONIDES, *King of Pentapolis*
CLEON, *Governor of Tharsus*
LYSIMACHUS, *Governor of Mytilene*
CERIMON, *a lord of Ephesus*
THALIARD, *a lord of Antioch*
PHILEMON, *servant to Cerimon*
LEONINE, *servant to Dionyza*
Marshal
A Pandar
BOULT, *his servant*
The Daughter of Antiochus
DIONYZA, *wife to Cleon*
THAISA, *daughter to Simonides*
MARINA, *daughter to Pericles and Thaisa*
LYCHORIDA, *nurse to Marina*
A Bawd
DIANA
Lords, Ladies, Knights, Gentlemen, Sailors, Pirates, Fishermen, *and* Messengers

THE SCENE: *Dispersedly in various countries*

Act I

Antioch: Before the palace

Enter GOWER

To sing a song that old was sung,
From ashes ancient Gower is come,
Assuming man's infirmities,
To glad your ear and please your eyes.
It hath been sung at festivals,
On ember-eves and holy-ales;
And lords and ladies in their lives
Have read it for restoratives.
The purchase is to make men glorious;
Et bonum quo antiquius, eo melius.
If you, born in those latter times,
When wit's more ripe, accept my rhymes,
And that to hear an old man sing
May to your wishes pleasure bring,
I life would wish, and that I might
Waste it for you, like taper-light.
This Antioch, then, Antiochus the Great
Built up, this city, for his chiefest seat;
The fairest in all Syria—
I tell you what mine authors say.
This king unto him took a fere,

Who died and left a female heir,
So buxom, blithe, and full of face,
As heaven had lent her all his grace;
With whom the father liking took,
And her to incest did provoke.
Bad child! worse father! To entice his own
To evil should be done by none.
But custom what they did begin
Was with long use account no sin.
The beauty of this sinful dame
Made many princes thither frame
To seek her as a bed-fellow,
In marriage-pleasures play-fellow;
Which to prevent he made a law—
To keep her still, and men in awe—
That whoso ask'd her for his wife
His riddle told not, lost his life.
So for her many a wight did die,
As yon grim looks do testify.
What now ensues to the judgment of your eye
I give, my cause who best can justify.

Exit

SCENE I—*Antioch: The palace*

Enter ANTIOCHUS, PRINCE PERICLES, and Followers

ANTIOCHUS: Young Prince of Tyre, you have at large received
The danger of the task you undertake.

PERICLES: I have, Antiochus, and, with a soul
Embolden'd with the glory of her praise,
Think death no hazard in this enterprise.

ANTIOCHUS: Bring in our daughter, clothed like a bride

Music

For the embracements even of Jove himself;
At whose conception, till Lucina reign'd,
Nature this dowry gave to glad her presence:
The senate-house of planets all did sit,
To knit in her their best perfections.

Enter the Daughter of ANTIOCHUS

PERICLES: See where she comes, apparell'd like the spring,
Graces her subjects, and her thoughts the king
Of every virtue gives renown to men.
Her face the book of praises, where is read
Nothing but curious pleasures, as from thence
Sorrow were ever razed, and testy wrath
Could never be her mild companion.
You gods that made me man, and sway in love,
That have inflamed desire in my breast
To taste the fruit of yon celestial tree,
Or die in the adventure, be my helps,
As I am son and servant to your will,
To compass such a boundless happiness!

ANTIOCHUS: Prince Pericles,—

PERICLES: That would be son to great Antiochus.

ANTIOCHUS: Before thee stands this fair Hesperides,
With golden fruit, but dangerous to be touch'd;
For death-like dragons here affright thee hard.
Her face, like heaven, enticeth thee to view
Her countless glory, which desert must gain;
And which, without desert, because thine eye
Presumes to reach, all thy whole heap must die.
Yon sometimes famous princes, like thyself,
Drawn by report, adventurous by desire,
Tell thee, with speechless tongues and semblance pale,
That without covering, save yon field of stars,
Here they stand martyrs, slain in Cupid's wars;
And with dead cheeks advise thee to desist
For going on death's net, whom none resist.

PERICLES: Antiochus, I thank thee, who hath taught
My frail mortality to know itself,
And by those fearful objects to prepare
This body, like to them, to what I must;
For death remember'd should be like a mirror,
Who tells us life's but breath, to trust it error.
I'll make my will then, and, as sick men do
Who know the world, see heaven, but, feeling woe,
Gripe not at earthly joys as erst they did;
So I bequeath a happy peace to you
And all good men, as every prince should do;
My riches to the earth from whence they came;
But my unspotted fire of love to you.

To the Daughter of ANTIOCHUS

Thus ready for the way of life or death,
I wait the sharpest blow, Antiochus.

ANTIOCHUS: Scorning advice, read the conclusion then;
Which read and not expounded, 'tis decreed,
As these before thee thou thyself shalt bleed.

DAUGHTER: Of all say'd yet, mayst thou prove prosperous!
Of all say'd yet, I wish thee happiness!
PERICLES: Like a bold champion, I assume the lists,
Nor ask advice of any other thought
But faithfulness and courage.

He reads the riddle

I am no viper, yet I feed
On mother's flesh which did me breed.
I sought a husband, in which labour
I found that kindness in a father.
He's father, son, and husband mild;
I mother, wife, and yet his child.
How they may be, and yet in two,
As you will live, resolve it you.
Sharp physic is the last. But, O you powers
That give heaven countless eyes to view men's acts,
Why cloud they not their sights perpetually,
If this be true, which makes me pale to read it?
Fair glass of light, I loved you, and could still,

Takes hold of the hand of the Daughter of ANTIOCHUS

Were not this glorious casket stored with ill.
But I must tell you, now my thoughts revolt
For he's no man on whom perfections wait
That, knowing sin within, will touch the gate.
You are a fair viol, and your sense the strings;
Who, finger'd to make man his lawful music,
Would draw heaven down, and all the gods, to hearken;
But being play'd upon before your time,
Hell only danceth at so harsh a chime.
Good sooth, I care not for you.
ANTIOCHUS: Prince Pericles, touch not, upon thy life.
For that's an article within our law,
As dangerous as the rest. Your time's expired:
Either expound now, or receive your sentence.
PERICLES: Great king,
Few love to hear the sins they love to act;
'Twould braid yourself too near for me to tell it.
Who has a book of all that monarchs do,
He's more secure to keep it shut than shown;
For vice repeated is like the wandering wind.
Blows dust in other's eyes, to spread itself;
And yet the end of all is bought thus dear,
The breath is gone, and the sore eyes see clear
To stop the air would hurt them. The blind mole casts
Copp'd hills towards heaven, to tell the earth is throng'd
By man's oppression; and the poor worm doth die for't.
Kings are earth's gods; in vice their law's their will;
And if Jove stray, who dares say Jove doth ill?
It is enough you know; and it is fit,
What being more known grows worse, to smother it.
All love the womb that their first being bred,
Then give my tongue like leave to love my head.
ANTIOCHUS: [*Aside*] Heaven, that I had thy head! he has found the meaning.
But I will gloze with him.—Young prince of Tyre,
Though by the tenor of our strict edict,
Your exposition misinterpreting,
We might proceed to cancel of your days;
Yet hope, succeeding from so fair a tree
As your fair self, doth tune us otherwise.
Forty days longer we do respite you;
If by which time our secret be undone,
This mercy shows we'll joy in such a son;
And until then your entertain shall be
As doth befit our honour and your worth.

Exeunt all but PERICLES

PERICLES: How courtesy would seem to cover sin,
When what is done is like an hypocrite,
The which is good in nothing but in sight!
If it be true that I interpret false,
Then were it certain you were not so bad
As with foul incest to abuse your soul;
Where now you're both a father and a son,
By your untimely claspings with your child,
Which pleasure fits an husband, not a father;
And she an eater of her mother's flesh,
By the defiling of her parent's bed;
And both like serpents are, who though they feed
On sweetest flowers, yet they poison breed.
Antioch, farewell! for wisdom sees, those men
Blush not in actions blacker than the night,
Will shun no course to keep them from the light.
One sin, I know, another doth provoke;

Murder's as near to lust as flame to smoke.
Poison and treason are the hands of sin,
Ay, and the targets, to put off the shame.
Then, lest my lie be cropp'd to keep you clear,
By flight I'll shun the danger which I fear.

Exit

Re-enter ANTIOCHUS

ANTIOCHUS: He hath found the meaning, for which we mean to have his head.
He must not live to trumpet forth my infamy,
Nor tell the world Antiochus doth sin
In such a loathed manner;
And therefore instantly this prince must die;
For by his fall my honour must keep high.
Who attends us there?

Enter THALIARD

THALIARD: Doth your highness call?

ANTIOCHUS: Thaliard, you are of our chamber, and our mind partakes
Her private actions to your secrecy;
And for your faithfulness we will advance you.
Thaliard, behold here's poison, and here's gold;
We hate the Prince of Tyre, and thou must kill him.
It fits thee not to ask the reason why,
Because we bid it. Say, is it done?

THALIARD: My lord,
'Tis done.

ANTIOCHUS: Enough.

Enter a Messenger

Let your breath cool yourself, telling your haste.

MESSENGER: My lord, Prince Pericles is fled.

Exit

ANTIOCHUS: As thou wilt live, fly after; and like an arrow shot from a well-experienced archer hits the mark his eye doth level at, so thou ne'er return unless thou say Prince Pericles is dead.

THALIARD: My lord, if I can get him within my pistol's length
I'll make him sure enough. So, farewell to your highness.

ANTIOCHUS: Thaliard, adieu!

Exit THALIARD

Till Pericles be dead
My heart can lend no succor to my head.

Exit

SCENE II—*Tyre: The palace*

Enter PERICLES with his Lords

PERICLES: Let none disturb us

Exeunt Lords

Why should this change of thoughts,
The sad companion, dull-eyed melancholy,
Be my so used a guest as not an hour
In the day's glorious walk, or peaceful night,
The tomb where grief should sleep, can breed me quiet?
Here pleasures court mine eyes, and mine eyes shun them,
And danger, which I fear'd, is at Antioch,
Whose arm seems far too short to hit me here.
Yet neither pleasure's art can joy my spirits,
Nor yet the other's distance comfort me.
Then it is thus: the passions of the mind,
That have their first conception by mis-dread,
Have after-nourishment and life by care;
And what was first but fear what might be done
Grows elder now, and cares it be not done.
And so with me. The great Antiochus,
'Gainst whom I am too little to contend,
Since he's so great can make his will his act—
Will think me speaking, though I swear to silence;
Nor boots it me to say I honour him,
If he suspect I may dishonour him;
And what may make him blush in being known,
He'll stop the course by which it might be known.
With hostile forces he'll o'erspread the land,
And with the ostent of war will look so huge
Amazement shall drive courage from the state;
Our men be vanquish'd ere they do resist,
And subjects punish'd that ne'er thought offence;
Which care of them, not pity of myself—
Who am no more but as the tops of trees
Which fence the roots they grow by and defend them—
Makes both my body pine and soul to languish,
And punish that before that he would punish.

Enter HELICANUS, and all the Lords

FIRST LORD: Joy and all comfort in your sacred breast!

SECOND LORD: And keep your mind till you return to us,

Peaceful and comfortable!
HELICANUS: Peace, peace, and give experience tongue.
They do abuse the king that flatter him,
For flattery is the bellows blows up sin;
The thing which is flatter'd but a spark,
To which that blast gives heat and stronger glowing;
Whereas reproof, obedient, and in order,
Fits kings, as they are men, for they may err.
When Signior Sooth here does proclaim a peace,
He flatters you, makes war upon your life.
Prince, pardon me, or strike me if you please;
I cannot be much lower than my knees.
Kneels
PERICLES: All leave us else; but let your cares o'erlook
What shipping and what lading's in our haven,
And then return to us.
Exeunt Lords
Helicanus, thou
Hast moved us. What seest thou in our looks?
HELICANUS: An angry brow, dread lord.
PERICLES: If there be such a dart in princes' frowns,
How durst thy tongue move anger to our face?
HELICANUS: How dare the plants look up to heaven, from whence
They have their nourishment?
PERICLES: Thou know'st I have power
To take thy life from thee.
HELICANUS: I have ground the axe myself;
Do but you strike the blow.
PERICLES: Rise, prithee, rise.
Sit down. Thou art no flatterer.
I thank thee for it; and heaven forbid
That kings should let their ears hear their faults hid!
Fit counsellor and servant for a prince,
Who by thy wisdom makest a prince thy servant,
What wouldst thou have me do?
HELICANUS: To bear with patience
Such griefs as you yourself do lay upon yourself.
PERICLES: Thou speak'st like a physician, Helicanus,
That ministers a potion unto me
That thou wouldst tremble to receive thyself.
Attend me, then: I went to Antioch,
Where, as thou know'st, against the face of death,
I sought the purchase of a glorious beauty,
From whence an issue I might propagate
Are arms to princes, and bring joys to subjects.
Her face was to mine eye beyond all wonder;
The rest—hark in thine ear—as black as incest;
Which by my knowledge found, the sinful father
Seem'd not to strike, but smooth. But thou know'st this,
'Tis time to fear when tyrants seem to kiss.
Such fear so grew in me I hither fled
Under the covering of a careful night,
Who seem'd my good protector; and, being here,
Bethought me what was past, what might succeed.
I knew him tyrannous; and tyrants' fears
Decrease not, but grow faster than the years;
And should he doubt it, as no doubt he doth,
That I should open to the listening air
How many worthy princes' bloods were shed
To keep his bed of blackness unlaid ope,
To lop that doubt, he'll fill this land with arms,
And make pretence of wrong that I have done him;
When all, for mine, if I may call offence,
Must feel war's blow, who spares not innocence;
Which love to all, of which thyself art one,
Who now reprovest me for it—
HELICANUS: Alas, sir!
PERICLES: Drew sleep out of mine eyes, blood from my cheeks,
Musings into my mind, with thousand doubts
How I might stop this tempest ere it came;
And, finding little comfort to relieve them,
I thought it princely charity to grieve them.
HELICANUS: Well, my lord, since you have given me leave to speak,
Freely will I speak. Antiochus you fear,
And justly too, I think, you fear the tyrant,
Who either by public war or private treason
Will take away your life.
Therefore, my lord, go travel for a while
Till that his rage and anger be forgot,
Or till the Destinies do cut his thread of life.
Your rule direct to any; if to me,
Day serves not light more faithful than I'll be.

PERICLES: I do not doubt thy faith;
But should he wrong my liberties in my absence?

HELICANUS: We'll mingle our bloods together in the earth,
From whence we had our being and our birth.

PERICLES: Tyre, I now look from thee then, and to Tharsus
Intend my travel, where I'll hear from thee;
And by whose letters I'll dispose myself.
The care I had and have of subjects' good
On thee I lay, whose wisdom's strength can bear it.
I'll take thy word for faith, not ask thine oath:
Who shuns not to break one will sure crack both.
But in our orbs we'll live so round and safe
That time of both this truth shall ne'er convince,
Thou show'dst a subject's shine, I a true prince.

Exeunt

SCENE III—*Tyre: The palace*

Enter THALIARD

THALIARD: So, this is Tyre, and this the court. Here must I kill King Pericles; and if I do it not, I am sure to be hanged at home. 'Tis dangerous. Well, I perceive he was a wise fellow and had good discretion that, being bid to ask what he would of the king, desired he might know none of his secrets. Now do I see he had some reason for't; for if a king bid a man be a villain, he's bound by the indenture of his oath to be one. Husht! here come the lords of Tyre.

Enter HELICANUS, and ESCANES, with other Lords

HELICANUS: You shall not need, my fellow peers of Tyre,
Further to question me of your king's departure:
His seal'd commission, left in trust with me,
Doth speak sufficiently he's gone to travel.

THALIARD: [*Aside*] How! the king gone!

HELICANUS: If further yet you will be satisfied
Why, as it were unlicensed of your loves,
He would depart, I'll give some light unto you.
Being at Antioch—

THALIARD: [*Aside*] What from Antioch?

HELICANUS: Royal Antiochus, on what cause I know not,
Took some displeasure at him; at least he judged so;
And doubting lest that he had err'd or sinn'd,
To show his sorrow, he'd correct himself;
So puts himself unto the shipman's toil,
With whom each minute threatens life or death.

THALIARD: [*Aside*] Well, I perceive
I shall not be hang'd now although I would;
But since he's gone, the King's seas must please
He 'scaped the land, to perish at the seas.
I'll present myself—Peace to the Lords of Tyre!

HELICANUS: Lord Thaliard from Antiochus is welcome.

THALIARD: From him I come
With message unto princely Pericles;
But since my landing I have understood
Your lord has betook himself to unknown travels,
Now message must return from whence it came.

HELICANUS: We have no reason to desire it,
Commended to our master, not to us;
Yet, ere you shall depart, this we desire—
As friends to Antioch, we may feast in Tyre.

Exeunt

SCENE IV—*Tharsus: The Governor's house*

Enter CLEON, the governor of Tharsus, with DIONYZA his wife, and Others

CLEON: My Dionyza, shall we rest us here,
And by relating tales of others' griefs
See if 'twill teach us to forget our own?

DIONYZA: That were to blow at fire in hope to quench it;
For who digs hills because they do aspire
Throws down one mountain to cast up a higher.
O my distressed lord, even such our griefs are!
Here they're but felt and seen with mischief's eyes,
But like to groves, being topp'd, they higher rise.

CLEON: O Dionyza,
Who wanteth food, and will not say he wants it,
Or can conceal his hunger till he famish?
Our tongues and sorrows do sound deep
Our woes into the air; our eyes to weep?
Till tongues fetch breath that may proclaim them louder;
That, if heaven slumber while their creatures want,

They may awake their helps to comfort them.
I'll then discourse our woes, felt several years,
And wanting breath to speak help me with tears.

DIONYZA: I'll do my best, sir.

CLEON: This Tharsus, o'er which I have the government,
A city on whom plenty held full hand,
For Riches strew'd herself even in the streets;
Whose towers bore heads so high they kiss'd the clouds,
And strangers ne'er beheld but wondered at;
Whose men and dames so jetted and adorn'd,
Like one another's glass to trim them by;
Their tables were stored full, to glad the sight,
And not so much to feed on as delight;
All poverty was scorn'd, and pride so great,
The name of help grew odious to repeat.

DIONYZA: O, 'tis too true!

CLEON: But see what heaven can do! By this our change
These mouths who but of late earth, sea, and air,
Were all too little to content and please,
Although they gave their creatures in abundance,
As houses are defiled for want of use,
They are now starved for want of exercise.
Those palates who, not yet two summers younger,
Must have inventions to delight the taste,
Would now be glad of bread, and beg for it.
Those mothers who to nouzle up their babes
Thought nought too curious are ready now
To eat those little darlings whom they loved.
So sharp are hunger's teeth that man and wife
Draw lots who first shall die to lengthen life.
Here stands a lord, and there a lady weeping;
Here many sink, yet those which see them fall
Have scarce strength left to give them burial.
Is not this true?

DIONYZA: Our cheeks and hollow eyes do witness it.

CLEON: O, let those cities that of Plenty's cup
And her prosperities so largely taste,
With their superfluous riots, hear these tears!
The misery of Tharsus may be theirs.

Enter a Lord

LORD: Where's the Lord Governor?

CLEON: Here.
Speak out thy sorrows which thou bring'st in haste.
For comfort is too far for us to expect.

LORD: We have descried, upon our neighbouring shore,
A portly sail of ships make hitherward.

CLEON: I thought as much.
One sorrow never comes but brings an heir
That may succeed as his inheritor;
And so in ours: some neighbouring nation,
Taking advantage of our misery,
Hath stuff'd these hollow vessels with their power,
To beat us down, the which are down already;
And make a conquest of unhappy me,
Whereas no glory's got to overcome.

LORD: That's the least fear; for by the semblance
Of their white flags display'd, they bring us peace,
And come to us as favourers, not as foes.

CLEON: Thou speak'st like him's untutor'd to repeat:
Who makes the fairest show means most deceit.
But bring they what they will and what they can,
What need we fear?
Our ground's the lowest, and we are half way there.
Go tell their general we attend him here,
To know for what he comes, and whence he comes,
And what he craves.

LORD: I go, my lord.

Exit

CLEON: Welcome is peace, if he on peace consist;
If wars, we are unable to resist.

Enter PERICLES, with Attendants

PERICLES: Lord governor, for so we hear you are,
Let not our ships and number of our men
Be like a beacon fired to amaze your eyes.
We have heard your miseries as far as Tyre,
And seen the desolation of your streets;
Nor come we to add sorrow to your tears,
But to relieve them of their heavy load;
And these our ships, you happily may think
Are like the Trojan horse was stuff'd within
With bloody veins, expecting overthrow,
Are stored with corn to make your needy bread,

And give them life whom hunger starved half dead.
ALL: The gods of Greece protect you!
And we'll pray for you.
PERICLES: Arise, I pray you, rise.
We do not look for reverence, but to love,
And harbourage for ourself, our ships, and men.
CLEON: The which when any shall not gratify,
Or pay you with unthankfulness in thought,
Be it our wives, our children, or ourselves,
The curse of heaven and men succeed their evils!
Till when—the which I hope shall ne'er be seen—
Your grace is welcome to our town and us.
PERICLES: Which welcome we'll accept; feast here awhile,
Until our stars that frown lend us a smile.

Exeunt

Act II

Enter GOWER

GOWER: Here have you seen a mighty king
His child, I wis, to incest bring;
A better prince and benign lord,
That will prove awful both in deed and word.
Be quiet then as men should be,
Till he hath pass'd necessity.
I'll show you those in troubles reign,
Losing a mite, a mountain gain.
The good in conversation,
To whom I give my benison,
Is still at Tharsus, where each man
Thinks all is writ he speken can;
And, to remember what he does,
Build his statue to make him glorious.
But tidings to the contrary
Are brought your eyes. What need speak I?
DUMB SHOW

Enter at one door PERICLES talking with CLEON; all the train with them. Enter at another door a Gentleman, with a letter to PERICLES; PERICLES shows the letter to CLEON; gives the Messenger a reward, and knights him. Exit PERICLES at one door, and CLEON at another

Good Helicane, that stay'd at home,
Not to eat honey like a drone
From others' labours; for though he strive
To killen bad, keep good alive;
And to fulfil his prince' desire,
Sends word of all that haps in Tyre:
How Thaliard came full bent with sin
And had intent to murder him;
And that in Tharsus was not best
Longer for him to make his rest.
He, doing so, put forth to seas,
Where when men been, there's seldom ease;
For now the wind begins to blow;
Thunder above and deeps below
Make such unquiet, that the ship
Should house him safe is wreck'd and split;
And he, good prince, having all lost,
By waves from coast to coast is tost,
All perishen of man, of pelf,
Ne aught escapen but himself;
Till fortune, tired with doing bad,
Threw him ashore, to give him glad.
And here he comes. What shall be next,
Pardon old Gower,—this longs the text.

Exit

Scene I—*Pentapolis: An open place by the sea-side*

Enter PERICLES, wet

PERICLES: Yet cease your ire, you angry stars of heaven!
Wind, rain, and thunder, remember, earthly man
Is but a substance that must yield to you;
And I, as fits my nature, do obey you.
Alas, the sea hath cast me on the rocks,
Wash'd me from shore to shore, and left me breath
Nothing to think on but ensuing death.
Let it suffice the greatness of your powers
To have bereft a prince of all his fortunes;
And having thrown him from your watery grave,
Here to have death in peace is all he'll crave.

Enter three FISHERMEN

FIRST FISHERMAN: What, ho, Pilch!

SECOND FISHERMAN: Ha, come and bring away the nets!

FIRST FISHERMAN: What, Patch-breech, I say!

THIRD FISHERMAN: What say you, master?

FIRST FISHERMAN: Look how thou stirrest now! come away, or I'll fetch thee with a wanion.

THIRD FISHERMAN: Faith, master, I am thinking of the poor men that were cast away before us even now.

FIRST FISHERMAN: Alas, poor souls, it grieved my heart to hear what pitiful cries they made to us to

help them, when, well-a-day, we could scarce help ourselves.

THIRD FISHERMAN: Nay, master, said not I as much when I saw the porpus how he bounced and tumbled? They say they're half fish, half flesh. A plague on them, they ne'er come but I look to be washed. Master, I marvel how the fishes live in the sea.

FIRST FISHERMAN: Why, as men do a-land; the great ones eat up the little ones. I can compare our rich misers to nothing so fitly as to a whale; a' plays and
tumbles, driving the poor fry before him, and at last devours them all at a mouthful. Such whales have I heard on o' the land, who never leave gaping till they've swallowed the whole parish, church, steeple, bells, and all.

PERICLES: [*Aside*] A pretty moral.

THIRD FISHERMAN: But, master, if I had been the sexton, I would have been that day in the belfry.

SECOND FISHERMAN: Why, man?

THIRD FISHERMAN: Because he should have swallowed me too: and when I had been in his belly, I would have kept such a jangling of the bells, that he should never have left, till he cast bells, steeple, church, and parish up again. But if the good King Simonides were of my mind—

PERICLES: [*Aside*] Simonides!

THIRD FISHERMAN: We would purge the land of these drones, that rob the bee of her honey.

PERICLES: [*Aside*] How from the finny subject of the sea
These fishers tell the infirmities of men;
And from their watery empire recollect
All that may men approve or men detect!
Peace be at your labour, honest fishermen.

SECOND FISHERMAN: Honest! good fellow, what's that? If it be a day fits you, search out of the calendar, and nobody look after it.

PERICLES: May see the sea hath cast upon your coast.

SECOND FISHERMAN: What a drunken knave was the sea to cast thee in our way!

PERICLES: A man whom both the waters and the wind,
In that vast tennis-court, have made the ball
For them to play upon entreats you pity him;
He asks of you that never used to beg.

FIRST FISHERMAN: No, friend, cannot you beg? Here's them in our country Greece gets more with begging than we can do with working.

SECOND FISHERMAN: Canst thou catch any fishes, then?

PERICLES: I never practised it.

SECOND FISHERMAN: Nay, then thou wilt starve, sure; for here's nothing to be got now-a-days unless thou canst fish for't.

PERICLES: What I have been I have forgot to know;
But what I am want teaches me to think on:
A man throng'd up with cold; my veins are chill,
And have no more of life than may suffice
To give my tongue that heat to ask your help;
Which if you shall refuse, when I am dead,
For that I am a man, pray see me buried.

FIRST FISHERMAN: Die quoth-a? Now gods forbid! I have a gown here! Come, put it on; keep thee warm. Now, afore me, a handsome fellow! Come, thou shalt go home, and we'll have flesh for holidays, fish for fasting-days, and moreo'er puddings and flap-jacks; and thou shalt be welcome.

PERICLES: I thank you, sir.

SECOND FISHERMAN: Hark you, my friend; you said you could not beg.

PERICLES: I did but crave.

SECOND FISHERMAN: But crave! Then I'll turn craver too, and so I shall scape whipping.

PERICLES: Why, are all your beggars whipped, then?

SECOND FISHERMAN: O, not all, my friend, not all! For if all your beggars were whipped, I would wish no better office than to be beadle. But, master, I'll go draw up the net.

Exit with Third Fisherman

PERICLES: [*Aside*] How well this honest mirth becomes their labour!

FIRST FISHERMAN: Hark you, sir; do you know where ye are?

PERICLES: Not well.

FIRST FISHERMAN: Why, I'll tell you: this is called Pentapolis, and our king the good Simonides.

PERICLES: The good Simonides, do you call him?

FIRST FISHERMAN: Ay, sir; and he deserves so to be called for his peaceable reign and good government.

PERICLES: He is a happy king, since he gains from his subjects the name of good by his government. How far is his court distant from this shore?

FIRST FISHERMAN: Marry, sir, half a day's journey; and I'll tell you, he hath a fair daughter, and to-morrow is her birth day, and there are princes and knights come from all parts of the world to oust and tourney for her love.

PERICLES: Were my fortunes equal to my desires, I could wish to make one there.

FIRST FISHERMAN: O sir, things must be as they may; and what a man cannot get he may lawfully deal for—his wife's soul.

Re-enter Second and Third Fishermen, drawing up a net

SECOND FISHERMAN: Help, master, help! Here's a fish hangs in the net, like a poor man's right in the law; 'twill hardly come out. Ha! Bots on't. 'Tis come at last, and 'tis turned to a rusty armour.

PERICLES: An armour, friends! I pray you let me see it.

Thanks, Fortune, yet, that after all my crosses,
Thou givest me somewhat to repair myself;
And though it was mine own, part of my heritage
Which my dead father did bequeath to me,
With this strict charge, even as he left his life:
'Keep it, my Pericles. It hath been a shield
'Twixt me and death;' and pointed to this brace
'For that it saved me, keep it. In like necessity—
The which the gods protect thee from!—may't defend thee!'
It kept where I kept, I so dearly loved it;
Till the rough seas, that spare not any man,
Took it in rage, though calm'd have given't again—
I thank thee for't. My shipwreck now's no ill,
Since I have here my father's gift in his will.

FIRST FISHERMAN: What mean you, sir?

PERICLES: To beg of you, kind friends, this coat of worth,
For it was sometime target to a king;
I know it by this mark. He loved me dearly,
And for his sake I wish the having of it;
And that you'ld guide me to your sovereign's court,
Where with it I may appear a gentleman;
And if that ever my low fortune's better,
I'll pay your bounties; till then rest your debtor.

FIRST FISHERMAN: Why, wilt thou tourney for the lady?

PERICLES: I'll show the virtue I have borne in arms.

FIRST FISHERMAN: Why, do'e take it, and the gods give thee good on't!

SECOND FISHERMAN: Ay, but hark you, my friend; 'twas we that made up this garment through the rough seams of the waters; there are certain condolements, certain vails. I hope, sir, if you thrive, you'll remember from whence you had them.

PERICLES: Believe 't, I will.
By your furtherance I am clothed in steel;
And spite of all the rapture of the sea
This jewel holds his building on my arm.
Unto thy value I will mount myself
Upon a courser whose delightful steps
Shall make the gazer joy to see him tread.
Only, my friend, I yet am unprovided
Of a pair of bases.

SECOND FISHERMAN: We'll sure provide. Thou shalt have my best gown to make thee a pair; and I'll bring thee to the court myself.

PERICLES: Then honour be but a goal to my will;
This day I'll rise, or else add ill to ill.

Exeunt

SCENE II—*Pentapolis: A public way or platform leading to the lists. A pavilion by the side of it for the reception of King, Princess, Lords, & c*

Enter SIMONIDES, THAISA, Lords, and Attendants

SIMONIDES: Are the knights ready to begin the triumph?

FIRST LORD: They are, my liege;
And stay your coming to present themselves.

SIMONIDES: Return them, we are ready; and our daughter here,
In honour of whose birth these triumphs are,
Sits here like beauty's child, whom nature gat
For men to see, and seeing wonder at.

Exit a Lord

THAISA: It pleaseth you, my royal father, to express
My commendations great, whose merit's less.

SIMONIDES: It's fit it should be so; for princes are
A model which heaven makes like to itself:
As jewels lose their glory if neglected,
So princes their renowns if not respected.

'Tis now your honour, daughter, to entertain
The labour of each knight in his device.

THAISA: Which, to preserve mine honour, I'll perform.

Enter a Knight; he passes over, and his Squire presents his shield to the Princess

SIMONIDES: Who is the first that doth prefer himself?

THAISA: A knight of Sparta, my renowned father;
And the device he bears upon his shield
Is a black Ethiope reaching at the sun;
The word, 'Lux tua vita mihi'.

SIMONIDES: He loves you well that holds his life of you.

The Second Knight passes by.

Who is the second that presents himself?

THAISA: A prince of Macedon, my royal father;
And the device he bears upon his shield
Is an arm'd knight that's conquer'd by a lady;
The motto thus, in Spanish, 'Piu por dulzura que por fuerza'.

The Third Knight passes by.

SIMONIDES: And what's the third?

THAISA: The third of Antioch;
And his device a wreath of chivalry;
The word, 'Me pompae provexit apex'.

The Fourth Knight passes by.

SIMONIDES: What is the fourth?

THAISA: A burning torch that's turned upside down;
The word, 'Quod me alit, me extinguit.'

SIMONIDES: Which shows that beauty hath his power and will,
Which can as well inflame as it can kill.

The Fifth Knight passes by.

THAISA: The fifth, an hand environed with clouds,
Holding out gold that's by the touchstone tried;
The motto thus, 'Sic spectanda fides'.

The Sixth Knight, PERICLES, passes by.

SIMONIDES: And what's the sixth and last, the which the knight himself
With such a graceful courtesy deliver'd?

THAISA: He seems to be a stranger; but his present is
A wither'd branch, that's only green at top;
The motto, 'In hac spe vivo.'

SIMONIDES: A pretty moral;
From the dejected state wherein he is,
He hopes by you his fortunes yet may flourish.

FIRST LORD: He had need mean better than his outward show
Can any way speak in his just commend;
For by his rusty outside he appears
To have practised more the whipstock than the lance.

SECOND LORD: He well may be a stranger, for he comes
To an honour'd triumph strangely furnished.

THIRD LORD: And on set purpose let his armour rust
Until this day, to scour it in the dust.

SIMONIDES: Opinion's but a fool, that makes us scan
The outward habit by the inward man.
But stay, the knights are coming. We will withdraw
Into the gallery.

Exeunt

Great shouts within, and all cry 'The mean knight!'

SCENE III—*Pentapolis: A hall of state. A banquet prepared*

Enter KING SIMONIDES, THAISA, Ladies, Lords, Attendants, and Knights, from tilting

SIMONIDES: Knights!
To say you're welcome were superfluous.
To place upon the volume of your deeds,
As in a title-page, your worth in arms
Were more than you expect, or more than's fit,
Since every worth in show commends itself.
Prepare for mirth, for mirth becomes a feast;
You are princes and my guests.

THAISA: But you my knight and guest;
To whom this wreath of victory I give,
And crown you king of this day's happiness.

PERICLES: 'Tis more by fortune, lady, than by merit.

SIMONIDES: Call it by what you will, the day is yours;
And here I hope is none that envies it.
In framing an artist, art hath thus decreed,
To make some good, but others to exceed;
And you are her labour'd scholar. Come, queen o' the feast—
For, daughter, so you are—here take your place.
Marshal the rest as they deserve their grace.

KNIGHTS: We are honour'd much by good Simonides.

SIMONIDES: Your presence glads our days. Honour we love;
For who hates honour hates the gods above.

MARSHAL: Sir, yonder is your place.

PERICLES: Some other is more fit.

FIRST KNIGHT: Contend not, sir; for we are gentlemen
That neither in our hearts nor outward eyes
Envy the great nor do the low despise.

PERICLES: You are right courteous knights.

SIMONIDES: Sit, sir, sit.
[*Aside*] By Jove, I wonder, that is king of thoughts,
These cates resist me, he not thought upon.

THAISA: [*Aside*] By Juno, that is queen of marriage,
All viands that I eat do seem unsavoury,
Wishing him my meat.—Sure, he's a gallant gentleman.

SIMONIDES: He's but a country gentleman;
Has done no more than other knights have done;
Has broken a staff or so; so let it pass.

THAISA: [*Aside*] To me he seems like diamond to glass.

PERICLES: [*Aside*] Yon king's to me like to my father's picture,
Which tells me in that glory once he was;
Had princes sit like stars about his throne,
And he the sun, for them to reverence;
None that beheld him but, like lesser lights,
Did vail their crowns to his supremacy:
Where now his son's like a glow worm in the night,
The which hath fire in darkness, none in light.
Whereby I see that Time's the king of men;
He's both their parent, and he is their grave,
And gives them what he will, not what they crave.

SIMONIDES: What, are you merry, knights?

FIRST KNIGHTS: Who can be other in this royal presence?

SIMONIDES: Here, with a cup that's stored unto the brim—
As you do love, fill to your mistress' lips—
We drink this health to you.

KNIGHTS: We thank your Grace.

SIMONIDES: Yet pause awhile.
Yon knight doth sit too melancholy,
As if the entertainment in our court
Had not a show might countervail his worth.
Note it not you, Thaisa?

THAISA: What is it
To me, my father?

SIMONIDES: O, attend, my daughter:
Princes, in this, should live like gods above,
Who freely give to every one that comes
To honour them;
And princes not doing so are like to gnats,
Which make a sound, but kill'd are wonder'd at.
Therefore to make his entertain more sweet,
Here, say we drink this standing-bowl of wine to him.

THAISA: Alas, my father, it befits not me
Unto a stranger knight to be so bold:
He may my proffer take for an offence,
Since men take women's gifts for impudence.

SIMONIDES: How!
Do as I bid you, or you'll move me else.

THAISA: [*Aside*] Now, by the gods, he could not please me better.

SIMONIDES: And furthermore tell him we desire to know of him
Of whence he is, his name and parentage.

THAISA: The King my father, sir, has drunk to you.

PERICLES: I thank him.

THAISA: Wishing it so much blood unto your life.

PERICLES: I thank both him and you, and pledge him freely.

THAISA: And further he desires to know of you
Of whence you are, your name and parentage.

PERICLES: A gentleman of Tyre—my name, Pericles;
My education been in arts and arms;
Who, looking for adventures in the world,
Was by the rough seas reft of ships and men,
And after shipwreck driven upon this shore.

THAISA: He thanks your Grace; names himself Pericles,
A gentleman of Tyre,
Who only by misfortune of the seas,
Bereft of ships and men, cast on this shore.

SIMONIDES: Now, by the gods, I pity his misfortune,
And will awake him from his melancholy.
Come, gentlemen, we sit too long on trifles
And waste the time which looks for other revels.

Even in your armours, as you are address'd,
Will very well become a soldier's dance.
I will not have excuse, with saying this
Loud music is too harsh for ladies' heads,
Since they love men in arms as well as beds.

They dance

So, this was well ask'd, 'twas so well perform'd.
Come, sir;
Here is a lady that wants breathing too;
And I have heard you knights of Tyre
Are excellent in making ladies trip;
And that their measures are as excellent.

PERICLES: In those that practise them they are, my lord.

SIMONIDES: O, that's as much as you would be denied
Of your fair courtesy.

The Knights and Ladies dance

Unclasp, unclasp.
Thanks, gentlemen, to all; all have done well,
[*To Pericles*] But you the best. —Pages and lights, to conduct
These knights unto their several lodgings! —
Yours, sir,
We have given order to be next our own.

PERICLES: I am at your Grace's pleasure.

SIMONIDES: Princes, it is too late to talk of love,
And that's the mark I know you level at.
Therefore each one betake him to his rest;
To-morrow all for speeding do their best.

Exeunt

SCENE IV—*Tyre: The Governor's house*

Enter HELICANUS and ESCANES

HELICANUS: No, Escanes; know this of me—
Antiochus from incest lived not free;
For which, the most high gods not minding longer
To withhold the vengeance that they had in store,
Due to this heinous capital offence,
Even in the height and pride of all his glory,
When he was seated in a chariot
Of an inestimable value, and his daughter with him,
A fire from heaven came and shrivell'd up
Their bodies, even to loathing; for they so stunk,
That all those eyes adored them ere their fall
Scorn now their hand should give them burial.

ESCANES: 'Twas very strange.

HELICANUS: And yet but justice; for though
This king were great, his greatness was no guard
To bar heaven's shaft, but sin had his reward.

ESCANES: 'Tis very true.

Enter two or three Lords

FIRST LORD: See, not a man in private conference
Or council has respect with him but he.

SECOND LORD: It shall no longer grieve without reproof.

THIRD LORD: And cursed be he that will not second it!

FIRST LORD: Follow me, then. Lord Helicane, a word.

HELICANUS: With me? and welcome. Happy day, my lords.

FIRST LORD: Know that our griefs are risen to the top,
And now at length they overflow their banks.

HELICANUS: Your griefs! for what? Wrong not your prince you love.

FIRST LORD: Wrong not yourself, then, noble Helicane;
But if the prince do live, let us salute him,
Or know what ground's made happy by his breath.
If in the world he live, we'll seek him out;
If in his grave he rest, we'll find him there;
And be resolved he lives to govern us,
Or dead, give's cause to mourn his funeral,
And leave us to our free election.

SECOND LORD: Whose death indeed's the strongest in our censure;
And knowing this kingdom, is without a head,
Like goodly buildings left without a roof,
Soon fall to ruin, your noble self,
That best know how to rule and how to reign,
We thus submit unto—our sovereign.

ALL: Live, noble Helicane!

HELICANUS: For honour's cause, forbear your suffrages.
If that you love Prince Pericles, forbear.
Take I your wish, I leap into the seas,
Where's hourly trouble for a minute's ease.
A twelvemonth longer, let me entreat you

To forbear the absence of your king;
If in which time expired he not return,
I shall with aged patience bear your yoke.
But if I cannot win you to this love,
Go search like nobles, like noble subjects,
And in your search spend your adventurous worth;
Whom if you find, and win unto return,
You shall like diamonds sit about his crown.

FIRST LORD: To wisdom he's a fool that will not yield;
And since Lord Helicane enjoineth us,
We with our travels will endeavour it.

HELICANUS: Then you love us, we you, and we'll clasp hands:
When peers thus knit, a kingdom ever stands.

Exeunt

SCENE V—*Pentapolis: The palace*

Enter SIMONIDES, reading a letter, at one door. The Knights meet him

FIRST KNIGHT: Good morrow to the good Simonides.

SIMONIDES: Knights, from my daughter this I let you know,
That for this twelvemonth she'll not undertake
A married life.
Her reason to herself is only known,
Which yet from her by no means can I get.

SECOND KNIGHT: May we not get access to her, my lord?

SIMONIDES: Faith, by no means; she has so strictly tied her
To her chamber that 'tis impossible.
One twelve moons more she'll wear Diana's livery;
This by the eye of Cynthia hath she vow'd,
And on her virgin honour will not break it.

THIRD KNIGHT: Loath to bid farewell, we take our leaves.

Exeunt Knights

SIMONIDES: So,
They are well despatch'd. Now to my daughter's letter.
She tells me here she'll wed the stranger knight,
Or never more to view nor day nor light.
'Tis well, mistress; your choice agrees with mine;
I like that well. Nay, how absolute she's in't,
Not minding whether I dislike or no!
Well, I do commend her choice;
And will no longer have it be delay'd.
Soft! here he comes: I must dissemble it.

Enter PERICLES

PERICLES: All fortune to the good Simonides!

SIMONIDES: To you as much, sir! I am beholding to you
For your sweet music this last night. I do
Protest my ears were never better fed
With such delightful pleasing harmony.

PERICLES: It is your Grace's pleasure to commend;
Not my desert.

SIMONIDES: Sir, you are music's master.

PERICLES: The worst of all her scholars, my good lord.

SIMONIDES: Let me ask you one thing:
What do you think of my daughter, sir?

PERICLES: A most virtuous princess.

SIMONIDES: And she is fair too, is she not?

PERICLES: As a fair day in summer—wondrous fair.

SIMONIDES: Sir, my daughter thinks very well of you;
Ay, so well that you must be her master,
And she will be your scholar; therefore look to it.

PERICLES: I am unworthy for her schoolmaster.

SIMONIDES: She thinks not so; peruse this writing else.

PERICLES: [*Aside*] What's here?
A letter, that she loves the knight of Tyre!
'Tis the king's subtlety to have my life.—
O, seek not to entrap me, gracious lord,
A stranger and distressed gentleman,
That never aim'd so high to love your daughter,
But bent all offices to honour her!

SIMONIDES: Thou hast bewitch'd my daughter, and thou art
A villain.

PERICLES: By the gods, I have not.
Never did thought of mine levy offence;
Nor never did my actions yet commence
A deed might gain her love or your displeasure.

SIMONIDES: Traitor, thou liest.

PERICLES: Traitor!

SIMONIDES: Ay, traitor.

PERICLES: Even in his throat—unless it be the King—
That calls me traitor, I return the lie.

SIMONIDES: [*Aside*] Now, by the gods, I do applaud his courage.

PERICLES: My actions are as noble as my thoughts,
That never relish'd of a base descent.
I came unto your court for honour's cause,
And not to be a rebel to her state;
And he that otherwise accounts of me,
This sword shall prove he's honour's enemy.

SIMONIDES: No?
Here comes my daughter, she can witness it.

Enter THAISA

PERICLES: Then, as you are as virtuous as fair,
Resolve your angry father if my tongue
Did e're solicit, or my hand subscribe
To any syllable that made love to you.

THAISA: Why, sir, say if you had,
Who takes offence at that would make me glad?

SIMONIDES: Yea, mistress, are you so peremptory?

Aside

I am glad on't with all my heart.—
I'll tame you; I'll bring you in subjection.
Will you, not having my consent,
Bestow your love and your affections
Upon a stranger?—

Aside

who, for aught I know,
May be, nor can I think the contrary,
As great in blood as I myself.—
Therefore, hear you, mistress: either frame
Your will to mine—and you, sir, hear you,
Either be ruled by me—, or I will make you—
Man and wife.
Nay, come, your hands and lips must seal it too;
And being join'd, I'll thus your hopes destroy,
And for a further grief—God give you joy!
What, are you both pleased?

THAISA: Yes, if you love me, sir.

PERICLES: Even as my life, or blood that fosters it.

SIMONIDES: What, are you both agreed?

BOTH: Yes, if it please your Majesty.

SIMONIDES: It pleaseth me so well that I will see you wed;
And then with what haste you can get you to bed.

Exeunt

Act III

Enter GOWER

GOWER: Now sleep yslaked hath the rout;
No din but snores the house about,
Made louder by the o'er-fed breast
Of this most pompous marriage feast.
The cat, with eyne of burning coal,
Now couches fore the mouse's hole;
And crickets sing at the oven's mouth,
Aye the blither for their drouth.
Hymen hath brought the bride to bed,
Where, by the loss of maidenhead,
A babe is moulded. Be attent,
And time that is so briefly spent
With your fine fancies quaintly eche.
What's dumb in show I'll plain with speech.

Dumb Show

Enter PERICLES and SIMONIDES at one door, with Attendants; a Messenger meets them, kneels, and gives PERICLES a letter. PERICLES shows it SIMONIDES; the Lords kneel to PERICLES. Then enter THAISA with child, with LYCHORIDA, a nurse. The KING shows her the letter; she rejoices. she and PERICLES takes leave of her father, and depart with LYCHORIDA and their Attendants. Then exeunt SIMONIDES and the rest.

By many a dern and painful perch
Of Pericles the careful search,
By the four opposing coigns
Which the world together joins,
Is made with all due diligence
That horse and sail and high expense
Can stead the quest. At last from Tyre—
Fame answering the most strange inquire—
To the court of King Simonides
Are letters brought, the tenor these:
Antiochus and his daughter dead,
The men of Tyrus on the head
Of Helicanus would set on
The crown of Tyre, but he will none.
The mutiny he there hastes t' oppress;
Says to 'em, if King Pericles
Come not home in twice six moons,
He, obedient to their dooms,
Will take the crown. The sum of this,
Brought hither to Pentapolis,
Y-ravished the regions round,
And every one with claps can sound
'Our heir-apparent is a king!
Who dream'd, who thought of such a thing?'
Brief, he must hence depart to Tyre.
His queen with child makes her desire—
Which who shall cross?—along to go.
Omit we all their dole and woe.
Lychorida, her nurse, she takes,
And so to sea. Their vessel shakes
On Neptune's billow; half the flood
Hath their keel cut: but fortune's mood
Varies again; the grizzled north
Disgorges such a tempest forth
That, as a duck for life that dives,
So up and down the poor ship drives.
The lady shrieks, and, well-a-near,
Does fall in travail with her fear;
And what ensues in this fell storm
Shall for itself itself perform.
I nill relate, action may
Conveniently the rest convey;
Which might not what by me is told.
In your imagination hold
This stage the ship, upon whose deck
The sea-tosed Pericles appears to speak.

Exit

Scene I—*Enter Pericles, a shipboard*

PERICLES: Thou god of this great vast, rebuke these surges,
Which wash both heaven and hell; and thou that hast
Upon the winds command, bind them in brass,

Having call'd them from the deep! O, still
Thy deafening, dreadful thunders; gently quench
Thy nimble, sulphurous flashes! O, how, Lychorida,
How does my queen? Thou stormest venomously;
Wilt thou spit all thyself? The seaman's whistle
Is as a whisper in the ears of death,
Unheard. Lychorida!—Lucina, O
Divinest patroness, and midwife gentle
To those that cry by night, convey thy deity
Aboard our dancing boat; make swift the pangs
Of my queen's travails!

Enter LYCHORIDA, with an Infant

Now, Lychorida!

LYCHORIDA: Here is a thing too young for such a place,
Who, if it had conceit, would die, as I
Am like to do. Take in your arms this piece
Of your dead queen.

PERICLES: How, how, Lychorida!

LYCHORIDA: Patience, good sir; do not assist the storm.
Here's all that is left living of your queen,
A little daughter. For the sake of it,
Be manly, and take comfort.

PERICLES: O you gods!
Why do you make us love your goodly gifts,
And snatch them straight away? We here below
Recall not what we give, and therein may
Use honour with you.

LYCHORIDA: Patience, good sir, even for this charge.

PERICLES: Now, mild may be thy life!
For a more blustrous birth had never babe;
Quiet and gentle thy conditions! For
Thou art the rudeliest welcome to this world
That ever was prince's child. Happy what follows!
Thou hast as chiding a nativity
As fire, air, water, earth, and heaven can make,
To herald thee from the womb: even at the first
Thy loss is more than can thy portage quit,
With all thou canst find here. Now, the good gods throw their best eyes upon't!

Enter two Sailors

FIRST SAILOR: What courage, sir? God save you!

PERICLES: Courage enough: I do not fear the flaw;
It hath done to me the worst. Yet, for the love
Of this poor infant, this fresh-new sea-farer,
I would it would be quiet.

FIRST SAILOR: Slack the bolins there! Thou wilt not, wilt thou? Blow, and split thyself.

SECOND SAILOR: But sea-room, an the brine and cloudy billow kiss the moon, I care not.

FIRST SAILOR: Sir, your queen must overboard: the sea works high, the wind is loud, and will not lie till the ship be cleared of the dead.

PERICLES: That's your superstition.

FIRST SAILOR: Pardon us, sir; with us at sea it hath been still observed, and we are strong in custom. Therefore briefly yield her; for she must overboard straight.

PERICLES: As you think meet. Most wretched queen!

LYCHORIDA: Here she lies, sir.

PERICLES: A terrible childbed hast thou had, my dear;
No light, no fire. The unfriendly elements
Forgot thee utterly; nor have I time
To give thee hallow'd to thy grave, but straight
Must cast thee, scarcely coffin'd, in the ooze;
Where, for a monument upon thy bones,
And e'er-remaining lamps, the belching whale
And humming water must o'erwhelm thy corpse,
Lying with simple shells. O Lychorida,
Bid Nestor bring me spices, ink and paper,
My casket and my jewels; and bid Nicander
Bring me the satin coffer. Lay the babe
Upon the pillow. Hie thee, whiles I say
A priestly farewell to her. Suddenly, woman.

Exit LYCHORIDA

SECOND SAILOR: Sir, we have a chest beneath the hatches, caulked and bitumed ready.

PERICLES: I thank thee. Mariner, say what coast is this?

SECOND SAILOR: We are near Tarsus.

PERICLES: Thither, gentle mariner.
Alter thy course for Tyre; When canst thou reach it?

SECOND SAILOR: By break of day, if the wind cease.

PERICLES: O, make for Tarsus!
There will I visit Cleon, for the babe
Cannot hold out to Tyrus; there I'll leave it
At careful nursing. Go thy ways, good mariner:
I'll bring the body presently.

Exeunt

SCENE II—*Ephesus: A room in Cerimon's house*

Enter CERIMON, with a Servant, and some Persons who have been shipwrecked

CERIMON: Philemon, ho!

Enter PHILEMON

PHILEMON: Doth my lord call?

CERIMON: Get fire and meat for these poor men.
'T has been a turbulent and stormy night.

SERVANT: I have been in many; but such a night as this,
Till now, I ne'er endured.

CERIMON: Your master will be dead ere you return;
There's nothing can be minister'd to nature
That can recover him.

To PHILEMON

Give this to the 'pothecary,
And tell me how it works.

Exeunt all but CERIMON

Enter two Gentlemen

FIRST GENTLEMAN: Good morrow.

SECOND GENTLEMAN: Good morrow to your lordship.

CERIMON: Gentlemen,
Why do you stir so early?

FIRST GENTLEMAN: Sir,
Our lodgings, standing bleak upon the sea,
Shook as the earth did quake;
The very principals did seem to rend,
And all to topple. Pure surprise and fear
Made me to quit the house.

SECOND GENTLEMAN: That is the cause we trouble you so early; 'Tis not our husbandry.

CERIMON: O, you say well.

FIRST GENTLEMAN: But I much marvel that your lordship, having
Rich tire about you, should at these early hours
Shake off the golden slumber of repose.
'Tis most strange,
Nature should be so conversant with pain,
Being thereto not compell'd.

CERIMON: I hold it ever,
Virtue and cunning were endowments greater
Than nobleness and riches: careless heirs
May the two latter darken and expend;
But immortality attends the former.
Making a man a god. 'Tis known, I ever
Have studied physic, through which secret art,
By turning o'er authorities, I have,
Together with my practise, made familiar
To me and to my aid the blest infusions
That dwell in vegetives, in metals, stones;
And I can speak of the disturbances
That nature works, and of her cures; which doth give me
A more content in course of true delight
Than to be thirsty after tottering honour,
Or tie my treasure up in silken bags,
To please the fool and death.

SECOND GENTLEMAN: Your honour has through
Ephesus pour'd forth
Your charity, and hundreds call themselves
Your creatures, who by you have been restored:
And not your knowledge, your personal pain, but even
Your purse, still open, hath built Lord Cerimon
Such strong renown as time shall ne'er raze.

Enter two or three Servants with a chest

FIRST SERVANT: So; lift there.

CERIMON: What is that?

FIRST SERVANT: Sir, even now did the sea toss upon our shore this chest.
'Tis of some wreck.

CERIMON: Set't down, let's look upon't.

SECOND GENTLEMAN: 'Tis like a coffin, sir.

CERIMON: Whate'er it be,
'Tis wondrous heavy. Wrench it open straight.
If the sea's stomach be o'ercharged with gold,
'Tis a good constraint of fortune it belches upon us.

SECOND GENTLEMAN: 'Tis so, my lord.

CERIMON: How close 'tis caulk'd and bitumed!
Did the sea cast it up?

FIRST SERVANT: I never saw so huge a billow, sir,
As toss'd it upon shore.

CERIMON: Wrench it open;
Soft! it smells most sweetly in my sense.

SECOND GENTLEMAN: A delicate odour.

CERIMON: As ever hit my nostril. So, up with it.
O you most potent gods! What's here? A corse!

FIRST GENTLEMAN: Most strange!

CERIMON: Shrouded in cloth of state; balm'd and entreasured with full bags of spices! A passport too!
Apollo, perfect me in the characters!

Reads from a scroll

Here I give to understand,
If e'er this coffin drive a-land,
I, King Pericles, have lost
This queen, worth all our mundane cost.
Who finds her, give her burying;
She was the daughter of a king.
Besides this treasure for a fee,
The gods requite his charity!
If thou livest, Pericles, thou hast a heart
That even cracks for woe! This chanced tonight.

SECOND GENTLEMAN: Most likely, sir.

CERIMON: Nay, certainly to-night;
For look how fresh she looks!
They were too rough
That threw her in the sea. Make a fire within.
Fetch hither all my boxes in my closet.

Exit a Servant

Death may usurp on nature many hours,
And yet the fire of life kindle again
The o'erpress'd spirits. I heard of an Egyptian
That had nine hours lien dead,
Who was by good appliance recovered.

Re-enter a Servant, with boxes, napkins, and fire

Well said, well said; the fire and cloths.
The rough and woeful music that we have,
Cause it to sound, beseech you.
The viol once more. How thou stirr'st, thou block!
The music there!—I pray you, give her air.
Gentlemen.
This queen will live; nature awakes; a warmth
Breathes out of her. She hath not been entranced
Above five hours. See how she gins to blow
Into life's flower again!

FIRST GENTLEMAN: The heavens,
Through you, increase our wonder and set up
Your fame forever.

CERIMON: She is alive; behold,
Her eyelids, cases to those heavenly jewels
Which Pericles hath lost,
Begin to part their fringes of bright gold;
The diamonds of a most praised water
Do appear, to make the world twice rich. Live,
And make us weep to hear your fate, fair creature,
Rare as you seem to be.

She moves

THAISA: O dear Diana,
Where am I? Where's my lord? What world is this?

SECOND GENTLEMAN: Is not this strange?

FIRST GENTLEMAN: Most rare.

CERIMON: Hush, my gentle neighbours!
Lend me your hands: to the next chamber bear her.
Get linen: now this matter must be look'd to,
For her relapse is mortal. Come, come;
And Æsculapius guide us!

Exeunt, carrying her away

SCENE III—*Tharsus: Cleon's house*

Enter PERICLES, CLEON, DIONYZA, and LYCHORIDA with MARINA in her arms

PERICLES: Most honour'd Cleon, I must needs be gone;
My twelve months are expired, and Tyrus stands
In a litigious peace. You, and your lady
Take from my heart all thankfulness! The gods
Make up the rest upon you!

CLEON: Your shafts of fortune, though they hurt you mortally,
Yet glance full wanderingly on us.

DIONYZA: O your sweet queen!
That the strict fates had pleased you had brought her hither,
To have bless'd mine eyes with her!

PERICLES: We cannot but obey
The powers above us. Could I rage and roar
As doth the sea she lies in, yet the end
Must be as 'tis. My gentle babe Marina, whom,
For she was born at sea, I have named so, here
I charge your charity withal, leaving her
The infant of your care; beseeching you
To give her princely training, that she may be
Manner'd as she is born.

CLEON: Fear not, my lord, but think
Your grace, that fed my country with your corn,
For which the people's prayers still fall upon you,

Must in your child be thought on. If neglection
Should therein make me vile, the common body,
By you relieved, would force me to my duty.
But if to that my nature need a spur,
The gods revenge it upon me and mine
To the end of generation!

PERICLES: I believe you;
Your honour and your goodness teach me to't,
Without your vows. Till she be married, madam,
By bright Diana, whom we honour all,
Unscissor'd shall this hair of mine remain,
Though I show ill in't. So I take my leave.
Good madam, make me blessed in your care
In bringing up my child.

DIONYZA: I have one myself,
Who shall not be more dear to my respect
Than yours, my lord.

PERICLES: Madam, my thanks and prayers.

CLEON: We'll bring your Grace e'en to the edge o' the shore,
Then give you up to the mask'd Neptune and
The gentlest winds of heaven.

PERICLES: I will embrace
Your offer. Come, dearest madam. O, no tears,
Lychorida, no tears.
Look to your little mistress, on whose grace
You may depend hereafter. Come, my lord.

Exeunt

SCENE IV—*Ephesus: Cerimon's house*

Enter CERIMON and THAISA

CERIMON: Madam, this letter, and some certain jewels,
Lay with you in your coffer; which are
At your command. Know you the character?

THAISA: It is my lord's.
That I was shipp'd at sea, I well remember,
Even on my eaning time; but whether there
Deliver'd, by the holy gods,
I cannot rightly say. But since King Pericles,
My wedded lord, I ne'er shall see again,
A vestal livery will I take me to,
And never more have joy.

CERIMON: Madam, if this you purpose as ye speak,
Diana's temple is not distant far,
Where you may abide till your date expire.
Moreover, if you please, a niece of mine
Shall there attend you.

THAISA: My recompense is thanks, that's all;
Yet my good will is great, though the gift small.

Exeunt

Act IV

Enter GOWER

GOWER: Imagine Pericles arrived at Tyre,
Welcomed and settled to his own desire.
His woeful queen we leave at Ephesus,
Unto Diana there a votaress.
Now to Marina bend your mind,
Whom our fast-growing scene must find
At Tharsus, and by Cleon train'd
In music, letters; who hath gain'd
Of education all the grace,
Which makes her both the heart and place
Of general wonder. But, alack,
That monster Envy, oft the wrack
Of earned praise, Marina's life
Seeks to take off by treason's knife.
And in this kind hath our Cleon
One daughter, and a wench full grown,
Even ripe for marriage-rite; this maid
Hight Philoten; and it is said
For certain in our story, she
Would ever with Marina be.
Be't when she weaved the sleided silk
With fingers long, small, white as milk;
Or when she would with sharp needle wound
The cambric, which she made more sound
By hurting it; or when to the lute
She sung, and made the night-bird mute,
That still records with moan; or when
She would with rich and constant pen
Vail to her mistress Dian; still
This Philoten contends in skill
With absolute Marina. So
The dove of Paphos might with the crow
Vie feathers white. Marina gets
All praises, which are paid as debts,
And not as given. This so darks
In Philoten all graceful marks
That Cleon's wife, with envy rare,
A present murderer does prepare
For good Marina, that her daughter
Might stand peerless by this slaughter.
The sooner her vile thoughts to stead,
Lychorida, our nurse, is dead;
And cursed Dionyza hath
The pregnant instrument of wrath
Prest for this blow. The unborn event
I do commend to your content;
Only I carry winged time
Post on the lame feet of my rhyme;
Which never could I so convey
Unless your thoughts went on my way.
Dionyza does appear,
With Leonine, a murderer.

Exit

Scene I— *Tharsus: An open place near the sea shore*

Enter DIONYZA and LEONINE

DIONYZA: Thy oath remember; thou hast sworn to do't:
'Tis but a blow, which never shall be known.
Thou canst not do a thing in the world so soon,
To yield thee so much profit. Let not conscience,
Which is but cold, inflaming love i' thy bosom,
Inflame too nicely; nor let pity, which
Even women have cast off, melt thee, but be
A soldier to thy purpose.

LEONINE: I will do't; but yet she is a goodly creature.

DIONYZA: The fitter, then, the gods should have her.
Here she comes weeping for her only mistress' death.
Thou art resolved?

LEONINE: I am resolved.

Enter MARINA with a basket of flowers

MARINA: No, I will rob Tellus of her weed,
To strew thy green with flowers. The yellows, blues,
The purple violets, and marigolds,
Shall as a carpet hang upon thy grave,
While summer days do last. Ay me! poor maid,
Born in a tempest, when my mother died,
This world to me is like a lasting storm,
Whirring me from my friends.

DIONYZA: How now, Marina! Why do you keep alone?
How chance my daughter is not with you?
Do not
Consume your blood with sorrowing: you have
A nurse of me. Lord, how your favour's changed
With this unprofitable woe! Come. Give me your flowers. On the sea margent.
Walk with Leonine; the air is quick there,
And it pierces and sharpens the stomach.
Come,
Leonine, take her by the arm, walk with her.

MARINA: No, I pray you;
I'll not bereave you of your servant.

DIONYZA: Come, come;
I love the king your father, and yourself,
With more than foreign heart. We every day
Expect him here. When he shall come and find
Our paragon to all reports thus blasted,
He will repent the breadth of his great voyage;
Blame both my lord and me that we have taken
No care to your best courses. Go, I pray you,
Walk, and be cheerful once again; reserve
That excellent complexion which did steal
The eyes of young and old. Care not for me;
I can go home alone.

MARINA: Well, I will go;
But yet I have no desire to it.

DIONYZA: Come, come, I know 'tis good for you.
Walk half an hour, Leonine, at the least.
Remember what I have said.

LEONINE: I warrant you, madam.

DIONYZA: I'll leave you, my sweet lady, for a while.
Pray walk softly, do not heat your blood:
What! I must have care of you.

MARINA: My thanks, sweet madam.

Exit DIONYZA

Is this wind westerly that blows?

LEONINE: South-west.

MARINA : When I was born, the wind was north.

LEONINE: Was't so?

MARINA: My father, as nurse said, did never fear,
But cried 'Good seaman!' to the sailors, galling
His kingly hands, hauling ropes;
And, clasping to the mast, endured a sea
That almost burst the deck.

LEONINE: When was this?

MARINA: When I was born.
Never was waves nor wind more violent;
And from the ladder-tackle washes off
A canvas-climber. 'Ha!' says one, 'wolt out?'
And with a dropping industry they skip
From stem to stern; the boatswain whistles, and
The master calls, and trebles their confusion.

LEONINE: Come, say your prayers.

MARINA: What mean you?

LEONINE: If you require a little space for prayer,
I grant it. Pray; but be not tedious,
For the gods are quick of ear, and I am sworn
To do my work with haste.

MARINA: Why will you kill me?

LEONINE: To satisfy my lady.

MARINA: Why would she have me kill'd?
Now, as I can remember, by my troth,
I never did her hurt in all my life.
I never spake bad word, nor did ill turn
To any living creature. Believe me, la,
I never kill'd a mouse, nor hurt a fly;
I trod upon a worm against my will,
But I wept for it. How have I offended,
Wherein my death might yield her any profit,
Or my life imply her any danger?

LEONINE: My commission
Is not to reason of the deed, but do it.

MARINA: You will not do't for all the world, I hope.
You are well favour'd, and your looks foreshow
You have a gentle heart. I saw you lately
When you caught hurt in parting two that fought.
Good sooth, it show'd well in you. Do so now:
Your lady seeks my life; come you between,
And save poor me, the weaker.

LEONINE: I am sworn,
And will dispatch.

Seizes her

Enter Pirates

FIRST PIRATE: Hold, villain!

LEONINE runs away

SECOND PIRATE: A prize! a prize!

THIRD PIRATE: Half-part, mates, half-part!

Come, let's have her aboard suddenly.

Exeunt Pirates with MARINA

Re-enter LEONINE

LEONINE: These roguing thieves serve the great pirate Valdes;

And they have seized Marina. Let her go;

There's no hope she will return. I'll swear she's dead

And thrown into the sea. But I'll see further.

Perhaps they will but please themselves upon her,

Not carry her aboard. If she remain,

Whom they have ravish'd must by me be slain.

Exit

SCENE II—*Mytilene: A brothel*

Enter Pandar, Bawd, and BOULT

PANDAR: Boult!

BOULT: Sir?

PANDAR: Search the market narrowly.

Mytilene is full of gallants.

We lost too much money this mart by being too wenchless.

BAWD: We were never so much out of creatures.

We have but poor three, and they can do no more than they can do; and they with continual action are even as good as rotten.

PANDAR: Therefore let's have fresh ones, whate'er we pay for them.

If there be not a conscience to be used in every trade, we shall never prosper.

BAWD: Thou sayest true; 'tis not our bringing up of poor bastards—as, I think, I have brought up some eleven—

BOULT: Ay, to eleven; and brought them down again.

But shall I search the market?

BAWD: What else, man? The stuff we have, a strong wind will blow it to pieces, they are so pitifully sodden.

PANDAR: Thou sayest true; they're too unwholesome, o' conscience. The poor Transylvanian is dead that lay with the little baggage.

BOULT: Ay, she quickly pooped him; she made him roast-meat for worms. But I'll go search the market.

Exit

PANDAR: Three or four thousand chequins were as pretty a proportion to live quietly, and so give over.

BAWD: Why to give over, I pray you? is it a shame to get when we are old?

PANDAR: O, our credit comes not in like the commodity, nor the commodity wages not with the danger; therefore, if in our youths we could pick up some pretty estate, 'twere not amiss to keep our door hatched. Besides, the sore terms we stand upon with the gods will be strong with us for giving over.

BAWD: Come, other sorts offend as well as we.

PANDAR: As well as we! Ay, and better too; we offend worse. Neither is our profession any trade; it's no calling. But here comes Boult.

Re-enter BOULT, with the Pirates and MARINA

BOULT: [*To Marina*] Come your ways.—My masters, you say she's a virgin?

FIRST PIRATE: O, sir, we doubt it not.

BOULT: Master, I have gone through for this piece, you see. If you like her, so; if not, I have lost my earnest.

BAWD: Boult, has she any qualities?

BOULT: She has a good face, speaks well, and has excellent good clothes: there's no further necessity of qualities can make her be refused.

BAWD: What's her price, Boult?

BOULT: I cannot be bated one doit of a thousand pieces.

PANDAR: Well, follow me, my masters; you shall have your money presently. Wife, take her in; instruct her what she has to do, that she may not be raw in her entertainment.

Exeunt Pandar and Pirates

BAWD: Boult, take you the marks of her—the colour of her hair, complexion, height, age, with warrant of her virginity; and cry 'He that will give most shall

have her first.' Such a maidenhead were no cheap thing, if men were as they have been. Get this done as I command you.

BOULT: Performance shall follow.

Exit

MARINA: Alack that Leonine was so slack, so slow!

He should have struck, not spoke; or that these pirates,

Not enough barbarous, had not o'erboard thrown me

For to seek my mother!

BAWD: Why lament you, pretty one?

MARINA: That I am pretty.

BAWD: Come, the gods have done their part in you.

MARINA: I accuse them not.

BAWD: You are light into my hands, where you are like to live.

MARINA: The more my fault

To scape his hands where I was like to die.

BAWD: Ay, and you shall live in pleasure.

MARINA: No.

BAWD: Yes, indeed shall you, and taste gentlemen of all fashions. You shall fare well; you shall have the difference of all complexions. What! do you stop your ears?

MARINA: Are you a woman?

BAWD: What would you have me be, an I be not a woman?

MARINA: An honest woman, or not a woman.

BAWD: Marry, whip thee, gosling! I think I shall have something to do with you. Come, you're a young foolish sapling, and must be bowed as I would have you.

MARINA: The gods defend me!

BAWD: If it please the gods to defend you by men, then men must comfort you, men must feed you, men must stir you up. Boult's returned.

Re-enter BOULT

Now, sir, hast thou cried her through the market?

BOULT: I have cried her almost to the number of her hairs;

I have drawn her picture with my voice.

BAWD: And I prithee tell me, how dost thou find the inclination of the people, especially of the younger sort?

BOULT: Faith, they listened to me as they would have hearkened to their father's testament. There was a Spaniard's mouth so watered, that he went to bed to her very description.

BAWD: We shall have him here to-morrow with his best ruff on.

BOULT: To-night, to-night. But, mistress, do you know the French knight that cowers i' the hams?

BAWD: Who, Monsieur Veroles?

BOULT: Ay, he; he offered to cut a caper at the proclamation; but he made a groan at it, and swore he would see her to-morrow.

BAWD: Well, well; as for him, he brought his disease hither: here he does but repair it. I know he will come in our shadow, to scatter his crowns in the sun.

BOULT: Well, if we had of every nation a traveller, we should lodge them with this sign.

BAWD: [*To Marina*] Pray you, come hither awhile. You have fortunes coming upon you. Mark me: you must seem to do that fearfully which you commit willingly; to despise profit where you have most gain. To weep that you live as ye do makes pity in your lovers; seldom but that pity begets you a good opinion, and that opinion a mere profit.

MARINA: I understand you not.

BOULT: O, take her home, mistress, take her home. These blushes of hers must be quenched with some present practise.

BAWD: Thou sayest true, i' faith, so they must; for your bride goes to that with shame which is her way to go with warrant.

BOULT: Faith, some do, and some do not. But, mistress, if I have bargained for the joint—

BAWD: Thou mayst cut a morsel off the spit.

BOULT: I may so.

BAWD: Who should deny it? Come, young one,

I like the manner of your garments well.

BOULT: Ay, by my faith, they shall not be changed yet.

BAWD: Boult, spend thou that in the town; report what a sojourner we have; you'll lose nothing by custom. When nature flamed this piece she meant thee a good turn; therefore say what a paragon she is, and thou hast the harvest out of thine own report.

BOULT: I warrant you, mistress, thunder shall not so awake the beds of eels as my giving out her beauty stir up the lewdly inclined. I'll bring home some to-night.

BAWD: Come your ways; follow me.

MARINA: If fires be hot, knives sharp, or waters deep,

Untied I still my virgin knot will keep.

Diana, aid my purpose!

BAWD: What have we to do with Diana? Pray you, will you go with us?

Exeunt

SCENE III—*Tharsus: Cleon's house*

Enter CLEON and DIONYZA

DIONYZA: Why, are you foolish? Can it be undone?
CLEON: O Dionyza, such a piece of slaughter
The sun and moon ne'er look'd upon!
DIONYZA: I think
You'll turn a child again.
CLEON: Were I chief lord of all this spacious world,
I'ld give it to undo the deed. O lady,
Much less in blood than virtue, yet a princess
To equal any single crown o' the earth
I' the justice of compare! O villain Leonine!
Whom thou hast poison'd too.
If thou hadst drunk to him, 't had been a kindness
Becoming well thy fact. What canst thou say
When noble Pericles shall demand his child?
DIONYZA: That she is dead. Nurses are not the fates,
To foster it, nor ever to preserve.
She died at night; I'll say so. Who can cross it?
Unless you play the pious innocent,
And for an honest attribute cry out
'She died by foul play.'
CLEON: O, go to. Well, well,
Of all the faults beneath the heavens the gods
Do like this worst.
DIONYZA: Be one of those that thinks
The petty wrens of Tharsus will fly hence,
And open this to Pericles. I do shame
To think of what a noble strain you are,
And of how coward a spirit.
CLEON: To such proceeding
Who ever but his approbation added,
Though not his prime consent, he did not flow
From honourable sources.
DIONYZA: Be it so, then.
Yet none does know, but you, how she came dead,
Nor none can know, Leonine being gone.
She did distain my child, and stood between
Her and her fortunes. None would look on her,
But cast their gazes on Marina's face;
Whilst ours was blurted at, and held a mawkin
Not worth the time of day. It pierced me thorough;
And though you call my course unnatural,
You not your child well loving, yet I find
It greets me as an enterprise of kindness
Perform'd to your sole daughter.
CLEON: Heavens forgive it!
DIONYZA: And as for Pericles,
What should he say? We wept after her hearse,
And yet we mourn; her monument
Is almost finish'd, and her epitaphs
In glittering golden characters express
A general praise to her, and care in us
At whose expense 'tis done.
CLEON: Thou art like the harpy,
Which, to betray, dost, with thine angel's face,
Seize with thine eagle's talons.
DIONYZA: You are like one that superstitiously
Doth swear to the gods that winter kills the flies;
But yet I know you'll do as I advise.

Exeunt

SCENE IV—*Before the monument of Marina at Tharsus*

Enter Gower.

GOWER: Thus time we waste, and longest leagues make short;
Sail seas in cockles, have an wish but for't;
Making, to take your imagination,
From bourn to bourn, region to region.
By you being pardon'd, we commit no crime
To use one language in each several clime
Where our scenes seem to live. I do beseech you
To learn of me, who stand i' the gaps to teach you
The stages of our story. Pericles
Is now again thwarting the wayward seas,
Attended on by many a lord and knight,
To see his daughter, all his life's delight.
Old Escanes, whom Helicanus late
Advanced in time to great and high estate.
Is left to govern it, you bear it in mind,
Old Helicanus goes along. Behind
Well-sailing ships and bounteous winds have brought
This king to Tharsus—think his pilot thought;

So with his steerage shall your thoughts grow on—
To fetch his daughter home, who first is gone.
Like motes and shadows see them move awhile;
Your ears unto your eyes I'll reconcile.

Dumb Show

Enter PERICLES, at one door, with all his Train: CLEON and DIONYZA at the other. CLEON shows PERICLES the tomb of Marina, whereat PERICLES makes lamentation, puts on sackcloth, and in a mighty passion departs. Then exeunt CLEON and DIONYZA

See how belief may suffer by foul show!
This borrow'd passion stands for true old woe;
And Pericles, in sorrow all devour'd,
With sighs shot through and biggest tears o'ershower'd,
Leaves Tharsus and again embarks. He swears
Never to wash his face nor cut his hairs;
He puts on sackcloth, and to sea. He bears
A tempest which his mortal vessel tears,
And yet he rides it out. Now please you wit.
The epitaph is for Marina writ
By wicked Dionyza.

Reads the inscription on MARINA's monument

'The fairest, sweet'st, and best lies here,
Who wither'd in her spring of year.
She was of Tyrus the King's daughter,
On whom foul death hath made this slaughter;
Marina was she call'd; and at her birth,
Thetis, being proud, swallow'd some part o' the earth;
Therefore the earth, fearing to be o'erflow'd,
Hath Thetis' birth-child on the heavens bestow'd;
Wherefore she does—and swears she'll never stint—
Make raging battery upon shores of flint.'
No visor does become black villainy
So well as soft and tender flattery.
Let Pericles believe his daughter's dead,
And bear his courses to be ordered
By Lady Fortune; while our scene must play
His daughter's woe and heavy well-a-day
In her unholy service. Patience, then,
And think you now are all in Mytilene.

Exit

SCENE V—*Mytilene: A street before the brothel*

Enter, from the brothel, two Gentlemen

FIRST GENTLEMAN: Did you ever hear the like?

SECOND GENTLEMAN: No, nor never shall do in such a place as this, she being once gone.

FIRST GENTLEMAN: But to have divinity preached there! Did you ever dream of such a thing?

SECOND GENTLEMAN: No, no. Come, I am for no more bawdy-houses. Shall's go hear the vestals sing?

FIRST GENTLEMAN: I'll do any thing now that is virtuous; but I am out of the road of rutting for ever.

Exeunt

SCENE VI—*Mytilane: A room in the brothel*

Enter PANDAR, BAWD, and BOULT

PANDAR: Well, I had rather than twice the worth of her she had ne'er come here.

BAWD: Fie, fie upon her! She's able to freeze the god Priapus, and undo a whole generation. We must either get her ravished or be rid of her. When she should do for clients her fitment, and do me the kindness of our profession, she has me her quirks, her reasons, her master-reasons, her prayers, her knees; that she would make a puritan of the devil, if he should cheapen a kiss of her.

BOULT: Faith, I must ravish her, or she'll disfurnish us of all our cavaleria and make our swearers priests.

PANDAR: Now the pox upon her green-sickness for me!

BAWD: Faith there's no way to be rid on't but by the way to the pox. Here comes the Lord Lysimachus disguised.

BOULT: We should have both lord and lown, if the peevish baggage would but give way to customers.

Enter LYSIMACHUS

LYSIMACHUS: How now! How a dozen of virginities?

BAWD: Now, the gods to-bless your Honour!

BOULT: I am glad to see your Honour in good health.

LYSIMACHUS: You may so; 'tis the better for you that your resorters stand upon sound legs. How now! Wholesome iniquity have you that a man may deal withal, and defy the surgeon?

BAWD: We have here one, sir, if she would—but there never came her like in Mytilene.

LYSIMACHUS: If she'ld do the deed of darkness, thou wouldst say.

BAWD: Your Honour knows what 'tis to say well enough.

LYSIMACHUS: Well, call forth, call forth.

BOULT : For flesh and blood, sir, white and red, you shall see a rose; and she were a rose indeed, if she had but—

LYSIMACHUS: What, prithee?

BOULT: O, sir, I can be modest.

LYSIMACHUS: That dignifies the renown of a bawd no less than it gives a good report to a number to be chaste.

Exit BOULT

BAWD: Here comes that which grows to the stalk—never plucked yet, I can assure you.

Re-enter BOULT with MARINA

Is she not a fair creature?

LYSIMACHUS: Faith, she would serve after a long voyage at sea.

Well, there's for you. Leave us.

BAWD: I beseech your Honour, give me leave: a word, and I'll have done presently.

LYSIMACHUS: I beseech you, do.

BAWD: [*Aside To Marina*] First, I would have you note, this is an honourable man.

MARINA: I desire to find him so, that I may worthily note him.

BAWD: Next, he's the governor of this country, and a man whom I am bound to.

MARINA: If he govern the country, you are bound to him indeed; but how honourable he is in that I know not.

BAWD: Pray you, without any more virginal fencing, will you use him kindly? He will line your apron with gold.

MARINA: What he will do graciously I will thankfully receive.

LYSIMACHUS: Ha' you done?

BAWD: My lord, she's not paced yet; you must take some pains to work her to your manage. Come, we will leave his Honour and her together. Go thy ways.

Exeunt BAWD, PANDAR, and BOULT

LYSIMACHUS: Now, pretty one, how long have you been at this trade?

MARINA: What trade, sir?

LYSIMACHUS: Why, I cannot name't but I shall offend.

MARINA: I cannot be offended with my trade. Please you to name it.

LYSIMACHUS: How long have you been of this profession?

MARINA: E'er since I can remember.

LYSIMACHUS: Did you go to 't so young? Were you a gamester at five or at seven?

MARINA: Earlier too, sir, if now I be one.

LYSIMACHUS: Why, the house you dwell in proclaims you to be a creature of sale.

MARINA: Do you know this house to be a place of such resort, and will come into 't? I hear say you are of honourable parts, and are the governor of this place.

LYSIMACHUS: Why, hath your principal made known unto you who I am?

MARINA: Who is my principal?

LYSIMACHUS: Why, your herb-woman; she that sets seeds and roots of shame and iniquity. O, you have heard something of my power, and so stand aloof for more serious wooing. But I protest to thee, pretty one, my authority shall not see thee, or else look friendly upon thee. Come, bring me to some private place. Come, come.

MARINA: If you were born to honour, show it now;
If put upon you, make the judgment good
That thought you worthy of it.

LYSIMACHUS: How's this? how's this? Some more; be sage.

MARINA: For me,
That am a maid, though most ungentle fortune
Have placed me in this sty, where, since I came,
Diseases have been sold dearer than physic—
That the gods
Would set me free from this unhallow'd place,
Though they did change me to the meanest bird
That flies i' the purer air!

LYSIMACHUS: I did not think
Thou couldst have spoke so well; ne'er dream'd thou couldst.
Had I brought hither a corrupted mind,
Thy speech had alter'd it. Hold, here's gold for thee:
Persever in that clear way thou goest,

And the gods strengthen thee!
MARINA: The good gods preserve you!
LYSIMACHUS: For me, be you thoughten
That I came with no ill intent; for to me
The very doors and windows savour vilely.
Fare thee well. Thou art a piece of virtue, and
I doubt not but thy training hath been noble.
Hold, here's more gold for thee.
A curse upon him, die he like a thief,
That robs thee of thy goodness! If thou dost
Hear from me, it shall be for thy good.

Re-enter BOULT

BOULT: I beseech your Honour, one piece for me.
LYSIMACHUS: Avaunt, thou damned door-keeper!
Your house, but for this virgin that doth prop it,
Would sink and overwhelm you. Away!

Exit

BOULT: How's this? We must take another course with you.

If your peevish chastity, which is not worth a breakfast in the cheapest country under the cope, shall undo a whole household, let me be gelded like a spaniel. Come your ways.

MARINA: Whither would you have me?

BOULT : I must have your maidenhead taken off, or the common hangman shall execute it. Come your ways. We'll have no more gentlemen driven away. Come your ways, I say.

Re-enter BAWD

BAWD: How now! What's the matter?

BOULT: Worse and worse, mistress; she has here spoken holy words to the Lord Lysimachus.

BAWD: O abominable!

BOULT: She makes our profession as it were to stink afore the face of the gods.

BAWD: Marry, hang her up for ever!

BOULT: The nobleman would have dealt with her like a nobleman, and she sent him away as cold as a snowball; saying his prayers too.

BAWD: Boult, take her away; use her at thy pleasure. Crack the glass of her virginity, and make the rest malleable.

BOULT: An if she were a thornier piece of ground than she is, she shall be ploughed.

MARINA: Hark, hark, you gods!

BAWD: She conjures. Away with her! Would she had never come within my doors! Marry, hang you! She's born to undo us. Will you not go the way of women kind? Marry, come up, my dish of chastity with rosemary and bays!

Exit

BOULT: Come, mistress; come your ways with me.

MARINA: Whither wilt thou have me?

BOULT: To take from you the jewel you hold so dear.

MARINA: Prithee, tell me one thing first.

BOULT: Come now, your one thing.

MARINA: What canst thou wish thine enemy to be?

BOULT: Why, I could wish him to be my master, or rather, my mistress.

MARINA: Neither of these are so bad as thou art,
Since they do better thee in their command.
Thou hold'st a place, for which the pained'st fiend
Of hell would not in reputation change;
Thou art the damned doorkeeper to every
Coistrel that comes inquiring for his Tib;
To the choleric fisting of every rogue
Thy ear is liable; thy food is such
As hath been belch'd on by infected lungs.

BOULT: What would you have me do? Go to the wars, would you, where a man may serve seven years for the loss of a leg, and have not money enough in the end to buy him a wooden one?

MARINA: Do any thing but this thou dost. Empty
Old receptacles, or common shores, of filth;
Serve by indenture to the common hangman:
Any of these ways are yet better than this;
For what thou professest, a baboon, could he speak,
Would own a name too dear. That the gods
Would safely deliver me from this place!
Here, here's gold for thee.
If that thy master would gain by me,
Proclaim that I can sing, weave, sew, and dance,
With other virtues which I'll keep from boast;
And I will undertake all these to teach.
I doubt not but this populous city will
Yield many scholars.

BOULT: But can you teach all this you speak of?

MARINA: Prove that I cannot, take me home again,
And prostitute me to the basest groom
That doth frequent your house.

BOULT: Well, I will see what I can do for thee. If I can place thee, I will.

MARINA: But amongst honest women.

BOULT: 'Faith, my acquaintance lies little amongst them. But since my master and mistress have bought you, there's no going but by their consent. Therefore I will make them acquainted with your purpose, and I doubt not but I shall find them tractable enough.

Come, I'll do for thee what I can; come your ways.

Exeunt

Act V

Enter GOWER

GOWER: Marina thus the brothel scapes and chances
Into an honest house, our story says.
She sings like one immortal, and she dances
As goddess-like to her admired lays;
Deep clerks she dumbs; and with her needle composes
Nature's own shape of bud, bird, branch, or berry,
That even her art sisters the natural roses;
Her inkle, silk, twin with the rubied cherry;
That pupils lacks she none of noble race,
Who pour their bounty on her; and her gain
She gives the cursed bawd. Here we her place;
And to her father turn our thoughts again,
Where we left him on the sea. We there him lost;
Whence, driven before the winds, he is arrived
Here where his daughter dwells; and on this coast
Suppose him now at anchor. The city strived
God Neptune's annual feast to keep; from whence
Lysimachus our Tyrian ship espies,
His banners sable, trimm'd with rich expense;
And to him in his barge with fervour hies.
In your supposing once more put your sight
Of heavy Pericles, think this his bark;
Where what is done in action, more, if might,
Shall be discover'd; please you sit and hark.

Exit

Scene I—*On board Pericles' ship, off Mytilene: A pavilion on deck with a curtain before it; Pericles within it, reclining on a couch. A barge lying beside the Tyrian vessel*

Enter two Sailors, one belonging to the Tyrian vessel, the other to the barge; to them HELICANUS

TYRIAN SAILOR: [*To the Sailor of Mytilene*] Where is Lord Helicanus? He can resolve you.
O, here he is.
Sir, there's a barge put off from Mytilene,
And in it is Lysimachus the Governor,
Who craves to come aboard. What is your will?

HELICANUS: That he have his. Call up some gentlemen.

TYRIAN SAILOR: Ho, gentlemen! my lord calls.

Enter two or three Gentlemen

FIRST GENTLEMAN: Doth your lordship call?

HELICANUS: Gentlemen, there's some of worth would come aboard; I pray greet them fairly.

The Gentlemen and the two Sailors descend, and go on board the barge

Enter, from thence, LYSIMACHUS and Lords; with the Gentlemen and the two Sailors

TYRIAN SAILOR: Sir,
This is the man that can, in aught you would,
Resolve you.

LYSIMACHUS: Hail, reverend sir! The gods preserve you!

HELICANUS: And you, sir, to outlive the age I am,
And die as I would do.

LYSIMACHUS: You wish me well.
Being on shore, honouring of Neptune's triumphs,

Seeing this goodly vessel ride before us,
I made to it, to know of whence you are.
HELICANUS: First, what is your place?
LYSIMACHUS: I am the Governor of this place you lie before.
HELICANUS: Sir,
Our vessel is of Tyre, in it the King;
A man who for this three months hath not spoken
To any one, nor taken sustenance
But to prorogue his grief.
LYSIMACHUS: Upon what ground is his distemperature?
HELICANUS: 'Twould be too tedious to repeat;
But the main grief springs from the loss
Of a beloved daughter and a wife.
LYSIMACHUS: May we not see him?
HELICANUS: You may;
But bootless is your sight—he will not speak
To any.
LYSIMACHUS: Yet let me obtain my wish.
HELICANUS: Behold him.
PERICLES discovered
This was a goodly person
Till the disaster that, one mortal night,
Drove him to this.
LYSIMACHUS: Sir King, all hail! The gods preserve you!
Hail, royal sir!
HELICANUS: It is in vain; he will not speak to you.
FIRST LORD: Sir,
We have a maid in Mytilene,
I durst wager,
Would win some words of him.
LYSIMACHUS: 'Tis well bethought.
She questionless with her sweet harmony
And other chosen attractions, would allure,
And make a battery through his deafen'd parts,
Which now are midway stopp'd.
She is all happy as the fairest of all,
And, with her fellow maids is now upon
The leafy shelter that abuts against
The island's side.
He whispers a Lord, who goes off in the barge of LYSIMACHUS
HELICANUS: Sure, all's effectless; yet nothing we'll omit
That bears recovery's name. But, since your kindness
We have stretch'd thus far, let us beseech you.
That for our gold we may provision have,
Wherein we are not destitute for want,
But weary for the staleness.
LYSIMACHUS: O sir, a courtesy
Which if we should deny, the most just gods
For every graff would send a caterpillar,
And so afflict our province. Yet once more
Let me entreat to know at large the cause
Of your king's sorrow.
HELICANUS: Sit, sir, I will recount it to you.
But, see, I am prevented.
Re-enter, from the barge, First Lord, with MARINA, and another Girl
LYSIMACHUS: O, here is
The lady that I sent for. Welcome, fair one!
Is't not a goodly presence?
HELICANUS: She's a gallant lady.
LYSIMACHUS: She's such a one that, were I well assured
Came of gentle kind and noble stock,
I'ld wish no better choice, and think me rarely wed.
Fair one, all goodness that consists in bounty
Expect even here, where is a kingly patient.
If that thy prosperous and artificial feat
Can draw him but to answer thee in aught,
Thy sacred physic shall receive such pay
As thy desires can wish.
MARINA: Sir, I will use
My utmost skill in his recovery, Provided
That none but I and my companion maid
Be suffer'd to come near him.
LYSIMACHUS: Come, let us leave her;
And the gods make her prosperous!
MARINA sings
LYSIMACHUS: Mark'd he your music?
MARINA: No, nor look'd on us.
LYSIMACHUS: See, she will speak to him.
MARINA: Hail sir! my lord, lend ear.
PERICLES: Hum, ha!
MARINA: I am a maid,
My lord, that ne'er before invited eyes,
But have been gazed on like a comet. She speaks,

My lord, that, may be, hath endured a grief
Might equal yours, if both were justly weigh'd.
Though wayward fortune did malign my state,
My derivation was from ancestors
Who stood equivalent with mighty kings;
But time hath rooted out my parentage,
And to the world and awkward casualties
Bound me in servitude.

Aside

I will desist;
But there is something glows upon my cheek,
And whispers in mine ear 'Go not till he speak'.

PERICLES: My fortunes—parentage—good parentage—To equal mine!—was it not thus? What say you?

MARINA: I said, my lord, if you did know my parentage
You would not do me violence.

PERICLES: I do think so. Pray you, turn your eyes upon me.
You are like something that—What country-woman?
Here of these shores?

MARINA: No, nor of any shores.
Yet I was mortally brought forth, and am
No other than I appear.

PERICLES: I am great with woe, and shall deliver weeping.
My dearest wife was like this maid, and such a one
My daughter might have been: my queen's square brows;
Her stature to an inch; as wand-like straight;
As silver voiced; her eyes as jewel-like,
And cased as richly; in pace another Juno;
Who starves the ears she feeds, and makes them hungry,
The more she gives them speech. Where do you live?

MARINA: Where I am but a stranger. From the deck
You may discern the place.

PERICLES: Where were you bred?
And how achieved you these endowments, which
You make more rich to owe?

MARINA: If I should tell my history, it would seem
Like lies, disdain'd in the reporting.

PERICLES: Prithee, speak.
Falseness cannot come from thee; for thou look'st
Modest as Justice, and thou seem'st a palace
For the crown'd Truth to dwell in. I will believe thee,
And make my senses credit thy relation
To points that seem impossible; for thou look'st
Like one I loved indeed. What were thy friends?
Didst thou not say, when I did push thee back—
Which was when I perceived thee—that thou camest
From good descending?

MARINA: So indeed I did.

PERICLES: Report thy parentage. I think thou said'st
Thou hadst been toss'd from wrong to injury,
And that thou thought'st thy griefs might equal mine,
If both were open'd.

MARINA: Some such thing
I said, and said no more but what my thoughts
Did warrant me was likely.

PERICLES: Tell thy story;
If thine consider'd prove the thousandth part
Of my endurance, thou art a man, and I
Have suffer'd like a girl. Yet thou dost look
Like Patience gazing on kings' graves, and smiling
Extremity out of act. What were thy friends?
How lost thou them? Thy name, my most kind virgin?
Recount, I do beseech thee. Come, sit by me.

MARINA: My name is Marina.

PERICLES: O, I am mock'd,
And thou by some incensed god sent hither
To make the world to laugh at me.

MARINA: Patience, good sir,
Or here I'll cease.

PERICLES: Nay, I'll be patient.
Thou little know'st how thou dost startle me
To call thyself Marina.

MARINA : The name
Was given me by one that had some power,
My father, and a king.

PERICLES: How! a king's daughter?
And call'd Marina?

MARINA: You said you would believe me;

But, not to be a troubler of your peace,
I will end here.
PERICLES: But are you flesh and blood?
Have you a working pulse, and are no fairy?
Motion! Well; speak on. Where were you born?
And wherefore call'd Marina?
MARINA: Call'd Marina
For I was born at sea.
PERICLES: At sea! what mother?
MARINA: My mother was the daughter of a king;
Who died the minute I was born,
As my good nurse Lychorida hath oft
Deliver'd weeping.
PERICLES: O, stop there a little!
Aside
This is the rarest dream that e'er dull sleep
Did mock sad fools withal. This cannot be:
My daughter's buried—Well: where were you bred?
I'll hear you more, to the bottom of your story,
And never interrupt you.
MARINA: You scorn; believe me, 'twere best I did give o'er.
PERICLES: I will believe you by the syllable
Of what you shall deliver. Yet, give me leave—
How came you in these parts? where were you bred?
MARINA: The King my father did in Tharsus leave me;
Till cruel Cleon, with his wicked wife,
Did seek to murder me; and having woo'd
A villain to attempt it, who having drawn to do't,
A crew of pirates came and rescued me;
Brought me to Mytilene. But, good sir,
Whither will you have me? Why do you weep?
It may be,
You think me an impostor. No, good faith;
I am the daughter to King Pericles,
If good King Pericles be.
PERICLES: Ho, Helicanus!
HELICANUS: Calls my lord?
PERICLES: Thou art a grave and noble counsellor,
Most wise in general. Tell me, if thou canst,
What this maid is, or what is like to be,
That thus hath made me weep?
HELICANUS: I know not; but
Here is the regent, sir, of Mytilene
Speaks nobly of her.
LYSIMACHUS: She never would tell
Her parentage; being demanded that,
She would sit still and weep.
PERICLES: O Helicanus, strike me, honour'd sir;
Give me a gash, put me to present pain,
Lest this great sea of joys rushing upon me
O'erbear the shores of my mortality,
And drown me with their sweetness. O, come hither,
Thou that beget'st him that did thee beget;
Thou that wast born at sea, buried at Tharsus,
And found at sea again! O Helicanus,
Down on thy knees, thank the holy gods as loud
As thunder threatens us. This is Marina.
What was thy mother's name? Tell me but that,
For truth can never be confirm'd enough,
Though doubts did ever sleep.
MARINA: First, sir, I pray,
What is your title?
PERICLES: I am Pericles of Tyre; but tell me now
My drown'd queen's name, as in the rest you said
Thou hast been godlike perfect,
The heir of kingdoms and another like
To Pericles thy father.
MARINA: Is it no more to be your daughter than
To say my mother's name was Thaisa?
Thaisa was my mother, who did end
The minute I began.
PERICLES: Now blessing on thee! Rise; thou art my child.
Give me fresh garments. Mine own, Helicanus—
She is not dead at Tharsus, as she should have been
By savage Cleon. She shall tell thee all;
When thou shalt kneel, and justify in knowledge
She is thy very princess. Who is this?
HELICANUS: Sir, 'tis the Governor of Mytilene,
Who, hearing of your melancholy state,
Did come to see you.
PERICLES: I embrace you.
Give me my robes. I am wild in my beholding.
O heavens bless my girl! But hark, what music?
Tell Helicanus, my Marina, tell him

O'er, point by point, for yet he seems to doubt,
How sure you are my daughter. But, what music?

HELICANUS: My lord, I hear none.

PERICLES: None!
The music of the spheres! List, my Marina.

LYSIMACHUS: It is not good to cross him; give him way.

PERICLES: Rarest sounds! Do ye not hear?

LYSIMACHUS: My lord, I hear.

Music

PERICLES: Most heavenly music!
It nips me unto listening, and thick slumber
Hangs upon mine eyes: let me rest.
Sleeps

LYSIMACHUS: A pillow for his head.
So, leave him all. Well, my companion friends,
If this but answer to my just belief,
I'll well remember you.

Exeunt all but PERICLES

DIANA appears to PERICLES as in a vision

DIANA: My temple stands in Ephesus. Hie thee thither,
And do upon mine altar sacrifice.
There, when my maiden priests are met together,
Before the people all,
Reveal how thou at sea didst lose thy wife.
To mourn thy crosses, with thy daughter's, call,
And give them repetition to the life.
Or perform my bidding or thou livest in woe;
Do it, and happy—by my silver bow!
Awake and tell thy dream.
Disappears

PERICLES: Celestial Dian, goddess argentine,
I will obey thee. Helicanus!

Re-enter HELICANUS, LYSIMACHUS, MARINA, & C

HELICANUS: Sir?

PERICLES: My purpose was for Tharsus, there to strike
The inhospitable Cleon; but I am
For other service first: toward Ephesus
Turn our blown sails; eftsoons I'll tell thee why.

To LYSIMACHUS

Shall we refresh us, sir, upon your shore,
And give you gold for such provision
As our intents will need?

LYSIMACHUS: Sir,
With all my heart; and when you come ashore
I have another suit.

PERICLES: You shall prevail,
Were it to woo my daughter; for it seems
You have been noble towards her.

LYSIMACHUS: Sir, lend me your arm.

PERICLES: Come, my Marina.

Exeunt

SCENE II— *Ephesus: Before the temple of Diana*

Enter GOWER

GOWER: Now our sands are almost run;
More a little, and then dumb.
This, my last boon, give me,
For such kindness must relieve me—
That you aptly will suppose
What pageantry, what feats, what shows,
What minstrelsy, and pretty din,
The regent made in Mytilene
To greet the King. So he thrived,
That he is promised to be wived
To fair Marina; but in no wise
Till he had done his sacrifice,
As Dian bade; whereto being bound,
The interim, pray you, all confound.
In feather'd briefness sails are fill'd,
And wishes fall out as they're will'd.
At Ephesus, the temple see,
Our king and all his company.
That he can hither come so soon,
Is by your fancies thankful doom.

Exit

SCENE III—*The temple of Diana at Ephesus; Thaisa standing near the altar as High Priestess; a number of Virgins on each side; Cerimon and other Inhabitants of Ephesus attending*

Enter PERICLES, with his Train; LYSIMACHUS, HELICANUS, MARINA, and a Lady

PERICLES: Hail, Dian! to perform thy just command,
I here confess myself the King of Tyre;
Who, frighted from my country, did wed
At Pentapolis the fair Thaisa.
At sea in childbed died she, but brought forth
A maid-child call'd Marina; who, O goddess,
Wears yet thy silver livery. She at Tharsus
Was nursed with Cleon; who at fourteen years
He sought to murder; but her better stars
Brought her to Mytilene; 'gainst whose shore
Riding, her fortunes brought the maid aboard us,
Where, by her own most clear remembrance, she
Made known herself my daughter.

THAISA: Voice and favour!
You are, you are—O royal Pericles!
Swoons

PERICLES: What means the nun? She dies! Help, gentlemen!

CERIMON: Noble sir,
If you have told Diana's altar true,
This is your wife.

PERICLES: Reverend appearer, no;
I threw her overboard with these very arms.

CERIMON: Upon this coast, I warrant you.

PERICLES: 'Tis most certain.

CERIMON: Look to the lady. O, she's but o'erjoy'd.
Early in blustering morn this lady was
Thrown upon this shore. I oped the coffin,
Found there rich jewels; recover'd her, and placed her
Here in Diana's temple.

PERICLES: May we see them?

CERIMON: Great sir, they shall be brought you to my house,
Whither I invite you. Look, Thaisa is recovered.

THAISA: O, let me look!
If he be none of mine, my sanctity
Will to my sense bend no licentious ear,
But curb it, spite of seeing. O, my lord,
Are you not Pericles? Like him you spake,
Like him you are. Did you not name a tempest,
A birth and death?

PERICLES: The voice of dead Thaisa!

THAISA: That Thaisa am I, supposed dead
And drown'd.

PERICLES: Immortal Dian!

THAISA: Now I know you better.
When we with tears parted Pentapolis,
The King my father gave you such a ring.
Shows a ring

PERICLES: This, this. No more, you gods! your present kindness
Makes my past miseries sports. You shall do well,
That on the touching of her lips I may
Melt and no more be seen. O, come, be buried
A second time within these arms.

MARINA: My heart
Leaps to be gone into my mother's bosom.
Kneels to THAISA

PERICLES: Look who kneels here! Flesh of thy flesh, Thaisa;
Thy burden at the sea, and call'd Marina,
For she was yielded there.

THAISA: Blest and mine own!

HELICANUS: Hail, madam, and my queen!

THAISA: I know you not.

PERICLES: You have heard me say, when I did fly from Tyre,
I left behind an ancient substitute.
Can you remember what I call'd the man?
I have named him oft.

THAISA: 'Twas Helicanus then.

PERICLES: Still confirmation.
Embrace him, dear Thaisa; this is he.
Now do I long to hear how you were found;
How possibly preserved; and who to thank,
Besides the gods, for this great miracle.

THAISA: Lord Cerimon, my lord—this man

Through whom the gods have shown their power—that can
From first to last resolve you.

PERICLES : Reverend sir,
The gods can have no mortal officer
More like a god than you. Will you deliver
How this dead queen re-lives?

CERIMON: I will, my lord.
Beseech you, first, go with me to my house,
Where shall be shown you all was found with her;
How she came placed here in the temple;
No needful thing omitted.

PERICLES: Pure Dian, bless thee for thy vision! I
Will offer night-oblations to thee. Thaisa,
This Prince, the fair-betrothed of your daughter,
Shall marry her at Pentapolis. And now,
This ornament
Makes me look dismal will I clip to form;
And what this fourteen years no razor touch'd,
To grace thy marriage-day I'll beautify.

THAISA: Lord Cerimon hath letters of good credit, sir,
My father's dead.

PERICLES: Heavens make a star of him! Yet there, my queen,
We'll celebrate their nuptials, and ourselves
Will in that kingdom spend our following days.
Our son and daughter shall in Tyrus reign.
Lord Cerimon, we do our longing stay
To hear the rest untold. Sir, lead's the way.

Exeunt

Enter GOWER

GOWER: In Antiochus and his daughter you have heard
Of monstrous lust the due and just reward:
In Pericles, his queen, and daughter, seen,
Although assail'd with fortune fierce and keen,
Virtue preserved from fell destruction's blast,
Led on by heaven, and crown'd with joy at last.
In Helicanus may you well descry
A figure of truth, of faith, of loyalty;
In reverend Cerimon there well appears
The worth that learned charity aye wears.
For wicked Cleon and his wife, when fame
Had spread their cursed deed, and honour'd name
Of Pericles, to rage the city turn,
That him and his they in his palace burn;
The gods for murder seemed so content
To punish them—although not done, but meant.
So, on your patience evermore attending,
New joy wait on you! Here our play has ending.

Exit